Freedom's Sword

Freedom's Sword

The NAACP and the Struggle Against Racism in America, 1909-1969

GILBERT JONAS

With a Foreword by JULIAN BOND

ROUTLEDGE
NEW YORK AND LONDON

Published in 2005 by
Routledge
270 Madison Avenue
New York, NY 10016
www.routledge-ny.com

Published in Great Britain by
Routledge
2 Park Square
Milton Park, Abingdon,
Oxon OX14 4RN U.K.
www.routledge.co.uk

Routledge is an imprint of the Taylor & Francis Group.

Printed in the United States of America on acid-free paper.

10 9 8 7 6 5 4 3 2 1

Library of Congress Cataloging-in-Publication Data.

Jonas, Gilbert.
Freedom's sword : the NAACP and the struggle against racism in America, 1909-1969 / Gilbert Jonas.
p. cm.
Includes bibliographical references and index.
ISBN 0-415-94985-8 (hb : alk. paper)
1. National Association for the Advancement of Colored People—History. 2. African Americans—Civil rights—History—20th century. 3. Civil rights movements—United States—History—20th century. 4. African Americans—Politics and government—20th century. 5. Racism—United States—History—20th century. 6. United States—Race relations. I. Title.

E185.5.N276J66 2005
323.1'196073'006073—dc22 2004014112

First and foremost, this book is dedicated to the tens of thousands of African Americans who placed their lives on the line to confront and defeat the cruel and oppressive forces of Jim Crow.

They are the true heroes of our nation's long struggle to attain civil rights for every citizen.

The public face of the civil rights struggle was necessarily the leadership, national and local, of the NAACP and its sister organizations. This book, hopefully one of many, pays tribute to the unparalleled assemblage of stellar leaders during the NAACP's first six decades, many of whom I was fortunate enough to count as friends and colleagues. They include Roy Wilkins, Walter White, Thurgood Marshall, John Morsell, Robert L. Carter, William Hastie, Charles Hamilton Houston, Charles and Medgar Evers, Kivie Kaplan, Henry Lee Moon, Buell Gallagher, Herbert Hill, Gloster Current, Julian Bond, June Shagaloff Alexander, Daisy Bates, Alfred B. Lewis, Clarence Mitchell, Ruby Hurley, Ralph J. Bunche, Vernon Jordan, Mildred B. Roxborough, Matthew Perry, Nathaniel Jones, Franklin Williams, James Farmer, Richard McClain, Robert C. Weaver, and Aaron Henry. No private American association has even come close to assembling such luminous leadership. Folk wisdom has it that each constituency receives the leadership it deserves. The foregoing list is indeed a reflection of the vast but devoted and disciplined membership of the NAACP during the years of its greatest struggles.

Acknowledgments

I am indebted to Judge Robert L. Carter, Herbert Hill, June Shagaloff Alexander, and Dr. Eugene Reed for generously sharing their experiences, recollections, and/or files with me. The material they provided could not have been found in any library or collection. I am also grateful to other former colleagues and friends who provided me with background and anecdotal material for some of the episodes in this book, including Judge Jack Tanner, Vernon Jordan, Benjamin L. Hooks, Rochelle Horowitz Donahue, Mildred Bond Roxborough, Gloster Current, and Mabel Smith.

My lonely burden was greatly eased by Adrian Cannon, who manages the vast NAACP collection at the Library of Congress, and by Mary Mundy of the Library of Congress's Prints and Photographs Department, who helped me to locate many of the photos in this book. Also of invaluable assistance were staff members of the Presidential Libraries of Harry S. Truman, John Fitzgerald Kennedy, and Lyndon B. Johnson.

This book would probably not have achieved publication without the perseverant commitment and professional counsel of Farley Chase. It would not have reached final manuscript form without the technical computer skills of John Whyms, who rescued me from despair on more than one occasion. The Routledge team, led by Bill Germano, provided invaluable advice and assistance in the final stages.

Last but by no means least, I wish to thank three long-time friends who suffered through innumerable drafts with constructive criticisms while never failing to support my labors. Their faith sustained me despite numerous setbacks. They are Stanford Whitmore, Elliot Schrier, and Seymour Reisin.

Lift Ev'ry Voice and Sing

Lift ev'ry voice and sing
Till earth and heaven ring.
Ring with the harmonies of Liberty:
Let our rejoicing rise
High as the list'ning skies,
Let it resound loud as the rolling sea.
Sing a song full of the faith that the dark past has taught us,
Sing a song full of the hope that the present has bought us.
Facing the rising sun of our new day begun,
Let us march on till victory is won.

First Verse of The Negro National Anthem
Words by James Weldon Johnson
Music by Rosamond Johnson

Contents

Foreword

Gilbert Jonas has taken on an enormous challenge. How does an author grasp an institution, a behemoth, especially one whose immensity has thwarted every comprehensive effort to place all its history between the covers of a book?

The National Association for the Advancement of Colored People (NAACP) is a venerable organization populated largely by people whose history has been taken seriously only in the last half-century. It is a democratic association that has been at war—nonviolently—with American racism for nearly 100 years. It has 2,000 branches today, scattered across the nation and the world, each engaging in a wide range of complementary activities. It is a grass roots organization, meaning that tens of thousands have had a hand in guiding it at various levels over nearly a century. How is that extensive and over-populated story best told?

Gilbert Jonas' inside look at the NAACP is more than welcome. He writes as an insider, a former employee, an intimate of NAACP leadership, a white man in an overwhelmingly black institution. He writes from inside the organization, not looking down from the top, but from within the bureaucracy. From that vantage point, he looks upward at the leadership and he looks outward at the hostile climate the NAACP has always faced. He looks backward, too, at the NAACP's founding, and like some of the NAACP's founders, brings the perspective of a lifetime spent in progressive politics.

For these reasons, this volume is likely to be the most personal and most political account of the organization whose acronym is as familiar to most as FBI or CIA.

Yet for all its familiarity, the NAACP presents a daunting and difficult subject for anyone trying to write about it.

The NAACP's scope is too large, with membership over 95 years in the hundreds of thousands and activities in every state and three foreign countries. Its papers at the Library of Congress are among the largest of any nongovernmental organization.

Its accomplishments are too great—ranging from multiple lawsuits advancing the cause of civil rights, including the landmark decision in *Brown v. Board of Education,* to boycotts, sit-ins, and marches, including the massive 1963 March on Washington. To date, the organization's place in the history of American reform movements has been considered too encompassing to be set down in manuscript.

Its leadership played important and leading roles in every civil rights struggle of the twentieth century, and continues to do so today. Much of that leadership merits volumes of their own, and several have been written. Executive Secretaries Walter White and Roy Wilkins wrote autobiographies, and White recently was the subject of a new biography. My predecessor as board chair, Myrlie Evers-Williams, has written an autobiography, and other NAACP personalities—Robert Williams, Thurgood Marshall, Rosa Parks, W.E.B. DuBois—have had their lives examined in print.

But there has been no single overall chronicle. Nonetheless, there has been vast documentation of the NAACP. Printed works about discrete chapters in its history constitute a small library.

This library includes poet Langston Hughes' 1962 paperback, *Fight for Freedom: the Story of the NAACP,* and encompasses a lengthy bibliography. Also included in lists of NAACP literature must be the many biographies of civil rights personalities not primarily associated with the NAACP, as well as studies done of other civil rights organizations. These include Taylor Branch's magisterial three-part series on America in the Martin Luther King Jr. years; David Garrow's King biography; studies by August Meier and Elliot Rudwick of the Congress of Racial Equality (CORE); Adam Fairclough's history of the Southern Christian Leadership Conference (SCLC); Linda Reed's history of the Southern Conference Educational Fund (SCEF); Jesse Moore's study of the National Urban League (NUL), and many more.

The organizations were formed, in part at least, in reaction to the NAACP, and the NAACP plays an important role in each organization's history. Most of them became its partners. While many also became competitors with the NAACP for influence and the allegiance of African-Americans, it was the NAACP that created space for each to exist and grow. Some challenged its approach as too timid, its policies too closely tied to prevailing powers, its strategies unlikely to achieve timely results. But while several of these organizations have since vanished and others are now only shadows of their former selves, the NAACP persists.

Despite critics both loud and numerous, it is universally respected by African Americans. In an April 1998 poll conducted by the Foundation for Ethnic Understanding, 81 percent of blacks reported a favorable opinion of the NAACP. An October 1995 *US News & World Report* poll reported 90 percent of blacks supported the NAACP. A 1993 leadership study by Brakeley, John Price Jones, Inc., showed 75 percent of blacks believed the NAACP to be the leader among groups with civil rights, social justice, and race relations agendas. In this study, 75 percent of all respondents believed the NAACP adequately represented the black community.

The NAACP has been so central to the story of the fight against racial discrimination in the United States that that story can hardly be discussed without reference to the NAACP. A biography of Malcolm X, the NAACP's antithesis, has 12 index references to the organization.

The NAACP is central to American popular culture as well. Biographies of many twentieth century popular culture heroes contain references to the NAACP or to NAACP actions. Examples include biographies of James Brown, Miles Davis, Muhammad Ali, Paul Robeson, and Richard Wright.

Today, a Google search for "National Association for the Advancement of Colored People" produces 85,000 listings; the "NAACP" produces 412,000. It is in today's newspaper, on yesterday's television news, and on tomorrow's blog.

The NAACP is profoundly democratic. As political scientist Adolph Reed has written, "Nationally, (only) the NAACP (of all black civil rights/political organizations) is governed by its individually based membership."

It is the "democratic" nature of the NAACP that gives it vitality and accounts for its long life. A bottom-up organization that regularly elects its leadership at the local, state, regional, and national levels insures regular regeneration of its leaders and a constant renewal of commitment to organizational values.

By creating board seats reserved for youth and elected only by youth members, the NAACP feeds a constant stream of new, young faces into its leadership stream. Today the NAACP has the largest number of youth members of any secular organization with both youth and adult members.

The NAACP continues to fight today on many fronts—some depressingly similar to battles waged when the organization was brand new. It fought and won protections for voters in the aftermath of the theft and suppression of black votes in Florida and elsewhere in 2000. In 2004, it helped convince legislators in several states to pass restrictions on the predatory lending industry that targets minority populations. In mid-2004 it was fighting an upsurge in police–minority clashes across the United States and trying to insure independent investigations and punishments for police who violate standards of behavior. It registers voters in every state and runs get-out-the-vote campaigns in every election cycle. Its legal staff—which provided the model for today's many public interest law firms—remains active on a variety of fronts.

In considering and repudiating the challenge to affirmative action at the University of Michigan during the Supreme Court's last term, Justice Ruth Ginsburg directly confronted the realities of our past and present, saying:

> [W]e are not far distant from an overtly discriminatory past, and the effects of centuries of law-sanctioned inequality remain painfully evident in our communities and schools. In the wake 'of a system of racial caste only recently ended,' large disparities endure.[1]

She acknowledged what we all know to be true—and gave ample reason why the NAACP's task is so great today:

> Unemployment, poverty, and access to health care vary disproportionately by race. Neighborhoods and schools remain racially divided. African-American and Hispanic children are all too

> often educated in poverty-stricken and under performing institutions. Adult African-Americans and Hispanics generally earn less than whites with equivalent levels of education. Equally credentialed job applicants receive different receptions depending on their race. Irrational prejudice is still encountered in real estate markets and consumer transactions.[2]

Just as the NAACP's task is great, so was Gilbert Jonas's. He has risen to it.

Julian Bond

(Julian Bond has been chairman of the NAACP Board of Directors since February 1998. He is a Distinguished Professor in the School of Government at American University in Washington, D.C., and a Professor of History at the University of Virginia.)

Endnotes

1. *Gratz v. Bollinger* (Ginsburg, J., dissenting) (citation omitted).
2. *Id.* (footnotes omitted).

Introduction

I set out to write the story of the National Association for the Advancement of Colored People (NAACP) for several reasons. First, my participation in the NAACP began in 1949 as a college student and continued with few interruptions until 1999. Thus, for half a century the Association has been my major allegiance, and in many ways, my extended family. Second, because of this involvement I have been privileged to work with many of the era's greatest Americans and social activists, and to have earned the trust of men and women for whom I have great respect and admiration. Few white Americans have had this enviable opportunity, which has helped to shape me as a human being and as a professional in my fields.

After I formally retired in 1997, I was struck by the awareness that few Americans had the slightest notion of how important the NAACP has been to our nation's fabric. It took me some time to realize that at least two generations—about four decades—had transpired since the peak of the civil rights struggle, during which a great deal of history has been lost and an even greater amount has been revised. For example, of that small minority still interested in the civil rights struggle, many believe that the so-called Civil Rights Movement began in 1955, when Dr. Martin Luther King Jr. led the Montgomery bus boycott inspired by the NAACP's Rosa Parks, and ended with the tragic assassination of Dr. King in 1968. Within that minority are those who believe that the Student Non-Violent Coordinating Committee (SNCC) was the key organization, and there are those who still believe that the Committee on Racial Equality (CORE) played the most important role. And, of course, many Americans—black and white—continue to regard Dr. King and the Southern Christian Leadership Conference (SCLC) as the agency most responsible for changing the nation. Indeed, dozens of books have been written on these three organizations and

Dr. King during the past 30 years, each claiming the subject organization has been preeminent in the struggle. The mass media, including television, has buttressed some of these notions with dramatizations and docudramas asserting they are reconstructing history as it really was.

But it wasn't that way. To begin with, the modern civil rights movement began in 1909 with the call to create a new organization to achieve for Negroes the rights guaranteed by the Constitution and to protect them from lynchings and pillagings by white Americans. That organization became known the following year as the NAACP, which immediately entered the public life of our nation by defending Negroes against injustice and by seeking to outlaw lynching. From that meager beginning, with a few hundred members and less than a dozen local units, the NAACP became the largest, most powerful, most feared, and most respected civil rights organization in the nation's history and perhaps in the history of the world. Even during the 13 years when CORE, SNCC, and SCLC were at their most vigorous, the NAACP remained the only mass organization capable of producing the desired crowds, while mounting crucial litigation in the courts and effectively lobbying Congress and the White House for landmark legislation. And, despite all of its recent travails, it still remains the sole national agent for civil rights change today.

Astoundingly, no general history of the NAACP has been published since 1967, when Dr. Charles Kellogg wrote about the NAACP's first 20 years but was unable to complete further volumes. Before that, in 1962 Langston Hughes wrote a short, poetic history for the Association called "Fight for Freedom." To be sure, several scholars have written compelling books about a single achievement or a self-contained story within the long history of the NAACP. Genna Rae McNeil has produced the definitive biography of Charles Hamilton Houston. Richard Kluger has written the most complete account of how the NAACP's lawyers won *Brown v. Board of Education*. Richard C. Cortner brought to life the NAACP's strenuous efforts to save Arkansas farmers from execution in "A Mob Intent on Death," and Kenneth W. Goings presented the definitive account of the NAACP's campaign to block Judge John Parker's ascent to the Supreme Court in "The NAACP Comes of Age." Mark V. Tushnet has written a critical account of "The NAACP's Legal Strategy Against Segregated Education, 1925–1950." Several good biographies of Thurgood Marshall are available, as is Denton Watson's thorough biography of Clarence Mitchell. There are a number of valuable autobiographical works, from James Weldon Johnson's and Mary Ovington's accounts of the early years, to Walter White's of the middle years, to those of Roy Wilkins and Jack Greenberg later on. But nowhere today can a youngster, white or black, or for that matter, any adult, read a single book that chronicles the achievements and the importance of the NAACP during its halcyon years.

That is what I have set out to do by writing the story of its first six decades—from 1909 to roughly 1969. I have sought to demonstrate that no private American organization has contributed as much to the realization of the American Dream during the twentieth century as the NAACP. Nor has any private organization served as the model for so many other ethnic and interest groups since the NAACP showed the way by winning *Brown* in 1954. Populations as diverse as women, Hispanics, Italo-Americans, gays, environmentalists, anti-war advocates, the disabled—to name but a few—have patterned themselves after the NAACP in their struggles for justice and identity. Nor have so many Americans—in addition to African Americans—benefited from the numerous Supreme Court decisions won by the NAACP's lawyers. All of these conclusions struck me most when the Association was mired in difficulty and nearly broke financially a decade ago. To those old enough to remember, it suddenly became clear what all Americans were in jeopardy of losing if the Association permanently lost its way.

Lastly, I believe it is vitally important for Americans of all races to know and to appreciate that virtually all of the NAACP's achievements were the product of the effort, intellect, commitment, and courage of African Americans in every corner of this nation, but most especially in the Jim Crow South. It is true that a few whites—a very few—participated in the struggle from the very beginning and their contributions, though valuable, represent a modest proportion of the total struggle. At each phase of the NAACP's evolution it was African Americans who, in increasingly substantial numbers, placed their safety, their economic future, and their very lives on the line to move the civil rights struggle another notch forward. These were mostly ordinary people of every possible vocation—school teachers and postal workers, dirt farmers and housemaids, mechanics and storekeepers, and a small but effective group of professionals, including lawyers, ministers, and doctors.

From the very beginning a tiny percentage of the white population —mostly progressives and reformers—joined the fray and provided financial help but, thereafter, the overwhelming membership—in the mid-ninety percentile—was comprised of African Americans. After the first decade the staff was also mostly African American and by the second decade so were the majority of the officers and governing board. What is most striking about that condition is that every year from about 1912 until 1969, most of the funding for the NAACP's work came from black Americans through modest dues, contributions, and the proceeds of local events. No other African American secular organization can make that statement and only black churches can make similar boasts.

As this book traces the rise of the NAACP, the reader should bear in mind that the NAACP had to invent itself in 1910 and then reinvent itself numerous times thereafter at crucial historical junctions. In 1910 no model existed that the NAACP's founders could replicate in their determination to overturn America's most imbedded social disease—racism. There was no template for the founding white Americans, other than minor facets of the abolitionist, suffragette and prohibition movements, each of which was comprised of white upper and middle class Americans, most of whom had means and education. As for African Americans in that same year, only the Christian church in its many varieties had become established institutionally in virtually every Negro community. Until the twentieth century, however, Negro churches, for the most part, refrained from the struggle, at least openly, while simultaneously nurturing faith and optimism, both of which helped to sustain the mostly secular NAACP. As it took shape and multiplied throughout its first 60 years, the NAACP increasingly received moral support, desperately needed funds, and numerous members from many black churches.

This volume traces the NAACP's organizational development from a few hundred committed members in half a dozen cities, mostly white reformers at the beginning, to more than 450,000 members, mostly black, in every African American community in every state, organized into over 2,000 local units, adult and youth, as well as dozens of statewide groupings. As the organization emerged physically, its members accepted as their primary mission the role of advocacy, initially to publicize the evils of lynching and, thereafter, to expose each manifestation of racial injustice within American society. Within this overarching role, the keystone has been *The Crisis* magazine edited and promoted by one of the twentieth century's foremost geniuses, W.E.B. DuBois, whose own writings became an integral part of the struggle.

From advocacy the NAACP soon leaped into litigation, providing legal representation for Negro victims of racism. These court experiences, which rolled back restrictive residential covenants and marginally increased Negro voting, led the Association to the realization, in large measure because of the vision of Charles Hamilton Houston, that the American judicial system could become the anvil on which to hammer out the Constitutional rights of black Americans. From that understanding, the NAACP's lawyers, under Thurgood Marshall and Robert L. Carter, devised the strategy and tactics that successfully overturned the separate but equal imperative proclaimed by the 1896 Supreme Court decision *Plessy v. Ferguson.* Ultimately, that 20-year effort resulted in the Supreme Court's most important decision, *Brown v. Board of Education.*

A quarter of a century earlier, however, the NAACP's leaders, led by Walter White, plunged into American political life in 1930 by helping to deny approval of President Herbert Hoover's nominee to the Supreme Court. That success proved so heady that White undertook to defeat every U.S. Senator who voted in favor of Hoover's choice. The NAACP's venture into the national electoral process was fortuitously synchronized with the overwhelming popularity of FDR and the New Deal, enabling the NAACP to boast of numerous victories throughout the rest of the decade. By the end of the 1930s the NAACP was well on its way to institutionalizing its branch voter registration and get-out-the-vote capabilities, with periodic assistance from the National Office. Thus, in the 1960s, the NAACP's electoral clout, combined with professional lobbying and patient coalition building by Roy Wilkins and Clarence Mitchell, produced the greatest civil rights legislative victories of the twentieth century—the 1964 Civil Rights Act and the 1965 Voting Rights Act. (President Lyndon B. Johnson's support and commitment were not insignificant either.) An equally vital part of this story is the crucial role played by the relatively short-lived

"Southern Movement"—Dr. King and SCLC, CORE, and SNCC—in confronting Southern brutality and intransigence, which through the mass media, marshaled public opinion on behalf of the civil rights activists. Another aspect of this event-filled era is the interaction of these confrontational organizations with the more strategy-directed NAACP.

Lastly, one of the mostly untold stories of the post-World War II era is the NAACP's confrontations and direct actions against labor unions and employers in a long and frustrating campaign to open up the nation's workplace to Negroes. Because that prolonged battle under the command of Herbert Hill lasted a quarter of a century—and ended with his retirement—it is narrated here until its conclusion in 1977. Thereafter, organized labor prevailed in its stubborn refusal to obey the laws of the land until, so weakened by the economy's vicissitudes and the catastrophic decline in membership, labor unions began to succumb to the process of desegregation that in many workplaces later became a function of necessity, not choice. By then the NAACP was no longer in the fray.

By the end of the 1960s however, the Association had earned the respect of most white leaders and the vast majority of blacks. It became, for the first time, the recipient of large grants and gifts from corporations and foundations, enabling it to expand its staff and programs significantly. It effectively exploited its legacy from DuBois to James Weldon Johnson to Walter White to Wilkins and Marshall, a roster of eminent activists and thinkers unparalleled in any other private organization. It was the preferred African-American organization of Presidents Truman, Kennedy, Johnson, and Carter, as well as of Eleanor Roosevelt, Ralph Bunche, Walter Reuther, A. Philip Randolph, Karl Menninger, Herbert H. Lehman, Clarence Darrow, Lincoln Stephens, Ida B. Wells, Lillian Wald, Jane Addams, and Ralph Ellison, not to mention hundreds of highly achieving African Americans in many fields of endeavor.

Here then is the NAACP's story. May its legacy live on.

1. Creating a Change Agent: The NAACP's Early Years

Necessity is the mother of invention.
Anonymous

A (True) American folk tale

It was exactly a century ago this year that Sam Hose left his home in rural Georgia for Atlanta. A literate and hard-working black man needing money to help care for his ill mother and his mentally retarded brother, Hose ended up laboring for a white landlord on a plantation outside the city. In the spring of the next year, the two had a falling out over wages. The white man threatened the black man with a pistol and the black man defended himself with the ax he was using to chop wood. Hose accidentally killed his employer and fled to his mother's cabin.

The white-owned newspapers of the South had long gorged themselves with exaggerated or fabricated accounts of such violence. In the papers' version, the fight between Sam Hose and his boss became transformed into the most enraging crime of them all: the rape of the white man's wife. White Georgians tracked Hose down and prepared for his lynching. Two thousand people gathered for the killing, some taking a special excursion train from Atlanta for the purpose. The leaders of the lynching stripped Hose, chained him to a tree, stacked wood around him, and soaked everything in kerosene. The mob cut off Hose's ears, fingers and genitals; they peeled the skin from his face. They watched, a newspaper reported, "with unfeigning satisfaction," as the man's veins ruptured from the heat and his blood hissed in the flames. "Oh, my God! Oh, Jesus," were the only words Hose could manage. When he finally died, the crowd cut out his heart and liver from his body, sharing the pieces among themselves, selling fragments of bone and tissue to those unable to attend. No one wore a disguise, no one was punished. Subsequent investigation showed that Hose had never entered the white home, much less committed a rape there.

Edward L. Ayers on *Trouble in Mind: Black Southerners in the Age of Jim Crow,* by Leon F. Litwack, *The New York Times Book Review,* May 3, 1998

On February 12, 1909, the NAACP was born, on the one hundredth anniversary of Lincoln's birthday. The choice of the date was no accident. The popular literature of the period still displayed a strong interest in Lincoln's life, 44 years after his assassination. Ida Tarbell's classic biography had been published only 14 years earlier—in *McClure's Magazine*—and was still widely read in book form. Perhaps most important of all, on August 14, 1908, Springfield, capital of Illinois, Lincoln's home town for most of his adult years, had been devastated by racial riots during which two Negroes had been lynched, six killed, more than fifty injured, and several thousand forced to flee the city, as a militia of 4,200 struggled to control the chaos.

Neither the NAACP nor the Springfield riots arose in a vacuum. Throughout the first decade of the twentieth century, Americans of African descent had been growing increasingly alarmed at the steadily escalating level of violence directed against them by segregationists. Fueled by racial and religious hatred, the Ku Klux Klan (KKK) was spreading throughout the Midwest and South while creating pockets of influence in the North and West. Four months after the riots—on December 26, 1908—Jack Johnson defeated Tommy Burns for the heavyweight boxing championship of the world, the first black man to hold that crown, though not the first black boxing champion.[1] The audaciousness of Johnson, who had publicly consorted with a white woman, further inflamed the minds of whites, especially men, throughout the nation, and thus was born the search for the "Great White Hope." For the next decade, the inability of white challengers to unseat Johnson helped to focus white enmity toward Negroes.

By way of contrast, the most popular Negro of the period, especially among whites, was Booker T. Washington. His accommodationist message to his people—eschewing agitation and political action in order to learn a vocation or a trade as the path to freedom—was comforting to white Americans and transformed him into a respected White House guest. His autobiography, *Up from Slavery,* was perhaps the Negro equivalent of the Horatio Alger stories, assuaging the consciences of the white majority even as the number of lynchings increased.[2]

The Springfield riots produced shock waves among the republic's intellectual and spiritual leaders, primarily because of William English Walling's graphic and stirring article "The Race War in the North," which described the scope and brutality of the Springfield violence and was published in *The Independent* magazine. Walling and his wife, Anna Strunsky, were well-known and well-respected progressives who had recently returned from Russia, where they had opposed the Czar's blatant attacks on the Russian Jews. In Walling's view, the attacks on Springfield's Negroes were even worse than the Czar's anti-Semitic pogroms. After the riots, he could find no regret or shame among the white citizens of the state capital of Illinois. At least in Russia, he observed, a pogrom was the product of the Czar's active manipulation. Walling expressed deep distress over the sanguine white response to the increasing attacks on Negroes and predicted that, without active intervention, the ubiquitous lynching of Southern blacks would spread to the North. He called upon all Americans to join hands in a new campaign to halt the attacks on Negroes and to punish the perpetrators. The prestige of both Walling and the magazine, which was a prominent human rights advocate, combined with the increasing incidents of violence against Negroes, not only got the attention of liberals and intellectuals but also impelled them to act.[3]

Prior to the Springfield riots, prominent Negro leaders had sought to form an organized campaign to protect and advance African Americans.

Four years before the NAACP's inception, 29 Negro professionals and leaders, led by the activist and scholar Dr. W.E.B. DuBois, responded to the increased violence against blacks by attempting to form a new organization, the Niagara Movement, to lead the racial struggle in the twentieth century. They met July 11 to 13, 1905, without evident result except for agreeing to meet again. The objectives set forth by DuBois at the second meeting in 1906 were unequivocal: "We shall not be satisfied with less than full manhood rights . . . . We claim for ourselves every right that belongs to a free-born American—political, civil and social—and until we get these rights, we shall never cease to protest and assail the ears of America with the story of its shameful deeds towards us."[4]

Unfortunately, the Niagara Movement failed to attract enough adherents or financial support; but the initiatives DuBois and his colleagues set forth reflected the emergence of Negroes in many fields of endeavor and accomplishment. At the onset of the twentieth century, Negro men and women were making their mark in almost all the professions and the arts, albeit in tiny numbers. In addition to DuBois and scores of doctors and lawyers, such professionals included Booker T. Washington, the scientist George Washington Carver, the poet Paul Laurence Dunbar, the composer Scott Joplin, and the crusading journalist Ida B. Wells.

In spite of these advances, the Negro gains from the decade of the Reconstruction, which followed the Civil War, had been virtually extinguished, exchanged for an entrenched pattern of repressive Jim Crow laws, which legally required segregation in almost every aspect of life in the South and in many of the border states. The Abolitionist sentiment of the North and Midwest had greatly dissipated and was replaced by growing humanitarian and political concerns for the massive influx of vulnerable European immigrants, who were to fuel the industrial revolution in the post–Civil War years. Causes like the right of trade unions to organize; the right of dissidents (Marxists, anarchists, even utopians, who were later joined by pacifists during World War I) to exercise free speech, as guaranteed by the First Amendment; municipal reform; and the Suffragette movement, which led the struggle to enfranchise women, were front-burner issues during the first decade of the twentieth century. For the most part, the disappearing gains of the freed Negro slaves were of lesser concern to the liberal and progressive forces outside the South—that is, until the Springfield riots.

Then, early in 1909, in response to Walling's eloquent plea, a fascinating group of American intellectuals, mostly white, together with Protestant and Jewish religious leaders, activist social workers, muckrakers, and veterans of the Abolitionist struggle, came together with individuals from DuBois's lapsed Niagara Movement to found what was later to be called the National Association for the Advancement of Colored People. Recounting the fresh assaults on Negroes in every sphere of life, 60 distinguished Americans, including several Negro leaders, signed a historic document written by Oswald Garrison Villard of the renowned Abolitionist family and editor of the *New York Evening Post* and its weekly supplement, *The Nation*,[5] calling for the formation of an organization to "renew the struggle for political and civil liberty." Known in civil rights lore as "The Call," this stirring manifesto described what a resurrected Lincoln would have seen in 1909: "If Mr. Lincoln could revisit this country in the flesh, he would be disheartened and discouraged." "The Call" enumerated the forms of segregation, oppression, and deprivation to which Negroes were again subjected 44 years after the Emancipation Proclamation.

Though later critics, especially black nationalists and radicals, would read negative meanings into the word "colored," those who chose it in 1910 had no ideological tinge, nor did anyone perceive the NAACP as a moderate or less militant organization because of this word. Later, the word's utility was accepted as an umbrella defense for the rights of "all peoples of color."[6]

"The Call" itself was not a concrete agenda for action, except by implication. It lamented the oppressive conditions under which most Negroes subsisted, arguing that the nation needed to assure "each and every citizen, irrespective of color, equality of opportunity and equality before the law." Again by implication, it urged the elimination of Jim Crow state laws, including those that barred Negroes from mixing publicly with whites; the reversal of Negro disenfranchisement throughout the South; and the eradication of segregated transportation and other public institutions. Above all, "The Call" demanded an end to the "spread of lawless attacks upon the Negro, North, South, and West . . . often accompanied by revolting brutalities, sparing neither sex nor age nor youth." Although "The Call" did not set specific goals or spell out a long-term plan, it did identify the critically important areas of human endeavor on which the NAACP would focus for the next half-century: voting rights, employment opportunity, equality before the law, desegregation of key civil institutions such as public schools and public services, and the same property rights enjoyed by the white majority. Each of these general objectives would at various times emerge as a specific public organizational goal for the NAACP. They comprised, after all, the commonsense aspects of decent living for all free men and women.

In conclusion, "The Call" appealed to "all believers in democracy to join in a national conference for discussion of present evils, the voicing of protests, and the renewal of the struggle for civil and political liberty." Given that "The Call"'s author was a newspaper editor during the age of muckraking journalism, as well as an heir to a great Abolitionist family, it is no surprise that the obvious means for furthering the Negro's cause would be that of advocacy—what Garrison termed "the voicing of protests." Garrison and his supporters were eager to get a new organization up and running and to publicize the founding of the NAACP, as it later became known.

More than 1,000 individuals were invited to sponsor the initial meeting, and some 150 agreed. At this first National Negro Conference, which was held at the Charity Organization Hall on New York City's Lower East Side from May 31 to June 1, 1909, more than a 100 attendees responded enthusiastically to the reformer's rhetoric. Villard concluded reading his "Call" with this admonition: "Silence under these conditions means tacit approval. The indifference of the North is already responsible for more than one assault upon democracy, and every such attack reacts unfavorably upon whites as upon blacks."[7]

This persuasive rhetoric and the cause itself resulted in an endorsement from W.E.B. DuBois and such leaders of the Niagara Movement as George W. Crawford, George W. Cooke, William Monroe Trotter, New York clerics Hutchins Bishop and Walter H. Brooks, and Dr. V. Morton Jones, a black woman physician. This support would be vital in reaching the nation's Negroes.[8]

The signers of "The Call," including DuBois and his followers and the original founders of the NAACP (these groups were not totally identical), were a virtual *Who's Who* of progressive American thinkers and activists, white and black. They included the Abolitionist William Lloyd Garrison; the famed social workers Jane Addams and Lillian Wald; Livingston Ferrand, the president of Cornell University; Mary

E. Wooley, the president of Mount Holyoke College; the philosopher John Dewey; the muckraking newsman Lincoln Steffens; Brand Willock, the mayor of Toledo; the philanthropist J.G. Phelps Stokes; the journalist and Southerner William English Walling and his firebrand wife, Anna Strunsky, both socialists; the Boston Brahmins Moorefield Storey and Albert E. Pillsbury; Alexander Walter, Bishop of the African Methodist Zion Church; Rabbi Stephen E. Wise; the journalists Mary White Ovington and Ida Wells Barnett; the social reformers John Haynes Holmes and Henry Moscowitz; Charles Edward Russell; and the Spingarn brothers (the academic Joel and the attorney Arthur). Together, they were to attract many more.

Conspicuously absent from this list of names was that of Booker T. Washington. The individuals composing the small committee that organized the founding conference debated whether to invite Washington, concerned that his absence would discourage fundraising among white sympathizers. Villard himself was engaged in distancing himself from Washington, whom he had come to regard as too conservative. The tepid invitation he issued to Washington was designed to be rejected, and it was. However, some of the committee members were apprehensive about the consequences of Washington's absence, since the Tuskegee sage was close to President William Howard Taft and the leaders of the Republican Party as well as to many of the leading philanthropists of the day. Ultimately, principle carried the day: the committee members understood that the race riots and lynchings were now so widespread that they had invalidated Washington's accommodationism. The founders were staking the future of the new organization, and of the nation's Negroes, on the radical demands outlined by DuBois and his associates.[9]

The initial conference adjourned and instructed a smaller committee to reconvene when it had completed a plan for a permanent organization and compiled a list of officers to direct it. Implicit in "The Call," the 1909 conference, and the follow-up conference that officially founded the organization on May 12 to 14, 1910, at the same site in New York City, was the notion of mobilizing grassroots support for the NAACP. This would serve both as a means of proliferating its advocacy mission and as a way of establishing a solid financial structure to underpin its activities and its growth. During its first three decades, the leadership was intent on building the largest, most powerful organization possible. This meant exploiting every opportunity to recruit members and, where they were clustered, to organize active branches. Later, these branches would form state conferences, and, still later, major regional groupings, every phase enhancing the organization's political and social power. Each of these acts, from the simplest, an individual paying his or her annual dues of one dollar, to the organization of massive interracial rallies, during which the staff literally passed the hat around to raise thousands, to the staff leader's strong solicitation of the local units for contributions and assessments, involved the generation of funds to maintain the engine of racial change.[10] Not until the mid-1960s—more than a half century after its inception—would the NAACP become the beneficiary of corporate gifts, foundation grants, and large contributions from wealthy individuals; virtually all these funds were dispensed by white Americans. Until then the nickels and dimes of African Americans provided almost all the NAACP's financial support.

In addition to agreement on the name—National Association for the Advancement of Colored People—the 1910 conference established a 100-member National Committee to raise money, an Executive Committee of Thirty (derived from the interim Committee of Forty) to conduct the organization's affairs and set policies, and a series of officers to run the organization between meetings. These were Morefield Storey, president; William E. Walling, chairman; John Milholland, treasurer; and Oswald G. Villard, disbursing treasurer. In the only significant clash among the committee members, the so-called radicals overcame conservatives by electing Dr. W.E.B. DuBois the full-time paid executive committee chairman, whose principal jurisdictions were education and publicity. (At the new organization's first executive committee meeting, DuBois's title was changed to director of publicity and research, a more appropriate title for a full-time paid staff executive. His salary was guaranteed for at least the first year. Meanwhile, Frances Blascoer, the white woman who had been in charge of administrative functions, was named acting executive secretary, with responsibility for organizing work and fund-raising.)[11] Dues were set as one dollar for the basic membership, escalating in steps to the highest category, life membership, at $500. (This lofty sum remained in place for the next seven decades.)[12] In 1911 (when the NAACP's membership was a meager 179), the executive committee adopted formal by-laws, establishing the association's permanent governing structure. The governing body became a 30-member board of directors. Virtually the same leadership that guided the new organization from "The Call" onward became the national officers—president (Moorefield Storey), vice presidents (John Milholland and Bishop Alexander Watts), chairman (Oswald Garrison Villard), secretary (Mary Ovington), and treasurer (Walter Sachs). DuBois was kept on as director of publicity and research. At that time, the total membership of the NAACP was 329, ensuring imminent financial distress.[13]

At the same time, several Negro branches were opposed to including white members. Villard and DuBois, among others, rose to the challenge and insisted that all branch memberships be open to whites. They reasoned that, in addition to the public relations and fund-raising values that white membership offered, it was essential at that time to counteract the widespread Southern notion of racial superiority and to promote understanding between the races by maximizing personal contact. That principle informed the NAACP's policies and programs for some eight decades.[14]

But before the NAACP could, in its early years, begin to resemble the powerful institution it would later become, it would have to demonstrate to African Americans that it could produce a noticeable impact on their lives. The two issues that most gripped black Americans in the second and third decades of the twentieth century were lynching and segregation, especially within the armed forces during World War I. Hardly a week went by that some black American—almost always a male in his prime years—was not hung from a tree or burned at the stake by an angry mob of white men, women, and children. These transgressions were almost always a way of circumventing the nominal legal system; all too often, a black man would be accused of a crime that involved the honor or person of a white woman. While awaiting trial, he would be dragged from his cell by armed vigilantes who meted out their own brand of justice. More often than not, the Ku Klux Klan (KKK) was behind these outbreaks of violence directed at helpless individuals. (The local law enforcement personnel either actively assisted the mobs or conveniently found themselves absent from the scene at the very moment of the mob's break-in.)

In a book published by the NAACP in 1919, the author Franklin Morton found that during the 30 years between 1889 and 1918, a total of 3,224 black people were lynched by angry white mobs. Of this number 61 were women.[15] It is not surprising, therefore, that until 1945, the relentless priority objective of the NAACP was the passage of a federal law prohibiting lynching. Although the organization came close on several occasions, especially in the House of Representatives, it never succeeded in persuading the majority of both houses of Congress to outlaw lynching. By the end of World War II, however, the number of lynching incidents had declined dramatically and the NAACP decided to cease pressing for the law because other issues of greater consequence had emerged by then.

But the low esteem in which most Negroes were held by the white majority (and their concomitant fear of Negro resistance) was illustrated most vividly during World War I. Despite the noble military achievements of black soldiers during the Civil War and afterwards in the "pacification" of the West, as well as admirable efforts during the Spanish-American War, the nation's political and military leaders were reluctant to accept Negro men into the services.[16] The Great War thrust new questions on the NAACP—whether Negroes ought to be allowed to serve their nation under Negro officers during a war of critical importance and, if so, whether they could be entrusted with the skills and knowledge of arms and military tactics.

Unhesitatingly, the young NAACP undertook a campaign to include Negroes among those men recruited for service during the war and to train Negroes to become officers.[17] The leadership's thinking behind this strategy was simple: If white Americans could witness the ability and courage of black soldiers, then the general level of respect for all blacks would rise. In 1917 black Americans were acutely aware of the positive combat roles of black troops during the Civil War, but antagonistic whites and demagogues warned of the imaginary dangers during wartime of arming black men, who might use their training and arms against the white majority later on. (The same argument had carried considerable weight during the Revolutionary and Civil Wars.) In classic contradiction, other bigots argued that blacks lacked both the intelligence and the competence to make good soldiers; to add insult to injury, many also alleged that black soldiers would cut and run at the first sign of danger.[18]

The NAACP's pleas to desegregate the U.S. armed forces fell upon the selectively deaf ears of President Wilson, a Virginia patrician and former president of Princeton University. A few years later, the same Wilson would proclaim his historic Fourteen Points, which, among other things, called for the self-determination of subjugated peoples throughout the world, except of course for Americans of African descent.

Eventually, the U.S. Army's staff generals, short of able-bodied draftees, agreed to accept a few hundred thousand Negro recruits for active service, with the unwritten understanding that most would be relegated to support functions. These military leaders hardly imagined how much the overseas service of the Negro soldiers, one-fourth of whom eventually saw combat in Europe, would inspire them to confront Jim Crowism on their return, adding a new thread to the fabric of the early civil rights movement. As soldiers, they performed effectively and courageously during World War I, but their many exploits were all but ignored by the American military establishment and the politicians. Paradoxically, it was our French and Belgian allies who most appreciated (and decorated) them. One black officer, Charles Hamilton Houston, who rose to the rank of Captain in the U.S. Army while serving in France, credited his wartime experiences, including the benign treatment he received from French people, as helping to focus his energies on the pursuit of liberation for his fellow Negroes. The war itself seems to have contributed to Houston's determination to return home to fight for the same kind of equitable treatment he and other Negroes received at the hands of the French and other Europeans. Already familiar with home-bred racism, Houston encountered a steady stream of racial discrimination among his fellow officers and enlisted men within the American Expeditionary Force. These experiences led almost in a straight line to Houston's selection as the NAACP's first legal counsel, and to his pioneering efforts as the architect of the NAACP's assault on segregation in education, which provided the groundwork for the *Brown v. Board of Education* decision. Houston selected a youthful Thurgood Marshall to assist him in the early stages of the education litigation campaign.[19]

While a minority of Negroes were assigned to combat zones in Europe, the vast majority were either trained or posted to Army bases at home and, as is still the case, many if not most of these bases were in the South. The gravest challenge to Negro soldiers was not the segregated and often unfair treatment received within the Army itself; it was the palpable enmity and hate directed at Negro soldiers when they left their bases to stroll through nearby towns (true during World War II as well). Nor was the Army particularly concerned with their well-being, whether or not they were in uniform, while being subjected to the most objectionable forms of Jim Crow behavior. It was inevitable that some Negro soldiers, especially those unfamiliar with Southern customs, would resist the local practices and respond in kind. On numerous occasions the NAACP was urgently called upon to provide these soldiers with legal assistance, further establishing itself as the guardian of African-American safety and well-being.

The most notorious of the World War I incidents was what the U.S. Army would later describe as a large-scale mutiny at a Texas military base. In 1917, following a series of explosive racial incidents, the majority of a 636-member all-black battalion of the 21st Infantry stormed into downtown Houston, and in the subsequent rioting, 17 people lost their lives. The Army charged 34 black soldiers with murder and executed 13. The remainder were imprisoned and received legal help from the NAACP, whose attorneys ultimately negotiated their discharge from the Army. The NAACP's role in defending these black soldiers was widely covered by the weekly black newspapers and played a significant role in establishing the organization as the voice and defender of black servicemen and servicewomen. (The incident is believed to have been the basis of the 1984 motion picture "A Soldier's Story," though the latter is set during World War II.)

Ultimately, some 200,000 Negro men were enlisted in the U.S. Army during World War I. The three-fourths who were consigned to all-black labor battalions performed outstandingly as stevedores, road builders, and in other logistic roles. The remaining 50,000 received combat roles, but some arrived after the Armistice—too late for action. Of those who did see combat, however, the record was exemplary. Among the most cited for combat were New York's 369th and 366th Infantry, Massachusetts's 167th Field Artillery, Illinois's 370th Infantry, and the 325th Signal Corps. The 371st Infantry of the

Ninety-third Division formed the apex of attack, earning 123 *Croix de Guerre* for displaying "unflinching conduct in the face of withering machine-gun fire." Of the 2,384 men attacking, 1,165 were killed.[20]

Front-line bravery notwithstanding, the Negro soldiers both in Europe and at home were subjected to a constant barrage of racial discrimination and vituperation from white American officers and soldiers. The NAACP was frequently called upon to intercede, represent, or protest on behalf of these soldiers, as they had earlier pleaded with an unsympathetic President Wilson to provide a place for them in the war effort. These early experiences with the U.S. military led to the NAACP's increasingly greater role in subsequent wars and to the NAACP's preeminent position as the single most important private force in desegregating the American military services, especially during the period of the Korean and Vietnam wars.

Returning from service in World War I, black soldiers were met with an outbreak of urban anti-Negro riots that superseded lynchings in the number of black victims whom the riots claimed. Perhaps the worst took place in Tulsa, Oklahoma, on June 1, 1921, when a rumor spread throughout the city that a black shoeshine man had tried to assault a white girl. Though the accused was subsequently cleared by the police, the rumor took on a life of its own, as a heavily armed mob of white men surrounded the Tulsa courthouse and threatened a lynching. Blacks responded by arming and marching to the jail, where shots were fired, leading to massive bloodshed, including the destruction of a thriving 30-block black neighborhood.

The town authorities maintained that the number of fatalities was 76 in the hostilities that ensued. Blacks were convinced that whites had used airplanes to bomb the black neighborhoods. The town fathers denied it. With NAACP prodding, a new investigation was opened in 1998 into the actual number of casualties and other damage done to the Tulsans of both races. It now appears that as many as 300 people, mostly blacks, had died during the Tulsa riots, and that virtually all of the property in the black neighborhood of Greenwood, some of it owned by whites, was destroyed.[21] The investigative commission appointed by the legislature proposed that the victims of the massacre, some 80 of whom survive, and the heirs of others receive some form of reparations. Rejecting the first proposal for $33 million in reparations, the commission agreed on the sum of

$12 million, but as of this writing the state legislature has not actually disbursed this sum.

Hand in hand with its proliferating activities in defense of Negroes attacked because of their race were the expanding efforts of the predominantly white officers and board to build a professional staff. Their twin goals were to improve the NAACP's advocacy efforts and to build a solid and broadly based grassroots structure. Initially, the NAACP's only Negro staff member was the scholarly W.E.B. DuBois, who edited *The Crisis* magazine, directed research, and served as the organization's public information arm. Five years after its birth, the Association's leadership consciously opted for recruitment of Negro staff members whose principal mission would be to recruit Negro members and build Negro chapters across the nation.[22]

In 1916, a talented protégé of Booker T. Washington, James Weldon Johnson—writer, diplomat, and composer—joined the staff and after a year was appointed field secretary. That same year the first issue of the *Branch Bulletin* appeared, and the first regional conference of branches was organized by the Cleveland affiliate. Johnson proved immediately successful in organizing local units: in his first year he organized 13 new branches in the South. Over a three-year period he increased the number of NAACP branches from 68 to 310.[23] By 1919, the tenth anniversary of the founding of the NAACP, Johnson as field director reported to the delegates at the annual meeting in Cleveland a total membership of 56,345 and 220 branches. Circulation of *The Crisis* had surpassed 100,000 as well.[24] His organizational acumen, together with his gift for verbal and written expression, led the board to appoint him as the first Negro executive secretary of the NAACP in 1920.[25] He and each of his successors could rightfully be called Renaissance men because of their many gifts in a variety of fields.

Of all of the men who have held the NAACP's chief executive position, Johnson may well have been the most interesting. Born in Jacksonville, Florida, in 1871, to a father who had educated himself and worked as a headwaiter at an exclusive hotel and to a mother who taught at an all-black school, Johnson was imbued from birth with the notion that he could do or achieve anything if he set his mind on it. (So positive was this upbringing, Johnson revealed later, that he had developed a sense of racial *superiority.)* NAACP members best remember him as the lyricist of the Negro National Hymn, "Lift Ev'ry Voice and Sing," which the NAACP adopted as its own anthem. Johnson wrote the words in one day, while in his twenties. He had been asked to deliver a speech on Lincoln's Birthday while serving as principal of the Negro school at which his mother had taught. Instead, he wrote the now-famous lyrics and then gave them to his brother Rosamond, who composed the stirring music. The Johnson brothers became highly successful songwriters, writing such Broadway show hits as "My Castle on the Nile," "The Congo Love Song," and the resilient "Under the Bamboo Tree."

James Weldon Johnson spent much of his leisure time as a youth reading law books; after 20 months of such reading, he took the Florida state bar examination and became the first Negro to pass it. His life is said to have changed when, as an undergraduate student at Atlanta University, he taught the children of former slaves, which according to his autobiography "marked the beginning of my knowledge of my own people as a 'race,' and it no doubt influenced his lifelong devotion—as a man of letters, an educator, and a political activist—to the folk."[26]

While in graduate studies at Columbia University, he began writing a work of fiction. For the next five years, he served in the U.S. diplomatic service as consul in Venezuela and then in revolution-racked Nicaragua, until 1912, when he completed the acclaimed novel of a Negro passing for a white man, *The Autobiography of an Ex-Colored Man,* although he was not identified as its author. It was by Anonymous until a second edition identified him as its author in 1927. The year prior to joining the NAACP, he directed the editorial page of the *New York Age,* a pro–Booker T. Washington paper.

During World War I, the NAACP's income declined, forcing temporary staff reductions. As early as 1914, Kellogg reports, "more than half of the income of the NAACP came from eighteen individuals" (presumably whites). Gradually, however, the growth of the membership and solicitations within it created a new fiscal reality: Between 1912 and 1917 the NAACP's average annual income ranged between $11,000 and $15,000. Besides field secretary, Johnson became acting (executive) secretary when John Shillady joined the U.S. Army. In urgent need of assistance for fieldwork, Johnson hired Walter White in February 1918. Thereafter membership increased almost fourfold to 43,094, with 165 branches in 38 states, including 85 new branches. Membership in the South soared to 18,701, twice the size of the entire national membership in 1917. NAACP branches were chartered in every Southern state. These developments placed the Southern Negro—and his acute problems—in the forefront of the Association's agenda. In 1918 the largest NAACP branch was that of the District of Columbia with almost 7,000 members, many of whom held federal government posts. This burst of growth under James Weldon Johnson's leadership amply demonstrated that African Americans had the skills and discipline to conduct the affairs of the NAACP. Thereafter the Association's staff became preponderantly Negro.[27] At that point the membership growth broke out of its constraints, and by 1919 some 62,300 members raised the NAACP's income to more than $44,000 in dues and contributions.[28] The following year the membership increased by 62 percent to 91,203, and the number of branches leaped by 70 percent to a total of 310. Perhaps of greater importance, the outset of 1920 marked the first time that the NAACP's membership in the South (42,588) exceeded that in the rest of the nation (38,420). Moreover, the proportion of white members declined to 10 percent of the total and never again exceeded this percentage.[29] Thus in a single decade, the most powerful civil rights organization in American history had become a stable, self-sustaining, and enduring African-American institution.

As the NAACP's CEO from 1920 until 1930, Johnson directed the fight to outlaw lynching through the Dyer Anti-Lynching Bill, which was passed by the House of Representatives but failed in the filibuster-prone Senate. He tirelessly traveled from local branch to local branch, urging greater activism upon the members, pleading for financial support, and building the institutional edifice that was to overshadow all its sister groups in the future. Most significant for the NAACP's future course, he recruited and directed the NAACP's first field staff, which became the prototype for its renowned professional staff. Johnson also proved to be an effective advocate among congressional sympathizers to the Anti-Lynching Bill, though powerful Southern senators, cushioned by the seniority system, perennially succeeded in blocking Senate approval of this measure. He left a mark of erudition and oratorical effectiveness, as well as a forceful written style, on the post of executive secretary, the NAACP's highest staff position, and the growing membership came to expect its foremost leader to maintain or better those standards.

After leaving the NAACP in 1930, he published his impressive cultural study, *Black Manhattan.* Having earlier edited *The Book of American Negro Poetry,* he published volumes of his own verse, then began a teaching career at Fisk University in Nashville until his death in an auto accident in Maine in 1938. In a newspaper essay, novelist Charles Johnson described him as a man with a "restless intellect, elegant, gentleman's charm and protean talents."

James Weldon Johnson would have been a tough act to follow under any set of circumstances. Add to that the hostile racial climate in the U.S., and the task becomes even more difficult. Yet each of the men selected later to fill the post of chief executive of the NAACP was, in his own way, also a man of diverse talents, skills, and achievements.

Shortly after Johnson was hired, the board agreed to add another Negro, William Pickens, to the staff, himself a man of many dimensions. When Johnson became executive secretary in 1920, Pickens succeeded him as field secretary for the next decade. As already noted, at Johnson's behest,[30] the board in 1918 authorized the hiring of a light-skinned, blue-eyed young man who could easily have passed for white. His name, coincidentally, was Walter White, and in 1930 he would succeed Johnson as the association's CEO. The extraordinary caliber, remarkable intellect, and obvious talents of each of these Negro men undoubtedly convinced the predominantly white board and officers to give the reins of control over the staff to Negroes themselves, following a decade of tutelage that some critics described uncharitably as paternalism. Since the financing of the Association's structure and activities still depended heavily on the generosity of the mostly white officers, board members, and their friends, the financial reins were not released for at least another decade.

As urgent as the NAACP's objectives were and as welcome as their assistance became, the NAACP found, in its first two decades, that it was no small task to balance its priorities with a relatively meager annual income. In the early years, an annual organizational income of $20,000 was regarded as a considerable sum. By the mid-1930s, annual revenues reached the $40,000 range. The initial membership dues were one dollar for an adult and fifty cents for a student. (The National Office shared the membership dues with the branches.) From its inception until 1930, the Board devoted most of its staff time and resources to the systematic effort to organize and build local branches of dues-paying volunteers. It was this effort that paid visible and material rewards, so that by the end of the 1930s, the membership reached about 200,000 and the number of local branches approached 1000. In the early decades, the standard adult dues did not include an annual subscription to *The Crisis* magazine, the highly respected monthly journal edited and directed by Dr. DuBois. Nevertheless, the magazine boasted of over 10,000 subscribers by the end of its first full year (1911), and 10 years later its subscription list exceeded 100,000.[31] Over the long term, no black-produced journal had earned as much prestige and credibility as *The Crisis*. Throughout these early decades, the NAACP and *The Crisis* magazine were considered synonymous. Until DuBois resigned as editor over organizational policy differences in 1934, he had imposed his high standards and expectations on the content of the magazine, which had become the single most influential journal dealing with the affairs of American blacks. Under Roy Wilkins, DuBois's successor as editor and later as the NAACP's executive secretary, the journal continued to reflect the intellectual ferment among black and civil rights thinkers and practitioners. Throughout its initial half-century, the magazine attracted most of the important thinkers and writers in the fields of civil rights and race relations. They included Dr. Kenneth Clark, Ralph Ellison, Thurgood Marshall, Judge Leon Higgenbottom, Dr. Martin Luther King Jr., Bayard Rustin, A. Philip Randolph, Robert C. Weaver, James Baldwin, and many other leading thinkers from the African-American community.

The magazine was also an integral part of the NAACP's national program. There were many things that made the NAACP unique, and one of them was its primary mission—advocacy. No other organization in the field had this mission as its foremost priority. For the NAACP, advocacy included public education and persuasion, lobbying, influencing the media, educating the general public, bringing about political and social change, and indoctrinating its volunteer base with the knowledge and know-how needed to fight for the achievement of civil rights goals locally and nationally. In this context, the magazine was crucial for nurturing thought among a broad spectrum of Americans. It served as a lightening rod in providing a respectful outlet for dissident ideas and for criticisms of the prevailing views. It was also an excellent tool with which to prepare individuals, branches, and entire black communities for new initiatives and new ideas that the organization was determined to advance.[32]

The most dramatic of these efforts was the groundwork done to desegregate the nation's universities and later its public schools. Almost every new legal initiative met resistance from the Negro communities' most conservative elements, as well as from those professions whose members feared that change, if it were too radical or too rapid or both, might jeopardize their means of support and safety. Indeed, important segments of black communities throughout the nation, including the media, expressed outright hostility to or serious reservations about Thurgood Marshall's strategy to go for broke by demanding the total desegregation of U.S. public schools. They preferred to continue the assault on the "separate but equal" doctrine proclaimed by *Plessy v. Ferguson.* Some Negroes were simply opposed to school desegregation as too radical a change; some saw the loss of their livelihoods if schools were desegregated; still others (the "realists") feared that if the NAACP lost, the clock would be turned back on the few gains already achieved.

Walter White carefully prepared the ground (and the membership) for these seminal changes, typically employing state conferences, regional meetings, and the annual national convention's workshops. As the campaigns became more sophisticated, White and later Roy Wilkins sought to share with the local branches the national office's plans, strategy, and methodology and to appraise frankly the consequences of the steps being undertaken that would, after two decades of struggle, ultimately result in the *Brown v. Board of Education* decision.[33] In the late 1930s and throughout the 1940s, Thurgood Marshall, Robert L. Carter, and the other lawyers working on the school desegregation cases tirelessly addressed NAACP local branch meetings to explain the strategies and generate both political and financial support among the membership. They were also constantly nurturing potential plaintiffs—NAACP members whose children attended segregated schools—for future litigation. All the while, the NAACP's field staff was gradually decentralizing, reflecting its geographical regions. From its early years, the staff was recruited from veteran NAACP members, those who had started as volunteers and worked their way up to paid staff. They had learned by doing and in the process acquired the skills to deal with a broad range of problems, subjects, and issues.

A few later went on to specialize in such areas as voting rights, youth work, employment, lobbying, and education.

The beauty of this flexible system was that it provided a training ground for staff advancement (to such posts as field organizers, program officers, state or regional directors, and department heads) while the system served as an important part of the advocacy function. Generating memberships and contributions from the local branches and the state conferences, as well as from outside sympathizers and organizations that were allied in coalitions with the NAACP, were also key responsibilities of the field staff. In this respect, their success derived more from the effectiveness of their advocacy and leadership on specific and immediate issues, either local or national, than from institutional appeals. Whenever it appeared to black Americans that the NAACP was articulating their most pressing grievances or demands, the membership increased significantly. Roy Wilkins and his associates understood this clearly; his successors often did not.

Beginning with the formal selection of Walter White as executive secretary in 1931, the direction of the overall field staff came from the NAACP's national office. There the director of branches, serving immediately under the executive secretary (later executive director), enforced the policies adopted by the volunteer leadership (the national board and national officers) through the executive secretary.

Even during this period of unprecedented growth, the NAACP leadership was compelled to divert precious time, energy, and resources to combat predators of the right and left. It very success in its early decades made it the target of both hostile opponents and competitors for the hearts and minds of American Negroes. The hard-line segregationists, exemplified best by the Ku Klux Klan and later the White Citizens Councils, attempted to thwart the NAACP's advances by violence and the perpetual threat of it, while on the left the NAACP appeared most vulnerable to insidious infiltration by members of the Communist Party USA. World War II stalled this tactic because the Kremlin ordered its proxies abroad, including the American Communists, to cooperate fully in the war effort against the Nazis and Fascists. Following the defeat of the Axis Powers, the Kremlin ordered its agents to resume their efforts to take over vulnerable democratic organizations and institutions throughout the Western world. Within the United States, one of the Communist Party's principal objectives was to gain influence in and ultimately control of the NAACP in order to win the loyalty of African Americans to the Soviet agenda.

It is significant that during the 1930s and 1940s, when the Communist Party USA and its subsidiaries were at their peak, a relatively small number of African Americans found these to be attractive revolutionary alternatives. With the exception of sporadic Communist efforts and an occasional statement by the Socialists,[34] the NAACP owned the monopoly on civil rights from 1909 until the beginning of the 1960s, a half-century after it was founded. Throughout the half-century of disputation with the KKK, Garvey's Back-to-Africa Movement, and the U.S. Communists, the NAACP steadfastly held that the salvation of the American Negroes was the U.S. Constitution and that, rather than taking any cues from separatists or revolutionaries, the NAACP and Negroes in general would seek to compel American society to comply with its own laws as defined by the Constitution, or, more accurately, as suggested by it.

More than any other institution in American society, the judicial system has been the principal bastion of the status quo during the years between the establishment of the republic and the first four decades of the twentieth century. Indeed, by its very nature, upholding the law, which had codified all of society's race-based inequities—legal, economic, and social—was its principal purpose. Thus, from 1789 until the Civil War, the judicial system had no difficulty sustaining slavery as a perfectly legal and acceptable way of life. After the imposition of the thirteenth, fourteenth, and fifteenth Amendments following the Civil War, and despite a brief interlude, called the Reconstruction, which was designed to redress the imbalance between former slaves and former masters, the law, the courts, and virtually all the practitioners—judges, prosecutors, and lawyers—found it fitting to return to a system of inequity based on race (and class).

Attorneys who used the law in *defense* of the oppressed—most particularly the four million people of African descent who had been born or raised as slaves—were opposing a system which, after 1865, still regarded Negroes as chattels for white men to use and discard as they saw fit. For the most part, Negroes were compelled by circumstances to rely upon white attorneys to defend them in court because the number of blacks who had achieved the status of an attorney was so small. The 1890 census, the first to provide lists by occupation, reports that "there were only 431 African-American lawyers" throughout the country.[35] It was not until 1869 that the first African Americans attended formal law school—at Harvard. It was not until 1930, when Charles Hamilton Houston reorganized and upgraded the Howard University Law School (Howard University is a federally supported institution in Washington D.C.), that black students in any significant numbers could hope to attend a full-fledged, full-time law school.

During the early decades of the century, a handful of white attorneys on special occasions provided blacks with legal representation. The NAACP itself, given its gravely limited resources, could not afford to establish a legal department to represent itself and its membership whenever desirable, or even whenever necessary. Beginning in 1913, Arthur C. Spingarn, brother of board chairman Joel, and Arthur's colleague, Charles H. Studin, provided volunteer (i.e., *gratis*) legal counsel for the association. NAACP President Moorefield Storey of the Boston Back Bay Storeys also contributed his renowned legal skills to the cause, and subsequently two famous liberal lawyers—Louis Marshall and Felix Frankfurter—also served as NAACP counsels on a *pro bono* basis.[36]

Meanwhile, the NAACP national office began to develop a roster of local attorneys, black and white, who courageously agreed to take on cases *ad hoc* in their communities when requested by the NAACP. This process grew to become one of the most important weapons in the NAACP's arsenal because it rendered the organization's litigation outreach many times greater than its limited resources might have otherwise permitted. Later on, the NAACP organized its Legal Defense and Education Fund, which followed a similar pattern; decades later, agencies like the ACLU, the Anti-Defamation League, and the NOW Legal Defense Fund modeled their own relationships with volunteer lawyers after that of the NAACP.

It remained for Charles Hamilton Houston to conceive of a larger vision, first for himself, and then for his people. During his military service in France, Houston had for the first time received respectful treatment from white people. Following his return home from the war in 1919, Captain Houston witnessed a major race riot in the nation's capital, during which an innocent young black man was convicted of murder and executed. The tragic event confirmed Houston's decision to pursue a career in the law. At Harvard Law School, Houston dazzled his professors and fellow students, earning both an LL.B. and a Doctorate of Laws. He then spent a year abroad studying law at the University of Madrid, an experience that opened his eyes even further to a range of social and economic possibilities not easily apparent in the strictly segregated society of Washington D.C. After a brief stint at civil law with his father, Houston expanded his vision to coincide with his already raised consciousness: with glowing recommendations from Harvard law professors Roscoe Pound and Felix Frankfurter, Houston was appointed a full-time professor at the Howard University Law School.[37] That institution was never to be the same. Gradually Houston set about to transform a good law school into a great one, dedicated to the mission of liberating his people from second-class status.

One of his first assignments was to head a survey in 1927 of black lawyers around the country, analyzing both their training and the kind of service they afforded each local black community. The study, funded by a grant from one of the Rockefeller philanthropic institutions, laid the basis for the elevation of standards at Howard Law and for the acceptance by the school's graduates of the obligation to use their training and skill for the betterment of their fellow African Americans. After the charismatic Mordechai Johnson became Howard's chancellor, Houston was appointed vice-dean of the law school in charge of a new three-year day school. (Previous candidates for the Howard law degree had but one option—four years of night school—an arrangement that remained in place until 1930. The night school arrangement permitted law students to hold full-time jobs during the day. The new day school transformed the Howard law students into full-time students.)

Supreme Court Justice Louis D. Brandeis had been pressing the Howard Law School dean to raise teaching standards, admission levels, and the overall quality of the legal education. Charles Houston was chosen to implement these objectives and to make the law degree from Howard a sought-after document. Over the next decade he succeeded in realizing this transformation. Just as importantly, he attracted and developed a corps of able black attorneys who were more than just lawyers; they were committed soldiers in the struggle of the American Negro for justice and equality.

In Genna Rae McNeil's excellent biography of Houston, his goals are effectively summarized in his own words:

> [The] Negro lawyer must be trained as a social engineer and group interpreter. Due to the Negro's social and political condition . . . the Negro Lawyer must be prepared to anticipate, guide and interpret his group advancement . . . . [Moreover, he must act as] business adviser . . . for the protection of the scattered resources possessed or controlled by the group . . . . He must provide more ways and means for holding within the group the income now flowing through it.[38]

It is no exaggeration to say that Charles Houston turned the Howard Law School into an incubator of progressive black lawyers who became the phalanx in an ever-broadening wedge of activist attorneys that carried out the lion's share of the civil rights struggle in the middle decades of the twentieth century. One consequence of Houston's determined mission was the creation of the legal department of the NAACP, of which Houston was the first Special Counsel.

Despite Houston's efforts, the number of African-American lawyers, especially throughout the South, remained small during the first half of the twentieth century. Even smaller was the pool of black civil rights attorneys in each Southern state—they could be counted upon the fingers of one hand by the early 1950s.[39]

The devotion to high legal and academic standards and the total commitment to the betterment of African Americans in all aspects of their being were to take hold and flourish within the NAACP's legal department and its tax-deductible spin-off, the Legal Defense and Education Fund. Enormously talented lawyers maintained this continuity of quality and commitment for roughly 50 years after Houston showed the way. Houston was followed by Thurgood Marshall, who in his own right demonstrated a degree of brilliance rarely displayed within the legal profession. The NAACP was determined to transform the U.S. into a just and equal society by using the same legal system that had kept Negroes in bondage since the founding of the republic. The route before them was expedited greatly by the African-American lawyers, most of whom were educated in Houston's Howard University Law School, who would win so many of the landmark decisions handed down by the U.S. Supreme Court during the twentieth century.

2. The Law as a Weapon Against Unjust Laws

[Civil] rights are not self-enforcing. Making them a reality requires individuals with the skill and determination to use the law's majestic machinery by bringing cases that expose the great gulf between the high-mindedness of the Constitution and the injustices of everyday life. Thus it was that in the 1930s the legal arm of the National Association for the Advancement of Colored People began plotting a litigation strategy to force the courts to confront the evils of official racism. Propelled by Charles Houston, William Henry Hastie and Thurgood Marshall, this effort eventually led to a momentous Supreme Court decision, *Brown v. Board of Education*, that finally broke the back of official segregation. From Brown v. Board flowed a robust civil rights movement and, in time, a giant wave of equal rights legislation that even a Congress disproportionately influenced by old-guard Southerners could not resist.

Editorial, *New York Times*, December 24, 1999

There is a school that holds that these legal victories are empty. They are not. At the very least, they provide the ground upon which we make a stand for our rights.

James Weldon Johnson, *Negro Americans, What Now?* New York, 1934, p. 39

> True, the [NAACP] strategy was to attack segregation in education, but the real agenda was the removal of the basic barrier to full and equal citizenship rights for blacks in this country. With segregation eliminated, blacks, it was thought, would have an unrestricted opportunity to function in the United States on equal terms with whites. We know now, of course, that the NAACP lawyers erred. The lawyers did not understand then how effective white power could be in preventing full implementation of the law; nor did they realize that the basic barrier to full equality for blacks was not racial segregation, a symptom, but white supremacy, the disease.
>
> **Federal Judge Robert L. Carter,**
> ***Michigan Law Review*, May 1988, p. 1095**

An ancient East Indian children's tale speaks of the nine blind men who, upon touching different parts of an elephant, came to different conclusions regarding the shape of the animal. Similarly, individual perceptions regarding the nature of the NAACP vary according to each individual's personal experience with the organization. Of the many possibilities, perhaps the most common is the perception that the principal activity of the NAACP is litigation. Probably because of the *Brown* decision, many Americans perceive the NAACP as a master of legal strategy and skill. In addition, the highly publicized activities of the NAACP Legal Defense Fund, whose public relations skills were preeminent among civil rights agencies from 1954 to the end of the 1980s, added to the inaccurate perception that most of the NAACP's resources were expended on court cases. Indeed, the NAACP has done more than any other institution in our nation to legitimize the employment of litigation to resolve disputes peacefully. Therefore, to many Americans, the NAACP has become synonymous with legal activism.

Certainly, no other private organization has won more cases before the Supreme Court nor expanded citizens' rights more widely than the NAACP through its legal victories, with the possible exception of the ACLU. Moreover, the model that the NAACP employed both as a citizens' pressure group and as a rights litigator has inspired many other demographic subgroups within U.S. society to take up their own cudgels for greater freedom and justice. Insiders used to say that the

NAACP demonstrated to the average citizen that you could fight City Hall (or the state or federal government) if you organized effectively and worked in a unified manner. Thus, in the decades after *Brown*, citizens of many walks of life created their own pressure groups and litigation arms to expand the rights of women, students, other racial and ethnic minorities, the disabled, veterans, and senior citizens. Among the broad spectrum of causes, the NAACP's example was also followed by the antiwar movement, opponents of nuclear proliferation, environmentalists, abortion rights advocates and their opponents, proponents of immigrant and human rights, and so forth.

It may be difficult to believe today, but during the first half of the twentieth century, with the exception of political movements (Socialists, Progressives, Bull Moosers, Prohibitionists) and the emergence of the trade union movement, there were few important citizens' organizations seeking to change the face of the nation. For the most part, individual Americans tended to accept the authority of their leaders and even of their seniors. Some Americans may mourn the demise of such knee-jerk obedience among the contemporary citizenry, but they do so out of ignorance of the realities of the past experienced by most Americans, or out of venality and ideological prejudice. With all of its warts, the U.S. today is far freer and far more democratic than it was at any earlier time, especially in the years prior to the 1920s, when all but a small percentage of white men were second- or third-class citizens.

In showing the way to black Americans and their white supporters, and then to the United States itself, the NAACP was instrumental in achieving a higher degree of political freedom. It used the courts effectively and efficiently, applying the Constitution (often for the first time) to daily practices of everyday living. However, because lawsuits were and are extremely expensive, the NAACP initiated court action only as a last resort, that is, when all other methods proved futile. Nevertheless, as time passed, especially after the 1960s, the very threat of a court action made many of the NAACP's other initiatives more effective—initiatives such as persuasion, negotiation, arbitration, public exposure, political pressure, and direct action.

As already noted, it helped considerably to be represented by very able and intelligent attorneys. A sizable proportion of the generation of African-American lawyers trained in the 1930s and 1940s, in part because of the severely limited opportunities then offered to them by a Jim Crow society, invested some or most of their energies and lives in the civil-rights struggle, and that was for the most part with or through the NAACP and its wholly owned subsidiary, the Legal Defense Fund (LDF).

In reality, the legal program of the NAACP began very modestly in 1910 when the new organization retained an outside attorney to represent a black man who was falsely accused of murder in Asbury Park, New Jersey. Unfortunately, the local police had already subjected that individual to the third degree when the NAACP-appointed attorney arrived. He nevertheless quickly obtained the individual's release. A few months later, a similar situation arose in nearby Lakewood, New Jersey. This time the NAACP's attorney arrived quickly and, before any harm could be done, this accused was also released. On this occasion, an early NAACP leader had written that the local authorities were already expecting the NAACP to intervene.[1] Presumably for that reason alone, they behaved in a more restrained manner.

The first attempt by the NAACP to use the judicial system in a lynching occurred the following year in Coatesville, Pennsylvania. A black man, Zach Walker, had been charged with shooting and killing a police constable after a fight broke out between them. Severely wounded, Walker was seized by a mob which chained him to his hospital bed and dragged him through the town's streets. After the bed broke in half, Walker was dragged for a half mile on the ground, then "thrown upon a pile of wood drenched with oil, and burned alive . . . . All attempts to indict members of the mob failed. They were given an ovation by their fellow citizens when they returned from the grand jury," according to an eye-witness journalist.[2]

At Oswald Garrison Villard's insistence, the NAACP agreed to conduct its own investigation of the tragic event. Having no trained investigators on the staff, it hired the well-known private detective William Burns, whose expensive fee was covered in large part by millionaire Jacob Schiff. Despite the considerable efforts of Burns and others, the investigation failed to turn up any new evidence that would warrant reopening the case. "We learned," said Mary Ovington, a well-to-do white journalist and an original founder of the NAACP, "the difficulty in getting an indictment against a lyncher whether he lived in Pennsylvania or Georgia."[3] (In 1914 Ovington became the NAACP's executive secretary and in 1917 its board chairman.)[4]

After a rash of bombings and other forms of violence against Negroes who had purchased homes in white neighborhoods in more than 20 border cities like Baltimore, Kansas City, and Louisville, the NAACP decided to challenge the Louisville housing ordinance which upheld racial exclusions in parts of the city. NAACP President Moorefield Storey agreed to serve *pro bono* as the NAACP's counsel in litigating the case. Storey's challenge proved brilliant: on November 15, 1917, the U.S. Supreme Court declared that such racial exclusionary laws were unconstitutional, citing the fourteenth Amendment to the Constitution as inherently limiting the extent to which local legislatures could deprive Negroes of their rights for whatever reason.

The Louisville housing segregation case was not the Association's first Supreme Court victory: in 1915 Moorefield Storey had already successfully argued the NAACP's initial victory before the highest court when the state of Oklahoma's grandfather clause was declared unconstitutional. Five years earlier the Oklahoma State Constitution had been amended to bar any person from registering to vote unless he could read and write, with one significant exception—that an illiterate person would be allowed to vote if he were a lineal descendant of a person who had been eligible to vote prior to January 1, 1866—hence the term "grandfather clause." It was on that date that the Civil War amendments to the Constitution took effect. The Oklahoma amendment's purpose was totally transparent: it was designed to prevent illiterate blacks from voting while enfranchising illiterate whites. Even a majority of the Supreme Court could see through this subterfuge. In fact, the Chief Justice based his decision on the fifteenth Amendment, the nullification of which was the specific objective of the Oklahoma provision.[5]

Bad as relations between the races had been before and during World War I, they deteriorated even further as the war was winding down. Racial rioting began to sweep the nation in the summer of 1919. Negro resistance and rebellion followed. The most famous instance took place in Elaine in Phillips County, Arkansas, where militant black farmers had been organizing a farmers' union. Fed up with their brutal treatment at the hands of their landlords, some farmers not only rioted but shot down their landlords. Before the first farmers' riot at a church in Hoop Spur, Arkansas, Negroes had rioted in Longview, Texas, in Chicago, Illinois, and in Omaha, Nebraska, where federal troops had been called in to restore order.[6]

The impetus for this rebellion in Elaine was the sudden rise in the price of cotton. The dirt-poor black tenant farmers realized that their white landlords were not about to share their newly found wealth with the (black) men and women who toiled the earth, bearing the brunt of the hardship. They decided to organize a union and hired a courageous white progressive lawyer, U.S. Bratton, to negotiate on their behalf. It was at the Hoop Spur church that the farmers presented Bratton with his $50 retainer, followed by a round of songs to spur further organization. At that point, as some curious whites were looking through the church window, somebody fired a shot into the church, and a few of the black farmers inside retaliated by firing back. This set off days of rioting which cost a great many Negro lives, as well as the lives of a few whites. Overall, Kellogg wrote, as many as 200 lost their lives in these riots.[7]

When the NAACP first turned its attention to the case, 12 jailed Negroes in Helena, a short distance form Hoop Spur, were awaiting execution for actions committed during the riots. (No white men had been convicted.) After receiving a report from its Arkansas state branch, the NAACP national office decided to send light-skinned, blue-eyed Walter White to Arkansas as a "white man" to investigate further. Then an NAACP field worker, Walter White, actually succeeded in interviewing the governor of Arkansas, who gave him his official reassurances and an autographed photo. In the small town of Helena, however, the climate was not nearly as hospitable, and the anti-Negro sentiment became palpable to White. When he was recognized, he was forced to flee for his life, barely escaping on the next train to Memphis.

His investigation at an end, White returned to New York to report that the 12 Negroes sentenced to death in Helena in effect had received no legal defense and that the jury had deliberated for about five minutes, while a mob raged outside the court house. At the same time, 17 other black farmers had been sentenced to prison, some for as many as 21 years. The 12 death sentences were scheduled to be carried out a few weeks later, on December 27.

The NAACP leadership decided to act quickly against this legal lynching. To pay for the legal defense of the convicted black farmers, NAACP headquarters launched a fund drive, tying the black farmers to the growing efforts of workers to unionize. The pitiful economic status of the tenant farmers was described by the NAACP as peonage, and the act of organizing a union was characterized as an effort to hire a lawyer to improve the tenants' share of their labor from the landlords. Checks and cash poured in.

After the original lawyer, U.S. Bratton, left the state, the NAACP retained a respected but elderly white lawyer to represent the Helena 12, with an able middle-aged Negro attorney to assist him, as the code of the day prescribed. They filed and won an appeal that postponed the executions. However, the case was split into two parts: six defendants were tried in somewhat cosmopolitan Little Rock, the other six in grimly bigoted Helena (where earlier four visiting Negroes had recently been shot to death while hunting. Nobody was ever indicted for these murders). At the onset of the Helena trial, the elderly white attorney became ill, and the burden of the defense fell on his black associate, Scipio Africanus Jones, who, despite meager resources and insufficient time, presented a flawless defense. To add to his difficulties, each night during the trial he was compelled to sleep in a different Negro home because of the ever-present danger to his life. (Not one Negro resident denied him a bed during the trial.) It was no surprise that in this inflamed atmosphere, the six men in Helena were again convicted of murder and sentenced to death. The case was appealed to the U.S. Supreme Court and, while Scipio Jones was trying to get the court to take the case of the six being tried in Little Rock as well, the court reversed the Helena court decision because no Negroes had served on the jury. The case was sent back to be retried in another venue.

Meanwhile, white demagogues and some so-called respectable white leaders demanded the execution of the six Little Rock defendants. The Governor set their execution for June 18, 1921, but that date passed without event and, after several legal maneuvers, the NAACP's counsel in September obtained an appeal before the U.S. Supreme Court based on new evidence. Once again the masterful New England patrician Moorefield Storey represented the NAACP before the Supreme Court. He recounted how the defendants had been tortured in jail to try to get some to testify against the others. While the court was deliberating its decision, the state released the six defendants in Helena; they were spirited away by Scipio Jones to safer turf in Little Rock where they were now free. Then on February 19, 1923, three and one-half years after the initial riot, the Supreme Court reversed the convictions of the Little Rock defendants and stayed the sentencing, ordering a new trial instead. In a decision written by Justice Oliver Wendell Holmes, the court's majority ruled that the defendants' right of due process had been denied by the intimidating presence of a bloodthirsty mob and that the state had failed to provide the necessary corrective measures to protect their due process right.[8]

The state of Arkansas never retried these Little Rock defendants. They were released and granted a conditional pardon the following January, more than four years after they had originally been convicted. The victory, however, propelled the NAACP into the major leagues of legal and political social change. The great constitutional lawyer Louis Marshall, who had lost a similar case in Atlanta involving the lynching of a Jewish man, Leo Frank, joined the NAACP's growing legal committee and made a substantial cash contribution because of this victory. Other important constitutional lawyers began to find the NAACP attractive both as a cause and as an effective, expanding institution.

The Phillips County farmers' union never recovered from the earlier events. But many of its farmers joined with poor white farmers in Arkansas to found the historic Southern Tenant Farmers' Union in July 1934, a biracial union that fought against the most overwhelming odds throughout the Great Depression for the dignity of labor, black and white, even as organized labor—hardly a partisan of integration—shunned it.

The legal, political, and financial success of the NAACP during and after the defense of the Phillips County farmers began to demonstrate a strategic point on which, in future years, experienced NAACP leaders would build. For the most part, cause organizations do not generate a great deal of support or membership from institutional efforts. Rather, the most effective and successful efforts are based on dramatic and immediate issues with real, credible people suffering injustice or oppression. Today, this may sound tautological, if not self-evident. It is not. Throughout the rest of the century, this argument needed to be made periodically by staff members, and not always to a receptive audience. As a result, time, energy, and resources that were better spent on critically important needs were allotted to institutional efforts (often self-serving) that either lost money or barely made their costs. And the persons who most needed the help often failed to receive it because the wrong strategic approach had been undertaken.

One of the most dramatic examples of this organizing principle arose a few years later when a black man in a Northern city was tried for murder because he sought to defend his family and home against a Klan-inspired white mob. The issue, which hit home hard for Negroes on both sides of the Mason-Dixon line, transformed a substantial number of African Americans across the nation into NAACP activists.

To understand the significance of this case, it is necessary to appreciate the way in which the mounting repression of Southern Negroes, including dramatic increases in the number of lynchings, impelled many blacks in the South to view the North and Midwest as the new Promised Land. That and the rapid industrialization of many Northern and Midwest cities promising decent jobs during the first 25 years of the twentieth century produced a massive migration of Negroes northward, especially to St. Louis, Chicago, Cleveland, Detroit, Philadelphia, Pittsburgh, and even New York. Unfortunately, poor bigoted whites—often for similar reasons—were also migrating to the same destinations in sizable, though smaller, numbers. These whites brought their racial prejudices with them.

Wherever the two migrant groups collided—the workplace, recreational sites, public transportation, and especially residential neighborhoods previously all-white—the impact produced a highly charged flashpoint. Thus, in 1926 in Detroit, a black medical doctor, O.H. Sweet, bought a house in a lily-white neighborhood. Shortly after he moved his family into the house, a mob of whites gathered ominously on the street outside his new home. A sudden volley of stones shattered the windows of the Sweet house. Then gunshots from the mob outside were fired into the house. Fear swept the Sweet family. One of them returned the gunfire, killing a white man later identified as a local mobster.

Detroit police, their force already riddled with Klansmen, promptly arrested Dr. Sweet, his wife, his two brothers, and seven friends. They were all charged with murder in the first degree. To defend them, the NAACP retained the services of the legendary Clarence Darrow, who had recently concluded the Scopes trial in Tennessee in which he locked horns with the celebrated William Jennings Bryan, a perennial Democratic Party candidate for president.

In his seven-hour closing statement to the jury, Darrow transformed the Sweet murder trial into a searing indictment of racial prejudice. "You are twelve white men trying a colored man," Darrow said to the jury. "I want you to be on your guard. I want you to do all you can to be fair in this case—and I believe you will." And then he hurled his rhetorical bombshell: "How would you like, gentlemen, to wake up one morning and find yourself colored?"

Before any of the jurors could begin to contemplate that seminal question, Darrow proceeded to detail the daily litany of denial, insult, and oppression afflicting Negroes in Detroit and throughout the nation. Underscoring the commonly accepted double standard of the day, Darrow said, "if white men had shot and killed a black while protecting their homes, no one would dream of having them indicted." With those words echoing in their ears, the jury retired the next day, deliberated for several hours and came back with a verdict of not guilty.[9] The outcome helped to reassure Negroes across the country that the *Sweet* decision had established the precedent, in the words of Langston Hughes, that a man's home is his castle. The case also contributed to the dramatic rise in Negro support for and confidence in the NAACP. The *Sweet* case did not involve highly abstract philosophic or legal principles; the right to defend one's home and family against a hate-filled mob constituted the nitty-gritty of daily life for many American Negroes during the third decade of the twentieth century. The NAACP, African Americans came to see, was fighting for *them*.

The *Scottsboro* case, which is dealt with later, consumed a good deal of the NAACP's time and energy during the decade of the 1930s, but it is doubtful if the organization came out the better for it. Part of the problem was the growing perception among NAACP leaders and white liberals that the Communist Party USA and its appendages possessed a different agenda from that of the democratic forces, domestically and worldwide. All too often that agenda was beginning to demonstrate that it was antithetical both to U.S. and to prodemocratic interests, even though party members were at times relentless and courageous in the struggle against racism.

Moreover, the NAACP itself was now coming into its own as a respected, prominent national organization with a sizable grassroots base, a strong media following, and the regard of a growing number of elected officials at the federal and local levels. Perhaps, it was thought, the Communist Party needed the NAACP more than the NAACP needed the support of the Communists. Further, the only real competition for Negro support that the NAACP faced as the activist phalanx in the struggle for racial justice was from the front groups that periodically sprung up as appendages of the Communist Party, often for propaganda value abroad. Nor could the NAACP leadership ignore the fact that most Negroes were as patriotic as most whites.[10] And, lastly, the NAACP itself still lacked a permanent legal department and a legal strategy for the next decade, which made it difficult to pursue broader objectives or to mount campaigns on a grander scale.

These problems began to change when, on October 26, 1934, Charles Hamilton Houston presented to the joint committee of the NAACP and to the Garland Fund's American Fund for Public Service a document that over the next 20 years would change the face of the United States of America. What Houston had written and effectively defended before a group of the finest liberal minds in America was a plan and budget for a national legal campaign against racial discrimination in education and transportation.[11] The committee approved the Houston plan, and Houston accepted its offer to direct the NAACP's first legal campaign. With that act, the legal department of the NAACP was born.

Houston followed, and was to build upon, the work of a white attorney and former fellow student at Harvard Law School—Nathan Margold—who had been selected in 1930 to direct a study of the state of the law in regard to blacks' civil rights and to direct part-time the NAACP's legal campaign, which was then still ad hoc after having received the Garland Fund's first installment of a grant of $100,000.

The original plan had been for the NAACP, with the Garland Fund grant,[12] to file a number of taxpayer suits against offending states, attacking their dual school systems on the grounds that they were separate but not equal. However, Margold studied the issue in depth and came to the conclusion that they had underestimated the number of suits and the amount of funding that would be needed to file a sufficient number of suits to change the status quo significantly. Instead, Margold proposed a "direct constitutional attack on segregation when coupled irremediably with discrimination." He urged that the assault be based on the 1888 Supreme Court decision *Yick Ho v. Hopkins,* which, he asserted, implied that discrimination permitted by a state was just as much a violation of the Constitution as discrimination arising from segregation mandated by a state. In short, he planned to focus on the *effect* of discrimination within segregated school systems, whether or not there was a requirement to segregate in a discriminatory fashion by the laws of the state in question.[13] The subsequent unexpected reduction of the Garland grant to $20,000 compelled Houston to rethink the original proposal and to conclude that, given the limited funds, he preferred to concentrate on a single major issue, namely, discrimination in education. His first targets were those states that apportioned their educational funds in an unequal manner, as a result of which black children were scandalously short-changed in the provision of books, supplies, equipment, library resources, building facilities, the number of teachers, and so forth.

Houston thereupon fashioned his suits against those institutions that, under the guise of separate but equal, were guilty of providing separate but highly unequal services to black school children. The NAACP's objective was to force, through the courts, a more equitable division—in short, to support dual but equal systems throughout each state—of the public resources for schools, which would in turn result in a monumental drain on the Southern state and local treasuries, particularly during the Great Depression. At the same time, Houston would prepare and provide model local briefs that lawyers associated with local NAACP branches could file against their elected officials and local school boards to force the latter to provide greater services to the separate black-attended part of each school system. Again, the burden of carrying two separate systems was being made heavier, in an attempt to weigh down each locality with financial burdens it could hardly afford.

Upon arriving in New York City in 1935, Houston quickly recognized that the resources at his disposal were even more limited than he had thought, obliging him to pare down his original program proposal. Instead, he decided to reduce the volume of the litigation by focusing on judicial precedent building in order to erode both the principle of separate but equal and the unconstitutional discrimination to which it usually led. His three targets for litigation became the significant pay differential between white and black teachers with the same qualifications; the glaring racial disparities in publicly provided transportation, mostly busing, which prevented the unification of rural school systems; and, in the state-supported professional and graduate schools, the substantial racial differences in opportunities provided, with white students generally on the receiving end of state funding while black college graduates had reached their ceiling: their pursuit of higher education was terminated at the bachelor's degree level because of their race.

The NAACP campaign against the inequities in higher education began in 1935 when Houston filed a suit on behalf of the NAACP, the legwork for which had been undertaken by Thurgood Marshall, then in private practice, on behalf of Donald Gaines Murray, a graduate of Amherst, who was seeking admission to the University of Maryland Law School in his home state. With high grades and glowing recommendations, Murray's credentials were impeccable. He entered the university conditionally while the case was argued. After hearing the testimony, Maryland's chief judge ordered the University of Maryland to admit Murray. A month later the university's appeal was heard, in which it argued that by providing scholarships for Negroes to study out of the state, it was meeting its constitutional obligations. The Maryland Court of Appeals ruled unequivocally that the scholarships provided to Negro students by the university failed to provide Murray with equal protection as guaranteed by the fourteenth Amendment. The Law School was ordered to permit Murray's unconditional attendance. The state of Maryland declined to appeal the decision to the Supreme Court, but with the favorable decision, Houston had established a major precedent for future decisions regarding state-funded graduate school discrimination against Negroes. The campaign towards *Brown* was underway.

The next building block began to take form in 1936 when Lloyd L. Gaines, an exceptionally qualified black college graduate, applied for admission to the University of Missouri Law School. Lily-white for a century, the University of Missouri some 15 years earlier had authorized the expansion of all-black Lincoln University as the separate but equal institution for Negroes aspiring to postgraduate or professional training. The legislature, of course, never appropriated sufficient funding to achieve such an equivalence. In the interim, the university offered out-of-state scholarships to Negro college graduates seeking entry into its graduate schools who could not find a satisfactory option at Lincoln. Attorneys for the university argued that the scholarships complied with the requirement of *Plessy v. Ferguson*'s separate-but-equal provisions and, in any event, Gaines, being a Negro, had applied to the wrong institution: he should have sought admission to Lincoln University. When the Missouri State Supreme Court upheld the university, Houston gathered a team of black lawyers to craft an appeal to the U.S. Supreme Court. With cocounsels Sidney Redmond and Henry Espy and later Thurgood Marshall, they constructed a persuasive and historic argument that won over the Court in December, 1938.

Writing for the majority, the eminent Chief Justice Charles Evans Hughes declared:

> The equal protection of the laws is a pledge of the protection of equal laws. Manifestly, the obligations of the State to give the protection of equal laws can be performed only where its laws operate, that is, within is own jurisdiction. That obligation is imposed by the Constitution . . . . [Furthermore,] the essence of the constitutional right is that it is a personal one . . . . It was as an individual that he [Gaines] was entitled to the equal protection laws, and the State was bound to furnish him within its borders facilities for legal education substantially equal to those which the State afforded for persons of the white race, whether or not other negroes [*sic*] sought the same opportunity.[14]

Once again the fourteenth Amendment had prevailed; the NAACP victory produced another vitally important precedent towards the objective of determining that racial separation, even with theoretically equal facilities, would be declared unconstitutional. Meanwhile, *Missouri ex rel. Gaines v. Canada (*or the *Gaines* decision, in short form) not only prevented a state from automatically denying a qualified Negro admission to its graduate schools but also it further imposed on the state the obligation to provide completely equal graduate school facilities to any qualified Negro applicant, regardless of the burden of cost, even if only one such student applied. To compel such an applicant to receive equivalent training through a scholarship outside the state, the Supreme Court had concluded, would be a direct violation of that individual's right to equal protection as required by the fourteenth Amendment. One of the NAACP's principal objectives—to make the cost of *Plessy* so great that it would threaten the economic viability of the Southern states—received a significant impetus with *Gaines*. It was hardly likely that any state would actually construct a full-fledged law school or any other professional graduate school solely to benefit the Negro citizens of its state. In reality, the Southern states during the Great Depression of the 1930s were usually the states ranked as the poorest in the Union.

The *Murray* and *Gaines* cases were undertaken as campaigns; the costs to the NAACP strained its resources almost to the breaking point. As part of Houston's total plan to assault segregated education, the full resources of the organization and its *The Crisis* magazine were drawn into the fray. National fundraising campaigns were undertaken that sought funds from sympathetic black organizations and white supporters, while the rapidly growing branch structure was tapping the membership as hard as it could. Black parents of school-age children were solicited in terms of their obvious self-interest. For the first time, the black fraternities and sororities were persuaded to organize their own national drives, producing heated competition for top honors. A national photo contest focusing on black school children was organized by Roy Wilkins at Houston's suggestion. Walter White as national executive secretary since 1931, Roy Wilkins as *The Crisis* editor, and the other staff members worked closely with Houston and Thurgood Marshall, assistant special counsel since 1938, to generate national public awareness and support for the long-term objectives of the NAACP attack on school segregation.[15]

Like the other NAACP departments, in the 1940s the branch department was devising and adopting new techniques both to generate membership support for the campaign and to attract new members because of the campaign. A special issue of *The Crisis* was published around the single subject of the campaign. In addition to several national drives, many branches launched their own local drives in support of the national campaign. Nevertheless, the NAACP continually approached the financial abyss, operating from hand-to-mouth between campaign appeals. That it survived financially after the *Gaines* victory was considered a minor miracle by the leadership. In 1943, for example, the total income of the NAACP barely exceeded $182,000, much less than a dollar per member.[16] Something had to change, the leadership concluded.

The change came in 1939 when the NAACP organized the NAACP Legal Defense and Educational Fund, Inc. as a vehicle to receive tax-deductible contributions from individuals, foundations, corporations, and other donors. The attraction of this status (commonly known as 50l(c)3 status) to wealthy donors became immediately apparent. With the federal government in effect paying for a sizable part of the deductible gift, regular donors began to increase the size of their gifts; the status attracted new donors as well. In addition, a number of wealthy families had created personal or family foundations that, with the LDF's new status, made grants to it from foundations legal. The same opportunity eventually applied to corporations as well, though in 1939 there was no rush by the Fortune 500 to participate in the Negro struggle for racial justice. Even so, a number of progressive small business owners who agreed with the NAACP's agenda were now able to make corporate gifts from their profits to the NAACP through the LDF.

A steady and gradually increasing stream of funds poured in, and before the year's end it was clear to Houston, Marshall, and Walter White that the legal program would enjoy ample support while it pursued Houston's long-range plan. Nevertheless, the LDF was neither a separate nor an independent entity: its policies and programs were in the final analysis determined by the NAACP national board, often through the national law committee. For example, the 1943 NAACP *Annual Report* clearly stated (in italics) at the beginning of the chapter "Education and Legal Defense" that "the majority of the [NAACP's] legal cases have been handled jointly with the NAACP Legal Defense and Education Fund, Inc."[17] Subsequent annual reports of the NAACP included summaries of cases financed by contributions to the Legal Defense Fund, without in any way distinguishing such litigation as outside of the NAACP's regular and ongoing activities.

Houston, and later Marshall, were of course highly respected by the board members, and many of the law committee's members were their friends and colleagues. Nevertheless, there were times when disagreements arose. It was generally understood by the LDF staff that the NAACP Board through its legal committee ultimately made the final policy decisions—that is, until 1961, when Thurgood Marshall resigned to become a federal appeals court judge.

The rapid and long-term financial success of the LDF was a result, in great measure, of the skills and commitment of a white fund-raiser from the coal-mining region of Pennsylvania, Harold L. Oram. Oram had initially learned some tough fundraising techniques as a member of the Communist Party, with which he later broke. In the mid-1930's he achieved great success, especially with the early use of direct mail, on behalf of the Republican cause during the Spanish Civil War. One of the early pioneers of cause fundraising, Oram drew on all of his experiences and contacts with the liberal left, including deft use of the classic front group—the LDF's Committee of 100 was comprised of prominent white liberals and mainstream Negro figures—to organize and develop a constituency for the LDF. Smith College President William Allan Neilson, Oram's father-in-law, served as its chairman. Jewish philanthropists shared prominence with the descendants of wealthy Yankee abolitionists in this unique endeavor. Many of the great names of letters, theology and humanism participated both as letter signers and as members, including Carl Van Doren, Harry Emerson Fosdick, Reinhold Neibuhr, Allen Knight Chalmers, Will Durant, and Episcopal Bishop Paul Moore.

While the advent of the LDF promised adequate resources for the NAACP to pursue its courtroom campaign to end school segregation and to attack discrimination in other areas, scant progress had been made through the courts during the World War II period (1941–45). The year 1944, however, saw the publication of Gunnar Myrdal's seminal study of the status of the American Negro, *An American Dilemma: The Negro Problem and Modern Democracy*, on which many important figures in the civil rights movement had worked, including Ralph Bunche and Kenneth Clark. The study was of paramount importance in spotlighting and documenting the second-class status and chronic oppression of America's black citizens. More than any other study of the mid-century, this work permeated the consciousness of countless Americans of influence and decisionmaking power, ultimately playing a critical role in the rise of public policy proposals designed to reduce or eliminate almost every facet of Jim Crow in the overall society. It provided the intellectual underpinning for much of the association's proposals and initiatives over the next decades.

Although deeply impressed by the Association, and by its membership, intellectual capabilities, and leadership, Myrdal expressed concern with the slow pace of the NAACP's efforts as the primary change agent in the field: He suggested that the NAACP was insufficiently militant, especially in its campaign to desegregate the nation's public schools. Whether this criticism in any way altered the nature or tempo of the NAACP's subsequent strategy is impossible to determine. The eyes of the NAACP's leadership had already turned to supporting the national war effort against racist Nazism and Fascism while seeking to ensure a greater role for Negro Americans in the armed forces and in the defense factories at home, activities that will be discussed in a later chapter.

Early in 1946, the NAACP's campaign through the courts resumed when a 24-year-old daughter of a black clergyman—Ada L. Sipuel—was summarily denied admission to the University of Oklahoma Law School. After she lost the appeal to the Oklahoma Supreme Court, Thurgood Marshall, in January 1948, filed an appeal with the U.S. Supreme Court. For the first time, the NAACP attacked the entire doctrine of separate but equal. Noting that Oklahoma had never undertaken even a gesture toward the establishment of a genuine all-black law school, Marshall declared that public school segregation by itself "helps to preserve a caste system . . . based upon race and color . . . designed . . . to perpetuate the slave tradition." Concluding that separate could never be equal, Marshall in effect characterized separate equality as an oxymoron.[18]

The Supreme Court took all of four days to declare unanimously that, under the fourteenth Amendment, Oklahoma was obliged either to admit Ms. Sipuel to the state university law school or to build a separate one with equal facilities for her and any other qualified Negroes who applied. Failing this, Oklahoma would be compelled to close its presently all-white law school until an equivalent law school for Negroes was opened.[19]

The university's response hardly fell within the letter or spirit of the separate but equal decision: it arranged to cordon off a section of the state capitol as a Negro "law school," thereby circumventing the Oklahoma law prohibiting whites and blacks from attending school together, and assigned three law school teachers (part time) to instruct Sipuel and "others similarly situated." Despite widespread protests among Oklahoma University's students and faculty, the U.S. Supreme Court bought this fraudulent solution by a 7-to-2 vote. Thus, because it failed to provide Ms. Sipuel with a legitimate law school education and, even more so, because it failed to advance the NAACP's strategy, *Sipuel* constituted a setback for Marshall, his fellow lawyers, and the NAACP, in the considered judgment of Richard Kluger, author of *Simple Justice,* the definitive text on the NAACP's campaign that culminated in *Brown.*[20]

During this period, Charles Hamilton Houston died, having suffered through a long illness. One of his protégés and the first black appointed to the U.S. Court of Appeals, William Henry Hastie, described Houston as the Moses of the legal struggle. The huge debt that Americans, especially black Americans, owe to Charlie Houston is incalculable: It had fallen to him to create and begin to implement a strategy of nonviolent but hard-nosed action, using the Constitution as his guide, that incrementally brought about the most sweeping revolution in U.S. social history. He did so with such skill and sufficient success that he gradually persuaded the lion's share of black Americans and a growing minority of whites of the rectitude of his course, including the dictum that violent alternatives were both self-defeating and more harmful to blacks than to whites.

There were voices that challenged Houston's thesis—the thesis of the NAACP in fact—and called either for armed struggle or for racial separation into an all-black nation (at one time a goal of the Communist Party) or for a return to Africa (the objective of Marcus Garvey, whose following was larger than that of the NAACP in the 1920s and early 1930s). Houston gave the NAACP its first effective modern weapon and taught a generation of talented black lawyers how to use it. It remained for Thurgood Marshall, Robert Carter, and their colleagues and successors to refine and improve Houston's techniques.

Anticipating by three decades the NAACP contention that desegregated schools are linked in part to racial residential patterns, in 1947 Marshall opened a new front for the NAACP by resuming the attack on restricted housing covenants, arrangements between realtors and homeowners to bar the sale of their homes to African Americans (and in some cases also to Jews and/or Catholics), this time in the private sector. The legal staff organized a conference of lawyers and sociologists in New York City to help map a campaign to have restricted covenants declared unconstitutional by the Supreme Court.

The immediate catalyst was a Detroit resident—Orsel McGhee—who bought a home in a white neighborhood only to be taken to court by his new neighbors seeking to enforce a restricted covenant. When the Michigan Supreme Court upheld the covenant, McGhee appealed to the NAACP to intervene. The NAACP lawyers argued successfully that these contracts were unconstitutional, with the Supreme Court concurring that the restrictions were therefore unenforceable. Joining in the suit in support of the NAACP were a broad range of liberal organizations—including the American Jewish Committee, both the AFL and the CIO, and the ACLU—each of which filed *amicus curiae* briefs, that is, briefs filed as friends of the court. Wilkins recounts that this coalescing of institutional and organizational interests, together with the growing struggle to enact a permanent FEPC and the mobilization of the National Committee Against Violence, an antilynching group, resulted in a formation of a "powerful coalition that fought sturdily for civil rights throughout the 1950s and 1960s."[21] These were the roots of the massive organizational lobby that Wilkins and Clarence Mitchell founded in 1951, which came to be known as the Leadership Conference on Civil Rights.

At the same time that Ada L. Sipuel was seeking admission to Oklahoma's state law school in 1946, Herman Marion Sweatt, a black letter carrier, was trying to enter the all-white law school at the University of Texas in Austin. Initially, under a local court order, Texas had tried to escape its legally ordained fate by producing a makeshift arrangement to patch together a law school with Prairie View State Normal College, an all-black college with very limited academic credibility. Sweatt's argument before the state appellate court was heard just as the Texas legislature had appropriated the princely sum of $100,000 to build an all-black law school in Austin itself. That law school was composed of three rooms in a basement, two part-time faculty, and a small law library. It came as no surprise that Sweatt rejected this alternative as less than equal.

In 1947, Marshall argued Sweatt's appeal before the Supreme Court and, for the first time, summoned a battery of legal and academic experts to buttress his arguments. He succeeded in creating a record that demonstrated that official segregation "was both scientifically unjustifiable and socially destructive."[22] In the *Sweatt* case, he was planting the seeds of the sociological arguments that the NAACP lawyers and social scientists would make in *Brown* and this, to the surprise of many, with the permission of the Supreme Court. Leading the witnesses who helped to construct this record was Professor Robert Redfield, chairman of the University of Chicago's Anthropology and later Social Sciences departments and a former lawyer of national renown himself.[23]

In addition to his dazzling courtroom achievements, Marshall also worked hard with the NAACP field staff to organize community support for Sweatt's entrance into the Texas law school. One result was an all-white NAACP branch with over 200 members at the University of Texas, "the first white southern college to organize an NAACP college chapter."[24] When the *Sweatt* trial began in May, 1947, NAACP staff and friends organized a mass rally on the university campus attended by more than 2,000 students, faculty, and friends—all supporting the desegregation of the university.[25] The techniques learned during this period helped greatly in later years to prepare communities for court orders that were highly unpopular but that, because of this preparation and the wise use of the media, reduced the level of violence or eliminated it completely. As observers became accustomed to the NAACP's *modus operandi,* they also came to understand why the organization was known for its constructive and responsible approaches.

While the court weighed the merits of *Sweatt,* another vitally important case was developing in Oklahoma, where George W. McLaurin, a 68-year-old black teacher with a master's degree, was seeking admission to the state School of Education to obtain his doctorate. When the university rejected McLaurin's application, Marshall chose to appeal through the federal courts in the hope of expediting the appeal. The state court route had proven both time-consuming and expensive. Marshall was bent upon setting more precedents through Supreme Court decisions. Thus, he brought *McLaurin v. Oklahoma State Regents for Higher Education* directly to a three-judge federal court in 1948—a route permitted only when a constitutional issue is at stake. A month later the special three-judge court upheld the NAACP's appeal, declaring that "the state is under the constitutional duty to provide the plaintiff with the education he seeks as soon as it does for applicants of any other group."[26] (Meanwhile, President Harry S. Truman in June had made his historic procivil rights declaration before the NAACP's 38th Annual Convention in Washington, D.C., sending an eloquent signal to the Supreme Court, the Congress and the U.S. public.)

While this decision was being appealed to the Supreme Court, McLaurin entered the University of Oklahoma in November 1948, only to learn that his admission provided for segregated locations outside his classroom, and at separate stations within the library and cafeteria. Rejecting these arrangements as unequal, McLaurin returned to federal court where Marshall and the NAACP argued on his behalf that the segregated arrangements humiliated him with "a badge of inferiority" that negatively affected all of his university relationships.[27]

Despite Marshall's eloquence, the three-judge court rejected McLaurin's appeal shortly afterwards, enabling Marshall to expedite his appeal to the Supreme Court. As fate would have it, *McLaurin* caught up with *Sweatt:* arguments for both were to be heard on the same April day in 1950. Two of the most important cases on the road to *Brown* were about to be decided simultaneously by the highest court in the land. The ball was once again in the NAACP's court, but the NAACP's lawyers (and many of its friends in academia) were divided. Some felt that Marshall's strategy was too militant; others believed that now was the moment to escalate the degree of militancy. They were also divided on tactics, especially whether this was the time to raise the ante by attacking segregation in education head-on, instead of continuing to demonstrate the failure of the Southern and border states to provide separate but equal facilities.

So divided were the civil rights and Negro attorneys and educators that Marshall organized a conference at Howard University Law School to give the legal and educational experts the opportunity to air their disagreements. The target of most of the criticism was Marshall's decision to represent McLaurin, because it raised the stakes beyond the relatively simple separate but equal equation. Influential Negro journalists, judges, and lawyers felt that if the NAACP lost *McLaurin,* then it would be jeopardizing many of the recently won gains in public education.[28] *Sweatt,* on the other hand, presented no problem because it was a logical extension of the effort to overturn *Plessy.*

After considerable give-and-take, during which few opinions were changed, Marshall assigned the brief-writing for *McLaurin* to his deputy, Robert L. Carter, whose recollection is that he had decided a few years earlier while writing an *amicus* brief for a California case to ratchet up the ante in *McLaurin* by going beyond the separate but equal contradictions in *Plessy*.[29] The escalated argument by Carter now contended that *Plessy* itself should be reversed by the Supreme Court because it had never provided equality or equal facilities. While he agreed with this construction, Marshall was not yet ready to argue that segregation was *ipso facto* a violation of the U.S. Constitution, though it appears that he very much wanted this argument tested.

He succeeded in persuading his friend, Professor Thomas Emerson of the Yale Law School, to draft a friend-of-the-court brief, which was ultimately signed by 187 of the nation's most prominent law professors. Their *amicus* brief went much further than that of the NAACP by declaring that the separate but equal doctrine itself, as a result of past decisions, had deprived black Americans of their basic rights and that it was now necessary to restore their rights immediately. Discrimination based on race, the law professors argued, was unreasonable and therefore automatically violated the fourteenth Amendment. In their conclusion, the law professors appealed to the justices of the Court as the custodians of the American conscience to free the white majority of its moral responsibility for the unfair treatment of the nation's Negro minority since the founding of the republic, if not before.[30] Not surprisingly, every one of the Southern states joined in *amicus* briefs in support of the state of Texas.

The *amicus* brief drafted by Emerson actually coincided with Marshall's own full acceptance of the premise that segregated schools were *ipso facto* unequal and therefore unconstitutional. He was now persuaded that this ought to be the central core of the NAACP's arguments before the court. In a letter to a Texas lawyer, Carter Wesley, in 1950 he wrote:

> A segregated school can never be the equal of any school which has all other racial and ethnic groups in it . . . even if the two schools were practically identical as to plant, library, curriculum, and faculty.[31]

At this juncture, Marshall appears to have experienced an internal crisis. He had agreed to write the brief for *Sweatt* after assigning Carter the *McLaurin* brief. The crosscurrents of opposing views by so many in the civil rights field quite possibly resulted in a form of temporary paralysis. The night prior to the Supreme Court appearances scheduled for both Marshall and Carter, Marshall informed Carter he had not written a brief and asked Carter to patch one together on short notice, which Carter was barely able to do, given the time constraints.[32] The last-minute extemporizing on a matter of such importance seems to have proven highly annoying to Carter, who may have experienced a case of the emperor wearing no clothes.

As the NAACP lawyer with the greatest experience in the education field, except possibly for Marshall, Carter had directed the 1949 suit that secured equal salaries for Mississippi's black teachers and the suit that opened the University of Kentucky to black students. He led off the doubleheader that day before the court by presenting the arguments for *McLaurin*. Afterwards Marshall presented the NAACP's arguments in respect to *Sweatt*. The NAACP's A-team was about to move from making precedents to making history.

On June 5, 1950, Chief Justice Fred M. Vinson, a moderate from Kentucky, read the court's unanimous decision on both *McLaurin* and *Sweatt*. Although narrower than the NAACP's brief, the court ruled that, under *Plessy*, the state of Texas's provision of a new but more modest law school for Negroes failed to provide an equivalent legal education. Texas was therefore ordered to admit Sweatt immediately. The court's ruling on *Sweatt* never questioned *Plessy*, which continued to survive as the law of the land, governing all constitutional matters related to race.

On *McLaurin*, the court shamelessly avoided the issue of whether racial discrimination produced unconstitutionally segregated schools. Instead it acknowledged that Oklahoma's treatment of and facilities for McLaurin were unequal, thereby causing him substantial harm. The justices concluded that Oklahoma's restrictions on McLaurin after his admission were unconstitutional and therefore must cease. Notwithstanding this indictment, the court declined to assign the blame for McLaurin's treatment to racial segregation. It failed to use the term even once in its decision. For the moment, it had chosen to dodge the big bullet by issuing the narrowest of opinions.

In a third decision on that same day, however, the court declared that segregating Negro interstate train passengers in dining cars violated the Constitution because, by its nature, this type of segregation emphasized the second-class nature of the service provided to Negroes. This case—*Henderson v. United States*—was one of the few dealing with civil rights prior to the 1960s not brought by the NAACP. A Negro federal employee, Elmer Henderson, had been unable to obtain his dinner at the single table provided for Negroes by the Southern Railway's dining car. He retained private Negro attorneys Belford Lawson of Washington, D.C., and Jawn Sandifer of New York, to represent him. The Negro fraternity Alpha Phi Alpha raised several hundred dollars to pay for the case. Through an extraordinary instance of favorable timing, *Henderson* reached the Supreme Court at the same time as *Sweatt* and *McLaurin*. The court scheduled it to be argued by Lawson immediately after both of the NAACP cases. Even more felicitous was that two key federal government lawyers, Solicitor General Philip Pearlman and his civil rights deputy, Philip Elman, both of whom had previously argued against restrictive covenants, had now decided to file *amicus* briefs in support of the *Henderson* appeal. The Justice Department also added its own briefs charging that *Plessy* violated the 14th Amendment in respect to both *Sweatt* and *McLaurin*. This novel federal intervention by the Truman Administration on behalf of Negro rights was welcomed by the NAACP and was eventually to become an important new weapon in the civil rights arsenal. The combination of the *Sweatt, McLaurin,* and *Henderson* decisions firmly established a framework of important precedents to round out the cornerstones of Charles Hamilton Houston's grand strategy.

In retrospect, these three decisions handed down on June 5, 1950, provided Marshall and his NAACP colleagues with the necessary foundation on which to build a new legal edifice over the next four years.[33] Its 15-year campaign had resulted in a precedent-building string of vitally important Supreme Court decisions that seriously impaired the *Plessy* decision. The NAACP attorneys had established decisively that *Plessy* could survive only insofar as each Southern state could prove that the instruction and facilities it provided were substantially equal for both races and available immediately to Negroes who sought admission to them. The Supreme Court established that segregation that caused individuals and groups to experience public humiliation and/or embarrassment also violated the Constitution both in state-supported institutions of higher learning and in interstate transport. Marshall and the NAACP at last possessed the ammunition they needed to obliterate *Plessy's* hold on public school education.

Marshall, however, was acutely aware of the resistance at the grassroots level to his determination to move from separate but equal to wholesale desegregation of the public schools. With the agreement of White and Wilkins, the NAACP proceeded to deploy every facet of its sizable apparatus to prepare the rank-and-file-membership and their Negro neighbors for the escalated objectives. At virtually every level from the national apex to the local branch base, the NAACP's leadership vigorously sought to explain their plans and strategy, and to motivate the membership to fan out within each black community to gain new adherents.

Realizing that the existing staff structure fell short of their needs, in April 1950, the NAACP's leaders, on Marshall's recommendation, employed two field workers assigned to the NAACP legal department. They were June Shagaloff and Daniel Byrd, and they worked under Marshall's direction to prepare the adults in each black community (especially the parents of school-age children) for the struggle wherever a suit was being filed against a prevailing segregated school system. It was the first time the NAACP had hired field workers for a program purpose—school desegregation—instead of simply for membership building and fundraising drives. Shagaloff, who a decade later became the NAACP's first National Director of Education, had the nerve-racking job of visiting many of the cities and towns—North and South—where the NAACP had, in effect, flung down the gauntlet, which in turn had generated counterreactions on the part of the segregationists, including the Klan. Byrd was assigned full-time to the South to encourage black educators—at both college and high-school levels—to support the NAACP's school desegregation initiatives.

Shagaloff recalled how she first had to explain the strategy step-by-step to the local branch and to black parents of the children involved. Then she had to elicit participation by enough parents so that the NAACP suit could gain standing in the court as representative of a sufficient number of actual parties (children) to the controversy. Thereafter, she went public with the local suit, using the local media, after which new pressures were put on those parents who had become plaintiffs in the suit. Many were subject to frightening threats of physical violence; some lost their jobs. Yet it was Shagaloff's job to persuade enough of them to hold the line, to stay the course, through the long years that it took to bring the case all the way to the U.S. Supreme Court. Where possible, she forged alliances with sympathetic whites, especially among the clergy, who also needed periodic bolstering.[34]

When the opportunity arose, Shagaloff encouraged the local branch and the general community to ease the financial burden on the national NAACP, which usually provided the legal and court costs. Later on, after each victory, Shagaloff helped the local leaders, often of both races, to prepare the ground for the school changes with a minimum of disruption, at the same time encouraging liaisons with the local school authorities, who were most often resistant to the coming changes.[35] Hers was one of the most important and heroic actions in the NAACP's history—24 years—during which there was little time for a personal life; all too often it meant enduring weeks or months of enormous stress from the sheer danger of the work. By the 1960s, June Shagaloff was already a legendary figure—soft-spoken, committed, tough, and intelligent. Virtually all the NAACP members who knew her firsthand (and that was a healthy proportion), as well as most of the press covering the developing school desegregation cases, believed she was a women of African descent in part because of her olive complexion, general features and short dark hair, but mostly because of the job she was doing. She rarely bothered to inform anyone that she was a white woman of Russian Jewish descent who came to this work out of personal experiences with racism and out of sheer conviction.[36]

Two decades after the initial campaign had been inaugurated, the NAACP was ready to target the nation's segregated public school systems from kindergarten to high school. For more than two years, psychologist Kenneth Clark and his professional colleagues had been developing and refining their tests measuring the damage done to school children by segregated schools, including his famous doll tests. NAACP staff researchers, led by June Shagaloff, had been gathering, collating, and evaluating national data not only on the effects of segregated classrooms on children but also on the impact of segregated housing, employment, voting, health care, and other aspects of human life on the health, welfare, and learning abilities of Negro and white children. Armed with an arsenal of knowledge never before available to the NAACP's legal department, the NAACP leadership signaled a green light to Marshall, Carter, and their associates to take the next giant leap forward.[37]

On June 26 and 27, 1950, the NAACP staff and volunteers, including 43 lawyers and 14 branch and state conference presidents, came together at a historic meeting in New York City to concur on a fateful decision: after serious deliberation, they agreed "to attempt a bold, all-out frontal attack upon educational segregation."[38] Negro children, they declared, could no longer wait three or four decades for discrimination to disappear: too many were already being irremediably harmed by the physical and psychological damage caused by racial segregation.

Instead of continuing to press for equal facilities under *Plessy,* from this date forward the NAACP aimed to obtain "education on a non-segregated basis and . . . *no relief other than that will be acceptable*" (my italics). In addition, every NAACP lawyer was instructed to "urge their client[s] and the branches of the Association involved to insist on this final relief." It is apparent that Marshall and his colleagues were concerned about the degree of resistance to the new and far more radical strategy among the NAACP's members and branches. With so many victories against *Plessy* already recorded, not a few NAACP branches and local leaders were ready to settle for separate but reasonably equal facilities and support in their communities. Robert Carter had been pressing for the use of testimony and supporting data from social scientists to demonstrate the grievous harm to Negro children produced by segregation. After intensive debate among the members of the legal staff and cooperating attorneys, Carter persuaded Marshall to venture down this path. Marshall convened a series of meetings and conferences with the cream of academia in America: the nation's leading sociologists, psychologists, anthropologists, educators, and other social scientists of both races who offered to help by critiquing and testing the range of arguments that the NAACP would employ in the federal courts in fighting its case against segregation. These sessions were invaluable in preparing the NAACP's legal team for the difficult questions which members of the Supreme Court were expected to pose.

Meanwhile, suits against school systems in Kansas, South Carolina, Virginia, Delaware, the District of Columbia, and elsewhere were undertaken by the NAACP, attacking the constitutionality of segregated public schools and seeking to reverse or undermine *Plessy*. By June 1952, the Topeka, Kansas, and Clarendon County, South Carolina cases had reached the appellate stage when the Supreme Court decided to join them and hear them together in early October of 1952. In July the NAACP filed an appeal with the Supreme Court on its Virginia case. At the end of August, the State Supreme Court upheld the NAACP's position on appeal in the Delaware case, thereby making it eligible for U.S. Supreme Court consideration. Just days prior to the scheduled hearing for the Kansas and South Carolina cases, the Supreme Court postponed argument until December 8th and joined the Virginia case with the earlier two.

In addition, the court clerk phoned Howard Professor James Nabrit, who headed the NAACP team arguing the District of Columbia case, to pass on Chief Justice Vinson's suggestion that the NAACP petition the D.C. Court of Appeals to send up the school discrimination case before them to the Supreme Court to be argued on December 8th as well. As expected, the Chief Justice's request was acted upon expeditiously, and in November the District of Columbia case was scheduled for argument after the Virginia case. A few days later Delaware's Attorney General petitioned the Supreme Court to hear his appeal of the decisions that rejected Delaware's defense of the status quo. Despite his objections, the court scheduled its hearing on the Delaware case immediately following the time set for the District of Columbia. Delaware was left with only a few weeks to prepare, but the Justices of the Court were clearly determined to hear cases representative of the various regions of the nation and, at last, to confront the American dilemma.

After hearing arguments on December 8th from both sides to each of the five cases, the justices met the following week to discuss their own views at some length without making any final decisions. From the presentations, it was apparent that most of the justices were uncertain about the degree to which they supported or opposed the decision to overturn *Plessy.* For the next six months, their discussions helped somewhat to narrow the differences but not to arrive at the end of the road. By almost every authority's evaluation, it was still a very close call. Justice Felix Frankfurter decided in June 1953 to seize the initiative. Together with his law clerk, Alexander Bickel, he drafted five questions both to help the members of the court to focus and rethink the issues, while instructing the litigants on both sides to discuss them when the case was reargued in the autumn of 1953.

The first question sought to ascertain whether Congress and the various state legislatures understood, when ratifying the fourteenth Amendment, that it would be used to abolish segregation in public schools. Second, if neither of these legislative bodies understood that compliance with the fourteenth Amendment would immediately abolish segregated schools, did the framers of the fourteenth Amendment intend that segregated schools would be abolished, as a result of the 14th Amendment, at some time in the future? Third, assuming neither of the above answers settled the issues before the court, does the court have the power to abolish segregated public schools under the fourteenth Amendment? Next, if the court decided to abolish segregated schools, was it compelled to do so summarily or could it permit an "effective, gradual adjustment" from segregated to integrated systems? Finally, should the court itself formulate specific decrees and, if so, what decrees, or should the Court appoint a special master to hold hearings to determine the terms of such decrees, or should the court remand to the initiating courts the responsibility for drafting decrees after receiving general instructions from the court, and, if so, what should those general directions be?

Very carefully, Frankfurter and Bickel were articulating, through these questions, all of the major issues causing doubt or concern among the justices. At the same time, Frankfurter was correctly reading the sentiment of the majority that the fourteenth Amendment to the Constitution overrode all other considerations, but several who held this view also feared the undesirable social consequences of a decision that would abruptly change the segregated public schools into integrated schools. Some of the foot-dragging also centered around the dilemma of the central authority dictating the terms of public policy at the lowest level of government, the school district, especially since the administration of education was one of the powers the Constitution reserved for the states. At the very least, Frankfurter's tactic moved the Court and the five cases off square one: reargument before the Court was scheduled for October 12, 1953.[39]

The NAACP, through the LDF, immediately launched a fundraising drive directed at its wealthiest supporters by sending telegrams to underscore the nature of the emergency. The telegraph appeal was to become a signature of the LDF-retained fundraising counsel, Harold L. Oram, who used it again successfully on several occasions. The telegram was signed by both the LDF's Director/Counsel Thurgood Marshall and the NAACP's Executive Secretary Walter White, demonstrating clearly that in 1953, at least, there was no separation between the NAACP national office and the Legal Defense Fund, except for the narrowly legal distinction that funds sent to the LDF were deductible against federal income taxes. Indeed, the NAACP's annual reports for the period from 1948 until 1956 failed to distinguish between the legal department staff of the NAACP and the staff members of the LDF. Marshall was listed as special counsel of the NAACP, under the listing for the executive secretary, which was Walter White until 1955 and Roy Wilkins thereafter.

Later on, Robert L. Carter, who had held titles like assistant special counsel and deputy counsel, became general counsel of the NAACP and was also listed beside Marshall's name but under that of the executive secretary. Since the publication of the NAACP annual report came under the jurisdiction of the executive director through his director of information, Henry Lee Moon, it is fair to assume that the table of organization implied by these listings was decided first by White, later by Wilkins, and that both regarded the legal counsels, the legal department, and the LDF as entities subordinate to their authority.[40]

The Marshall/White telegram, in effect, pleaded poverty, indicating that the LDF had spent $58,000 on the cases before the Supreme Court over the past three years, funds generated from supporters like those who had received the latest telegram. The Court's decision to postpone the argument and to insist upon bringing in "historical constitutional factors, sociological data and authoritative opinion" placed the "decent" education of three million Negro children in jeopardy because the LDF had no money to meet the emergency. The appeal sought the sum of $15,000 immediately.

Marshall immediately accepted the challenge presented by the Court. He recruited an old friend and colleague, the Lincoln University political scientist John A. Davis, who had coincidentally taught Robert L. Carter and recommended him to William Hastie, dean of the Howard law school. On a shoestring, Davis arrived at the LDF's new headquarters on West 43rd Street—described by some as shabby, seedy and overcrowded—and proceeded to organize one of the most massive research undertakings of its kind, although the academic summer break had already begun. Initially, Davis received rejections from several major scholars, including Columbia's Henry Steele Commager, who doubted that the framers of the fourteenth Amendment had any intention of abolishing segregation. However, Davis soon recruited a number of the profession's luminaries, including Horace Mann Bond, president of Lincoln University, historian C. Vann Woodward of Yale, and Professor John Hope Franklin, later the chairman of the History Department of the University of Chicago.

Eventually more than 200 scholars and lawyers participated in the task force, most of them *pro bono,* including lawyers recruited by attorney William Coleman in each of the 37 states that had ratified the fourteenth Amendment almost nine decades earlier. Franklin became the coordinator of the research answering the first two questions, which were historical in nature and delved into the intent of Congress and the state legislatures regarding the segregation of public schools during their consideration and adoption of the fourteenth Amendment. Shagaloff was assigned by Franklin to research the congressional debates and spent several months at the New York Public Library perusing the Congressional Record. Later she assisted Franklin in examining the state records researched by local historians in a desperate effort to find evidence that the adopters of the Amendment had no intention of perpetuating segregated schools.[41]

The stickiest of the questions were the final two, which in effect dealt with what methods and timing were to be recommended for the transition from segregated to nonsegregated schools. The psychologist Kenneth Clark, recruited by Robert Carter, directed this research, and eventually Marshall assigned June Shagaloff full-time to assist Clark in both conducting the research and drafting the findings.[42]

Clark's study found that gradual desegregation "not only does not ensure the 'effectiveness' of desegregation, but has been found to increase the chances of resistance and resentment." According to Clark's findings, clear leadership advocating change coupled with clear public enforcement of the new desegregation policies were the determining factors to achieve desegregated schools with maximum local public support. To minimize public resistance, the Clark study asserted that five conditions were essential: "(1) clear and unequivocal statement of policy; (2) firm enforcement of policy in the face of initial resistance; (3) a willingness to deal with violations with strong enforcement; (4) refusal of authorities to tolerate evasions of desegregation; and (5) appeals to fair play and justice."[43] The entire project, including the findings, were published over Dr. Clark's name in the *Journal of Social Issues* in 1953.[44]

Despite massive amounts of research and countless hours of dissection and debate, the historical evidence turned up by the task force was at best ambiguous. No clear-cut proof had been uncovered to validate the NAACP hypothesis that the framers of the fourteenth Amendment anticipated that its ratification would abolish school segregation, either immediately or at some future date. The traditional view of the fourteenth Amendment in 1953 was that it was meant to reenact and therefore ensure the constitutionality of the 1866 Civil Rights Act (even shorn of its "no discrimination" language).[45]

Then, in November, after the court had postponed the hearing until December at the request of U.S. Attorney General Herbert Brownell, who sought more time to conclude the federal government's brief, a member of the task force discovered the crucial piece of evidence urgently required by the NAACP lawyers. Deep within the stodgy confines of the Congressional Record, the researcher uncovered the words of Rep. John Bingham, the abolitionist who had agreed to remove the key "no discrimination" clause from the 1866 Civil Rights Bill, almost certainly because he feared that it lacked the authority of the Constitution. This defect, task force legal experts posited, was intended by Bingham and his supporters to be rectified through the adoption of the fourteenth Amendment. A later speech by Rep. Thaddeus Stevens, who supported Bingham's draft, carried the premise to its logical conclusion: Wherever the states discriminate against a class of individuals, the fourteenth Amendment gives "Congress . . . the power to correct such discriminations and inequality."[46]

Suffice it to record that with this and other evidence produced by the Davis task force, Marshall, Carter, Spottswood Robinson, Robert Ming, William Coleman, Jack Greenberg, and the other NAACP lawyers fashioned both a persuasive brief and an eloquent testimony during the arguments before the Supreme Court. Then, on September 8th well before dawn, in what was to become the most determining factor amidst a complicated cluster of forces and events, Chief Justice Fred M. Vinson died in his sleep. Vinson of Kentucky and Stanley Reed were the two Court justices most certainly opposed to overturning *Plessy*. By the end of the month, with Congress in recess, California Governor Earl Warren was named by President Eisenhower to replace Vinson as chief justice. A moderate with a hard-won reputation as an honest politician, Warren was sworn in on October 5th in time to chair the Court's new session. Of all the acts of fate or circumstance attached to this long struggle, none was more critically important than the death of the man who had consistently blocked the Court's resolution of the issues posed by the NAACP and his replacement by the man who would bring about, albeit with Justice Frankfurter's manipulative assistance, a unanimous decision.

The dramatic events, both public and behind the scenes, which produced the May 17, 1954, Court decision known as *Brown v. Board of Education et al.* are perhaps the best known of the NAACP's achievements. They have been dramatized twice on television (with Sidney Poitier cast as Thurgood Marshall in one version) and written about in hundreds of articles, feature stories, and books. To most authorities, *Brown* has been the most important landmark decision wrought by the NAACP and, in the opinion of some, the most important decision of the Supreme Court in U.S. history.[47] It effectively revoked *Plessy*, declaring that the racial segregation of U.S. public schools was inherently unconstitutional and ordering that they be desegregated.[48]

One year after the Court pronounced *Brown*, it heard arguments by the NAACP and the Southern states in respect to the time frame and jurisdictions in implementing the 1954 landmark decision. The NAACP's legal staff was divided over the course it would urge the Court to follow. Supported by social scientists who had played important roles as witnesses in the five court cases composing *Brown*, both sides were adamant in their positions. Citing the results of his published research, psychologist Kenneth Clark, whose doll studies had contributed greatly to persuading the nine justices about the harmful consequences of racial segregation, urged in the strongest possible terms that the NAACP insist that the Court order immediate nationwide desegregation.[49] Renowned social scientists such as Yale's Gordon Allport, joined with NAACP staff lawyers from the South in arguing against any immediate compulsion to desegregate, recommending instead that no time limits be established by the Court and that the Court be pressed to empower the local federal district courts to devise their own approaches based on local conditions and facts to carry out the Court's decision.

Nevertheless, each of the NAACP's six lawyers arguing their cases before the Court—Marshall, Carter, Jack Greenberg, Spottswood Robinson, Louis Redding, and James Nabrit—pressed for rulings that called for immediate desegregation not only within the four states mentioned and the District of Columbia, but throughout the nation as well. The Court itself was divided, more or less, but virtually all of the justices agreed that the need for another unanimous decision was paramount over the details. In the end, Chief Justice Earl Warren came up with a phrase that had been used earlier by Justice Felix Frankfurter, who apparently discovered it in the writings of justice Oliver Wendell Holmes. This phrase, which for the moment appeared to be a brilliant compromise but which over the next three decades would prove to be the Achilles heel of the *Brown* decision, was "all deliberate speed." The Court intended that this phrase should describe the pace with which the states and lower courts were ordered to implement the 1954 decision. The civil rights community, including the NAACP's leadership and supportive white liberals, while somewhat disappointed that the order was not to desegregate immediately or very soon, still believed that the trade-off—a unanimous Court decision in exchange for an indeterminate timetable—was well worth the decades of struggle, that this Court decision was a watershed event in U.S. history, and that, as a result of *Brown,* the desegregation of America's public schools was inevitable. There was at this moment virtually no negative characterization of *Brown* from this side of the civil rights aisle.[50]

Known later as *Brown II,* this masterpiece of judicial diplomacy did indeed weld a unanimous court, but only by avoiding the hard choices. Its very imprecision created enough loopholes to inspire throughout the next 20 years a small army of clever Southern lawyers and politicians bent upon the undoing of the *Brown* decision. Instead of preparing public opinion for the inevitable, most of the South's governors, members of Congress, mayors, and other elected officials—spurred on by inflammatory newspaper editorials—swore to the white citizenry that they would and could resist the law of the land, to use the tepid phrase with which President Eisenhower expressed his unenthusiastic view of the *Brown* decision. Thus followed a variety of mean-spirited but often imaginative initiatives by Southern legislatures, such as nullification, interposition, massive resistance, and when all else failed, lily-white private academies. Besides temporarily thwarting legitimate efforts to implement *Brown,* these measures also promised ill-advised hope and encouragement to the fired-up white majority who seemed bent upon fighting the Civil War all over again.

Exploiting this angry zeal, the Ku Klux Klan gained new prominence as well as numerous new adherents. For those more worldly Southerners whose taste levels were offended or embarrassed by the prospect of hooded vigilantes, the White Citizens Councils proved to be a satisfactory alternative in the cities and towns of the South, fomenting racial hatred above and below public view, all too often with local governmental support. Law enforcement officials were often organically related to these councils in many towns, assuring that racial justice—and the law of the land—would be thwarted for decades.

3. Southern Retaliation Against Negro Determination

What makes *Brown* historic . . . is its fall-out effect. It transformed and radicalized relations in this country, removing blacks from the status of supplicants to full citizenship under law, with entitlement by law to all the rights and privileges of all other citizens. Equal citizenship is not yet a reality, but blacks can now contend that the reality is contrary to law. This a powerful argument—a potent force that an equal facilities victory could not have produced.

Federal Judge Robert L. Carter,
***Michigan Law Review*, 1094–1095, May 1988**

You are not required to obey any court which passes out such a ruling [as *Brown*.] In fact, you are obligated to defy it.

U.S. Senator James Eastland of Mississippi,
Speech, August 12, 1955, in Senatobia, Mississippi

You can only create a resistance movement when people don't care about [losing] their lives.

Alan Furst, *Kingdom of Shadows*, New York, 2000, 102

Following the Court's pronouncement of *Brown* on June 17, 1954, 14 of the citizens of Indianola, Mississippi, met secretly to found the White Citizens Council as a loose confederation of upstanding Southerners who "condemned the traditional night-rising violence of the past and pledged that opposition to school desegregation would be carried out by lawful means," according to Harry S. Ashmore, a respected white journalist and a Southerner.[1] Reflecting the lead of the first White Citizens Council Chairman, planter Robert P. Patterson, the founders' legal expert, Judge Thomas Pickens Brady, "specifically disavowed the Ku Klux Klan." Respected white citizens of every other Southern state were to follow Mississippi's lead in subsequent years as they responded to the call to preserve their revered heritage from the imagined evils of desegregation.

On August 12, 1955, shortly after *Brown II* was delivered by the Supreme Court, the South's foremost exponent of resistance, Senator James Eastland of Mississippi, exhorted an audience in Senatobia: "You are not required to obey any court which passes out such a ruling. In fact, you are obligated to defy it." Later on the president of the Mississippi Bar Association, John C. Satterfield, told a Greenville audience that though it was "abhorrent . . . the gun and the torch." one of the three methods open to vigilant citizens to maintain segregation.[2]

Thus, the contrived public face of the White Citizens Councils and of those so-called respectable Southerners was a device for creating a benign image, while the private face had only the slightest reluctance to using "whatever means necessary," in the later words of Malcolm X, to gain their objectives. However, in the marginal possibility that there are those today who still perceive the members of the White Citizens Councils as patriots bent on preserving the genteel manners and practices of the pre–Civil War South, it is useful to examine exactly what these Southern gentlemen regarded as appropriate and acceptable behavior towards those Negroes in their home towns who dared to seek their constitutional rights.

Few since have said it better than a young, white Mississippi writer, Willie Morris, who happened to attend a White Citizens Council meeting in his home town of Yazoo City in the summer of 1955. Morris was then on his summer break from attending that supposedly liberal bastion, the University of Texas. Morris described the atmosphere of the meeting, attended by his father and most of his close friends, as "the pent-up hysteria of organized crowds . . . a kind of claustrophobic terror." Men shouted from the back of the hall, "Let's get the niggers!" in response to the attempt by local black parents (and the NAACP branch) to desegregate the local schools.

Morris detailed the subsequent course of the meeting in a brilliantly written narrative in his memoir, *North Toward Home*. Newsman and editor Harry S. Ashmore adeptly summarized Morris' rapierlike insights into two devastating paragraphs in his own memoir:

> The chairman quickly stilled the clamor. The white citizens of Yazoo City, he said firmly, would neither commit nor condone violence. He then outlined the procedure to be followed in preserving the Southern way of life: employers of blacks who signed the [school desegregation] petition would fire them. If they were tenants [on farms] their landlords would evict them. Wholesalers would cut off supplies and credit to the black retailers who had signed. And white merchants would refuse to sell their goods to the petitioners.
>
> The chairman, obviously on the advice of counsel, noted that this action was not being undertaken by the Citizens Council, but represented the spontaneous reaction of the white community as a whole. The combination of outrage to his sense of justice and insult to his intelligence marked the end of innocence of Willie Morris, who, like many a sensitive Southerner before him, was launched on the road that would take him . . . *North Toward Home*.[3]

This cold-blooded plan of action was, to be sure, merely violence in another form—violence in which massive economic and political power combined to crush any Negro who had the courage and temerity to stand up for his rights. The Council agenda was simple: starve them and their families until they leave, die, or comply. Surely, these white gentlemen of the Old South needed only to lift their blinders to perceive the inhumane character of their plan.

With massive resistance permeating the Southern air and the threat of violence almost always close to the surface of daily life, the NAACP was compelled to face its first serious test of the enforcement of the

Brown decision in Little Rock, Arkansas, as the 1957 school term began that fall. The site of the initial showdown came as a surprise, because at least three other Arkansas school systems—Fayetteville, Charlestown, and Hoxie—had produced voluntary desegregation plans after the 1954 decision by the Court. In addition, the University of Arkansas had earlier begun accepting Negro students to its graduate schools as a result of the Texas and Oklahoma decisions. None of these actions had caused a stir within the state. In Little Rock, a federal court order resulted in a negotiated plan with the school board—a plan which, by the way, was so conservative that the NAACP had gone back to federal court to oppose it. When the federal judge ruled against the NAACP's arguments, the Association and its Arkansas State Conference decided to withdraw their opposition and see how things worked out.

However, in 1957 the publicity-hungry Governor of Arkansas, Orville Faubus, seizing the opportunity, scuttled the arrangement worked out between the city's community leaders and the school board by obtaining an injunction from a local chancery court to halt the plan. He argued that to proceed with the plan would be to invite violence, a contention rejected even by the local police chief and sheriff. Little Rock leaders of both races had worked hard to persuade the citizenry to support the plan. Suddenly all bets were off.

The focal point of the desegregation impetus became the NAACP's Arkansas State Conference President, Mrs. L.C. Bates, known to her friends and ultimately to the nation as Daisy. During the prolonged crisis, a number of economic measures by white supremacists were directed at Mrs. Bates and her husband, owners of the militant *Arkansas State Press,* the voice of local Negroes pressing for change. It was no coincidence that the local power and telephone companies withdrew their important advertising from the paper; then the local politicians followed suit. When these tactics failed, the supplier of newsprint was prevailed upon to deny credit to the Bates. Still, they managed to hang on. It took little imagination to ascertain who had instructed the Arkansas Department of Internal Revenue to review the Bates' tax returns and to come up with a claim of $1,200 due in back taxes. Daisy Bates barely avoided a lien on the newspaper's presses by raising the demanded sum at the last minute.

When Governor Faubus openly launched his campaign to prevent the entry of the initial nine black children to Little Rock High School by calling up the Arkansas National Guard to block them, the showdown escalated dramatically. The Bates home was attacked, first with a burning cross, after which rocks were hurled through their front windows. The Bates phone rarely stopped ringing as it conveyed a steady stream of hate calls, larded with obscenities and threats. None of these acts succeeded in intimidating Daisy Bates, who stubbornly endured the siege surrounding her home as she propped up the resolve of the nine Negro students and their parents to continue with the scheduled entry. After U.S. District Court Judge Ronald Davies ordered the school board to ignore the chancery court order and continue with the desegregation move, Daisy Bates led the nine youngsters to the perimeter of Little Rock High School where 270 fully armed National Guard soldiers blocked their entry and sent them packing. This was the first time in modern history that a federal court order had been defied by armed troops, which were still under orders by Faubus himself.[4]

Roy Wilkins received the news that Faubus's troops had blocked the students' entry with extreme alarm. He realized what a precedent this could become throughout the South if Faubus were allowed to nullify the Supreme Court's historic decision. He fired off a message to President Eisenhower, noting that this act constituted a state's defiance of the authority of the federal government and asked the President to crush the rebellion. Ironically, the general who had commanded the largest military force in history appeared to have lost his resolve during this test. He dawdled for three weeks, sending the FBI to ascertain whether Faubus' claim of threatened violence had any merit. Meanwhile, the U.S. attorney general followed Judge Davies's advice and obtained an injunction against Gov. Faubus. Then Eisenhower invited Faubus to meet with him in Newport, Rhode Island, after which both men issued some placatingly innocuous statements that failed to satisfy the NAACP. Its board of directors immediately urged the president to federalize the Arkansas Guard and order his attorney general to implement the law of the land by thwarting Faubus' insurrection.

Wilkins meanwhile tried assiduously to arrange his own meeting between the president and a group of black leaders. It seemed to him and his board that leaders of the Southern forces of resistance had no trouble meeting with the president, who not once had met with Negro leaders. Finally, the president's aide, Sherman Adams, returned Wilkins's calls to arrange a meeting of not more than 10 black leaders, "six if possible." However, events overtook the planned meeting. The next day the federal judge dismissed the last of Faubus's arguments and ordered the Negro youngsters admitted immediately. Three hours later Faubus called off the troops, and the local and state police took over for the weekend.

On Monday morning, Mrs. Bates found a way through a side door to gain entry to the high school for the nine youngsters. Immediately a crowd of 800 coarse and potentially lethal men, women, and high school students surrounded the school, threatening the lives of the black children. The police made no effort to disperse them. After three hours, Bates marched them out of the school, the vocal threats and racist obscenities ringing in their ears, and delivered them to their homes. Then she proceeded to inform the President of the United States publicly that she would not return them to Little Rock High until she had Eisenhower's word that the government of the United States would protect them. The next day the president not only federalized the Guard but also ordered 1,200 tough troops from the 101st Airborne to Little Rock to carry out the federal court's order and keep the peace. According to Wilkins, each of these decisions was made by Daisy Bates herself, denying the white supremacists the grounds to charge that the crisis had been caused by the supposedly ubiquitous outside agitators.[5]

With the arrival of the federal troops, the Little Rock Nine reentered the high school and endured eight more months of harassment and vilification at the hands of a small minority of race-crazed white students, egged on by outside adults. The Guard soldiers did nothing to interfere with these continuous attacks, which Wilkins was told amounted to at least 42 during the school year, not to mention scores of others not reported. One student—16-year-old Minnie Jean Brown—was the most frequent target because she was the tallest. She restrained herself until December when she spilled her cafeteria tray on two white boys who had mercilessly baited her. She was suspended and later readmitted by the school authorities after she promised to endure any torment without striking back. As the attacks became more frequent, her resolve dwindled. In February, a white girl followed her in the hall and called her a "nigger bitch." Minnie Jean responded by calling her tormentor "white trash." For this incredible crime, she was suspended for the rest of the term. None of the white tormentors was ever suspended.

The remaining eight continued to endure the hate-filled harassment by a small white minority, while the rest of the students, roughly 1,950 of them, and the school authorities failed to lift a finger to punish the tormentors. In June, Ernest Green graduated from Little Rock High School, the first Negro to do so. Slowly over the ensuing years, the students and the community itself came to accept the black students until today, the school is thoroughly desegregated and generally incident-free, thanks to the heroic sacrifices of nine teenage children in 1957 and the dauntless leadership of the NAACP's Daisy Bates.

Following the Little Rock experience, Southern attorneys general also devised a variety of legal maneuvers to deflect, retard, or defeat court-directed initiatives to desegregate public schools within their jurisdictions.[6] To the NAACP Legal Defense and Education Fund fell the major responsibility of litigating throughout the South, school system by school system, usually on behalf of plaintiffs recruited by the local NAACP branches, as the campaign slowly proceeded to break down the segregation laws and practices in the region.

Even though there had been a significant degree of tension between Marshall and Wilkins during the last half of the 1950s, until Thurgood Marshall retired as director/counsel of the LDF in 1961 to become a federal appellate judge, the LDF generally coordinated its strategy with the national NAACP, its executive secretary Roy Wilkins, and the national board. The last was represented by its legal committee, which oversaw the legal program of the Association. Where conflicts arose, the LDF under Marshall tended to align its strategies with the policies crafted by the NAACP national board or its legal committee. However, he generally ignored Wilkins's conviction that the LDF director ought to report to the NAACP's chief executive.[7]

After Southern Members of Congress had begun to realize in 1952 that the NAACP had been financing the litigation that ultimately produced *Brown* in 1954 with tax-deductible contributions through its Legal Defense Fund, their anger was manifest. Under Representative Cox of Tennessee, a subcommittee of the Ways and Means Committee launched a series of hearings to investigate whether the NAACP had committed any illegal act. Mostly sound and fury "signifying nothing," the hearings, however, produced a monumental loss of nerve in Eisenhower's Treasury Department, in which resides the Internal

Revenue Service. Surrendering to Southern demagoguery and pressure (at the time most of the congressional committee chairmen were Southerners), the IRS in 1957 insisted that the NAACP divest itself of the tax-deductible Legal Defense Fund.

The LDF moved to its new offices on Columbus Circle, while removing from the NAACP's payroll any LDF employees, and vice versa. In addition, Marshall took with him those NAACP board members loyal to him to serve on the initial board of the LDF. The Wilkins/NAACP loyalists remained on the latter's national board and, for the first time, overlapping of members was prohibited. The LDF continued with its own professional fund-raising and developed its own bookkeeping and accounting capabilities. And it retained its entire legal and secretarial staff, except for Robert L. Carter and his secretary. (It continued, however, to identify itself as the NAACP Legal Defense and Education Fund.)

When Thurgood Marshall originally hired Robert Carter in 1945, it was with the understanding that Carter would do the deep thinking in respect to policy and strategy while Marshall would continued to perform the high-visibility duties as the NAACP's highest ranking lawyer. In Carter's view, Marshall afforded him the greatest possible latitude to explore the most radical or unconventional approaches to the law and to debate them freely with the entire legal staff, as well as with the NAACP board's legal committee, while Marshall listened to, absorbed, and even synthesized opposing views. It was in this manner that Carter had initially proposed and subsequently defended (on numerous occasions) the premise that historical and social science evidence could help to persuade the Supreme Court justices that racial segregation in schools was in itself unconstitutional because of the damage it did to Negro children. With the imaginative participation and research of renowned psychologist Dr. Kenneth Clark and scores of assisting social scientists, Carter marshaled the evidence so successfully that, in the end, it produced a unanimous court decision.

Carter was also assigned the responsibility for producing most of the important briefs on behalf of the NAACP legal department and the LDF. His late-night sessions to meet the court-designated deadlines were legendary within the Association. Even to this day, those who worked with the NAACP or the LDF who are still alive describe Carter as the mainstay of the office, holding the staff to difficult schedules and grinding out with his colleagues the briefs required by numerous deadlines. While Carter and several legal secretaries were burning the midnight oil, however, Marshall was usually addressing a public gathering for the cause, or holding a press conference, or traveling to another city to argue a case the next morning, often from notes prepared by Carter. As the LDF's chief executive, it was a given that Marshall would develop an admiring public, adding to his celebrity with each legal victory, all of which generated the publicity and fundraising so vital to the success of the legal campaigns. Even though Carter argued three of the five cases that ultimately led to *Brown,* the popular notion to this day credits the *Brown* decision solely, or very largely, to Marshall.

When the bookish and introverted Carter first joined Marshall, the latter was already the acknowledged kingpin among African-American lawyers, and it is no great leap to suggest that the young novice Carter stood in awe of him and of his reputation. Over the next six or seven years, however, Carter began to develop his own persona and a sense of self-confidence that resulted in a more realistic and human view of Marshall.

Marshall was gregarious, extroverted, and a raconteur with a remarkable gift of gab (ranging from Oxfordian English to down-home Southern dialect). Carter's skills were both analytical and written, combined with a discipline and commitment that carried him through the long nights at the office. Carter eventually began to realize that he had become a serious player and not just a second fiddle to Marshall. As Carter's legal acumen and skills progressed and he matured into a major legal force within the civil rights community, he very naturally began to view himself differently from the novice who had received his big break from the NAACP's legal giant. With no patience for intra-office politics and convinced that his only concern was performing the legal work that he did so well, Carter was probably unaware of the change in his overall persona. Nor did Marshall ever confront him directly to voice any dissatisfaction.[8]

However this might have manifested itself in their relations, Carter had a pivotal friend in court—Marshall's first wife, Vivian, known to her friends as Buster—who became a big sister to Carter and whose pillow talk regularly reassured Marshall that not only was Carter loyal to him but also that Marshall needed him very much. Suddenly, in

1955, Buster contracted cancer and, within a few months, passed away. In the following years, the relationship between Marshall and Carter deteriorated further, though Carter insists even today that he was not aware of the widespread perception among the staff that one was obligated to take sides in this schism. With no friend in court, Carter was more vulnerable than ever. At this juncture, a few fellow lawyers carried tales to Carter of Marshall's alleged negative assessments of him, at which Carter periodically erupted and sent the messenger back with a few well-chosen epithets. In the years that followed, Carter came to appreciate that these self-appointed Iagos were deliberately exacerbating the tension between the two top civil rights lawyers in black America, probably in order to advance their own careers.[9]

Carter had argued three of the five cases that ultimately came before the Supreme Court and were later known as *Brown v. Board of Education*, so it was natural that he would come to expect greater public visibility and recognition than that previously accorded him. It is likely that Marshall began to wonder how ambitious Carter had become. The civil rights and legal communities were already acknowledging that Carter himself had originated the concept that the social harm done to black children in segregated schools was in itself unconstitutional; and that he was the original proponent of the notion that sociological evidence could be amassed to persuade the Supreme Court that segregated schools were inherently unconstitutional. By opening the door to this combination of sociological, historical, political, economic, and anthropological evidence, he was to begin a new era in which these factors were weighed by each successive Court in determining the rights and welfare of the majority of Americans. The impact on the texture of U.S. life from this pioneering strategy is still being felt.

The backgrounds of these two men were very different. Marshall had grown up in Baltimore, then still a full-fledged component of the old South. He had learned to survive through a studied deference combined with fast-talking humor—in low-down Southern dialect, when advantageous. In his relations with powerful whites, he played the game with great finesse, telling them what they expected to hear rather than what he or other Negroes actually thought. (The game was and is known as "jiving.") He revered the law and sought to comply with it while he tried to change specific laws to conform to the U.S. Constitution, which to him was the ultimate law. He was a heavy-drinking, card-playing, earthy, and garrulous man with a sizable appetite for life. Wherever he went, Negroes idolized him in a manner never experienced by Walter White, Roy Wilkins, or their successors.

Carter, by way of contrast, was slender of build, academic in manner, and very much the product of a Northern upbringing. He deferred to no one, even as early as high school in New Jersey, when he refused to accept the school's policy segregating its swimming pool. His college degree was earned at the all-Negro Lincoln University in Pennsylvania, after which he graduated from Howard Law School and Columbia University. His experiences in the U.S. armed forces during World War II, where he challenged the Army's segregationist practices, contributed to his independent thinking and to his skepticism that the law stood above all else. It required a background such as this to develop a legal theory based on evidence from the social sciences and history. It required a background such as this to recommend later on—when Southern courts ordered the NAACP to turn over its membership rolls to state authorities—that these court orders be defied for the greater good of African Americans. Where Marshall was a loud-voiced, whiskey-drinking extrovert, Carter had developed into a soft-spoken gourmet and wine maven whose greatest delight was a night at the Metropolitan Opera. One could argue that these opposites complemented each other; others might insist they were the living contradictions of each other.

In 1957, in conjunction with the separation of the LDF from its parent, the NAACP selected Carter to become its first general counsel. At the time, Marshall reassured Carter that the new assignment would not change a thing in their relationship. In fact, Carter's office remained within the LDF's suite on West 43rd Street after the LDF had moved from the NAACP headquarters at Freedom House on West 40th Street a year earlier. By this juncture, Carter recollects, the tenor of their relationship had begun to alter substantively. The close, symbiotic relationship between Marshall and Carter began to cool.

In 1958, Marshall remarried. His new wife was called Gloria; she was an LDF staff member who was not a partisan (or opponent) of Carter's. The following year, as Carter was preparing to leave for a London vacation with his wife, Marshall handed him a sealed envelope which, he instructed, was not to be opened until the Carters had reached their destination. Robert Carter waited until the plane had reached its maximum altitude and was cruising across the Atlantic before reading Marshall's note. It stated briefly that since their relationship was no longer "viable," Marshall instructed Carter to leave the LDF's offices and move back into the NAACP headquarters proper. The substance of the letter, Carter later said, came as no surprise to him, although he had thought at the time that Marshall ought to have had the courage to tell him this to his face. On his return, Carter moved back to the association's headquarters at Freedom House on West 40th Street; he remained the full-time general counsel to the NAACP.[10] He came to the conclusion that there was life after serving as Thurgood Marshall's deputy.

Marshall continued as director/counsel of the LDF until President Kennedy tapped him to be a federal appellate court judge in 1961. While awaiting congressional approval for his appointment, Marshall alone selected white attorney Jack Greenberg to succeed him as the Legal Defense Fund's director/counsel. The decision was then ratified by the LDF's trustees, now independent of the NAACP and not elected even indirectly by the black communities around the nation.[11] Roy Wilkins and NAACP Board Chairman Bishop Stephen Gill Spottswood also agreed to Greenberg's appointment, according to Carter.[12]

Despite the inevitable tension that would color the relationship between the two legal groups carrying the NAACP's initials in future years, they both maintained the Houston/Marshall/Carter tradition of high professional standards and unparalleled commitment to the advancement of Negro Americans. Under Carter, who became a federal judge in 1972; his successor, Nathaniel Jones, who became a federal appeals judge in 1977;[13] and Thomas Atkins, who came up from the ranks as a student and then an adult NAACP leader in Boston, the NAACP legal department became the organization's proudest jewel. The younger associates were renowned for their zeal and competence as they expanded the scope of the association's legal forays into employment, housing, voter rights, gerrymandering, suburban zoning, veteran's rights, and free speech exercises while launching a new nationwide onslaught against *de facto* school segregation in almost every state outside the South, a decade after the *Brown* decision.

Robert Carter began to shape a cohesive new legal strategy after it became clear that the Legal Defense Fund was investing most of its resources in the school desegregation fight throughout the South. The seeds of this new strategy—an assault on the segregated schools *outside* the traditional South—actually went back to the early part of the 1950s, before the NAACP attorneys had begun to distinguish between Southern and non-Southern school cases. In 1951, when Marshall hired June Shagaloff as one of the first two program field workers in the Association's history, her first assignment was to research and analyze the school system in Amityville, a town on New York's Long Island. Earlier, the NAACP legal department had filed a suit in federal court challenging the town's proposed site for a new junior high school. Breaking ground as she proceeded, Shagaloff pored through the local board of education records from 1920 to 1951. The payoff was almost total: She unearthed so many blatant instances of the school board's use of race, as the sole basis for pupil assignments and school site selections, that the local board, upon being presented with its history, promptly agreed to change the site of the new junior high school (to the benefit of minority students) and to desegregate its elementary schools. After the school board agreed to adopt Shagaloff's plan to desegregate its elementary schools, the NAACP withdrew its suit.[14]

The NAACP had not previously challenged local or state laws that required segregated schools—the so-called *de jure* form of segregation. Instead, the NAACP's lawyers had uncovered and proven that in fact the school board of Amityville, on its own initiative, had collectively decided to segregate its students by such devices as assigning white pupils to one school and black pupils to another, or by locating a new school in a neighborhood which was virtually all-white or all-black. Because no local or state law required the board to segregate in this way, its practice came to be known as *de facto* segregation. Thus almost every case brought in the South resulted from strict state and/or local laws requiring segregation, whereas almost every case brought in the North was a result of deliberate practice or custom and not required by local and/or state laws. The methods of proof in the South, especially after *Brown,* were clear-cut because the racially motivated laws remained on the books until the very end of the era. In the North, more imagination and unconventionality became necessary if NAACP attorneys were to develop the legally effective forms of proof that would persuade juries and judges that black students were being segregated unconstitutionally.

Shagaloff, trained as a social scientist, played a critically important role in helping the NAACP's lawyers to craft strategies that would be persuasive in court. After the Amityville victory, Marshall assigned her to investigate and evaluate the segregated schools in communities across southern Illinois, a hotbed of the Ku Klux Klan. From the beginning, the situation was explosive, so much so that the Cairo, Illinois, branch of the NAACP pleaded with the national office for immediate assistance to end the segregated school system, in which all of the black students attended certain schools and all of the whites others. The system alarmingly mirrored those in Mississippi or Alabama.

At the same time, Shagaloff investigated similar conditions in Alton, East St. Louis, Centralia, Mt. Vernon, and Carbondale, all in the same region. In the winter of 1952, after the NAACP made the decision to demand the end of segregation not only in the schools but also public accommodations, transportation, and public housing in Cairo, Shagaloff returned to that city to assist the local NAACP branch in an all-out campaign. She and the local leadership immediately encountered an outbreak of racial violence, apparently led by local white town officials. The homes of NAACP leaders were bombed, several were shot at by anonymous individuals, and, finally, the segregationist town police arrested the NAACP's local leaders, several black parents seeking desegregated schools for their children, and Shagaloff herself, a total of eight individuals. They were charged with "disturbing the peace and dignity of the people of Illinois."

All except Shagaloff were freed on bail after they posted property bonds. Since she did not reside in Illinois, Shagaloff owned no property there and thus remained in jail. Thurgood Marshall lost no time in flying from New York to St. Louis, then to Cape Giradeaux, from which he drove to Cairo to negotiate Shagaloff's release. He persuaded the local judge to accept a property bond from a resident black peddler, Mr. Enix Mason, on Shagaloff's behalf, and she was finally permitted to leave.[15]

During the entire confrontation between the town's white officials and the local NAACP, Illinois Governor Adlai Stevenson rejected requests from the NAACP's state and local units for an immediate investigation of the violence. He even refused to assign state police to the town to prevent further violence, ending up sending one black state policeman to Cairo near the end of the confrontation.[16] Only months prior to Stevenson's nomination as the Democratic Party's 1952 presidential candidate, the NAACP was receiving a candid preview of his core attitudes on race.

The NAACP did file a school desegregation suit in federal court, but before it could be heard, the town of Cairo took the bull by the horns and peacefully desegregated not only the schools but also restaurants, movies, buses, and other public accommodations. A year later, *Time* magazine observed:

> When the NAACP went into action in Cairo, in southern Illinois, in the winter of '52 to fight segregation in the schools, some citizens decided to take the law into their own hands. One band of whites lit a cross on the levee, another fired a shotgun at the house of a Negro dentist, and still another tossed a dynamite bomb into a Negro physician's backyard. But, in spite of such hooliganism, Negro children began enrolling in white schools. In the last year there have been a few fist fights, but gradually Cairo is learning to take some kinds of desegregation in stride. For the first time, Negroes have begun to appear at meetings of the P.T.A.[17]

Other local NAACP units began to clamor for assistance from the national office to compel their local officials to desegregate the schools. In late 1952 and for several months into the following year, Marshall sent Shagaloff to southern New Jersey and Pennsylvania to advise local leaders on how to go about achieving desegregation. The NAACP was becoming adept at the utilization of a combination of weapons: court suits or threats of suits, local agitation, publicity, recruitment of local allies among white and black residents, especially clergymen and business leaders, strikes by school children, marches downtown by concerned parents, and so on. When several counties in southern Delaware were targeted for a major suit by Marshall, he assigned Shagaloff to that region for several months to prepare the local NAACP leadership and the black community for the pressures they were to face as the suit moved successfully (and fairly rapidly) through the state courts to the Supreme Court, where it was merged with four others to become

Brown v. Board of Education.[18] (Another of the five cases—the famous *Brown* case itself—attacked the segregated schools in Topeka, Kansas, which was also considered non-South.) Most of these suits, including the pre–Supreme Court arguments in Delaware, were formulated by Robert Carter. Not yet consciously labeling them as such, Carter was evolving a courtroom approach to *de facto* school segregation in the North, Midwest, and West, in no small part based on Shagaloff's field experiences. The largest effort took place in New York City's Brooklyn and Bronx in 1953, when Shagaloff was assigned by Marshall to aid the local branches in those boroughs to attack discriminatory pupil assignment, school zoning, and site selection—devices that most often accompanied non-South school segregation (but which were later copied by resistant Southern school systems).

Dr. Kenneth Clark and his psychologist partner and wife, Dr. Mamie Clark, had for several years demonstrated that the pupil assignment policies of many New York City schools were discriminatory in tests conducted by their Harlem-based Northside Center for Child Development, the first child development institution founded by Negroes. In a dramatic challenge to these policies, Dr. Clark and June Shagaloff organized the local New York City NAACP branches and the local Urban League unit to sponsor a citywide conference entitled "Children Apart." In response to the embarrassing allegations made at the conference, the New York City board of education appointed a "Committee on Integration."[19]

A year later, when the board had failed to rectify its own municipal shortcomings and on the heels of the May 17 decision of the Supreme Court in *Brown,* Dr. Clark and Shagaloff mobilized the NAACP and the Urban League of New York to call a second conference—"Children Together"—to pressure the board, but again they had no success. In 1955 race-based student assignments, zoning practices, and feeder patterns to a Brooklyn junior high school were exposed by the NAACP, and they escalated into an explosive citywide controversy, leading to a variety of further initiatives that sought to compel the school board to change its racially motivated assignment practices. These NAACP initiatives included professional conferences, mass petitions, and street demonstrations.[20]

It was not until the 1960s that black parents succumbed to the idea that the NYC board of education would never reform the system and forbid discriminatory practices while raising educational standards. Open conflict erupted throughout the city school system as minority parents defied the authority of the school board and the political establishment, disrupting classes and surrounding affected schools. Spurred on by a new generation of local leaders, including a few demagogues, the minority parents turned their anger against the teachers' union as well, demanding school decentralization on the premise that local control by the parents could compel the reforms that the citywide board of education and the United Federation of Teachers had resisted.

With its national headquarters in New York City, the NAACP leadership was intimately aware of the nature of these conflicts and of the issues involved. They fully appreciated the potential for similar outbreaks in cities across the nation unless they could begin to meet the aspirations of Negro parents long frustrated by the dual school system practices that not only continued to separate black children from white but also failed to provide a decent level of education. The NAACP's ability to forge a broad and effective campaign to attack school segregation in the non-South cities was clearly to become a priority of the highest magnitude. It was impelled in part by rapidly moving events and in part by a renewed sense of mission.

It received a taste of what was to come in nearby New Rochelle, a suburb less than a half hour from New York City by commuter train. Long a bedroom community for professionals and executives in Manhattan, New Rochelle had, during the 1950s experienced a gradual influx of African Americans, initially as domestics and other servants to the more affluent white majority. Eventually a sizable downtown Negro enclave grew from these modest beginnings, with an economic system of support services and shops as well as churches and clubhouses.

The response of the town fathers was to devise a segregated system of education for the children of the Negro help in this town, which paradoxically had been founded by Huguenots fleeing from religious oppression in France. The antiquated and largely unrepaired Lincoln School in downtown New Rochelle had for many years been assigned the role of the Negro elementary school; black youngsters seeking admission to the white schools were systematically rejected. Spurred on by NAACP branch activists, Negro parents began to protest publicly the segregation of their children in the public school system. Calling for a referendum, the town fathers proposed both to tear down the antiquated Lincoln School and to build a new school on the same site, presumably to perpetuate the segregated system. The referendum was passed. Then the NAACP branch and the parents hired a lawyer, Paul Zuber, to challenge the system in federal court. The NAACP parents also attempted to place 13 black children in the white schools to test the intentions of the school board. All the children were rejected. They then employed a series of sit-down demonstrations, which served to focus considerable publicity on New Rochelle, none of it favorable.

The NAACP was largely ignored in the substantial and growing media coverage of the federal trial, in which attorney Zuber's articulate and dramatic performance made excellent visual copy. During 1960 and early 1961, when the controversy was at its height and the trial had reached its climax, in the words of June Shagaloff, the NAACP national office was floundering without an articulated policy on the growing number of non-South school crises.[21] Negro communities throughout the North and Midwest, frustrated by their own encounters with segregated and second-rate educational facilities for their children, were taking a lesson from their Southern brethren. A new militancy began to arise throughout the ghettoes of the Northern and Midwestern urban centers, which had grown much since the beginning of the migration that was spurred initially by World War II. By 1960 a sizable proportion of the African-American population—between 33 and 40 percent—had left the South, largely for the big cities of the North, the Midwest, and the West. These new demographics began to be reflected in the composition of the NAACP's own membership. While Southerners still were the majority of the association's members, they were no longer as dominant as they had been in the past. The Midwest membership was growing rapidly, followed by the Northeast and the Mid-Atlantic. These changes would produce new political demands to which the Wilkins leadership, including his board and staff, would have to adjust in order to retain power.

Then on January 24, 1961, almost at the same moment that John F. Kennedy was being inaugurated, a federal district court ordered the New Rochelle public schools to desegregate. Almost like a hurtling rocket, the struggle undertaken by the Negro community of New Rochelle, the participation of the local branch, and the favorable court decision exploded into the consciousness of Negroes throughout the urban North and Midwest. The best that the national office could do at this juncture was to send a congratulatory letter over Wilkins's signature to the local branch president, warning that the court decision would "have only symbolic value unless it is implemented in good faith by the New Rochelle Board of Education." Wilkins urged the board to "move promptly and in full accord with the spirit of the decision." He suggested that the board would find "invaluable the constructive support and cooperation of all of the parents, Negro and white, whose children make up the present Lincoln School population."[22]

What is most illuminating about this communication from Wilkins is what it does not say: there is, for example, no offer of support, in technical advice, legal assistance, or funds to help the branch, totally composed of volunteers, to monitor and pressure the board for full implementation. There is no suggestion by Wilkins that the national office was considering a policy outside the South to pursue school desegregation. At this juncture in the early days of 1961, Wilkins and his colleagues were focused elsewhere as a new, young, and reputedly liberal president of the U.S. was taking office in Washington, D.C.

However, the focus of the NAACP's grassroots was largely on itself after six difficult years struggling to implement *Brown* in the South in the face of renewed violence and widespread hostility. Paradoxically, the NAACP branches and members throughout the rest of the nation —and especially in the great urban centers of the Midwest and Northeast—were expressing their dissatisfaction that the organization was still investing almost all of its resources on the blatant racial injustices of the South. Demands among the non-Southern branches were growing for a greater allocation of staff and funds to the large metropolitan areas of the North, Midwest, and West. By July 1961, the voice of the membership was heard loud and clear in the annual convention in Philadelphia: The delegates overwhelmingly demanded that the NAACP intensify its national and branch activity to attack segregated school systems nationwide.

In 1960 June Shagaloff had persuaded Wilkins's Deputy Director, Dr. John Morsell, that the NAACP should explore a broadscale campaign to desegregate public school systems outside the South. After the outburst of delegate support for this course at the July 1961, convention, Morsell received the go-ahead from Wilkins and in September, 1961 he hired Shagaloff as the NAACP's first special assistant for education, a title later changed to education secretary. In a paraphrase of the convention resolution, she was charged specifically with launching the new campaign to "end . . . all segregated education in fact or by law by all means available."[23] By this point, General Counsel Robert L. Carter was well along in his development of the legal theories and strategies that would underpin such an initiative. Together, they began a collaboration that was to lead to one of the NAACP's most important achievements.

The LDF, meanwhile, was expanding its efforts throughout the South to implement *Brown* against region-wide and often ferocious resistance. For the most part, the LDF had carried the huge burden of implementing the Court's 1955 "all deliberate speed" order in the border and Deep South states. Political and other civic leaders in those states demonstrated alarming resilience and imagination in coming up with new pseudo-doctrines and strategies designed to thwart the Court's intentions in *Brown,* including the broad-based defense of states rights followed by the doctrine of massive resistance. For the most part representing NAACP local branches, the LDF battled in the courts throughout the South to overcome widely popular efforts to circumvent the Supreme Court's rulings, by now accepted outside the South as the law of the land. Backing these various resistance measures were not only the legally constituted local law authorities and populist governors like George Wallace, Ross Barnett, Orville Faubus, and Lester Maddox, associated with the patently illegal violence committed by the white-robed Ku Klux Klan, but also the quasi-respectable though equally nefarious White Citizens Councils. These councils were financed and supported by some of the South's so-called respectable citizens, including businessmen, professionals, academics, and journalists. Local NAACP branches from Louisville and Memphis to as far South as Miami, New Orleans, Birmingham, and Jackson became the front lines of the massive battles that were taking place simultaneously, stretching the resources and personnel of both the NAACP and the LDF to the breaking point.

As the LDF's leading education specialist during the 1950s, June Shagaloff had been assigned to cities throughout the South shortly after the *Brown* decision was handed down (for most of 1954 and 1955) to help black parents and NAACP branches to challenge what they deemed to be ineffective or token school desegregation plans after the Brown decision. At the same time, she patiently aided the local leadership in pressing for more effective plans, many of which were eventually accepted by the federal judges presiding over these cases. Her work in the South took her to Nashville, Tennessee; Charlottesville, Virginia; Atlanta, Georgia; and the Texas cities of Dallas, Houston, and Corpus Christi, to name just a few. This fieldwork played an important role in the Association's acceptance of and later demand for professional field workers in a variety of disciplines besides education, such as voter education, employment, housing, and urban affairs. Local branches came to appreciate that the most effective form of assistance from the national office was the expertise and advice that such experienced and trained field personnel could offer them to solve local problems. By the mid-1960s the NAACP was to find the resources to apply these lessons broadly in assisting local branch leaders, almost all of whom were volunteers, to become even more effective change agents in their communities.[24]

Under Jack Greenberg's leadership, the LDF attracted widespread financial and media support throughout the North, Midwest, and Far West, generating more than a dozen local sponsoring committees between Boston and Princeton in the East and Los Angeles and Denver in the West. The committees attracted committed whites, for the most part, together with a small number of upper-income blacks, providing sizable gifts to expand the struggle to implement *Brown* in the South. As the principal tax-deductible civil rights vehicle during the 1950s and early 1960s, the LDF had established strong relationships with those foundations, large and small, that had become important players in the civil rights struggle. For the most part, they remained LDF partisans, especially as a result of intensive personal and professional cultivation by LDF's director/counsel, Jack Greenberg.

Greenberg remained at the helm of the LDF for almost a quarter of a century, expanding its activities into such controversial areas as welfare rights, poverty law, equal job opportunities, and a long-standing campaign against capital punishment. He also endeavored to become the legal counsel for the entire civil rights movements, gestures toward which had already been made by Thurgood Marshall between 1957 and 1961. Greenberg no doubt perceived the advantages of cultivating such people as Martin Luther King Jr., the Freedom Riders of Congress on Racial Equality (CORE), and the courageous semiguerrilla tactics of Student Non-Violent Coordinating Committee (SNCC). Empathetic whites, already guilt-ridden by the daily televised dangers faced by civil rights workers from the NAACP and the other organizations and, for the most part, mistakenly believing that the LDF was still organically connected to the NAACP but simply providing a tax write-off alternative for their gifts, rallied to the LDF. The old-line wealth that had been assiduously recruited since LDF's founding in 1939, including most of the wealthy Jewish supporters, also chose to remain with the LDF after the two agencies separated. Whites, including many Jews, were generously represented in the LDF's leadership and board, which no doubt raised the comfort level of the donors and encouraged them to attend LDF parties, luncheons, and dinners.

At the same time, the LDF downplayed its separation from the NAACP, continuing throughout the 1960s to publish photos of Wilkins and other NAACP leaders in its annual reports. The LDF also continued to represent NAACP branches, especially in school desegregation suits, even when denied permission by the national office of the NAACP to do so.[25] Wilkins was completely aware of these activities and chose to tolerate them.

The underlying issue between the two organizations had earlier been articulated in 1960 by intellectuals like Dr. John Morsell, Wilkins's respected and trusted deputy, and by General Counsel Robert L. Carter. They understood that the NAACP's national board of directors was then the only secular legislative body democratically chosen by rank-and-file black Americans organized within several thousand local branches in virtually every black community in America. Each year one-third of the 64 board members turned over, so that fresh grassroots expressions of policy were possible annually. That board, imperfect as the selection process might be, was still the most widely representative body of African Americans in the nation, based on geography, class, income, education, age, political persuasion, religious affiliation, and so on. Its three or four full board meetings a year were attended by 80 percent or more of its members. For the most part, getting elected to the board required having a sizable constituency within the association, especially during the last two decades. It had become extremely difficult, indeed almost impossible, for an unknown without a constituency to win election. As the number of leaders increased whose ambitions had risen high enough to seek National Board membership, the number of outside celebrities, largely white, declined precipitously. By contrast, during the NAACP's first 50 years, prominent whites like Eleanor Roosevelt, Herbert H. Lehman, Joseph Rauh, Karl Menninger, and Walter Reuther were board fixtures. By 1994, when the NAACP faced its foremost crisis, only three whites remained on the 64-member board, and one of them was Walter Reuther's successor four times removed—the then current leader of the United Auto Workers.[26]

The LDF's independent course was in no way determined by the orderly expression of the will of African Americans as institutionalized within the structure of the NAACP, with its broadly elected board of directors (and their elected executive committee between board meetings) and its annual convention of delegates elected locally each spring by the entire branch membership throughout its 2,500 branches and youth and student chapters.

The NAACP regularly holds one of the nation's five largest annual conventions; each year between 1965 and 1995 the NAACP conventions drew between 3,000 and 6,000 elected delegates and alternates every July. Meeting in convention, these delegates had the power to determine every aspect of policy, structure, and program. Through these mechanisms, the majority views of the nation's African Americans came to be articulated annually (as well as periodically at board meetings throughout each year). If the U.S. political system prevented African Americans from fully determining their own destiny, then through most of the twentieth century the NAACP at least (and probably alone) had provided the best mechanism, which in turn determined the strategies and initiatives that the majority of black Americans would undertake and support.[27]

The LDF, on the other hand, has always been a public interest law firm specializing in civil rights for African Americans. Its only members are its legally constituted board of directors, roughly 48 men and women, who perpetuate themselves by nominating and electing the board's composition. In effect, they select each other. Among them are some of the brightest and most committed men and women in the civil rights struggle, but few of them have an institutional connection to any grassroots constituency, which, of course, provides LDF with enormous freedom of action and flexibility. It can decline a case, regardless of the merits, because no grassroots membership in (say) Mississippi demands that it help. It can choose to fight on an issue of little impact on the total African-American community, such as capital punishment. It can experiment with an idea and discard it if it does not prove advantageous in the courts or financially, such as the campaign to expand welfare rights and services. And it can continue to exploit its earlier antecedents with the NAACP, 50 years after the two entities had separated. These were the real underlying differences that resulted in a prominent court battle later on, when the NAACP sought unsuccessfully to compel the LDF to drop the use of its initials.

Nor should one hold against the LDF its lack of accountability to an institutionalized constituency. Virtually all of the players in the civil rights and civil liberties fields (as well as the National Urban League) are similarly structured—their legal members are their boards of directors and these boards are self-perpetuating. They have no other authority to which they must report and account for their actions, except in strictly defined ways to the IRS, state regulators, and major foundation and corporate donors. Among these public interest law firms are the Lawyer's Committee for Civil Rights Under Law; the Mexican, Puerto Rican, and Asian-American Legal Defense and Educational Funds; the Natural Resources Defense Council; the NOW Legal Defense Fund; the Indian Law Resources Center; and the Lambda Legal Defense Fund.

Most of these are highly effective firms acting for a specific segment of the public, but they should not be confused with the NAACP, which first conceived the idea of a tax-deductible public interest law firm in 1939 (that went on to win *Brown)*. More significantly, for most of the twentieth century, the NAACP had been the nation's premier grassroots citizens, change agent, using the courts as one of its primary vehicles, but buttressing its legal efforts with pressure by organized citizens, almost all of whom were black, at every level of the political structure as well. To this day no other ethnic or racial group has been able to construct an apparatus of local chapters and members on the scale and with the level of effectiveness of the NAACP—not the B'nai Brith Anti-Defamation League, not La Raza of the Mexican-American community, not the Italo-American Anti-Defamation League, not Aspira, which serves Puerto Ricans, nor any other racial or ethnic group. Perhaps this is because no segment of the U.S. population (other than Native Americans, who still rely more on tribal mechanisms than on outside activity) has had such an extensive and long history of oppression and unfulfilled aspirations as have Americans of African descent.

Until the 1960s, virtually every civil rights case involving African Americans was litigated by the NAACP or its subsidiary, the LDF. As Robert L. Carter noted recently, at no time did the NAACP possess enough funds or personnel to undertake all of the legitimate civil rights cases presented to its legal staffs during its first half century.[28] The NAACP lawyers were always practicing a form of triage by deciding who among the many calling upon them would be represented in court.

By the Kennedy and Johnson years—with half a dozen activist national agencies and scores of local agencies agitating for racial justice, followed by a prolonged period of congressional legislation in voting rights, education, employment, housing, and public accommodations—the number of legal cases grew astronomically, and the number of cases for which there were no resources was even larger. By the end of the 1960s, there was simply not enough money or personnel to represent the majority of legitimate rights cases springing up almost daily. Together, the NAACP and the LDF could not respond to more than a fraction of the demands on them. Formation of the Lawyer's Committee for Civil Rights Under Law, the Southern Poverty Law Center, and some regional rights law centers, together with occasional forays into civil rights by the ACLU and its civil rights subsidiary, could not make much more than the slightest dent in the backlog.

There is no question that, a decade earlier, hard feelings, both political and personal, had resulted from the LDF's decision to select Greenberg to succeed Marshall. Yet both sides, and their partisans, refused to permit the controversy to interfere with their civil rights work or to prevent collaboration between the two entities, when events demanded it.

Moreover, Carter—after returning physically to the NAACP's headquarters as the Association's General Counsel—put aside his disappointment and channeled his emotions into a new approach. He began to formulate and then create a new and formidable NAACP legal department, now that the LDF was independent of the NAACP. To fund it, completely on his own initiative, Carter devised a groundbreaking approach to the Internal Revenue Service, arguing that tax deductibility was warranted for that portion of the NAACP's programs that were inherently educational or charitable. In the past, a nonprofit was either fully tax-deductible or not at all. Now, Carter wrote, the IRS under the law and its own regulations had the power and the obligation to accord tax-deductible status for those functions that inherently merited such status, while continuing to rule that the remainder of the organization's programs and activities were denied that status because they comprised lobbying, political activities, and so forth. Under Lyndon B. Johnson's administration, the IRS agreed with Carter's premises and approved the NAACP's application in March 1964, enabling it to establish the NAACP Special Contribution Fund (SCF) as a wholly owned subsidiary of the NAACP national office with the capacity to accept tax-deductible gifts and grants from foundations and corporations.

Carter then presented the IRS decision to Wilkins as a *fait accompli.* He later recalled that Wilkins was far from enthusiastic about the new IRS ruling. With the schism caused by the departure of the LDF fresh in his mind, Wilkins was determined that this new tax-deductible entity would never be able to run off on its own. To overcome Wilkins's reluctance, Carter organized the new entity so that its trustees were appointed annually by the NAACP national board. To attract foundation and corporate funding, virtually all the NAACP's programs, including those based upon litigation, were placed under the SCF's umbrella, thereby enjoying tax-deductible status. Thus the NAACP could now seek foundation, corporate, and large individual gifts on an equal footing with the LDF, the National Urban League, and other nonprofits.[29] The structure crafted by Carter also designated the NAACP's executive secretary (then Wilkins) as the corporate secretary of the SCF so that the latter could control both entities. Then in 1965 Carter began to recruit his own legal staff; by 1969 he was directing 11 of the most committed, talented, and experienced civil rights lawyers in the nation, all of whom were working for the NAACP.

Given the magnitude of the racial challenges before them, there was hardly any point to continuing earlier rivalries. Carter and Greenberg recognized that there was plenty of room for both the LDF and the NAACP to conduct their legal programs without their stepping on each other's feet. The same applied to some of the other public interest law firms. There was almost no friction, at least on the staff level, as the LDF continued to carry out its region-wide campaign to desegregate Southern schools. Meanwhile, with the rapid growth of new income from the Special Contribution Fund, the NAACP, under a strategy conceived by Robert Carter and substantially expanded by his successor, Nathaniel Jones, in 1970 launched a massive campaign to desegregate the public schools in the North, Midwest, and Far West. For the first time since before *Brown,* the NAACP could anticipate sufficient funding to launch such a grand campaign.

As the LDF continued to carry almost the entire burden of school desegregation cases throughout the South, Carter's legal department began to expand its outreach and staff, rapidly becoming a major courtroom player in the civil rights struggle. In theory, every one of the NAACP's 1500 to 2000 adult branches was obliged in the early 1960s to obtain approval from the NAACP legal department if it sought or required legal representation or assistance. In practice, the legal department chronically lacked the resources, including attorneys, to respond to one-fourth of the legitimate, even urgent, requests made of it. Not long after the LDF formally separated itself from the NAACP, a *modus operandi* of sorts evolved whereby the LDF continued as the primary litigant on behalf of school desegregation plaintiffs throughout the South—the so-called *de jure* cases—even when a local NAACP branch or its members were the plaintiffs.

Meanwhile, as the 1960s drew to a close, General Counsel Carter and Education Director Shagaloff expanded their attack against *de facto* school segregation in urban and suburban systems throughout the North, Midwest, and Far West. Based on the experience of the past decade, they combined community action with litigation to a degree unheard of previously. In city after city outside the South, the NAACP argued that, based upon *Brown,* state and local school officials were obliged by law to end as quickly as possible the racial segregation of their schools, regardless of the cause.

Simultaneously, NAACP staff and attorneys attacked the practices that resulted in segregated black schools that were overcrowded, underfunded, taught by inexperienced and incompetent teachers (often substitutes), and low in educational standards; moreover both teachers and administrators had low expectations. (The patterns described by the NAACP almost four decades ago have a highly contemporary ring in the year 2004.) These conditions were, on their face, unconstitutional as well, the NAACP charged, and subject to immediate remedy.[30] Between these two lines of attack, the NAACP had no choice but to fight both for maximum desegregation and for improved educational standards, school by school, where it was not possible in the foreseeable future to desegregate. No rigid ratios by race were proposed by the NAACP so long as school systems adopted measures to bring about further desegregation.

The arsenal of potential remedies possessed by the NAACP was substantial. If a school district was plagued by segregated residential patterns, the NAACP recommended rezoning school attendance areas to cut across or to divide segregated neighborhoods. If a segregated school district assigned different grades to different schools, the NAACP proposed what came to be known as the Princeton Plan—all children regardless of race would be in each grade level, with grades 1 to 3 in one school and grades 4 to 6 in another. In other school systems the NAACP proposed to desegregate by having three four-year schools, one for primary, one for intermediate, and one for senior high schools.

To thwart another growing practice that sustained racially segregated schools, the NAACP proposed to some districts that they reorganize their feeder patterns, which assigned grade school students to middle schools and middle school students to high schools. One of the most successful options that came into more frequent use in later decades, especially when school budgets were enhanced by the state and/or federal government, was the specialized or magnet school, which was permitted to draw students from a wider-than-normal area, and which offered desirable course concentrations, such as art, science, and computer skills. Such opportunities persuaded white parents to overcome their reluctance to send their children to school with African-American children because of the potential career rewards for their own children.

When a pattern of school site selections was determined to be the primary cause of segregation, the NAACP insisted that new criteria be adopted by the school board for future sites. In the most extreme cases, the NAACP proposed that an inferior school be closed and its students reassigned to schools with better records, or it pressed for recalcitrant school districts to merge with educationally superior ones.

The one option that the NAACP opposed, because it was the least effective, was the voluntary pupil transfer plan, or open enrollment. This was, not surprisingly, the most preferred option by white parents, especially when the major burdens fell on the shoulders of black children. Since most white parents made certain that the funding, plant, instruction, and educational materials, such as books, were more than satisfactory for their own children (and they possessed the income to pay for these), it was inevitable that the predominantly white school would be the magnet, instead of the poorly financed, run-down, and inferior black school. Thus, when a federal judge ordered that school transportation would be necessary to effect desegregation, the NAACP was often the only important institutional voice to argue that busing was simply a means to desegregate and not a plan in itself, that the real issue was the destination of the bus, since throughout the South and elsewhere it was common for white children to be bused longer distances past all-black schools every single school day. Nor was it uncommon throughout the North for white parents to demand more buses to expedite their children's transportation to school, so long as desegregation were not the issue. As the Reverend Jesse Jackson was later to declare in the face of white resistance to busing, "It's not the bus, it's us." In fact Chief Justice Warren Burger, in a 1967 landmark Supreme Court ruling that permitted busing to achieve desegregation, observed that each day about 40 million American children, mostly white, are bused to school without the slightest outcry.

Another line of attack by those who opposed school desegregation centered around the so-called neighborhood school. This became a code word for those parents who demanded that all-white schools be preserved and that the introduction of black children into them was somehow an assault on God, motherhood, morals, and the American Way. (In fact, each day millions of white children and others are assigned by their own school districts to schools that are not the closest to their residence.) In response, NAACP staff argued that neighborhoods were now defined by color and class, not by geography and distance from the nearest school. In any competition between desegregated schools and neighborhood preservation, the NAACP insisted, the Constitution only demanded desegregated schools.

To prepare its branch members with the know-how and understanding necessary to monitor their own local schools' practices and policies, the NAACP education department issued a running series of policy statements and guidelines, blueprints for local action, and manuals explaining how to examine the pupil assignment and school zoning practices. The members were taught how to approach school officials, how to formulate recommendations and demand changes, how to mobilize community support, and, in the face of resistance, how to organize protests, mass meetings, marches, boycotts, and picket lines, as well as when to initiate legal action.

With the cooperation of the branch department, which had made the school issue its top priority, throughout the 1960s Shagaloff worked with several hundred branches, counseling and providing technical assistance, as they moved to seek change. She and General Counsel Robert Carter undertook a coast-to-coast call to action, starting with a joint trip to the West Coast and the Southwest to spur branch activity on schools. They met with state commissioners of education in the North and West, and during the first half of the 1960s they persuaded statewide authorities—including educational commissioners, governors, and legislatures—to move to desegregate their schools in New York, California, New Jersey, Massachusetts, Connecticut, Illinois, and Indiana.

The NAACP campaign organized by its education department and run jointly with the legal department reached over 200 school systems, large and small, throughout the North, Midwest, and Far West during the 1960s and early 1970s. It reached into 18 states, including the border states of Delaware, Maryland, and Missouri, where segregated housing patterns were the most significant causes of segregated schools, despite their formal compliance with orders based on *de jure* segregation.[31]

Ultimately, the record of achievements of this phase of the NAACP's effort was, at best, mixed. A few school districts, recognizing the educational harm resulting from segregated schools regardless of cause, adopted district-wide plans either to end segregation or to reduce significantly its extent. A larger number of school systems simply adopted voluntary student transfer plans, the option that the

NAACP least preferred. Still other school systems established citizens' committees to study the NAACP's charges and to suggest reforms. Although a few of these committees actually proposed far-reaching desegregation plans, most proposed token recommendations that barely altered the segregated-school landscape. Lastly, a group of systems, in place of desegregation, adopted compensatory education programs for their predominantly black schools. Few major changes were accomplished by this massive NAACP effort, except that tens of thousands of grassroots members had become adept school activists and would in future years shoulder the major burdens of change advocacy in their own backyards.

By the late 1960s, however, it was apparent to the NAACP board and to Carter and Shagaloff that dismantling *de facto* school segregation outside the South would require the NAACP's use of its heaviest artillery—major and well-crafted litigation. This would become possible when some of the nation's most prestigious and wealthiest private foundations pledged to underwrite a major court campaign without any termination date in sight. Carter and his staff, using data and experiences derived from Shagaloff and her enhanced field staff, began the new phase by filing a dozen suits in the last years of the 1960s, but the major research and witness development was targeted for Detroit. With most of the brief-writing completed before Carter resigned in September 1968, his successor, Nathaniel Jones, was formally to file the first major *de facto* suit in 1969 against the school system of Detroit. That would launch yet another era in the rich legal legacy of the NAACP.

Now that the NAACP's legal staff had grown to 10 or more attorneys, with an equal number of support personnel, through the tax-deductible SCF, General Counsel Carter expanded the range of cases this staff was permitted to undertake until they covered almost every important aspect of civil rights, as well as defending the NAACP itself from litigation. With a full-fledged legal staff, the NAACP was no longer so dependent upon other public interest law firms, most pointedly the LDF, although General Counsel Carter had no desire to supplant the LDF's school desegregation cases in the South. However, protocol among sister nonprofit agencies, as well as NAACP national office rules, required that the LDF formally request permission from the NAACP in order to solicit plaintiffs from among NAACP branches or members. This, however, was honored more in the breach, as Jack Greenberg himself affirmed in his own memoir,[32] though most often cordial relations continued between the LDF and the NAACP staff, especially among the attorneys. On the other hand, the volunteer leadership—the national officers and board of directors of the NAACP—periodically took umbrage at the LDF. During the post–*Brown* decades, the best that could be said of the overall relationship between the two civil rights stalwarts was that it usually remained correct.[33]

Despite the underlying tensions between the NAACP and its former subsidiary, the record achieved by the LDF in the decades following *Brown* throughout the South was extraordinary. (In all fairness, the civil rights struggle received marginal assistance from other public interest entities, such as the ACLU Southern Office and the Lawyer's Committee for Civil Rights Under Law during the 1960s, but the LDF was the litigation heavyweight in the region during this period.) After winning its most important post-*Brown* victory, the 1971 decision which approved the use of busing to bring about desegregation in *Swann v. Charlotte-Mecklenberg School District of North Carolina*, the LDF was able to build on this ruling to persuade courts throughout the South to permit similar plans.[34] As a direct result, by the school year 1972–1973, 46.3 percent of the region's black public school students were attending schools in which the student majority was white. A few years later that figure exceeded 50 percent, the apex of racial school-desegregation progress, after which the mood of the nation and of the judiciary began to change for the worse.

The association's sister agency and closest institutional ally, the National Urban League, had been founded a year after the NAACP (1910) as a social welfare organization for city-dwelling Negroes. It was never a civil rights agency, although for about 15 years (from the early 1960s until the mid-1970s), its presidents, first Whitney Young and then Vernon Jordan, took part in the summit meetings of the national civil rights leaders. Whitney Young inserted himself by force of personality: an able negotiator, he used his position to bring the rival civil rights leaders together. He depended heavily on his clout with white moneyed interests, both major corporate leaders and wealthy individuals. Somehow, it was thought that he could deliver such interests to the civil rights cause when needed, but it rarely happened.

In any event, his organization's actual members never totaled more than 5,000, consisting solely of the board members of the more than one hundred local Urban Leagues. In all probability, the majority of these board members were local white corporate leaders, at best middle-of-the-roaders, but willing to give Whitney Young his head to see if order could be imposed on the natural chaos of five or six organizations competing for preeminence among the mass of black Americans. Programmatically, with the exception of a relatively modest voter registration/education campaign, the Urban League's efforts were restricted to social and economic initiatives, all quite serious and relevant but involving very modest numbers of individuals being intensively assisted and/or trained. The League's financial base was largely from business, with a smaller but important level of foundation support. In the late 1960s it began to experience a noticeable growth in, and eventual dependence upon, governmental grants and contracts, mostly federal. The League never succeeded in developing a grassroots base, either black or white.

Under Whitney Young, the National Urban League and a great many of its hundred-odd local units also became adept at generating sizable amounts of government funding so that when the worm turned under Ronald Reagan, about 80 percent of the National Urban League's income was dependent upon government funding. Reagan terminated this federal largesse, not the least because of the sharp criticisms he and his party had received from Vernon Jordan and his successor, John Jacobs. These massive funding reductions forced the Urban League to drastically curtail its program staff both at the national and at the local levels. Two decades later, the League had still not fully recovered from this wholesale retrenchment. (In 1998, it was compelled by financial pressures to sell its much-admired East River headquarters building adjacent to the United Nations, both of which were financed mostly by the Rockefeller family. The league then moved its headquarters to Washington, D.C.)

As Young's successor, Vernon Jordan himself possessed some strong civil rights credentials. Coming from the ranks of the NAACP, he served as field secretary in Georgia from 1961 to 1963 and gained both prominence and visibility there. He accompanied the first black students into the University of Georgia in 1961 before nasty, screaming crowds. One of those students was Charlene Hunter (now Gault) of PBS celebrity. From there Jordan moved on to become the director of the Voter Education Project (VEP), a subsidiary of the prestigious Rockefeller-backed Southern Regional Council, which had gradually evolved into a major force supporting change in the South. The Voter Education Project, a private fund encouraged by the Kennedy Justice Department and several wealthy Northerners to help finance voter registration in the South, became an independent entity several years later.

Thereafter, Jordan headed almost every short list of successors to Roy Wilkins, who was known to be especially fond of him.[35] His next promotion brought him to New York City in 1970 as executive director of the United Negro College Fund (UNCF). It was here that Vernon Jordan finally attained national exposure, considerable polish, and close ties to the nation's corporate leaders. His efforts helped the UNCF to grow substantially during that term of office as corporate America began to discover the nation's "invisible" population—black Americans. And, quite naturally, significant support to a college fund for deprived Americans, even black ones, would hardly generate many internal corporate fights or attacks from the shareholders. In short, giving to UNCF was safe yet positive, from the corporate point of view.

In 1972, Jordan was selected by the National Urban League Board (its only legal national members) to succeed Whitney Young, who had died suddenly from a heart attack while swimming in the Atlantic off an African beach. Now Jordan had reached the senior ranks of both black America and the civil rights movement; he inherited Whitney Young's mantle as a civil rights leader without a civil rights constituency, and he brought real civil rights experience to the table. Roy Wilkins never objected to the high-level roles played by either Whitney Young or Vernon Jordan, in part because they were close to him personally and in part because they almost always supported Wilkins's positions vis-à-vis the other civil rights leaders and organizations.

Moreover, while the Urban League in 1972 provided no competition to the NAACP for the latter's members or for its traditional financial support, later on the two organizations would compete head-to-head for corporate and foundation funding. But in the Wilkins era, that was still not a problem. More to the point, both Young and Jordan fully understood and deferred to the NAACP's preeminent role within the overall movement. This became increasingly important as

Dr. King's influence grew during the 1960s, along with that of CORE and SNCC, especially among younger activists.

By 1961, several new civil rights organizations had emerged to supplement and occasionally to challenge the NAACP. Dr. Martin Luther King Jr.'s ascension to the national stage, for example, came initially as a result of acts taken in 1955 by leaders of the NAACP's Montgomery (Alabama) branch, whose secretary was Rosa Parks, a 42-year-old married seamstress. When Mrs. Parks decided not to leave her seat at the front of the municipal bus and subjected herself to arrest, a veteran leader of the NAACP branch and a senior organizer for the Brotherhood of Sleeping Car Porters, E.D. Nixon, provided the initiative and strategy that produced the Montgomery Improvement Association (MIA), which organized the historic bus boycott.[36] In order to broaden support within the black community, E.D. Nixon persuaded the local black ministers to form this *ad hoc* group so that, through the pulpit, virtually every black resident of Montgomery could be reached without depending on white media or institutions. As the new boy on the block as pastor of a church in the downtown area, Dr. King, recently arrived in Montgomery, was drafted to lead the ministerial group (which later expanded to include secular members and white ministers and rabbis).

From the early days, the boycott proved successful, inadvertently aided and abetted as it was by the local Montgomery newspapers, which put on the front page the details and the names of the leaders, as well as the times and places for planned meetings. By so doing, they kept every local Negro informed to an extent that would have been impossible if undertaken solely by the boycott leaders. Early every morning, long processions of Negro domestic workers—cooks, gardeners, maids, drivers, nannies, and cleaning women who took care of the home life of white families, together with a much smaller number of Negroes employed elsewhere—traversed the main streets of Montgomery from the Negro neighborhoods to the white center, ignoring the municipal buses. Every night the procession was reversed. Without enough paying customers, the bus company was forced to shut down its four lines running through the black community. Wilkins and his national board decided to leave the direction and leadership of the boycott to the local leaders, so that the white supremacists could not argue that outside agitators were behind the campaign. He instructed the

NAACP field secretary for Alabama, a taciturn individual named W.C. Patton, to work with the Montgomery leadership.

Within weeks, the local leadership requested support, including funds, from the NAACP. However, Wilkins felt obliged to hold back because the initial demands made by the King-led MIA to the city government were, in the NAACP's opinion, simply too timid. In the early negotiations with the city's white leaders, Dr. King initially sought agreement for a highly moderate set of objectives: courteous behavior on the part of the white drivers towards black riders, the appointment of a few black bus drivers, and a new seating arrangement, with blacks who took the rear seats permitted to move forward on a first-come, first-served basis, while whites in the front seats would be permitted to move to the back. With the NAACP already having filed suit involving a similar bus case in South Carolina in which its lawyers were arguing an appeal calling for the complete abolition of segregation on the bus lines, Wilkins saw no way in which he could involve the national NAACP in such a moderate endeavor.

"I wrote Patton," Wilkins said in his autobiography, "that the NAACP could not enter the case or use its legal staff to support such a mild protest. The Montgomery Improvement Association seemed to be talking about improving segregation, making it more polite. The NAACP wanted to knock it out completely."[37]

Montgomery's white town fathers were incapable of digesting even this degree of timidity. Instead of exploring what common ground might exist, they decided to crack down hard on the boycott leaders, beginning with an epidemic of arrests and traffic tickets, followed by bombing of the homes of Dr. King and Mr. Nixon. The boycott's attorney, Fred Gray of the NAACP, was threatened with an indictment and disbarment, which prompted his draft board to remove his deferment as a part-time minister.

In response to these tactics, the NAACP finally provided some modest direct funding to the MIA, and Wilkins also agreed to assume the responsibility for all the legal work and costs incurred to defend every person rounded up by the city who was connected in any way with the bus boycott.[38] In addition, the NAACP took on the suit on behalf of Montgomery's black citizens to void the segregated bus system. General Counsel Robert Carter drafted the original suit for the MIA, seeking to overturn the state's laws requiring segregated seating on the local buses. The NAACP increased its national publicity mechanisms and media contacts to publicize the determined efforts of Montgomery's black citizens to thwart the public and private forces defending segregated buses. The tag line of the NAACP's successful efforts was an appeal for funds to underwrite the legal costs of the campaign.

When Dr. King wrote to Wilkins expressing concern that the NAACP's promotional activities were overshadowing those of the MIA nationally, Wilkins responded by pledging again to cover all the legal costs of those who had been arrested and jailed, the costs of the lawsuit challenging the state segregation laws, and the cost of Mrs. Parks's appeal. Wilkins wrote that the NAACP had assumed "the entire cost of the defense for those persons arrested and indicted and thus to relieve the MIA of a burden in that respect."

Wilkins also wrote to King that the NAACP expected to "carry the major part, if not the entire cost, of the bus segregation case challenging state law," which compelled segregated seating, adding that the NAACP anticipated that the case would have to be argued all the way to the Supreme Court. Lastly, Wilkins reiterated that "the NAACP would pay all the costs of the appeal of the Rosa Parks conviction." Because of rumors that King and his colleagues were questioning the way the NAACP was handling the funds it was raising for the Montgomery campaign (and the MIA no doubt feeling that it was entitled to a greater share than it had received), Wilkins also warned King in the same letter that the NAACP could not contribute towards the MIA's operating expenses except in an emergency. He also firmly warned King against any public hint of a rift between them over fundraising and what expenses the NAACP funds should cover.[39] It was an early example of the growing tensions between King and Wilkins and their respective staffs. A few years later the national press was writing about the schisms, but both men, despite such problems, continued to collaborate.

After a year of steadfast boycotting by the Negro community, which was constantly subjected to physical and legal harassment, Montgomery's municipal authorities refused to surrender or to compromise. Then in 1956 the U.S. Supreme Court determined that the state laws requiring segregated seating by race on public buses were unconstitutional and ordered the bus lines to be desegregated immediately, another historic case that was argued successfully by the NAACP's lawyers. Ultimately, "it was the NAACP's legal efforts," concluded the civil rights activist Julian Bond, "that integrated Montgomery's busses . . ., not the year-long bus boycott, which thrust young Martin Luther King into prominence."[40]

Capitalizing on his national prominence and the explosion of popular support for his nonviolent agenda, Dr. King decided to create his own national organization for civil rights, restricting membership to ministers, priests, and rabbis. A disaffected NAACP national staff member, Ella Baker, proved to be the invaluable King aide who actually pulled the organization together, but the chemistry between Dr. King, who viewed Baker as a mere secretary because of her gender, and the single-minded organizer who would not countenance any gender discrimination, led to the appointment of a male minister at the SCLC's top staff post.[41]

By 1957, with the NAACP's help and blessing, the Southern Christian Leadership Conference (SCLC) came into its own with Dr. King as its head. King had moved from Montgomery to Atlanta where he recruited a staff, mostly of able and committed black ministers, reflecting the vast majority of his membership. These included his old Montgomery friend, Reverend Ralph Abernathy, and some new ones whom he had met in seeking to expand the nonviolent influence of the Montgomery movement, such as Reverends Fred Shuttlesworth, Wyatt Tee Walker, and Andrew Young. Wilkins had always been uncomfortable around and impatient with the style and even the content of the rhetoric employed by most ministers, especially those who were Baptists; it usually clashed with his low-key, intellectual style. King and his circle were impatient with Wilkins's caution, his measured rhetoric, his insistence on the primacy of the NAACP and its vast organizational network, and its heavy reliance on the courts for social change. King and his lieutenants came to believe that they themselves had the answers to the long unresolved racial dilemma in America.

The Congress of Racial Equality (CORE), headed by former NAACP Program Director James Farmer, had long been a proponent of nonviolent change; in the late 1950s it had come of age as it refined its tactics of direct action. Even more militant than CORE and SCLC was the Student Nonviolent Coordinating Committee (SNCC), which had arisen out of the student sit-ins, the first of which emerged on February 1, 1960, in Greensboro, North Carolina, when four black students, all NAACP youth members from North Carolina A&T, decided to demand food service at the lunch counter of the local Woolworth's. Their example, eventually televised, spread like wildfire across the South and border states, attracting white student support from the rest of the nation as well as thousands of Southern black students who challenged the Jim Crow public accommodations laws. The vast majority were arrested, and massive legal and financial assistance wase needed. The NAACP drew down its reserves—over $2 million from life memberships—to provide bail to thousands of sit-in and other demonstrators. Like a broken record, scores of Southern judges sang the same refrain, fining these students amounts equivalent to the bail posted for them. The NAACP never recovered these sums.

Meanwhile, SNCC began to draw memberships from many of the NAACP's youth councils and college branches. During the 1960s, the more radical appeal pronounced by SNCC proved highly attractive to a few thousand younger activists, white and black. Wilkins and the NAACP board were quite happy to let SNCC siphon off the most militant youth from the Association's college chapters and youth councils. The adult branches in those communities, where local youth units had become more outspokenly militant, were for the most part ill-prepared to deal with this new generation of post-*Brown* young men and women who had seemingly failed to "learn their places" in the New South.

It served the NAACP's strategy quietly to support, financially and legally, the more strident and radical SNCC, because in the long run, when reality finally set in for local white Southern leaders, negotiating a settlement with the NAACP was almost a welcomed alternative to conducting talks with SNCC's leaders, who in the early days included James Foreman, Robert Moses, John Lewis, Julian Bond, and a young Angela Davis, before she broke with them to join the Communist Party in 1968. Like many young activists, the SNCC leadership found compromise difficult, demanding instead immediate social and political change.

At the same time, a much larger number of black youth, especially in the South, avoided involvement with SNCC and opted to remain active within the NAACP's ranks. At its peak, it is doubtful whether SNCC at any moment in time could count upon 2,000 adherents, including staff, volunteers, and members, whereas the NAACP's college and youth division numbered between 15 and 20 times that figure, and each was a paid member, albeit with modest dues.

Employing various deliberate techniques to ignite confrontations with Southern intransigence, SCLC, SNCC, and CORE required periodic cataclysms of a highly dramatic nature—dramatic enough to make the 6:30 P.M. network television news as well as the front pages of the dailies the next day—in order to continue generating support from liberals outside the South. None of these groups had the vast staying power and organizational base that the NAACP, after five decades, brought into the 1960s. Such cataclysms often produced direct challenges to local or state law enforcement, resulting in large numbers of arrests. These in turn required costly bail and courtroom representation later. They were excellent fundraising and public relations events, and more importantly, they helped greatly to inform the rest of the nation about the oppressive nature of the Jim Crow system and its brutality. Rarely did the income from these event-driven appeals cover the long-term legal costs, much of which were contributed to by the NAACP and the LDF.

Since none of the three new civil rights agencies possessed its own legal staff, Jack Greenberg, the new director/counsel, extended the LDF's mission to become, in its own view, the law firm for the entire civil rights movement. Wilkins never objected to this expanded role for the LDF and collaborated with Greenberg in defending a vast number of men and women arrested during the 1960s for challenging the Jim Crow laws. As already noted, Wilkins persuaded his board to use the NAACP's only reserves—its life membership dues—to post bail for many of those arrested, hundreds of whom came from other parts of the nation to show their solidarity with the victims of U.S. apartheid. The new organizations challenged the NAACP for the support of contributors (mostly white) outside the South and for the loyalties of the black masses, North and South. Thus the NAACP's virtual monopoly (as the main U.S. civil rights organization) was quite suddenly altered within a short time. The more confrontational the tactics became (and the more violent), the greater the media coverage was generated by CORE, SNCC, and SCLC, to which monetary contributions sharply increased. Nevertheless, the movement's overall muscle still came from the NAACP, with its 2,000-odd local units and its membership of half a million. All the other civil rights groups together could not account for 50,000 followers, including duplicates, throughout the1960s, about one-tenth the NAACP's membership during the peak years of that decade.

Jack Greenberg and the LDF understood these realities; they had no intention of severing their identification with the NAACP, which was still the best known and most respected agency in the field.[42] During the 1960s the LDF prominently displayed its NAACP identification as the *NAACP* Legal Defense and Education Fund. Later on, when NAACP leaders began to express anger over the dual claims, the LDF experimented with identifications that played down the association with the NAACP. At other times, it broadcast the connection as loudly as possible. It tended to use whichever approach produced the most revenue at the time; until the NAACP's catastrophic collapse in 1993–4, there was no question that linking the LDF to the NAACP proved to be the most lucrative approach. It should be noted that Roy Wilkins, a former newspaperman, always believed that the NAACP received much of the credit for the achievements of the LDF, since the newspapers covering a case won by the LDF always included the NAACP identification and, once in a while, simply described the LDF's attorneys as NAACP lawyers.

4. Leading the African-American Quest for Political Power

Of the nearly 4000 persons known to have been lynched in the United States, the great majority have been Negroes. White mobs have lynched Negroes for offenses so trivial that the mob-murders seems absolutely incomprehensible, if the social background is not understood. In some Southern communities, for example, possession of any automobile other than a Ford by colored people, is frowned upon. It is a breach of the social code for a colored man driving an automobile to pass a white. For violation of these articles of the unwritten law, colored men have actually paid the death penalty, have been lynched by a mob. They have been lynched for not turning out of the road for a white person driving an automobile; for "talking back" to white people; and one negro who came to the door of a house for a drink of water, was lynched because the white woman, being hysterical, ran screaming from the house claiming the negro had come to attack her.

James Weldon Johnson, NAACP Executive Secretary, in "The Price of Lynching," *Century* Magazine, 1927, 67

I am, then, both visibly and legally the descendant of slaves in a white, Protestant country, and this is what it means to be an American Negro, this is who he is—a kidnapped pagan, who

> was sold like an animal and treated like one, who was once defined by the American Constitution as "three-fifths" of a man, and who, according to the Dred Scott decision, had no rights that a white man was bound to respect. And today, one hundred years after his technical emancipation, he remains—with the possible exception of the American Indian—the most despised creature in his country.
>
> **James Baldwin, *The Fire Next Time*, New York, 1963, 98–99**

If the American public's image of the NAACP's method of operation has been characterized by litigation alone, then it has failed to appreciate one of the critical elements in the association's nine-decade saga: by 1930 winning parity at the polls was perceived by the NAACP leadership as *the* key to attaining equality in every other sphere. It has been a virtual given among most NAACP leaders since World War II that the ballot box offered the most direct route to the realization of full freedom and dignity. Further, the more sagacious NAACP leaders understood fully that most Americans held the right to vote as the most sacrosanct of all rights and that they would be hard-pressed as a people to deny *any* citizen that right (except, of course, where Americans were being directly challenged in the Deep South. Even there, numerous white voices became aroused during the critical years to support the African American's "dangerous" campaign for full enfranchisement).

No private agency (or combination thereof) has amassed such a record of achievement in extending the franchise to more people than the NAACP. Nor has any organization suffered more harm and death among its members, staff and leaders in the long quest to achieve the right to vote. Only the federal government, following the Voting Rights Act of 1965, has helped to register as many black citizens as the NAACP; very often since that year, they have worked in consort toward this goal.

However, in its earliest period, the founders of the NAACP were compelled to view efforts to register Negro voters as marginal activities, considering that the vast majority of Negroes prior to 1940 lived in the South, where *any* form of Negro voter activity was regarded as suicidal. Voter initiatives until the end of World War II were locally initiated and took place in the North and Midwest, in the main within the large urban concentrations. It is no accident that its antilynching campaign *preceded* any significant campaigns by the NAACP to register Negro voters. Indeed, in many locales and not necessarily in the South, far less dramatic behavior by Negroes was regularly "discouraged" by lynching.

During its first two decades—roughly between 1909 and 1929—the NAACP's solitary political focus (and primary programmatic theme) was the campaign to outlaw lynching nationally. In Congress, this took the form of bills designed to make participation in or commission of the act (of lynching) a federal criminal offense, which was most notably embodied in the Dyer Anti-Lynching Bill, a measure that garnered majorities in the House of Representatives but consistently failed to clear the Senate (even as late as the years immediately following World War II, after which the NAACP finally abandoned the effort).

Prior to the formation of the NAACP in 1909, significant numbers of Southern black citizens had registered to vote during the post–Civil War decade of Reconstruction. Thereafter, the rapidly growing system known as Jim Crow, which was imposed upon Negroes throughout the South, had systematically and thoroughly diminished black voter rolls amassed during the decade following the end of the Civil War. With the departure of the Union Army and the white Northerners,[1] derogatorily called carpetbaggers by the defeated Southerners, the latter deftly replaced the occupation force's attempt at democratization with a new system much closer in spirit to slavery but without the burdens of economic responsibilities felt by a number of the slave owners. The new order was built upon the fiction that the Negro was now (after 1865) free and thus responsible for his own material needs and welfare, as well as those of his wife and children. However, the wealth-producing resources of the South—the land, the businesses, and the savings—remained almost totally in the hands of the defeated whites. In no mood to coddle their former slaves after such an expensive and humiliating defeat, the opinion molders and political leaders replaced the Northern-imposed Reconstruction with a system that legalized a racial caste order that effectively denied the newly freed slaves most of their recently won rights.[2] What distinguished the Jim Crow system from its predecessors was that the long list of forbidden activities imposed on the Negro were now backed by specific state and local laws and ordinances that prohibited Negroes from a variety of occupations as well as a very broad range of other activities. Rule 1 was that Negroes were denied contact with whites unless they were performing a servile role attending to the needs or interests of white persons. Thus the superiority of whites and the concomitant assertion of Negro inferiority were rapidly codified into a web of laws, requiring their observation by both resident and traveler. By the turn of the century, all of the Reconstruction's gains in both voting and electing blacks to public office had been eradicated. Racism—the notion that Negroes are inherently inferior to whites—again became the official ideology of the South; local governments codified the Negro's second-class status into a straightjacket of laws and rules governing almost every aspect of human existence from education to enfranchisement to public transportation to intermarriage.

Absent any significant outcry from the rest of the American populace—at the very least, that Union majority that had won the Civil War—the South's leaders became increasingly emboldened in their retrogressive slide toward the imposition of the American version of apartheid. By 1890, white leaders in the state of Mississippi felt sufficiently secure to establish a poll tax and literacy requirements as conditions for voter registration of its own citizens. Over the next 75 years these and similar devices effectively blocked meaningful Negro voter registration in any of the Southern states, all of which followed the example of Mississippi. It came as no surprise that none of these former Confederate states attempted to apply the same restrictions to poor, illiterate white Southerners. It was to become a common paradox for some Southern polling places, wherein educated Negroes were systematically denied the right to register to vote, while coarse white illiterates were granted that right.

With the U.S. Supreme Court's 1896 ruling in *Plessy v. Ferguson* that segregation was constitutionally legal as long as it resulted in equal facilities, the circle was closed. Jim Crow had emerged victorious 31 years after the Confederacy had surrendered at Appomattox. America's law of the land once again coincided with its received wisdom—that Negroes were inferior in all essential characteristics and, in order to survive and prosper, they required white guidance and direction, as God had supposedly so intended in his Biblical revelations.

The seeds of violence were inherent in this mix: white bigots, including some law-enforcement agents, unhesitatingly applied brute force to discourage "uppity niggers." Lynching became one of the most effective means to enforce Jim Crow; its threat was ever-present and it effectively produced a generalized climate of fear and subservience among the Negroes of the South (as well as in some locales throughout the North and Midwest.)[3] Between 1882 and 1932, over 5,000 Negroes were lynched. According to the 1919 NAACP report, in 1892 the highest annual toll was recorded—155 slain blacks—and there were 128 such murders in 1895. By 1933 the annual toll had declined substantially—to a total of 24. The first year that failed to record a death from lynching was 1952—the year General Dwight D. Eisenhower was elected President (which was also Harry S. Truman's last year in the White House).

Given the violence-charged atmosphere pervading Southern society during the 50 years between 1882 and 1932, it should not be difficult to comprehend how dangerous it was for Negroes to undertake *any* form of political activity, especially in the South, including the elementary act of registering to vote. Nor should it be forgotten that virtually no white participating in a lynching had ever received serious punishment during the same five decades: in almost every instance white Southern male juries refused to convict *any* white accused of lynching. Indeed, lynching in the United States between 1875 and 1955 —a total of eight decades—proved to be the ultimate weapon in the armory of white racists to discourage Negro political participation in any form, regardless of the Constitution and the fourteenth and fifteenth Amendments.[4]

The last decades of the nineteenth century and the early decades of the twentieth were noteworthy as well for the public dichotomy between black America's two most prominent leaders—Booker T. Washington and W.E.B. DuBois. Washington argued strenuously against Negro agitation and political action; he believed that acquiring vocational skills would be the principal route to Negro advancement. White conservatives warmly embraced his accomodationist philosophy, providing him with substantial funding and often lionizing him, much as his black spiritual successors were rewarded during the Reagan–Bush years.

Always the combatant, DuBois endorsed agitation, protest, and confrontation. By the early twentieth century, the failure of Booker T. Washington's approach to reduce the frequent use of violence against Negroes not only helped to discredit his status but also buttressed the philosophy and strategy advocated by DuBois. Even Negroes who had attained college or professional degrees as well as financial success were unable to enjoy their political rights (a condition analogous to the grievances of the French merchant and professional classes that emerged prior to the French Revolution).

When DuBois brought the remnants of his Niagara Movement to the newly organized entity in 1909 that was to become the NAACP, he brought with him a strategy that projected agitation through advocacy and other means. (Washington's decision to decline the invitation to attend the NAACP's founding conference was both a relief to the callers of the conference and an assurance of the primacy of DuBois's strategy.) By the second annual conference of the NAACP in 1910, which settled on the organization's present name, the Association's principal mission of advocacy had been effectively established, and DuBois appropriately became the NAACP's public voice as its first director of publicity and research.[5]

Whites directed the NAACP staff for the entire initial decade. Serving as secretary—in effect, the staff director—until 1920 were a series of five white men and women, including Frances Blascoer (1910–1911), Mary White Ovington (1911–1912), May Childs Nerney (1912–1916), Roy Nash (1916–1917), and John R. Shillady (1918–1920). (The first person to use the title of executive secretary appears to have been Shillady.) In 1916, after Booker T. Washington's death and the absorption of many of his followers into the NAACP, the organization established its first field staff when James Weldon Johnson was hired as a branch organizer (field secretary), followed shortly thereafter by the employment of Walter White and William Pickens as associate field secretaries. They were the NAACP's first Negro staff members after DuBois himself. However, with the exception of DuBois, whites remained firmly in control of the organization by holding on to the post of executive secretary, in effect the staff CEO, until 1920. Thereafter, whites continued to control policy by monopolizing the key volunteer offices—chairman, president, executive committee chairman, and treasurer. With these positions, whites governed the Association's policy and finances for another decade. During the NAACP's first 25 years, its white board chairmen included Oswald Garrison Villard, Joel Spingarn, Mary White Ovington, and Arthur Spingarn. Finally, in 1935, the NAACP leadership determined that it was time for a board chairman of African-American heritage. The first was famed medical doctor Louis T. Wright, who held the post until 1952. He was followed by such luminaries as Channing Tobias, Robert C. Weaver, and Bishop Stephen Gill Spottswood. On the latter's death, Margaret Bush Wilson became the first black woman to fill that post in 1975.

Villard and Ovington served as the association's earliest treasurers; in 1948 Ovington was succeeded by Allan Knight Chalmers, who in turn was succeeded by Alfred Baker Lewis—all of them white. Not until Lewis's retirement in 1972 was the NAACP to name an African American as treasurer. (The first was Jesse Turner Sr.)

Similarly, after the first black board chairman was elected, the post of NAACP president remained reserved for whites, including Moorfield Storey, Joel and then Arthur Spingarn, and Kivie Kaplan. Following Kaplan's death in 1975, the board selected Dr. Montague Cobb, renowned Professor of Anatomy at Howard University, as its next president. Thereafter, all of the NAACP's three highest posts—chairman, president, and treasurer—were filled by African Americans, reflecting the gradual growth of both independence and ethnocentrism within the association.

Aside from perfunctory initiatives by some local branches to foster voter registration in their communities, the NAACP's first foray into political action was a national campaign to secure adoption of the Dyer Anti-Lynching Bill between 1919 and 1923. Despite its ultimate failure in Congress, the process enabled the NAACP to begin crafting and honing an array of techniques and processes that effectively served its substantial political activities in future years. These included lobbying at the federal and state levels, the marshaling of publicity to buttress its objectives, and the effective use of its prestigious journal, *The Crisis* (edited by DuBois) to educate and mobilize the troops—the widespread rank-and-file membership, which was in its own right learning how to effect change locally.

As a precursor of later voting rights activity, the NAACP as early as 1914 began to question congressional candidates on their attitudes toward race, especially in regard to outlawing lynching. In 1917, the NAACP launched its first national investigation of lynching, establishing a pattern for future decades of careful staff investigation before making policy decisions at the board level. Another pattern was established when the NAACP made a direct appeal to President Woodrow Wilson for support of its antilynching crusade during World War I as a means of helping to pacify the home front. Unfortunately, the appeal fell on deaf ears.[6] Wilson himself was viewed by many Negroes at the time as an unreformed racist, despite his internationalist pretensions.[7]

In 1919, at James Weldon Johnson's initiative, the NAACP and friends organized the National Conference on Lynching, an early coalition model, and held a two-day conference in New York City, May 5–6. The participants, both liberal whites and Negro leaders, presented a number of legislative and law-enforcement proposals to the conference participants. Moorfield Storey served as the conference chairman. A sizable public meeting at Carnegie Hall, addressed by NAACP leader James Weldon Johnson and presidential candidate Charles Evans Hughes, later to serve on the Supreme Court, among other notables, concluded the conference. These techniques became standard operating procedure for the NAACP as it continued to polish its advocacy skills.[8]

Another major event was the "monster mass meeting" (the NAACP's own descriptive term), which the association organized on March 1, 1922, at New York's Town Hall, West 43rd Street and Broadway, to "memorialize the United States Senate" in support of the Dyer Anti-Lynching Bill. Besides NAACP Executive Secretary James Weldon Johnson, the speakers included Congressman Dyer himself and former U.S. Attorney General George W. Wickersham. Despite a rash of dilatory tactics employed by Southern Democrats and Northern Republicans over a four-year period and a failed appeal to President Warren Harding to support the legislation, the House of Representatives had finally passed the Dyer Anti-Lynching Bill on January 16, 1922, by almost a two-to-one margin, 231 to 119. The Republican Senate leadership, however, continued to collude with Southern Democrats to delay consideration of the measure by various parliamentary devices. Led by Borah of Idaho and Lodge of Massachusetts, the Republican leaders sidestepped consideration throughout the life of the 67th Congress. Thus, when the 68th Congress convened in 1923, its rules required that the process begin all over again in the House, producing widespread discouragement among the NAACP's staff and leaders, both of which had waged a heroic and exhausting fight to obtain House passage of the bill. Nevertheless, the experience and contacts accumulated by the NAACP staffers, notably by Walter White, provided the foundation for the eventual establishment of a permanent (and universally admired) lobbying capability on Congressional Hill in years to come.

During the late summer of that same year—1923—the NAACP organized a major conference on race relations in Kansas City attended by 500 delegates from 28 states. It was Roy Wilkins's first glimpse of the NAACP and its emerging Negro leaders, including DuBois, James Weldon Johnson, Walter White, and William Pickens. The experience proved inspirational for Wilkins and presumably for many others who attended. Besides a silent march against Jim Crow and injustice, journalist Wilkins covered the presentation of the Spingarn Medal to botanical scientist George Washington Carver and a mass meeting on the final day attended by "10,000 black people from Kansas City and nearby towns into Convention Hall . . . . I had never seen anything like it," Wilkins said. "On the platform, the old accomodationist ways of Booker T. Washington were swept away by DuBois."[9]

However, an unexpected incident occurred that helped to illuminate the mission of the NAACP in eloquent terms: a representative of the Missouri governor rose to read the latter's message to the delegates. As Wilkins described it, before the speaker had uttered a few sentences, somehow the word "darkey" emerged from his lips, sending the huge crowd into a prolonged and disruptive uproar. Finally, Arthur Spingarn, one of the NAACP's founders and principal leaders, managed to restore order so that the governor's representative could finish reading his letter, which infelicitously had urged the NAACP delegates to pursue "industry, thrift, individual achievement, rather than the perusal of so-called equality."

In the eerie silence that followed these patronizing sentiments, NAACP Executive Secretary James Weldon Johnson rose in rebuttal. This is how Roy Wilkins remembered the next few minutes:

> "His Excellency advised patience, industry, thrift and intelligence," Johnson said softly. Then his voice rose: "Patience? We know that patience is a foundation upon which we have built. Who has been more patient than we? Who has endured more hardships, suffered more insults, bent to more humiliation than we? Thrift and industry?" he said, looking at [the governor's representative]. "Look around you, sir, at these thousands who by thrift and industry, by study and by devotion to church, have

> made themselves worthy to enjoy the rights of American citizens. But, sir, do they enjoy them?"
>
> There was a tremendous roar of applause. Johnson turned. Facing the governor's man squarely, he pounded his hand down upon the table before him and said, "We are here to serve notice that we are in a fight to the death for the rights guaranteed us as American citizens by the Constitution." Ten thousand black people rose to their feet. They cheered and clapped until their voices were hoarse and their hands stinging with pain. As they cheered, a soft sunlight streamed down around James Weldon Johnson, and I knew I had seen a great leader—and found my cause.[10]

In the closing years of the decade, NAACP lawyers won two widely publicized decisions before the Supreme Court, the first further outlawing residential segregation by ordinance in New Orleans. The second victory had implications for the further expansion of Negro voting rights: Argued by Arthur Spingarn and his colleague, the NAACP victory slightly opened up the political process when the court struck down the state of Texas's law that barred Negro participation in the Democratic Party primaries. Employing the fourteenth Amendment, Justice Oliver Wendell Holmes's opinion forthrightly stated that race or color alone could not be used to deprive Negroes of their right to vote.

As expected, Texas immediately circumvented the Court's ruling when the state transferred responsibility for setting voter qualifications to the state Democratic Party, which thereupon adopted a resolution "restricting primary voting to white Democrats."[11] The court left this maneuver untouched because the Democratic Party was regarded as a private entity.

Then in 1930 another residential segregation case came before Judge John J. Parker of the Fourth Court of Appeals. In this case, the City of Richmond had sought to establish residential segregation by employing the state's law against racial intermarriage, which had yet to be declared unconstitutional. The Richmond ordinance barred anyone from residing in a neighborhood in which the same individual could not legally marry its residents. In January 1930, Parker ruled that the ordinance was unconstitutional, and in May the Supreme Court upheld its ruling. Judge Parker and the NAACP would meet again at a historic turning point, because earlier that year an associate justice of the Supreme Court (Edward Terry Sanford of North Carolina) had died suddenly, providing President Herbert Hoover with an opportunity to appoint a new justice to the Court.

Nevertheless, these new court victories continued the evolving process and expanded the NAACP's credibility, especially among Negroes; growth in memberships and in the number of branches followed. By the beginning of 1930, however, the NAACP was being battered on all sides—black nationalists led by Marcus Garvey as well as left-wing ideologues, including the Communists and socialist labor leader A. Philip Randolph, accused the NAACP of excessive caution and lack of militancy. Locally, conservative Negroes with material gains at risk urged the NAACP to move more deliberately. Some white intellectuals even argued that the NAACP was too occupied with generating publicity: they failed to appreciate the linkage between publicity and the generating of resources, including memberships and cash, which then translated into political muscle.

Before mundane politics raised its formidable head, President Hoover is believed to have included on his initial list of candidates for the open Supreme Court seat such legal luminaries as Benjamin Cardozo, Learned Hand, and Owen J. Roberts,[12] as well as some staunch segregationists like Georgia's Walter George. However, party politics ultimately determined the choice: Hoover decided on John J. Parker, in part because he was a North Carolinian and a Southerner like Sanford. Moreover, Parker had accumulated a significant political record as a leader in the Republican Party's effort to build a viable lily-white party in the South to challenge the lily-white Democrats. That required a break with Negroes, who had been drawn to the Republicans because of Abraham Lincoln. Since the end of Reconstruction, however, the Republicans had systematically distanced themselves from the cause of Negro advancement, in effect repudiating Lincoln and the Republicans' rich Abolitionist credentials.

Half a century before Republican presidential candidates launched their "Southern Strategy," the Republican Party had already sown the seeds of this calculated appeal to white racists. By 1920, John Parker was heading the Republican ticket in North Carolina as the candidate for governor, "receiving 230,000 votes, which was 63,000 more than the candidate for Governor of either party had received prior to that time."[13] Although he lost the contest, Parker had helped his party to make substantial inroads across the entire region. As a result, he received several appointments from Presidents Harding and Coolidge, the latter sending him to the U.S. Court of Appeals in 1925.

In 1928 Herbert Hoover himself had courted white Southern voters and is regarded by some as the originator of what was later to be called the "Southern Strategy." At first this strategy was moderately progressive—it was conceived to attract those who believed in the "New South"—the modernization of the agricultural, largely rural, post–Civil War society through universal public education, improved transportation, attracting of industry, protecting workers, and taxing the affluent to support the region's development. Only on the subject of race were the Republican advocates of the New South retrogressive; Judge Parker was no exception. During his 1920 gubernatorial campaign, he repeatedly declared his opposition to Negro participation in politics, including voting. "Participation of the Negro in the political life of the South," Parker warned, "is harmful to him and to the community, and is a fruitful source of . . . racial prejudice . . . . As a class he has learned that lesson. He no longer desires to participate in politics. The Republican Party of North Carolina does not desire him to participate in the politics of the state."[14]

When Parker's nomination was announced, the NAACP's acting executive secretary, Walter White, initiated a routine investigation of Parker, in line with the Association's practice in regard to all high-level federal appointees. In response, a key North Carolina NAACP member transmitted a newspaper clipping generated by the 1920 Parker gubernatorial campaign, in which the candidate was quoted as affirming that Negroes had been effectively excluded from the state's Republican Party since 1908. Endorsing that policy, Parker was reported by the news article to have said: "The participation of the Negro in politics is a source of evil and danger to both races and is not desired by the wise men in either race or by the Republican Party in North Carolina."[15]

In Walter White's opinion, these words were sufficient to launch a serious campaign to block senatorial approval of the Parker nomination. As acting executive secretary, White's first act was to write to 177 NAACP branches "in selected states, asking them to contact their senators requesting that the nomination be rejected." The NAACP national office wrote directly to the same U.S. senators in these states with the same request.

What is remarkable about this opening shot across Parker's bow is that the 21-year-old NAACP in the year 1930 could identify 177 local units "in selected states" to mobilize for practical political action. Implicit in this strategy is that these 177 branches were the most effective and were located in states in which grassroots political pressure from Negroes could be expected to yield a positive result. (Less effective branches and/or those located in other states, namely the Southern states, it was implied, had not been directed by Walter White to pressure their senators as yet.)

White's request to President Hoover to withdraw the nomination because of Parker's alleged anti-Negro positions was summarily rebuffed. White then appeared before the Senate Judiciary subcommittee considering the Parker nomination. His was a less-than-stellar performance in the face of intense and hostile interrogation: having failed to do his homework, White's case against Parker was substantially deficient in documentation.

Prior to White's testimony, the president of the American Federation of Labor—William Green—appeared before the subcommittee to register organized labor's vehement opposition to Parker because, as a federal judge, he had ruled in favor of yellow-dog contracts. Green and his colleagues, however, carefully sought to distance themselves from Walter White, the NAACP and the race issue.

After the subcommittee voted two to one to recommend Parker's nomination to the full Judiciary Committee, White stepped up the campaign, now bent on mobilizing every NAACP branch in the nation to pressure their senators. At the same time, he appealed to the entire NAACP membership both for their activism on this issue and for crucially needed funds to carry the campaign forward. Through the media —notably the black press—White broadened the drive for funds and memberships to Negroes and white sympathizers throughout the nation. Once again, offering an issue of substantial importance to African Americans, the NAACP found its membership and financial support rising exponentially.

Parker's supporters, mostly within the Republican Party, fought back by creating some ersatz Negro support from political nonentities in North Carolina. Overall, Negroes were neither impressed nor fooled by this subterfuge, and they rallied almost without exception behind the NAACP. When the full Judiciary Committee finally polled its members on the nomination, 10 members, including several Progressive Republicans, opposed the nomination while six supported it. The full committee therefore advised the Senate to reject the Parker nomination, which greatly heartened White and the NAACP.

Now Parker began running scared. Breaking with precedent, he organized a major lobbying effort on behalf of his own nomination, while publicly defending his views on labor and race. By April 28, when the Senate debate began, Parker's views on race were considered as important as his views on labor rights. Nevertheless, many of Parker's Democratic opponents in the Senate, including liberals, limited their remarks in the debate to Parker's antilabor record in order not to provoke fellow Democrats from the South who might be planning to vote the party's line against the Republican nomination. Separately, labor and NAACP representatives twisted every senatorial arm they could access. Every NAACP branch was directed by Walter White to generate telegrams to its senators opposing the nomination. NAACP field staff fanned out across the nation, addressing branches and community rallies, recruiting new members, and initiating local petitions for the defeat of Parker. As the confirmation fight deepened, general news coverage greatly increased. DuBois, Arthur Spingarn, and Walter White spoke repeatedly before mass rallies, generating even more coverage and support. The Negro press almost unanimously urged support for the NAACP and defeat of Parker's nomination.

By May 7th, when the entire Senate took up the nomination, the tide had clearly turned. Repudiating President Hoover, the Senate rejected his nominee, 41 to 39. The voting majority was comprised of 23 Democrats, 1 independent, and 17 Progressive Republicans.[16] While the NAACP did not defeat Parker by itself, most historians now credit the organization with having played a major and perhaps decisive role, possibly equaling in importance the role played by organized labor, which together with the Senate liberal Democrats and the Progressive Republicans produced the coalition capable of defeating the nomination. It is generally recognized now that neither a bloc of senators nor organized labor alone could have succeeded if the NAACP had not effectively exposed Parker's anti-Negro views and mobilized black and liberal voter opposition to Parker. The elements of future coalition building on behalf of civil rights positions were becoming apparent to the NAACP leadership following the Parker fight.[17]

The Parker victory catapulted the NAACP into the preeminent leadership role of African Americans, leaving behind the Garvey separatists, the socialist agitators, and the Communist ideologues. The victory demonstrated to many blacks what their potential political power could become through activism and a unified effort. White politicians in the North and Midwest began to pay serious attention to attracting black voter support. Local political clubs began to court support from NAACP branches. With the Great Depression deepening, a new alignment of have-nots and have-littles was being forged across regional, ethnic, and racial lines, and for the first time Negroes were considered players. By the 1932 election, FDR't,s New Deal had broken the Republican hold on black voters, whose allegiance thereafter was firmly Democratic.

By this time, NAACP leaders had come to appreciate fully the interaction between its leadership of dramatic and relevant campaigns, on the one hand, and generating new members and financial support, on the other. Meanwhile, scores of private black organizations and institutions, ranging from Negro women to the Associated Negro Press to black fraternities and sororities to church denominations, consciously chose to ally themselves with the NAACP and its continuing struggles and to spread the Association's messages among its members, who were also then called upon to provide financial support.

Perhaps most extraordinary of all, the NAACP achieved these results on an annual budget of less than $50,000 in 1930. The value of its volunteer effort was, however, incalculable. In dollars, it was worth several million. The activity of the volunteers more than made up for the small size of the professional staff leading the fight.

Had the NAACP paused after the Parker fight to catch its breath, it would still have been entitled to wear with pride the slogan of its 1930 annual convention marking its 21st birthday—"The NAACP Comes of Age." The Parker experience marked the permanent entry of the NAACP into the nation's political life: Voting rights then became one of the cornerstones of the Association's policies and programs for the next sixty years, joined shortly by the quest for desegregated quality education for all Negro children. (It was not until the early 1950s that employment and housing were elevated to equivalent status by the board of directors, thus shaping the four cornerstones of the enduring foundation for Negro advancement.)

Fortunately, Walter White refused to rest on his laurels after the intense six-week struggle that denied Parker a seat on the court. Recognizing the momentum among the nation's Negroes stirred by Parker's defeat, White persuaded his board to exploit the new fervor by targeting for defeat those senators who had voted in favor of Parker's nomination. One staff member—Branch Director Robert Bagnall—was already campaigning against Senator Allen in Kansas, presumably without official NAACP authorization. Then W.E.B. DuBois, entirely on his own initiative, published a list of the names of the senators who had supported Parker in the next issue of *The Crisis* and, without prior approval, encouraged NAACP members to bring them down in the forthcoming elections.

While in general agreement with both sentiments, White recognized that with the recent death of Board Chairman Moorfield Storey, with the prestige White had garnered from the Parker fight, with his own unsurpassed popularity among the branch leaders, and with the fact that a sizable number of board members owed their advancement (and allegiance) to him, it was the perfect moment for him to seize full control of the staff and the organizational apparatus. Regardless of his affinity for DuBois and Bagnall's unauthorized initiatives, they *were* unauthorized to act: no effective chief executive could tolerate such freewheeling behavior among his staff. He thereupon moved decisively to centralize the NAACP's decisionmaking throughout the rapidly growing organization, including control over *The Crisis*, which by then had become the NAACP's official organ and which now depended on the NAACP for its funding. DuBois promptly resigned in a huff, thereby temporarily solving one of White's major internal problems.(However, DuBois was to return soon to challenge White directly for the overall leadership of the NAACP and of the civil rights movement.)

On July 14th, White, having consolidated his position, obtained the board's approval to target two specific senators—Allen of Kansas and McCulloch of Ohio—for defeat in the elections scheduled for the following November. Fully appreciating the limitations of the NAACP's resources, White created a second category for "special attention"—

Senators Baird of New Jersey and Watson of Indiana—with the understanding that the NAACP would organize more limited campaigns against them. All except Watson were up for reelection that November. Four other Parker supporters were also running for reelection in November, 1930—Gillette of Massachusetts, Hastings of Delaware, Grundy of Pennsylvania, and Goff of West Virginia. They were all on DuBois's original hit list. However, because of sparse resources, the NAACP restricted its opposition of these four to publicity and the provision of a few speakers to their opponents.

Sound strategy underpinned the NAACP's choice of its prime targets. Its objective was to defeat the pro-Parker incumbents, not merely to gain moral victories. White and the NAACP leadership settled on Allen, McCulloch, and, later, Baird (of New Jersey) as the prime targets in part because the Negro vote in Ohio and New Jersey, at least, was large enough to affect the outcome, in part because all three had become vulnerable politically, and in part because effective NAACP state conferences were already in place or about to be created because these states had so many active local branches. Though Baird chose not to run for reelection as a senator and instead accepted the nomination of his party to run for governor of New Jersey, the NAACP remained steadfast in opposing him for that post as well. In Kansas a young Roy Wilkins, editor of the *Kansas City Call,* persuaded White that even though the black population in his state was relatively small, the political conditions existed for Allen's defeat.

Astonishingly, considering the NAACP's lack of electoral experience on a statewide level, its lack of funds, and the short time remaining until the November election, Senators Allen and McCulloch and gubernatorial candidate Baird were defeated. Almost half of the NAACP's available resources had been invested in these three campaigns. In the races where the NAACP had limited its opposition to publicity, two Parker supporters won—Gillette of Massachusetts and Hastings of Delaware—while Grundy of Pennsylvania was defeated. (The fourth, West Virginia's Goff, ultimately decided not to run for reelection.)

The defeat of Allen in Kansas proved to be an important feather in Roy Wilkins's cap. Having argued vociferously for an all-out campaign in Kansas, his judgment had been vindicated. George McGill, the Democrat who defeated Allen, later acknowledged publicly that the NAACP had played a crucial role in electing him by mobilizing a sizable number of Negro votes on his behalf. (At the same event McGill took out a $10 membership in the NAACP, which at the time was a considerable amount of money.) Impressed by Wilkins's talents, White recruited Wilkins to join the national staff the following year to edit *The Crisis* and to direct the publicity department.

Branch Director Bagnall had crisscrossed Kansas several times during the summer preceding the election, organizing successful membership drives in conjunction with the campaign against Allen. The interaction of these two objectives was soon to become a classic pattern for the NAACP—its outspoken opposition to anti-Negro candidates regardless of party affiliation generated intense interest and support among Negroes, which in turn translated both into memberships and votes.

In the same November 1930 election, Ohio's Sen. Roscoe McCulloch proved to be an easier target, having only served as an appointee for a short period. More importantly, even before the final Parker vote, McCulloch's bid for reelection had become a priority concern of AFL President William Green, himself a former Ohio state legislator. After Parker's defeat, Branch Director Bagnall began molding the organization of the state conference of branches in Ohio, modeled after the successful state conferences in New Jersey and Indiana, but with the additional mission of defeating Sen. McCulloch. The developing NAACP campaign against McCulloch was inextricably intertwined with the formation of the Ohio State Conference, as well as the organization of new branches and the generating of new memberships. Bagnall and the NAACP's local leaders took extra precautions, however, to avoid involvement with or funding from the Ohio political parties or candidates, a standard which was to be followed in all subsequent political campaigns. Another important aspect of the Ohio campaign was the national office's decision to delegate the direction of the campaign to the state conference, while providing some financial support and speakers. Eventually, the anti-McCulloch campaign was transformed into an effort to elect his opponent, despite heated opposition from some black Republicans in Ohio. As the Ohio campaign became increasingly sophisticated, it devised techniques that served as models for future NAACP electoral campaigns.

Sensing a possible victory in Ohio, White called an unprecedented second statewide conference one month before the general election.

Chairing the meeting himself, White sought to rally the troops while assessing each branch 1 cents per member to pay for the final push, which placed heavy emphasis on a number of rallies across Ohio. The national office sent each of the Ohio branches an innovative instructional memorandum, setting forth six important assignments each branch was urged to undertake: producing campaign literature to explain why the NAACP opposed McCulloch as well as organizing public meetings for the same purpose; house-to-house canvassing of all prospective voters; persuading local ministers and heads of local organizations to put the NAACP's case before their congregations or members; widespread local publicity; and generating sizable membership attendance at mass rallies. These tactics have provided much of the content for local NAACP voter drives ever since. The same national office memo emphasized the need to maintain accurate records of how the funds were spent for each voter drive, a theme that would recur frequently over the next six decades, at times in vain. Altogether, the national office expended the princely sum of $1,213.21 in cash contributions for the four 1930 senatorial campaigns, of which two-thirds was invested in Ohio.[18] The time and effort of thousands of local volunteers, on the other hand, was incalculable.

The 1930 victories served to whet Walter White's appetite once more for additional political campaigns. In 1932—the year FDR swept Hoover out of office—the NAACP invested in a major campaign against Sen. Watson in Indiana, who was defeated; it also conducted a sizable publicity campaign against Sen. Shortbridge of California, who also lost his seat. (Another pro-Parker target, Connecticut's Bingham, decided not to run for reelection.)

Two years later, in the 1934 elections, during which FDR's supporters were elected to Congress in a landslide, the NAACP targeted six pro-Parker senators—each on DuBois's original hit list. All six were defeated. With the Great Depression squeezing the organization's resources, White was compelled to limit the NAACP's electoral efforts to intensive publicity in each of these races. A seventh potential target —Maryland's Goldsborough—also chose not to seek reelection.[19]

Of the 17 pro-Parker senators on DuBois' original list, 12 were defeated, two were reelected, and three decided not to run again. The NAACP had a hand in the defeat of all 12, though its role was decisive in none. The electoral fallout from the Great Depression begun under Republican President Herbert Hoover had impacted Negroes disproportionately, but it also caused near-universal havoc among whites, producing an avalanche of anti-Republican votes as early as 1930, from local and state posts to those in Congress all the way up to the presidency. Undoubtedly, the defeat of the 12 Republican senators owed more to the Depression and to their identification in most voters' minds with the party of Herbert Hoover than to any other factor.

But the significance to the NAACP leadership of such a victorious sweep in their first foray into electoral politics cannot be overestimated. If the figures had been reversed—12 pro-Parker senators victorious and only two defeated—who can tell whether these initial electoral experiences would have been regarded by the NAACP's leaders so positively? As it turned out, the NAACP proceeded to incorporate within the organization's collective psyche and future programs the commitment to electoral politics as a permanent mission. From 1930 onward, the inclusion of voting rights became the programmatic equal of litigation. As a perennial duty, each branch was obliged by the NAACP's Blue Book—containing the Association's by-laws—to maintain a permanent voter education committee of its members, as indeed it was obliged to maintain both a legal and an education committee.

White continued to expand the Association's voter capabilities in 1936 when he targeted the NAACP's resources against the candidacy of Senator William Borah of Idaho for the Republican nomination for president. As Roy Wilkins acknowledged in his autobiography, Borah was "a decent senator and a distinguished internationalist," but he "had developed a blind spot about the Fourteenth Amendment and the rights of Negroes" and had "for years opposed our campaign for a federal anti-lynching law." During his campaign, Borah pledged to veto "any anti-lynching law which passed his desk."[20] The NAACP national office organized a substantial campaign against Borah, which commenced when Borah decided to kick off his candidacy in Brooklyn. An alliance of local NAACP branches, churches, and the Young People's Socialist League (YPSL) of Brooklyn produced such massive opposition that the Borah campaign remained severely handicapped thereafter. In the early Idaho primary, a sizable turnout of black voters helped to defeat him and toppled his candidacy. The NAACP's reputation for political clout continued to grow.

White's burgeoning success and expanding power within the association, however, led to a head-on collision with DuBois, who in Wilkins's view had nurtured a long antipathy for White and his policies. Under James Weldon Johnson and his white predecessors, DuBois had a freer hand and was treated with considerably more deference than by White after he became executive secretary. Indeed, White consistently sought to consolidate control and power in his hands, starting within weeks after his appointment. DuBois's initial foray against White was to call for a reorganization of the NAACP "from top to bottom, an argument aimed at getting rid of Walter," Wilkins has suggested.

When this and other attempts failed, DuBois' next initiative proved to be very strange, if not bizarre: in a *Crisis* editorial in January, 1934, DuBois placed himself in support of racial segregation. Arguing that "the thinking colored people of the United States must stop being stampeded by the word segregation," DuBois declared that the "race conscious black man . . . will eventually emancipate the colored race . . . if he cooperates with like-minded others to form and work through segregated institutions and movements." He urged the formation of segregated farms and communities "to accomplish his economic emancipation through voluntary, determined [and segregated] co-operative effort."[21]

For the foe of accommodationist Booker T. Washington to advocate voluntary segregation was almost unthinkable, especially at NAACP headquarters. As the criticism came back to the Association in buckets, some thought DuBois had lost his mind. Others were simply furious. A young William Henry Hastie, a cousin of Charles Hamilton Houston and then a novice attorney who had recently joined the team of NAACP lawyers, launched a vitriolic rebuttal, concluding with this multiedged barb:

> In theory there can be segregation without discrimination, segregation without unequal treatment. But any Negro who uses this theoretical possibility as a justification for segregation is either dumb, mentally dishonest, or else he has, like Esau, chosen a mess of potage.[22]

Hastie, it should be noted, became the nation's first black federal judge.

While White never wavered in his commitment to desegregation and integration, this incident would not be the last in which NAACPers, both leaders and followers, would resort to the race card, call for a form of segregation, seek to expel whites, and otherwise deviate from the core of the NAACP's philosophy: the attainment of total and complete integration in every facet of U.S. life. Many times when reason failed and no other approach seemed to bear fruit, some NAACP leaders would make the basest appeal of all—that of blood or of skin color. Regardless of the race or ethnic group, it is the most difficult of all demands for loyalty to reject, whether in the U.S., or Bosnia, or Rwanda, or Sri Lanka.

Thus DuBois, in throwing down the segregationist gauntlet, provided White and the young NAACP with a major test. White wanted not only to expel DuBois from the NAACP but also to thwart DuBois's claim to philosophic preeminence among African Americans. "Against this backdrop," Wilkins wrote, " I suspect Dr. DuBois's sudden interest in segregation was a declaration of independence, a test of Walter's power, and an assertion of Dr. DuBois' claim to be the intellectual leader of the race—a line in the dust." For the next six months the two titans battled relentlessly, in the pages of *The Crisis,* before the membership, and at Board meetings. Finally, in June, DuBois drafted and released a wholesale indictment of the NAACP under White and declared that his labors to correct its shortcomings internally had failed and that his program proposals had been ignored and his protests characterized as petty jealousy or disloyalty. After all this, DuBois said he had "but one recourse, complete and final withdrawal, not because all is hopeless . . . but because evidently I can do no more."[23]

Characterizing this farewell manifesto as a "blast of anger, sorrow, and self-pity," Wilkins, who had sympathized with DuBois to some degree, was shocked to learn that DuBois's reorganization plans included the firing of both White and Wilkins. No effort was made to persuade DuBois to reconsider his resignation. His departure aided White in gaining total control of the staff operations and publications. Wilkins was appointed editor of *The Crisis,* in addition to his other duties, with no increase in pay, which clearly disturbed him. (This bit of irony will not be lost on Wilkins's own NAACP staff: after he was named executive secretary, he became notorious for holding down staff salaries.) Finally, the NAACP rejected DuBois's advocacy of voluntary segregation and reaffirmed its commitment to integration. In the years ahead, this commitment would be frequently tested and not always favorably.

If there was a particular moment when the NAACP and Walter White achieved national celebrity and respect, it probably occurred when White became the subject of *Time* magazine's cover on January 24, 1938. White was portrayed on the cover in front of a graphic painting of the lynching of a Negro man. The cover story that week was about the filibuster in the U.S. Senate blocking passage of the Wagner-Van Nuys Anti-Lynching Bill, which had already been adopted by the House of Representatives. The *Time* article quoted South Carolina's Senator James Byrnes, who identified Walter White as the awesomely powerful force behind the bill. Byrnes, later both a Supreme Court Justice and a Secretary of State, bellowed in angry terms to his fellow solons: "The South . . . has been deserted by the Democrats of the North . . . . One Negro . . . has ordered this bill to pass and if a majority can pass it, it will pass . . . . If Walter White should consent to have this bill laid aside, its advocates would desert it as quickly as football players unscramble when the whistle of the referee is heard."[24]

Walter White, who was present in the Senate gallery when these remarks were made, was credited with having produced the senatorial support for the antilynching bill and described as "the most potent leader of his race in the U.S." The article included a lengthy history of the NAACP's initial three decades and asserted that White had promised that 73 of the 96 senators would vote for the bill, if it ever reached the floor for a vote. Unfortunately, many of those same senators refused to vote to override the filibuster, which required two-thirds of those present. According to the *Time* article, White had made several trips to the Senate gallery to confer with the bill's supporters, prompting Senator Byrnes to utter "with *sotto voce* sarcasm, [Majority Leader Alben] Barklely can't do anything without talking to that nigger first." (This was the article's second use of the word *nigger*.)[25]

Following the anti-Parker electoral victories, most black voters would take their cues from the NAACP's leadership—locally, statewide, and nationally. The vast network of volunteers, composed of paid-up NAACP members, could quickly be mobilized (with appropriate legal, political, and/or financial assistance from the national staff) to launch an all-out voter registration drive, to generate support or opposition for a Supreme Court nominee, or to pull out the vote on election day for those candidates whose records were most supportive of civil rights and black interests. Each year thereafter, local branches and/or state conferences weighed the pros and cons of various candidates and, after determining their own resources, voted to determine in which campaigns to participate and which candidates appeared to serve their interests best. For the most part, however, their choices were limited to white politicians; it was not until after the 1965 Voting Rights Act, when black voter registration surged, that the prospect of electing black officeholders emerged. Indeed, when John F. Kennedy was elected president in 1960, there were only three black congressmen in the House of Representatives—Adam Clayton Powell, Jr. of New York, Charles Diggs of Michigan, and William Dawson of Illinois. There were no black U.S. senators until the progressive citizens of Massachusetts elected Edward Brooke, a Republican, in 1966.

The rise in the number of black registered voters was vitally important for its own sake in the electoral process; as the numbers grew, the Association's lobbying clout on Capitol Hill and in the legislatures of most states grew commensurately. Elected officials, especially legislators, need no special instruction when it comes to the arithmetic of votes. Each electoral success posted by the Association produced more Senators and congressmen ready to listen to its agenda. The executive Branch of the federal government was less responsive in the decade prior to the Great Depression, in part because of the quality and character of the three Republican presidents elected during that period. During a decade when Negro voters were few, no one of the three, Harding, Coolidge, or Hoover, had ever exhibited any compassion for or interest in Negroes. Hoover had even sought to craft his own Southern strategy to attract white voters in the South away from the Democratic Party.

Franklin D. Roosevelt, always dependent on Southern Democrats in Congress for passage of a vast array of New Deal legislation, proved no more responsive to the appeals of the Negro leadership than did his predecessors. He refused to jeopardize what he regarded as the nation's only chance to recover from the Great Depression by in any way accommodating the pleas of the NAACP. Walter White, therefore, undertook to lobby the president and the executive branch through Eleanor Roosevelt. White began soon after FDR took office in 1933, bombarding "Mrs. Roosevelt with letters and telegrams and appeals for interviews, . . . especially on behalf of an anti-lynching bill."[26] In

1934 Wilkins was directed to invite Mrs. Roosevelt to address the silver anniversary of the NAACP at its 25th Annual Conference (later called a convention) in Oklahoma City. His invitational letter observed that in a quarter of a century the NAACP had grown to 375 branches in 40 states and the District of Columbia.

Even after Mrs. Roosevelt's secretary declined for her, White steadfastedly continued to seek her support. Through these efforts, her own education in respect to "the Negro problem" grew substantially. She is reported to have continually needled FDR to support the antilynching legislation, though he appears never to have wavered. Ultimately, after FDR's death, Mrs. Roosevelt became an important, influential, and active member of the NAACP's national board of directors.

In 1939 the Daughters of the American Revolution refused to rent Constitution Hall in Washington for a concert performance by Negro soprano Marian Anderson. Interior Secretary Harold Ickes offered Ms. Anderson the Lincoln Memorial for the concert. On April 9, 1939, Easter Sunday, a vast crowd of 10,000 converged on Washington from almost every point on the compass, including a sizable number of Negroes. In this pretelevision age, the event was widely covered by the mass media, most conspicuously by all of the newsreel agencies.[27] Like the March on Washington 24 years later and the Selma-to-Montgomery March a few years after that, the Marian Anderson concert became a watershed moment in the long racial struggle in the U.S. It was one of the first important manifestations of support for civil rights from the executive branch of the U.S. government. To most observers Mrs. Roosevelt was considered to have been a primary force behind the scenes, which added to the importance of the event or at least to the legend that grew around it. Black Americans came to believe in Mrs. Roosevelt as their friend in court, and her popularity rubbed off on the president. The truth is that the person most responsible for Ms. Anderson's Lincoln Memorial concert was NAACP Executive Secretary Walter White, who marshaled all the necessary forces, including Ickes, Mrs. Roosevelt, and impresario Sol Hurok, to bring about the event. It was to White's credit that he allowed Mrs. Roosevelt to bask in the glory in order to draw her closer to the NAACP's inner circle.[28]

As the Great Depression began to wind down and the struggle for Negro liberation inched forward, momentous global forces were playing out in Europe and Asia. In Europe totalitarian dictatorships of the right and left were rapidly gaining ground while Japan's militaristic imperialism was systematically decimating China. The Fascist forces of General Francisco Franco had won the brutal Spanish Civil War and destroyed the Republican government. Hitler and Stalin shocked the civilized world by signing a nonaggression pact in 1939 and simultaneously invading Poland. The giant Soviet Union invaded its diminutive neighbor, Finland, whose overmatched forces resisted defeat for more than a year. The Nazi ideology, which threatened all of Europe, became the world's foremost proponent of racism. The NAACP's leaders comprehended the ultimate threat that Hitler posed to all non-Aryans and to civilization itself. America began slowly and reluctantly to mobilize for the inevitable war. Into this whirlpool flowed the decade-long struggle between the Communist Party USA and the NAACP for the hearts and minds of American Negroes.

5. Comes the Revolution: The Struggle Between the NAACP and the Communist Party USA

We remember that in the Scottsboro case the NAACP was subjected to the most unprincipled vilification. We remember the campaigns of slander in the Daily Worker. We remember the leaflets and the speakers and the whole unspeakable machinery that was turned loose upon all those who did not embrace the "unity" as announced by the Communists. We want none of that unity today.

Roy Wilkins, Letter to W.L. Patterson, Executive Secretary of Communist-dominated Civil Rights Congress, March 22, 1950

There is no place in this organization for Communists or those who follow the Communist line.

Thurgood Marshall, NAACP Special Counsel, to the Plenary of the 1956 NAACP convention, San Francisco

The Communist Party supports the right of self-determination for the Negro people, that is, their right to realize self-government in the Negro majority area in the South.

"The Communist Position on the Negro Question," Pamphlet, New York, 1947, 12

The year 1939 will be remembered not only for Marian Anderson's historic performance at the Lincoln Memorial; it was also the year in which the Soviet Union betrayed its anti-Fascist posturing by signing a pact with Nazi Germany, after which it invaded diminutive Finland and occupied the eastern half of Poland. To many Americans who sympathized with the Kremlin's pronounced objectives, Stalin's decision to sign a pact with Hitler came as an inexplicable shock. To the leadership of the NAACP, it came as no surprise. Indeed, the struggle for the hearts and minds of American Negroes had pitched the NAACP into direct opposition to the Communist Party USA (CPUSA) almost from the latter's formation after the Third Internationale met in 1919.

The initial strategy of the CPUSA was to compete directly with the NAACP for Negro support by projecting itself as the proletariat savior of the worker, by opening its doors to Negroes during an era in which such racial mixing was still considered taboo, by elevating a few Negro members to visible positions of leadership, and by advocating the establishment of a separate Negro nation-state carved from a swath of the South's Black Belt.

Tactically, the American Communists sought to denigrate the NAACP by questioning its integrity and its ideological commitment to civil rights. The Communist description of the NAACP often began with such pejoratives as "Uncle Tom," "capitalist tool," or "bourgeois." In the black ghettoes of the nation's major cities, the local Communist units often engaged in verbal combat with the local NAACP branch as they competed for membership and financial support. The Great Depression of the 1930s had radicalized a significant segment of the American populace; over all one in five American wage earners was unemployed. In black communities the jobless rate was twice that of whites. Communist organizers, often at great physical risk, challenged both the capitalist and the racist practices of the nation. They were especially prominent in the organizing of the new industrial unions, such as the United Auto Workers and the Steel Workers, during which they insisted that Negroes enjoy the same membership rights as whites. To a minority of Negroes confronting relentless desperation, such activism was compelling. Despite the steady stream of attacks on the NAACP, the Communists were able to recruit an impressive group of black intellectuals and artists, including

Richard Wright, Max Yergan, Ralph Ellison, Paul Robeson, and NAACP co-founder W.E.B. DuBois.

Eventually, however, writers such as Wright and Ellison became disillusioned with the party after a few years, refusing to conform to a rigid party line and increasingly aware of the CPUSA's subordination to the strictures of the Kremlin.

One of the earliest heated confrontations between the two forces took place in January 1933. That month Roy Wilkins and newsman George Schuyler had returned from a dangerous mission to the Mississippi Delta to expose depression-era exploitation of black men working for pittances constructing levees and other forms of flood control on America's mightiest river. Their employer was the Corps of Army Engineers. The organization's annual meeting was being held at the Abyssinian Baptist Church in Harlem—the ministry and power base of Rev. Adam Clayton Powell Senior and later of his illustrious son. Walter White had labored for days to produce an enormous crowd to hear Wilkins' first-hand report. After Wilkins finished his narration and sat down, Communist provacoteurs in the audience leaped to their feet to denounce Wilkins and Schuyler, falsely charging that neither had even gone to Mississippi and that the Wilkins report was fiction. The Communists further claimed that the investigation was an attempt by the NAACP to "trick" the Negro people. Mindful of the extreme danger faced by Schuyler and himself, Wilkins was deeply angered by the false charges and recalled the episode a half century later with uncharacteristic bitterness.[1]

Throughout the 1930s, the Communists continued their attacks on the NAACP, feeding upon the national malaise produced by the Great Depression. The party, however, had greater success among the majority white population than it managed to achieve among African Americans. Meanwhile American awareness of their invisible countrymen reached a new plateau in 1936, when Negro sprinter Jesse Owens won an unprecedented four gold medals at the 1936 Olympics in Berlin in defiance of the avowed racism of Nazi dictator Adolf Hitler and his ubiquitous black-shirted storm troopers. At home Owens' victories transformed him into an overnight hero.

The following year—1937—Hitler's favorite pugilist, Max Schmeling, earned a match with the heavyweight division's primary challenger,

Joe Louis, a Negro. The bout took place in New York and, to the surprise of most Americans, the experienced German fighter and former champion knocked out the young Brown Bomber. The racists were jubilant.

With newspapers and radio commentators frequently reminding Americans and Germans of the bout's significance—both racial and nationalistic—Louis found himself brooding about the loss and increasingly eager for a rematch. That opportunity came on June 22, 1938, at Yankee Stadium. As the bell rang to open the initial round, Louis exploded from his corner and, with a series of furious blows, knocked out Schmeling in the first round. The people of New York's Harlem, wedded to radios covering the fight blow-by-blow, were reported by the media to have erupted in a loud, joyous, and effusive celebration which lasted for two days. (According to contemporary accounts, Jewish neighborhoods in Brooklyn and the Bronx also shared in the celebrations on the city streets.) Louis himself, soft-spoken and carefully correct, became the new Negro hero of the American people for the next decade. Like Owens, he conveyed the image of the "good" Negro—that is, the Negro who chose not to challenge the system and who expressed his gratitude to God and Country for the opportunities accorded him. That mission—to challenge the Jim Crow system—was left to the NAACP.

While most of its energies and attention remained focused on dismantling America's segregated institutions, the NAACP was compelled to stand up to the challenges from the extreme Left as well. The NAACP's most dramatic confrontation with the CPUSA arose during the mid-1930s over the handling of the famed Scottsboro Boys case. In 1931 nine young Negro men and boys between the ages of 13 and 20 were arrested in Alabama for the alleged rape of two white teenage girls.[2] At first, the NAACP dragged its heels over the question of entering the fray by hesitating to provide legal counsel to the accused because of the rape allegations. This was a period in which the NAACP had no permanent legal staff as yet. Consequently, the organization's fact-finding had been egregiously slow to such a degree that there was serious uncertainty about the merits of the case and the nature of the charges, notably the alleged rape of white women. To some NAACPers, accepting a case involving a violent crime, such as rape or murder, appeared to compromise the organization's basic civil rights mission.

Moreover, several nationally-prominent lawyers had already been recruited by the CPUSA to represent the young men. Cognizant of the impact the Scottsboro affair was beginning to have throughout black communities in the American heartland, Wilkins pressed Walter White into taking a role in the case even before he reported to New York to work as White's aide. The Communists had succeeded in making sizable inroads into the black community through the publicity generated by the case and several important Negro newspapers were championing their efforts. When Wilkins arrived in New York in 1931, Walter White told him that the Scottsboro Case was "your baby." To Wilkins' enormous regret, by then the Communists' lawyers had signed up the defendants as their clients and fully controlled their defense.[3]

> "In the Scottsboro case . . . the Reds found a drum they could thump with might and main" . . . attacking the NAACP, savaging the black bourgeoisie, raising money for other causes—doing everything, in short, but getting the Scottsboro Boys out of jail. I suppose the Party tried, but it looked to me as if the [Scottsboro] group was far more valuable to them as martyrs than as free men. From the point of view of those nine boys staring at the execution chamber, working out dialectics and the future of communism and capitalism wasn't the real issue. Their lives were the important thing, not abstract issues of Marxism, historical determinism, or even race, and I wanted to see them safe and free.[4]

Later, some observers contended that because the trial had become an international *cause celebre,* it generated an important source of funding for the CPUSA; for this reason and for propaganda purposes, they argued, the Communists needed to keep the case alive.

According to Roy Wilkins, after several years of monopolizing the case, the Communists' front group, the International Labor Defense (ILD):

> . . . disgraced itself thoroughly enough to allow the NAACP and other civil rights groups to re-enter the case. At precisely this time Joseph Stalin ordered his international outriders to form united fronts with liberal groups. Overnight we capitalist tools

> became potential comrades-in-arms. I became the NAACP's representative on a new Scottsboro defense committee, made up of the NAACP, . . . ACLU, Methodists, ILD, and League for Industrial Democracy (LID) . . . Dr. Allen Knight Chalmers, chairman and pastor of the Broadway Tabernacle of New York City, became head of the new committee, and we set out as quickly as we could to save the boys from the Communists and the white juries of Alabama.[5]

After persuading flamboyant defense counsel Sam Liebowitz to take a back seat in the defense of the nine, a capable white Alabama lawyer, Clarence Watts, took over and slowly began to make progress.[6] He persuaded an Alabama judge to sentence one of the nine, Haywood Patterson, to 75 years in jail instead of the electric chair. In less than two years, Watts managed to get the state to acknowledge insufficient evidence to convict four of the young men—Roberson, Williams, Montgomery, and LeRoy Wright—and granted them their freedom. Nevertheless, with the same evidence, the state refused to free the remaining five. It took 13 more years of legal work before the last of the five was freed in 1950. By then most of the world had experienced so many other horrors that few remembered the Scottsboro Boys. (Decades later, the NAACP provided the funds and support for the remaining Scottsboro Boys to live out their lives in relative peace.)

Black poet and activist Langston Hughes recalled that the Communists:

> . . . seeking to exploit the matter for their own ideological purposes, misrepresented the NAACP as being in league with "the lyncher bosses" and persuaded the boys to abandon NAACP-provided counsel, which included Clarence Darrow and Arthur Garfield Hayes. Later, as a participant in the Scottsboro Defense Committee, the Association helped raise funds for strictly legal expenses. Death sentences were imposed, appealed, reversed, reimposed, and appealed once more. None of the boys were executed; eventually, as the result of NAACP negotiations, they were successively released.[7]

Today, other than specialists and historians, few Americans remember one of the most influential race-based cases in our history. In addition to permanently establishing the Communists and the NAACP as bitter enemies, the case had a significant impact on the American psyche (and on the worldwide perception of race in America.) In 1975, Roy Wilkins wrote:

> The Scottsboro affair was a milestone in establishing the Negro as a human being entitled to all the rights and privileges of a citizen. The most telling ruling that came out it was Judge James Horton's setting aside of the conviction on the ground that it was contrary to credible evidence. This was a body blow at the system of [Southern] jurisprudence as it affected Negroes accused of crime.[8]

It did not go unnoticed, at least among Negro leaders of the period, that a disproportionate number of American Jews had established close working relationships with Negroes in many walks of life. Joe Louis's own promoter was Jewish (much to the dismay of Hitler himself). The lead attorney in the Scottsboro case, Sam Liebowitz, was Jewish. Many of the music publishers and club owners of the period were also Jewish and closely intertwined with Negro musicians and song writers. A significant number of labor organizers and activists, including many Communists, were Jewish and were active in pressing for full Negro participation in the newly formed industrial unions comprising the Congress of Industrial Organizations (CIO). One of the nation's most popular Sunday night radio programs, though by no means too far ahead of its time, was the Jack Benny Hour, in which a skinflint white comedian, who was also Jewish, parried funny one-liners with his black man-servant, Rochester (Eddie Anderson).

Further cementing the popular perception that their interests were inextricably connected, another Negro-Jewish collaboration began in 1937. That year a left-wing Jewish schoolteacher, Abel Meeropol, who also used the name Lewis Allen, wrote a poem, and then the music, for what was to become the most celebrated American anthem comprising barbed social commentary, "Strange Fruit." Meeropol later sang the song for the legendary Negro singer Billy Holiday, who promptly annexed it as her own. In 1939 she began singing it in public and recorded it with Commodore Records after her own record company, Columbia, refused it as too controversial. Later Holiday encouraged the myth that the song had been written especially for her. The substantial success of the Holiday recording, which closely identified the singer with the song, reached millions of mainstream Americans who were followers of jazz, swing, and popular ballads. "Strange Fruit" became their portal to the otherwise unspoken American dilemma—the nagging, painful unresolved stresses of race.[9]

During the late 1930s, the Communists surfaced as a key component of the first National Negro Congress in Chicago, where Roy Wilkins gave an address on lynching. Wilkins was there also to observe what role the Communists were trying to forge within the congress. Party members popped up in every discussion group but, uncharacteristically, refrained from trying to dominate them. One of the leaders of the congress—a radical named John Davis—told Wilkins afterward that the congress would replace the NAACP as the nation's leading Negro and civil rights organization, but promised Wilkins a job when that took place. Wilkins lost no sleep over the threat, and in the ensuing months ideological struggles among the Communists, Socialists, and liberals so weakened the congress that the Communists, having lost patience, openly took it over and transformed into a formal front group.[10]

Although the CPUSA benefited from the alliance of the United States, Britain, and the Soviet Union during the Second World War, this collaboration appears to have produced far more white conversions to the Soviet brand of socialism than Negro ones. With over a million Negroes serving in the U.S. armed forces and hundreds of thousands employed gainfully in the defense industries, the Communist solution to the Negro Question—a separate state carved out of the Black Belt—became an increasing source of political embarrassment for the CPUSA. That it stuck to its failed political formula for so long is no doubt a function of its intellectual source—Joseph Stalin.

By 1946, however, even the American Communists were aware that the separate state formula was a deadweight in courting Negro members. Early that year a debate was conducted among the Communist leaders over the Negro question—a debate inextricably involved with the hard-line leadership of Earl Browder, who was replaced by William Z. Foster as national chairman. From December 3 to December 5,

1946, the CPUSA held a plenum in New York City to consider, and ultimately adopt, a resolution in which the CPUSA retreated from the separate state formula, while reaffirming Joseph Stalin's view that the Negroes of the United States were a separate nation.

In calling for the "full realization of Negro nationhood, whether it be achieved under capitalism or socialism," the resolution declared:

> The Communist Party supports the right of self-determination for the Negro people, that is, their right to realize self-government in the Negro majority area in the South. Only on this basis will the relation of the Negro people to the State and Federal governments be determined on the basis of freedom .... Its form will be determined by the relationship of social forces in the country as a whole and by the relation of the Negro people to the progressive coalition.[11]

The new approach of the CPUSA on Negro liberation rested heavily on voter registration and participation and, ultimately, office-holding which, by the Party's new definition, constituted self-government leading to self-determination. This common sense victory over ideology brought the CPUSA much closer to the every-day pragmatism of the NAACP and its strategy of advancing Negro voter registration wherever possible. It also offered an ideological passport for the Communist leaders to urge their members to join the NAACP on a broad scale, since they were at this moment so compatible. Their objective, however, was far less benign than comradely affiliation; the CPUSA hoped to infiltrate into local NAACP branches sizable numbers of party members under its discipline who would gain disproportionate influence, if not control, over the NAACP's policies and programs. It was genuinely believed at the time, and much evidence then and later supported the notion, that the CPUSA was basically under the control of the Soviet Union.[12] Aware of both dangers, Walter White, Roy Wilkins, and the NAACP national board were determined to resist by battling the infiltrators at the grassroots level, triggering a barrage of Communist attacks on the NAACP's leadership.

In the spring and summer of 1947, NAACP regional and national meetings condemned "the attempts of various groups, particularly

Communists, either to secure control of our branches outright, or to use the branches as sounding boards for political or other ideas" and later rejected "the attempts of any organized clique, political party, or religious group to seize control of the branches or national office for the purpose of undermining the program to which the Association is dedicated."[13]

In 1949, after the NAACP decided to organize a new coalition of organizations termed the "Civil Rights Mobilization," the NAACP received a letter from William L. Patterson, the Negro Executive Secretary of the Civil Rights Congress, an outright front for the CPUSA. The latter offered to "cooperate" with the NAACP in this endeavor, while lamenting the fact that it had not been invited to participate.

Roy Wilkins, then Walter White's deputy, responded for the NAACP by noting that the Civil Rights Congress had been deliberately excluded, because the NAACP had not forgotten the behavior of the Communists and their various fronts toward the NAACP since the Scottsboro case. "We remember," Wilkins wrote, "that in the Scottsboro case the NAACP was subjected to the most unprincipled vilification. We remember the campaigns of slander in the *Daily Worker*. We remember the leaflets and the speakers and the whole unspeakable machinery that was turned loose upon all those who did not embrace the 'unity' as announced by the Communists. We want none of that unity today."

The most telling indictment of the Communist behavior, however, was not in regard to its relentless attacks on the NAACP. In the same letter, Wilkins charged the CPUSA with hypocrisy and abandonment of civil rights whenever it served the interests of the Soviet Union. In one of his most eloquent passages, Wilkins asserted:

> We of the NAACP remember that during the war when Negro Americans were fighting for jobs on the home front and fighting for decent treatment in the armed services we could get no help from the organizations of the extreme Left. They abandoned the fight for Negro rights on the ground that such a campaign would "interfere with the war effort." As soon as Russia was attacked by Germany they dropped the Negro question and concentrated all effort in support of the war in order to help the Soviet Union. During the war years the disciples of the

> extreme Left sounded very much like the worst of the Negro-hating southerners.
>
> American Negroes, and especially the NAACP, cannot forget this. It seems to us to prove conclusively (even if there were not mountains of additional proof) that the organizations of the extreme Left, when they campaign for civil rights, or in behalf of a minority, do so as a secondary consideration, activity upon which is certain to be weighted, shaped, angled, or abandoned in accordance with the Communist Party "line."[14]

In addition, Wilkins reminded Patterson of a list of failures on the part of Communists to support civil rights or civil liberties causes in recent years, noting that during a meeting on a case in Trenton, New Jersey, Patterson himself had stated that "the NAACP should be put out of business."

The NAACP's leaders, however, were determined to both defeat the efforts of the CPUSA and to retain their commitment to democratic values and the promises inherent in the U.S. Constitution. At the same time, given the rapid rise of anti-Communist hysteria, the NAACP believed it vitally important to demonstrate its total independence from ideology of any extreme. Immediately after World War II, under instructions from Walter White, then Roy Wilkins and Thurgood Marshall, Gloster Current became the field general in the nationwide campaign to block the efforts of the CPUSA to infiltrate the NAACP's ranks, especially among the youth and college chapters, where any young person could join if he had the $1 for annual membership dues.

The NAACP leaders had additional reasons for concern because, by that time, two giants among American Negroes had become major symbols for the CPUSA: the legendary actor, singer, and athlete Paul Robeson and the militant scholar and former *Crisis* editor W.E.B. Dubois. The CPUSA appreciated how vast the grassroots structure of the NAACP had evolved: by 1949, the NAACP reported 1,457 local branches, youth councils, and college chapters, 63 percent of which were located in the South.[15] No other mass organization, outside of the labor movement, offered such a tempting target for the CPUSA.

The Communists early on had targeted American Negroes as the most likely demographic group for conversion to their ideology on the obvious premise that, having been the longest and most oppressed segment of American society, they would be the most vulnerable to the appeals of the CPUSA. However, they were chronically unable to grasp the essential truth that, despite their long and horrific ordeal, most African Americans were not only patriotic, especially during the first half of the twentieth century; but also they wanted above all to share in the rights and rewards of American citizenship. They wanted what most Americans had and took for granted. The centerpiece of the Communist program for Negroes—to carve out a swath of territory in the South's Black Belt to establish a separate state for Negroes—would not achieve these goals or fulfill Negro aspirations. A separate Negro state—either in Africa as Garvey had proposed or in the American South as the Communists advocated—failed to resonate with the vast majority of American Negroes.

After the Second World War many of the liberal and left-leaning labor unions, especially among those comprising the CIO, were also targeted by the Communists during that brief period of Comintern-ordered world-wide "brotherliness" in which party members were directed to "join like-minded organizations."[16] These unions were, in the main, newly formed, purportedly open to any worker regardless of race, and organized among the nation's hourly-wage industrial workers. Major efforts to stop the Communists and expel their leaders were undertaken by the United Auto Workers, the Electricians Union (UE), the Mine Workers, and the Men's Clothing Workers as well as by the American Federation of Labor's (AFL) Ladies Garment Workers. The West Coast Longshoremen and the New York-based Furrier Workers, on the other hand, remained loyal to the Communists.

The Communist post-war takeover of the American Labor Party, combined with the Progressive Party's nomination of Henry Wallace, provided voters with a left-wing alternative to Harry Truman in 1948. Truman, at the same time, had to fight the Southern segregationists who had bolted from the Democrats to form their own Dixiecrat Party. Both made Truman's race for the presidency against the favored Republican standard bearer, Thomas E. Dewey, a totally uphill battle. Liberals, with Hubert Humphrey among the most visible, rallied behind Truman. These liberals formed their own anti-Communist political action association—the Americans for Democratic Action (ADA)—which also adopted a membership card barring Communists and all other followers of totalitarian organizations—right or left—

from joining. The American Civil Liberties Union (ACLU) leadership also cleaned house and supported several federal government measures suppressing the Communists, which, in later years, the next generation of its leaders came to regret.

Part sheer patriotism, part adept public relations, part succumbing to the hysteria of the period—the actions by the NAACP to separate itself from the Communists were important facets of its overall advocacy mission. As the Cold War and the hysteria against domestic Communists grew, it became increasingly difficult to get Americans to listen with open minds to the grievances and assertions of the NAACP, especially among those who believed that the NAACP itself was part of the Communist conspiracy. Racists from the South and radical conservatives from the rest of the country denounced as Communist initiatives every effort to remove or ameliorate Jim Crow or to increase opportunities for Negroes. Immediately after World War II, both houses of the U.S. Congress were Republican-controlled and dominated by archconservatives, including powerful Southern committee chairmen. The Supreme Court—moderate to liberal at the time—was largely comprised of appointees from the four-term tenure of Franklin Delano Roosevelt, but headed by a moderately conservative Southern chief justice. On a national level, the only reliable friend of civil rights within the federal government was the Truman Administration in 1948.

Truman's near-miraculous victory came despite the bitter enmity of the far right and the far left. He owed his second term to liberals and left-of-center moderates and to Negro and other minority voters. Given this background, the direction in which Walter White, then Roy Wilkins, steered the NAACP made both strategic and tactical sense; in in no way could be the cause of racial justice helped by an alliance with the political extremes. The NAACP's success in separating its views, policies, and membership from those of the CPUSA established the Association as a responsible, constructive force, committed to internal democracy, as well as to democracy throughout the nation and abroad. Its bona fides thus established, the NAACP was able to command the respect and the growing support of the huge middle-of-the-road electorate and of the liberals who began to listen both with open minds and hearts as the NAACP spelled out the compelling case for first-class citizenship for Negroes to the American people in the decade following the end of World War II. Its message would also resonate well with the vast majority of American Negroes who were wedded to the goals of the American Dream and the values of the Constitution.

By 1950 the NAACP was compelled to face its internal Communist problem head on. At its annual convention in Boston in June, the leadership placed a resolution before the delegates condemning the attacks on the NAACP and it officers by the Communists and their fellow travelers. It directed the national board to take "necessary steps to eradicate Communist infiltration and, if necessary, to suspend, reorganize, lift the charter of, or expel any branches that came under Communist control . . . . Wilkins recalled. "After the delegates passed the resolution by a 6-to-1 margin [309 to 57], our more radical friends rose in high dudgeon and stormed out of the room," Wilkins recalled in his autobiography. "I was happy to see them go," he wrote.[17] Director of Branches Gloster Current was charged with the mission of carrying out these resolutions, which he implemented with energy and thoroughness.

According to the NAACP 1950 *Annual Report,* "The vote followed two hours of acrimonious debate. The outcome, however, was never in doubt. The convention went on record as unequivocally condemning 'attacks by Communists and their fellow-travelers upon the Association and their officials.'"[18]

Thurgood Marshall's biographer, Juan Williams, revealed in 1998 that Marshall began collaborating with FBI Director J. Edgar Hoover in 1956 at the latter's invitation to share information regarding the Communist infiltration of civil rights organizations, especially their efforts to gain control of NAACP local units. Williams reported almost a half century later that Marshall had kept Hoover and his associates abreast of news of Communist infiltration of branches; Hoover and the FBI reciprocated by allowing Marshall to read the most secret and unexpurgated intelligence files compiled from reports by FBI agents and informers on the latest tactics and techniques employed by the Communists, especially as directed toward NAACP branches. In the period after 1956, one of the most effective was the formation of labor front groups, which in turn sought to obtain NAACP assistance in fighting employer discrimination. Their efforts proved futile, however, because of the vigilance of Labor Director Herbert Hill and Branch Director Gloster Current.

A veteran correspondent of the *Washington Post,* Juan Williams reported that the FBI permitted Marshall to take written notes and, if he desired, to copy verbatim whatever he wished from the FBI files. Marshall intimated to a few close associates during that period that he was providing Hoover only with information the FBI already had. Those who were familiar with Marshall's demeanor appreciated how he could appear to be agreeing with the views of white people while playing them for contrary reasons. The suggestion of these old associates is that Marshall was "jiving" Hoover, while the FBI director believed he was the recipient of genuine intelligence. Since both principal figures are deceased, it is impossible to state with any certainty which version is more accurate.

Privy to the latest intelligence, Thurgood Marshall gave the keynote address to the 1956 NAACP national convention in San Francisco, where he "sounded the alarm" to the assembled delegates. "Whatever the name, whatever the avowed purpose, we know them for what they are," Marshall roared from the podium to the plenary. "There is no place in this organization for Communists or those who follow the Communist line," he added.[19]

One of the most regrettable aspects of this period was the NAACP's disassociation from Robeson and DuBois. In 1948 and in response to federal government harassment, DuBois had moved to Ghana to map out a strategy for Pan-Africanism. As a bone to the extreme right and the racists, DuBois was no longer mentioned by the NAACP and Robeson was occasionally vilified, especially when he returned from one of his Moscow sojourns.[20] Both men had been authentic African-American heroes and their political predilections hardly disqualified their other deeds from either recognition or approbation.[21]

6. World War II and Its Consequences for Race

Currently [in 1944] there are 481 branches of the Association . . . 77 youth councils and 22 college chapters. The total membership . . . is approximately 85,000. . . . Few similar organizations have reached the organizational stability and the membership size of the NAACP. It should be stressed that, while the lack of a mass following is a weakness, the high intellectual quality of the membership is an asset. Few organizations in the entire country compare with the NAACP in respect to the education and mental alertness of the persons attracted to it. In a study of 5,512 Negro college students . . . , Charles Johnson found that 25 percent of them were members of the NAACP. No other organization of Negroes approached that percentage. The quality of the membership is reflected in the National Office.

Gunnar Myrdal, *An American Dilemma,* New York, 1944, 821

The pattern of life for the Negro in the armed services of the United States, unhappily, is the familiar one in civilian life. Even more unhappily, this military pattern follows the way of race relations in the most backward states of the Deep South instead of the patterns Negroes know in the more enlightened states in the north. . . . Before it is too late, America needs to realize that

> the roots of this treatment of her own Negro minority are also the roots of a condition, almost wholly unrelated to the Negro, of deep concern to all of us who see that an Axis victory is far from impossible and that such a victory would mean actual slavery for men and women of all races all over the world.
>
> **Walter White, NAACP Executive Secretary, "The Right to Fight for Democracy"** ***Survey Graphic*****, November 1942, 472–474**

The December 7, 1941, attack on Pearl Harbor, which triggered American involvement in the actual fighting, was noteworthy in terms of race as well. The Roosevelt Administration, determined to forge the maximum degree of national unity to pursue the global war, initiated a string of ethnic and racial war heroes in the early days of the war, including an Irishman, a Jew, and a Negro. The latter was 22-year-old Dorie Miller of Waco, Texas. Relegated to a noncombatant post as a steward or officer's mess servant, Miller had never been instructed on the firing of guns. Nevertheless, during the Pearl Harbor attack aboard the ill-fated USS *Arizona,* Miller dragged his mortally wounded captain to safety, and then manned a machine gun and, according to U.S. Navy information personnel, he shot down five Japanese planes. (He died two years later when the aircraft carrier to which he had been assigned was sunk by a Japanese submarine.) Miller's feats ascended to a level of legend and were retold often, especially in publications read by American Negroes, the majority of whom experienced an understandable pang of pride in his heroism.

During World War II the NAACP's political activity was largely confined to pressuring Washington for a fair employment practices act, a diluted version of which had been promulgated by FDR as an executive order;[1] to insisting on the hiring of Negroes in the nation's defense plants; and to pressing for the desegregation of the armed forces, including the assignment of Negro units to combat roles. At one point, the NAACP demanded that the War Department permit mixed white and black units of volunteers, including mixed officers, but Secretary of War Henry Stimson refused.[2] The organization walked a narrow line between constant pressure for further desegregation and for increasing the role of Negroes in the war effort—civilian and military—on the one hand, and the careful avoidance of impairing the rapidly-growing American juggernaut that was vital to the defeat of the racist Nazis, on the other.

Having received a large number of complaints from Negro servicemen, the NAACP also pressed for improved treatment of Negro personnel, both on active duty and in the communities surrounding the military bases. Since most of the stateside bases were in the South, Negro personnel were receiving the undiluted Jim Crow treatment from civilians as well as from Southern servicemen and officers. It goes without saying that virtually every aspect of military life in this period was segregated, including such red-blooded American institutions as the Red Cross and the United Service Organizations (USO). Both of these quasi-private institutions, though chartered by Congress, continued to exclude Negro servicemen from receiving most of their services and, in the exceptional cases where assistance was provided to Negroes, these institutions tended to treat them as second-class warriors long after the military services were desegregated. In addition to its civil rights functions, therefore, the NAACP also provided Negro servicemen with the social and economic assistance that the Red Cross and the USO denied them, including notifications from families of medical emergencies that would justify short leaves for the servicemen, hospitality while away from home, communication between servicemen and their loved ones, assistance for wives and parents entitled to monthly support, and so forth.[3]

Closer to its central mission, the NAACP provided lawyers to defend Negro servicemen who had resisted assaults by civilians and uniformed personnel. To no avail, the Association during wartime pressed for federal intervention on behalf of black servicemen murdered by civilians and local law enforcers. The NAACP's lawyers actually won a not guilty verdict for a Negro private accused in 1943 of raping a 50-year-old woman. To the astonishment of almost everybody, the verdict was arrived at by an all-white jury.[4] So appreciative were Negro troops of the NAACP's efforts that they contributed a total of $7,000 to the Association in 1943 alone.

Walter White and Charles Hamilton Houston vigorously lobbied the administration to compel employers and unions to hire Negro workers in the defense industries as well, which gradually bore fruit as the war deepened. One result of the constant NAACP pressure was the experiment known as the Tuskegee Airmen, which despite innumerable obstacles helped to demonstrate the skill, acumen, and courage of black pilots in combat.[5] The NAACP was less successful in its fight against the Red Cross's practice of segregating the blood plasma contributed by white and Negro donors, even though scientifically there was no medical reason to do so.

Throughout the war years, the NAACP also made its voice heard in numerous congressional committees on social and economic policies and federal programs, often calling upon Charles Hamilton Houston, once again residing in Washington, to appear on behalf of the Association to present its views. Walter White and his assistant, Roy Wilkins, constructed an evolving network of official and unofficial relationships and political contacts that provided the underpinnings on which to build a much-admired lobbying mechanism that would influence the thinking and behavior of future congressional lawmakers.

In turn, as the NAACP expanded its vaunted Washington Bureau in 1950 under the sagacious direction of Clarence Mitchell, whose Baltimore family was a political powerhouse within the NAACP, the organization's clout would also be greatly enhanced by its ability to mobilize large numbers of voters in each of the congressional districts and states. With guidance from the national staff, these voters pressed upon their elected representatives the views and needs of the Association, nationally and locally. It was this classic two-way street—lobbying at the top in Washington (or the state capitol) and generating grassroots sentiment at the bottom—which became the model for other citizens' organizations in the years ahead.

One by-product of the Allied victory was the rapid growth of political interest and understanding among the hundreds of thousands of Negro troops who had been enlisted in the struggle to preserve democracy while they themselves were being consigned to second-class status because of their race. Thousands vowed that if they returned home alive, they would fight for first-class citizenship. In the Jim Crow South, that battle began almost the week following the surrender of Japan as scores of courageous Negro veterans, having faced the worst the Nazis and Japanese could deal out, now squared off with their domestic oppressors by actively seeking the right to vote. The noble South, however, was not the least bit inclined to honor these servicemen who had returned from defending their nation. The violence that had remained close to the surface throughout the war years sprang forth with eloquent vengeance after the war and victimized countless returning Negro veterans who were bullied, beaten, forced to flee, or even murdered in cold blood.[6]

Slowly however, counter forces were beginning to emerge among intellectual and religious groups outside the South. Several of the Jewish secular agencies and a sizable number of rabbis began to speak publicly about the immorality of racism. Some of the less established Protestant ministers, especially Unitarians, Universalists, and Quakers, openly condemned the Jim Crow practices of the South. Perhaps the most unexpected voices came from a Jesuit priest in the Catholic Church, Rev. George H. Dunne, who branded segregation a sin in an article published in the influential lay Catholic periodical *Commonweal* in 1946. Father Dunne became a reliable activist in the civil rights demonstrations and protests of the 1960s and 1970s.[7] He also inspired a generation of Roman Catholics to fight racial injustice, especially during the 1960s in the South.

One major impetus to the NAACP's growing political activity and clout came in June 1947 when President Harry S. Truman broke with precedent by addressing the NAACP's 38th annual convention in the nation's capitol and making the most radical presidential statement in support of civil rights since Lincoln's Emancipation Proclamation. Placing himself squarely in support of racial equality and the duty of the federal government to participate in the struggle, Truman effectively broke with his powerful Dixiecrat wing in his reelection bid in 1948 by telling the cheering NAACP delegates:

> We can no longer afford the luxury of a leisurely attack upon prejudice and discrimination. There is much that state and local governments can do in providing positive safeguards for civil rights. But we cannot, any longer, await the growth of a will to action in the slowest states or the most backward community. *Our national government must show the way.* (emphasis added)[8]

The political ferment created by returning Negro servicemen in the South resulted in more than a dozen lynchings in the years immediately after the war. As a result, the NAACP pushed for hearings before the House of Representatives' Judiciary Committee, which were held in early 1948, possibly the last specifically to seek adoption of an antilynching bill.[9]

Not content to depend solely on the NAACP's membership and lobbying apparatus in Washington, Wilkins and Washington bureau chief

Clarence Mitchell formally organized the Leadership Conference on Civil Rights (LCCR) in 1951. It was Wilkins's unwavering contention that, given the status of African Americans as a permanent minority of 11 or 12 percent of the population, the only way to significantly move American society was to develop strong and committed allies from among other demographic and occupational groups, and most especially from among the white majority. Wilkins believed firmly that positive change either from Congress and/or the executive branch depended upon rallying a sufficient number of whites to the cause at any given moment, so that the nose-counting politicians would perceive that their self-interest was connected with the civil rights proposals then on the table. Wilkins rejected separatism not only as the other side of the coin from segregation, and not only because he regarded it as morally wrong, but also because, in pragmatic terms, he was convinced that it was self-defeating. He had no faith in the notion that the majority of white Americans would support the claims of Negroes if the latter chose to sever their connection with the larger society.

As a result of these deeply held philosophical views that Wilkins shared with Mitchell, they invested much of their energy and resources in the process of welding an effective, and predominantly white, national coalition. The seeds of this process were planted in the 1947 appeal before the Supreme Court to bar restrictive covenants, when a score of sympathetic organizations filed *amicus curiae* briefs; in the formation of the National Committee Against Violence; and in the 1946 campaign headed by Wilkins, Mitchell (then NAACP labor secretary) and A. Philip Randolph, the leading black trade union leader. Under Randolph's aegis, but with substantial assistance from the NAACP, an interracial group known as the National Council for a Permanent FEPC (Fair Employment Practices Commission) was formed to make permanent the war time FEP law that had lapsed that year. Altogether, 70 groups joined the council, directed by Wilkins and its secretary, Arnold Aronson, a leader of the Jewish secular community. Despite support from the Truman Administration and energetic lobbying conducted by the broad-based coalition, the conservative Congress failed to adopt the proposed legislation.[10]

Faced with stubborn opposition on Capitol Hill, Wilkins and Aronson issued a call for a massive interracial lobbying effort in 1949 to be conducted by representatives of all sympathetic national organizations.

Dubbed the National Emergency Civil Rights Mobilization, this gigantic citizens lobby comprised of some 4,000 representatives from approximately 100 black and white groups—religious, political, and civil rights—convened on January 15, 1950, for a three-day conference combined with the largest lobbying effort in the history of the nation. The participants spread out on the Hill and its environs, buttonholing senators and congressmen in support of civil rights, especially the FEPC. Wilkins led a delegation to meet with President Truman, who cut Wilkins short when he tried to list their demands, advising them to concentrate on the Congress, where the real roadblock existed. Truman, Wilkins recollected, was firmly in their camp and *he* could count noses.

The coalition's organizational representatives meeting in Washington agreed to form a permanent umbrella group whose purpose would be to effect the passage of civil rights laws. Its member organizations and unions would pay dues and educate their own constituencies about the proposed civil rights laws, while its Washington staffs would help the newly formed entity to lobby for passage of the proposed laws. In effect, the NAACP remained in control of the organization for the next 45 years. Although Walter White's name appeared as the first LCCR director, he was indisposed because of failing health and Wilkins, acting in his stead, exercised full control. The next most important post was legislative chair, the vanguard lobbying position, and the NAACP's Clarence Mitchell was appointed to fill it. Arnold Aronson was elected secretary and labor attorney Joseph L. Rauh, long an NAACP board member and leader of the ADA, was named LCCR counsel. A. Philip Randolph begged off because he decided to focus all of his efforts on behalf of an FEPC. The official name—Leadership Conference on Civil Rights, or LCCR—was adopted in 1951 after another organizing conference.

Wilkins was formally elected LCRR director when he became the permanent executive secretary of the NAACP in 1955. He retained that powerful post until 1977, when he retired from both organizations. (Mitchell headed the organization until his own retirement in 1978, after which the new NAACP CEO, Benjamin L. Hooks, was elected its director in 1981. Hooks retired from both posts in 1995.) The coalition grew incrementally over time with about 185 member organizations at its peak, adding groups that represented women, Hispanics, Asian-Americans, gays, and the disabled. It became a vitally important and potent weapon in the NAACP's armory and was instrumental in the adoption of almost every civil rights law passed by Congress and signed by the sitting president from 1957 until 1995, as well as the principal vehicle for defeating Supreme Court nominations of candidates perceived as hostile to civil rights.

The promulgation of *Brown* in 1954 impacted on the political realm in both positive and negative ways. Initially, *Brown* became the battle cry in reverse for the segregationists throughout the South. They became more determined to thwart any Negro initiatives in the electoral process by blocking—legally and illegally—most of the voter drives spurred by the NAACP and, when they perceived that the NAACP was nearing success in a given locale or state, the extremists hardly hesitated to kill, maim, or wound the black activists leading the drives. Martyrs to the cause of voter registration were nothing new to the NAACP activists. As early as June 23, 1940, the body of local NAACP leader Elbert Williams had been found floating in a local river in Brownsville, Haywood County, Tennessee. Williams had been publicly and energetically urging Negroes in the county to vote. On Christmas Day, 1951, NAACP state leader Harry T. Moore was murdered in a bombing attack in Florida for his courageous leadership of the statewide NAACP apparatus as the first paid full-time state executive director in the NAACP's history. Expanding Negro voter registration had been one of his major priorities, and by the year of his death Florida's roll of Negro voters far exceeded that of any of the other Southern states. Although a white witness emerged during the 1990s and a state newspaper sought to reopen the case, it remains unsolved.[11]

As if *Brown* were not enough of a red flag for the violence-prone Southern segregationists, the Supreme Court's historic school decision served also to embolden Southern blacks in their quest for their voting rights. Throughout the South, individual local leaders began to take the initiative to gain access to the ballot box, despite the fact that the Eisenhower Administration equivocated over where it stood in the face of the Supreme Court's decision. Fearless Negroes seeking the vote in 1955 could expect no assistance or protection from the federal government. The gravest showdown came in one of the most regressive counties in the state of Mississippi—Humphreys County, which was the home of 16,012 Negroes eligible to vote. With enormous effort and daring, Rev. George W. Lee and Gus Courts, the NAACP branch president, had persuaded some 400 Negroes to register. Using the cover of darkness on the night of May 7, 1955, a heroic representative of the Confederacy on May 13 gunned down Rev. Lee on a main street of the county seat, Belzoni. The chilling murder failed to muster any investigation by the local police. The shotgun pellets found in Rev. Lee's mouth caused one local sheriff to speculate as to whether they had been fillings from his teeth. A few weeks later, on May 31, 1955, the U.S. Supreme Court ruled in *Brown II* that America's public schools must be desegregated "with all deliberate speed." Another red flag unfurled before the eyes of hate-filled, gun-toting white Southern manhood.

Two months after Rev. Lee's assassination, on August 13, NAACP leader Lamar Smith of nearby Brookhaven was murdered. Smith was gunned down at midday on the courthouse lawn before scores of white witnesses. Despite that, the local grand jury failed to indict any individual for lack of evidence. What was Lamar Davis' crime? He had the temerity to urge blacks to use absentee ballots to register to vote.[12] As expected, no person was ever apprehended or punished for Smith's murder either.

Following the two murders, every registered Negro except Gus Courts dropped off the registration rolls. The local members of the White Citizens Council, in what today would be regarded as an out-and-out conspiracy, applied escalating forms of economic pressure on Gus Courts. His landlord tripled the rent of his grocery store, forcing him to move. When that failed to halt his voter activity, by "coincidence" all of his suppliers refused to advance him the customary credit for the goods he sold. On the brink of disaster, Gus Courts held out until, emboldened by the failure to apprehend or convict anyone for the murder of Rev. Lee and Lamar Smith, another son of the Confederacy gunned down Gus Courts on November 25. Courts survived the attempted assassination—barely—but he was never the same again. Not unexpectedly, his assailant was never identified either.

Furious at the U.S. Supreme Court's decisions, the South's elected leaders egged on its most vociferous and violence-prone elements. Governor Talmadge of Georgia pledged that he would resist the Supreme Court's decision in every one of the state's 159 counties. The White Citizens Councils by then virtually in command of Mississippi's official power structure stepped up their race-baiting.[13] Roy Wilkins, less than two months after being elected executive secretary, was besieged with reports from his no-nonsense Southern regional director, Ruby Hurley, and the field secretaries from each of the NAACP's Region Five states, that the most extreme elements were organizing to employ intimidation and violence against any Negroes who stood up to Jim Crow. Dr. T.R.M. Howard and war veteran Charles Evers (Medgar's brother and successor as field secretary in 1963) were terrorized after trying to register in Philadelphia, Mississippi, forcing both men to flee the state. (Charles Evers did not return to Mississippi until after his brother's murder eight years later.)

On August 28, 1955, a 14-year-old boy from Chicago, Emmett Till, was kidnapped and murdered in Money, Mississippi, allegedly for whistling at a white woman. His beaten and shackled corpse was recovered from a local river and helped to produce a public outcry outside the South against the epidemic of brutality unleashed in response to *Brown*. The NAACP organized a series of mass meetings across the nation to protest the murder of Emmett Till, whose grief-stricken mother at each gathering pleaded with the civilized world to end Jim Crow and lynching.[14] Nevertheless, none of those suspected of killing Till were convicted in a trial atmosphere of unparalleled arrogance and outright bigotry. Again, the federal government under wartime hero Dwight David Eisenhower remained silent and noncommittal, although Herbert Brownell's Justice Department expressed anger and dismay. Blacks wondered aloud how the leader of the Allied forces in Europe that freed the world from heavily armed Nazi and Fascist racism could fail to provide protection for citizens of his own country who happened to be black.

In 1955, the same year that Rev. Lee, Lamar Smith, and Emmet Till were murdered and Gus Courts was crippled for life, the National Press Club in Washington, D.C., admitted its first Negro to membership. He was Louis Lautier, a reporter for the black *Atlanta Daily World*. Lautier had been one of the first blacks admitted to the U.S. congressional press galleries on March 18, 1947. Now at least, Negro reporters could cover lynchings from the nation's capital on the same terms as white reporters. Against this morsel of progress, the 1955 NAACP *Annual Report* stated that, because of the reign of terror throughout the state of Mississippi in 1955, the number of registered Negro voters had declined from 22,000 to less than 8,000.[15]

Not only did the federal government during this era fail to protect the lives and bodies of black Americans in the South, it also refused to enforce the law of the land—the *Brown* decision—as the Deep South states systematically nullified almost every effort to desegregate public schools. The spread of the White Citizens Councils from Mississippi to its neighboring states and then as far north as Virginia meant that many of the South's "respectable" white leaders were condoning the use of coercion to halt Negro progress as well as enforcement of court decisions on race. The Bill of Rights itself was flouted at every opportunity by those sworn to uphold the law. In 1956 the attorneys general of Louisiana and Alabama launched all-out attacks on the NAACP, seriously crippling its ability to function. Violating a number of rights guaranteed by the First Amendment, including free speech, association, and assembly, both states succeeded in halting the respective NAACP state conferences and their branches by obtaining court orders for the NAACP units to divulge their membership lists to both state authorities. In the interim, Virginia also obtained an injunction against any further NAACP activities until the latter complied with *its* orders.

Fighting now for its very survival, the NAACP ultimately decided to refuse these demands, but only after a heated discussion between Thurgood Marshall and Robert L. Carter, the association's top two lawyers, at a meeting also attended by Roy Wilkins.[16] Carter opposed any effort to provide the authorities in any of the Southern states with the NAACP's membership lists on First Amendment grounds, one of his specialties, whereas Marshall argued with equal vehemence that the NAACP could not ignore a court order, regardless of the underlying motives. Carter also expressed the view that compliance with the court orders would result in the destruction of the NAACP in the affected states and, perhaps, over a wider jurisdiction. After an extended argument, Marshall, according to Carter, threw up his hands and offered to leave the decision to Wilkins, who had carefully listened to both sides without murmuring a word. At this point, Wilkins picked up a phone and began to systematically call each of the NAACP Board members to explain the dilemma and to seek their opinions. As it turned out, the majority supported Carter's position to refuse to comply with the court order.

As Carter recollects the vote, every lawyer on the board except Loren Miller of California voted to comply with the court order by turning over the membership lists to the state authorities. On the other hand, every other board member reached, none of them lawyers, voted to defy the court order. Whatever his personal views might have been, Wilkins followed the board majority and instructed the NAACP's lawyers to defy the court orders. The board majority had recognized that the safety, even the lives, of those members exposed publicly would be gravely jeopardized by any other course of action. Once the NAACP Board arrived at its position, Thurgood Marshall fully supported the National Board when they voted to resist.[17]

The NAACP fought these measures by Louisiana and Alabama all the way to the Supreme Court where, under General Counsel Robert Carter's direction, the NAACP was vindicated. However, almost an entire decade transpired before this victory. Meanwhile, the organizational apparatus in both states went underground, making it extremely difficult to conduct its normal activities, including membership solicitation and renewal.

Shortly after Alabama and Louisiana tightened the screws on the NAACP, the state of Virginia passed seven separate laws against the NAACP, including prohibiting it from raising funds to support litigation in antidiscrimination cases, barring it from advocating desegregation of public schools in Virginia, and preventing it from financially aiding any person involved in law suits against the state. It also required the NAACP to turn over its membership lists. The state of Texas followed suit shortly thereafter with its own brand of unconstitutionality. In none of these nor in any other state did the NAACP succumb to the demands for their membership lists.[18]

On June 1, 1964, the Supreme Court unanimously struck down the unconstitutional measures employed by Alabama against the NAACP. The Association immediately resurfaced and, as early as July 23, delegates form Alabama branches were participating in the 1964 national convention in Washington, D.C. On September 11–12, 1965, the NAACP conducted a mini-convention and national board meeting in Birmingham, attended by 350 delegates. The board members, delegates, and staff attending exhibited a mixture of anxiety and exuberance, the latter hardly encouraged by white-robed Klansmen filming the entry and exit of the participants. Disappointingly, white hotel guests failed to exhibit the traditional hospitality and graciousness for which the South (in its own mind at least) was best known. The small number of whites attending the NAACP meeting frequently heard loud whispers of "nigger lover" whenever they walked through the lobby or out on to the street entrances. The KKK tactics and the inhospitable behavior, however, failed to intimidate the Alabaman NAACPers. By the end of 1965, their membership had reached almost 7,000 with 36 branches, more than two-thirds of the level of organization enjoyed by the NAACP eight years earlier when the state banned its activities.[19]

Despite the relentless harassment and attacks, the *Brown* decision had visited a seminal change in the South, if not the nation: It had persuaded, indeed inspired, a sizable portion of the Negro population to cast off subservience and ignore fear in order to transform their status. No longer would black Americans passively accept their lot without a struggle; the threat of violence would ultimately fail to intimidate the black majority. This transformation would in the long run be the most important and lasting achievement of *Brown.*

Sensing this sea change of attitude, white segregationists escalated their violent responses to the increasing number of forays by local black leaders in the struggle over the ballot box. In the early 1960s, a string of new NAACP martyrs in Mississippi fell to the bullets and bombs of the Klan and the White Citizens Councils: Medgar Evers in Jackson, George Metcalf in Natchez, Vernon Dahmer in Hattiesburg when a fire bomb was thrown into his bedroom window while he and his wife slept, and Korean war veteran Wharlest Jackson in Natchez. Dozens of NAACP leaders suffered savage attacks because of their voter activities, resulting in fatalities or crippling wounds.

As each NAACP leader fell, however, others stepped forward to take their places. Unquestionably, large numbers of Negroes were still being intimidated and frightened away from the voter registration or polling places by the violence of the Klan and the White Citizens Councils. Despite the palpable fear and the virtual monopoly of the weapons of violence in the hands of their oppressors, thousands of other Negroes continued to risk everything to gain the right to vote. Many lost their jobs or livelihoods—farmers found their loans called in by the local banks; maids and laundresses were summarily dismissed; schoolteachers were not rehired. Youngsters in school and students in college were expelled, dismissed, or suspended, even by historically black colleges, for participating in legal, constitutionally guaranteed voter rights activities. Ministers were harassed and local churches, often the only possible meeting places for the activists, firebombed. For those identified as "troublemakers" (which was equated with activism in the NAACP or with seeking to register to vote), credit at the local general store or food market dried up. And then there were those who were the targets of violence: a small mob attacking one or two unarmed Negroes, or a visit from the hooded night riders who tossed gasoline-fueled firebombs on the homes and barns of Negro families, or the hysteria-whipped crowds surrounding the local jail and kidnapping a Negro accused of a crime but not yet tried, in order to impose vigilante justice at the end of a rope.

The growing violence by itself should have given Congress and the White House sufficient incentive in 1957 to enact a halfway respectable civil rights law. Instead, the lawmakers and the executive branch interpreted the massive white resistance, including the violence toward African Americans, as the will of the majority of white Americans generally. Members of Congress, even those outside the South, saw little on the "up" side for their political careers, should they support a strong civil rights bill. The general *laissez faire* philosophy of President Eisenhower and most of the elected Republicans worked against any significant federal intervention. With Southerners controlling most of the House and Senate chairmanships and the potency of Rule 22 (the measure designed to promote filibusters) unchallenged, not too many of the non-South Democrats in Congress had the stomach to fight what was almost certainly a losing battle.

Nevertheless, in 1957 a respectable civil rights bill was passed by the House, calling for a civil rights commission, setting up a civil rights division under its own assistant attorney general in the Justice Department, empowering the Attorney General to "correct abuses of any constitutional rights," and directing that voting rights be protected by the federal government. Senate Majority Leader Lyndon B. Johnson, perhaps realizing that some day he would require the support of African Americans in his own run for the presidency, informed Wilkins and Mitchell that he was only interested in the voting rights provision of the House bill. He was dead set against submission of the third section—Title III—because the Southern legislators feared that its enactment would be used to implement the Court's order to desegregate public schools. He accepted the proposals to establish a civil rights commission and to create a civil rights division within the Justice Department.

In a disingenuous effort to sweeten the pot, Johnson added a jury trial provision that was hollow from the start: it required that civil rights violators cited for contempt could be tried but only by a jury trial, knowing full well that a Southern jury (usually one lily-white) would never convict a white defendant so charged. The gutted bill passed the Senate in August 1957. The liberal Republicans, led by supportive Vice President Nixon, turned around and urged that the LCCR and the NAACP oppose the final passage and wait until 1958, after the congressional elections, to produce a "better" bill. Within the civil rights movement, and especially within the NAACP, tempers flared on both sides of the argument. Joe Rauh persuaded Wilkins to call a meeting of LCCR leaders and argued that after waiting 87 years for the passage of a civil rights bill, they had no alternative but to accept the one before them because it would break the logjam and open the way to other and better bills.

In the midst of the struggle, Wilkins later recalled, "Hubert Humphrey took me aside and said, 'Roy, if there's one thing I have learned in politics, it's never to turn your back on a crumb.' He knew what he was talking about. The crumb of 1957 had to come first before the civil rights acts that followed," Wilkins observed in his autobiography.[20] With the coalition leadership following his lead, Wilkins decided to support passage of the bill, in the face of vitriolic criticism, especially from blacks within and outside the Association. As he often told his close associates and later noted in his autobiography, he never regretted it.

In 1959, Wilkins organized a coalition of 17 civil rights organizations to fight for the modification of Rule 22 to end the South's stranglehold on the levers that could bar senatorial filibusters. Rule 22 required a two-thirds majority of the senators to override a filibuster. Illinois Senator Paul Douglas and New York Representative Emanuel Celler introduced fairly strong civil rights bills, but neither Eisenhower nor Lyndon Johnson gave them any support. In fact, Eisenhower seemed pleased that the bills were once again gutted by amendment. The final bill, otherwise even more pallid than its 1957 predecessor, did include a diluted version of a Justice Department proposal for federal referees to supervise voting rights challenges. However, the watered-down version still required Negroes denied the vote to run the traditional local obstacle courses common to the South.[21] The bill passed by a wide margin—71 to 18—proof that it appeared to represent no threat to the antediluvian interests of the die-hard South. Yet, the measure contained the kernel of a new idea—the use of federal marshals to oversee voting rights challenges—which would emerge a few years later in a voting rights bill with teeth.

At the same time that Wilkins and Mitchell were pressing Congress for desperately needed legislation and gaining less than half a loaf, the NAACP's General Counsel Robert L. Carter was completing the argument before the U.S. Supreme Court on October 19, 1960, which would permanently alter the political landscape of the United States. The case involved the Negro residents of Tuskegee, Alabama, whose homes had been removed from the city proper by the white mayor and council, which changed the city's shape from a square to a 28-sided figure. All but a few Negroes were eliminated from the city, thus assuring white political domination in perpetuity.

The NAACP agreed to represent the Negro residents expelled by the city and sued the Tuskegee mayor, Phil M. Lightfoot, and the town's other elected officials to nullify the local act that had also been passed by the Alabama state legislature. Noted Alabama civil rights attorney Fred D. Gray had called upon Carter and the NAACP to work with him in seeking to declare the act passed by the state legislature as unconstitutional. Carter eventually took over the entire case on behalf of the Association. The complaint he filed was dismissed by the U.S. District Court in Alabama. The U.S. District Court of Appeals for the Fifth Circuit upheld the dismissal, after which the Supreme Court granted *certiorari,* thereby agreeing to take up the NAACP's complaint. Four weeks later on November 14, 1960, the Court rendered its unanimous decision upholding the NAACP's complaint that the action of the local elected officials that had been ratified by the state legislature did in fact deny 400 Negro residents their constitutional right to vote in the municipal elections of the city of Tuskegee. The Court ruled that, regardless of the other powers a state may have over its municipalities, it is forbidden by the fifteenth Amendment "from passing any law that deprives a citizen of his vote because of his race." That rule applies even in cases where a state is exercising its power to realign its political subdivisions.

Thus, the Court found that the "Alabama legislature had not merely redrawn the Tuskegee city limits with incidental inconvenience to the petitioners; it is more accurate to say that it has deprived the petitioners of the municipal franchise and consequent rights," which was its true intention when it redrew the city boundaries.[22] The case, known as *C.G. Gomillion et al. Petitioners v. Phil M. Lightfoot, as Mayor of the City of Tuskegee et al.* was also labeled the "One Man, One Vote" decision of the Court. Hereafter, the right of every eligible American to vote and for each vote to be counted equally would prevail. This decision provided the juridical foundation for future challenges by Negroes and other minorities of the numerous clever and imaginative efforts by white Southerners to deprive Negroes of their voting rights, especially in local elections ranging from city council to school board to local sheriff.

By 1964, even without a federal voting rights act, the number of registered Negro voters had soared to six million because of accelerated voter drives, largely conducted by local NAACP branches, although various brave acts of field workers from SNCC, CORE and SCLC often paved the way by arresting the attention and bolstering the courage of local Negroes in the Southern states. In 1964 alone, NAACP branches claimed to have compiled a record of adding 800,000 Negro voters to the electoral rolls nationwide.[23] (By 1965, that year's *Annual Report* claimed, the NAACP had doubled the number of registered Negroes in the South to about 1.5 million *even before a federal law had been passed to safeguard the Negro's right to vote.*) As the numbers of registered black voters soared, the votes of African Americans became increasingly a potent force in determining statewide races and in the election of virtually every manner of local official, from mayor to dog catcher. To nullify or vitiate the black vote, white local and state political forces concocted various schemes and subterfuges. One of the most widely used involved the replacement of district representation in municipalities and counties to countywide or citywide representation. This measure enabled white majorities to elect every city council or county commission member, and freeze out any Negro representation, despite heavy geographic concentrations of Negro voters. Because of *Gomillion,* virtually all of these end runs were ultimately doomed to failure as the federal courts ruled them to be unconstitutional.

The long-term significance of this Court decision is difficult to exaggerate. More than any other Court decision, *Gomillion* opened the door wide to the exercise of political power by African Americans and other minorities. In July 1992, at a luncheon honoring the noted federal jurist Leon Higgenbottom Jr., the latter told Robert L. Carter, himself a federal judge, that, "although the world celebrates you [Judge Carter] for your role in *Brown,*" in his opinion "*Gomillion v. Lightfoot* is by far your most important victory, at least in terms of its contribution to the freedom of blacks and other minorities." Many civil rights lawyers concur.

7. The Politics of Political Advancement

If an American, because his skin is dark, cannot eat lunch in a restaurant open to the public, if he cannot send his children to the best public school available, if he cannot vote for the public officials who represent him, if, in short, he cannot enjoy the full and free life which all of us want, then who among us would be content to have the color of his skin changed and stand in his place? Who among us would then be content with the counsels of patience and delay? One hundred years of delay have passed since President Lincoln freed the slaves, yet their heirs, their grandsons, are not fully free. They are not yet freed from the bonds of injustice. They are not yet freed from social and economic oppression, and this nation, for all its hopes and all its boasts, will not be fully free until all its citizens are free.

President John F. Kennedy, Televised Nationwide Civil Rights Address, Washington, D.C., June 12, 1963

For what is justice? It is to fulfill the fair expectations of man. American justice is a very special thing. We have pursued it faithfully to the edge of our imperfections and we have failed to find it for the American Negro.

President Lyndon B. Johnson, Commencement Address to the Graduating Class of Howard University, June 5, 1965

During the closing years of the Eisenhower Administration, Wilkins, Mitchell, and the other NAACP leaders had become fed up with the retrogressive tactics of the president and the Senate leaders, especially of Lyndon B. Johnson. They were looking forward to the possibilities of significant political change that the 1960 election promised. Meanwhile, as the racial hardliners faced off against the NAACP over the next few years, new civil rights allies entered the fray, even more impatient with the slow rate of change during the Eisenhower years. Each of these new organizations made its own important contributions, eloquently demonstrating the new militance adopted by African Americans in the five or six years since *Brown*.

Led by former NAACP staffer James Farmer, in May 1961 CORE (Committee on Racial Equality) launched seminal Freedom Rides throughout the South,[1] forcing confrontations with the most extreme segregationists on their own ground. These Freedom Riders, many of whom were originally NAACPers, challenged especially in Alabama and Mississippi the illegal segregation practices in public transportation—the bus stations, airports, and train depots where Negroes had been denied access to rest rooms, water fountains and food services, while physically separating them in different, usually inferior, waiting rooms. Federal law and Supreme Court decisions, many won by the NAACP itself, had made these practices illegal in interstate transportation, but the Southern states passed their own laws contradicting the federal laws, which they were bent upon ignoring. Although few outsiders knew at the time, the NAACP National Office and many local branches provided funds, legal assistance, volunteers, and moral support to the Freedom Riders, while the Legal Defense Fund eventually became their legal counsel whenever they were arrested.

The Student Non-Violent Coordinating Committee, popularly known as SNCC, focused on developing young cadres, often philosophically radical, while targeting voter registration targets in ultra-hostile locales. Each event usually resulted in a dramatic confrontation attracting national coverage on the nightly television news. Through his Southern Christian Leadership Conference (SCLC), Dr. Martin Luther King Jr., employing a unique oratorical gift and a keen sense of drama, heightened national public awareness of the magnitude of segregationist oppression and the extent of its cruelty through six carefully orchestrated events. The mass media fed ravenously on the specter of this moral man of the cloth besieged by red neck barbarians bent on denying him and his people their basic human rights, if not their very right to live.

The average white television viewer in regions other than the South could readily understand and comprehend this personalized struggle, even if the abstractions proved too great a challenge. Even decent Southerners, deprived of the facts by a local press subjugated to the censorship of the segregationists, found themselves moved or confused by the factual and dramatic narrative that the Northern-based television and radio networks were able to broadcast. Perhaps more than any other single event, King's 1965 march on Selma, Alabama, and the rabid opposition of the white majority, including the state government and police, served to transform the white majority outside the South into temporary partisans of the civil rights movement and its goals. Thousands of white volunteers poured into the movement's organizational components, and many risked their lives and health by participating in the increasingly besieged South. White racists reserved their most potent venom for these "nigger lovers from the North" especially those suspected of being Jews.[2]

Ever since the Montgomery bus boycott had succeeded in unifying much of the national African-American community and forcing a highly visible showdown with the local manifestations of Jim Crow, the NAACP—and Wilkins in particular—had come under increasing criticism for refusing to abandon the organization's historic dependence upon using the courts and political pressure, including lobbying, to bring about change. It seemed to a sizable minority within the NAACP that direct action—as employed in Montgomery, and later in the Freedom Rides, Selma, Birmingham, and some other locales—was becoming the most effective weapon available to the civil rights movement.

Later on, leaders of other civil rights groups and their partisans added their voices and weight to the almost constant criticism of the NAACP as "the giant that chose to go slow" or for its preference for the long-term route over short-term successes. Although Wilkins was never adverse to direct action and had utilized this method often in the past as one of many available weapons, he nevertheless remained committed to the association's legal and political priorities. In his view, "there were . . . limitations to what the tactics of Montgomery could achieve. My own view was that the particular form of direct action used in Montgomery was effective only for certain kinds of local problems and could not be applied safely on a national scale . . . . Such tactics could work in the South, but only in cities like Montgomery, where Negroes were in the majority or in sufficient numbers to make their weight felt." Citing the failed boycott in San Francisco that same summer of 1956, Wilkins observed that the number of blacks seeking to boycott the local cab company for refusing to hire black drivers was simply too few to intimidate the company's owners.

"The danger I feared," he recorded three decades later in his autobiography, "was that the Montgomery model would lead to a string of unsuccessful boycotts where conditions were not so favorable at a time when defeats could only encourage white supremacists to fight harder."[3] Nevertheless, he agreed with the delegates to the 1956 annual convention that the NAACP's national program should be broadened by all lawful means and the Montgomery model was recommended to the national board for consideration. (He also reminded them that an NAACP lawsuit, not the boycott, had desegregated Montgomery's buses.) When the student sit-ins erupted across the South in 1960, Wilkins did not hesitate to support them with the full strength of the Association and to devise his own counterpart campaign for the adult members of the NAACP and black communities in general. The consensus among the NAACP's senior staff at the time was that the white press had been responsible for reenforcing the false image of the NAACP as an organization of middle-class Negroes who were reluctant to employ direct action. Some staff members believed that the white-dominated media furthered this canard as part of an overall worldview that portrayed the NAACP as bourgeois in contrast to the romanticized portrayal of SNCC, CORE, SCLC, US, the Black Panthers, and a variety of others as "truly revolutionary" black organizations. (All of them would disappear as effective agents of change by the next decade.)[4]

Wilkins, perhaps more than any of his contemporaries among the so-called movement's leadership, was capable of taking a very broad view of the struggle and saw that there was a useful and even catalytic role for each of the movement's components. For the most part, he ceded the turf of direct action to SCLC, CORE, and SNCC, ready to provide them with manpower, resources, and moral support when necessary, but not at the expense of the strength, visibility, and power of the local NAACP branches. He also appreciated that it would take several lifetimes to achieve the desired level of national change through localized direct action alone. Yet he greatly valued the national publicity generated by the courageous acts of the Freedom Riders, the marchers, and the sit-in students. He realized that many white hearts and minds had been altered by the images transmitted by the national media, especially television, and that in turn worked its way into the psyches of the federal executive branch and Congress, perhaps even into the minds of the nine Supreme Court justices as well. Therefore, he sought to orchestrate the overall scenario as much as possible, while continuing to press for far-reaching national legislation and court decisions that would serve to dismantle Jim Crow throughout the Southern and border states.

Thus, when the 1956 NAACP convention voted to broaden the national program and use the Montgomery model as a guide, Wilkins diplomatically accepted the modified program. Nevertheless, he "remained convinced that the best division of labor was for us [the NAACP] to support Reverend King and direct action down South while devoting our resources to keeping the White House and Congress honest on desegregation. The benefits of what we could attain through our legal campaign in the courts and our lobbying with the executive and legislative branches would ultimately come down to Negroes in the South and the rest of the country. Reverend King could do his work, we could do ours, and all black Americans would be better off for it."[5]

Only two years later—in 1958—two NAACP youth councils in Wichita and Oklahoma City deployed the first lunch counter sit-ins against local stores that denied Negroes food service. By mid-1959, more than 50 local NAACP youth councils and college chapters were conducting their own sit-ins. That same year at the NAACP's 50th Annual Convention, the Wichita and Oklahoma City youth councils were honored for their initiatives and the NAACP delegates voted to expand youth representation from one to three representatives on the national board.[6] Inexplicably, the national media chose to ignore these dramatic sit-in initiatives by NAACP youth, whereas the local media in Wichita and Oklahoma City, for example, provided extensive coverage. No national television crew was assigned to cover the NAACP's youth sit-ins, which at the time seemed par for the course to the

NAACP staff. Most of the latter came to believe during the 1960s that there was an unstated agreement among many of the national media's decision-makers that most NAACP initiatives were inherently not newsworthy.

However, it was not until six months later that this new strategy would cause the dam of Jim Crow prohibitions on Negro access to lunch counters, restaurants, department stores, and other local merchants to burst and result in a flood of changes throughout the South.[7]

To college students, black and white, the most inspirational act of defiance was the 1960 Woolworth's lunch counter sit-in in Greensboro, North Carolina, initiated by four black North Carolina A&T students—Ezell Blair Jr., David Richmand, Joseph McNeil, and Franklin McCain. Two of them—Blair and McNeil—were officers of the Greensboro NAACP youth council and the other two members, a secret well-kept by the national press.[8] The television news coverage of these four brave young men refusing to leave, despite the brutal bullying of outraged white men and hostile local police, took on the drama of a biblical story. The dignity with which these and other civil rights activists stood their ground could hardly fail to move any fair-minded witness. The four original lunch counter protesters had the good judgment to seek the advice and counsel of James Farmer, CORE's national director, in keeping the local protest viable. Meanwhile, CORE volunteers began their own peaceful protests throughout the South, demanding the end to segregated restaurants, sports facilities, movie theaters, swimming pools, and other facilities that relied on a sizable Negro customer base.

Because the sit-ins were simple, direct, and inexpensive to mount, they ignited a nationwide outbreak of direct action led by black college students against the South's Jim Crow practices and laws requiring the separation of the races in public accommodations. Outside the South hundreds of integrated picket lines, formed in the main by local NAACP branches and members, as well as their coalition partners among unions, churches, synagogues, liberal organizations, and political figures, took to the streets of cities to vigorously protest the Jim Crow practices of national retail chains—especially Woolworth's, Kress, Kresge, and Sears. The picket lines were so successful that, in conjunction with boycotts instituted by the student sit-ins and the NAACP branches in the South, they substantially reduced the national and local sales of these chains to the point where each of them was compelled to reverse course and abandon the segregated practices not only at lunch counters but in their retail and employment practices as well.

As the student lunch-counter sit-ins spread across the South and began to achieve local successes, the NAACP launched a "selective buying" campaign in Southern cities, which was in effect a boycott of those local retailers, restaurants, and other merchants who continued to adhere to such Jim Crow practices as refusing to hire Negro employees, prohibiting Negroes from eating at stores that otherwise sold their merchandise to Negroes, or that prevented Negroes from trying on clothing. Merchants were also the target of selective buying in cities or towns that continued to segregate public accommodations, such as requiring Negroes to ride in the backs of local buses, or prohibiting Negroes from using public parks, swimming pools, or rest rooms in local bus terminals and train depots. Though it was no surprise to Wilkins and his colleagues, the national press virtually ignored the NAACP's campaign and, when they did cover some aspect of it, more often than not simply failed to identify the NAACP's involvement.

Because federal laws did not apply to private enterprises or to local public facilities (unless they also involved interstate commerce), the NAACP and the other civil rights organizations felt compelled to force the issue in most localities throughout the South. The NAACP's strategy employed economic pressure based on the premise that the "quest for green," that is, the elevation of profits above most other values, would impel the local merchants, bankers, and even media owners to pressure the local political leaders to desegregate public facilities rather than continue to lose money. The same theory, in a more direct dose, applied to the boycotts of recalcitrant local merchants.

To enforce the boycotts, the local NAACP branches usually established picket lines around the targeted stores, calling out the names of local Negroes who attempted to pass through the lines. In other instances, they organized sit-ins, not only in stores, but also in targeted public facilities (for example, those organized in parks were called picnic-ins). These acts generated unprecedented publicity for local NAACP branches, but the local press coverage also often carried the names of participants, which frequently led to the loss of their jobs, harassment of their children and spouses, telephone threats, and even a visit from the night riders. However, none of these traditional methods of white intimidation succeeded in halting a single selective buying campaign or sit-in. That, to many observers, constituted the real revolution.

Despite the full force of the local and state law combined with the virtual monopoly of wealth held by the local white merchants, bankers, and planters, the NAACP branches across the South together with the widespread student sit-ins wrought a degree of unprecedented local change that, for all intents, became permanent. In town after town, African Americans had by their sacrifices, courage, and unity wrested change from a recalcitrant white-dominated society—change that would never again be reversed. Although only the beginning of the beginning, to paraphrase Churchill, it opened up access to an array of possibilities that had never before seemed available. It compelled a degree, however minimal, of racial mixing upon which other changes could begin to be contemplated. And it was achieved by black men, women, and children for the most part, vividly demonstrating to Negroes across the nation (as well as to other minorities) what could be accomplished through unity and teamwork in the future.

If the truth is ever fully told, the number of local black men, women, and children who seized the day in their communities during this period—the first five years of the 1960s—was legion. For example, Mrs. Mercedes Wright (then a volunteer but later to become the NAACP's second education director) directed the Savannah drive that would end Jim Crow in public facilities and buses, integrate the lunch counters, and provide jobs to Negroes for the first time in some occupations. Youth council leader John Edwards chaired a drive in Durham, North Carolina, which integrated the sales staffs of 23 local retailers. He was 18 years old at the time. Las Vegas Branch President James McMillan, a medical doctor, led a successful campaign to open up the hotels and gambling casinos to Negroes. Before that, even prominent black performers like Sammy Davis Jr., Dorothy Dandridge, Dinah Washington, and Nat "King" Cole could not sleep in the hotels in which they performed to standing-room only crowds. NAACP boycotts permanently shook the status quo in Jacksonville, Louisville, New Orleans, Memphis, Greenville, South Carolina, and Jackson, Mississippi. In Miami, attorney G.E. Graves won a suit on behalf of the local NAACP to open up the local municipal swimming pools to Negroes, while the powerful Atlanta branch won a long fight to desegregate the city's buses.[9] These successes are merely illustrative—not exhaustive. The achievements of the NAACP's Southern and border state branches —where more than half of the organization's membership has always resided—during this period alone would easily fill a volume, and that is without including the gains locally won by units of the other civil rights agencies.

Since the *Brown* decision in 1954, one of the questions most frequently asked by white Americans is: "Why don't blacks help themselves?" It is a question based almost totally on ignorance, or at the very least, lack of information. With the exception of service in the armed forces, few Americans have had to fight as much for the most elementary opportunities our society has to offer as those of African descent. These struggles, pursued on a shoestring and conducted by men and women of the most modest means imaginable, have been exhausting to most Negroes—and they seem never to be over. In the present era, from the prosperous 1950s to the close of the century, most Americans, and in recent years that also includes a sizable portion of blacks, have had to worry only about themselves and their immediate families. They have not been compelled to struggle against a resistant society to open up the doors as those before them had been forced to do. Succeeding in life is hard enough for almost any individual without adding the larger societal burdens thrust by time and fate on the generations of black Americans who have lived during the twentieth century. Only some of their children, those fortunate enough today to have parents with middle class means or better, have been exempted from the struggle, or so they believe.

The fact is that, as the 1993 attack on Rodney King illustrated, enough racism persists in this nation so that no person of color is truly free from its specter. But at least one-third or more of the nation's black youngsters today have been afforded the material means to pursue life with a reasonable chance of success. That began to become possible in the early years of the decade of the 1960s, when hundreds of thousands of American Negroes, blacks, and African Americans decided they were no longer going "to take it" and ignited the process of revolutionary change in America.

For most of the 1960s the NAACP shared the media spotlight with CORE, SCLC, SNCC, and even the National Urban League (NUL), at the same time providing the major share of the know-how, organization, resources, manpower, political and media contacts, and a degree of level-headedness (which its critics described as hidebound conservatism) that kept the diverse efforts relatively well-coordinated. As the nation's temperature rose in the face of such broad-scale civil rights agitation and resistance, the NAACP's membership climbed dramatically in 1961 to almost 400,000, with slightly less than 1,300 adult, student, and youth units. Its income that year topped $1 million (for the first time), as it began a steep ascent, especially after 1965, when its tax-deductible program subsidiary, the Special Contribution Fund (SCF), became operative. That year the total income to the NAACP was slightly under $2 million, including the sum of $352,521 produced by the new entity in 1965.[10] In 1969, the SCF itself had raised $1,356,191. In 1970, only five years after its inception, the SCF's total income had already climbed to almost $2 million, virtually all of it newly found money.

The ferment produced by such unprecedented activism in so many different locales from Virginia to Mississippi to Texas quickened the nation's pulse and heightened its consciousness; perceiving this, Roy Wilkins and the national board decided to escalate the ante.[11] With a young and vibrant new president—John F. Kennedy—in office in 1961, Wilkins, King, Farmer, A. Philip Randolph, and Whitney Young began to press the new administration to redeem its electoral pledge to issue, "with the stroke of a pen," a new and strong fair housing policy executive order.[12] Perhaps because of its razor-thin margin of victory in 1960, the Kennedy team proved unexpectedly timid, even though his own architects of the sizable black voter turnout were able to argue with persuasive evidence that Negroes had provided the margin of votes needed to elect him. As impatience turned to hostility among much of the Movement's leadership and that of white liberals, the pressure for change during its first two years was met by tart intransigence by the Kennedy Administration's point man on civil rights, Robert Kennedy, the attorney general and the president's brother.[13]

The president's special counsel, Harris Wofford, who virtually alone within the White House constituted the civil rights lobby, came to realize that neither the president nor his brother intended to put forth any serious civil rights measures during the Administration's initial years and that they had relegated Wofford's role to deflecting pressure from the civil rights leadership. Wofford's access to JFK became limited to about one meeting a month; he encountered great difficulty with the so-called Irish Mafia surrounding Kennedy to arrange for the president to meet with Dr. King.[14] After 15 months, Wofford resigned his post and joined the Peace Corps as head of the Ethiopian program.[15] That left the White House without a strong civil rights advocate, a signal that was not missed by the civil rights leadership, especially King, Bayard Rustin, and James Farmer. By the end of 1961, King, A. Philip Randolph, and the SNCC leaders began to openly criticize the Kennedy Administration for its failure to initiate any serious civil rights measures and for breaking its "stroke-of-the-pen" campaign pledge for a strong fair housing executive order.

Wilkins, more than any of the other leaders, appreciated the global problems besetting the new president and, for the time being, tempered his public statements. In his capacity as head of the LCCR, Wilkins had early in the new administration submitted to the White House a lengthy memorandum, urging it to withhold federal funds—then exceeding $1 billion—from those Southern states that refused to guarantee that they would be distributed in a nondiscriminatory manner. A $2 million grant to Mississippi for the new airport outside Jackson had already been awarded, despite the fact that all of its public facilities remained segregated.

The president emphasized during his few meetings with the civil rights leaders that the problem he faced was with the Congress, most especially with the Senate, where Rule 22—the rule to close debate—still required a two-thirds vote to overturn it in order to avoid a filibuster. With sufficient votes, Southerners together with arch-conservative Republicans had historically blocked cloture, enabling them to shut down the Senate's work by employing the filibuster until the opposition relented and dropped the measure to which the Southerners and arch-conservatives objected. In addition, Attorney General Robert F. Kennedy and his colleagues accepted the notion that the Justice Department was prevented by the federal division of powers from enforcing constitutionally guaranteed individual rights denied by a state to its own citizens, except where law and order had broken down and violence had become widespread. At the time, the Justice Department's thinking was that congressional action was required in order to empower it to intervene in a wide range of civil rights areas, including enforcement of the *Brown* decision, prohibition of racially segregated public accommodations required by state laws, and the compelling of the states to permit Negroes to register and vote, at least in federal elections.

A number of dramatic events during 1961 and 1962 helped to transform the reluctance of the Kennedy brothers and their subordinates to place civil rights change on the front burner. The turmoil stemming from the student lunch-counter sit-ins and the NAACP's selective buying campaigns, as well as CORE's Freedom Rides, and SNCC's string of confrontations in places like Albany, Georgia, repeatedly placed new demands upon the top Justice Department personnel. Meanwhile, Wilkins, King, Randolph, Farmer, and others kept pressing for federal protection of civil rights activists and other forms of intervention in the face of local law enforcement personnel who refused to protect either their own citizens or those from out-of-state, including whites, who dared to challenge the South's Jim Crow laws. Thousands of arrests were being made of men and women and even children who were simply exercising their First Amendment rights of speech, assembly, and protest against laws that violated the U.S. Constitution. Much of this brand of Southern justice was heavy-handed, often violent and cruel—and most of it was televised for the first time on the networks' evening news programs.

The president and the attorney general were greatly surprised to encounter defiance from Southern governors, mayors, sheriffs, and police chiefs to their personal pleas for restraint. A watershed moment came on May 19, 1961, when the Freedom Rider Greyhound bus, supposedly protected by state troopers after the governor of Alabama had pledged that the riders would be safeguarded the day after considerable bloodshed in Birmingham, entered the Montgomery bus station. As the riders disembarked, a white mob attacked them with clubs, cattle prods, and stanchions, beating unconscious Robert F. Kennedy's personal representative and close friend, former newsman John Seigenthaler. Three of the riders were savagely beaten before the local Negro reception committee was able to rescue them. The local police, deliberately, failed to show up for at least 15 minutes, allowing the weapons-wielding Klansmen the opportunity to run amok.

When he came to, Seiganthaler had the presence of mind to phone Robert Kennedy from the hospital—after another federal employee had described to the Justice Department leadership the bloody state of Seiganthaler's face and shirt. This detailed description is alleged to have turned the attorney general's face pale, after which he burst into a loud tirade asserting that this constituted an attack on *him* as attorney general. His anger impelled him into the civil rights circle, joining his already committed deputies, including Burke Marshall, Ramsey Clark, Nicholas Katzenbach, and John Doar.[16]

The attorney general now ordered federal marshals into Montgomery to protect the Freedom Riders. The Justice Department obtained a federal injunction against the local Klansmen and their ilk, barring them from harassing the Freedom Riders. It was rather too late but it *was* the kind of action that Wilkins and King had been urging upon the federal government. In fact, forcing the Justice Department's hand was precisely the goal of James Farmer and CORE when the Freedom Rides were launched.[17]

A wave of new incidents followed the Freedom Rides, but the most decisive, in terms of the attorney general's transformation, was the NAACP's effort to register James Meredith as a student at the University of Mississippi—"Old Miss"—which had begun in January 1961, the same month that JFK had been inaugurated as president. The resistance and double-dealing of that state's governor, Ross Barnett, over the next 18 months, finally brought matters to a head in September 1962, when violence erupted, which the state government not only refused to control but was believed to be encouraging. The violence spread through the town of Oxford, where the university is situated, ultimately compelling Robert Kennedy to order federal marshals twice to accompany Meredith, NAACP Field Secretary Medgar Evers and LDF attorney Constance Motley through the uncontrolled mob to the administration building. But the mob, encouraged by former Major General Edwin A. Walker,[18] won the day. RFK ordered the marshals to retreat.

After Barnett was found guilty of contempt of court and fined $10,000 a day, President Kennedy then instructed his brother to federalize the National Guard and order them and regular army troops to converge on Oxford to restore and maintain order and to ensure the admission of James Meredith to the university.[19]

In the midst of this crisis, the nation celebrated on September 22 the centennial of the Emancipation Proclamation. The irony was not lost on the president, who ordered the Interstate Commerce Commission on that day to desegregate all interstate transportation facilities by November 1.[20] The objectives of the Freedom Rides, the sit-ins, SCLC's efforts in Birmingham, and the NAACP's selective buying strategy, insofar as they involved interstate commerce, had finally been met. Meanwhile, the NAACP, operating on another track, had begun the longer-range effort on Capitol Hill to overturn Rule 22 and to encourage the Kennedy Administration to propose a meaningful civil rights bill that would deal effectively with public accommodations, voting rights, and school desegregation.

Wilkins and Mitchell were in the process of nurturing strong relationships with organized labor, initially through the old CIO industrial unions that in 1955 had merged with the more conservative craft-union-dominated AFL. Mitchell's persistent efforts began to open doors, at least legislatively, with George Meany and some of the craft unions. (Paradoxically, at the same time, NAACP Labor Secretary Herbert Hill was stepping up the NAACP's campaign against the lily-white policies of many of the same craft unions.) High-level collaboration was now taking place between the NAACP and the National Council of Churches and many of its Protestant denominations, especially the Methodists, Lutherans, Episcopalians, and Presbyterians. The major Jewish secular organizations concerned with civil rights—the Anti-Defamation League, American Jewish Congress, and American Jewish Committee—were providing the NAACP with legal help, access to funding, and targeted political support, as rabbis from the reform and conservative movements intoned their support from synagogue and temple pulpits. A number of lay Catholic groups, together with liberal priests, nuns, and monsignors, added their support and, in mufti, began joining in the marches, North and South.

Clarence Mitchell began welding these organized groups into a highly effective lobbying force in the halls of Congress. (It often became difficult to ascertain where the NAACP line ended and the LCCR began, but none of the members seemed to mind, given the vast store of trust and confidence they had in both Wilkins and Mitchell, as well as in John Morsell, Wilkins's deputy, who very often stood in for Wilkins in coalition meetings.) Mitchell succeeded in bringing Hispanic and Asian organizations into the LCCR, as well as every one of the predominantly black civil rights organizations.

That there were conflicting agendas as a result of the wider net spun by the LCCR to broaden the legislative coalition was inevitable. The delicate task of producing consensus and maintaining harmony under these circumstances was monumental. For example, many unions and black organizations opposed the efforts of the various nationality groups, including Hispanics and Asians, to open the doors of immigration much more widely. Their obvious fear was that the new arrivals would undercut their own constituents in the job market (and to a great degree, that did occur, especially in the low-end occupations like restaurant and hotel work, the needles trades, and building maintenance services). Clarence Mitchell himself energetically opposed any public policy for requiring dual language provisions, both on general principle and on the pragmatic grounds that such expenditures depleted public funds available to the nation's native poor, black and white. When the NAACP convention voted, in the late 1970s, in favor of bilingualism (as a political compromise to hold the national coalition together), an agitated Mitchell opposed the motion from the floor.

After the women's movement emerged in the early 1970s and its major constituents joined the LCCR, Bayard Rustin (who later succeeded Wilkins in the LCCR's highest post) and Mitchell encountered difficulty holding member groups from bolting over the issue of choice in abortions; the views of the Catholic groups and some Protestant and Jewish fundamentalists were directly opposed to the feminist views. So vital to the passage of key legislation was this coalition in the view of the NAACP leadership that it was willing to compromise on some important issues in order to sustain the support for its priority agenda among the members of the coalition. Mitchell and Wilkins also viewed the LCCR and other coalitions as critically important vehicles for public education on behalf of the goal of integration in every aspect of American life.

Thus, in line with President Kennedy's admonitions, the NAACP in 1962 focused its sights (and that of its coalition) on defeating Rule 22 by recruiting the support of those senators who had little or no stake in the outcome of the struggle over civil rights legislation. For the most part, these senators represented states west of the Mississippi with small Negro populations and no philosophical ties to the segregationists of the South. JFK had also warned the civil rights leaders to avoid threatening these senators by demonstrations in their home states or in Washington itself, on the grounds that such tactics would backfire because the senators would regard such demonstrations as "a gun to their heads."[21] JFK, with Lyndon Johnson's support, even tried to persuade the civil rights leaders to call off their most confrontational Southern demonstrations during 1962 on the grounds that they would harm his efforts to persuade Congress to pass civil rights legislation.[22] Although none of the civil rights leaders was buying this position, it was all CORE, SNCC, and SCLC could do simply to conduct small programs in a few locales. None of the three had the capability to lobby effectively in Congress, except perhaps King, who had made effective congressional appearances as a witness testifying on proposed legislation. The NUL, and its president, Whitney Young, were helpful in bringing to bear the support of key business leaders allied with the organization or with one of its 100 urban affiliates. The moderate senators were especially receptive to Young and the League. The brunt of the lobbying campaign, however, fell on the shoulders of the NAACP, and especially upon those of Clarence Mitchell, who labored so hard and so successfully that he eventually came to be known as the "101st Senator." Even the hard-line segregationists begrudgingly expressed their respect and admiration for Mitchell, a life-long Republican who had changed his affiliation during the Kennedy years. His reliability and trustworthiness were such that both White House and Justice Department senior executives came to rely heavily on his judgment and knowledge.

Sensing the changes in the attorney general after the mob riot in Montgomery and then the civil disorder in Oxford, Mississippi, Mitchell and Wilkins began to press the administration for a strong civil rights bill in early 1963. On February 28, the president's message to Congress carried his most eloquent call to date for the elimination of racial inequality, particularly stressing the disparities in voting, education, public accommodations, and employment. He listed the grave social and economic costs to the nation of discrimination, and noted how it jeopardized the American position abroad. "Above all, it is wrong," he concluded, the first American president in history to make such a declaration. Just when the civil rights leaders thought JFK had finally crossed the line, however, he presented his proposals—a weak set of suggestions calling for public aid to those school districts voluntarily desegregating, piecemeal voter reforms, and extending the life of the Civil Rights Commission, an agency that had been established during the Eisenhower Administration and was hardly on the cutting edge of change.

This time not only were the black leaders of the civil rights organizations deeply disappointed, their chagrin was joined by liberal white groups, such as the ADA, and even the U.S. Civil Rights Commission and its staff, mostly Kennedy appointees. The commission issued a hard-hitting condemnation of civil rights violations in Mississippi and the total failure of the law enforcement agencies, state and local, to protect the constitutional rights of American citizens in that state. The report concluded, without a single dissent among the commissioners, that "only further steps by the federal government can arrest the subversion of the constitution in Mississippi."[23] After reading the final draft, President Kennedy unsuccessfully sought to persuade the commission chairman, John Hannah, and the executive director, Berl Bernhard, to suppress the report. They refused and it is to the president's credit that he accepted their decision as an honest difference of opinion and left it at that.

Meanwhile, in the South a series of new and influential developments began to take place against a backdrop of massive resistance to either public school desegregation or the efforts of Negroes to register and vote. By the end of 1963, for example, fewer than 13,000 black children in the South were attending schools with white children, nine years after *Brown*. More than 2,000 Southern school districts were still totally segregated while the rate of segregation in the North was growing rapidly.

Only a tiny percentage of Negroes had succeeded in registering to vote, despite the unprecedented widespread efforts of the civil rights organizations. In a speech to the Bar Association of St. Louis in 1973, Wilkins reported *Congressional Quarterly* figures that only 6.1 percent of Mississippi's Negroes—25,821 of the 421,866 Negroes of voting age—had been registered to vote in 1961.[24] Of Mississippi's 82 counties, 76 had registered less than 15 percent of the eligible Negroes. He compared that ratio with 33 of 67 counties in Alabama with less than 15 percent black registration, 22 of 254 in Texas, and only 2 of 75 in

Arkansas. In Mississippi's Tallahatchie County (where Emmett Till had been lynched in 1955), of 6,483 Negroes eligible to register, only five individuals had succeeded in registering to vote. Throughout the South in 1961, only about 60 percent of all eligible whites had registered, largely because until then Negro voters presented no threat to the Jim Crow system. By contrast, the combined Southern state authorities had permitted only one-fourth of the eligible Negroes in the South to register in the same year.[25]

At the same time, poverty among the nation's Negro population was deep and endemic. Virtually no significant progress had been made in terms of employment because trade unions had become even more intransigent than employers, both North and South, in opening up Negro access to the workplace or to membership by Negroes in their unions, which was often a prerequisite for employment in a craft.

As black rage grew, individuals as disparate as James Baldwin and Malcolm X articulated this rage. For his next project, King decided to lead a new campaign in April in Birmingham, directly confronting the city's notorious public safety director, Eugene "Bull" Connor. The anticipated violence came swiftly, with Connor brutally employing police dogs and fire hoses to subdue the Negro demonstrators, arresting large numbers, and insisting upon high bail. Despite the efforts of Robert Kennedy and his colleagues to work out a compromise with local white merchants and political moderates, Connor maintained heavy-handed control of the local conditions. Gov. George Wallace backed him to the hilt and refused to succumb to the president's pleas. The nation watched in horror as photos and newsreels of teeth-gnashing police dogs strained on their leashes to attack unarmed Negro protesters. The excessively cruel behavior of Connor and his troopers transformed the nation's largely apathetic mood to that of sympathy for the demonstrators. It transformed President Kennedy as well. He was fed up with Wallace and Connor.

Then, on May 2l, a federal district court ordered the admission of two Negro students represented by the NAACP—James Hood and Vivian Malone—to the University of Alabama. After a few weeks of posturing by Governor George Wallace about barring the door to these students, Kennedy federalized the Alabama National Guard, Wallace retreated from the open door, and that afternoon, without violence, the students were registered.[26]

That night—June 12—Kennedy addressed the nation with the most moving and persuasive speech of his Presidency, graphically describing the plight of the Negro in America and daring any white American to imagine what it was like to have black skin. If we white Americans were subjected to the oppression and indignities that Negroes suffered daily, Kennedy asked, "who among us would then be content with the counsels of patience and delay?" He linked the second-class status of black Americans to the victims of those who advocated a master race. Civil rights veterans and Negroes throughout the nation wept with pride and joy that, at last, a president of the United States both understood and had the courage to state the true plight of the American Negro.[27]

The joy was short-lived; minutes after the president's speech ended, NAACP Field Secretary Medgar Evers was shot to death outside his home by a concealed assassin. He had been leading Mississippi's first statewide voter registration campaign. The attorney general attended his funeral at Arlington National Cemetery, where Medgar Evers was buried with honors amongst his fellow World War II veterans. Robert Kennedy took Medgar's brother Charles aside after the funeral, handed him his card with his direct phone lines, and told him to feel free to call at any time. Charles Evers had just assumed Medgar's mantle as NAACP field secretary in Mississippi and he was bent upon completing Medgar's work as the sweetest form of revenge possible. Meanwhile, RFK was forging a new alliance that in subsequent years would have crucial significance for him and Charles Evers.

Prior to the funeral, the nation's civil rights leaders and their prominent allies gathered in Jackson, Mississippi's capital, to participate in a march in memory of Medgar Evers down Lynch Street, where the NAACP's headquarters were located. The event attracted some of the most zealous racists in the state, as well as a variety of law enforcement personnel with Klan sympathies. It was not known whether the state troopers lining the way would intervene to prevent—or to promote—violence. Relentlessly, the confrontation was building up when one of Robert Kennedy's deputies, John Doar, leaped into the street between the opposing forces and eloquently pleaded for a temporary truce, successfully defusing the explosive situation.

President Kennedy, on the night of Medgar Evers' assassination, had described the plight of the American Negro as a "moral issue . . .

as old as the Scriptures . . . and as clear as the American Constitution." He referred to the change about to take place as a "revolution" and urged all Americans to help him and the government to make it "peaceful and constructive." He then proceeded to use the White House to mobilize opinion makers and leaders in various fields, including business, labor, academia, and religion, to explain why he was now compelled to act and how much he needed their support. Then on June 19 he sent a civil rights bill with teeth to Congress, calling for the authorization of the attorney general to initiate court cases to compel school desegregation, enforcement of equality in public accommodations, the eradication of racial bias in employment in which federal contracts or funds were involved, the power for the federal government to withhold federal funds when the recipient was guilty of discrimination, support for the FEPC, and the establishment of a Community Relations Service in the Justice Department to anticipate racial disputes and provide mediation and conciliation services to resolve these disputes. Some around the president, including Vice President Johnson, believed it was not the right time to submit such a strong bill. The civil rights leaders, as might be expected, wanted even more than this unprecedented powerful bill offered, especially the power to deploy federal marshals to register Negro voters and the immediate establishment of an FEPC.[28]

From early March, Wilkins had dragged his heels in responding to A. Philip Randolph's call for a march on Washington. Meanwhile, King, Rustin, and Farmer had become strong supporters of the proposal. Wilkins' primary focus was on the means required to circumvent Rule 22 and bring about passage in the Senate of a strong civil rights measure. He had a number of reservations about such a march, including concern that it might produce a boomerang effect on the swing senators needed under Rule 22 to close debate and bring the matter before the Senate to a vote. Another major concern was whether the NAACP would once again have to bear most of the costs, as it had in recent years for projects to which SCLC, CORE, or SNCC had become committed but were unable to fulfill alone. The NAACP had already depleted its reserves from life memberships—almost $2 million—as bail money for thousands of activists who were arrested during demonstrations conducted by not only the NAACP, but also its sister organizations. Very little of this money was ever returned to the Association, which endured without any reserves for the next decade. That meant it was obliged to live on its irregular cash flow and how cleverly its financial staff could manage it.[29]

Given the events of the past three months, including the murder of Medgar Evers, the violent confrontation in Birmingham that catapulted King to the forefront and turned Bull Connor into a national symbol of evil, the use of federal troops to thwart George Wallace and register two black students at the University of Alabama, and the transformation of the Kennedy brothers into pro-civil rights advocates, Wilkins perceived that, in this charged atmosphere, the chances for passage of a civil rights bill had greatly improved. However, he felt that the nation needed one major, positive event to provide sufficient momentum for the national mood to move behind the banner of the civil rights movement long enough to bring about passage of the bill. In June, he was informed by Kennedy's staff that a strong bill was about to be proposed, containing many provisions for which the NAACP had been lobbying.

At two meetings of the movement's organizational heads with some wealthy white civil rights funders[30] a few weeks after Medgar's death, Wilkins extracted a series of assurances from Randolph, King, and the other leaders, including their agreement to withdraw both their plan to conduct demonstrations and sit-ins in the capital and the plan to hold a day of direct lobbying by demonstrators of their elected representatives, which, in Wilkins' opinion, would have produced counterproductive resentment on the part of the members of Congress. He also received assurances that the tab for the march would be shared satisfactorily and, in fact, was informed by the white donors present that a sum in excess of $500,000 would soon be distributed to the civil rights organizations, with the largest shares to the NAACP and the NUL. Lastly, Wilkins approved of the proposal to recruit black New York policemen to serve as marshals for the march and to deprive radical groups of a presence there.

Though personally friendly with Bayard Rustin, who had recently served on his own program staff,[31] Wilkins placed on the record his objection to naming Rustin as the director of the march. Wilkins referred to Rustin's status as a conscientious objector in World War II, his membership in the Young Communist League as a college student, and his arrests as a homosexual. Wilkins made it plain that he personally had no problem with Rustin but he feared that segregationist senators would trash the march and the movement because of Rustin's past. This was, after all, 1963.

None of the other civil rights leaders agreed with Wilkins but, in their desire to ensure full participation by the NAACP, they approved a proposal to make Randolph the march director and to permit him to choose whomever he wanted as his deputy. Wilkins agreed to this device, knowing full well that Randolph would name Rustin as his deputy. With these concessions, Wilkins now supported Randolph's proposal for a massive march on Washington to press for jobs and freedom, the latter regarding the quest for voting rights. (A few days prior to the march, South Carolina's racist Senator Strom Thurmond attacked Rustin from the chamber floor, denouncing him as a Communist and a "pervert." Rustin brushed off the attack by charging that Thurmond was simply attempting to discredit the march. Because it was Thurmond who attacked Rustin, many moderate and even conservative Negroes, as well as white supporters, rallied behind Rustin, ignoring Rustin's sexual orientation, which, at the time, was itself a startlingly advanced rights position.)

Next Wilkins prevailed on UAW President Walter Reuther, the nation's second most powerful labor leader, to join the leadership. Together, Wilkins and Reuther and their respective staffs and organizations unleashed the manpower, finances, and other resources required by Bayard Rustin to guarantee its success. Rustin initially budgeted for $65,000 in order to attract 100,000 marchers. With very little assistance from other civil rights organizations, the brilliant Rustin-directed undertaking marshaled the professional personnel and members of the NAACP and UAW and their allies to take part in an event literally unprecedented in the history of the civil rights struggle. Shortly before the march, President Kennedy attempted to persuade the civil rights leaders to call off the march but came away pleased that the confrontational proposals had been eliminated and that the leadership had assured him of a peaceful event.

On August 28, 1963, over a quarter of a million Americans of a both races (about three-fourths Negro) marched from the Washington Monument past the reflection pool to the steps and lawn before the

Lincoln Memorial where, for the next six hours, they listened enrapt and with swelling pride to some of America's greatest moral and political leaders demand of their government the rights and freedoms guaranteed by the Constitution for those citizens still denied them. Late in the afternoon, Rev. King, whose participation in the organization of the march was minimal, concluded the speeches with his now-famous "I Have A Dream" speech, which at the time, ironically, was not especially singled out for unusual attention by the media (it was too late for most of the evening television news shows).[32] It received coverage comparable to that of the addresses of such other speakers as Roy Wilkins, A. Philip Randolph, Whitney Young, James Farmer,[33] John Lewis and, of course, Walter Reuther.

To the utter amazement of local District of Columbia law enforcement personnel, the march was orderly and respectful, virtually without incident, as the marchers comported themselves with a bearing and dignity until then rarely witnessed by most of white America.[34] Live television coverage brought the monumental event into the homes of almost every family. From every section of the nation busloads of committed Americans had arrived early on that sun-washed, humid morning. Hundreds of buses streamed into Washington from the North, especially from New York; scores came from the Deep South, the Midwest, and even the Pacific Coast. As they marched slowly from the starting point to the Lincoln Memorial, its white marble facade glistening in the sunlight, total strangers grasped hands in a show of solidarity, singing movement songs and gospel hymns.

No person who was present on that day came away untouched. For some the degree of personal commitment was escalated. For others the resolve to press on was confirmed. For still others the pride of being part of a truly liberating process would help to sustain them for the rest of their lives. The 1963 March on Washington with its universalistic philosophy and its commitment to one integrated society was quite possibly the high point of the modern American civil rights movement, not that the years that immediately followed represented in any sense a decline.

August 28, 1963, and its manifestations, produced an elixir of pure belief in the fullest possibilities represented by the American Dream. For a few more years that pinnacle was sustained on the shoulders of tens of thousands of activists, as more and more Americans put the past behind them and decided to be part of much-needed change. Even in the South, white men and women—once again representatives of the New South—began to accept changes long overdue. The pace of desegregating Southern public schools increased exponentially. The NAACP's efforts to desegregate public schools in the North, Midwest, and Far West were gaining momentum as well. More and more jobs were opening up to Negro workers and in desegregated settings. Even the polling places began to reflect change.

As a harbinger of the changes, President Kennedy had nominated Thurgood Marshall in 1961 to serve on the U.S. Court of Appeals in Washington, D.C., the second most important court in the land. He had also named the NAACP's Board Chairman Robert C. Weaver, a prominent authority on housing, to head the Housing and Finance Agency, which would become the Department of Urban Affairs (later HUD). The new department head would be raised to cabinet-rank by President Johnson, making Weaver the first black to serve in the Cabinet.

In sports, Jackie Robinson, Jesse Owens, Joe Louis, and a young Cassius Clay were no longer isolated icons. A courageous television producer even tried to broadcast a weekly network variety show featuring Nat "King" Cole, but Southerners felt so threatened by this talented visitor to their living rooms that the locals station often refused to broadcast the program. Nevertheless, Oscar-winner Sidney Poitier was about to come to a memorable dinner less than a decade after he and Tony Curtis, bound by handcuffs, had cinematically escaped from a chain-gang and embarked on a long chase in which, while fleeing from a posse, they had discovered each other's humanity. To the surprise of almost every one, both groundbreaking films, despite their racial dimension, proved commercially successful—even in the South. And perhaps even more significantly, the nation's white youth were almost unanimously converted to a new musical form directly derived from Negro rhythm and blues. (Conservative whites, including ministers, referred to R&B as "Nigger Music.") The rapid rise in the popularity of rock and roll would by the 1960s effectively blur the boundaries between black and white popular culture.

The euphoria produced by the late summer march on Washington was transformed into horror on the morning of September 15—a peaceful late summer Sunday—when a bomb was hurled at the 16th Street Baptist Church in Birmingham, resulting in the death of four young Negro girls.[35] If the racists who detonated the bomb thought they were interrupting the momentum of the nation's determined drive to fulfill the new civil rights agenda, they were dead wrong. For a few months, the vast majority of Americans, profoundly moved by the wanton murder of these children, coalesced behind JFK's initiatives, providing significant impetus in Congress for bipartisan collaboration. On October 2, 1963, the Judiciary Committee of the House passed the Kennedy civil rights bill and reported it to the full House on November 20. Two days later John F. Kennedy was dead. Nevertheless, in February 1964 the bipartisan leadership of the House of Representatives fulfilled its promise to JFK and passed his civil rights bill. It then remained for President Lyndon Baines Johnson and the leadership of the civil rights movement to find the way to achieve senatorial approval in the wake of the national tragedy that had befallen the American people.

Profoundly moved by JFK's death, Roy Wilkins and Clarence Mitchell, working through their grief over the assassination of the youthful president, pressed on with the implementation of their strategy to achieve passage of this strong, substantial federal legislation that, they believed, would set in motion nationwide revolutionary change—the 1964 Civil Rights Bill. In the wake of Kennedy's death, which black Americans deeply mourned with virtual unanimity, the NAACP's state conferences determinedly geared up for a major push on the entire Senate membership, with special attention to those regarded as the swing voters. Coalition allies, particularly among the labor unions and religious alliances, were prevailed upon to press the swing vote senators "to do the right thing" when they came face-to-face with the vote on cloture. It was unnecessary to articulate the sentiment common to almost every participant: The most appropriate memorial to the late president would be passage of the civil rights bill he had proposed and for which he had fought. (To this day, many Negroes continue to believe that his views on race could well have contributed to his assassination.)

Two months before the march on Washington, Mitchell had determined that the passage of the civil rights bill required a strategy that separated Republican moderates and some conservatives from the Southern wing of the Democratic Party. Building on his relationships with Republican legislators that had brought about passage of the 1957 Civil Rights Act, Mitchell went to work to cultivate support from among Republicans in both houses. Illinois Representative Clarence Brown, a Republican with whom Mitchell had established a close association since 1957, proved especially helpful in the House. Mitchell realized, however, that he again needed the intervention and support of Republican Senate Minority Leader Everett Dirksen, whose leadership in 1957 and 1960 proved critically important to then Majority Leader Lyndon Johnson. Mitchell had no qualms about using younger Republican stalwarts within the NAACP, such as Sam Jackson, Sam Simmons, and Stanley Scott (all of whom later received key appointments in the Nixon Administration) to lobby Republican members of Congress. In August 1963, shortly after the march on Washington, an NAACP legislative meeting extended the lobbying for the bill to the Republican congressional membership, many of whom were visited by NAACP Republicans as well as by others.

In the wake of the Kennedy assassination, President Lyndon B. Johnson addressed a joint session of Congress on November 27 and pledged his full support for a civil rights bill. He rarely wavered in the subsequent months, twisting arms among recalcitrant Southerners, including his own Texas delegation. In December Johnson reached out to NAACP board member and LCRR Vice Chairman Joseph Rauh, who was leading the lobbying campaign for the bill, seeking his advice and assuring him of the full support of the White House. Rauh persuaded LBJ to invite Clarence Mitchell to subsequent strategy meetings for the bill.

The initial obstacle in the House was the control of the Rules Committee by arch-segregationist Howard W. Smith—known as "Judge Smith"—who, as its powerful chairman, was blocking the bill from reaching the floor. Mitchell prevailed on the president to use his considerable influence to move the bill out of the Rules Committee. As committee votes began to change, Speaker of the House John McCormack of Massachusetts met with Mitchell and Rauh on January 21, after which he pledged to move the bill out of the Rules Committee by mid-February. With McCormack's permission, Mitchell and Rauh informed both the president and the press of McCormack's commitment. That development prompted representatives of both parties to press Judge Smith for a committee vote, which took place on January

30. The bill was approved by the committee majority by a vote of 11 to 4 and sent to the House floor.

Former NAACP Public Information Director Denton Watson, whose biography of Mitchell remains the definitive work on the subject, describes the lobbying effort called for by Roy Wilkins at the end of January with these words:

> An army of LCRR and NAACP lobbyists with carefully crafted instructions greeted lawmakers upon their return from the Christmas recess and maintained direct contact with them to ensure that they "voted the right way."[36]

Watson reported that Wilkins instructed his NAACP branches to send influential branch leaders who knew their congresspersons first hand. NAACP representatives from 10 states joined the LCRR's professional lobbyists under Mitchell's direction. Watson noted that they "used carefully focused organizational and other forces of pressure to target lawmakers in order to achieve well-defined objectives."

Meanwhile, CORE, SCLC, and SNCC continued to ignite mass demonstrations, mostly in the South, which kept the civil rights struggle in the news and continued to impact on the psyches of the nation's white majority. A squad of LCRR staffers and volunteers were organized in the House gallery as watchers to ensure that every representative known to favor the bill was present when each critical vote was to take place. The tactic helped to ensure maximum attendance on the floor. Back at the House office buildings, representatives of the Amalgamated Clothing and Textile Workers—known as "O'Grady Raiders" in honor of the union's lobbying director—responded to the reports from the gallery and sped to the offices of the truant representatives to impel them back to the House floor for each pending vote.

Back in the boondocks, local coalition leaders, spurred by NAACP branch stalwarts, were writing letters to the editor, making statements on radio and television, and visiting the local newspapers to plead for editorial support of the voting rights bill. Each congressman was obliged to pay considerable attention to the sentiments being expressed back home, should he or she have any doubts. The overall strategy was being coordinated in the office of New Jersey Democratic Congressman Frank J. Thompson, who played a major role in

JFK's campaign as the prime coordinator of voter registration initiatives, especially among minorities.[37]

For nine days the House soberly and extensively debated the provisions of the bill, with the majority holding fast against amendments designed to weaken its provisions. The closest the pro-civil rights forces came to a crisis was when Virginia's Judge Smith, a hardened reactionary, craftily sought to divide the civil rights majority by proposing an amendment that for the first time included gender among the types of discrimination prohibited by the bill. The Democrats were unprepared for this maneuver and, afraid that this new criterion might weaken support among Republicans, argued vehemently against it. Even Representative Edith Green, the consummate liberal and feminist precursor, reminding her colleagues of her credentials in the long struggle for gender equality, pleaded with the House to drop or defeat the Smith amendment. In a frank statement perhaps too long forgotten, Green observed that the degree of discrimination suffered by American [white] women could in no way be compared to that which Negroes of both genders had experienced. The House ignored her plea and passed the amendment, despite the opposition of the Johnson Administration as well.

Mitchell, on the other hand, reluctant to oppose any provision that prohibited discrimination in any form, had quickly announced his support of Smith's amendment, unconcerned that it might in any way jeopardize the bill. Thus, with a casual wave of the hand, so to speak, a provision was inserted into the most important civil rights law in American history, expanding the law's jurisdiction to more than half of the nation's population and by implication equating the discrimination experienced by majority women with that of minority African Americans and Native Americans. By so diluting the federally legislated definition of what constituted minority status that would entitle millions of persons to special protection by federal law and to special benefits from those ameliorative programs springing from it, the House virtually assured that the main beneficiaries of federal assistance for minorities would not be the two historically most deserving as well as most critically in need—blacks and Native Americans. Instead the other demographic groups entitled by this law to also call themselves minorities would absorb the lion's share of the benefits, including the various forms of affirmative action.

For the next three decades women—mostly white and middle class —leap-frogged over blacks and Native Americans to fill most of the new job openings, garner most of the business subsidies and set asides, take up most of the college admissions provided by federal and state programs and by affirmative action, all of which were originally intended for the most extreme victims of historic American racist oppression.

Paradoxically, the pie comprising all of these mandated opportunities grew much more slowly than the number of individuals eligible for the benefits of the Civil Rights Act and its programmatic offspring, as well as the decisions of the courts. Head to head, white middle-class women, the vast majority of the 1964 law's beneficiaries, soaked up the majority of the opportunities, reaching parity with males in college admissions after a little more than two decades, and surpassing male admission totals before the end of the third decade. Further, the private sector rushed to meet the unspoken but very real federal numerical objectives in hiring for white (and even other) females but failed to come close to any reasonable percentage for black males, many of whom, because of various pathologies, were largely unprepared or unqualified to fill these positions and who for the most part lacked sound educational underpinnings as well as job skills.

Certainly, no leader, including Joseph Rauh and Clarence Mitchell, could in 1964 have predicted this unwanted and unexpected result, but the fact is that liberals and moderates of both parties, races, and genders made it possible when they permitted the gender category to be added to the bill, as well the overall category of color, for such groups as Hispanics and Asians, most of whom had recently immigrated to the United States. Two decades later the federally legislated definition of minority was further expanded when Congress enacted a bill guaranteeing equal rights to the handicapped. Without any further contemplation of the possible fallout from this exceedingly broad, ultra-liberal definition of who constitutes an historically aggrieved minority in the United States, categories had been (arbitrarily) legislated which ultimately designated some 70 percent of the nation's population as minorities eligible for special protection and assistance under federal (and many state and local) laws.

On February 10, 1964, the House approved by 290 to 130 the strongest civil rights bill in our history, including those passed during the four decades since the 1964 bill was adopted. Repeating their vaunted House lobbying assault on the Senate, Mitchell and Rauh mobilized the LCCR troops for the long final push. Key to their success was the deep commitment and involvement of President Johnson, who discussed the bill's progress in the Senate with Mitchell almost every day. At Mitchell's request, LBJ took responsibility for eight recalcitrant Senators, including Minority Leader Everett Dirksen. Given Dirksen's ties to sizable corporate interests, Mitchell and LBJ were cognizant of the problems a liberal bill presented to Dirksen. Nevertheless, the president set out to court the Illinois Republican, while Majority Leader Mike Mansfield, a Democrat, provided the minority leader with every opportunity for public attention and media coverage. Although Mansfield adopted a low-key, almost nonpartisan posture for this struggle, thereby keeping the door open to working with Dirksen and some of the most zealous opponents of the bill, he appointed Hubert Humphrey—no doubt the most knowledgeable, committed, and deserving Democrat for the job—as floor leader. Fortuitously, Dirksen named California moderate Thomas Kuchel as the Republican floor manager, presenting strong bipartisan leadership for the prolonged fight. Kuchel was especially influential with his party's moderates and liberals, although he was considered the *bête noir* of the ultra-right wing forces.

President Johnson made it absolutely clear that he would tolerate no amendments to the bill drafted and presented by his own Justice Department. Senator Edward Kennedy implored his colleagues to vote for this bill without change as a monument to his late brother. It caused a considerable strain on Mitchell and Rauh to avoid opportunities to strengthen the bill, knowing they had the votes.

The first challenge was to prevent the Judiciary Committee headed by segregationist Mississippi Senator Jim Eastland from bottling up the approved House bill in his committee and thereby preventing a vote. Quite reluctantly and despite the tempestuous opposition of Oregon's Wayne Morse, Mansfield invoked Senate Rule XIV, the same rule invoked successfully in the adoption of the 1957 Act, which enabled Mansfield to bypass the Judiciary Committee and place the bill on the calendar for the consideration of the entire Senate. The Southern challenge led by Georgia's Richard Russell was easily dispatched, 54 to 37.[38]

More than a week later, as Mansfield vacillated, the Southerners undertook what was to be a 17-day filibuster on the motion to consider the bill. Although the tone and substance of the debate remained extremely cordial, almost unctuous at times, the flagrant distortions of fact and history spewed by the 18 Southern senators desperately striving to hang on to the last vestiges of white supremacy in the states of the Old Confederacy could not long remain unanswered.

Reversing their original strategy to refrain from rebutting the Southern spokesmen, Humphrey and Kuchel took to the floor to counter the race-based rubbish being enunciated by their opponents with hard facts and solid evidence of the systematic violations of the rights of the South's Negro citizens. A few of the Southern diehards actually conceded the validity of these charges by the procivil rights speakers. Finally, on March 26 the filibuster ended and Mansfield's motion to consider the bill passed overwhelmingly, 67 to 17. For the next two months most of the maneuvering took place behind the scenes, with Dirksen offering a series of amendments that helped bolster his ego without seriously changing the substance. The most important attempt to change the House bill dealt with the proposal to require jury trials for those charged with criminal contempt. A number of variations on this theme were rejected, including one sponsored by Mansfield and Dirksen. Throughout, Humphrey gave his opponents every opportunity to express their views and to be listened to carefully. He pledged that no surprise tactics would be foisted on the bill's opponents, who learned that he was as good as his word.

Although Mitchell and Rauh were now beginning to display impatience with the slow grinding progress in the Senate, Humphrey came forth on May 26 with a compromise worked out with Dirksen that essentially altered the House's original language without seriously changing the bill's substance. Basically, the compromise, which Mitchell had already resigned himself to accept as inevitable, gave the states and localities the first opportunity to resolve racial complaints. Individuals claiming they were victims of racial discrimination in public accommodations or at their jobs would be required to first file their complaints with appropriate state agencies. Since such agencies did not exist in most Southern states, Southern senators were correct in charging that this change was actually aimed at them by not really altering the reality of the House provision. The federal government's power to file suits to end specific racial violations or patterns of racial discrimination would now rest with the attorney general, who was barred from suing on behalf of individuals but still had the power to intervene in their cases.

Mansfield filed the cloture petition on June 6, preparing for a vote on it on June 9, but three important fence-sitting Republican senators —Hickenlooper, Cotton, and Morton—demanded a chance for their amendments to be considered, barring which they threatened to defeat cloture. Those amendments failed on June 9, except for Morton's latest version of a jury trial amendment, which barely passed 51 to 48. With the cloture vote scheduled for the next day, Humphrey confidently counted noses that the LCCR under Mitchell and Rauh had lined up so effectively during the previous days; he was able to assure the president that he had the requisite two-thirds.

After Senator Robert Byrd of West Virginia carried out the session's only all-night filibuster, on June 10 the Senate voted before a packed gallery to invoke cloture by 71 to 29—the first time in modern history that debate over a civil rights bill had ever been cut off. Despite this overwhelming margin, some senators continued to try to alter the bill further. The NAACP, and Mitchell personally, were besieged with powerful pressure to back down on parts of the bill, especially on Title VII, which barred employment discrimination and caused many corporate employers to worry about the ultimate cost of the measure.

One year to the day (June 19) after JFK had submitted his draft of a civil rights bill, the Senate approved the compromise with amendments 73 to 27. The House approved the bill on July 2 by 290 to 130. Shortly thereafter President Johnson signed the 1964 Civil Rights Act into law, effectively removing the civil rights issue from the 1964 election campaign, which was about to begin. First, however, President Johnson felt compelled to squash the relatively modest effort of the Mississippi Freedom Democratic Party (FDP) to be seated in place of the traditional lily-white regular delegation at the Democratic convention in Atlantic City.[39] Then, days after the Republican convention, racial rioting broke out in a number of cities across the nation. The specter of a truly reactionary president represented by the Republican nominee—Barry Goldwater—led Roy Wilkins and the NAACP Board of Directors to oppose Goldwater in a radical departure from the NAACP's past record of nonpartisanship. Negro rights may have been removed from the formal agenda of the election campaign by the Civil Rights Act, but underlying almost every political confrontation the issue smoldered, as many whites, including growing numbers outside the South encouraged by an unrepentant George Wallace, began to fashion their own response to the winds of change.

Nevertheless, by impelling passage of the 1964 Civil Rights Act—the strongest in American history—the NAACP had reached the zenith of its political influence, producing a legislative achievement comparable to its 1954 Supreme Court victory in *Brown v. Board of Education* only 10 years earlier.

8. Revolution at the Ballot Box

Representatives and direct Taxes shall be apportioned among the several States which may be included within this Union, according to their respective Numbers, which shall be determined by adding to the whole Number of free Persons, including those bound to Service for a Term of Years, and excluding Indians not taxed, *three fifths of all other Persons.* (emphasis added)

Article 1, Section 2, Paragraph 3,
Constitution of the United States of America

The spoken lie is of no consequence. The silent colossal national lie that is the support and confederate of all the tyrannies and shams and inequalities and unfairness that afflict the peoples—that is the one to throw bricks and sermons at.

Mark Twain, in a written attack on slavery (date unknown)

The single biggest flaw of the 1964 Civil Rights Act, in the minds of the civil rights leaders, was the failure to secure the right to vote for Negroes and other minorities with adequate enforcement features. As soon as the celebrations over the 1964 victory subsided, the NAACP's leaders began preparing for the renewed struggle for a voting rights act. Without question, the violent encounters across the South during 1964, many sparked by the thousands of young volunteers from other regions of the nation, arrested the attention and imagination of a sizable—and growing—proportion of white Americans.

The disappearance in June 1964 of three young activists—Andrew Goodman, Michael Schwerner, and James Chaney—during a CORE voter drive near Philadelphia, Mississippi, produced widespread apprehension, tragically confirmed a few months later when their bodies were discovered in a local lake by FBI agents, who announced that they had been murdered. The fact that two white youths from the North, together with a local black youth, had been singled out for execution contributed to a further sense of outrage at the unfairness of the racist system still governing so much of the South. After all, many white Americans asked, what was their crime? Registering American citizens to vote? Who among us would settle for less? Did not NAACP Mississippi director Medgar Evers die for the same crime a year earlier? And were not scores of local NAACP leaders being harassed, beaten, shot, and worse because they also refused to abandon the voting rights weapon?

The singular problem of the civil rights organizations during this period was sustaining the attention, concern, and sympathy of the nation's citizenry. In 1965 the Vietnam War had already begun to heat up after LBJ ordered several hundred thousand American troops in division strength to the rice paddies of Southeast Asia, diverting attention, funds, and volunteers from the civil rights struggle. Now the burgeoning environmental movement was beginning to attract followers. The nation's many new diversions, combined with the birth pangs of the "Age of Aquarius," were proving tough competition for the hearts and minds of American youth. In this context, King and his associates, in urgent need of a strong, salable program that could regain national focus and preeminence, targeted the city of Selma, Alabama, a stubborn community of Jim Crow adherents in total political control of the levers of power and law enforcement. It was in this city that a local judge, following passage of the 1964 Civil Rights Act, prohibited all public gatherings in the wake of local efforts to desegregate public accommodations, thereby attacking the very core of the new national legislation.

The sporadic efforts of SNCC in Selma to marshal Negro resistance to this and other manifestations of Jim Crow had petered out by 1965. Fully aware of the local establishment's capability for extreme responses to any demonstration of Negro resistance, the SCLC leadership not only expected confrontation on a significant scale, but also almost certainly welcomed it. Given the record of reckless and hot-tempered acts by the city's sheriff, James G. Clark Jr., during previous tests of local law enforcement, Dr. King, Rev. Fred Shuttlesworth, his Alabama lieutenant, and others were virtually assured of an excessively brutal response to their planned initiatives.[1]

With this expectation in mind, SCLC provoked a local crisis over voter registration. Prospective black voters in Selma were being compelled to answer a long list of questions, many of them complex, in place of a simple literacy test required by state law. Few, if any, whites had been subjected to the same test. As expected, most of the prospective black registrants were eliminated by such tests. Frustration and resistance among local black citizens began to pour out into the streets. King called for federal assistance, meeting with President Johnson, Vice President Humphrey and Attorney General Katzenbach to press for a voting rights bill that would prohibit such unconstitutional obstacles to the right to vote. The administration, although sympathetic, offered no commitments either on the proposed bill or on local intervention. In fact, LBJ perceived King's efforts as a grandstanding play to embarrass the presidency.

The SCLC leaders thereupon decided to organize a march of demonstrators from Selma over the Pettus Bridge to Highway 80, aware of the expected response: state troopers halted the marchers with billy clubs and tear gas, wounding more than 70 men and women. The bleeding and injured marchers were forced to retreat but the entire bloody tableau was captured under the glare of television cameras and sped to the networks, which flashed the dramatic images to almost every American household—often at dinner time. The television footage illuminated the explosive employment of violence by local Southern law enforcement against unarmed American citizens exercising their First Amendment rights of free speech and assembly in order to protest the state's refusal to permit them to exercise their constitutionally guaranteed right to vote. The unrestrained brutality of the troopers and local police further damaged whatever shred of sympathy might have prevailed for their position. Once again Americans of every station and region were faced with clear-cut moral choices, regardless of their personal views on race.

Attorneys for Dr. King and the SCLC immediately appealed for relief to federal Judge Frank Johnson Jr. Judge Johnson's response was to issue an order barring any further marches until he had conducted a hearing in which the arguments of both sides would be articulated, after which he would render judgment. King's inclination was to wait for Judge Johnson's decision, but more militant colleagues within SCLC, as well as such movement allies as the SNCC, pressed him to resume the marches even before the hearings proposed by Judge Johnson had begun. Legal Defense Fund Director Jack Greenberg, one of SCLC's attorneys in Selma, advised against defying a federal judge. Just as it appeared that matters would get out of hand, a federal official, the Justice Department's Community Relations Service Director Leroy Collins (a former governor of Florida) worked out a deal between both sides, permitting King and his followers to march to the far end of Pettus Bridge and back, including penetration of the line formed by the state troopers, who were instructed to part to enable the marchers to pass unharmed. The prearranged scenario was accomplished without a major hitch.

At the same time the Justice Department had completed its draft of the proposed voting rights bill, obtained White House approval, and within days had won the support of Democratic Senate Majority Leader Mike Mansfield and Republican Minority Leader Everett Dirksen, guaranteeing a sizable bipartisan majority in the upper house. Impetus to the speeded-up process came from the murder that day of white volunteer James Reeb, a Massachusetts Universalist minister who had journeyed to Selma to stand up for the Negro cause. Meanwhile, the proposed civil rights bill was speedily transmitted to the chairman of the House Judiciary Committee, Emanuel Celler, a feisty partisan of civil rights from Brooklyn with substantial seniority.

Possibly fearing that events were outracing him, President Johnson called a hastily organized press conference and, with Alabama's anti-civil rights governor, George Wallace, at his side, vigorously denounced the attacks on the Negro demonstrators by local law enforcement personnel and expressed his sorrow over the death of Rev. Reeb. LBJ also deplored the denial of the Negro's right to vote almost a century after the Constitution had been amended to guarantee this very act.[2] Describing the bloody events in Selma as "an American tragedy," the President lectured his constituents:

> Ninety-five years ago our Constitution was amended to require that no American be denied the right to vote because of race or color. Almost a century later, many Americans are kept from voting because they are Negroes.[3]

He thereupon announced that he had submitted his own proposal for a voting rights bill to Congress, urging Governor Wallace to support the right of Negroes to vote and to assemble peacefully. He also pressed the recalcitrant governor to defuse the tension by conducting biracial meetings in Alabama to confront the state's race-based problems.

Three days later, on March 15, 1965, President Johnson addressed a special session of Congress but his eyes were fixed, through television, directly on the American people. Gazing purposefully at the camera, the President spoke with uncharacteristic candor and with a degree of sincerity rarely captured by camera in the demeanor of any public official. "It is wrong—deadly wrong," he drawled in measured phrases, "to deny any of your fellow Americans the right to vote in this country." Asserting that the courage of Negro protesters in Alabama had "awakened the conscience of this nation," LBJ then compared events at Selma with those at Lexington, Concord, and Appomattox. With his words heavily accented by generations of Southern heritage, and to the utter astonishment of partisans and foes across the land, the President of the United States then pledged to the Negro men, women, and children of America that "we shall overcome," repeating the historic movement's mantra again and again. Upon those utterances by an American president with Southern roots, the civil rights movement had attained its pinnacle in terms of national support, influence, and acceptance.[4]

The immediate struggle in Alabama, however, was far from achieving resolution. While SCLC leaders and their Legal Defense Fund attorneys worked to bring closure to the Selma episode, the SNCC leadership, having bitterly split with King over the strategy employed in Selma, hastily moved its focus to Montgomery, the state capital. There, local white thugs, backed by colluding police, brutally beat SNCC demonstrators in downtown Montgomery. As if the besieged forces bent on preserving white dominance did not have enough difficulties with which to contend, the Montgomery assault on unarmed protesters was also filmed by television and still cameras employed by the nation's networks, news services, and print media. The press coverage was enormous, further fanning the outrage of the American people.

These events, however, further radicalized the ranks of SNCC, which began the process of expelling its moderates and integrationists. SNCC's radical leaders became infuriated with King for his alleged failure to arrange for their protection in Montgomery. King was restrained from reaching out to SNCC in part because of the unflattering names they had called him, but more importantly because he feared that SNCC's new radical appeals for confrontation with state and federal powers would boomerang against the entire civil rights movement and possibly reverse the hard-won support of Congress, the administration and the American people, which he, the NAACP, CORE, and the Urban League had painstakingly fashioned.

The day following the Montgomery debacle, federal District Judge Frank Johnson, after holding hearings, handed down his order. He authorized a march to Montgomery and ordered the state of Alabama to provide protection for the participants' right to protest peaceably on public highways and streets. He even prescribed the route on Highway 80 from Selma's Pettus Bridge. Predictably, an unreconstructed Governor Wallace took to the airways to decry Judge Johnson's decision, alleging that the state of Alabama did not possess sufficient personnel to protect the marchers over the 70-mile route. Later, Wallace declared that the state could not afford to call up the Alabama unit of the National Guard, whereupon LBJ nationalized 1,800 Alabama guardsmen under the direction of Deputy Attorney General Ramsey Clark, another Texan, to protect the marchers.

On March 21, 1965, the historic march from Selma to Montgomery began, but not until King privately appealed to Roy Wilkins for a large number of bodies and financial help to make the march successful. Despite his personal problems with King, Wilkins agreed, appreciating how important the march's outcome would be to the bill now before the House Judiciary Committee, on which Clarence Mitchell was devoting his complete attention and influence. NAACP branches organized busloads of members and friends to beef up the local contingent. Individuals from all of the civil rights organizations, and from many of its allies, appeared in time to join the march. In a show of unity before the cameras recording history for the American public, all of the major civil rights leaders, including Roy Wilkins, Whitney Young, and A. Philip Randolph, joined Martin Luther King Jr., a badly bruised John Lewis, and their fellow leaders in the front ranks of the march, leading over 3,000 men and women before massive press coverage on the final day as they marched down Highway 80 and entered Montgomery.

With young Alabamians comprising the National Guard unit assigned to provide what was to become airtight protection, the marchers reached Montgomery in four days without serious incident. Awaiting them in front of the Alabama State Capitol was a huge crowd —estimates ranged as high as 25,000. Weary but exuberant, Dr. King addressed the crowd and the nation with a moving speech that reaffirmed his belief that, after "a season of suffering," America's Negroes would reach their goal of a "society at peace with itself."[5]

That night the jubilant civil rights activists learned of the murder of Viola Gregg Liuzzo, a white volunteer who had journeyed from the Midwest to stand up at Selma. The wife of a Detroit teamster, Mrs. Liuzzo had apparently raised the ire of local bigots by volunteering to drive black and white marchers back to Selma on Highway 80. The next day, President Johnson announced that the FBI had taken four suspects into custody. It was later revealed that one of the four was an FBI informant who had informed his controlling agent of the shooting a few hours after the crime was committed. That accounted for the speedy apprehension of the murderers, but it also reminded every participant in the struggle that despite the string of victories, chronic danger remained.

The true significance of the Selma March was not, of course, what King and his colleagues achieved in Selma itself, where few significant changes took place over the next two decades. It was the national public perception of Selma, transmitted by the mass media and most especially by the young and still awesome medium of television, which moved millions of Americans to raise their voices on behalf of the civil rights goals which so many ordinary black people were risking everything to attain. As the sympathy for the courageous Negroes standing in harm's way mushroomed beyond any previous level, the nation's political leaders responded to the intense pressure by publicly supporting the King-led marchers.

In the halls of Congress, Clarence Mitchell lost no time in exploiting this coast-to-coast support. Following Wilkins' direction, Mitchell organized grassroots pressure through the Branch department on behalf of a voter rights bill. He then capitalized on this pressure by face-to-face visits with senators and representatives. Both Wilkins and Mitchell mobilized the member organizations of the LCCR, almost 150-strong, and many of the component organizational leaders in turn instructed their rank-and-file members to generate local support for the voting bill. The more repressive and violent the Southern response to the activist initiatives in Selma, the greater the success of the Mitchell lobbying campaign to convert new congressional support. The primitively brutal responses of sheriffs like Jim Clark and Bull Conner, as JFK once observed, were the civil rights proponent's most effective weapons. Even some white segregationists found themselves repelled by the lawlessness of those entrusted with upholding the law.

Leading the fight in the Senate were long-time civil rights stalwart Paul Douglas of Illinois and the newly elected Senate Whip, Russell Long of Louisiana, to the surprise of Mitchell and almost everyone else except Senator Douglas, who backed Long as the successor to Hubert Humphrey—now vice president—for the post. Besides the cataclysmic struggle of the intensively televised events in Selma, the nation had already begun to experience what was to become an epidemic of urban riots. Long-neglected and smoldering, the despair-ridden big-city ghettoes, mostly black, had entered into a tailspin of disintegration comprised of so many pathologies, it was difficult to know where to begin. The explosion began with the 1964 summer riot in Harlem, followed by violent conflagrations in Rochester, the New Jersey cities of Elizabeth, Jersey City, and Paterson, then Philadelphia and Rexmoor, Illinois.

Nothing in the 1964 Civil Rights Act or the hoped-for Voting Rights measure promised a shred of relief or hope for the sizable inner-city minority populations. Among urban blacks, half of the children were born into poverty. Unemployment among black men averaged two to three times that of whites and in some places it was five times greater. Jobs had begun to flee to the predominantly white suburbs. Drug abuse was on the rise and with it the growth of street violence. It was in this context that Congress was to take up the Voting Rights bill presented by Lyndon Johnson, who had modified the original proposal submitted by John F. Kennedy six months before he was assassinated.

The Justice Department had been involved in four voting rights cases when 1965 began. All had crept through the federal court system at a snail's pace, thwarting the zeal of Attorney General Nicholas Katzenbach. Southern attorneys had learned quickly how to nullify the previous civil rights acts' voting rights provisions through legal maneuvering, shameless delays, and bold-faced defiance. The Twenty-Fourth Amendment, adopted in 1964, might well prohibit the poll tax in federal elections, but in local and state elections, where the raw power of the state displayed itself eloquently, the poll tax remained.

Even though Title I of the 1964 Civil Rights Act all but outlawed unfair literacy tests, discrimination by the state against potential black registrants, and oral literacy tests, it also established the completion of a sixth-grade education as a national standard for literacy. Nevertheless, Southern judges and public officials for the most part still refused to enforce the new provisions. Mitchell and Rauh expressed the will of virtually the entire civil rights community when they pressed for even stronger federal protection of Negro voting rights.

Since the late 1920s, the NAACP had promoted voter education, including registration and getting out the vote, among its branches. Throughout the non-South, the NAACP had become the single major force year after year in the registration of Negro voters. In turn, the reasonably high ratio of Negro voters in certain key states—Illinois, Michigan, Ohio, New York, New Jersey, and Pennsylvania—helped to elect statewide officials more sensitive to their interests, as well as some local legislators and congressmen. Virtually all of these elected officials were, of course, white men and, infrequently, white women. The NAACP Blue Book, containing the organization's by-laws, mandated a voter education committee for each branch. During the Great Depression and following the defeat of Judge Parker's nomination to the Supreme Court, huge numbers of Negro voters switched from the Party of Lincoln to the Democratic Party because they believed in FDR's compassion for every one of the nation's "little people." At the local level both parties often vied for the support of NAACP branch leaders in close contests.

Under Wilkins, the national office established the Voter Education Department led by a diminutive but dynamic Alabamian, W.C. Patton.

The department produced a variety of how-to guides, provided direction on key electoral issues, and distributed small sums of money to selected branches each year to increase registration or voting. The major criteria applied by the national office for these awards were, first and foremost, the importance of the election, followed by the quality of the written presentation by the branch, including a reasonable budget, coupled with the branch's record in living up to its commitments.

In 1961, as part of an effort by wealthy white philanthropists to craft an unattainable degree of unity among the major civil rights groups, the Voter Education Project (VEP) was organized in New York by Harold Fleming, Steve Currier, and Jack Kaplan, together with representatives of the Kennedy Administration, the latter anxious to deflect criticism from some of the organizational leaders for its tepid approach to civil rights. Given the size of the promised dollar support, it is no small wonder that SCLC envisaged a significant organizational expansion into the voter field. On the other hand, the NAACP was represented by more than 2,000 adult branches in virtually every black community in the nation. Most of those branches sustained some degree of voter activity, depending on their size, resources, and quality of leadership.

Wilkins and Mitchell were not at all exultant over the prospect of SCLC (or for that matter, later SNCC and CORE) setting up voter drives in competition with local NAACP branches. However, in locales where the NAACP branch was inactive or suffering from poor and/or compromised leadership, they made no fuss about sister organizations moving in on these branches, while expressing the hope that local units would find ways to collaborate. In the major cities, the Urban League units collaborated closely with the NAACP, whose members lived in the African-American communities often targeted by an Urban League drive operating from the downtown business hub. On August 31, the concept of the VEP was agreed upon as a subsidiary of the Southern Regional Council, which had enjoyed lavish Rockefeller support and the participation of moderate white Southern leaders, journalists, and professionals. The VEP began operations on April 1, 1962, with a prominent black attorney, Wiley Branton, as its first director. The NAACP and the NUL received the largest grants from the VEP, which helped to persuade Wilkins to accept the VEP's proposal to assign responsibility for registration geographically, with the VEP deciding which organization would become the lead entity in each locale. Within the next two years, however, King's SCLC had eroded its credibility to a serious degree with the VEP by failing to mount voter campaigns in cities assigned to it and for which it had received VEP funding. Moreover, its financial reports were either not forthcoming or in such disarray that even SCLC's personnel could not explain them.[6] The original support for the VEP came from donors more interested in assisting Dr. King and possibly SNCC than in across-the-board support of the more established civil rights organizations. SCLC's critical defaults in such important cities as Chattanooga, Tallahassee, and Montgomery, as well as northeastern North Carolina and a sizable segment of Georgia, made it clear that its program capacity was extremely limited—more often than not it could sustain only one important event at a time and no more.

Added to this discovery was the mounting concern over its finances—even SNCC's leaders argued with Dr. King over what was their appropriate share of fund-raising income designed to support them jointly. More seriously, outsiders expressed concern that some of the unaccounted VEP funds, a highly restricted grant, might have been used for SCLC's general upkeep.

The VEP faded into inactivity until 1966, when the NAACP's field secretary in Georgia and one of its brightest young stars, Vernon Jordan, was named director of a revitalized VEP. Long one of Wilkins' favorite staffers, Jordan was not well-known nationally except among civil rights professionals. The VEP post thrust him into the national spotlight. Jordan changed the VEP's grant-making method so that the grants no longer went to the national organizations but to their local units, which were obliged to submit written proposals with competent budgets and a written *modus operandi.* Ultimately, the bulk of the grants were made annually to NAACP local units throughout the South, which, with the help of the NAACP's national director of voter education, were able to submit successful applications and later satisfactory financial and program reports.[7]

Paradoxically, a few years after the VEP began making grants to the NAACP in 1962–1964, the Internal Revenue Service (IRS) accorded the NAACP's program arm, the Special Contribution Fund (SCF), tax deductibility.[8] The SCF proceeded to raise an increasingly large stream of voter education grants from the Ford, Carnegie, and Rockefeller

Foundations, as well as occasional grants from the New World, Stern, and Taconic Foundations, and, near the end of its existence, the Field Foundation. The latter proved to be a major source of satisfaction because it, more than any other entity, had kept the VEP alive long after it had become clear that it had little reason to continue. Because most of its grants wound up in the coffers of NAACP branches, first Wilkins, then Ben Hooks, questioned whether the need for a separate organization, with a separate overhead and separate fund-raising activities. Almost half of the VEP's annual expenditures went for administrative and fund-raising line items, and the remainder for its program —voter education. The NAACP leaders argued that the administrative funds were being wasted in order to maintain the fiction of another independent agency.

The Field Foundation, however, insisted on directing all of its funds for voter education in the South to the VEP. For reasons that were never explained to the NAACP, the Ford Foundation, at Field's request, matched Field's grants almost dollar for dollar. However, the IRS held up a steadfast rule that no tax-deductible charity could receive more than 25 percent of its regular support from one source. Even with Ford's contribution, each foundation would be providing half of the income. To circumvent this rule, the VEP undertook an expensive and unrewarding direct mail campaign, costing roughly the same dollars as the combined grants the VEP received from Ford and Field. So long as the mail campaign reached a break-even point at the end of each year, VEP was in formal compliance with the IRS regulation, despite the fact that its direct mail campaign produced little or no surplus income over the costs of mailing. The magnitude of the annual volume of letters mailed by the tiny VEP almost equaled that of the NAACP, with both competing for the same gifts from virtually the same donors.

When the Field Foundation ultimately decided to close its doors by giving away its capital, it became a heavy supporter of the NAACP's voter education program, most particularly of the state and regional efforts of Ms. Carolyn Coleman who, based in North Carolina, worked tirelessly throughout the Deep South in very difficult and dangerous circumstances during the 1970s and 1980s, becoming almost a legend during her own lifetime.

As the SCF grew, more and more opportunities for grants relating to voter activities arose. In the early 1970s, special grants were made by a fund established from a controversial fund-raising dinner organized on behalf of LBJ's candidacy. The proceeds were placed in a special account outside of the Johnson campaign and later distributed to the NAACP and other minority organizations for voter registration and vote pulling. Directing the fund was attorney Wiley Branton, the first executive director of the VEP. During the same decade, following a controversial grant to CORE by the Ford Foundation that appeared to aid the campaign of Cleveland Mayor Carl Stokes, however indirectly, Congress legislated some restrictions on the use of tax-deductible funds for voter registration and generating voter turnout. It limited the use of tax-deductible grants specifically for these purposes to three national organizations that had maintained national voter education programs —the NAACP, the Urban League, and the League for Women Voters —in order to reduce the opportunities for partisan funding of these activities that might result in aiding specific candidates.

Despite the millions of dollars in grants made by the VEP or by foundations through the national office for local voter drives, the largest amount came from the branches themselves, including those that also received outside help. The local units became increasingly sophisticated and efficient in wringing funds from the community, both black and white. The NAACP was never able to introduce an accurate retrieval system on local branch programs and expenditures, but in the national office it had become an accepted fact that local units raised between two and five times the amount that the national office disbursed in voter education grants annually. The volunteer manpower recruited by the NAACP, most especially by the local branches, college chapters, and youth councils, for each November election was certainly unrivaled among minority organizations; senior NAACP staff members estimated that the total man-hours contributed by volunteers to register and pull the vote exceeded that of any white voluntary organization, including the League for Women Voters.

The NAACP volunteers covered the entire spectrum of voter activity, starting with basic door-to-door canvassing to identify unregistered voters, to educate voters on the current election, to convert through persuasion if necessary, and then make certain that the converted actually voted. Phone banks were set up in larger branches for that purpose. Members and voters identified as favorable might receive one or more mailings conveying the NAACP's positions on those issues regarded as of greatest importance to African Americans. The night prior to the election, NAACP volunteers employed the phone bank to remind the favorable voters to actually vote and to respond to any last minute reservations about the candidates. Arrangements would also be made by the branches for those who required transportation to the polls the next day or who might need assistance to vote by absentee ballot.[9] Many volunteers served on transportation committees that drove voters to the polls on election day, especially in rural areas. The more experienced volunteers often became poll watchers or members of the election board to ensure that the interests of African-American voters were protected throughout the process. Others canvassed the community, handing out literature, at the same time reminding adults to vote and at what hour the polls would close.

The voter education apparatus of the NAACP was not only the preeminent electoral mechanism among the nation's minorities; it was also the most cost-effective and thorough ballot box mechanism among America's private nonprofit agencies and it answered most calls to arms, especially during important national elections. From the mid-1960s until the end of the 1970s, the average cost to the NAACP for registering a new voter was roughly one dollar, because such a high proportion of the effort was undertaken by volunteers, usually within their own communities, thereby reducing or eliminating any room-and-board bills.

Over the three key decades—roughly 1960 to 1990—the NAACP registered more Negro voters than all of the other private agencies combined—close to six million by one internal estimate—and probably registered as many Negroes as did the federal marshals after passage of the 1965 Voting Rights Act. Had the voter education program of the NAACP been the sole program of a separate organization, it would have received unstinting acclaim and credit. Given the collective antipathies toward the NAACP of so many within and outside the civil rights community, the permanent NAACP nationwide voter education network was rarely accorded the credit it merited (except by professional politicians); instead, it was grudgingly acknowledged as merely another consequence of the NAACP's unique and vast grassroots membership. Few on the outside appreciated the degree of organization and staff hours involved in shaping and directing such an extensive system of volunteers in almost every state and in several thousand predominantly black communities.

By the summer of 1965, the NAACP and its sister organizations had put in place an elaborate and often effective voter registration network, especially throughout the South. These locally led cadres were in the position of butting heads with the full force of local law enforcement agencies, backed throughout the South by diehard state governments less interested in protecting or expanding the rights of their black citizens than in holding on to their centuries-old positions of privilege and power based in large measure on the color of their skin. Every possible subterfuge was being employed by local and state election boards to deny or discourage blacks from registering to vote. The most obvious was the broad-scale use of intimidation—murdering civil rights workers sent the most eloquent message possible to activists, black and white, involved in voter drives. Local employers refused to give their workers time off to register; if any of their employees managed to find a way to register, they were often summarily fired. Some local election boards opened only for two hours every other week, resulting in long lines of black prospective voters, most of whom never reached the door to the election board before it was closed until the next registration period. With white supremacists monopolizing the predominant power—political, legal, and economic—while hiding behind the overwhelming legal firepower in the hands of the local sheriffs, state police, and National Guard, the odds were greatly stacked against the NAACP's cadres and those of its sister groups.

Into this confrontation heavily weighted against the civil rights forces, the federal government was preparing to inject itself through the proposed voting rights bill. It was no secret that a voting rights bill with real teeth enforced by the full power of the federal government could redress the imbalance and even change the momentum in favor of those demanding the vote for African Americans in the South.

With the groundswell of public opinion growing daily because of the events in Selma, Clarence Mitchell moved his operation into high gear on Capitol Hill. Aided by NAACP board member Joe Rauh and Washington bureau staff attorney Frank Polhaus, Mitchell proceeded to line up the needed Senate votes to break the cloture deadlock. Though he kept the names secret until the vote, several were senators from the South. On one side he was obliged to contend with obstructionism from what was then called "the Southern contingent" of the civil rights organizations—King and SCLC, SNCC, CORE, and the Freedom Democratic Party in Mississippi, which had lost its bid to be seated at the 1964 Democratic Convention in Atlantic City. Largely because of misinformation, these four civil rights organizations, devoid of real experience in lobbying Congress, came to believe mistakenly that the bill being promoted by the Justice Department would apply only when less than 15 percent of eligible black voters were registered. They also vehemently opposed the NAACP's efforts, energetically led by Mitchell, to include a total bar of the poll tax in the proposed act. They were not only wrong about the facts, but they implied that Mitchell and the NAACP, as well as the supporters of the Justice Department proposal, were guilty of tokenism, while they themselves alone constituted the true Civil Rights movement.[10] In his autobiography, Wilkins suggests less noble reasons for their opposition to the efforts led by Mitchell to fashion a strong and encompassing voter rights bill. Years later, he observed:

> Three groups seemed willing to sacrifice the poll tax ban to win quicker passage of the bill. The Mississippi Freedom Democratic Party and SNCC wanted to get the bill behind us quickly so publicity could focus on their campaign to purge the House of its white Mississippi congressmen. Dr. King was running a student project down South that summer; he believed that his work would be adversely affected if he didn't have the Voting Rights Act behind him by July. There were also the advocates of LBJ's other Great Society programs who had hoped to put social welfare and labor legislation proposals to Congress before civil rights. When Selma switched the timetable on them, they argued that a long fight over the poll tax in a House-Senate conference would only threaten the rest of the Great Society.[11]

Mitchell persuaded the liberal senators of both parties, led by Ted Kennedy of Massachusetts, to hold the line against these pressures. He maneuvered between the Justice Department and Capitol Hill to strengthen by stages the drafts of the proposed provisions, backing the maximum version submitted by Representative Celler in the House as chairman of the Judiciary Committee. Except for its omission of a ban on the poll tax, the total package submitted by the administration (largely the work of the Justice Department under Attorney General Nicholas Katzenbach) was so sweeping it covered almost every base. Encompassing elections at every level from local to national, including primaries, the administration proposed to ban virtually every device and unfair test used to deprive minorities of the vote and to outlaw state-imposed registration requirements that discriminated against any minority. Any restrictions on eligibility to vote were banned, except for age, residence, a past felony conviction, or lack of mental competence. To ensure that the bill's measures were applied fairly, the draft proposed that federal examiners be assigned where necessary to administer registration. The main responsibility for enforcing the law rested with the executive branch, which could seek stiff civil and criminal penalties against those convicted of violating the law. Geographically, the proposed measure covered Alabama, Georgia, Louisiana, Mississippi, South Carolina, and large portions of North Carolina and Virginia, where Negro populations ranged from 20 percent to one-third of the total adult population.[12]

Overall, Mitchell and Wilkins strongly approved of these provisions, but continued, as Wilkins put it, to lobby "hard to get rid of the poll tax." Even President Johnson disagreed with the NAACP on this strategy, as did many of the Southern and Republican conservative senators. Representative Celler greatly assisted Clarence Mitchell when he "inadvertently" dropped a letter from Dr. King on the floor of the House, urging the congressman not to support the NAACP-proposed ban on the poll tax. This "accident" made the King position public, much to his embarrassment,[13] and effectively checkmated King from further lobbying against the NAACP position.

The principal problem before Mitchell, he recollected in later years, was how to determine what set of circumstances should trigger the executive branch's appointment of federal examiners when the voting rights of blacks had been violated, and how long these examiners should be appointed to serve. There were a myriad number of political considerations to be weighed among the various congressional groupings before these issues could be resolved. Mitchell dealt with each faction with the skill of a United Nations diplomat. As early as February 1965, the NAACP and the liberal House Democrats had adopted a strategy of avoiding endorsement of a specific bill in order to discourage the opposition from coalescing against any single measure. Wilkins then visited LBJ and urged that his proposal include federal registrars and the banning of all literacy tests at the federal and local levels. On March 11, the Justice Department agreed in a meeting with Mitchell to include a trigger mechanism that could be invoked by the attorney general after he certified that a jurisdiction had denied citizens the right to vote, thus permitting the appointment of federal registrars. The other provisions of the Justice Department proposal were less than satisfactory to Mitchell, since they called for continued collection of poll taxes but only by voting registrars and the right to use literacy tests in areas not affected by discrimination. The proposal also called for the expiration of the act in 10 years.

Using these measures as a starting point, Mitchell and his associates joined with a bipartisan Senate group to develop a more acceptable draft, which Senators Paul Douglas (Democrat) and Clifford Case (Republican) of New Jersey introduced on March 15 as S. 1517. The administration, through the Justice Department, agreed to accept most of the stronger features of the Douglas-Case measure, but still refused to accept a ban on the poll tax. Mitchell's skill as a diplomat was best demonstrated at this juncture; instead of railing against the administration and the attorney general, Mitchell expressed the view that they were comprised of men and women of good will who simply had an honest disagreement with him and the NAACP over this measure. That permitted the administration's forces to lobby in support of the bill's other measures, while Mitchell kept his own cards close to his vest; in his own mind he was convinced he had the votes to expand and liberalize the provisions of the administration's bill once it reached the floor of the House and Senate. Just to make certain, he once more polled his supporters and found them solidly in his corner. Appearing before a House subcommittee wearing the hat of the LCCR, Mitchell won quick approval to further strengthen the drafts that would now totally eliminate the poll tax in state and local elections, at the same time removing the requirement for an aggrieved party to appear before a state official before seeking help from a federal registrar.[14]

Despite dilatory tactics by the hostile chairman of the Senate Judiciary Committee, Mississippi's James Eastland, the chair's capacity to obstruct was circumvented when 67 senators (42 Democrats, including

5 Southerners, and 25 Republicans) transmitted the administration's bill to the Senate Judiciary Committee on March 18 with instructions to report it out no later than April 9. Eastland loaded up the hearings with hostile witnesses, compelling Mitchell to withdraw most of his supporters' testimony and to settle with their written testimony submitted to the House by Wilkins and Joe Rauh. When the entire Judiciary Committee proceeded to a vote on the administration's proposal, nine liberals voted to include a ban on the poll tax and to include other strengthening measures, against five opponents.[15]

When the House Judiciary Committee followed suit and included a ban on the poll tax in its final draft, the Justice Department's leaders became openly hostile, seeking to convince senators and congressmen to remove the poll tax ban from their measures. Mitchell fought back, appealing directly to President Johnson to intervene. In a detailed letter to LBJ, Mitchell not only documented his case for the ban, but accused the attorney general of "working overtime to extirpate the anti-poll-tax provision from the [bills]." He then issued a press release, revealing that he had sent the letter to the president to "ensure that it not get lost in the mail," but withheld the details of the letter itself. Even friends of the NAACP outside the Congress, as well as such liberal publications as the *Washington Post* and the *New Republic,* were accusing the NAACP of "rocking the boat" in terms of getting the voting rights bill approved. Justice Department officials were privately telling senators and press contacts that they believed that the anti-poll-tax provision was unconstitutional. Without replying to Mitchell's letter, President Johnson allowed himself to be quoted as opposing the anti-poll-tax measure and stating that he had instructed the attorney general to work with like-minded members of Congress to defeat the ban.

Three weeks into the Senate debate Majority Leader Mike Mansfield and Minority Leader Everett Dirksen introduced a substitute bill removing the ban on the poll tax and some of the strengthening language added by the Judiciary Committee. In response, Senator Ted Kennedy offered an amendment to ban the poll tax, which failed by four votes, 45 to 49, on May 11. The margin of defeat could be credited to a letter from Attorney General Katzenbach to Mansfield, read by the latter from the floor, questioning the constitutionality of the amendment.

In an episode that triggered his underestimated temper, Clarence Mitchell angrily attacked the Mansfield-Dirksen substitute that, he charged, had "emasculated" the voting rights bill before the Senate. He also attacked the Senate leadership for buckling under to Dirksen's conservatism, while ignoring the landslide victory by President Johnson less than six months earlier over the nation's guru of conservatism (Barry Goldwater), as well as the fact that the majority of the Senate clearly supported a stronger bill than Dirksen proposed. He pointedly challenged the diehard Southern senators to mount a filibuster, observing that their leaders were either too old or too sick to sustain one long enough to be effective. He mounted a new lobbying effort through the LCCR, but the arm-twisting and the public relations effort were to no avail. Mansfield and Dirksen, probably with the president's tacit support, retained control, and instead of banning the poll tax, they amended their own bill to include a statement that the poll tax infringed on the constitutional rights of citizens to vote. Aside from some additional wording making some language stronger than before, the only other improvement from the NAACP's viewpoint was an amendment that assigned federal poll watchers in areas where voter rights had been violated.[16]

On May 25, the Senate voted by 70 to 30 for cloture for the second successive year, just as Mitchell had forecast, ending the filibuster. The next day, by an even greater margin—77 to 19—it passed the Voting Rights Act and sent it back to the House. Mitchell mobilized the combined lobbying forces of the NAACP and the LCCR to keep the lawmakers' feet to the fire—hundreds of volunteers from outside the District of Columbia joined with the Washington professionals in lobbying the representatives. The House bill was passed overwhelmingly on July 9 and contained Mitchell's hoped-for ban on the poll tax. However, the bipartisan Mansfield-Dirksen Senate combine possessed the majority of votes in the conference committee set up to resolve the differences between the two bills. Ever a realist, Mitchell and his civil rights colleagues let their House allies off the hook by urging them to give up the ban on the poll tax in order to avoid any further delays. Instead Mitchell concentrated the NAACP-LCCR effort on extending the bill's coverage to every aspect to state and local elections as well as the federal ones. He was successful; the final bill approved by both houses of Congress—S. 1564, otherwise known as the Voting Rights

Act of 1965—became the most powerful voting instrument in the history of the United States.[17]

The final bill, containing a trigger to activate it, included the stronger versions of the Douglas-Case proposal, covering the same geographical scope in the South, authorizing the appointment of federal voting examiners in those states and counties, and requiring that any change in voting laws in the entire region under the Voting Rights Act's jurisdiction would require the prior approval of either the attorney general or the federal district court in Washington. The Voting Rights Act also suspended the use of literacy tests and other voter qualification devices throughout the region covered by it.

In addition to the declaration that state and local poll taxes infringed upon the rights of citizens, the Voting Rights Act directed the attorney general to bring lawsuits against the poll tax "forthwith," a time frame far more desirable than that of "all deliberate speed" which had been formulated to implement *Brown v. Board of Education*. That was exactly what Attorney General Katzenbach had sought because, as he explained years afterwards, "I was absolutely persuaded that we would get rid of the poll tax faster by a decision of the Supreme Court than we would have if we had included the provision [in the Voting Rights Act.]"[18] Subsequently, Mitchell treated Katzenbach and his associates with considerable respect, conceding that their position on this issue had been sincere. Later, the Supreme Court did rule in suits brought by the Justice Department that poll taxes enacted by localities and states were unconstitutional.

Upon signing the Voting Rights Act, President Johnson shared with the American people his reasons, moral and political, for fighting for its passage. He said:

> The Act flows from a clear and simple wrong. Its only purpose is to right that wrong. Millions of Americans are denied the right to vote because of their color. The law will insure them the right to vote. The wrong is one which no American in his heart can justify. The right is one which no American true to our principles can deny.
>
> You will find that the vote is the most powerful instrument ever devised by man for breaking down injustice and destroying the terrible walls which imprison men because they are

> different from other men. Today what is perhaps the last of the legal barriers is tumbling. And then the promise: It is not enough just to give men rights. They must be able to use those rights in their personal pursuit of happiness.[19]

Because they appreciated the role of compromise in the process of legislation and because their idealism was firmly based in reality, Wilkins, Mitchell, and the NAACP settled for three-fourths of a loaf that, as it turned out, was meaningfully more than they had originally hoped to achieve. They exploited every advantage presented to them, whether it was the brutal response of Sheriff Clark in Selma, or the highly televised acts of courage by hundreds of African Americans confronting their racist nemeses in Selma, Montgomery and scores of other Southern cities and towns, or the president's friendship, or the respect of the congressional majority of both parties, or the debilitated condition of the Southern leaders in Congress, or the mammoth volunteer mechanism developed by the NAACP's leaders and staff that effectively deployed many of its 500,000 members and 2,500 local units, or the unprecedented coalition of more than 150 national organizations in the LCCR. Each one of these factors contributed to the passage of the 1965 Voting Rights Act that, together with the 1964 Civil Rights Act, still remains today the greatest legislative achievement by a nongovernmental organization in the history of civilized humanity.

It has been said by admirers of Dr. King that without Selma there would have been no 1965 Voting Rights Act. Possibly that is true, but without the NAACP's determination, skills, and leadership, as exemplified by Clarence Mitchell and his associates, even with Selma there would have been no Voting Rights Act in 1965. The vision and knowhow of King, Farmer, Lewis, and the other leaders of the Southern part of what was then regarded as the civil rights movement ended with direct confrontation. They had hardly a clue as to how to translate the massive publicity and support into a positive and constructive national legislative endeavor. This in no way minimizes their courage or commitment; it is simply a bald historical fact.

It required the wisdom and experience of Mitchell and Wilkins, backed by Whitney Young, A. Philip Randolph, Dorothy Height, Bayard Rustin, and labor leaders like Walter Reuther and James Carey, to maneuver through the battlefields of Congress and the White House and craft the most liberating pieces of legislation in modern American history. It required the steadfast support of the coalitions built by the NAACP, most importantly the members of the LCCR, because it was essential for the centrist members of Congress and the Senate to perceive that the measures demanded by the NAACP were also supported by multitudes of white Americans from every walk of life, every part of the country, every religion, every class, and every national heritage. In this regard, the active participation of moderate Republican senators, such as Kuchel, Javits, Cooper, Case, Scott, Smith, and Keating made it possible for the Senate to both vote for cloture and produce a powerful and broadly encompassing voting rights bill that was clearly bipartisan.

The opposition, comprised of hard-line Southern Democrats and extreme right-wing Republicans, was also bipartisan. Thus, it was impossible for either party to exploit the bill's passage for purely partisan gain. Tragically, today such a bipartisan congressional alliance is virtually impossible because the moderate Republican elements of both the House and Senate are all but invisible, having been systematically eradicated by extreme right wingers within the party since the election of Ronald Reagan to the presidency. It took only two decades for the plantation-based Dixiecrats to migrate from the Democratic Party of FDR and become the rock-solid base of the contemporary Republican Party, which can now almost automatically count on the electoral votes of the South in a presidential election.[20]

The 1965 passage of the Voting Rights Act also required the massive support of the media—print and broadcast—not only through very gripping, objective news coverage, but also on the editorial pages. Yet, in the final analysis, what made the Voting Rights Act politically palatable and editorially supportable was the rapid transformation of white American attitudes over the first half of the 1960s. A poll by the highly respected George Gallup published just two weeks before the Senate vote revealed a startling degree of white support and a sea change of attitudes. Whereas in 1959, Dr. Gallup reported, only 5 percent of Americans regarded integration as "the most important problem facing the United States, . . . [T]oday nearly five times as many Americans consider integration their country's major concern, second only to peace." Although many whites remained wary of federal enforcement of desegregation laws, the poll found, the dramatic civil rights events in the South had produced both a widespread "sense of inevitability" among whites, as well as "a sense of guilt." As a result, the 1968 Gallup poll reported, 63 percent of American adults and 71 percent of youth favored federal intervention in the South to enable Negroes to register and to vote. Only in the South, where 48 percent favored this federal role, did less than a 60 percent majority support such intervention. Almost as surprising, "eight in 10 white Americans said they would not move . . . if a Negro family moved next door to you." In fact, only 23 percent of Southern whites said they *would* move.[21]

The transformed attitudes of white Americans were a direct product of the talented, determined, and often courageous American journalists who, by their coverage of the historic events and the moral issues underlying them, educated the citizenry to such an extent that they abandoned old prejudices and overcame indifference to become sympathizers of the Negro struggle for first-class status. There are few, if any, other comparable eras in our history in which the American press "got it right" so consistently and to such a degree that mass attitudes were radically altered. Finally, all of these disparate pieces needed to be orchestrated to play one common melody and the fact that they did can only be credited to the conductor—the NAACP.

As one of the nation's foremost students of the civil rights struggle, Frank R. Parker, concluded 25 years later: "Few events in American political life have had as profound or as far-reaching consequences as has passage of the Voting Rights Act of 1965."[22] Within a few years, the entire electoral landscape in the South had begun to change drastically. The readiness and power of the federal government to intervene in state and/or local situations in which voting rights violations had been alleged proved to be an irresistible force, both in its own right and as a means of encouraging African Americans, Native Americans, Latinos, and Americans of Asian descent to act on their own and demand their constitutionally guaranteed voting rights.

In 1965 the total number of black Americans registered to vote was somewhere between two and three million; by 1990 that number exceeded 12 million. A direct consequence of the 1965 Voting Rights Act, the number of black elected officials multiplied about 14-fold between 1965 and 1989. From a figure of approximately 500 the year the Voting Rights Act was passed, that number had grown to about 7,200 in 1989, roughly two-thirds of whom were in the South. More than 300 mayors and 400 state legislators were black men and women in 1989. In the 1992 national elections, more than 40 members of Congress, including one black woman in the U.S. Senate, were elected.

Looking backward after a quarter century of struggle through the courts in Mississippi and other parts of the South, Frank R. Parker, who as much as any other individual in the private sector helped to expand black voter rights as a front-line attorney, characterized the Voting Rights Act's effect in these broad terms:

> The Voting Rights Act swept away the primary legal barriers to black registration and voting in the South, eliminating the literacy tests and poll taxes and allowing the Justice Department to dispatch federal registrars and poll watchers to ensure the integrity of the voting process.[23]

As Parker was quick to point out, however, the response of the Southern states to the Voting Rights Act was to shift their strategy from blocking the Negro' access to the vote to the adoption of measures to nullify the impending black vote. These state authorities adopted what Parker termed a "second generation of disenfranchising devices"—including at-large elections, racial gerrymandering, transforming certain previously elected officials to become office appointees, and raising the qualifications for candidates running for office. These measures, which replaced the earlier literacy tests, poll taxes, and other devices, cumulatively represented massive resistance to the Voting Rights Act in the hope of perpetuating—or at least prolonging—the white monopoly on elective office throughout the South.

For a time in some places, these tactics succeeded in discouraging the registration of black voters. However, times had changed and the nation's mood was different after 1965. Not only did the Justice Department itself file suit, conduct investigations (often through the FBI), and oversee changes in voter legislation, but also an unprecedented large number of civil rights attorneys went on the offensive, filing voter rights suits in the South and in every other section of the country, seeking immediate remedies that opened up the registration rolls and enabled black candidates (and those of other minorities) to be elected to office. In addition, major foundations had been persuaded to join the fray, supporting the NAACP's SCF, the Legal Defense Fund, the Southern office of the ACLU, and the Lawyers Committee for Civil Rights under Law as they crafted suits to attack the recalcitrant Southern obstructers.

Even with this sizable mobilization of legal talent, combined with the financial support of foundations, law firms, and others, there were never enough resources—human or financial—to provide legal representation for every legitimate need. In some cases, large private law firms sought to fill part of this void by providing *pro bono* help on voter rights cases, adding to the impact. Significant foundation funding gradually became available for voter registration and get-out-the-vote campaigns, given the new opportunities presented by the Voting Rights Act. Despite the foot-dragging by Nixon's Justice Department from 1969 until 1974, by the end of the first decade after the Voting Rights Act had been passed, so many black voters had been registered in the South that the black vote became crucial to winning statewide office in every Southern state—ranging from about 34 percent in Mississippi to about 20 percent in Alabama. Elected blacks began to join county commissions, school boards, and election boards locally, opening up their internal processes to public view and changing the way they had historically done business.

Given the premise that few people voluntarily give up power, it was to be expected that those who controlled the levers of Southern power, including control of the electoral process, would resist until they were defeated, either in court or at the polls. It should not surprise anyone that pockets of resistance continue to fight against the 1965 Voting Rights Act even today. Nevertheless, since the 1980s, the nationwide black percentage of registered voters has been, on average, only about 5 percent lower than that of whites; in many cities and towns in the South, the proportion of registered black voters is significantly higher than that of northern central cities. The difference is easily explained —the fundamental changes that the South has experienced since the 1960s continue to offer hope to its African-American citizens as they become increasingly desegregated in almost every aspect of life, as the economies of the South grow and offer better jobs to blacks, and as more and better housing is made available to blacks. The much harsher pathologies of non-South cities from New York and Philadelphia to Detroit and Chicago to Los Angeles and Houston have bred a substantial degree of hopelessness and despair among sizable numbers of urban, ghettoized African Americans, providing far less incentive for the exercise of the ballot. The almost overwhelming manifestations of violence—most of it black-on-black violence—in these large older cities contrast poorly with the more genteel milieu of many, but not all, Southern cities. That is why, for several years now, more blacks have been migrating back to the South than have been leaving the South for the North or West.

The Voting Rights Act played a crucial role in radically transforming the South from the land of Jim Crow to a more open, less segregated, and more modern society. The NAACP was the key player in bringing about the Voting Rights Act—it is a permanent monument to the great men and women who led the Association through that struggle, and to the black masses that steadfastly followed them despite endemic danger. In addition, more than any other private agency, the NAACP through its branches registered millions of African Americans and spurred even more to cast their ballots on election day. Lastly, NAACP lawyers, as well as attorneys from sister agencies, carried the burden of the struggle to remove the new barriers erected by Southern diehards to prevent blacks from benefiting from the provisions of the 1965 Voting Rights Act. One major result was the election of more than 7,000 blacks to elective office by 1989. Another was the registration of some 10 million new black voters nationwide, including decisively high percentages in most Southern states. With the light visible at the end of the tunnel in respect to political rights for black Americans, it became increasingly clear, however, that economic and social equality did not automatically follow political parity, that systemic racism had become deeply imbedded in our institutions, and that different strategies and tactics would, as we shall see, be needed for these challenges.

Postscript

President Johnson signed the 1965 Voting Rights Act on August 6 in the Capitol, dispensing scores of pens used by him during the signing ceremony to senators and congressmen who had played key roles in the Act's passage. (Clarence Mitchell, known as the "101st Senator," received none.) Six days later, the predominantly black Watts section of Los Angeles exploded with the fury of a volcano, unleashing thousands of angry and frustrated African Americans who rioted and looted for days before the ubiquitous "eyes" of the network television cameras. It took federal troops to quell the uprisings that, in the minds of many African Americans, were as much a political rebellion as they were a lawless outburst. Clearly, gaining the right to vote was not only not a priority in the eyes of urban blacks outside the South; but also it failed to promise the slightest succor to those whose lives were dominated by despair and hopelessness.

9. Black Workers, White Unions, and the Struggle for Job Equality

There is thus, unquestionably, room for more concerted action on the side of the Negro people, particularly there is need of an agency attempting to integrate Negro labor into the trade union movement . . . . The question is, however, whether or not this is the proper task for the NAACP. To an extent it is, undoubtedly, and the Association has, during the New Deal, become increasingly active in fighting discrimination in public welfare policy and in the labor market.

Gunnar Myrdal, *An American Dilemma,* 1944, 834–835

Even a casual look at the cause of racial unrest in America will discover that the job is the thing. A race has to believe that its members, if they qualify as well as any other applicants, will have a fair shake at employment opportunities. Moreover, if a race is to amount to anything at all, the breadwinner must have access to a pay check. This is the way to feed a family, pay rent to the landlord or make payments on a mortgage, buy health care, send the children to school, buy clothes and furniture, hold the family head up, and look after a dozen other items that require money . . . . Can one be a responsible, upstanding citizen when those who seek jobs are barred because of color, race and sex?

Roy Wilkins, "The Color of Television," nationally syndicated newspaper column of June 30, 1973

From the Great Depression and World War II forward, a critically important cornerstone of the NAACP's national program was its campaign to open up the workplace to African Americans. As early as 1910, the NAACP's founders had expressed their deep concern over the racially exclusionary practices of the AFL. According to Charles F. Kellogg, "throughout its existence, the Association made repeated attempts, in spite of the hostile climate, to secure admission of Negroes to unions on a basis of equality with white workers but without much success."[1]

For at least 25 years before the passage of the 1964 Civil Rights Act, the NAACP had been in the forefront of the struggle for what it termed "economic justice." Shortly before World War II, the Association undertook a legal campaign, crafted initially by Charles Hamilton Houston, to raise the salaries of Negro teachers to the level of their white counterparts in the South, in conjunction with the strategy to demand total equality of facilities and expenditures under the separate-but-equal doctrine set out by the *Plessy v. Ferguson* decision. Houston, and later Thurgood Marshall, hoped to pile on to the Southern states and townships an enormous burden of costs involved in financing a "separate but equal" school system for black children. NAACP attorneys won a number of important cases that resulted in increased salaries for Negro teachers, which was one more way to add to the financial burdens of the Southern states under *Plessy,* while helping to improve the economic status of African-American teachers who constituted a significant proportion of the full-time workers in almost every black community.

Another industry in which prewar Negroes filled a sizable number of stable and modestly remunerative jobs was that of the railroads. However, by the 1930s Negroes had been relegated to the least skilled and lowest paid of the railroad service occupations—porters and dining car waiters. Earlier, Negroes had comprised a sizable number of those employed as firemen, and on some Southern rail lines, made up a majority holding that post.[2] Hostile white unionists, however, systematically eliminated them from the fireman jobs. By the late 1930s, dozens of complaints of racial discrimination had been lodged by Negroes against the railroads and their unions, which resulted in widely publicized FEP hearings in 1943. The hearings revealed that the railroad companies and the railroad unions had signed an agreement in 1928, which, among other things, led to the wholesale removal of Negroes as firemen, while reserving virtually all of the other better-paying railroad posts for white union members.

The NAACP's Charles Hamilton Houston filed a number of lawsuits on behalf of African-American railroad workers, including *Steele v. Louisville & Nashville Railroad Co.* and *Tunstall v. Brotherhood of Locomotive Firemen and Enginemen.* In 1944 the Supreme Court rendered a narrowly constructed decision, which for the first time imposed on the union a duty of fair representation of all in a given craft. However, the Court left intact the union's power to exclude Negroes from union membership and union jobs. Thus, the Court denied the NAACP's contention that the union was required to accept Negro members under the Railway Labor Act. Although limited in their application, these cases were the beginning of a significant body of antidiscrimination labor law.[3]

Earlier, in 1935 the black workers and the NAACP suffered a major defeat when President Roosevelt and his New Deal supporters in Congress agreed to the passage of the National Labor Relations Act—widely known as the Wagner Act—from which an antidiscrimination provision had been deleted. The NAACP and the National Urban League had fought hard to retain this provision, which was in the original proposal. FDR withdrew his support after the AFL and its lily-white constituent unions threatened to defeat the entire bill unless the antidiscrimination provision was deleted.[4] With the advent of World War II, the NAACP joined forces with A. Philip Randolph, the most important black leader within the labor movement as the president of the Brotherhood of Sleeping Car Porters, then the sole "colored" union affiliated with the AFL. Their goal was to launch a campaign to pressure the federal government into proclaiming a FEP that would open up industries with government contracts, mostly defense-related, to Negro employment. FDR hesitated for as long as possible, but on the eve of a well-planned march on Washington in 1941 headed by Randolph and the NAACP under Walter White, FDR capitulated by signing a limited FEP executive order. That order, plus the rapidly growing shortage of able-bodied men, eventually opened up war-time assembly line jobs to both blacks and women, and both produced stellar records of skill and productivity until V-J Day in August 1945.

However, as the fighting men returned from the European theater during the second half of 1945, defense industry employers began releasing women and blacks from their jobs in order to return these jobs to white male war veterans. For the most part, women—about 3.5 million of whom had worked in defense industries—gracefully accepted the edict and voluntarily returned to home and hearth, though a small number, having tasted financial independence, remained in the job market throughout their productive years. They were the vanguard of the women's liberation movement that burst forth a quarter of a century later.

Black men (and a smaller number of black women), however, had experienced a long delayed and satisfying taste of not only well-paying jobs with increased benefits, but also many of the intangibles, such as enhanced self-worth based on performing well in high status jobs. In addition, most of the defense industries were located outside the Deep South where Jim Crow still ruled, which is not to say that the Midwest and the Pacific Rim were devoid of racist practices. Nevertheless, the overall climate for blacks outside the South was usually far more benign and hopeful than that of the South in the mid-1940s.

NAACP Executive Secretary Walter White, aided by Charles Houston, as well as the Association's assistant secretary, Roy Wilkins, and the NAACP's first labor secretary, Clarence Mitchell, had continually urged the Roosevelt and Truman Administrations from 1940 to 1945 to keep the pressure on the defense employers (as well as on the armed services) in order to sustain the momentum that resulted in opening up job opportunities for Negroes. Often this required the filing of complaints charging that the fair employment executive order issued by FDR was being violated. On occasion, it required some political intervention by senators and congressmen with sizable black constituencies (largely outside the South) to intervene on behalf of blacks seeking defense jobs within their jurisdictions. Clarence Mitchell became very effective at this exercise, forging dozens of personal relationships that would produce sizable political dividends decades later.

The NAACP job campaign had begun to emerge with the birth of the CIO during the turbulent 1930s, when labor violence, most often provoked by hired private police—too often a euphemism for unemployed thugs and scabs—characterized the auto industry in Detroit, the mining industry in Pennsylvania, West Virginia, and as far west as

Arizona, and the longshoremen on the West Coast, to identify a few. The CIO proved more militant and radical than its older counterpart, the AFL. The latter had been led by Samuel Gompers of the Cigar Makers Union, which excluded Negroes. Gompers displayed undiluted animosity towards Negroes and other workers of color. The unions that were affiliated with the AFL at that time were, for the most part, craft unions—carpenters, painters, plumbers, electricians, bricklayers, iron workers, masons, operating engineers, and so forth—that required one or more skills developed only through apprenticeship and work experience controlled by the unions. Virtually all of these craft unions were lily-white, in no small measure because of practices that stemmed from the belief that each existing membership was preordained to be inherited by a blood relative of the original member, not unlike the medieval practices of craft guilds in Europe.

In the last quarter of the nineteenth century, when freed slaves included sizable numbers of highly skilled craftsmen in most fields, many developed their job skills in the plantation economy. The AFL unions shut their doors tightly to any Negro applicant, while swelling their ranks with European immigrants recently arrived on American shores. The first waves of Europeans arrived with some of the necessary skills and quickly assimilated to the rampant American notion that it was acceptable to bar blacks with the same skills from competing for available work. Later waves of immigrants were even larger —in the millions annually—and they provided a vast and ever-increasing pool of cheap and unskilled labor that served as an effective damper on labor agitation for increased wages and benefits in the newly created factories of the Northeast and Midwest during the last third of the nineteenth century.

Had the entrepreneurial leaders of the American Industrial Revolution provided employment to the newly freed slaves, especially the males, after the Civil War, it is more than likely that much of the ensuing poverty and family disintegration borne by the freed slaves and their descendants could have been avoided. Tens of millions of immigrants were drawn to American shores between 1870 and 1910. In 1865, there were only 4 million Negroes in the United States, half of them children. Simple math would demonstrate that the burgeoning industrial base could provide more than 10 times as many jobs as there were adult Negroes to fill them. In their virtually total refusal to employ Negroes in the new American factories, most of which were in the North and Midwest, the owners of industry joined with the lily-white American labor movement in creating a pattern of racial exclusion with long-term consequences for the entire society.

By the 1930s, when the Great Depression had exposed the gravest injustices of capitalism as well as its enormous vulnerabilities, the AFL's approach to labor organizing proved highly inadequate and, in some quarters, suspect in respect to its policy towards organizing racial minorities. Out of this turbulent series of confrontations in industry after industry, a new labor federation, the CIO—led by John L. Lewis of the United Mine Workers—succeeded in capturing the imagination of the nation's dispossessed, including a sizable number of Negro workers. Many employers attempted, some successfully, to recruit unemployed blacks as scabs to replace striking white workers. CIO leaders recognized that if such a practice proved widespread, it could not only break the back of their strikes, but also lead to pervasive racial violence. The NAACP's leaders agreed. Thus was born a measure of cooperation between the CIO and the NAACP, which the NAACP leadership hoped would prove fruitful to both parties in later years.

The UAW became the most advanced labor union with a large integrated membership. In 1955, when the AFL and the CIO merged in a founding convention in New York City, Walter Reuther, its president, and his colleagues insisted on the designation of a black vice president of the labor federation—Willard Townsend of the CIO's United Transport Service Employees Union—to join the AFL's A. Philip Randolph, whose selection George Meany had already agreed to accept as the first black member of the merged union's executive council.[5] Although those elections marked the first time that blacks had reached the level of national leadership within organized labor's federations, many still perceived their presence on the labor movement's highest governing body as mere window dressing.

In the post of the NAACP's first labor secretary, Clarence Mitchell essentially served as the principal assistant to the NAACP's Washington Bureau Director, Leslie Perry, during the years after the war. Responsible for some legislative matters, Mitchell was assigned to respond to the continuous flow of complaints from black employees of federal agencies, especially within the District of Columbia. Early on, he perceived the value of coalition-building with organized labor and, in his capacity as the NAACP Labor Secretary during the 1940s, devoted a great deal of his time to that objective. He worked with Randolph in his postwar efforts to produce a permanent fair employment law and with some labor unions in the early campaigns for fair housing.

Expanding upon the 1948 *ad hoc* coalition of 22 national black organizations determined to maximize the black vote in the national elections of that year, the NAACP established the Joint Committee on Civil Rights in 1949 to press for passage of a fair employment act. The following year the NAACP brought more than 4,000 delegates from 100 organizations to Washington to press President Truman for civil rights support, which he pledged, and to gain enactment of a federal fair employment law. This national emergency civil rights mobilization evolved into the National Delegate Assembly for Civil Rights, which in 1956 brought 2,000 delegates from 32 states to Washington for a three-day mobilization, resulting in the official formation of the LCCR. At this historic meeting, the passage of a fair employment act still remained the highest priority of the interracial coalition, but Senate filibusters and their ever-present threat blocked passage of such a measure in the upper house.[6] This obstacle was not overcome until 1964, when passage of the Civil Rights Act included a major provision to open up jobs to Negroes.

This sustained lobbying experience proved invaluable in learning to pull the levers of decision making on Capitol Hill when Mitchell was named the NAACP's director of the Washington bureau in 1952. He undertook the courting of the more conservative AFL leaders, especially George Meany, and gradually recruited them to LCCR's ranks, which eventually became the most powerful coalition on Capitol Hill. No black leader in America was more trusted by the majority of trade union leaders than Clarence Mitchell—not Dr. King, not Roy Wilkins, not Thurgood Marshall, not even Bayard Rustin.

In addition to Walter Reuther, John L. Lewis, and A. Philip Randolph, Mitchell and the NAACP could often also depend upon several other union presidents to support and work hard for civil rights legislation, such as James B. Carey of the CIO's Electrical Workers Union, Fred O'Neal of Actor's Equity, Willard Townsend of the United Transport Service Employees Union, and Jerry Wurf of the State, County, and Municipal Workers. They remained, however, a distinct minority within the ranks of organized labor.

For the three decades beginning in the mid-1960s, George Meany and his deputy (and successor), Lane Kirkland, often responded to appeals from Mitchell, Wilkins, and later Ben Hooks to rally member unions in support of specific civil rights legislation. Labor lobbyists joining Mitchell became a familiar sight in twisting congressional arms to support the civil rights proposals of each period, often adding just enough muscle to change the minds of recalcitrant legislators whose constituencies numbered few Negroes.[7]

It often fell upon Roy Wilkins to balance the competing claims between those who urged the NAACP to forcefully press the case against the racial job practices of unions and those who sought to nurture the NAACP's friendship with labor in order to gain their support for civil rights legislation. It was never an easy or simple task but Wilkins never deviated from his primary responsibility to eliminate the racist job pattern.

The major flaw in this otherwise productive alliance was that labor's role as a legislative civil rights ally between 1955 and 1965 was restricted to the top leadership of the trade union pyramid. The national union presidents, the senior officials of the AFL-CIO, and the senior staffs of both the labor federation and the larger unions supported, with some exceptions, the civil rights bills proposed by the NAACP and its allies.[8] Unfortunately, this pro-civil rights support at the apex of the labor movement rarely translated into support for desegregation at the local workplace or plant site, nor did it generate support for the NAACP's efforts to eliminate employment discrimination on the shop floor.[9] The average local union leader continued to nurse his racial biases, perceiving blacks and other minorities as illegitimate competition for the jobs of his members. As will be demonstrated later, the hard fact is that change at the grassroots level was often barely perceptible in most unions and industries after 1955. Many of these same unions, including the UAW, were complicit in maintaining patterns of racial exclusion from well-paid skilled craft jobs, or of segregating Negroes either at the job site or within the union, or both. Almost universally, the international unions failed to enforce the formal antidiscrimination provisions or policies on their own books, relegating these provisions to the status of empty rituals.

Wilkins and Mitchell had little hands-on contact with such locals —their primary experience was with the upper-level leaders who invariably showed them formal respect, but most labor leaders lacked the vision of an interracial labor movement. For the most part, the union leadership remained committed to their white membership base, without the will to press their memberships to cease discriminating against blacks and to open up their various memberships to all minority workers. It was extremely rare for a recalcitrant local to be penalized for such failures either by the international union or by the AFL-CIO itself.

But rank-and-file black workers, beginning in the mid-1960s, experienced for the first time a federal law prohibiting job discrimination by both employers and labor unions. Known as Title VII, the employment section of the 1964 Civil Rights Act was to provide for a federal system of complaints by aggrieved minority workers who claimed they were prohibited from employment or promotion because of their race, religion, nationality, or gender. Barring a voluntary resolution of the complaint, the employee and his or her coworkers were authorized to file suits in federal court to resolve the charges.

In real life, however, very few workers had the resources, the know-how, and the time to begin such a process on their own, which was exactly what some of the employers and legislators—state and federal —had relied upon. What they failed to anticipate was the passion, the dedication, the energy, and the imagination of the NAACP's Labor Secretary—Herbert Hill. Hill had joined the national staff in 1948 and became labor secretary in 1952 when Clarence Mitchell was named director of the Washington bureau. Hill was to become a legendary figure in the struggle to eliminate racist job practices. Eventually, he came to be perceived by labor leaders and employers as a forceful combatant determined to break down racial barriers in the workplace and within the labor movement.

It did not take long for black workers throughout organized labor to receive the message that the NAACP, through Herbert Hill, was their most effective ally in attacking racial discrimination on the job, whether it stemmed from the employer or the union, or both. Under Hill's leadership, local NAACP branch labor committees sprang up in hundreds of communities, North and South, advising black workers of their rights after the start of Title VII in 1965.[10] Under prodding from the NAACP, the federal government issued executive orders during the same period prohibiting job discrimination by government contractors. Like a whirlwind, Hill and his staff began processing and filing hundreds of complaints on behalf of African-American workers in fields as diverse as construction, steel and paper manufacturing, railroads, and aircraft production. These complaints, containing extensive documentation, attacked the patterns of long-standing, large-scale discriminatory practices that had barred blacks from employment or from the better paying jobs, or locked them into segregated jobs on separate tracks for advancement only in dead-end positions. Numerous complaints were field against corporations with a record of consistently rejecting blacks for employment, or always relegating black employees to menial positions such as janitorial duties, or failing to advance any black employees to higher or better positions, often those regarded as "white" jobs. Quite often they attempted to stonewall the NAACP while dismissing the employees who had made trouble, that is, the ones who had filed complaints. It did not take long for business leaders to learn that this practice was in itself illegal and that the NAACP was able to back up its words with expert legal representation. Always prepared for action, Herbert Hill was ready to pounce on any recalcitrant major government contractors.

Hill was a unique combination of activist and intellectual, capable of solid and painstaking research as well as dramatic descriptions of racist practices.[11] In his youth, he had shown an interest in the anti-Stalinist left, where he made the acquaintance of C.L.R. James among other black intellectuals. Because he was always good copy with a talent for dramatizing his actions, he became a favorite of newsmen. The media had become familiar with the precise and restrained oratory of Roy Wilkins, the dry and factual presentations of Clarence Mitchell, and the careful, legalistic explanations presented by the NAACP lawyers. Hill came from a different school—he was consistently intense and combative—but the Herbert Hill they saw and heard at each press conference was the same person elsewhere. He was certain of his position, impatient with the pace of most events, and ready to do battle with the enemies of racial equality. His standing among the black rank-and-file union members rose year after year because they never doubted his sincerity or commitment. Nor was he antilabor; on the contrary, his zeal in attacking racial discrimination within trade unions stemmed from his earlier activism in labor struggles, and his belief that the fight against white working class racism was in the best interests of the labor movement.

Even before he had been elevated to the post of labor secretary by Roy Wilkins and the NAACP Board of Directors after serving for three years as assistant field secretary, Hill and the NAACP were fighting Jim Crow practices in labor unions. Perhaps the earliest NAACP act against a union and certainly the longest to be resolved was the complaint filed against New York City's Sheet Metal Workers Local 28. The original complaint was filed in 1948, at which time the New York State Commission Against Discrimination (SCAD) ordered the union to desist from excluding Negroes through its constitution or by-laws. Even though the noxious clause had been removed, no progress in admitting Negro members was recorded 16 years later, after numerous motions filed by both the NAACP and the union's lawyers, who proved expert at finding causes for delay acceptable to the commission, the name of which had in the interim changed to the New York State Commission for Human Rights (NYSHR).

At last, in March 1964, the commission found that the local union had automatically excluded blacks since its inception 78 years earlier. In a decision termed "revolutionary" by its chairman, the commission later issued a cease-and-desist order and demanded that the union undertake affirmative action measures to end its discriminatory practices.[12] Hill, who had brought the original complaint to the commission, explained that same year why the decision had been groundbreaking in nature:

> The decision was called "revolutionary" by the Commission's chairman, George H. Fowler, because "it takes into account a historical pattern of exclusion and not merely a specific complaint." Thus the commission ruled against the union as an institution functioning within a given racial situation and with a history, and not on the basis of the "validity" of an individual complaint . . . . The State Commission charged that Local 28's admission program bore "a remarkable resemblance to the medieval guilds" by maintaining a father-son admission standard. The Commission noted that in a provision of its International Union constitution, which was deleted in 1946, the union declared that "no Negro could ever become a full member."[13]

And for the next four decades, as the union resisted compliance with court order after court order and the NAACP filed suit after suit, the black sheet metalworkers continued to be denied their legal rights as citizens. As Herbert Hill later wrote in a *New York Times* op-ed article upon learning that the Supreme Court was about to hear oral arguments from the union's lawyers to reverse earlier federal court decisions, the local union, "a member of the AFL-CIO, has repeatedly defied municipal, state, and Federal orders to cease discriminatory practices that have been documented many times over."

In 1981, a federal judge found Local 28 in contempt for the "willful disobedience of a court order" and fined the local union $150,000. (This was not the first union cited for contempt under Title VII. That "honor" belongs to Plumbers Local Union 189 of Columbus, Ohio, which was also sued by the NAACP.[14]) Finally, on July 2, 1986, the Supreme Court upheld the imposition of numerical quotas by lower federal courts on Local 28—38 years after Hill filed the initial complaint against the local.[15] Because the Reagan Administration opposed quotas and refused to argue the case, New York State Attorney General Robert Abrams assumed the primary task, arguing on behalf of minority workers before the Supreme Court.

Hill—since 1977 a professor of industrial relations and African-American studies at the University of Wisconsin-Madison—made it perfectly clear that "Black workers were not denied jobs and membership by Local 28 as individuals but as a class—no matter what their personal qualifications. Correspondingly, whites as a class benefited from systematic discrimination. Local 28 and other labor unions engaged in activities that gave whites substantial advantages in the labor market at the expense of blacks. *The union became the institutional repository of whites' expectations based on the deliberate denial of nonwhite workers' rights. This pattern became the norm,*"[16] Hill concluded (emphasis added).

Hill's summary could easily be applied to almost every other complaint or suit brought by the NAACP against other unions, local and national, during the four decades following World War II. The core of his commentary provided the legal, moral, and political underpinning of the NAACP's virtually ceaseless campaign to achieve equality and justice in the nation's workplaces between World War II and the late 1970s.

At the same time, Hill also observed that in 1986 the Reagan Administration had chosen to become Local 28's ally, calling upon the Supreme Court to invalidate two separate orders by the U.S. Court of Appeals of the Second Circuit to remedy the long record of job discrimination by utilizing affirmative action. The appellate court remedies set numerical targets for the inclusion of minority workers in both the union's apprenticeship program and its membership. The Reagan Justice Department, reflecting the ultra-conservative views of Bradford Reynolds, an assistant attorney general, while admitting that Local 28 has "an ample record of inexcusable disobedience" to the court's order, opposed the use of affirmative action remedies because, in the reactionary views of the Reagan Administration's lawyers, they constituted quotas, which they viewed as "objectionable."[17] Presumably the court's insistence on such quotas was, to the law-and-order Reaganites, even more objectionable than chronic refusal to obey federal court orders, not to mention the even more egregious adherence to the unconstitutional application of racially biased practices.

Herbert Hill has further observed that the Sheet Metal Local 28 case and that of the Metal Lathers Local Union 46 in New York City,[18] both of which have taken more than 40 years in court to resolve, exemplified the power and wealth of most unions to delay the effective authority of the judicial and executive branches of government in cases involving job discrimination.[19] "Both Local 28 and Local 46, by paying substantial legal fees to evade the law, demonstrate the disparity of power between institutions with great resources, such as unions and corporations, as compared with individual workers. In the real world, this disparity results in the effective nullification of civil rights laws and judicial decisions," Professor Hill explained.[20]

We shall never know how many hundreds of thousands of black and other minority workers have been denied their rights since Title VII and other employment laws, court decisions, and executive orders have been promulgated, only to be defied by recalcitrant union lawbreakers. Almost equally at fault, of course, are the local, state, and federal executive branches of government that failed to enforce these civil rights laws, administrative rules, and court orders that would have opened doors to black workers.

As of late 2002, Local 28 had still not accepted the last verdict of the courts; the case remains under a master appointed by the federal court, who has been unable to compel the union to accept more than a token number of black members. Local 28's lawyers, meanwhile, were pressing the court to release the union from the earlier affirmative action decisions, even though the union has never substantially complied with any of the previous court orders and remains a virtually all-white union.

For the record, the saga of Local 46 of the Wood, Wire, and Metal Workers Union of Manhattan was also typical of the construction unions that succeeded in evading compliance with various court orders for almost four decades. The earliest federal court order against Local 46, a consent decree, was filed in 1970, requiring it to provide minority workers with intensive job-skill training and the report to the results of such training to the court. The union flatly ignored that and subsequent court orders, appealing to higher courts in order to forestall any resolution of the issues. In 1994 a new lawsuit was filed on behalf of minority workers by the Center for Constitutional Rights. Five years later, in 1999, Federal Judge Thomas P. Griesa approved a settlement between the parties, a settlement in which the local union refused to admit any wrong-doing, but that required Local 46 to provide the training ordered 20 years earlier and to pay $500,000 to 39 workers from minority groups who brought the suit charging that "white workers were consistently given more, and better, construction jobs" through the union's hiring hall. It has not been possible to ascertain whether any of the minority workers has yet received either his or her share of the cash award or the job-skills training ordered by the court.[21]

This pattern of defiance by construction unions has been repeated in many other cities in which the NAACP was active: pipe fitters in Chicago, bricklayers in Milwaukee, Wisconsin, operating engineers in Philadelphia, Pennsylvania, electricians in Cleveland, Ohio, and plumbers in Columbus, Ohio. This successful strategy of defiance by the local craft unions is a measure of the support the unions have been able to generate among white politicians, elected judges, and bureaucrats, one or more of whom have provided a substantial degree of protection for those local unions that have been actively discriminating along racial lines.

In the long-term campaign to end the patterns of racial discrimination in the construction industry, the NAACP and Hill used the law in combination with racial protest campaigns such as mass demonstrations at federally funded construction projects. Combined with relentless public exposure, these tactics punctured the liberal pretensions of labor union leaders. Those disputes that culminated in legal suits were all the more powerful for the community agitation and glaring publicity that the NAACP—as a mass membership organization—was able to generate in advance. The majority of confrontations were, however, resolved before actual court trials, in no small measure because of the embarrassing public exposure caused by the NAACP.[22]

As early as 1953, Hill began encouraging Negro union members, especially those in industrial unions where they were concentrated, to assert their strength and numbers within their respective unions. He pressed them to make demands of the union leadership for better representation of their interests, for more staff and officer slots, and for sensitivity to the problems encountered by Negro communities. Since few of the Negro trade unionists had much experience in written expression, Hill helped them to draft their demands and grievances both for the union leaders and the corporate employers. The NAACP staff conducted workshops to teach them to become empowered within their own unions by learning how to present their problems and how to up the ante when more congenial methods failed. For the next decade, black unionists, with Hill's encouragement, gradually enlarged their power bases within a score of major unions, forming Negro caucuses to maximize their strength, and, with the NAACP's help, getting their case to the union leaders, the employers, and the public at large.

One of the earliest targets was the Fisher Body Plant of General Motors Company in Grand Rapids, Michigan, where the local NAACP branch attacked a pattern of discriminatory employment practices by UAW Local 730. The 1955 branch campaign included workers at General Motors' Electro Motive Diesel Division represented by UAW Local 167. The NAACP demonstrated that Negro workers were denied advancement to lead operators on the assembly lines and could not advance to higher classifications or pay levels. The result was the opening up of a number of higher categories to Negroes, including crane operators and maintenance painters, as well as a number of better-paying production jobs. Hill conducted a series of conferences with local UAW officers, staff, grievance committee members, and executive board members, helping to make them more responsive to the interests of

Negro members. He drafted and filed their grievance complaints, which led to major changes and he restructured the branch's labor committee, transforming it into a significant trade union force in Grand Rapids as well as a showcase for improving the NAACP's standing within the community.[23] Throughout, Hill and the NAACP were fortunate to enjoy the backing of the UAW's regional director, Leonard Woodcock,[24] who later succeeded Reuther as UAW president.

That same year, the NAACP, at the request of President David Dubinsky of the International Ladies Garment Workers Union (ILGWU), intervened in a strike by ILGWU workers against a Delaware manufacturing plant to dissuade unemployed Negroes from scabbing as replacements for the striking unionists. The NAACP communicated its support of the strike among local blacks, and urged striking black unionists to stand with the union until the end of the strike.[25] The following year, Hill provided similar aid to the United Hatters, Cap, and Millinery Workers when their local struck the Hat Company of America in Norwalk, Connecticut. The company's recruitment of Negro scabs had led to violence and heightened racial tension. The national and local NAACP took the lead in defusing the tension, urging Negroes not to serve as strikebreakers and persuading black unionists on strike to refuse to defect.[26]

In 1956, the ILGWU asked Hill to collaborate with their Southeastern regional director in merging the union's white and colored locals in Atlanta, which enabled black women to obtain promotions and to seek less physically taxing jobs as sewing machine operators. Until then, black women had been hired solely to fill the strenuous presser jobs. The success of this endeavor led the ILGWU to invite the NAACP Labor Secretary to participate in the planning of similar ILGWU efforts throughout the South.[27]

At the same time, Hill collaborated with the AFL-CIO, especially after the merger of the AFL and CIO in 1955. He conducted workshops and seminars for the federation's staff and for the staffs of many of the international unions, sensitizing them to the claims for racial justice of black workers. Hill also represented the NAACP throughout the 1950s at the annual conventions, testimonial dinners, and workshops of dozens of international unions claiming to support the NAACP's work, including annual contributions of cash. For the most part, his passionate commitment was respected by his labor counterparts and his relationships with many national and local union leaders were cordial during the first years after the AFL-CIO merger in 1955, but this was to change by the end of the decade.

From the early 1950s onward, Hill also spearheaded the NAACP concern for the plight of the nation's migratory farm workers, a high proportion of whom were poverty-stricken Negroes from the South. Hill described the practices of the farm owners and food operators availing themselves of Negro migrant workers, including children, as a "system of inhuman economic exploitation" running through the Northeastern states along the Atlantic seaboard. Among the leading culprits were the farm owners of New York and Pennsylvania, states whose citizens otherwise boasted of their liberal proclivities. In these states, however, it was permissible to place "entire families—including women and children—[living] . . . in shacks, abandoned barns, and tents amidst indescribable squalor."

Hill charged that, "Unscrupulous labor agents deduct amounts from the meager earnings of the migrant workers and in several instances," an NAACP investigation revealed, "labor agents have vanished at the end of the season without paying any wages." Hill also served as point man in the lengthy NAACP campaigns to reform the laws covering agricultural workers in several states, confronting powerful farm interests that fought vigorously to prevent these changes. He was successful in thwarting the farm owners' campaign to change the child labor law to permit children to work long hours as migrant farm laborers. The NAACP stake in the plight of migrant farm workers was sustained for decades; then the composition of the migrants gradually changed from mostly Negro to mostly Hispanic.[28]

In 1955 New York State finally passed a number of reforms, including mandatory licensing and regulation of the hiring agents for migrant workers.[29] In 1957, Hill conducted investigations of migratory labor camps and worker conditions in the groves and fields along the Atlantic seaboard. Starting in Homeland, Florida, he followed a migratory labor caravan until it reached upper New York State, recording the conditions experienced by the migratory workers.[30]

Hill's investigations led to his testimony before the Pennsylvania and New York legislatures and to his prize-winning book, *No Harvest for the Reaper—the Story of the Migratory Agricultural Worker in the United States.*

On the heels of his migratory reform campaign, Hill began an NAACP investigation of the status of Negro workers in the Birmingham, Alabama, steel industry, the first step in a 25-year campaign, focusing initially on Tennessee Coal and Iron, a Southern subsidiary of U.S. Steel. After an extensive field investigation of the steel industry's employment practices in the South, Hill initiated the NAACP's campaign by documenting the racial job pattern before the national CIO's Committee Against Discrimination and the Steel Workers Union. This report documented in painful detail how the steel companies and the union relegated blacks to the lowest paying jobs, and maintained segregated job structures that prevented job mobility. The NAACP continued to apply pressure on the steelworkers union for decades until the law eventually produced promotions for a modest number of Negro workers in Birmingham steel plants.[31]

In April 1957, eight black steelworkers in Local 2401, after having exhausted every internal avenue to redress their grievances, met with the NAACP Atlanta branch's labor committee to seek assistance. The workers charged that their local employer—Atlantic Steel—paid whites more than double what blacks received, often for the same work, and that, in violation of their union contract, blacks with longer seniority were passed over for advancement by whites with less seniority. Herbert Hill was assigned by Wilkins to deal with their complaints. After an exhaustive investigation, Hill confirmed the black workers' allegations, leading to a tense confrontation between the steelworkers union and the NAACP.[32]

The NAACP sustained this effort for a decade, setting the stage for it to play a major role in a later struggle of black workers in the steel industry. After the 1964 Civil Rights Act was enacted, the NAACP filed scores of complaints under Title VII against many of the steel companies and the steelworkers union, North and South, attacking the continued segregation of black workers. Even after a court-supervised consent decree in 1974, the NAACP was compelled to press the case for equal promotional opportunities for black workers in the industry, charging both the employers and the steelworkers' union with maintaining and enforcing a rigid system of job promotion and assignment based upon race.

Around the same time (1957) Hill began discussions with the International Association of Machinists, which controlled access to work in major segments of the metal trades industry. Until 1948, Negroes had been barred from membership in this major union by a constitutional provision. To open up this industry, the NAACP leadership decided to make a long-term commitment. In 1956 the NAACP took on segregated employment practices in the oil industry, wrenching major concessions from the Oil, Chemical, and Atomic Workers Union, which pledged to enforce a new national policy by prohibiting discriminatory clauses in union contracts with employers, and called upon the locals to abolish segregated units. Complaints filed by Hill gained Negroes in many refineries the right to bid for vacant jobs on the basis of seniority and ability, at the same time eliminating segregated labor departments and opening up promotion for the first time to qualified Negroes.[33]

In 1954, Hill also investigated an anti-black outbreak in Shelbyville, Delaware, where 400 Negro poultry workers had gone out on strike. Several of the black unionists had been beaten and crosses had been burned on the front lawns of others. More than 100 Negro strikers had been imprisoned as well. Some of the striking workers were also evicted from their company-owned homes. The NAACP's intervention exposed the brutal repression imposed on the black workers by the company and, while they endured the strike, the NAACP provided emergency assistance to the strikers.

In 1955—the year following *Brown I*—Hill began to lay the groundwork for a broad-scale national campaign to open up the building trades industry, comprised largely of old-line craft unions belonging to the AFL, which in December of that year was to merge with the CIO. The craft unions operated from the principle that each member owned his membership slot, which was a passport to regular and high-paying work. Without a union card, no individual could be employed on a unionized construction job. Further, each member appeared to believe that with this ownership came the right to choose one's successor, normally a son, nephew, or other related male family member. Through a specially-tailored apprenticeship system, these male descendants, all white, would be able both to perpetuate the familial "franchise" in perpetuity while keeping out "strangers," which was often a way of keeping out Negroes. Most of the building trades occupations—masons, bricklayers, carpenters, painters, plumbers, operating engineers, and so forth—were relatively high paying and over the 1950s and 1960s became even more lucrative by strictly limiting the numbers of union-card members in each discipline in the face of ever-growing building booms. Each occupational shortage produced a new hourly wage increase. Not only that, by keeping the number of workers with each skill below the numbers needed by the open market, the craft union workers could spread out the work over longer periods of time, assuring them of full employment and even overtime at double the going rates.

The NAACP's efforts to reform this highly controlled market—the very opposite of *laissez faire* economics—were correctly viewed by the craft unions as a direct threat to their monopolistic practices and their lucrative sinecures. Of course, black skilled workers could form their own locals—after all, all of these skills were needed in local black communities as well—and some of the national unions were not hesitant in chartering all-black segregated locals. But this form of union membership usually continued to bar black building trades workers from the better paying opportunities available to their white counterparts. The mechanism controlling this door was the union hiring hall. Each craft local maintained a hiring hall for its members—and it members only. Contractors requiring so many carpenters, pipe fitters, metal workers, plumbers, and so forth, appeared each morning at the appropriate hiring hall to enlist the day's consignment of workers needed for their building projects. Since only white members were allowed into these hiring halls, the contractors left only with white workers.

The all-white union hiring hall would become one of Herbert Hill's principal targets for the next two decades as he sought to integrate white and black locals, to open up all white locals to new black memberships, to fashion apprenticeship programs that honestly integrated locals and led to real work, and to compel recalcitrant locals to comply with the new body of equal opportunity laws that was unfolding over these years. He employed every tool known to the NAACP—adverse publicity and exposure, advocacy for new state and federal laws, direct appeals to the national union leadership, direct action and confrontation, complaints filed with EEOC and under Title VII of the 1964 Civil Rights Act, and lawsuits when necessary. At times it appeared as if there were many Herbert Hills, his presence being felt in several localities at the same time as he energetically sped from place to place asserting the NAACP's demand for economic justice.

One of the earliest targets within the building trades was a Florida local. In 1954 the NAACP compelled Local 7 of the Bricklayers, Masons, and Plasterers Union in Florida's Dade County to admit 65 Negro mechanics, the first time this had happened in the history of the international union and in the Deep South. In a spate of optimism, the NAACP's Florida state conference formed a committee composed of representatives of 12 communities within the state to pursue further advances in the craft unions. The next year Hill initiated a number of meetings with union local and state AFL officials in an effort to persuade them to integrate other building trades locals, at the same time formulating complaints to file with federal agencies. The net result was a solid wall of resistance to change.

Progress within the building trades unions themselves proceeded at a snail's pace, despite the buildup of pressure from the NAACP and its labor department. More than a few Negro leaders regarded the segregation of white and black locals as a given, almost a permanent given, and urged that the Association's limited resources be focused on more vulnerable targets, such as the large industrial unions. Hill pointed out that, while the number of jobs within the industrial sector were rapidly disappearing, the jobs controlled by the craft unions within the building trades were expanding and offered some of the best opportunities for employment for both male and female black workers. Hill appealed to leaders of the AFL and the international unions comprising the building trades, but the response was uniformly negative. Even the powerful George Meany, a former plumber and then president of the merged labor federation, in a visit to a New York meeting defended the practices of the building trades councils. AFL-CIO Vice President Walter Reuther, long a friend of and advocate for the NAACP, failed to lift a finger during AFL-CIO council meetings on these abrasive issues, according to Herbert Hill.[34]

Nevertheless, Hill pressed relentlessly on, next targeting the Operating Engineers, which in 1956 admitted their first Negro member after a long struggle led by Hill. His following target was the International Brotherhood of Electrical Workers (IUEW), whose Cleveland local maintained a stranglehold on all electrical work at Cleveland area construction sites. This IUEW local adamantly refused to admit qualified Negro electricians to its membership or Negro novices to its apprenticeship programs. Despite the pressure of adverse publicity, pressure from local political figures, the urging of the AFL-CIO and national officers of the electricians union, the IUEW local stubbornly refused to surrender. The President's Committee on Government Contracts, moreover, denied that it had jurisdiction over the dispute. President Eisenhower displayed neither interest in the issue nor sympathy for the excluded black workers. Meanwhile, Negroes remained excluded from every construction site throughout greater Cleveland, including the six Nike launching sites being constructed for the U.S. Army.

Simultaneously, the NAACP attacked the Milwaukee Bricklayers Local Union 8, which had repeatedly denied membership to skilled Negro bricklayers. Among these were air force veteran James Harris and Randolph Ross. The NAACP's efforts to generate support for Harris and Ross from the bricklayers' international union and from the AFL-CIO proved futile. In fact, the former defended the Milwaukee local's refusal to admit Negroes, while AFL-CIO President George Meany pleaded with the Wisconsin state government to refrain from enforcing the state's antidiscrimination law. Defying the nation's most powerful labor leader, the state's fair employment practices division, charged with the responsibility for enforcing the fair employment statute, found the lily-white local union guilty of violating Wisconsin's law prohibiting racial discrimination and ordered the local to admit both Negro workers. The union adamantly refused, prompting the state legislature to enact a stronger and more enforceable law, which resulted in the admission of both Negro men and two others to the union. Eleven years after war veteran Harris had been fired from his construction job because he was not a union member (at a time when the union barred him from membership because of his race) and two years after litigation against the local union had been filed, Bricklayers Local 8 finally accorded Harris and his coplaintiffs membership on September 24, 1957. By so doing, the union was granting the four men their "licenses" to work on construction jobs and to feed, clothe, and house their families like other men were doing in 1957.

Despite this clear-cut record, the chairman of the AFL-CIO's Civil Rights Committee, Charles Zimmerman of the ILGWU, defended the local's exclusion of the two Negro bricklayers, mistakenly asserting that neither man was qualified to ply his trade as a bricklayer, an assertion that not only contradicted the wisdom of the Wisconsin courts, but also contradicted the testimony of former employers of both men.[35]

An observer might have thought that the NAACP leadership was compelled to walk on eggshells during the 1950s because the Association's foremost priority had necessarily been the implementation of the 1954 and 1955 *Brown* decisions throughout the Southern and border states. Given the tenacious and often violent resistance of the Southern state and local governments and of so many private entities and individuals, the NAACP might have been expected to adopt a more amicable demeanor towards many recalcitrant Southern locals, because nationally the AFL-CIO supported the Supreme Court's school desegregation decisions. Indeed, the more racist Southern labor union locals threatened to defect from the internationals because of the AFL-CIO's strong statements supporting civil rights. Although Clarence Mitchell deftly juggled the various interests of the NAACP in Washington, Wilkins gave Hill the green light to intensify the campaign against Southern local unions. Referring to the AFL-CIO's decision to oppose Representative Powell's amendment to the school construction bill that the NAACP strongly supported, Wilkins told Hill: "They can't afford to be wrong on both jobs *and* education. Keep the heat on them." Inevitably, conflicts would arise between Mitchell's national legislative and lobbying objectives, and Hill's energetic criticisms of trade union resistance, but neither Wilkins nor Hill backed down.[36]

Since late 1954, when the White Citizens Councils had been formed in response to *Brown*, many local unions, especially those in the South, had provided muscle, manpower, and funds to attack local NAACP branches and to try to intimidate local Negro parents of children serving as plaintiffs in school desegregation cases. In Front Royal, Virginia, Textile Workers Union Local 371 and others had organized white students to boycott their high school after the first Negro student was admitted. The textile local union then financed a lily-white private academy and used the local union's facilities to conduct classes for white students who were boycotting the county public school.

A number of local unions in the South threatened to organize their own independent federation of local unions if the internationals pressed desegregation upon them. Moreover, "the White Citizens Councils succeeded in taking control of certain AFL-CIO local union affiliates," the 1959 NAACP *Annual Report* noted. "Reluctance of the national leadership of organized labor to act affirmatively on racial practices in many places in the South permitted KKK and White Citizens Councils' forces, especially in Alabama, to transform some local unions into virtual extensions of segregationist organizations," it concluded.[37]

Dartmouth College history professor Bruce Nelson quoted a citizens council official who asserted that the white Tuscaloosa rubber workers and the Birmingham steelworkers were "the backbone of the [White Citizens] council movement in Alabama." Union leaders affirmed to Professor Nelson that, "many members of the United Steelworkers, as well as members of other labor organizations, are members of the councils." One estimate of the number of council members among the steelworkers ranged from 10 to 50 percent. Several Atlanta locals of the UAW "became bastions of the Ku Klux Klan; one of them even boasted of the Georgia Klan's grand dragon as a member," he noted. The response of Steelworkers officials to the widening racial gap was to seek to avoid placing any civil rights issues on the union's agenda, especially in the South, because "they recognized that the union was powerless to prevent such activity."[38]

Despite these pressures, Western Electric—a subsidiary of AT&T—bowed to NAACP appeals and opened up substantive jobs and promotions to Negroes in two North Carolina plants in Burlington and Winston-Salem. Burlington Industries, a textile giant, followed suit in its Greensboro plant, as did Douglas Aircraft in Charlotte. These advances turned out to be idiosyncratic; Southern union intransigence was growing, not shrinking. The economic effect on most Southern Negroes was approaching catastrophe. The modest gains won by Negro workers before *Brown* were rapidly melting away as the South's hard-liners adopted an increasingly vindictive policy towards all Negroes. Each civil rights success further unified and hardened the determination of the white majority in the South—one of the first casualties was Negro jobs. It was not illogical for blacks to turn inward and organize their own vehicles for advancement. After all, the previous route—following white labor leaders and their unfulfilled promises—had proven to be a grim mistake.

According to labor historian Bruce Nelson, following the civil rights victories in *Brown* and the Montgomery bus boycott, the "equilibrium on matters of race" had reached its limits and was falling apart. Professor Nelson observed,

> The second half of the 1950s was characterized not only by massive resistance to racial change but also by the shift from an era of black economic progress to one in which ambiguity, foreclosed opportunity, and major setbacks deepened the sense of apprehension and urgency among African Americans. In this context, the move toward black self-organization in the mills and other industrial workplaces was as inevitable as it was necessary. It was rooted in the growing disillusionment of a generation of black industrial workers and in their emerging recognition that justice for them would come not by following but by challenging the leadership of organized labor . . . they were learning the painful lesson that where issues of racial justice were concerned, union solidarity and the myth of working class interracialism were chains that bound them to an increasingly intolerable status quo.[39]

By the end of 1959, the NAACP and Labor Secretary Hill had abandoned hope that racial justice in the workplace could be accomplished under the leadership of white labor leaders. They had recognized that the merger of the CIO with the AFL had failed to reform the racial practices of the overall labor movement and that the leaders of organized labor, including the international presidents, were not able (and in many cases not willing) to expend precious political capital to convert recalcitrant locals, North and South, which continued to bar Negro members and/or opportunities.

Hill's own words, before and after, best illustrate the disenchantment. In 1956, the first year after the merger of the AFL and the CIO, Hill's chapter in the NAACP *Annual Report* emphasized optimism and cooperation:

> A close day-to-day working relationship between the NAACP and the organized labor movement was an important aspect of the Association's labor program. Mr. Hill sought to secure wide trade union support for the elimination of racial restrictions in the training and employment of Negro workers, assisted the ever-growing number of Negro workers to become an active and informed force within the ranks of organized labor, and sought trade union participation in the Association's civil rights programs. During the year a close relationship was established

> between the NAACP and the newly created National Civil Rights department of the AFL-CIO; the labor secretary worked with the director of the department and its staff members and was invited to participate in its conferences. Mr. Hill submitted memoranda and reports both to the department and to the civil rights committee of the AFL-CIO.[40]

Three years later—in 1959—the bloom had disappeared from the rose. Because of the intransigence of the international trade union leaders in refusing to pressure their racist locals to change their behavior, Hill had reversed course and was ready to confront organized labor's record of racist practices. Earlier in the year Hill carefully prepared a comprehensive statement, backed by affidavits that meticulously documented the complaints of Negro workers, North and South, charging a widespread pattern of racial discrimination by both AFL-CIO affiliated international unions and their locals. All of the practices described above, Hill maintained, continued among a broad number of unions, even those that had compelled their locals to remove lily-white exclusion clauses from their constitutions. Hill persuaded Roy Wilkins of the merits of his indictment, realizing full well how much of an awkward position this would place his colleague, Clarence Mitchell in, who was in charge of sustaining the coalition with organized labor and others in Washington, D.C. (There is no indication that Mitchell argued against the initiative by Hill against organized labor.)

In the 1959 NAACP *Annual Report,* the official record for the Association, Hill concluded his new attack on organized labor's racial practices with these powerful words:

> In the four years since the merger of the AFL and the CIO, the national labor organization failed to eliminate even the most obvious instances of racism within the affiliated unions. As for the Federation's civil rights committee its performance seemed to indicate that its major function was to create a "liberal" public relations image rather than to attack directly the broad pattern of anti-Negro practices.
>
> The executive secretary [Wilkins], together with the labor secretary, conferred with the president of the AFL-CIO after the

> Association's report was discussed at a quarterly executive board meeting of the Federation's executive council. NAACP action in this area received extensive national coverage in major newspapers and periodicals throughout the country.
>
> As of December, complaints of discrimination were pending against many of America's leading international unions with the President's Committee on Government Contracts and with state and municipal fair employment practices commissions.[41]

With this act, Herbert Hill had fired a serious warning shot across the bow of organized labor's vessel. The next shots would be more crisply targeted. Hill's defiant act was fully supported by Wilkins and the majority of the NAACP Board, but from that period on Hill became the target of increasingly acrimonious attacks by members of organized labor, including those on the NAACP Board. Their objective initially was to discredit him as an objective authority; Wilkins and other NAACP leaders, however, continued to support him although they were occasionally uncomfortable with his zeal.

One year later, after relations with the AFL-CIO deteriorated further, Wilkins took the unusual step of assigning Herbert Hill to address the NAACP's annual meeting on January 3, 1960, in New York City. (This is the same forum Wilkins himself addressed almost 30 years earlier, after he had returned from his undercover investigation of the Army Corps of Engineers' exploitation of black workers in the Mississippi Delta.)

The opportunity to spell out the case against the giant labor federation was seized by Herbert Hill; he delivered a finely documented but no less scathing attack on organized labor's racial practices, charging that five years after the well-hyped merger, "The national AFL-CIO has repeatedly refused to take action on its own initiative" to "eliminate discriminatory practices within trade unions." These practices "are not simply isolated or occasional expressions of local bias against colored workers, but rather, as the record indicates, a continuation of the institutionalized pattern of anti-Negro employment practices that is traditional with large sections of organized labor and industrial management." Hill added that this pattern of union responsibility is spread across the nation geographically and throughout the nation's industries and the unions that operate within them. The modest changes that *have* taken place, the NAACP leader noted, were solely the result of protests from "civil rights agencies acting on behalf of Negro workers."

The Hill report claimed that the few victories that forced unions like the Bricklayers, the Railway Clerks, and the IUEW to admit a few Negroes to membership were nothing more than tokens and could hardly be described as integration. The AFL-CIO's member unions were, Hill asserted, guilty of four types of racist practices: "outright exclusion of Negroes, segregated locals, separate racial seniority lines in collective bargaining agreements, and exclusion of Negroes from apprenticeship training programs controlled by labor unions." These four categories became the principal targets of Hill's efforts on behalf of the NAACP over the next two decades.

Much to the dismay of the labor federation's leadership, Hill charged that the principal function of the AFL-CIO's Civil Rights Department was "to create a 'liberal' public relations image rather than to attack the broad pattern of anti-Negro practices within affiliated unions." Meanwhile, as part of the federation's policy of avoiding internal controversy, Hill alleged, the KKK and the White Citizens Council have taken over many Southern union locals, especially in Alabama, "and made them, in effect, virtual extensions of segregationist organizations." The Klan and the Councils had been actively recruiting trade unionists; the segregationist organizations had been holding meetings in union halls, advertising the meeting place in local newspapers, and union officials had been photographed for local consumption as participants in such meetings. As a result, a very large number of Negro workers had been alienated by organized labor and had been voting to reject major contracts with local unions, often providing the margin of defeat against union representation.

The report at the 1960 NAACP annual meeting listed in detail those international unions of the AFL-CIO that maintained segregated local unions. They included the Railway and Steamship Clerks; the Railway Carmen; the Carpenters; the Hod Carriers, Building, and Common Laborers; the Papermakers and Paperworkers; and the Pulp, Sulphite, and Paper Mill Workers. The only positive notes cited in the report were the mergers of segregated locals in 16 cities by the Musicians Union and the merger of white and black sections of an

ILGWU local in Atlanta. Unions excluding Negroes from obtaining employment included the IUEW, the Iron and Steel Workers, the Plumbers, the Plasters, the Sheet Metal Workers, and the Boiler Makers. Some of these same unions and others were also accused by the NAACP of having negotiated contracts with separate lines of seniority promotion and/or excluding Negroes from their apprenticeship programs, which was tantamount to denying them work within their respective industries.

The NAACP now called for direct action by the AFL-CIO leadership and by the international unions involved to correct this mutually damaging situation. Speaking for the NAACP, Hill added, "At the very least what is required is that AFL-CIO members and local affiliates not be active participants in segregationist attacks upon the Negro's struggle for basic citizenship rights."[42]

Suffice it to say, the AFL-CIO failed to heed the public criticisms by the NAACP except to deny the realities. In fact, its overall racial practices actually deteriorated further, with a few notable exceptions.[43] Their disappointment in the intentions of the labor movement compelled the NAACP leaders to abandon any reliance on the white-dominated AFL-CIO and, instead, to encourage the development of black caucuses, locals, and other entities that were comprised of Negro workers belonging to the AFL-CIO's component unions. These organized groups of Negro workers within most of the international unions were to become the vanguard from the bottom up of the movement for racial reform in the AFL-CIO. Herbert Hill, acting on behalf of the NAACP, became the tutor and the prod in the evolution of these black centers of worker influence. His stock among Negro workers within organized labor never ceased to rise over the next 18 years. No NAACP official was more trusted or revered among black working men and women than Hill. When the efforts of organized labor's leadership failed to discredit Hill, labor leaders and staff directed their efforts to having him fired, but Wilkins steadfastly stood by him throughout the 1960s and 1970s. In the latter years, antagonistic labor representatives on the NAACP's Board pressured every labor union board member to oppose Hill's efforts, solely on the grounds of labor unity (which quite clearly trumped the notion of racial unity.) One of the few NAACP labor leaders to resist those pressures and to continue his public support for Hill's efforts was Horace Sheffield of the UAW.

In 1957 the NAACP had started a major campaign to desegregate airline and aircraft manufacturing industries, targeting the practices of both the employers and the industries' dominant union, the International Association of Machinists, whose discriminatory practices had been attacked by the NAACP as early as 1948. After concerted pressure from NAACP Labor Secretary Hill, the New York State Commission Against Discrimination persuaded the 18 airlines with a New York presence to sign an agreement to open up their employment opportunities to Negroes in all facets of the industry and to promote solely on the basis of merit.

The aircraft manufacturers proved more difficult. Despite numerous complaints filed by the NAACP on behalf of Negro workers before the President's Committee on Government Contracts, no action had resulted by year's end. Anticipating such stonewalling, Hill was compelled to devise new tactics to challenge one of the most insular Jim Crow manifestations among Southern industrial employers. His first target was the huge Lockheed plant in Marietta, Georgia, with 17,350 employees. Of this sizable sum, only 1,350 Negroes were employed and virtually all of them had been restricted to two departments designated as structural assembly helpers, a euphemism for janitorial and other menial classifications. Not a single Negro was employed in either clerical or personnel work and, although the plant employed some 2,400 women, not one was Negro. For the seven years ending in 1951, "no Negro was admitted to the apprentice training program conducted jointly by the company and the International Association of Machinists. Accordingly, these workers were barred from on-the-job training, and denied seniority promotions to more skilled and better paying jobs," according to an NAACP annual report.[44]

Hill commenced the NAACP's Lockheed campaign by meeting with black workers employed by the company in Marietta, Georgia. After presenting their grievances to the international president of the machinists union in Washington, Hill negotiated an agreement with the union to support the NAACP's efforts to open up the formerly lily-white job classifications to Negroes. In addition, both the machinists union and the Lockheed Corporation agreed, on paper, to recognize the seniority rights of Negro workers.

The next step was to eliminate the segregated locals within the machinists union nationally. So long as Hill kept up the pressure, small gains were recorded almost every year. By the early 1960s, however, the Jim Crow system at Lockheed had still not been dismantled. Lockheed was a major supplier of military hardware to the U.S. forces engaged in a difficult and long war in Vietnam. The national culture was undergoing enormous changes, including attitudes towards race. Lockheed's executives wanted to get on with their mission and not to be perceived as provincials or bigots. The bottom line was more important to the Lockheed Board of Directors than archaic local traditions. Not so with many of the local white assembly line workers in Marietta. They disapproved of the new cultural changes and of the efforts to desegregate their communities as a result of which they would lose their automatic privileges as white males They also perceived the potential growth in the number of black plant personnel as a threat to their jobs.

Precisely the appropriate leverage for the NAACP to open up a discussion of Lockheed's employment practices arose on March 6, 1961, when President John F. Kennedy issued an executive order establishing a presidential committee, chaired by Vice President Lyndon B. Johnson, prohibiting discrimination against Negro workers in government jobs or in jobs funded by government contracts. Known as the Committee on Equal Job Opportunities, the new mechanism was organized to receive complaints against employers who violated the ban against anti-Negro discrimination, to investigate charges of discrimination, and to recommend that government contracts be terminated if the facts warranted it. Directing the committee's work was Assistant Secretary of Labor Jerry R. Holleman, who also served as the committee's executive vice-chairman.

A week after JFK announced the establishment of the committee, the Pentagon announced that Lockheed had been awarded a $1 billion contract to produce jet transports at its Marietta, Georgia, aircraft plant, at that time the largest U.S. government manufacturing facility under private contract. That set the stage for a dramatic intervention by Herbert Hill and the NAACP on behalf of scores of black workers at the Marietta plant. Hill presented affidavits from more than 30 Negroes detailing the segregated job classifications that relegated Negroes to the bottom levels of unskilled and semi skilled work at the lowest hourly pay. Until March 24 of that year, even Lockheed's water fountains had been segregated. Lockheed integrated them at considerable cost by converting them to faucets that required devices that dispensed paper cups. Lockheed also relinquished segregated time clocks. The NAACP-generated affidavit also charged that the seniority rights of black workers had been denied, that blacks had been rejected for apprenticeship programs because of race, and that blacks had been denied equal pay for equal work.[45]

Terming the Kennedy Administration's decision to award the huge contract to Lockheed a "shameful mockery" of its executive order against racial discrimination in any government-funded workplace, Hill filed complaints and affidavits that day and the next to document the charges, according to *The New York Times*. Asserting that both Lockheed and its union had "clearly violated" the presidential order, Hill demanded that the contract be "reexamined" and, if Lockheed fails to change its policy of "overt discrimination" that has existed for "many years," then the contract should be canceled.[46]

The NAACP was especially incensed that "Lockheed absolutely refuses to admit competent Negro applicants into the apprenticeship program to develop higher-paid craft and technical skills." Hill cited the affidavit of one worker, James O. Watt, a graduate of Morehouse College, who had been trained by a series of unschooled and inexperienced whites receiving higher pay, while Watt had been "kept in low-grade, all Negro departments" ever since he had been hired six years earlier. Hill further noted that he had met with the machinists union's president, A.J. Hayes, and its Southern regional director, Jesse McGlon, and others, since January 1957, "But to no avail." The official spokesmen for the machinists, in a classic demonstration of stonewalling, denied that any cases of discrimination had occurred in recent years, suggesting that the last time such cases existed was before World War II.[47]

The political embarrassment that the NAACP's front-page attack caused the Kennedy Administration was palpable. On the same day that the story broke, the committee's chief executive, Assistant Secretary Holleman, speaking for Vice President Johnson who was traveling abroad, pledged that the Kennedy Administration would "cancel contracts with any employer who refused to comply with . . . anti-Negro discrimination in government work." According to *The New York Times'* follow-up story by Peter Braestrup, Holleman made the pledge directly to Herbert Hill after he had filed 31 complaints against Lockheed and the machinists union with Holleman's office. Stressing that the NAACP desired "equal job opportunities for Negroes" and not "contract cancellation for cancellation's sake," Hill filed complaints against two other private contractors as well as the South Carolina employment office. The *Times* noted that during fiscal year 1960 the 10 Southern states enjoyed military contracts valued at about $2.7 billion, a huge sum in those days.[48]

The new federal policy helped to spur the tempo of change at Lockheed, although the machinists union resisted many of the required changes, whereas management, more concerned with the bottom line than with maintaining obsolete local traditions, was more compliant, ready to make those changes that expanded the size, skills, and quality of its work force without, hopefully, causing disruptions. The Lockheed management conveyed its more constructive posture to the NAACP in succeeding years. JFK's executive order also proved helpful in pressing some corporations producing military hardware to open up their workplace to modest numbers of Negro workers over the next four years, but the order lacked enough teeth to make a marked difference. Still, it prepared the ground for a much more effective weapon against racially motivated job discrimination—Title VII of the 1964 Civil Rights Act, which took effect on July 5, 1965. Shortly thereafter, the NAACP filed a complaint with the EEOC and then filed a federal suit in Atlanta against both Lockheed and the machinists union in order to obtain further employment concessions from both. Not long after, the company and the union agreed to the demands incorporated in the NAACP suit.[49]

10. Head to Head with the Garment Workers Union

On Meany's watch at the helm of the AFL-CIO, . . . organized labor would find it increasingly difficult to relate sympathetically to a militant civil rights movement that challenged the existing relations of power through mass mobilization of the grassroots. Although AFL-CIO leaders spoke the language of racial equality, they were simply unwilling to launch a frontal assault on the deeply rooted patterns of inequality in trades and industries where labor's strength was greatest.

Professor Bruce Nelson, Labor Historian, Dartmouth College, *Divided We Stand: American Workers and the Struggle for Black Equality*, p. 232

No NAACP employment campaign better demonstrates the growing chasm between organized labor and the Association than that directed by Hill against the discriminatory practices of the ILGWU, whose president, David Dubinsky, was an icon and a legend among liberals, socialists, and trade unionists. Dubinsky had heroically led his constituency through the fires of employer violence and general obduracy for four decades, while backing numerous reformist causes with his union's substantial exchequer. By the late 1950s, however, the ILGWU's membership no longer consisted largely of Jewish immigrants, as it had been since the early twentieth century. It had become a membership of color, in which blacks, Latinos, and Asians increasingly took the jobs of sewing machine operators, the lowest paying occupation in the garment industry except for janitorial slots. The leadership at the national and local levels remained uniformly white, mostly Jewish, with a small carefully selected Italian leadership based upon the union's few Italian locals.

During the mid-1950s, Hill and the NAACP had been helping the ILGWU to desegregate their Southern locals and to attract Negro members, especially during strikes. By 1958, however, as already noted, Hill and Wilkins were coming to the conclusion that the labor movement would never order and enforce a policy of desegregation from the top down and that the potential for overall Negro economic advancement through jobs and decent incomes was significantly obstructed by the practices and obdurate posture of the unions, especially the locals. Meanwhile, the New York-based NAACP headquarters was minutes away from the nation's foremost garment district, where Negroes, Puerto Ricans, and other Latinos had come to comprise a majority of the union's central membership base in New York, the largest component within the ILGWU, which claimed about 450,000 members in 1960. Yet, as Hill was to convincingly demonstrate, not a single Negro or Puerto Rican was an officer or executive board member of the ILGWU, nor a manager of any of the locals. After scores of minority members of the ILGWU prevailed on the NAACP to intervene on their behalf against the union, Hill attempted to broker changes through negotiation with the union leadership, only to be totally rebuffed by his previous allies. Given the importance of the ILGWU both in electoral politics (it controlled New York's Liberal Party) and within the AFL-CIO, Wilkins and the Board urged Hill to move cautiously and deliberately, partly in the vain hope that the ILGWU would come around and begin to dismantle its own version of Jim Crow practices in New York City. It was not lost on the NAACP leadership that most of the ILGWU's officers, from Dubinsky down, were Jewish immigrants and no NAACP leader had any intention of turning the critique of the ILGWU into an anti-Semitic event, certainly not Hill who himself is Jewish.

Finally, in 1961 a young Negro veteran of the Korean War and an activist in the NAACP's sit-ins in Savannah, Georgia, came to Hill with a very compelling case. Ernest Holmes, a black cleaner employed by Primrose Foundations, a New York City ILGWU shop, had also been working as a cutter's helper without receiving additional compensation or the benefits that automatically accrued to other cutter's helpers, all of whom were white. On at least four occasions Holmes had been refused permission to join the cutter's union, Local 10. At this juncture he sought the help of the NAACP. White union members with whom he worked had informed him that he was entitled to higher hourly wages and such benefits as medical coverage. Since his wife was pregnant with two young children at home and his take-home pay was meager, his family needs compelled him to press for the improved employment status.

Before filing a formal complaint, Hill called his long-time friend, ILGWU Assistant President Gus Tyler, summarized the facts and asked Tyler to intervene on Holmes' behalf. Tyler told him he would look into it and phone him back. After several days without a response, Hill phoned Tyler again, who claimed he had been very busy and had not had a chance to follow up. But Hill was persistent; after another week, he phoned Tyler again. This time Tyler said he had spoken to the union's agent, and was informed that this was a situation in which, he suggested, that perhaps the local union official was "on the take."

"Herb," Tyler said, "my advice is to forget this one and don't make trouble. There's nothing to it." Hill assured Tyler he would not only *not* forget it; he would pursue it vigorously.[1] Consequently, in early 1961, Hill filed a complaint on behalf of Holmes with the New York State Commission for Human Rights, after an extensive investigation of Local 10 and other ILGWU practices. Hill charged that the union restricted its Negro and Puerto Rican members to low-paying jobs. (Cutters in the greater New York City area then received about $125 a week, twice the amount of workers in the semiskilled and unskilled classifications.) Hill outlined how the local and other ILGWU unions worked out private deals with the garment employers to keep most of the better paying jobs for whites, often relatives of the union leaders, while preventing Negroes and Puerto Ricans from filling those jobs when they became vacant.

In Ernest Holmes' case, not only had the ILGWU representative denied Holmes membership in the cutters' local after he was assigned to that post, but also he continued to receive the lowest possible wage —$1.25 an hour—even though cutters were supposed to receive twice that amount. In addition, he had been denied the union's health and welfare benefits, which went automatically with membership in Local 10, and which were especially crucial because of his wife's pregnancy. Hill's investigation of the Ernest Holmes case revealed unequivocally that the ILGWU—not the factory owner—controlled work assignments and promotions at most of its unionized plants. By denying Holmes membership in the cutters' local, the union was in fact preventing him from rising above the bottom rung, which would not only have raised his wages, but also would have covered the medical needs of his entire family.

At the same time that the state commission was weighing the evidence gathered from its investigation, Hill learned from an intermediary that the local union's manager, Moe Falikman, wanted to meet with him. A phone call revealed that Falikman felt it would undercut his authority for him to meet anywhere else but his own union headquarters. Hill agreed and met with Falikman in the presence of his union associates. In heavily-accented English, Falikman sought to explain the basis for the problem in Holmes' case by recalling that the garment manufacturer, a former ILGWU member, had been deluged with orders during the recent holiday season and had called Falikman to request additional workers because he was overwhelmed. He was informed that the local union had no unemployed workers to refer to Primrose, the employer, who then asked Falikman for permission to utilize Holmes, "a black man," as a helper on the cutting tables. Falikman said that as a favor to an old colleague, he had agreed to the temporary employment of Holmes in this capacity. "So you see, Hill," Falikman said, "it was all a misunderstanding, nothing to get excited about. Better to forget it and don't make me trouble," he concluded hopefully.

Hill rose up to his full height of six feet and leaned over Falikman's desk, replying in stentorian tones, "But Falikman, you gave an employer permission to violate your own contract." Falikman, alarmed at Hill's observation, replied, "Hill, don't get excited, nothing to get excited about. Don't make me no trouble." Hill, seizing the last word, shouted, "Falikman, you don't know what trouble is. I haven't even *begun* to make trouble," after which he stomped out of the union leader's office, slamming the door behind him.[2]

On July 1, 1962, after an extensive 15-month investigation by the state commission, an investigation that was obstructed in every way possible by the union and its political allies, ILGWU's Local 10 "was judged guilty of racial discrimination by the New York State Commission for Human Rights." According to a front-page press report in the *New York Herald Tribune,* "the commission found the union:

- Lacked 'good faith' to comply with the state anti-discrimination law.
- Was indifferent to a worker's charge of mistreatment.
- Lacked a clear policy through which minority-group members could gain union membership.
- Showed 'reluctance' to disclose the racial composition of its membership to the investigators."[3]

The commission ordered the union to provide Holmes with a job and pay equal to his skills on the cutting tables; to provide him with a written guaranty that if, after training, his skills were satisfactory, he would become a full union member; to instruct all of Local 10's supervisors and business agents to accept membership on merit alone, and to display the commission's work and rules in every one of the union's offices. At the time of the decision, Hill used the occasion to attack the union's discriminatory practices as well as the systematic exclusion of nonwhites in the ILGWU's leadership.[4]

In response to the NAACP's assault, the ILGWU marshaled all of its public relations resources to attempt to counter the understandable embarrassment produced by the commission's judgment and the NAACP's publicity. In liberal circles during the era of JFK, with whom the union and Dubinsky had been clearly aligned, the charge of racial discrimination against poor members of minority groups was in Yiddish terms, a *shonda,* a public disgrace. The union's response was, in effect, to deny the charges, to claim the charges stemmed from Republican partisanship (Rockefeller was then New York's governor and the commission appointees were his), and to do virtually nothing to remedy the situation.

The union's defense was coordinated and led by its house intellectual—the venerable Gus Tyler, who held the title of assistant president but who had no union constituency or internal political clout. It was Tyler's task to rebut the commission, to discredit Hill (and by indirection the NAACP), to generate union and other expressions of support, and to fill the pages of those publications financially supported by the union, such as the *New Leader* and the *Jewish Daily Forward*, with apologia in the form of denials. In addition, those organizations that depended heavily on the ILGWU's annual cash contributions, such as the Jewish Labor Committee, were encouraged to issue declarations of support. These techniques, including the establishment of seemingly independent front groups, had been developed and refined by the Communists in the 1930s and 1940s, such that socialists and liberals found it expedient to adopt similar techniques. (It was no accident that Dubinsky's major adviser on international affairs and later providing the same service to George Meany was former American Communist Party leader Jay Lovestone, who in the early Cold War era became a steadfast and effective anti-Communist.)

The Jewish Labor Committee sent a long letter to the NAACP, defending the ILGWU and criticizing Hill and the NAACP for bringing the affair into the public spotlight.

NAACP Executive Director Roy Wilkins responded in a letter reaffirming the NAACP's position against the ILGWU's racially discriminatory practices, declaring forcefully, "We do not feel that the general denials and outraged protests that have been the response of the ILGWU to our charges of discriminatory practices are in any way an adequate answer to those charges."[5]

The union compounded its guilt by inventing statistics out of thin air. Local 10's manager, Moe Falikman, told *The New York Times* a few weeks later that his cutters local union had "more than 500 Negroes and Puerto Ricans" as members.[6] Subsequently, the ILGWU reduced that total three times, until it had been reached 200. Gus Tyler wrote an article claiming that, "In Local 10, there are 199 Negro and Spanish-speaking members."[7] He later explained that this included members from a variety of Central and Latin American nations. Two decades later in a book of reminiscences, he asserted that there were 275 Negro members of Local 10 at that time of the confrontation with the NAACP. The ILGWU in late 1962 distributed a reprint of a column by the National Labor Service of the American Jewish Committee, another recipient of its largesse, which asserted that Local 10 had "250 Negro and Spanish-speaking cutters." As Herbert Hill was to conclude 30 years later when the ILGWU revived the controversy because of a doctored statement in a museum exhibition, "The evident disparity in these numbers and their apparently arbitrary nature needs no further comment."[8]

After roughly six months of disinformation on the part of the ILGWU, bolstered to a degree by the solidarity statements of the AFL-CIO and other union leaders, the NAACP's disappointment was palpable. Here was an old friend and civil rights stalwart within the Jewish community, the one white ethnic group that had generally supported the NAACP's agenda for the past half century, not only stonewalling the charges, but also actually fabricating data to defend itself.

On October 8, 1962, the NAACP Board of Directors overwhelmingly adopted a resolution declaring that:

> The ILGWU has made no adequate answer to our charges that Negro and Puerto Rican workers are concentrated in the lowest paying jobs ... that non-white workers are for the most part barred from entry into those ILGWU locals which control the well-paid stable jobs; that Negroes are not admitted into various informal and formal training programs where entry is controlled by the union .... Our members and the non-white community are shocked by the union leadership's repeated statement that "Negroes and Puerto Ricans are not ready for positions of leadership in the union." This pious hypocrisy that "Negroes are not ready" is an all-too familiar refrain and is no more acceptable coming from the mouth of a "liberal" union than from an avowed racist in the Deep South ... the NAACP calls upon its members who are members of the ILGWU to assert their rights within the *union.* The Association will *actively assist all garment workers in pressing for equality of opportunity within the ILGWU and within the industry.* [emphasis added][9]

Herbert Hill in subsequent years discovered a highly vindicating document in the ILGWU archives at Cornell University. It was an internal memorandum from an important union staff member, Will

Chasen, dated October 23, 1962, to ILGWU Vice President Charles Zimmerman, who was also the highest ranking local New York City leader of the union as manager of the union's New York City joint board. Chasen wrote, in reference to a letter Hill had sent to the American Jewish Committee, "The awful thing about Hill's letter is that, on the whole, it is probably an accurate summary, and it exposes the awful idiocy of the way the situation was handled."[10]

At the NAACP's insistence, an *ad hoc* subcommittee of the House Committee on Education and Labor held hearings on the racial practices in the garment industry in September 1962. Harlem's representative, Adam Clayton Powell Jr., the militant Negro minister, presided and later was falsely charged by the ILGWU with seeking vengeance because the union had not endorsed him for reelection. The charge was so absurd that no person of political significance repeated it because, first of all, Powell regularly won by huge majorities; second, there were almost no ILGWU members in his district; and, third, the union's political franchise in New York was the so-called Liberal Party, which, although it had no presence in Harlem, had chosen to run its own candidates against Powell.

The hearings had proved so damaging to the ILGWU that it expended serious political capital to have them recessed, never to be reconvened.[11] However, the lengths to which the ILGWU would go was revealed during the hearings when a black female member of the union testified that she had been warned by an official of Local 55 that if she testified, she would never again work in the garment industry. The union was true to its word; the woman was fired a few days later and was never again able to find a job in the industry.[12]

In addition to the substantiated charges of racial discrimination, the most damaging evidence revealed by Hill was the dictatorial manner in which Dubinsky had come to control the union. In his testimony before the House subcommittee on August 18, 1962, later published in the *Congressional Record* and other publications that same year, Hill described in detail how Dubinsky controlled every aspect of the union, thwarting the democratic process at each significant juncture. Hill noted that although 120,000 ILGWU members were Negro or Puerto Rican, almost one-third of the national total, not a single minority member held a national or local leadership position, including those in the New York locals, of which 52 percent were then non-white.

As the all-powerful union president, Dubinsky successfully throttled any minority voice—either political or racial—from arising by employing an array of manipulative measures built into the union's constitution and by-laws. Article three of the ILGWU constitution, for example, required that a candidate for the general executive board must have been a delegate to the current convention, a member for five years and a paid officer for at least three years, effectively barring all but 300 of the 450,000 members from running for the governing board. To run for union president or secretary-treasurer, a member must have been a delegate at the current convention and a member and paid staff for at least 10 years, thereby reducing the number of eligible individuals to less than 200 individuals, or less than one-twentieth of 1 percent of the membership. In addition, the union constitution barred members from any internal political activity, including caucuses, except for the three-month period prior to the biannual union convention, thereby preventing any meaningful opposition from rallying support for its positions.[13]

The justification for this blatant violation of the Bill of Rights, especially of free speech and association, was the union's avowed need to prevent Communist infiltration, but by the early 1960s that threat was virtually nonexistent and, in any case, reasonable men may well challenge the notion that throttling free speech and association is a worthwhile price to pay for the possible infiltration of a few dozen Communists. Certainly, no information garnered from the operations of the garment industry itself could be described as vital to the nation's security. Hill amply demonstrated to all but the union and its labor allies that not only was democracy absent from the ILGWU's affairs, but also that, in effect, every post was occupied by an individual appointed by Dubinsky and his followers, the actual election by the national or each local being a mere formality.

As if these measures were not sufficient to maintain tight control over the union, Dubinsky required all officers, board members, and local leaders to submit a signed and undated letter of resignation upon their appointment or election. Since virtually all of these posts were paid jobs by which each individual supported himself and his family, it was highly unlikely that any officer or staff member would buck "D.D.," as Dubinsky was commonly known. Even the retired members, all of whom voted in the union's elections, were controlled by the tight administration of their pensions, medical and other benefits dispensed completely by the union's headquarters.[14]

As a result, there were very few rebellions among the officers or members of the ILGWU. Even less likely to challenge the internal system were Negroes and Puerto Ricans, most of whom believed in the 1960s that they were completely without power or influence, and that they had few if any political levers to pull on their behalf. They looked at the leadership of their union and saw no faces like their own in any positions of responsibility or authority. Even after the NAACP took the necessary initiatives to challenge the union's practices, very few ILGWU members felt comfortable in challenging any injustices they had experienced. These injustices included the failure of the union to enforce its own contracts and to perform the basic responsibilities of any legitimate trade union in protecting the rights of every one of its members. As the NAACP had amply demonstrated, the union had been collaborating with many employers to exploit the Negro and Puerto Rican members of its union to ensure that they were low paid and remained that way, and to deny them any chance to advance beyond the minimum wage or a few cents an hour above it. The union's white members, especially those well-connected or related to any level of leadership, were accorded all of the privileges and opportunities to move upward and to fill the best paying jobs, both in the workshop and in the union.

One of the ILGWU's defenses was the oft-repeated line that the "union is not an employment agency." When Local 10 manager Moe Falikman sought to make this point before the House subcommittee investigating the NAACP's charges, Representative James Roosevelt contradicted him on this point, asserting that "you are" an employment agency. "I'd have greater faith in you [the ILGWU]," FDR's son stated, "if you would face the situation honestly and say, yes, this needs looking into." For public relations purposes, Falikman grudgingly agreed to do so.[15]

As the ILGWU's efforts to defend itself became less and less effective, particularly in respect to so many false claims of minority membership that it could not document, it resorted to a tactic commonly employed by oppressors when their backs are up against the wall: It accused the NAACP, and especially Hill's statements, of being anti-Semitic. Never mind that Hill himself was Jewish. On December 10, 1962, the *Jewish Daily Forward*'s J. Fogel accused Hill and writer Paul Jacobs, who had written an exposé of the ILGWU's practices in *Harper's* that month, of "spread[ing] anti-Semitic poison against the ILGWU and against President Dubinsky." The article noted that both men were Jewish. However, neither Hill nor Jacobs had raised the issue of religion in their critiques.[16] The charges were a low mark of desperation for the union and its subsidized supporters, such as the *Jewish Daily Forward,* by that date heavily dependent upon the ILGWU for substantial annual financial support (deriving, of course, from the membership's dues, including those of the one-third who were black or Puerto Rican.)

Through another union surrogate, the Jewish Labor Committee, the ILGWU continued the campaign to discredit the NAACP's efforts and Hill's leadership, by formally charging anti-Semitism in a letter to Roy Wilkins dated October 31, 1962. Wilkins was livid in response to the charges. He took them seriously and, with a grim and icy demeanor, he responded to Jewish Labor Committee Executive Director Emanuel Muravchik in the clearest of terms:

> We assert with the greatest emphasis that nothing, absolutely nothing, in Mr. Hill's recent or more remote statements can be construed as anti-Semitic. This is a grave charge to make. It requires more substantiation than your flip reference in a part of a statement. We do not deign to defend ourselves against such baseless accusations. Its inclusion in the resolution, as well as in the statements to the press by Mr. Zimmerman [Charles Zimmerman, the union's top official in New York City and earlier the leader of the Communist faction within the union] is unworthy of an organization like the Jewish Labor Committee, which in the very nature of things, must be conversant with the seriousness of such a charge and with the evidence required to give it substance. No such evidence has been submitted in this case beyond the citation of the use by Mr. Hill of one word, "ethnic," out of a total of 4,500 words in his testimony before the House subcommittee. The relevance of his comparison of the ethnic composition of the membership and the leadership of the ILGWU can hardly be questioned in this context.[17]

Most of those close to the civil rights and union movements recognized the union's move for what it was: a craven and dishonest last-ditch effort to justify the stranglehold with which whites strove to continue to control a union fast becoming nonwhite. It was also a cynical effort to intimidate the national black leadership if the latter wanted to keep the larger coalition of labor unions and rights organizations together. The ILGWU was actually implying that if the NAACP continued to pursue its attacks on the union, the coalition with organized labor would crumble.

Despite the thousands of hours invested in building this important coalition by Walter White, Roy Wilkins, and Clarence Mitchell, despite the not insubstantial sums that it cost the NAACP to sustain the coalition as the LCCR, and despite the vital importance to the NAACP of labor support in the halls of Congress for major civil rights legislation already being discussed in depth by Congress, Wilkins was not prepared to sacrifice the black and Puerto Rican minimum-wage workers in the garment industry. Indeed, he escalated the stakes by letting organized labor know through his reply to Muravchik that the NAACP would not abandon the interests of rank-and-file workers in the union. Thus, to Muravchik, he wrote in the same letter:

> We reject the proposition that any segment of the labor movement is sacrosanct in the matter of practices and/or policies that restrict employment opportunities on racial or religious or nationality grounds. We reject the contention that bringing such charges constitutes a move to destroy "unity" among civil rights groups unless it be admitted that this unity is a precarious thing, perched upon unilateral definition of discrimination by each member group. In such a situation "unity" is of no basic value and its destruction may be regarded as not a calamity, but a blessed clearing of the air.[18]

Wilkins had no hesitation in telling the ILGWU, and if necessary, the AFL-CIO where they could go if they sought to bargain their support of civil rights legislation in exchange for the NAACP's turning a blind eye to union racial practices. Wilkins also understood the political dynamics within the NAACP, especially among the National Board members, which included a number of trade unionists. With these considerations in mind, he concluded by establishing for both outsiders and insiders just who controlled the NAACP's staff, stating:

> [I]t is well to reiterate a facet of this discussion which appears to have escaped the attention of various reviewers and resolution writers. It is that Herbert Hill, our labor secretary, has but one duty and that is to serve the interests of the Negro workers through the NAACP. Other groups, including trade unions, have powerful machinery to protect their principal interests. Mr. Hill is employed to maintain antidiscrimination work in the employment field as his top and only priority. He is not for trade unions first and Negroes second. He has no divided loyalties.[19]

No more stirring testimonial could have been written for any civil rights activist. That this was written by the preeminent black civil rights leader of the era about a white staff member was both fitting *and* remarkable, given the role that Hill played.[20] It is of some importance to note the effort by the ILGWU's respected Washington lobbyist, Evelyn Dubrow, to suggest to House members and their staffs that Hill was not only anti-Semitic but also a Communist bent upon stirring up racial tensions. Coming from a left anti-Stalinist background with a long record of attacking the Communist Party, Hill was, to any knowledgeable person of the times, the least likely candidate for Stalinist activity or behavior. The ILGWU demonstrated that, eight years after the censure of Senator Joseph McCarthy, it had no qualms about employing McCarthy's methods to discredit its critics.[21]

In the years that followed, the union gradually made some cosmetic changes as here and there a black or Puerto Rican face emerged on the executive board of a local or joint board, and finally on the national executive board.[22] However, real change came much more slowly and only when Dubinsky stepped down at the age of 80 in 1966.[23] That the union had barely changed its spots was best demonstrated by the suit filed by Violett Putterman against the union's Knitgoods Local 55 in 1983, again charging the union with gender and racial discrimination. Dozens of complaints before the EEOC against the ILGWU's locals were filed during the 1970s and 1980s with the help of the NAACP in such cities as Kansas City, Missouri; Baltimore,

Maryland; Memphis, Tennessee; Chicago, San Francisco, Philadelphia, Pennsylvania; Cleveland, Ohio; and Birmingham, Alabama.

As a result of the NAACP's exposure of the Garment Workers' racist practices and the widespread publicity resulting from it, the union was also compelled to cancel substantial annual support for a Workmen's Circle home for retired union members in the Bronx that excluded black union members. The union had invested $1.3 million in the construction of the home in 1960–1961.[24] In another dispute, nonwhite union members rose up against the union leadership at that time because the union had also constructed the residential East River Houses for its white members, excluding blacks, Hispanics, and Chinese members. The union had invested $20 million in membership funds in this project. The nonwhite members filed suit in federal court before Judge Robert L. Carter (the former NAACP general counsel), whose decision found that there was a pattern of unlawful racial exclusions by the union in the East River Houses.

After the passage of Title VII of the 1964 Civil Rights Act, the NAACP filed scores of complaints on behalf of ILGWU minority members before both the EEOC and federal courts, usually succeeding in proving racial and gender discrimination by the union.[25] As a result of this relentless pressure and despite the ILGWU's prolonged resistance to the changes sought by the NAACP and often demanded by the law, the two-decade campaign by the NAACP did force the garment makers' union to adopt these changes:

1. Appointment of a black woman and a Puerto Rican man in 1962–1963 to the national general executive board;
2. For the first time the union actively solicited blacks and Puerto Ricans to join some skilled locals, such as Local 10 cutters' union, which resulted in immediate employment at double the bottom wages for the new members; and
3. Dubinsky and his successor, Louis Stulberg, actively recruited black, Puerto Ricans and Asian-Americans as white collar professional, secretarial, and clerical headquarters staff members.

These acts, however begrudgingly, were responses to court and other pressures but they did serve to widen the doors of opportunity for hundreds of minority workers who were eventually able to earn a halfway decent wage in the skilled and headquarters positions. None of these acts, of course, seriously diminished the power of the white leadership. In fact, a not disingenuous observer could well argue that these changes helped to forestall a rank-and-file rebellion and thereby to prolong the grip of the older white leaders over a union, the majority of whose membership was now comprised of men and women of color.[26]

11. The End of Pretense: Organized Labor Refuses to Desegregate

Who the hell appointed you as guardian of all the Negroes in America?

George Meany, AFL-CIO President, in a savage verbal attack against A. Philip Randolph, at the 1959 Convention Plenary

On the day Title VII of the Civil Rights Act became effective in 1965, reaction from organized labor was mixed. "The fact is we have a problem . . . . [We must] take them [Negroes] in . . . provided they are qualified."

Peter Schoemann, President of the Plumber's Union, *New York Times,* July 3, 1965

It's the law. We've got to take the niggers in.

Unnamed New Jersey building trades leader, *New York Times,* July 3, 1965

The foregoing examples of the NAACP's efforts to desegregate a broad range of labor unions demonstrate that neither the AFL-CIO nor the federation's constituent unions, with very few exceptions, have permitted any significant progress in opening the American workplace to blacks or other minorities. From its earliest days during the last quarter of the nineteenth century, the AFL under Samuel Gompers consisted of unions that barred blacks from membership or that relegated Negroes to second-class, segregated status or that simply controlled access to the job site and used this control to prevent the hiring of otherwise qualified Negroes for jobs. That pattern developed early in the history of the American labor movement and has been so impervious to attack and reform that it continues in a variety of overt, as well as subtle forms, today.

Its unsavory corollary is the profoundly held belief of many, if not most, American skilled workers (and on occasion even industrial workers) that somehow the job they presently hold permanently belongs to them and, therefore, it is they—and only they—who can determine to whom it may passed on.[1] This institutionalized nepotism that violates local, state, and federal laws has been pandered to by elected officials at every level of the American federal system and by the respective courts. It has become the anthem of the white building trades mechanic, or worker, who at the same time seeks to keep the availability of his skills—as a plumber or a carpenter or a bricklayer—in short supply by limiting membership in his craft union (and therefore license to work on the building site) to his own tight circle of humanity: family first, then friends, then the slightly wider ethnic community. By limiting the supply of his particular skills, the white mechanic can keep the price of his hourly wage many times that of the minimum wage while stretching out the available work so that he remains fully employed over long periods. Gompers' successor in 1924, the colorless William Green, continued the policy of excluding Negro workers, although he proved more adept at suggesting that the labor federation publicly eschew racial bias. This, however, is the same man who refused to be seen sitting in the same room with Walter White during the 1930 Senate hearings in which both men sought to defeat the nomination of Judge John Parker to the Supreme Court, but for different reasons.

After George Meany succeeded Green on November 25, 1952, a few weeks following the latter's death, the new labor chief—himself a former plumber—became the building trades' most effective opponent of demands to desegregate the unions and the job sites. Meany, however, had a better grasp of the measures and words needed to enhance the public's perception of the AFL and its image at home and abroad, where it sought to lead "the Free World's" trade unions in the struggle for the hearts and minds of the world's workers against its Communist counterpart, the World Federation of Democratic Unions (WFDU). For two decades, the CIO had bested the AFL in the battle for the minds of America's intellectuals, academics, writers, commentators, and most members of minority groups. Since the 1930s, the CIO had been the federation that reputedly kept its doors open to all workers, regardless of race, class, religion, or degree of skill. The CIO was the militant force organizing the unorganized. And the CIO was the honest federation, unmarred by corruption or other scandals.

These appeared to be widely held beliefs when Meany took office as the AFL's chief in 1952. Innately combative, with a thrust-out jaw and a tightly gripped, well-aimed cigar, Meany always seemed ready for a fight. And in his early years, he fought mostly with Communists and their adherents and with blacks and other minorities, occasionally confusing the two. It was Meany who in 1955 capitulated to the bruising public relations campaign by A. Philip Randolph who demanded that the merged labor organization adopt a formal policy of nondiscrimination. To silence the sharp-tongued and ubiquitous Randolph, at the time a guest on almost every local or national radio or TV talk show, Meany guaranteed Randolph's election as a federation vice president and a member of the executive board, in return for Randolph's silence in the months immediately prior to the merger.

It did not take long for Randolph to surmise that neither Meany nor the newly merged federation's number two leader, CIO chief Walter Reuther, were committed to any active antidiscrimination program within labor unions, especially since the merged labor federation admitted into affiliation railroad unions with racial exclusion provisions intact in their respective union constitutions. In 1959, after Randolph sharply attacked the AFL-CIO's discriminatory practices, including scores of segregated locals, it was George Meany who shouted hoarsely from the convention podium at the gentle-mannered Randolph: "Who the hell appointed you as guardian of all the Negroes in America?" Undeterred by Meany's bullying, Randolph made the Negro workers' case, repeating it chapter and verse, before the entire Executive Council. Then Randolph escalated the conflict in 1960 by forming the Negro American Labor Council (NALC), to which black workers flocked in defiance of Meany, Reuther and the other leaders of organized labor.

"The NALC reflects within organized labor the same rebellion that finds its expression in the student lunch counter demonstrations in the South," which had erupted only a few months earlier, Bruce Nelson observed. Randolph's initiative contributed to Meany's growing rage, which leaped another notch when the NAACP announced its support of Randolph and the NALC. Herbert Hill made it clear that the NAACP intended to work closely with the NALC units as they were formed. The NAACP continued its widely publicized actions against both the ILGWU and the United Steelworkers Union, two of Meany's most powerful backers. When Randolph invited Meany to address the 1961 NALC assemblage, Meany revealed his true colors (no pun intended) by railing against the NAACP, characterizing Hill's charges against the ILGWU as "smears" and "falsehoods," at the same time dismissing the allegations against the steel union as "fantastic." Nelson noted that *The New York Times* characterized the Meany address as "blunt, bitter and scornful."[2]

Later that year Meany ordered the AFL-CIO Executive Council to censure Randolph for creating "the gap that has developed between organized labor and the Negro community."[3] Neither Meany nor his aides had the slightest clue that the Meany attacks on Randolph, a lifetime socialist, contributed to Randolph's popularity among and support from the masses and the classes comprising black America, especially black workers within the labor federation.

When President John F. Kennedy's labor secretary, Willard Wirtz, sought to issue rules that would guarantee Negroes access to union-sponsored apprenticeship programs, it was George Meany who forced the federal government to withdraw its original directive on October 20, 1963—one month before JFK's death—and to replace it with a weakened version satisfactory to Meany and organized labor. The massive minority protests at construction sites throughout the summer of 1963, many of them organized by NAACP staff and local members, were characterized by Meany as attacks by "opponents of labor unions," at the same time denying that these AFL-CIO building local unions "refused to work with these men because of their color."[4]

Meany's growing paranoia had already begun to spread throughout the upper ranks of the labor federation.

As the Cold War deepened, Meany's extensive public relations operation burnished his image as a "statesman/warrior in defense of freedom."[5] Meany's close circle began to court public figures, including academics—men and women less concerned with labor's ties to organized crime, to corrupt politicians, or to Jim Crow than with the larger struggle against the Soviets. By the early 1960s, he had become an artist at public relations manipulation, no longer voicing implacable opposition—and choice quotations—against the efforts of minorities to gain access to decent jobs by joining unions or gaining all of the other rights enjoyed by white workers. Instead, he left the harsher words to others, including presidents of internationals and members of his executive council. Now his political fist was more often cloaked in silk. The labor federation's war chest included nominal gifts to minority organizations, such as the Urban League and the NAACP, but the sizable amounts were reserved for the entities under the AFL-CIO's direct control or influence, such as the Jewish Labor Committee, Frontlash, *The Jewish Daily Forward,* League for Industrial Democracy, Social Democrats USA, and the Urban Coalition, and, in a classic bit of irony, after Randolph's death, the A. Philip Randolph Institute led by Bayard Rustin, whose livelihood became dependent on the labor federation's quarterly gifts.

Throughout the remainder of the 1960s and well into the next decade, George Meany continued to insist, as did his colleagues and proxies, that none of the AFL-CIO's member unions practiced racially motivated policies or behavior. Nevertheless, Randolph's unrelenting attacks on racial discrimination within the member unions of the AFL-CIO, even after he was unanimously censured by the federation's Executive Board, continued to elevate Randolph's stature among rank-and-file minority union members as well as among civil rights groups and some white liberals. The constant barrage of antidiscrimination initiatives undertaken by NAACP Labor Secretary Herbert Hill further inflamed Meany, who is reported to have complained that Hill "was acting in an irresponsible manner that brought harm to the labor movement."[6] The same reporter added that Steelworkers President David McDonald and Garment Workers President Dubinsky, smarting from Hill's formal complaints and litigation backed fully by Wilkins and the NAACP board, launched public attacks on the NAACP itself. They declared that "criticism can no longer be confined to the labor secretary [Hill] but becomes the responsibility of the entire organization," according to the same journalist.

Meany followed these remarks with his own warning to Wilkins that, unless Hill was curbed, the NAACP's "working relationship" with the labor federation would be jeopardized. Indeed, in an effort to reduce the influence of both the NAACP and Randolph, Meany invited Martin Luther King Jr. to cochair a full-day meeting at the 1961 national convention. He also invited National Urban League President Whitney Young to speak before the Executive Council where Young offered to work with organized labor to eliminate racial discrimination in the workplace. Although Meany and his colleagues accepted Young's proposal, Young was not in the least bit fooled by the offers of cosmetic change made by some of the unions, whose sincerity remained perpetually in question.[7]

Nothing meaningful came from the Urban League initiative, nor from the platform accorded Dr. King, although his own organization, SCLC, benefited from the sudden rise in cash support from labor unions that had in the past contributed to the NAACP. King very selectively helped the organizing drives of local unions with sizable minority memberships or the potential thereof, such as the New York City hospital workers, the multipronged campaigns of the activist local District 65, and the sanitation men organized by the state, county, and municipal workers.

Profoundly influenced by the attacks from Meany and several executive council members who also headed international unions with sizable minority memberships, the NAACP decided to devote more and more of its energies and resources to the organization of massive local community protests, marches, sit-ins, and other means of expressing black demands that organized labor eliminate its racial barriers, the principal obstacle to the acquisition of decent paying jobs in many urban areas for minority workers. The stepped-up activity and resultant publicity finally persuaded Meany and other labor leaders that the barrage of public criticism would never disappear without at least some appearance of change within the ranks of organized labor. The dramatic public events—Freedom Rides, sit-ins, the opening of universities to blacks in Alabama, Mississippi, and Georgia, the brutal confrontations in Birmingham where "Bull" Conner employed attack dogs foaming at the mouth against protesters—had transformed American public opinion in support of the civil rights struggle. Labor's own members outside the South could hardly remain unaffected by these struggles.

Meanwhile, virtually all of the Southern locals and local labor federations continued to resist the winds of change well into the 1960s. The AFL-CIO needed a fig leaf, that is, a means to shift the blame from itself and its affiliated international unions for their failure to eliminate racist practices. At the same time, they had no desire to forfeit the reins of power. The answer was simple enough: Meany and the AFL-CIO executive council would support a fair employment practices proposal within the draft civil rights bill proposed by JFK and his deputies in 1963 and then pending before Congress. If Congress could pass such a provision backed by the full force of law, it would be the federal government, not the AFL-CIO leadership, which was demanding change in the traditional practices of obdurate locals and recalcitrant internationals, and would also be responsible for the lack of change. Such a law would literally take the labor federation off the hook, not only from growing domestic criticism, but also from the skeptics abroad who questioned the AFL-CIO's legitimacy to be the leader of the "Free World's" labor unions.

According to Meany's biographer, despite the almost uniform rejection of the FEP proposal by the White House staff and congressional leaders, Meany ordered his deputies—Andrew Biemiller and Lane Kirkland—to stand fast and threaten to jeopardize passage of the entire civil rights legislation if an FEP provision was not included in the legislation. On July 17, 1963, Meany presented dramatic testimony before the House Judiciary Committee on the plight of unemployed Negroes and their inability to join unions. "We have a selfish reason; in fact, we have two of them. First, we need the statutory support of the federal government to carry out the unanimously adopted principle of the AFL-CIO . . . (be)cause the labor movement is not . . . a monolithic, dictatorial, centralized body . . . we cannot dictate even in a good cause. Second, we want federal legislation because we are tired of being the whipping boy in this area. We have never at any time tried to gloss over the shortcomings of unions on the subject of equal opportunity.

Yes, some of our members take a wrong-headed view .... But we in the labor movement deplore these few holdouts against justice," Meany concluded defensively.[8]

These remarks demonstrated a selective memory on Meany's part, since in the past he had defended most of the member unions against charges of discrimination made by the NAACP and others. Further, his severest critics, such as the NAACP's Herbert Hill, consistently maintained that the overwhelming majority of the member unions belonging to the federation discriminated in one or more ways against minorities.[9] Tired of always taking the blame for the shortcomings of his member unions, Meany appeared to believe that federal compulsion would deflect criticism from him, both from the segregationist forces within the labor federation and the civil rights forces outside the labor federation.

An additional explanation for what seems to have been a dramatic temporary reversal of Meany's stubbornly held earlier position on race rests upon his refusal to accept the proposals of civil rights leaders to establish affirmative action programs for those minority workers long denied union membership or promotion on the job, as a form of compensation for past injustices. Meany opposed this and any other form of compensation for minority workers.[10]

Though apparently supporting an historic reform that promised to open the doors of employment nationally to Negroes and others, Meany was at the same time maneuvering to restrict the proposed bill so severely that it could take decades, if not generations, for Negro workers to achieve parity with whites in the factories, on the railroads, in the building trades, and elsewhere. On the one hand, he would receive widespread credit for insisting on an FEP provision in what was to become Title VII, but in reality he was hamstringing the legislation in such a way as to insure that minimal change would take place in the racial practices of labor unions for the foreseeable future.

Representative Richard Bolling of Missouri, a seasoned liberal, summed up the historical record when he stated that, "the AFL-CIO had to have the umbrella of the [FEP] law." Bolling also added that, "We never would have passed the Civil Right Act without labor. They had the muscle; the other civil rights groups did not."[11] Perhaps in respect of the FEPC provision, Bolling's statement has some merit. However, most historians who have examined the forces behind the

1964 Civil Rights Act (see Chapter 7) award the lion's share of the credit to the massive coalition organized by the NAACP and led by Clarence Mitchell who, together with Joseph Rauh, rallied the LCCR, including many AFL-CIO unions, to support the legislation. That organized labor played an important role, regardless of its motivations, is equally difficult to deny. Regardless of labor's role, the bill failed to pass until after the assassination of President Kennedy, when Lyndon B. Johnson as president exerted the influence of the White House upon his congressional allies on behalf of the civil rights legislation as a memorial to the slain president.

Even after Title VII—the employment section of the 1964 Civil Rights Act—was passed, its enforcement was postponed for a full year (until July 3, 1965) at the insistence of George Meany and the leaders of the member unions of the AFL-CIO, virtually all of whom paid nothing more than lip-service to compliance with the new law. In hundreds of cases and thousands of complaints into the 1980s, the NAACP herded the unions to hearings and to courts where symbolic victories were recorded years later. Even after unions were found to be in violation of Title VII by federal district courts, many unions appealed to higher courts, often devoting years to complex legal challenges that delayed justice to black workers. The disparity between the resources available to labor unions and to black workers became apparent in this context.

As Meany's protégé, Plumber's Union President Peter Schoemann, said to a *New York Times* reporter on July 3, 1965, when Title VII officially took effect, "We have a problem . . . . [We have to] take them [Negroes] in." However, he hedged this admission by adding, "provided they are qualified." That remark was a tip-off on how he planned to continue to exclude Negro applicants: by adding to the plumber's test a written examination that would stymie a majority of the Negro applicants, who were otherwise fully capable in their trade but, because of limited and defective basic education, had serious difficulties with reading and writing. The same device became widely used by the other craft unions as a means of excluding minority applicants.[12]

So well did George Meany (and his successor Lane Kirkland) learn the public relations skills then employed best by industry and political figures that he became an icon among liberals and even among some minority leaders and organizations, the latter more interested in the annual cash contributions from the labor federation than in social change. Now well received by some liberals and moderates of both parties, Meany was acclaimed abroad as the central figure in the global campaign to establish non-Communist unions. He allowed himself to be the recipient of numerous awards that also became a means to bolster the treasuries of nonprofit organizations. He added people of color, such as Bayard Rustin, to his circle. He met with an astounding array of non-Communist Third World leaders. His speeches were researched and prepared by the followers of Max Schactman, which produced an intellectual flair that burnished his working-class Bronx background.

The leaders of the NAACP, the Urban League, and what remained of the other "Movement" organizations were usually treated correctly by Meany and his subordinates, especially when the federation's vast lobbying apparatus was turned loose in the halls of Congress to generate support for civil rights measures, except for those that might enhance minority rights om the workplace. Organized labor was especially helpful in gaining majority support for the original 1965 Voting Rights Act and its subsequent revisions proposed by the NAACP and the LCCR, of which the AFL-CIO and many of its constituent unions were also full-fledged, paying members. At the polling place there was a virtual identity of interest between minorities and organized labor—the mostly white candidates usually gaining the support of the civil rights leadership were also strongly pro-labor.

Despite the improved public image, the points of friction between the NAACP and organized labor increased. Between 1965 and 1977, the NAACP staff and attorneys filed several thousand complaints with the EEOC and other agencies under Title VII and other laws, executive orders, and court decisions on behalf of minority workers against both labor unions and employers, private and public. It is no coincidence that the first two contempt citations filed under Title VII were against labor unions sued originally by the NAACP more than three decades earlier—Plumbers Local 189 in Columbus, Ohio, and Metal Lather Local 46 in New York City.[13] Because local, regional, and national unions openly violated the rights of thousands of minority workers, the resources of the NAACP and the hours each day available to Herbert Hill and his small staff were never sufficient to take on even one-third of the violators.

Scores of local, regional, and national public law firms came into existence from 1965 onward, joining such established players as the Legal Defense Fund,[14] the ACLU, and the Lawyers Committee on Civil Rights Under the Constitution, to assume part of the seemingly endless task of representing minority workers fighting for their employment rights. Because of limited resources, however, the campaign to open up the building trades unions to minorities was ultimately compelled to depend upon the government.

"It is, of course, an irony," Hill wrote later, "that the various voluntary programs in the building trades and elsewhere were created in response to the threat of court orders or other forms of government action. Without government pressure even the gesture of voluntarism would not have existed."[15] Four decades after passage of Title VII of the 1964 Civil Rights Act, however, the majority of the local unions in the building trades and the crafts continue to exclude black workers from their memberships and often from their apprenticeship programs, and/or to otherwise deny minorities the same rights and advantages as those enjoyed by whites.

One of Herbert Hill's most innovative contributions to the civil rights armory was necessitated by the negative responses within the construction trades industry to Hill's efforts to aid Negro building contractors, all of them small business enterprises, sometimes with just two or three workers. They were electricians, carpenters, painters, masons, plumbers, and other specialized artisans, or mechanics, with substantial skills to perform the smaller jobs in construction, but, because of their race, had been denied access to the bidding process in large construction projects. Many had no previous experience in producing a written bid for building contracts because they could not fulfill the insurance and bonding requirements to qualify for bonding. As a result, few were able to obtain the necessary bonding guarantees, particularly performance bonds, normally required by substantial construction companies.

Hill prodded them into organizing the National Afro-American Builders, Inc., (NAAB) in 1969 and generated enough foundation support to hire seasoned staff to expand the organization. NAAB's staff undertook to teach the members the basic skills necessary to bid for jobs and to collaborate amongst themselves to bid on even bigger jobs.

Hill had anticipated by two decades the rise of incubators for small businesses that provided the same training and skills development, but instead of requiring the participants to come to a central learning site, Hill's staff took the training to the local minority builders. Hill also anticipated the development of affirmative action practices that would vastly expand the opportunities for minority building contractors, both in terms of set asides and the mandatory participation of minority contractors in varying degrees at the local, state, and federal levels.[16] At Hill's insistence, at least a few percent of the earnings of each member contractor was contributed to a fund for apprenticeship training for minority youth to prepare them for construction jobs.

The black and Hispanic contractors organized by Hill, and their counterparts outside, faced one serious handicap that skills training could not solve. The companies that insured contractors for performance, surety, and other bonding requirements uniformly refused to provide the requisite insurance to minority contractors, few of whom had sufficient business experience to demonstrate their fiduciary soundness. After a number of personal efforts in which he met repeated failure with the larger insurance corporations, Hill was preparing to sue some of the major issuers of surety bonds when one of the medium-sized companies decided to enter the playing field and sell the needed insurance to minority contractors. This decision broke the logjam and eventually some of the others followed suit. As it turned out, the minority contractors' default experience fell well within the overall parameters for the industry as a whole. Over the decade that followed, Hill's arrangements produced several hundred million dollars' worth of bonding, which enabled the minority contractors to undertake construction projects valued at several times that sum. Thus was the minority construction industry brought into the twentieth century to help to form a reliable economic base within the black and Hispanic communities.

This enterprise proved to be a well-executed end run around the hard-hearted refusal of most of the building trades unions to open their doors to blacks without long and costly law suits, followed by specific orders from federal judges, which were then interminably appealed. The NAACP was prepared to follow the litigation route as well, but its limited resources compelled General Counsel Nathaniel Jones and Labor Secretary Hill to narrow their focus to a few crucially placed suits each year. Except for the NAACP and the Legal Defense Fund, the pursuit of civil rights employment law litigation in the 1970s by other public interest law firms was sporadic and well short of the needs of minority workers.

Thus, the growth of the minority building contractors not only provided local black communities with competent mechanics. It also bolstered their start-up years so that when opportunities arose to bid for parts of larger projects, residential and commercial, in the majority community, these black and Hispanic contractors now had a track record to recommend them. Moreover, the minority contractors were far more likely to hire young and unemployed black and Hispanic men (and later women), thereby contributing to the reduction of the community's unemployment rate, and doing so with jobs that often paid far more than the minimum wage. In fact, a number of entry-level minority males working for minority contractors became apprentices on the job, learning the requisite skills that would later enable them to earn hourly wages sufficient to sustain a middle-class life. And a few of these contractors grew into multi-million dollar enterprises that gave some of their profits back to the community.

Hill certainly did not endear himself to the AFL-CIO and the construction unions when, in the fall of 1972, he vigorously opposed Nixon's nomination of Peter J. Brennan, president of the New York City AFL-CIO Building and Construction Trades Council, to be Secretary of Labor. The only time that Hill and NAACP Washington Bureau Director Clarence Mitchell clashed was over Brennan's nomination. Mitchell pleaded with Hill, then with Wilkins, not to oppose Brennan's nomination because it meant so much to George Meany, who had proposed Brennan to Nixon. Hill proved more persuasive than Mitchell on this issue, pressing Wilkins to testify personally against the nomination (which of course precluded Mitchell's appearance in favor of it.) Wilkins, in testimony originally drafted by Hill but later revised by Wilkins himself, charged that Brennan had "done nothing" to help black workers gain acceptance in the craft unions, especially within the construction trades, adding that his nomination was "appalling in the nature of a disaster."[17] Wilkins' testimony systematically presented detailed data exposing the discriminatory practices of the New York building trades unions and Peter Brennan's decisive role in defending the racist pattern. As was to be expected, President Nixon defended Brennan and the Senate confirmed his nomination, the NAACP's objections notwithstanding.

In 1976, a year before Wilkins' retirement, an incident took place that was as revealing of Wilkins' character as it was of Hill's. It stemmed from a study Hill had conducted for the Institute of Urban Affairs and Research of Howard University, entitled "Labor Union Control of Job Training—A Critical Analysis of Apprenticeship Outreach Programs and the Home Town Plans." At the institute's behest, Hill had undertaken an investigation of the federally funded apprenticeship training programs of unions and private organizations from fiscal year 1963 to fiscal year 1972, the latest year for which he was able to obtain data and statistics, much of it from sympathetic inside sources at the U.S. Department of Labor.

Before publication of his 130-page monograph by the institute in 1974, Howard University organized a conference on black employment issues, at which Hill presented an extract of his work. At the conference, which was open to the public and the press, Hill delivered a sharply detailed exposé of the false claims made by organized labor as well as their satellite organization—the A. Philip Randolph Institute, which itself conducted an apprenticeship outreach program, known as Recruitment and Training Program (RTP).

Also included in the study was the program conducted by the National Urban League, which, like the AFL-CIO and many of its member unions and together with the various building trades groupings, and the Randolph Institute's RTP, had received sizable federal grants. Overall, grants totaling $104 million had been made by the Department of Labor to fund apprenticeship and outreach programs for the benefit of black and other minority workers over a 10-year period. The AFL-CIO itself received $5.8 million and the construction unions a total of $7.7 million, according to Hill's investigation, during the decade between 1963 and 1972. And yet, when Hill proceeded to track the funding and the results of the major programs, he discovered that the claims of the AFL-CIO, the other unions, and private agencies were baseless—instead of hundreds, if not thousands, of apprentices having been trained, Hill found that in reality the actual numbers were more often in the dozens, with few ever actually obtaining a union job.

In the District of Columbia, for example, Hill and a Department of Labor specialist attempted to identify the more than 800 apprentices claimed by the D.C. unions, including the local fire fighters union, which had initially received a grant of $465,000 from the Labor Department for a training program. Ultimately, Hill found a total of 12 individuals who actually received some apprenticeship training. He proceeded to interview each of them, only to conclude that not a single one had been referred by the union local to a union-controlled program for a job.[18] Yet, the average cost of the training of these apprentices came to somewhat over $20,000 per individual. Hill told the assembled audience at Howard University that, after studying the results of these grants in a selection of cities, he could only conclude that the union-sponsored apprenticeship programs supported by the Department of Labor "were designed to give the illusion of compliance with the law, but were in fact used to circumvent the law" by the construction unions.[19]

As it turned out, an able *Washington Post* reporter—Austin Scott—was in the audience when Hill made his candid presentation. The next day Scott's lengthy article was front-paged by the *Post,* followed a few days later by a shorter piece by Paul Delaney in *The New York Times.* In between, Hill was interviewed for a half hour on Washington's most watched television talk show. The response from the leadership of the AFL-CIO was predictable: George Meany erupted in anger, demanding that Hill and the NAACP feel the full wrath of organized labor. That eventually translated into a recommendation to Bayard Rustin, president of the A. Philip Randolph Institute, to convey organized labor's case to Roy Wilkins in the expectation that he could be prevailed upon to intervene on their behalf.[20]

Meanwhile, in the summer of 1974, Howard University's Urban Affairs Institute published Hill's monograph and distributed it widely. The publication contained meticulous detail, well documented by reference notes, supporting Hill's charges that the apprenticeship programs were, in effect, shams and fraud. Notwithstanding such rigid scholarly documentation, Hill was faced with a political problem of some magnitude: the three sponsoring organizations on which he had focused were the National Urban League, the AFL-CIO, and the Recruitment and Training Program of the A. Philip Randolph Institute. The leaders of each of these notable institutions, all allies of the NAACP, especially within the LCCR, were incensed. Eventually, Randolph Institute President Bayard Rustin picked up labor's ball and, claiming to speak for the AFL-CIO and the Urban League, urgently requested a meeting with Roy Wilkins to discuss Hill's allegations. His call was backed up by the director of the AFL-CIO's civil rights department, William Pollard (later a board member of the NAACP and after that the NAACP's deputy executive director.) Each of these organizations had political and other forms of clout.

The day prior to the meeting, Wilkins called Hill to his office to discuss his findings and go over the facts. Wilkins informed Hill that Washington "friends" of the NAACP had already confirmed that Hill's facts and charges were correct. Nevertheless, Wilkins asked Hill, "Are you really sure of all your facts?" Hill discussed his sources and described how he had researched and documented his case, after which Wilkins indicated he was satisfied with Hill's presentation. According to Hill, however, Wilkins said, "Herb, I want you to do me a favor. I don't want you to do any of the talking, no matter how exaggerated or outrageous the charges may be. Leave all of the talking to me."[21] Hill nodded in agreement, no doubt disappointed that his role in this confrontation would be restricted to a passive one.

With Wilkins and Hill already seated, Rustin, Pollard, Ernest Green, who directed the Randolph Institute's RTP and was one of the high school students comprising the Little Rock nine—and Napoleon Johnson, representing Vernon Jordan and the Urban League, filed soberly into the NAACP's meeting room at its headquarters at 1710 Broadway, just off Columbus Circle. As soon as the amenities were concluded, Rustin announced that he was chairing the meeting. Wilkins fired back that this was the headquarters of the NAACP and those attending were *his* guests—*any* meeting conducted in the NAACP's house would be chaired by Wilkins. Wilkins' acerbic reply embarrassed Rustin, who realized he had made a serious tactical error and, seeking to recover from it, offered a semi-apology.

With that out of the way, the visiting delegation was invited by Wilkins to state the reasons for their meeting. Except for Green, each of the three organizational representatives spoke for five or six minutes, charging Hill with inaccurate or misinformed statements, exaggerated conclusions, and general hostility towards these three institutional friends of the association. The complaints were made in broad, general terms, without the slightest effort to support their charges with specific examples or factual rebuttal. Instead, as if by chorus, they asked Wilkins to disavow Hill's monograph. Wilkins listened for about 20 minutes, until it was clear that the three speakers had completed their case.

Then Wilkins asked them which of Hill's statements they regarded as untrue. There was no response. Wilkins then referred to a series of specific pages in Hill's monograph on which he had underlined potentially controversial sentences, pausing after each to ask, "Is this statement true?" Not one of the Hill statements was challenged for veracity by any of the four-man delegation. Rustin complained that the overall tone of the Hill monograph was interpreted as being hostile to organized labor and that George Meany and other leaders were deeply disturbed by the intent behind it.[22] Another of the group argued that because the NAACP and the three organizations they represented were allies, it was unacceptable for an NAACP staff member to criticize the friends of his employer.

Wilkins stared at the three visitors for several seconds and said, "Herb Hill does not work for the Urban League, the AFL-CIO, or the Randolph Institute. He works for the NAACP. That means he works for me. He has no obligation to make George Meany or the AFL happy. I'm the only one he has to make happy. And I will be the one to decide whether anything he has done warrants my disavowal. So far today you have not given me a shred of evidence to justify such an action. Apparently everything in that article is accurate. As far as I am concerned, that closes the discussion. Now, if you have nothing further, *I* have a great deal of work to do."[23]

Knowing how little Wilkins cherished such confrontations and how strongly he sought to maintain the appearance of unity among all of the civil rights players, Hill appreciated how significant was Wilkins' support in the face of such pressure. The lesson was not lost on the rest of the staff either. It was how Wilkins played the game; he stood behind his troops. Hill, however, realized that without the maximum support and commitment of the NAACP executive director, he could never maintain his position in the Association as the gadfly of both the unions and the big corporations. That was to play a major role in his final career decision not much more than a year later, when Wilkins' successor took office.

One of the ironies revealed by Hill's study has never been examined: Although the Justice Department and the EEOC were filing suits against unions that discriminated against minority workers resulting in federal court findings that these unions had failed to comply with Title VII and other antidiscrimination laws,[24] the federal government through its Department of Labor was subsidizing these same unions, through the apprenticeship outreach program and the home town plans, as they continued to violate the equal opportunity laws. (In this way, Presidents Nixon and Ford were able to—in the most political of terms—have their cake and eat it, too.)

Well into the 1970s, Hill led the NAACP's campaign against those trade unions that continued to exclude black workers from union membership and union-controlled jobs. The majority of the unions of the AFL-CIO that were targets of Hill's effective campaigns on behalf of black workers were defeated defendants in litigation while some chose to settle out of court to avoid negative publicity.

Perhaps the largest settlement resulted from 20 years of pressure in the courts and elsewhere by the NAACP against the steel industry's second-class treatment of black and other minority workers. Anticipating a substantial defeat if it continued its intransigence, the steel corporations and steelworkers union in 1974 negotiated with the Nixon Administration to end the stalemate by agreeing to a "voluntary, nationwide plan to end racial and sexual discrimination in hiring, employment, and pay practices," according to *New York Times* correspondent Philip Shabecoff. Even before the plan was made public, Herbert Hill, having received an advance copy, denounced it as demonstrating that the federal government "is more concerned with protecting the treasuries of the corporations and the union than in protecting the integrity of the law." Hill was especially angered by the provisions that "require[d] any worker receiving back pay to sign a waiver stating he will not sue the company or the union for damages suffered as a result of infringements of his civil rights."

The plan also provided that if a worker declined the offer of back pay and chose to sue, the U.S. Department of Justice would be compelled under the plan to intervene on the side of the steel companies and the union against the worker. Hill also attacked the cash settlements, denouncing them as grossly insufficient; they only provided for "back pay ranging from $250 to $500 per worker with an average estimated at $400." Hill insisted that a fair settlement should involve thousands of dollars, instead of hundreds. Finally, he protested that the settlement failed to obliterate the separate racial seniority lines in union contracts. The NAACP Labor Secretary added that he was especially incensed that black workers and their representatives had been excluded from the negotiations.[25]

When Executive Director Ben Hooks inaugurated a full-fledged corporate fund-raising campaign in 1979, most of the steel companies, led by U.S. Steel, refused to participate, expressing their continued anger at the NAACP's success in having their employment practices judged discriminatory and imposing sizable financial penalties for these practices.[26] Only Inland Steel, led by a liberal chief executive officer, Joseph Block, broke ranks with its industry by making a small contribution to the NAACP campaign.

As the NAACP expanded its campaigns to open up jobs to Negroes in numerous crafts and vocations, the leadership of the AFL-CIO became increasingly antagonistic to Hill, especially the presidents of the international unions representing the building trades and the railway unions. By the 1960s even the influence of Walter Reuther within organized labor had so waned that he removed the UAW from the AFL-CIO and experimented with a futile collaboration with the giant Teamsters Union, the nation's largest international union. For a short time, the Teamsters, appreciative of Reuther's gesture, provided some financial support to the NAACP, though during the 1960s most of their largesse was directed to Dr. King and SCLC through their most liberal regional leader, Harold Gibbons of St. Louis, Missouri. The total amount of cash contributed to the NAACP by the overall labor movement became less and less significant during the 1960s as the latter's overall income, especially after 1965 when the tax-deductible SCF was formed, increased substantially, while labor's contributions remained stagnant.

Labor's influence within the NAACP, however, remained strong throughout the 1970s, both because of their important coalition role in Washington in support of civil rights measures through the LCCR and through direct lobbying, as well as their carefully nurtured hold on key NAACP board and officer positions. James Kemp of Chicago's Building Service Employees Union, Tom Turner of Detroit's AFL-CIO Council, William Oliver and Marc Stepp of the UAW, Maida Springer of the ILGWU, and Ponsie Hillman of the AFT, together with scores of other labor delegates at the annual convention and labor union members who served as officers of local NAACP branches, protected organized labor's agenda to the maximum possible extent during the annual conventions and at periodic board meetings. They increasingly operated from a pre-established united front, benignly described as labor solidarity, at the NAACP conventions. Their most important priority was to discredit or reduce the influence of Herbert Hill within the NAACP and to undercut his policy recommendations.[27] Hill, meanwhile, had become the nation's foremost expert on Title VII, the employment section of the 1964 Civil Rights Act. His work in developing and filing EEOC complaints against unions and employers exceeded the capacity of the NAACP labor department to such a degree that he felt compelled to call upon the Legal Defense and Education Fund to handle some of his department's suits.

The blossoming of civil rights law under Title VII persuaded more and more employers to reverse their discriminatory practices, since they were the entities most likely to be fined heavily if their hiring or promotion practices were determined to be illegal. In addition, with Negroes comprising 11 or 12 percent of the population, it did not take a math genius to comprehend that with a larger available labor pool, the overall cost of labor would decrease or not increase at the same rate as previously. Thus, most of the unions seeking to remain lily-white found themselves losing their most important industry allies, the well-heeled employers and their corporate lawyers.

The commitment of organized labor to its traditional racial practices, however, thwarted the overall employment objectives of the NAACP. By the mid-1970s Herbert Hill was expressing despair that the condition of black workers, especially of males, was steadily deteriorating with no respite in sight. He castigated the federal government for failing to act to ameliorate the employment crisis in black communities, where unemployment rates normally remained two to three times that of whites. In a June 2, 1974, interview with the *Washington Post,* he described the conditions of black unemployment as "explosive," citing EEOC figures for 1969 that reported that black workers made up "0.2 percent of the sheet metalworkers, 0.2 per cent of plumbers, 0.4 per cent of elevator contractors, 0.7 per cent of electrical workers, 1.6 per cent of carpenters, 1.7 per cent of iron workers, and 0.9 per cent of the asbestos workers union." Three years later, the article observed, the EEOC reported very little change in all categories except sheet metalworkers, which had risen to 5 percent, and carpenters, which reached 3.2 percent. Hill also reported that a good deal of falsification of progress reports characterized both state employment training programs and those of labor unions,[28] since these reports had been based on a self-reporting system with no independent monitoring by the U.S. Department of Labor.

In December 1974, at the same time the press was celebrating Hill for 25 years of service as the NAACP's labor secretary, Hill accused the labor movement of perpetuating racial discrimination in employment and especially attacked labor's role in developing the home town plans, which were voluntary agreements between employers and unions to comply with civil rights laws, and the union-sponsored apprenticeship outreach programs of the construction unions to create the illusion of their compliance with Title VII. But the unions continued to run sham programs that graduated very few of the enrollees; those few who did graduate either found no jobs or were confined to low-end menial work, despite the skills they had presumably learned in the programs.

In the NAACP's view, the court-ordered remedies that followed the suits based upon Title VII of the 1964 Civil Rights Act had driven the contractors, business owners, and unions into finding ways to appear to be adhering to the spirit and letter of the law, but in reality their efforts had been, for the most part, a mirage.[29]

W. E. B. DuBois

Mary White Ovington

Joel Spingarn

James Weldon Johnson

"A Man Was Lynched Yesterday" banner from window of the NAACP headquarters on New York's Fifth Avenue during the 1920s.

Howard University students protesting the Justice Department's failure to punish lynching outside a 1935 anti-crime conference.

Charles Hamilton Houston

Moorefield Storey

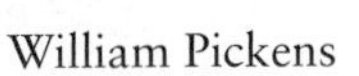

William Pickens

Walter White

Left: Dressed as a levee worker, Roy Wilkins returns from secret investigation of U. S. Army exploitation of black workers on Mississippi River levees; *right:* Jack Johnson as heavyweight champion.

Paul Robeson

Marian Anderson

Marian Anderson in the famed 1939 concert at the Lincoln Memorial.

President Harry Truman addressing 10,000 NAACP 1947 convention delegates and guests from the steps of the Lincoln Memorial.

Truman, Eleanor Roosevelt and Walter White on their way to the Lincoln Memorial.

Eleanor Roosevelt addresses the 1947 NAACP national convention. *Foreground:* Truman and Attorney General Tom Clark.

Roy Wilkins

Thurgood Marshall

Robert L. Carter

Gloster Current

Thurgood Marshall (right) jokes with NAACP Labor Secretary Herbert Hill at NAACP convention.

President Eisenhower greets NAACP delegation at the White House. They are (l. to r.)Arthur Spingarn, Pres. Eisenhower, Clarence Mitchell and Walter White.

Announcing new NAACP poster to "Stamp Out Mississippi-ism" are four of the Association's top executives (l. to r.) Public Information Director Henry Lee Moon, Executive Secretary Roy Wilkins, Labor Director Herbert Hill, and Special Counsel Thurgood Marshall.

The NAACP Brain Trust, circa 1950: Roy Wilkins, Walter White and Thurgood Marshall.

Robert L. Carter, June Shagaloff and Walter White at a press conference to discuss Cairo, Illinois, school crisis after Shagaloff's release from local jail for aiding local chapter.

NAACP leaders salute 1955 labor union merger: (l. To r.) A. Philip Randolph and Willard Townsend, organized labor's first Negro national vice presidents; Thurgood Marshall; Jim Carey, civil rights supporter and AFL-CIO Vice President; and Roy Wilkins.

Left: President John F. Kennedy reads proclamation to NAACP leaders Bishop Stephen Gill Spottswood, Arthur Spingarn, and Roy Wilkins during the 1961 convention. *Right:* At the White House, Kennedy welcomes NAACP delegates to the 1961 convention, including Mississippi State Chairman Aaron Henry at left and Ohio leader Ted Berry at right.

More than 250,000 stand up for civil rights at the 1963 March on Washington.

After the resoundingly successful 1963 March on Washington, Kennedy congratulates the nation's civil rights leaders in the White House. The assembled guests are Eugene Carson Blake, Floyd McKissick, unidentified man, Whitney Young, Martin Luther King Jr., John Lewis, Rabbi Joachim Prinz, Ashley Totten, A. Philip Randolph, Kennedy, Lyndon Johnson, Walter Reuther, and Roy Wilkins.

Left: Roy Wilkins and Thurgood Marshall counsel Autherine Lucy as she drafts a statement concerning her unsuccessful attempt to enter the University of Alabama; *right*: During White House summit of civil rights leaders, President Johnson tries out a new strategy with Roy Wilkins before signing the 1964 Civil Rights Act.

Johnson signs the 1964 Civil Rights Act surrounded by Congressional leaders and Judge Thurgood Marshall.

Ruby Hurley

Herbert Hill

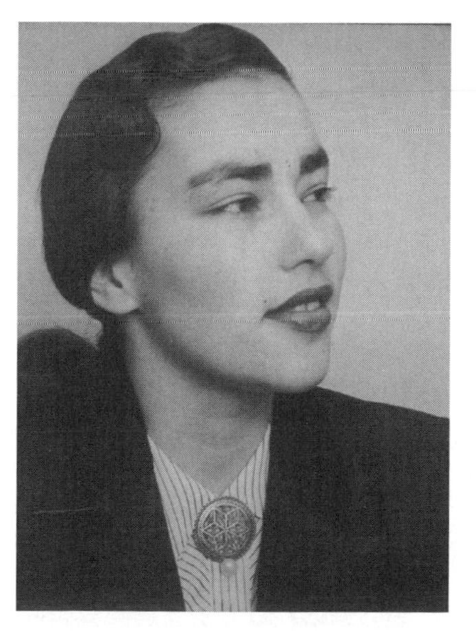

June Shagaloff

Medgar Evers

Left: In a well-earned celebratory moment at the White House after the signing of the 1965 Civil Rights Act are ADA's Joseph Rauh, who joined Clarence Mitchell in piloting the bill through Congress, and Roy Wilkins; *right:* Clarence Mitchell receives congratulations from Johnson for his stewardship of the 1968 Civil Rights Act.

During the Congressional struggle over passage of the 1965 Voting Rights Act, Johnson and Roy Wilkins discuss strategy and tactics.

Leaders of the biracial Loyal Democrats of Mississippi meeting to challenge the segregated "regular" Democratic delegation to the 1968 Convention in Chicago. The NAACP's state chairman Aaron Henry (hand raised) and Field Director Charles Evers joined with white leaders, including Hodding Carter III (chairing meeting), to unseat the segregated delegation and permanently change the party's politics.

In May 1969, Charles Evers informs black supporters in a Fayette church of his victory as first black to be elected mayor of a biracial town in the South since Reconstruction. He is joined by Gil Jonas, who organized national support for the campaign.

Dr. John Morsell

Dr. Kenneth B.Clark

Bayard Rustin

Dr. Ralph Bunche

12. Roy Wilkins: The Gentle Giant

Even if we did not believe steadfastly in making real, for black as well as white Americans, the great dream of equal opportunity for our young nation, tactically, for a numerical minority of about one-tenth, and an economic, political, and social minority of far less strength, integration is the only way to go. The word integration is not used here to mean assimilation. No one is advocating loss of identity, loss of color distinction, the burying of a culture, and a complete merging into the general population. The anti-integrationists have sought to give that impression of the integrationist position. We seek no elusive "melting pot." Instead, we use the dictionary definition of integration: "The making up of a whole by adding together or combining the separate parts or elements."

We seek to become a part of the whole, an equal part of that whole, to be on the inside with other Americans, rather than on the outside looking in. We want to make our country whole, to give it its missing teeth, to fill the ugly gap in its teeth, to enable it to throw away the crutches and hobbling gait of the color line and to replace the stuttered apology with strong straight talk.

Roy Wilkins, Address to the NAACP 61st Annual Convention, Cincinnati, Ohio, June 30, 1970

> For many decades, Roy Wilkins has been the conscience of America. His words have not always been welcome or pleasant to listen to, but it has been impossible to turn our backs on their truth.
>
> **Mrs. Ralph J. Bunche, Letter of September 7, 1976, to NAACP Supporters**

With the passage of the Voting Rights Act in 1965, Roy Wilkins had completed a decade in full control of the NAACP's helm. His apprenticeship had begun in 1931, shortly after Walter White consolidated his power as the national executive secretary of the organization. For more than two decades, he gained the invaluable experience of an insider at the very pinnacle of the organization, which was to prepare him for the NAACP's highest post even more thoroughly than his two Negro predecessors, James Weldon Johnson and Walter White. As director of public information and later editor of *The Crisis*, Wilkins had assiduously demonstrated his talents in articulating the grievances and aspirations of the nation's Negroes. He was greatly admired by intellectuals of both races and, as a former newsman, by the men and women of the working press. Later, as White's deputy, he gained stature from constant exposure before the Association's members and the branches across the country.

Wilkins first experience as *de facto* head of the NAACP came at the expense of his mentor's personal pain in 1949, when Walter White requested a one-year leave of absence. He was about to divorce Gladys, his Negro wife of several decades, in order to marry Poppy Cannon, a white woman. The traditionalists among the Association's membership, most notably the hard-working women who as volunteers carried out the difficult, often dangerous, day-to-day work of the NAACP locally—by generating memberships, conducting fund drives, and energizing church support to fight discrimination—demanded White's head on a silver platter.[1]

White had already been suffering from poor health. In 1947, shortly after Wilkins had recovered from cancer of the colon and Marshall had recovered from another severe illness, White was hospitalized with a severe heart attack. Wilkins took over temporarily until White's return, but in 1949, when White asked for a year's leave of absence, the Board of Directors appointed Wilkins as acting executive secretary. White finally returned in late 1951, though his health remained, in Wilkins' word, "delicate." Wilkins and Marshall took up much of the leadership slack during that period to relieve the pressure on White. A vociferous faction of the NAACP's leadership still opposed White's return and continued to try to force his resignation. However, Eleanor Roosevelt, then a Board member, intervened and persuaded the Board to permit White to remain at the helm. On March 21, 1955, a few hours after visiting the NAACP's headquarters, Walter White died.[2]

Several weeks later at the April 1955 meeting of the National Board, Wilkins was chosen to succeed White over the bids of Thurgood Marshall and Clarence Mitchell. As the occupant of the organization's highest staff position, Wilkins automatically became the foremost spokesperson for Negro America. Paradoxically, no private voluntary organization during the twentieth century, regardless of race, could boast of two persons of such eminent stature and ability equal to Wilkins, Marshall, or Mitchell. The NAACP could boast of three.

The competition during the previous four years for the top post may have been the origin of growing tensions between Marshall and Wilkins, which resulted in Marshall's decision to move the legal staff from the NAACP's headquarters in Freedom House, 20 West 40th Street, in Manhattan, to another building nearby. The official explanation was that the 40th Street offices were overcrowded. Marshall, of course, had gained control of the NAACP Legal Defense and Educational Fund (LDF) during the previous 15 years; most of the LDF's trustees were individuals he had personally selected who, not surprisingly, also supported him without reservation. Thus, while the LDF under Marshall continued to cooperate closely with the NAACP proper, this was no longer automatic, especially since the differences between the two leaders continued to multiply.

Those who observed at first hand the relationship between Clarence Mitchell and Wilkins appreciated that it was one of mutual respect. Mitchell's judgment on political matters, especially within Congress and the executive branch, almost always carried the day with Wilkins and the National Board. His cumulative experience, enormous intellect, and persuasive personality resulted in a level of professional success to which no other lobbyist of the era could attain. As a public speaker, he was one of the most effective within the civil rights movement. Senators and congressmen came increasingly to defer to him, especially during the 1960s and early 1970s, when the civil rights agenda was still on the front burner.

During his initial decade as the NAACP's chief executive, Wilkins had recruited, trained, and then surrounded himself with a staff of superior quality and integrity. Their commitment was never in doubt, nor was their loyalty to Wilkins, who rarely failed to back up his lieutenants when they were under attack by a faction of the Board or the membership, or by allies like those in the labor movement, as well as by forces who opposed integration or the NAACP's assault on racist institutions. In almost every important fight, there were those Board members, local leaders, and branches who counseled against a strategy designed to produce radical and hopefully rapid change. These persons were usually the ones who feared that, if the strategy failed, the boomerang effect would set the cause back or even wipe out recent advances or bring additional problems to the community. During the years prior to the NAACP's arguments before the Supreme Court that resulted in *Brown,* many Negro teachers and educators were afraid of losing their own jobs if segregation were abolished. They, as well as some lawyers, journalists, and community leaders, pleaded with the NAACP and Marshall not to press for a total prohibition of segregated public schools, also fearing that the Court's rejection would eliminate the marginal gains already won.

Neither Wilkins nor his senior staff was timid, though Wilkins demanded meticulous preparation for every initiative. Even after his mind was made up, he proceeded cautiously, even deliberately, to craft his new approach. He lined up as much support as was possible, while his staff fanned out to explain the new initiative to the troops—the rank-and-file—so that each branch could respond locally with, hopefully, informed support. In small towns and rural areas, many of the branch presidents were intelligent but uneducated; they found it difficult to produce a written report. However, in the crucible of civil rights activism from the early 1950s until the mid-1980s, thousands of such men and women learned the methodology of effective local activism. With guidelines from the National Office, they were able to organize branches, formulate local resistance, articulate their grievances or demands to the local power structure, sustain community support for the NAACP's agenda, and scratch out the most meager sums to keep the branch alive and functioning.

Back in the period before the civil rights explosion of the mid-1960s, even the NAACPs $1 annual dues were a hardship for a very large number of adherents. Before the dues were raised to $2 in the 1960s, it required a major internal struggle over several years until the measure was adopted by the delegates to the national convention. In the following year, the size of the national membership dropped off substantially (though it eventually recovered).

As soft-spoken and gentle as Wilkins appeared to be, his inner core was rock-hard. Those who tangled with him were often surprised at his toughness, especially after he had gathered the available facts and arrived at a conclusion. David Garrow, who has written the definitive book on Dr. King and the SCLC, notes that King would never confront Wilkins head-on, that he was actually reluctant to engage in any direct confrontations with Wilkins, and usually backed away from such face-to-face showdowns.[3] Most of the other civil rights leaders were equally respectful. Rustin in later years felt free to engage in frank discussions with Wilkins, and Farmer often disagreed with Wilkins's tactics, but rarely were these exchanges uncivil.

Roy Wilkins, John Morsell, Clarence Mitchell, Robert Carter, Gloster Current, and the other senior staff directors in the National Office and in the field were at home in every milieu. Patronizing from the top was infrequent; the most humble tenant farmer received the same regard as urban intellectuals. That spirit usually pervaded the staff from top to bottom and impacted positively on the membership that nevertheless chronically complained of the meager resources, delayed staff responses, unanswered correspondence, and so forth. The fact was that until 1968, the NAACP national office had a staff of less than 50 servicing a membership of 500,000 and the national programs. That means that the ratio of staff to members was about one to 10,000. With a sizable proportion of the membership actively involved during that period, it is clear that the NAACP was gravely understaffed. Only the life-commitment of the staff and the enormous energy, dedication, and broad-based participation of the volunteers made possible so many triumphs, locally and nationally.

Far more than his predecessors, Wilkins empathized with the local volunteer members. He had spent a decade as an active member and officer of the St. Paul, Minnesota branch and appreciated the shortcomings and strengths of most local units. Unlike both James Weldon Johnson and Walter White, his persona had not been nurtured in the adulation of the New York-based elite, black and white, neither when he joined the national staff nor when he succeeded White. He took very seriously the notion that his salary was paid by the modest annual dues paid by the membership.

His undercover assignment to expose the exploitation of black workers on the Mississippi Delta levees sensitized him to the dangers and vulnerabilities of the grassroots members, especially in the South. On his return to New York, he had made a persuasive and passionate case for the National Office's hiring of a full-time attorney to work with the volunteers, including the provision of legal protection for the membership and branches.[4] Until then, the attorneys—all outside retainers or white volunteers—dealt with cases at the apex of the struggle, cases with national implications and often those that would ultimately be decided by the Supreme Court. Wilkins' concern was for the humble members at the bottom of the pyramid who risked so much by merely belonging to the organization and who were thrust into jeopardy every time they were asked to undertake a public act, such as registering to vote or becoming a plaintiff in a suit to desegregate the local school district, or publicly condemning the behavior of a police officer or elected official. Wilkins never lost this abiding preoccupation, which accounted for his vast popularity among the overwhelming majority of the membership. He worked tirelessly to inculcate the same concern in his staff.

Under Wilkins, the staff's first duty was to train and educate the local leaders. This was accomplished through leadership training sessions conducted over a three- or four-day period each year at the national convention, as well as at the seven three-day regional conventions conducted annually, and at the 40 or so weekend state conventions scheduled throughout every year. The Branch Department under Gloster Current organized and directed these sessions, which dealt with conducting membership meetings, observing *Roberts Rules,* holding annual elections for convention delegates and biannual elections for the branch leadership, complying with the organization's rules, especially in respect to keeping financial records, organizing membership drives and events to raise funds, generating community support, communicating within and outside the branch, working in coalition with other groups and churches—in short, the nuts and bolts of nonprofit organizational know-how, the point of which was, in the volunteers' parlance, to learn "to fight City Hall."

The branch leaders were also supposed to attend workshops, seminars, and panel discussions at the same state, regional, and national meetings on each of the major action program areas supported by the NAACP: voter education, housing, employment, public education, youth activities, veterans affairs, and some of the key litigation initiatives being conducted by the NAACP during each time frame. The departmental directors, often joined by nationally recognized experts in the subject, conducted training sessions in their fields for local NAACP leaders and members, national board members, and guests from other agencies.[5]

Herbert Hill's meetings were often the most contentious, since he pressed his criticism of organized labor's discriminatory practices in employment with the same intensity that he attacked racial bias within big business. Occasionally, youth dissatisfaction became audible at some of these sessions because they were one of the few forums for such expression. Local leaders disagreeing with the NAACP's latest strategy in public education would make known their opposition at the workshops conducted by Shagaloff, who was often able to defang the opposition with clear explanations of the thinking behind the decisions of the national office.

General Counsel Robert Carter and his entire staff of lawyers (a dozen or so at its peak) held workshops on pending or new legal actions in each of the NAACP's major program areas. The legal department's newest legal strategies and concepts were usually explained to large audiences, including scores of guest attorneys from throughout the movement, by Carter and a panel of experts that would frequently include judges, law school deans, and top Justice Department officials.

The amount of information directed to the member-delegates at each national convention, buttressed by pounds of printed and mimeographed materials fashioned specifically for these sessions each year, were the equivalent of an intensive semester college course, but covered many disciplines. The state and regional meetings were designed to reinforce the information and concepts offered at the national convention's workshops or lectures, and to add to the skills of NAACP leadership on the state and local levels. All of this effort was geared to producing greater activism. Special program materials were mailed to every branch president. On major issues, *The Crisis* magazine carried lengthy articles by recognized authorities in these fields. Under Wilkins, this overarching system of education of the volunteer membership was finely crafted and polished to an extent never before equaled in comparable citizens' movements. Given the pitifully small budgets on which the Association managed to survive during its first half century, it is a miracle that so many tens of thousands of persons were trained in the skills and knowledge required to conduct successful civil rights campaigns locally, not to mention the hundreds who attained state and regional leadership every decade.

Wilkins' public persona, both before and after becoming the chief executive of the NAACP, had become familiar to the nation's decision makers, opinion molders, and activists. Getting to know the real Roy Wilkins was, however, a difficult task. Reticent and close-mouthed about his personal life and feelings, Wilkins often gave the appearance of a loner after he became the NAACP's "maximum leader." His only consistently close confidant, especially in his later years, was his wife, Minnie, to whom he was unequivocally devoted.

Professionally and personally, his closest colleague was Dr. John Morsell, who sacrificed his own promising academic career as a sociologist to become Wilkins' deputy and alter ego. So akin in thought were these two that they easily became interchangeable within the workings of the Association and the civil rights movement, especially within the LCCR, where Morsell frequently sat in for Wilkins and where he had developed extremely close relations with Arnold Aronson, Joe Rauh, Bayard Rustin, Jim Farmer, Walter Reuther, and other leaders of the coalition.

An examination of Wilkins' early years provides a revealing key to his makeup, temperament, and philosophy, especially to his unshakable commitment to an integrated society and his faith that ultimately enough fair-minded white Americans would place the provisions of the U.S. Constitution above all other considerations in achieving a truly color-blind society. Wilkins was born in St. Louis in 1901, a time when that Mississippi River port city was for all intents and purposes a segregated Southern town ruled by Jim Crow. His parents had fled from a much harsher and deadlier Mississippi shortly after his father repeatedly struck a white farmer, following the latter's humiliating verbal assault. A graduate of all-black Rust College, Roy's father Willie had already encountered the economic realities of Jim Crow when, despite his education, the only jobs he could find were menial and/or low-paying. Striking a white man in Mississippi at any time before the most recent past for whatever reason was a one-way ticket to a graveyard for a Negro. A white neighbor quickly warned Wilkins' grandfather of what was about to transpire and Roy's young parents were spirited out of Holly Springs to a railroad depot, where the next train took them to the sanctuary of St. Louis.

Willie Wilkins was, however, to find that life in the Missouri mecca was also extremely difficult for a Negro. The daily struggle to find enough work and make ends meet ultimately defeated him. He became distant and stern with his children, turning to religion as an empty pacifier. This escape from reality earned him the rejection of young Roy, who himself developed a jaundiced view of those who relied on religion to reach "the Promised Land." Roy himself was born a year after his parents arrived in St. Louis. The births of his sister, Armeda, and his brother, Earl, followed during the next four years. Then his mother fell ill and without warning died from consumption. Before she succumbed, however, Mayfield Wilkins, who was known to her friends as "Sweetie," called upon her sister Elizabeth to come from Minnesota to "rescue" the children from their father. Because Willie Wilkins was broke, "Aunt Elizabeth" arranged for the burial of her sister in Holly Springs and paid for it in installments.

Sweetie's body was eventually joined by those of her mother and father in the Mississippi graveyard. It was Roy's grandfather who had made the greatest impression on the youngster, especially later in his youth when he and his brother visited for the summer. Born a slave in 1851 and freed in 1865 but with almost no exercisable rights, Roy wrote in his autobiography that Grandfather Wilkins:

> [L]ike millions of other Negroes, . . . responded by becoming a stoic; he endured. I inherited his staying power, but not his patience. Chattel slavery and the damnable nineteenth century race rulings of the Court divided my people—Grandfather Wilkins along with them—into two camps: victims of bondage and segregation who abided their sufferings passively hoping for

> a better day and rebels who heaped coals of fire on everything that smacked of inequality. I have spent my life stoking the fire and shoveling on the coal. My grandfather had to keep his head down—or get his neck stretched.[6]

For a short time Wilkins attended a segregated school in St. Louis. When, after his mother's death, Aunt Elizabeth persuaded her extraordinary husband Sam to prevent the breakup of the three siblings by agreeing to have them live in his St. Paul home, the entire direction of Roy Wilkins' life changed—forever. From the age of five until he left St. Paul 18 years later for a journalism job in Kansas City, Roy Wilkins lived in an overwhelmingly white society encountering a bare minimum of racial prejudice. He went to integrated schools—often he was the only Negro or one of a very few in the classroom—and had little difficulty establishing his space and persona as a gifted student and a responsible young man. Roy's aunt and uncle became the surrogate parents (and later the legal ones) of all three Wilkins children, serving as their role models for hard work, thrift, compassion, honesty, and concern for their fellow Negroes.

The relatively open Minnesota society permitted Roy to develop friendships and trust with whites from childhood onward. In addition, the small black community of 7,000 in St. Paul was replete with achieving African Americans, including a smattering of lawyers, doctors, writers, and artists, but the black middle class was largely composed of relatively well paid waiters, Pullman car porters, and barbers. Missing were black politicians or teachers.[7] Though the realities of race rarely overwhelmed young Roy, he had become acutely aware of the "glass ceiling" of the period and of the limitations to the fulfillment of his people that racial discrimination imposed. It was, however, no accident that Roy Wilkins never turned to the ministry either for succor or as a calling. Even though Aunt Elizabeth tried assiduously to bring him to religion, young Roy appears to have merely gone through the motions solely to satisfy his aunt whom he loved and respected. His view of Christianity is summed up cryptically in his autobiography: The church "has sometimes sustained and sometimes subdued Negroes for more than 200 years" after John Wesley converted the first African American in 1758.[8] As anyone close to Wilkins during the 22 years he led the NAACP can attest, his patience with men of the cloth often wore thin. His own soft-spoken, erudite style of speaking was (perhaps deliberately) in utter contrast to the garrulous, gesticulating, rhythmic, and often fever-pitched style of Negro ministers, particularly those of the Baptist and evangelical denominations. His approach to ideas was persistently analytic, requiring evidence and proof to make a point. In his thinking, there was no room for an argument that rested on faith alone.

He was also a consummate wordsmith, a person who venerated the English language and used it with precision and style. He was unable to tolerate poor grammar, incorrect spelling, and improper diction among his aides because he had chosen them for their skills, among which was supposed to be the proper and effective use of the language. For the most part, his staff directors were among the most literate in the entire movement and several were frequently published in their fields as well as personal interests. Henry Lee Moon, the public information director, wrote the first definitive book on the Negro vote.[9] Herbert Hill wrote frequently for academic and professional journals about the status of black workers and the resistance of unions and industry to the integration of the work force. Hill also edited and wrote the introductions to several books of contemporary black literature and was an accomplished jazz commentator. As lawyers, Robert Carter and Nathaniel Jones both wrote frequently about legal subjects in the nation's most prestigious law journals, before and after becoming federal judges. June Shagaloff (for almost every facet of education) and Bill Morris (for housing) were frequently published, too. John Morsell was an accomplished writer of both academic and popular articles. A staff meeting comprised of these individuals and their other colleagues was often stimulating and replete with the cross-fertilization of ideas, suggestions, and commentaries. It was a quintessentially Wilkins creation, and one of its hallmarks was that the participants felt free to offer differing views, until Wilkins had made up his mind.

For the most part, Wilkins' anger was reserved for those who were careless, thoughtless, or plain dumb. In addition, he brooked no deviation once the internal "party line" was established by him. On the other hand, he would occasionally tolerate conflicting acts or positions, fully aware of their contradictions, because they served a larger purpose, at least for the time being. He was imbued with very high standards of performance, which he tried to pass on to those who worked for him and he demanded from them the same level of quality that he demanded from himself.

Wilkins' physical courage was not questioned, especially after he volunteered at the age of 31 to investigate reports from the AFL that the U.S. Corps of Army Engineers had been exploiting black men to build flood control dams and river levees along the Mississippi Delta for the princely sum of 10 cents an hour. A few months after he had been hired by Walter White and moved to New York, Wilkins proposed that he and George Schuyler, then a rebellious black reporter, pose as black field hands and go undercover to verify the reports. In an aura of great secrecy, Wilkins and Schuyler left New York a few days before Christmas in 1932 for Memphis, where they were briefed and then, each on his own route, made off to the dangerous Delta, the most oppressed section of Mississippi. Their initial fear was of being betrayed by what Wilkins later called "quislings" among Southern Negroes who informed on strangers and otherwise collaborated with white sheriffs. The NAACP staff in New York was officially muzzled during Wilkins's absence and instructed not to discuss his whereabouts.

White roughnecks patrolled the Mississippi levees, looking for black men who were seeking work on the Delta levees; these whites were angry that blacks were willing to undercut them and accept such low wages. Wilkins had a number of close calls—several Negroes he encountered looked with suspicion upon this well-spoken black man with no calluses on his hands. But it was Schuyler who experienced the gravest danger. He was jailed on suspicion of a robbery in Vicksburg after having been fingered by a local black informer. Schuyler was married to a white woman and kept a photo of her in his wallet. His greatest fear was that the police would inspect his wallet and find that incriminating photo. He bribed a guard to allow him to send a wire to Wilkins for help, but before Wilkins could respond, the real perpetrators were caught and Schuyler was released.

After that close call, they decided to stick together for the remainder of their investigation. (Walter White further endangered them by rushing out a press release on the incarceration of Schuyler.) For another week they crossed the region by foot, trying to find work and documenting the abject poverty of the Delta's Negroes which the U.S. Army Engineers were exploiting. As strangers, they were constantly threatened by the paranoid whites who feared outside troublemakers. But they gathered the necessary facts and, finally, in mid-January they took a bus back to Memphis and then another to New York. At the conclusion of his odyssey, Wilkins reported to the annual meeting of the NAACP and to its national board a few days after his return. His acute sense of injustice and resultant anger emerge even a half century later with the following evaluation of the Delta story:

> At the time the federal government was spending over $300 million building and improving the levees, . . . but these millions were dribbling out in nickels and dimes. Payday fell every two weeks when it came at all. Company commissaries plucked back most of what was paid out. I met one man who took home $12 for two months work. Anyone who complained was fired; anyone who complained too loudly risked a beating or worse. All this was under the supervision of the U.S. Army Corps of Engineers, in mockery of the American flags that flew on the staffs erected in the camps. It was a system of peonage organized by the federal government and paid with American tax dollars. The more I saw, the angrier I grew.[10]

The heckling by Communists of Wilkins' Delta journey report at the NAACP 1933 annual meeting in Harlem's Abyssinian Baptist Church was especially grating to Wilkins after such a prolonged exposure to danger. Walter White had beaten the bushes to generate a huge crowd to hear Wilkins' first-hand report. The Communists clearly feared that this dramatic and courageous venture by an NAACP executive was a threat to their drive to take over the movement for Negro "betterment." They seeded the audience with provocateurs who rose to their feet and denounced Wilkins and Schuyler as fakes who had never gone to Mississippi in the first place and were about to trick the people of Harlem with their phony report. Wilkins never forgot this incident, which permanently disposed him to conclude that the Communists were never truly interested in the liberation of American Negroes, placing the welfare of the Communist Party above all other loyalties.[11]

Another consequence of this nerve-rattling odyssey, in addition to the celebrity with which the Wilkins-Schuyler report was met, came a few months later when New York Senator Robert Wagner succeeded in circumventing Southern obstructionism and held Senate hearings on the NAACP report. The extensive public ventilation of the dire conditions in the work camps and the wage exploitation of the black workers compelled the U.S. Army Corps of Engineers to radically change its method of operation, not the least important result being the doubling of the wage scale, so that millions of additional dollars reached the pockets of the levee workers. This early foray into the hallowed halls of Congress and the impact on the executive branch produced by the public hearings resulted in the kernel of a new strategy in the minds of both Wilkins and White.

"For me," Wilkins said looking back almost 50 years later, "the reward was even more substantial; we had proved that if you pushed the government long enough, hard enough, and in the right places, change could be accomplished. I felt hope and renewed energy. If we could bring a few dimes to Mississippi, perhaps we could one day bring freedom."[12] That experience became one of Roy Wilkins' recurring mantras, to which he remained committed even when many of the other movement leaders were ready to abandon hope that the federal government could play the major role in producing the requirements of full freedom.

Wilkins' courage would be tested many times in the years following the journey to the Mississippi Delta, including a life-threatening bout with colon cancer in 1945 that resulted in a colostomy. Yet he managed to function effectively for the next 35 years, never once using that serious medical condition as an excuse. (Very few of his associates were even aware of the condition.) During the two decades following the *Brown* decision, when the danger of assassination from white supremacists was at its peak, Wilkins never flinched from marching in the front ranks of every major protest in the Deep South, including the funeral procession following the murder of Medgar Evers in 1963 and the march across the Pettus Bridge in Selma arm-in-arm with Dr. King.

Equally dangerous was the secret plan of the Revolutionary Action Movement (RAM), a small armed band of black ultra-militants, to assassinate Roy Wilkins, Whitney Young, A. Philip Randolph, Bayard Rustin, and other so-called moderate leaders within the movement. Persuaded that the national black leadership was pursuing liberation too slowly during the mid-1970s, the conspirators were bent upon triggering a violent uprising of African Americans by killing several popular leaders and making it appear that the murderers were white.

The New York Police Department had infiltrated RAM and informed Wilkins and the others face-to-face of the plot. The cops took it very seriously. They kept Wilkins and the others under full-time surveillance, assigned a full-time guard to him, then raided RAM's headquarters and uncovered an impressive cache of arms. Sixteen RAM members were arrested; two were tried for conspiring to kill Wilkins and the others in order to set off riots in the black ghettoes by blaming whites for the assassinations. They had already drawn maps of Wilkins' home and neighborhood and identified which shrubs would provide cover. After they were convicted, Wilkins refused further police protection, even though other RAM members were still at large. Minnie Wilkins was far from pleased.[13]

Given to understatement, often as a form of irony, Wilkins rarely raised his voice to a shout. Intellectually, he held his own with the best, yet he was relaxed and easily conversant with the least educated. Most important of all,[14] he was firmly wedded to the truth. Even when it might serve the cause by providing a momentary advantage, he refused to lie, insisting on the same commitment to honesty by his staff and the organization he served. Time after time over the decades, one recalls him addressing huge crowds of African Americans where his bluntness might have turned the crowd away from him. Instead, it had the opposite effect—the throng took to its feet to cheer and "amen" his honesty.

In the late 1960s, for example, he spoke before some 5,000 people at the open public meeting held during every annual convention to enable the local Negro population to share more than a glimpse of the NAACP's leaders. It was a time of great ferment, with urban riots beginning to flare up across the land. Black nationalists and separatists were reviling "whitey" as the cause of every problem confronting Negroes. One of the most urgent demands repeated like the chorus of a rhythm-and-blues recording was the constant 25-year-old cry for decent jobs. Title VII of the 1964 Civil Rights Act was just beginning to open doors to the workplace. In this setting, Wilkins raised the issue and talked about the exclusionary practices of both big corporations and big unions. He described the life-sustaining importance of good jobs and how blacks had either been bypassed or shunted to the unskilled, low-paying, and often dirty occupations. He once again asserted that the "best welfare project was a decent job." Then he reported on some of the changes wrought by the NAACP through the courts and by direct pressure.

Finally, he bore down on the work habits of "those Negroes who," he said, "call in sick on Monday, and start leaving for the weekend on Thursday afternoon." He talked about the frequency of black workers coming to work late or taking more than the allotted time for lunch, and the wide range of excuses they gave for such behavior. The crowd stamped their feet in approval, filling the hall with loud guffaws, but each and every one present knew that Wilkins was speaking the truth. He closed by telling them that changing this behavior was their responsibility because it would do Negroes no good if the NAACP opened the doors after so much struggle and sacrifice, only to have the men and women who passed through the doors throw away their hard-won opportunities by not adapting to the legitimate requirements of work.[15]

Roy Wilkins' quiet self-confidence was often contagious. In September 1955, the NAACP had organized a massive national campaign to protest the murder in Mississippi of a 14-year-old Negro boy from Chicago visiting relatives in the town of Money. In August of that year, a white woman told her husband that young Emmett Till had wolf-whistled at her. Shortly thereafter, Emmett was kidnapped but his body was not found for several weeks. It was raised from a local stream, by then almost unrecognizable because the youngster had been beaten so viciously by the lynchers. Nobody was ever convicted of the crime; a jury of 12 local white men exonerated all of the accused, who sat through the trial wearing arrogant smirks.[16]

The NAACP arranged with Emmett's mother, Mamie, to fill a schedule of appearances across the nation to protest her son's lynching and the federal government's inaction. Early one Sunday in September, Wilkins accompanied Mrs. Till to Harlem's huge Abyssinian Baptist Church ministered by Adam Clayton Powell Jr., U.S. Representative and Baptist theologian. The thousands of seats within the church on this hot, steamy day were filled early. Loudspeakers were set up outside on Lenox Avenue to accommodate the large overflow; as far as the eye could see, every inch of available space between the canyon walls of buildings were filled with Harlem Negroes. The heat made them testy. The rage over Emmett Till's unsolved murder continued to grow, both inside and outside the church. The warm-up speakers, including Rev. David Licorish, Powell's deputy minister, started rousing the crowd. Licorish began to emote a pulsating Baptist-style peroration, in which only a few of the words were comprehensible, but which was clearly directed against whites. Several other speakers picked up this theme and worked it roundly.[17]

Mrs. Till rose and in a low-key manner, punctuated with sobs, described what had befallen her "baby" Emmett. The crowd began to seethe but at least she didn't call for a crusade against all whites. Then Rev. Powell himself took the lectern, beautifully robed, his movie-star-handsome face impeccably shaven, his hair perfectly groomed, his moustache pencil thin. Powell was tall, broad-shouldered and among the most imposing men of the era. He was also a masterful speaker and manipulator of audiences. That afternoon he would forego his Oxford-perfect diction and "get down" with the crowd as a Baptist preacher. He denounced the state of Mississippi and its political leaders, some by name. He called for the punishment of every redneck and cracker in the state, stridently demanding that the murderers of Till be brought to justice. "An eye for an eye," he shouted, "the wrong must be righted!" Then, almost without thought, he began a lengthy cry for a march on Washington right there and then—with no preparation or contemplation of the consequences. The crowd began to respond with cries of "Amen" and "You tell 'em!" Then they started stomping their feet, after which some stood up encouraging Dr. Powell, until everybody was on his and her feet cheering and screaming, "March! March! March!"

Perspiring heavily and wiping his face every few seconds, Powell pounded on the podium to punctuate his points. Then, spent, he sat down to a tumultuous roar. The next and final speaker was Wilkins. He had absolutely no warning that Powell would propose a march on the capital. In fact, he realized that Powell himself may not have known when he stood up to speak that he would call for such a march. Nevertheless, he was facing about 5,000 whipped-up African Americans inside the church and maybe twice that number outside, all chanting "March! March!"

Wilkins walked very slowly to the podium, as if collecting his thoughts. He stood for more than a minute staring at the audience, waiting for the excitement to settle down, speaking not a word. He looked from side to side, then at the middle and the balcony, to give the impression he was looking at everybody present. Then, in his characteristically gentle but firm voice, he spoke with deliberate emphasis:

> Nobody's . . . going . . . anywhere.
>
> There's not going to be any march—to Washington or anywhere else. The minute we get down to 125th Street, we'll lose half of you because it's almost dinner time and you all will want to get some of that good Sunday dinner waiting for you. Get down to 116th Street, and half of the rest of you will drop out cause your feet hurt. By Ninety-sixth Street almost all of the rest will be remembering something else you were supposed to do and that'll be the last of that crowd. By Seventy-ninth Street, only ones left will be Dr. Powell, Rev. Licorish, and me. So hush this talk about a march.

To each assertion by Wilkins, the crowd let out a huge "Amen" followed by whoops and laughter. By the end of his mini-lecture, they were doubled up with laughter, because he had not only seen through their con but had helped them to see through it. The feverish temperature suddenly dropped to a manageable level; everything was back on track. Wilkins then took the opportunity to spell out in detail what he and the NAACP were going to do to avenge the murder of Emmett Till, translating that into acts by individuals like those present, both to give them a sense of participating in this blessed crusade, and to increase the membership rolls of the NAACP. To the relief of the whites in the press corps, and the few white staff members, Wilkins has transformed a short-lived mob into a respectful audience, no less angry about Till's lynching but departing with a feeling that not only could something be done of which they would be a part, but that hope still prevailed.

Acts such as these took more than physical courage; they required the highest form of moral and intellectual courage because the countermoves by any rabblerouser were so easy to employ. One never knew who among such large audiences was a disciple of Marcus Garvey or Malcolm X or Louis Farrakhan, poised to spew the venom that could ignite the tinder of violence. To his credit (and that of thousands of

NAACPers in similar circumstances), Wilkins barely hesitated before jumping into the maelstrom.

There was never any doubt that Wilkins was jealous of his prerogatives as head of the largest, oldest, most powerful, and most important Negro and civil rights organization in America, possibly in the world. An adept political strategist, he set about in 1955 to gradually build a National Board in his image—a Board with a substantial majority who reflected his own philosophy, a Board totally loyal to him. In this long-term effort, Gloster Current became his talent scout by identifying the men and women who met the standards and values set by Wilkins. These loyal Board members, who were obliged to earn their promotions, later constituted "the Caucus" that met in advance of important meetings and determined the outcome of pending matters. The National Board and the leadership caucus were chaired by Bishop Stephen Gill Spottswood of the AME Church, who was elected on April 10, 1961, to succeed Dr. Robert C. Weaver, after President Kennedy named the latter to head the federal housing bureau. That process enabled Wilkins to keep firm control of the organization until the death of Bishop Spottswood, followed four months later by the death of John Morsell.

Only once during Wilkins' long reign as the NAACP's chief did a group of dissidents attempt to unseat him on political grounds. A small band of dissident board members and local leaders called themselves the "Young Turks." Most of them were men in their prime and Wilkins enjoyed characterizing them as "neither young nor Turks." They surfaced for the first time in 1962 during a maelstrom of assaults on the NAACP and its leadership from the rapidly spreading tentacles of the White Citizens Council, which was trying to destroy the NAACP's organizational base in most of the Southern states. At the same time, and with considerable interaction, the NAACP's civil rights "partners" were employing a variety of confrontational tactics that garnered intensive publicity through the national media. The vast attention paid to the activities of SNCC, CORE, and SCLC resulted in a decline in publicity for the NAACP, and a reduction of the number of members and gifts it was to receive during the period. At this worrisome juncture that seemed to occupy every waking moment of Wilkins and his staff, the organization's internal opposition to Wilkins reached its zenith. The Young Turks, having challenged Wilkins' Southern strategy, in which the organization had invested the bulk of its personnel, resources and strategic moves to desegregate the South, demanded a reordering of the NAACP's priorities to cope with the rapidly rising Negro discontent in the cities throughout the North, Midwest, and Far West.[18]

In April 1964, at the NAACP's west coast regional conference in Palo Alto, California, one of the Young Turk leaders, Jack Tanner, called for the resignations of Wilkins and Spottswood, along with the members of the Spingarn family on the board. As the alternative to Wilkins, Tanner and his rebellious colleagues promoted the candidacy of Franklin H. Williams, former NAACP west coast director and then U.S. Ambassador to the United Nations Economic and Social Council. The internal challenge reached the general public the next day, starting with extensive newspaper coverage in the San Francisco Bay area. Wilkins' supporters were furious. The NAACP National Treasurer, Alfred Baker Lewis, a white socialist, described Tanner's attack as "seditious" and demanded that Tanner be expelled from the organization. In fact, a hearing was conducted at the next NAACP board meeting to determine whether Tanner was to be expelled. Tanner was defended by Board member Earl B. Dickerson, who following the vote, successfully moved that the entire debate be expunged form the minutes of the meeting.[19] Only Lewis voted to expel Tanner, whose Board term was not renewed at the end of the year.[20]

Tanner's departure from the Board, however, failed to terminate the Young Turk rebellion. At the close of 1964, Dr. Eugene Reed of Amityville, New York, then the head of the New York State Conference of NAACP Branches, initiated a new challenge to Wilkins by seeking to elect six Young Turks to the national board as at-large members. (Each year the NAACP branches select six at-large members through a weighted voting system based on the size of branch memberships. The results of this process are tabulated at the NAACP's annual meeting, which in that era took place on the first weekend after New Year's Day. It has since been moved to February.) The slate proposed by Reed included himself, attorney Earl B. Dickerson of Chicago, educator Evelyn H. Roberts of St. Louis, businessman Kenneth Guscott of Boston; Dr. Aaron Henry, president of the Mississippi State Conference; and Franklin H. Williams, then an ambassador to the United Nations.[21] Each was a prominent figure from his region as well as nationally.

The media perception was that Reed's group was "attempting to wrest control of the organization from Mr. Wilkins," words used by *The New York Times* reporter in paraphrasing pro-Wilkins board member Robert Ming, one of the nation's most important black attorneys. Dr. Reed denied this charge, instead stating that the Young Turks were seeking to give the branches "more power" that would result in "more militancy and aggressiveness" to meet the competition from the other civil rights groups and to improve the NAACP's financial position.[22] His subliminal message was that Wilkins and his colleagues, staff, and board were insufficiently militant, as a result of which many blacks were turning to CORE, SNCC, and SCLC to participate in the struggle physically and financially.[23] (The membership and contribution records of the period, however, completely contradict this assertion.)

Reed's election gambit, made possible because he was then chairman of the Board's nominating committee, failed to change the power balance on the NAACP Board. Although the dissidents diverted Wilkins and his circle from other important matters and even caused some slight embarrassment, the Young Turks never came close to attracting a majority of the board or of the membership. In fact, they probably never garnered more than 20 percent of the Board.

At the 1968 national convention, the Young Turks organized a vociferous and dramatic attempt to sway the 3,000 delegates assembled in Atlantic City. Although his supporters sought to suppress the outburst, Wilkins insisted from the dais that the opposition be permitted to dominate almost an hour of plenary session time during which dozens of television cameras and their klieg lights added to the drama and encouraged excessive acting out on the part of the Young Turks.[24] The convention delegates overwhelmingly rejected the Young Turks and resoundingly supported Wilkins.

In the fall of 1968, Tanner proposed that branches sympathetic to the Turks' views should withhold money to the National Office, arguing that an economic boycott was the only way to get the NAACP leadership to listen to the rebels' demands. Another Young Turk leader, Chester Lewis of Wichita, Kansas, threatened to form a new college and youth organization and to lead the younger members out of the NAACP.[25] Neither threat proved effective. After that, the Young Turk movement simply died out.

Despite their defeat, many of the Young Turk leaders—Reed, Dickerson, Roberts, as well as Pennsylvania State Conference President Henry Smith and attorney Sam Jackson of Topeka, Kansas—continued their activism as National Board members. Over the next few years the NAACP redirected its focus and resources to confront the pathologies attacking the cities of the North, Midwest, and Far West. General Counsel Robert Carter, who covertly maintained a supportive relationship with the Young Turks, crafted the strategy that resulted in the massive court attack on non-South *de facto* school desegregation. The new emphasis on fair housing and on expanding the housing supply under Housing Secretary William Morris' direction was funded more generously than any previous housing efforts. Labor Secretary Herbert Hill expanded his programs to reach black workers throughout the North and Midwest urban centers. The membership and branch campaigns formulated by Gloster Current devoted more staff and resources to organizing and aiding branches outside the South.

A number of other factors helped to spur this redirection of the NAACP to the North. One was the loss of patience among non-South urban blacks over so many unfulfilled promises by government, often spotlighted by days or weeks of rioting. A second was the dramatic rise both in the number of African-American voters and of black elected officials after the 1965 Voting Rights Act. Scores of Northern black mayors were elected after Carl Stokes won that office in Cleveland, Ohio in 1966.

Although thwarted in their bid for power, the Young Turks' forceful rebellion rhetoric also influenced the NAACP's choices during the remainder of the 1960s and the 1970s, as the civil rights giant balanced the competing demands for its energies, resources, and funds between the South and the remainder of the nation. In this sense, the otherwise ambiguous agenda of the Young Turks may well be regarded as successful since it helped push the Wilkins-led NAACP from a heavily Southern-weighted organization to one in which the South comprised about one-half of the NAACP's resources, reflecting the actual location of the Negro population during those decades. Although there is no evidence that the NAACP leadership ever developed a well thought-out plan or strategy to attack the causes of urban civil unrest, several times during the 1960s senior NAACP staff delivered public statements announcing programs directed towards the riot-riven cities outside the South. General Counsel Robert L. Carter, for example, flanked by program secretaries for labor, housing, education, and other disciplines, declared that he would coordinate a national legal campaign in collaboration with these colleagues to attack the underlying causes of the riots. Labor Secretary Herbert Hill later announced a new NAACP thrust to implement the federal Model Cities program. Carter and Education Secretary June Shagaloff had already begun the process of initiating a school desegregation campaign in cities and towns outside the South. Perhaps the single most decisive factor in the expansion of NAACP programs in the North, Midwest, and Far West was the collective decision making of the new SCF grant makers, in this case mostly foundations. The NAACP undertook only those programs that were assured of significant funding for two or more years. Virtually all of this new foundation funding throughout the 1960s and well into the next decade supported programs outside the South, programs that the senior staff believed to be effective in attacking one or more of the causes of the urban ferment. The Ford Foundation underwrote the most ambitious program—the creation of urban program officers in a number of cities throughout the regions outside the South.

Bishop Spottswood's successor as Board Chair was supposed to be long-time Board member, Wilkins loyalist, and UAW executive William Oliver. Just as the highly popular Oliver was preparing to be elected chairman by the Board in 1975, a nefarious letter was circulated to the board members and to influential African Americans both within and outside of the NAACP. In it the dark-skinned Oliver, whose social graces and diction were not exactly polished, was described as a field hand, a euphemism, one former board member told me, for "an uncultured (and dark-skinned) nigger." Board members were reminded that the NAACP's chairman had never come from the ranks of "field hands" but were exclusively of the lighter-skinned upper caste of Negro society.[26] They included Louis T. Wright, Channing Tobias, Robert Weaver, and Bishop Spottswood himself (before these three, the chairmen had all been white). When this message reached Oliver's ears, he decided to withdraw his unopposed candidacy and to help name the light-skinned, socially prominent, and long-time NAACP activist attorney, Margaret Bush Wilson of St. Louis, to

the
Board Chair. Wilson was elected to the chair at the annual meeting on January 13, 1975, the first African-American woman to hold the post.

There is some persuasive evidence that the men dominating the leadership caucus believed that they would be able to control Mrs. Wilson, largely because she was a woman. They were to learn to their dismay that she was as single-minded and independent as any of the men. Her initial goal was to increase her authority as board chair and to effect the retirement of Roy Wilkins. For the first time in two decades, his control of the NAACP through the Board had been shaken and his control of the organization itself was in question. Despite this turnabout, Wilkins refused to step down until he was ready, appealing to the membership over the heads of the officers and board. The Board Chair and many of the Board members, on the other hand, had concluded that Wilkins's age—75 years—and his declining health converged to produce the moment when Wilkins should step down. Mrs. Wilson and her supporters preferred a younger person to head the organization and, quite possibly, one who was less independent of the Board's will and less popular among the membership. They continued to press Wilkins to agree to a retirement date earlier than he had been inclined to accept.

On July 1, 1976, the fourth day of that year's annual convention being held in Memphis, Wilkins took to the podium of the plenary session to assert that a "campaign of vilification" had been launched against him by "certain members of the Board of Directors" a few days after the death of Chairman Spottswood in December 1974, and "continues to this day." In an address filled with bitter irony, he reported a list of "charges" made behind his back, from feebleness to incompetence to dishonesty to lack of achievement, all of which he vigorously denied. He noted that he had considered suing for defamation of character but was talked out of this course by a Board member whom he greatly respected. He then announced his determination to remain at his post until the next convention scheduled for St. Louis, his birthplace and the city where his mother died, as well the birthplace and hometown of his wife, Minnie. He directly threw down the gauntlet to Mrs. Wilson and her followers on the Board, concluding with these words: "If God is willing I shall be at the St. Louis convention as an active, directing member of the NAACP family. If the Board elects to fire me before that time, then I shall have to call upon you to let me represent your interests directly." The feisty address was met with huge applause, choruses of "We want Roy," and a long-standing ovation. There was no question of who owned the delegates.

Mrs. Wilson had left the auditorium well before Wilkins' remarks. She listened to a tape recording of them, then called an emergency meeting of those Board members she could quickly round up. She issued a statement on behalf of the Board's Executive Committee expressing "their shock and dismay at the statement read by Executive Director Roy Wilkins this morning. The allegations . . . are without foundation," the statement asserted.

The statement then recounted the Board's version of the negotiations between it and Wilkins, noting that originally they had agreed that Wilkins would step down on June 30, 1977, but, in order to better accommodate his successor, they had moved this up to January 1, 1977, believing they had Wilkins's acquiescence. Having made provision for Wilkins to receive a pension, medical coverage, and fringe benefits, the Executive Committee decided to name him Executive Director Emeritus. The statement paid homage to Wilkins's "illustrious career and contributions," recording its distress that he had gone over their heads to the delegates instead of meeting with them that afternoon to discuss his grievances.[27]

The National Board met that afternoon and, recognizing that Wilkins had outflanked them by exploiting his enormous popularity with the vast majority of the delegates, tabled the controversy until the September board meeting, when they would be less subject to pressure from the membership. Their calculations proved wrong; in the weeks following the convention, the membership became even more vociferous in their support of Wilkins, believing his charges that he had been vilified and that certain Board members were trying to push him out earlier than he wanted to leave. The decision was again postponed until the November board meeting when, in a face-saving gesture, the Board backed down. Then, and only then, Wilkins finally agreed to retire on his original timetable—in his wife's former hometown of St. Louis in the summer of 1977 during the NAACP's national convention. There he turned the levers of power over to Benjamin L. Hooks and went home to his modest apartment in Queens, New York, for good.

In connection with such challenges to his authority, Wilkins from time to time also had to face efforts by staff members to by-pass him or reverse his decisions by allying their efforts with Board members. Soon enough the staff came to learn that he brooked no disloyalty from staff members, whom he regarded as extensions of himself. He quickly disposed of disloyal staff members. By way of contrast, he permitted a vocal minority to remain on the National Board and to have their day in the sun at national conventions. He would endure the criticism from these quarters, rather than compel them to depart from the organization or the civil rights movement. As only a rationalist and a professional journalist can, he understood that no one individual is the receptacle of the entire truth.

Being a foe of ideology, he refused to construct his own ideology during his 22 years at the helm of the NAACP. He kept the Association unwaveringly on the path towards integration, at the same time consistently fighting the separatists of each generation. During the 1960s, he unhesitatingly denounced Black Power, the Black Panthers, the new breed of black nationalists, such as Stokely Carmichael, Huey Newton, and Floyd McKissack, as well as SNCC's James Forman, who on May 4, 1969, at the Riverside Church made headlines by demanding $500 million in reparations for African Americans from the nation's white churches and synagogues. ("That's $15 a nigger," Foreman observed.) Wilkins even resisted the vocabulary change from Negro to black that arose during the 1960s (and one may confidently speculate that he would have resisted Jesse Jackson's successful effort to change black to African American.) However, when the press ultimately accepted the change from Negro to black, he adopted it as well.

One of Wilkins' pet targets was so-called Black English, which he confronted with devastating logic and wit, affording countless school administrators and teachers the legitimization they needed to reject what Wilkins described as "suicidal reform." In the late 1960s and the early 1970s, hundreds of American colleges and universities opened their doors to blacks, often in the wake of the national mourning over the deaths of Dr. King and Robert Kennedy, as well as to other so-called minorities. An unprecedented number of scholarships were created for black high school graduates, resulting in a minor explosion of black college students on a high proportion of American campuses.

Parallel to this welcome phenomenon was the partial legitimization by the white-controlled media and some wealthy white supporters of the self-described revolutionary doctrines of such marginal players as Angela Davis, Huey Newton, Bobby Seale, Timothy Leary, Eldridge Cleaver, H. "Rap" Brown, Abbie Hoffman, Tom Hayden, and Ron Karenga. One would be hard pressed to identify a single significant contribution to the advancement of civil rights by any of these individuals or their collaborators. Unfortunately, unknowledgeable individuals of the period, as well as their confused successors in later generations, assigned disproportionate historical importance to them and their alleged achievements. At best, they merited a few footnotes.

Nevertheless, one of the consequences of this process—termed "Mau Mauing the Rich" by writer Tom Wolfe in describing the upper class celebrities who kowtowed before the Black Panthers—was the resurrection of the separatist notion among newly matriculated black college students. On the most basic level, the tendency to retreat to "one's own" was an expression of the sense of powerlessness experienced by a great many Negroes in the decade following *Brown*. Opting for a more restricted environment in a sea of otherness seemed to offer some black students the opportunity to at least control part of their daily lives. No doubt for other black beneficiaries of a more open enrollment policy, the idea of separatism was a means—conscious or otherwise—of self-preservation because of the fear among some black students that they were insufficiently prepared for the higher level of academic competition that the new enrollment policies made possible. For some it was social fear, since a sizable number of black students had never mixed socially, and some even academically, with white students. Given the South's history and customs even in recent times, it is not surprising that some Southern black males were especially cautious of the possible complications of social intercourse with white females. (Others exploited the novelty to the maximum.) Finally, a significant number simply wanted to enjoy the comfortable and safe milieu of an all-black social setting after experiencing the pressures of integrated classrooms all day.

In any event, a great many black students (and students of other ethnic and racial groupings) bought into the concept of segregated living quarters, dormitories, and eating facilities, followed by segregated cultural facilities, meeting places, and even course programs—Afro-

American studies limited to African Americans. Meanwhile, white self-proclaimed revolutionaries such as the Students for a Democratic Society (SDS) and the followers of Mao and Castro, as well as extremist antiwar groups, were already besieging college administrations, sitting-in on college presidents, blocking access to lecture halls and classrooms, calling for strikes that would bar classroom attendance, and so forth. Great institutions such as Columbia, Cornell, and the University of California at Berkeley were forced to shut down at various times.

Therefore, it came as no surprise to some that senior college administrators would knuckle under to the demands of the separatist black students for separate facilities and/or studies. NAACP leaders perceived this quick surrender as a form of racial discrimination, affirming the notion that "the interests of the black students were of little importance to the white campus administrators. Therefore, instead of resolving these confrontations on the grounds of principle or on grounds of the best long-term interests of the black students," they were ready to capitulate for short-term public relations gain. Wilkins dispatched a strong letter to every college and university president and chancellor, condemning this new form of segregation and urging the educational institutions not to surrender to "racial blackmail" either out of expediency or guilt.[28] Using the Wilkins statement to buttress their decisions, the majority of colleges resisted the separatist demands of their black students (often supported by white radicals). However, perhaps about 20 percent—several hundred institutions of higher learning—to their infinite disgrace capitulated to separatism in a vain endeavor to buy temporary peace by betraying principle, and the pattern continued for decades. Even today, some of the nation's most prestigious universities continue to underwrite separatist facilities—Stanford, MIT, and Cornell among them—which has led them almost in a straight line to their later crises of values over the primacy of "multiculturalism" and "politically correct" practices.

In July 1969, the NAACP held its first national convention in Mississippi, less than two months after Charles Evers, its former field secretary and brother of the murdered Medgar, was elected the first black mayor of a Southern biracial town since Reconstruction. (Three days after the NAACP convention concluded in Jackson, Evers was inaugurated mayor of Fayette, less than 100 miles south of the Mississippi capital.) Wilkins took the opportunity to address the NAACP's youth convention that summer, which traditionally runs parallel to the adult convention. The lure of separatism was very much on his mind. As was his wont, he tackled the subject head-on:

> Our young people who form the greatest asset of our race, must first decide to remain Americans and to fight unceasingly for all the rights and privileges of first-class citizenship. If we wander off and follow another star to a land of separatism and going-it-alone, we are charting a journey to a hazardous, even foolhardy future.
>
> And we must examine every invitation to deviate from our arduous and soul-testing task of integration to discover those booby traps which would lead us into the desert of separatism.
>
> Shall our young people give up on the U.S. Constitution and the Declaration of Independence in favor of the sayings of Chairman Mao? Does Chairman Mao know any more about the Delta country of Mississippi, the bayou country of Louisiana, about Easter, North Carolina, or the ghettos of Chicago, Detroit, and New York than we do? Does he have more than a saying with which to attack these conditions?[29]

Using every opportunity open to him, Wilkins energetically denounced those who demanded separation and those who surrendered to such demands. Before a packed audience of delegates and local guests at the 1970 national convention in Cincinnati, Ohio, Wilkins asserted:

> The young black separatists, including a small percentage of black students, are giving aid and comfort to the enemy by calling for separatism. Negroes are dismayed and whites cannot believe their good fortune. Just when white Americans thought they must at last give in and open the doors to opportunity and equality wider and wider, a small school of vociferous young Negroes, including, of all people, some Negro college students, are chanting, "We want to be alone."[30]

In the early 1970s, Wilkins extended the struggle by rejecting racially based studies, such as Afro-American studies. He argued that the major disciplines—that is, history, sociology, economics, anthropology, political science—were already broad enough to include the serious study of the African-American experience. He rejected the notion that a degree from a racially based field of studies could become a professional passport. Despite his reservations about the professional potential of African-American studies, in subsequent years it would manifest substantial growth potential in many American universities, including the most admired of all, Harvard.

On the other hand, Wilkins was not rigidly doctrinaire about the black power phenomenon. "The race pride aspect of black power is a good one," he told a civil rights seminar at the Lyndon B. Johnson Library in 1972, adding:

> The movement to implant classes and courses of black studies were all worthy attempts to make up for past neglect. But the black power harm to the ongoing crusade for citizenship rights of a small powerless minority spread. The slogan was willfully misunderstood by a considerable segment of whites. Worse still, it was flaunted by black folk who did not know that in any showdown at this stage, their group was armed only with a moral argument. So racial separation has grown out of the powerlessness of blacks. While it seeks to build group power, a small black minority has withdrawn unto itself. It seems to be losing devoted followers today, as the realization of the innate evil of racial segregation comes home to more black people, particularly to those who have had their 25th birthday.[31]

Almost sensing that he and the NAACP were swimming against the tide, Wilkins attacked the trend towards polarization, especially in many of the older urban centers. In 1974, he wrote in his syndicated newspaper column:

> The worst thing that could happen to a multi-racial nation like America is for public opinion to become ethnically polarized . . . . No American city can be racially polarized and remain

> American. The nonwhites are merely knocking on the door of American opportunity as have other ethnic groups before them. If a separate and unequal status is created for them, then it will be but a relatively short time before the superior ethnics will fight among themselves.[32]

Wilkins was keenly conscious of his African roots and his Afro-American heritage and, as an intellectual of the 1930s, he was involved with the leaders of the Harlem Renaissance, including his director, Walter White, and his journalistic companion, George Schuyler. Wilkins was especially interested in art produced by American Negroes. In 1968, I proposed to a prominent Madison Avenue commercial art dealer that he sponsor a show by black American artists. Aside from Romare Bearden and Jacob Lawrence, the art dealer—Lee Nordness—expressed doubt that there were enough talented Negro fine artists to warrant such a show. If we were able to identify some, he promised to mount a suitable show, no doubt leaving with the confidence that he would not hear from us again.

Admittedly, an element of bluff was involved, since my knowledge of African-American artists was very limited. But I reasoned that among 26 million American Negroes or, for that matter, any group of 26 million people, there had to be hundreds of talented artists in every field. Familiarity with white artists afforded appreciation of the difficulties encountered by any new artist to break into the Madison Avenue gallery world. I could well imagine how many times more difficult it would be for black artists. Therefore, I insisted at the outset that Nordness approach the project with a view to attracting commercial representatives or galleries for the participants. After he agreed, I cast about until I found an expert in the contemporary art field on whom we could rely for advice. His name was Carroll Greene, then curator of the Afro-American collections of the Frederick Douglass Institute in Washington, D.C. After spending four hours with Greene, I came away confident that there were more than enough talented artists for the proposed exhibit.

The next hurdle was the boss himself. Aside from the usual consideration of scarce resources and more than enough demands for civil rights actions from the field, Wilkins was concerned because of the public relations disaster surrounding the exhibition—"Harlem on My Mind"—earlier that year mounted by the Metropolitan Museum of Art. Not only were few blacks involved in the planning of that exhibit, but also many felt it was superficial, diluted the artistic values of a great museum, and conveyed a paternalistic demeanor by the hosts. Wilkins insisted that these errors were to be avoided, that the highest standards needed to be upheld. The plan was outlined to him and the credentials of Caroll Greene emphasized to show that, as a black art historian, he could carry out Wilkins' objectives.

With two caveats, Wilkins enthusiastically gave us the green light. The first caveat was that, in order to protect Wilkins and those working on the project from Board members and state conference presidents with relatives claiming to be artists who ought to be included in the exhibition, all artistic decisions and choices were to be made by Caroll Greene alone. Second, under no circumstances would this project involve the expenditure of the NAACP's hard-won general funds. In short, every penny for the project had to be raised separately. It proved quite easy to find the few thousand dollars we needed to commission Caroll Greene to undertake the assignment; ultimately, a gala opening night benefit on January 22, 1969, attended by such celebrities as Leonard Bernstein and Gardner Cowles, produced sufficient income to make the project profitable. After the Nordness gallery exhibit concluded, the show was exhibited at Gimbel's Department Store for a two-week "Salute to New York." Thereafter, an abridged edition was assembled for the Smithsonian Institution and shown at its Washington, D.C. museum, followed by a traveling exhibit across the United States for the next two years. With grants from a daughter and niece of Nelson Rockefeller, we were able to create and produce an attractive full-color catalogue. That catalogue accompanied the Smithsonian tour and was sold for the benefit of the NAACP. Immediately after the exhibition, 6 of the 12 artists represented received commercial representation.[33]

However, the *New York Times* reviewer, while according complimentary remarks to each of the artists in the show, objected to the concept that brought 12 Afro-American artists together under one (racial) umbrella, since their styles differed so greatly. (Years later the same critic could find no objection to a Metropolitan Museum of Art show of Latin American artists or another institution's exhibit of works by female artists.) He was not the only critic to be disconcerted by the fact that all but two artists failed to paint "Negro subjects." For example, one of the participating artists—Arthur Coppedge—was represented by two oil paintings of Italian-American women; he resided on Bleeker Street in Greewhich Village and often captured subjects for his painting from his window.

In his introduction to the catalogue, Wilkins repeated the criticism of the *Times* critic who said that "no doubt there are legitimate political reasons for imposing such racial categories on the public consumers these days, but esthetically they make no sense at all." To this early manifestation of "political correctness" Roy Wilkins responded as follows:

> I believe this critic was saying: "That is the way it *should* be," because in his field he is devoid of racial consideration. That, we of the NAACP believe, *is* the way it should be; but it is not that way yet . . . . We are working toward that goal, in part by showing white Americans what Negroes have already achieved as a measure of their potential. In the same way, we are trying to demonstrate to our fellow Negroes their indisputable achievements in all fields—thus, the unquestioned anthologies of Negro literature, poetry, and music; the recent rise of "black theatre;" the new consciousness of Afro-American history. For it is only on the basis of achievement that meaningful pride can be based; and only upon such pride as men and women that we can take our place as equal Americans.[34]

In terms of the range of his interests, Wilkins was the most "well-rounded" intellectual among the national civil rights leaders, followed only by John Morsell and Bayard Rustin. Throughout his 22 years leading the NAACP, Wilkins maintained a global view that impelled him to follow closely the Cold War, the struggle against traditional colonialism, indeed virtually every individual struggle for national freedom in the remotest corners of the planet. He always perceived the connection between the struggle of Negroes for full freedom and the globe's many other freedom struggles. While forcefully condemning Stalinism (to the dismay of some leading ACLU lawyers), he opposed McCarthyism in the 1950s with equal intensity. Early on, Wilkins recognized the twin evils of Nazism and Fascism for the racist threat they posed to most of the world's peoples. He was an eloquent supporter of an independent state for Israel but significantly also expressed support for an independent Arab state in Palestine during a period when few Americans gave the subject any thought.[35]

Wilkins' long-standing passion was, expectedly, the struggle for independence throughout the continent of Africa. He was an original Board member of the first truly successful American lobby for African independence—the American Committee on Africa (ACOA), founded by a pacifist minister, George Houser, who had been incarcerated with Bayard Rustin during World War II as a conscientious objector. The board included virtually all of the luminaries of the American "Old Left"—Norman Thomas, Roger Baldwin, A.J. Muste, A. Philip Randolph, George Haynes, Bayard Rustin, Rev. John Haynes Holmes, Rev. Donald Harrington, and Lester Granger—most of whom were either socialists or pacifists or both—and left-wing defense attorney Conrad Lynn.[36] Wilkins and Granger, his Urban League counterpart, were, of course, mainstream politically. Wilkins especially followed the independence struggles in Ghana, Nigeria, Kenya, and Tanganyika, becoming friends with such legendary leaders as Nkruma, Azikwe, Awolowo, Mboya, and Nyrere. Most importantly, Wilkins kept on the front burner the NAACP's long involvement in the struggle of South Africa's blacks to free themselves from white domination. Few Americans realize that the charter of the African National Congress, Nelson Mandela's party, was based upon that of the NAACP, circa 1910. DuBois sustained the NAACP's interest in the South African maelstrom, which had early influenced Wilkins, and when apartheid reared its ugly head at about the time Wilkins was chosen as the NAACP's leader, he became its implacable and energetic foe.

If his schedule permitted, Wilkins never turned down a chance to speak in support of Israel, the liberation of the captive nations of Eastern Europe, the struggles in Spain and Portugal to overthrow the dictators Franco and Salazar, and similar causes. He understood and appreciated the relationships between and among all of the ethnic and racial liberation struggles; he also appreciated the educational value of his personal appearances before groups of white ethnics who had little or no interest in the Negro's struggle in America, to which many of them had only recently emigrated.

On one memorable day during the 1960s Wilkins received an urgent phone call from me, informing him of a sizable rally of Irish Americans protesting before the British consulate. Irish Americans were not exactly the warmest supporters of African-American liberation, especially after the NAACP's campaign in the courts had resulted in the busing of South Boston children of Irish descent. I urged him to join the rally in support of the struggle of Catholics in Northern Ireland. Thirty minutes later he was being welcomed on the platform by the rally's organizers. He spoke eloquently of the freedom struggles in Ireland and America and how they were connected. Perhaps no convert was produced that day; still, a great many Irish Americans would have second thoughts in the future when they were confronted by black demands for greater equality or opportunity.[37]

It was virtually impossible to deny or ignore Wilkins' universalist approach to human rights—he personified it. At a 1968 human rights conference in Teheran as an American representative, marking the 20th anniversary of the Declaration of Human Rights, Wilkins told the distinguished gathering:

> We Americans are merely beginning to implement a full panoply of economic and social rights which will validate the promise of Americans life. There is not the slightest doubt in my mind despite the hard dialogue and the civil disorders of 1967, about my country's glittering future for all Americans—black men and white, Indians, Protestants, Catholics, Jews, and non-believers. Such a statement is justified by the confidence that the president of the nation, its court system, and belatedly its national legislature, are full committed towards this ideal. The whole country will surely follow, as many of its regions are now doing.

In the same address, Wilkins reaffirmed his commitment to the achievement of human rights wherever denied on the face of the earth, recognizing fully what obstacles stood in the way of their full realization:

> The fabric of human rights is never completed—and may its borders never be limited by the sights of one group, or one generation . . . . The Universal Declaration is properly named. Its

> ideals are universally accepted, but it remains a declaration and not a fact. In part, the problem is the unlimited claim of national sovereignty. I submit that under the United Nations Charter no nation is entitled to wrong its citizens. Either the Charter provisions dealing with human rights have meaning or they are a cruel fraud. If these provisions are meaningful, they must carry their thrust into the boundaries of member states. Human rights violations on this planet (except in Antarctica or outer space) occur in the territories of States.[38]

One of the most revealing facets of Wilkins' worldview came in the autumn of 1971 in, of all places, Mississippi. There former NAACP leader Charles Evers, then Mayor of biracial Fayette and Democratic candidate for governor of the state, was approached by a group of white woodhaulers, rugged outdoorsmen who cut the trees on the land owned by the big paper corporations and hauled the trees to the corporate mills for processing. These men, many by their own admission formerly with the KKK, had been dealt a bad hand by such corporate giants as the Crown Zellerbach, International Paper, and Masonite Company, which arbitrarily reduced the haulers' cash compensation by changing the method of measuring each truckload. Most of the woodhaulers, who owned their own truck and saws, netted barely enough—after expenses on average of about $5,000 a year—to feed their families in good times. Finally, they formed a union and went out on strike. As the strike progressed, some of the striking families were evicted from their homes, others lost their electricity and water, and still others were without food. The reaction of the white majority in the state, including the politicians, was to turn their backs on the strikers. The well-connected paper companies and Masonite somehow persuaded the state government to deny the strikers any benefits whatsoever, including food stamps.[39]

The strikers became desperate and reached out to Charles Evers, the only public figure who promised to aid them—if they welcomed into their union the black woodhaulers as well. The deal was struck. In October 1971, Evers addressed a racially mixed meeting in Hattiesburg covered by some of the national media. Evers then phoned Senator Ted Kennedy and arranged for the woodhaulers to send a delegation to the nation's capital to testify before a Senate subcommittee on the denial of food stamps by the state. Immediately, the Nixon Administration instructed the state to distribute stamps to the woodhaulers' families or risk losing the entire state program.

However, that breakthrough sustained the strikers for only a few weeks more. At this point Evers asked me, as the NAACP Director of Fund Raising, what help, if any, we could give the striking woodhaulers. I went directly to Roy Wilkins and suggested that the NAACP fill the breach with direct aid to the strikers. Wilkins leaped at the proposal and ordered that funds from the NAACP's Emergency Relief Program be distributed to the woodhaulers, white and black. The initial outlay was only $5,000, and when Rev. Kenneth Buford, who directed the emergency relief program in the South, had used up that sum, the NAACP contributed more. Almost 1,000 woodhaulers received a check, ranging from $15 to $40, in November 1971. At least 84 of them, without prompting, immediately joined the NAACP and publicly stated that this act of kindness had already altered their view of the Association and the civil rights struggle. Wilkins knew that this single act would not produce a populist alliance or contribute to the class struggle, but he had no hidden agenda in approving the assistance. It was solely an act of compassion for desperate men and women, who happened to be white and, more likely, on the wrong side of the struggle. We hastily produced a special emergency relief appeal and the NAACP continued to distribute checks to the strikers into the winter months.

As Charles Evers foretold, the new alliance would prove to be a giant step in the state's Olympian effort to overcome its racist past and begin to reconcile its racial divisions.

Evers flaunted his new alliance during his gubernatorial campaign, angering extremists among both whites and blacks. In so doing, he enlarged the moderate middle. The national publicity, which my staff and I orchestrated from New York, became a chronic irritant to the major paper companies with forest reserves in Mississippi, as well as to Masonite. And the addition of the black support, including black woodhaulers that widened the strike to 30 more mills, plus the intrusion of the NAACP into the fray, ultimately persuaded the companies to settle on terms satisfactory to the woodhaulers.

The NAACP's efforts to generate support from organized labor for the strikers' union—the Gulf Coast Pulpwood Association—came to naught, however, when the president of the retailers and wholesalers international union (AFL-CIO) met with the woodhaulers' leader, Jim Simmons, and rejected his request for admission. The grounds for rejection were as Marxist as one could possibly imagine: according to the AFL-CIO's evaluation of the request, the woodhaulers were ineligible for membership because they owned the means of their production—a run-down truck and a gas-powered saw. Ironically, the anti-black and ultra-right wing *Jackson Daily News,* which described itself as "Mississippi's Greatest Newspaper," claimed that the hidden truth behind the strike was that it was a "Communist conspiracy," editorially speculating that Moscow would be keeping a close watch on the strike and subsequent events. "We wonder if Moscow is pleased with such a turn of events down at Laurel," the newspaper asked editorially.

Although the alliance eventually frittered away, Wilkins was extremely pleased that the NAACP had unhesitatingly offered its hand to the down-and-out white woodhaulers. It was, he told staffers, "a lesson" for both blacks and whites.

Ultimately, it was this universal application of the human rights struggle that made the NAACP under Roy Wilkins' leadership so appealing to so many white Americans, as well as Americans of Asian, Native American, and Hispanic descent. From the 1960s forward, the NAACP recognized chapters that were predominantly comprised of individuals from each of those ethnic groups. This universality provided both the overall movement and the NAACP with its moral underpinning. It was what provided a respectable place at the table for those whites, like me, willing not only to support the struggle but also to become a part of it. Indeed, Wilkins' insistence on fostering a universal application of civil and human rights was what impelled appreciative blacks to extend a friendly hand or better to whites who joined them on the picket lines, the marches, the sit-ins, and the other dangerous manifestations of the struggle, and who sat through the long hours, the weekends, and the holidays in grimy motels, often sustained by third-rate food eaten at the wrong hours, while "taking care of business."

Rarely did NAACP staff or members behave with hostility towards white men and women (and those of any other race) within the Association's ranks or staff. Throughout the 1950s and 1960s, a sizable portion of the National Board and of the officers were white, including the president, the vice chairman and the treasurer. The staff heads of two major departments—education and labor—were white, although they were often mistaken as blacks by both whites and blacks. Also white were a number of staff attorneys, the deputy director of the Washington bureau and several other personnel. Because of the clear-cut direction and guidance provided by Wilkins and Morsell, the white staffers were hardly ever confronted by hostile blacks at annual conventions, regional meetings, or in the field.[40]

The other side of the universality coin was also important: Implicit in the NAACP message under Wilkins was that if the roles had been reversed, that is, if a white minority had been oppressed by a black majority, Roy Wilkins would be leading the fight to free white people. The NAACP was therefore counted on by Native Americans, by Japanese Americans whose internment during World War II the NAACP vigorously protested, by poor Appalachian whites weighed down by chronic poverty, by exploited immigrants from Mexico and the Caribbean, and by overlooked American citizens from Puerto Rico. During the White and Wilkins era, the NAACP was in the civil rights business; it was not therefore a lobby for the exclusive advancement of black Americans. The policies it advocated affected all Americans. Wilkins fought long and hard to maintain these distinctions. His successors either failed to understand these distinctions, did not care about them, or refused to expend political capital on such abstractions. The organization and the movement would ultimately pay the price for the abandonment of these values.

Perhaps from his journalism days, Wilkins possessed a sharp eye; he was an extremely keen observer of both the total picture and the details that comprised it. Wilkins was also a consummate charmer of women, his eyes glistening when appreciating a good-looking female.[41] His charm extended to all women and they always gathered around him, knowing how much he enjoyed their company. However, not once in his long tenure at the NAACP National Office did his behavior give rise to the slightest hint of impropriety.

Wilkins' enjoyment of female company, however, was deliberately compartmentalized—he restricted it to social settings. Quite a few female staff members, especially during the 1960s and 1970s, believed that Wilkins and most of his male colleagues were unable to fully accept women as equals, even though most of the Association's active members were women and most of the organizational work, including the nitty-gritty, was performed by women. Since the Board of Directors was overwhelmingly composed of men, and men occupied virtually all of the policy-level staff positions, there was no major outcry against such inequity. Men were more generously compensated to such a degree that the union representing the staff once urged some female members to file a formal protest,[42] which they declined to do (at the same time that Labor Secretary Herbert Hill was counseling ILGWU staff members to protest the union's refusal to permit the staff to organize a union shop that would enable them to bargain collectively).

It is no accident that only a handful of women achieved senior status under Wilkins. They included June Shagaloff as education secretary, Ruby Hurley as regional director of the densely populated Deep South, Althea Simmons as training and education director, Ina Boon and Verna Canson as regional directors in the Plains and Far Western states, respectively, several senior attorneys, and a number of able administrative managers who, in effect, ran the NAACP headquarters. In the mid-1970s, when the women's movement began to make itself heard and felt, the *New York Times* ran a long feature (on what was then considered the "women's page") interviewing female members of the NAACP staff, as well as Wilkins and his male colleagues. The dissatisfaction of the women staffers interviewed was palpable, even as they tried not to embarrass the NAACP or the struggle for racial justice. The awkwardness of the responses by Wilkins and the other men interviewed served mostly to validate the complaints of the female staff members and to demonstrate the deep-seated cultural lag among black civil rights leaders in accepting women as equals. (In later years, female activists wrote several books, revealing similar Neanderthal attitudes of black male leaders inside such progressive organizations as SNCC, CORE, SCLC, and the Black Panthers.) Within the NAACP transformation on gender happened very slowly, gaining considerable ground under Ben Hooks, then suffering a catastrophic setback in the 1990s.

Roy Wilkins had one hobby—his only distraction from his work and his wife. He loved vintage cars and read everything he was able to get his hands on about them. In fact, he loved automobiles in general. Walking down any street with him in the 1960s and 1970s was a memorable experience; almost everybody recognized him and the majority, of all races, greeted him with affection and respect. Network television, especially shows like "Today" and "Good Morning America" and later "Meet the Press" had made him a national celebrity, as did the three networks' evening news. That was a new experience for him and one that he took advantage of, but usually seemed surprised about. When Negroes came up to him to shake his hand, he would never respond abruptly; most of the time he would challenge them to show their NAACP membership card (which he was certain each possessed.) The majority pulled out dog-eared cards, with expirations from an earlier year or decade. They would then get the "50-cent lecture" on renewing their membership with the explanation that it had to be done every year. (It was Wilkins' contention that several million black folks considered themselves NAACP members because they had paid their annual dues once. The notion that those dues had expired was, he said, a difficult one to sell.)

Most whites outside the South admired and respected him as well. Rarely did one see any white person outside the South respond to him with antagonism. That was especially so when Wilkins would stop in mid-stride to regard an exquisite car parked at the curb. He would investigate every facet of it like a rare gem, on occasion kneeling down to look under the chassis. If the driver were in place, he would engage in a detailed inquiry of the vehicle's merits. If he showed any inclination, the driver would often ask him to sit at the wheel, pointing out the new features. The ultimate inquiry resulted in an examination of the motor under the hood. White car owners were extremely gracious in indulging him in these flights from his everyday reality. He clearly enjoyed these experiences, much as a gourmet savors exquisitely prepared food.

In the 1970s, *The New York Times* reported that the owner of Harrah's Hotel and Casino in Reno would soon be permitting visitors to his extensive personal collection of vintage cars. Later the staff was informed that Wilkins was planning a West Coast trip to speak before a number of branches. After his assistant provided a copy of the schedule, I phoned Mr. Harrah in Reno. Without hesitation, he took the call and listened patiently as I explained Roy Wilkins's obsession for vintage cars. Mr. Harrah immediately suggested that arrangements be made for Wilkins to stop off in Reno en route to Los Angeles where he would be the hotel's guest that night. Mr. Harrah said that he would personally conduct Wilkins through the car museum for as long as he wanted to stay. My gratitude was difficult to express, until Mr. Harrah said, "Young man, *I* am the one who is honored. Thank you for giving me this opportunity."

It took no persuasion to gain Wilkins's agreement to take this day off. He could barely wait to leave. When he returned from his speaking tour of the West Coast, he described in mind-numbing detail how he had been received and what he had seen. He sounded very much like a youngster who had been turned loose for a day in an FAO Schwarz toy store.

As already observed, not every characteristic of Roy Wilkins was positive. He was usually distant from his colleagues, except when dealing with business. John Morsell appeared to be "joined at the hip" with Wilkins and was familiar with his thoughts on almost everything, and in fact had made it possible for Wilkins to avoid most of the numbing responsibilities of administration, which he left to Morsell. However, when *The New York Times Magazine* published a cover story about Wilkins in the early 1970s, the NAACP chief told the interviewer that aside from his wife, he was close to nobody. For a time, Morsell felt deeply hurt by this oversight. In fact, Wilkins himself was not a good administrator at all but he delegated those chores to Morsell and others who over time made their boss look like an all-star administrator. Most of the staff tensions and personal fights were left to Morsell to resolve. Wilkins was free to travel for extensive periods, whether for the branches or to an important Washington meeting, because he had John Morsell as his deputy. However, Wilkins was never generous with accolades, possibly because he expected only the best performances from those who worked for him.

Although Wilkins paid considerable attention to detail, it was John Morsell, as his deputy, who was largely responsible for the day-to-day administration of the NAACP, including most of the nitty-gritty work. A former sociology professor at Columbia and a statistician, Morsell was an effective teacher. For example, he would pour over direct mail results of the mailings we organized in the decades before personal computers were available, and, as early as the 1960s, he was adept at identifying correlations and patterns that direct mail specialists did not usually grasp. He would also provide valuable critiques of the foundation proposals we prepared, as well as of the staff reports, in every field of endeavor in which the NAACP was involved. His observations enabled us to make stronger cases before the professional foundation staffs. He continuously briefed us on current and anticipated policies so that we could write and produce up-to-date letters and other materials reflecting the latest policy decisions and program initiatives determined by Wilkins and the Board. Among the senior staff directors, he served as the glue in a running effort to maximize coordination and even synergism, despite the background music from several jealously independent executives. He literally kept his door open to all staff members regardless of rank, and tried to find time to listen to all of their problems, big or small. Because the staff meetings devoted to policy discussions were infrequent, we depended greatly on John Morsell's guidance, as well as Wilkins's weekly newspaper columns and his major speeches for policy direction, including casual indications about what issues preoccupied him at the time. Each week or two, I also made the rounds of the senior staff, either by phone or in person, very similar to my earlier experiences as a city hall reporter, in order to extract from each program director the latest developments regarding their activities and planned initiatives.

Roy Wilkins was also notoriously tight-fisted with the NAACP's money and the staff usually suffered from it. It takes no exemplary imagination to realize that he saw his work at the NAACP as a calling, almost a religious one at that. In his own mind, it followed, therefore, that everyone else should see his and her NAACP work as a calling as well. In sharp contrast to his successors, he turned in to the NAACP every honorarium he received for speaking on the NAACP's behalf. Wilkins was shielded, however, from the day-to-day realities of the struggle for economic survival, especially as it related to the cost of living in New York City. First of all, Roy and Minnie Wilkins had very modest needs and interests—a nice, pleasant middle-class apartment in Queens; an annual trip, often abroad, in their later years; and a small vintage *Triumph* auto. They never had children so neither had a dollars-and-cents notion of what it cost to raise children in the second half of the twentieth century in America, much less in New York City, where most things were 50 percent higher than elsewhere. Finally, Minnie Wilkins herself had achieved a significantly high status within the city's welfare department, where she reached the post of assistant commissioner. Her salary was at least as high as Roy's was and she was eligible for a generous pension.

All of these factors made Roy Wilkins complacent about salaries for his staff and he routinely fought any increases beyond the cost-of-living indexed by a union contract. Because some of his executive staff were exempt from union membership, they were treated by Wilkins unsympathetically when it came to salaries and pensions. As for the latter, until the very last months of Wilkins' tenure in 1977, the provisions for staff pensions were abysmally small. Some senior staff members retired with more than a decade of service to receive a pension slightly exceeding $1,000 a year. However, when Wilkins agreed to retire in 1977, a special arrangement was made to provide him with a decent retirement.[43] It was not until his successor, Ben Hooks, revisited the subject that the NAACP's staff pensions approached the level of those in comparable outside occupations.

The chronically low salaries at the NAACP proved costly in terms of personnel—year after year staffers who had gained their expertise and experience on the NAACP payroll would leave for higher paying jobs in other organizations, corporations, law firms, and government. In the 1960s, a wave of mid-level staff personnel left for the various branches of the Johnson poverty program, usually at double or triple their NAACP salaries. In later years, the best staff lawyers wound up in large law firms for salaries four or five times that of the NAACP, or as federal judges with generous lifetime sinecures. The mediocre lawyers stayed on as long as possible, or until their less-than-satisfactory performances were discovered.

Nothing better illustrates Wilkins' hard-nosed commitment to low salaries than the confrontation he had with General Counsel Robert L. Carter in 1966. Carter had been responsible for creating the SCF, which opened up the door to sizable amounts of new money. With two young sons who would soon be entering college, Carter explained to Wilkins that he could not make it on his current salary of $23,000. He asked Wilkins for a $3,000 raise. Wilkins demurred, pointing out that only he received a greater annual compensation—$26,000. Wilkins said that he did not want a raise and that it would not be permissible for him, as the chief executive, to earn the same salary as Carter. Carter said he really did not care how Wilkins worked it out as long as Carter received the raise he needed. Otherwise, he insisted, he would resign. Either Wilkins thought he was bluffing, or he had already decided to accept Carter's resignation.

Into the fray entered Dr. Ralph Bunche, the former UN mediator and Nobel prizewinner who was a trustee of the SCF. He had learned of Carter's dilemma. As luck would have it, a trustee meeting of the SCF was scheduled for a few weeks hence. Bunche chaired the meeting. He inserted the salary issue on the agenda. Wilkins, an *ex officio* member of the trustees, objected. Bunche ruled him out of order. Bunche then proposed to raise Carter to $26,000 and Wilkins to $29,000. Wilkins objected again, stating he rejected the increase. Bunche ruled him out of order again and, when Wilkins tried to speak, Bunche silenced him by reminding him that he was a staff member who had no vote in such matters. The decision was solely that of the trustees, Bunche added. He quickly rammed the resolution home, leaving Wilkins in a rare state of speechlessness. The raises were adopted. Carter remained. The institution survived.

Wilkins was notorious for canvassing the desks of the staff and collecting errant paper clips for future use. He would periodically phone to harangue those responsible for the direct mail campaigns about the number of returned envelopes that the mass mailings produced because of bad addresses. No matter how many times it was explained to him, he refused to accept the direct mail industry-wide guideline of 5 percent or fewer bad addresses from each list as an acceptable level. Speedy trips were made to the NAACP headquarters to evaluate the "mountains of envelopes," only to find four or five boxes, amounting to a few thousand returns. After a few years of this time drain, our response to such complaints was to dispatch clerical staff who maintained the various lists to count the bad addresses.

Then Wilkins' administrative assistant, Mildred Bond Roxborough, and I devised a plan to make use of the returns as they came in. The NAACP had been producing fewer and fewer pieces of literature that dealt with current and substantive issues. The direct mail letters focused on immediate issues and spelled out the NAACP case for each one in a timely fashion. They were signed by Wilkins and accompanied by folders or newspaper reprints that documented the assertions found in the letter. They were perfect issue guides for the branches, some of which were already requesting copies of the letters for their own education. The headquarters staff proceeded to remove the contents of the returned letters, batch them, and recycle them to the branches, killing two birds with one stone. In the end, we often did not have enough returns to meet the rising branch demand and had to print extra copies of the letters or the enclosures for the branches.

Even this cost-effective solution failed to change the Wilkins crusade against waste. In 1969 Labor Secretary Herbert Hill made a major announcement in New Orleans about a new federally funded Model Cities program. Remembering that Public Information Director Henry Lee Moon mailed all of his press releases in a bundle every Thursday to accommodate the black weekly newspapers (he displayed only the slightest interest in placing stories in the majority media), Hill phoned the New York headquarters and dictated a press release to a secretary to include in Moon's package being mailed the next day. When Hill returned to New York City, he found a note on his desk, commending him on his achievements in New Orleans but taking strong issue with the $1.86 long distance phone charge he had incurred. Hill went to Wilkins to explain his reasoning. Wilkins told him the release could have waited another week; after all, he was "spending the members' money."

According to another former staffer, shortly before his death, Medgar Evers was attending an NAACP meeting in New York. He was obviously unhappy and explained to his staff colleague that Wilkins had reprimanded him in writing because his expense account addition was off by three cents!

During the peak years of the larger civil rights movement—the early and mid-1960s—the major press and broadcasting media adopted a journalistic formula that apparently was first employed by *The New York Times,* then the single most influential and admired publication in the nation. The radio and television networks and many of the national magazines, as well as other newspapers, seemed to take their cue from the "good, gray" *Times* on how and when to cover many of the most controversial public issues before the nation. The *Times* itself had recruited and trained the best collection of written media correspondents in the nation, perhaps in the world, and for the most part these job-tested, experienced, and well-educated men and women were given free rein to pursue their stories wherever they led. Their civil rights coverage as a whole was unequaled in the print media, though other print publications, including the *Christian Science Monitor,*

Chicago Sun-Times, Washington Post, Wall Street Journal, Time, and *Newsweek* at times also produced stellar and insightful reports.

But the *Times* remained the standard for all and, in a misguided effort to avoid favoring any of the major civil rights players, which they tended to equate with objectivity, the *Times* devised a format that, when an issue arose requiring comment from the Movement leadership, it would display across the top of a page photos and brief comments of roughly equal length from "The Big Five" or "The Big Six"—the NAACP's Wilkins, SCLC's King, Urban League's Young, CORE's Farmer, and SNCC's Lewis. (Occasionally they would add Randolph of the Sleeping Car Porters or Dorothy Height, president of the National Council of Negro Women, and later Rustin of the Randolph Institute.) In this way, the *Times* proclaimed that all five (or six) were of equal prominence, importance, and, by extrapolation of the readership, of equal power, competence, effectiveness, and worthiness. The other media often copied this format, again transmitting this arbitrary equality to the predominantly white audience. This in turn influenced foundations, individual donors, and later corporations in terms of their giving habits and preferences.

Wilkins had a difficult time accepting the mass media's overriding concentration of press coverage on Dr. King. He fully appreciated King's charismatic demeanor and speaking ability and welcomed it as another powerful weapon in the civil rights movement's arsenal. Wilkins also perceived how successful King had become in converting whites to the integration banner. However, Wilkins believed that the NAACP remained the single most important component of the struggle, the only one with a significant membership and outreach in every single African-American community in the nation, with a stellar record in the courts and in lobbying in the halls of Congress and the state capitols. With the possible exception of its sister agency, the National Urban League, the NAACP was the only proven long-distance runner.

When all was said and done, Wilkins' civil rights contributions covered at least 46 years (1931 to 1977), whereas King's not more than 13 (1955 to 1968). Yet, historians after King's death labeled King "the great leader"—the man who contributed the most to the struggle. These were difficult consequences for Wilkins to swallow, especially since Wilkins was acknowledged by his peers and most of the press to be the intellectual superior of all the key players and the one who wielded the most power. It is to Wilkins's credit that he managed to contain his dissatisfaction with this state of affairs by limiting it to his closest colleagues—in almost every dispute with another civil rights organization, Wilkins sought to keep it within the "family."[44]

There is no doubt, however, that King and some of his lieutenants tried Wilkins' patience on a half dozen or more occasions, when they gave the press highly critical or unkind statements about the NAACP or Wilkins. The written correspondence, some of which has already been cited, reveals that Wilkins answered in measured and careful language (almost as if he were writing for history), refuting the statement(s) he found erroneous, and avoiding name-calling and any other form of expression that would require a break with Dr. King or others.

Similarly, when his National Board and some staff members pressed him to confront the NAACP Legal Defense Fund head-on and demand that it abandon the use of the NAACP's initials, Wilkins avoided such showdowns, and continued to cooperate with the LDF and Jack Greenberg after Thurgood Marshall had left, even appearing at its annual convocation as if the NAACP were still being significantly served by LDF (land after several of his staff urged him not to attend). Despite the confusion of donors in every category over the status of the relationship between the two entities (there was no question that scores of donors every year made gifts to the LDF believing they were supporting the NAACP), Wilkins argued that most of those who read about the LDF's legal victories in the press thought that the NAACP had been responsible. This was certainly true among many local branches that were solicited by LDF attorneys to identify plaintiffs among their members or later to become their plaintiffs in court actions. All too often, these LDF lawyers neglected to explain to the branch leadership that they were no longer connected in any organic way with the NAACP and in fact were competing with the latter for support.

Beginning with the first NAACP General Counsel Robert L. Carter, the NAACP tried to halt this undiplomatic practice, which some regarded as ambulance-chasing, by forbidding branches to make such arrangements without the approval of the Legal Department, or by insisting to the LDF that it seek the NAACP's permission in advance of any arrangement with an NAACP branch.[45] None of these devices stood up over time, and Wilkins made no effort to enforce them through the Branch Department (which was a measure of his ambivalence on the subject). The LDF, its proponents have argued, had no choice but to pursue such a route because, having no membership and no built-in constituency, it needed to identify and recruit plaintiffs through the NAACP branches if it were to remain in business. The NAACP basically monopolized the African-American constituency, though not infrequently, the LDF would represent a local SCLC, CORE, or SNCC unit until virtually all of them disappeared as serious civil rights entities by the mid-1970s.

In the 1980s, the NAACP benefited from a landmark Supreme Court decision won by the UAW that, in effect, declared that membership organizations like the UAW (or NAACP) had automatic court standing in any community where they could demonstrate that they had a respectable number of members. Thereafter, essentially any locality where the NAACP had a branch provided it with automatic standing to go to court on its behalf without having to recruit individual plaintiffs or even to expose them to any reprisals. That decision greatly aided the NAACP's lawyers, and helped to reduce the cost and time required for suits.

It should also be noted that several other legal defense entities involved themselves in civil rights cases. The two most effective, after the LDF, were the ACLU and the Lawyers' Committee on Civil Rights, both of which maintained close and cordial relationships with the NAACP national office and with its legal department. They usually sought permission in advance to represent NAACP units and often shared the work on the suit with the NAACP.

Although Roy Wilkins often bridled at the attention accorded Dr. King in the mass media and bemoaned the presentation of all of the active civil rights groups as equals, he had very close relations with Whitney Young (and his successor Vernon Jordan) and John Lewis (of SNCC), and worked amicably with Jim Farmer of CORE, who had earlier worked for Wilkins. He openly admired A. Philip Randolph, who was his senior, and, despite his objections (mostly for the record) to naming Bayard Rustin the coordinator of the 1963 March on Washington, he and Rustin were increasingly close from that time onward. Randolph, Rustin, Young, Jordan, and at times Farmer, understood fully that the heart of the civil rights movement and its *only* muscle was the NAACP. They might be divided by tactical disagreements but they would never break publicly over them.

It would be a serious mistake to assume from these recollections that Roy Wilkins sought to be the sole leader of the only African-American organization struggling for the achievement of civil rights. A superb strategist, Wilkins saw the great value of having a number of serious "players" of varying degrees of perceived militancy within the movement. He provided financial and other support to both SCLC and SNCC, aided CORE with bail money and legal help, and took a back seat to Whitney Young's campaign to move the big corporations into the civil rights camp. He appreciated the advantages of occasionally having the players issue contradictory statements; he knew how to play off the militancy of SNCC or CORE to persuade conservative legislators that unless they adopted the NAACP's proposals, they would be faced with far more radical alternatives later.

He was especially angered when whites criticized African Americans for not speaking with a single voice, a condition that nobody ever suggested for white Americans. As far back as 1922, Congressman Leonides Dyer, the major sponsor of the antilynching law in the House, lectured the congregation of a black church in St. Paul that "colored people . . . instead of standing together . . . fight among themselves about who shall 'lead' or 'hold office.'"

In his autobiography, Wilkins angrily denounced this notion of one spokesperson or one organization for black America:

> The argument that blacks should entrust all their interests to a single organization has always been wrong; black interests are too broad and varied to be contained in such a tight compass. But there has always been a tendency among us to carve one another up over questions of leadership, when discrimination and inequality have provided more than enough targets to shoot at, more than enough work to go around.[46]

No statement better explains Wilkins' views on the validity of having a number of organizations in the struggle, nor of his common-sense commitment to the important priorities.

Lastly, it is impossible to define the Wilkins philosophy without understanding his initial premise—that blacks are a permanent American minority of 11 or 12 percent and therefore cannot effect the earth-shaking change required to eradicate racism and gain parity for blacks without the support and help of a sizable proportion of the white population. Wilkins was acutely conscious of the disproportionate distribution of power—economic, social, and political—in white hands. In 1975, he reaffirmed his commitment to an integrated struggle to achieve integration, for practical, as well as moral, reasons:

> Truth to tell, integration is the only philosophy that goes anywhere under the present circumstances where there is a minority of 10 to 90. Until black people build up the retail field, reduce their number of household domestics, improve their landholding class (farmers and non-farmers), find a way to employment in all brackets, fight their way to good solid education, and are housed freely in all kinds of neighborhoods, they might as well forget going it by themselves.
>
> Blackness is not enough. It helps by instilling knowledge and pride, but it falls short. When it gets down to the money-on-the-table stage and to the subsequent operating phases, there are few who will come up with the cash and have discipline enough to operate a business and see that costs are met.[47]

He never lost sight of the overwhelming amount of military power controlled by white leaders from the president on down. He viewed the use of arms to advance the struggle of blacks in this nation as a fantasy, and a suicidal one at that. While working as the editor of the Kansas City *Call* in the late 1920s, a black newspaper that he took over and transformed into a militant opponent of Jim Crow, Wilkins was so outraged by a particularly bloody lynching in a nearby town that he began to organize a group of young black men to retaliate with their own violence. Before he could carry out the scheme, however, he came to his senses:

> It didn't take me long to realize how ridiculous the idea was. We could not have made the fantasy work; we would have invited our own deaths instead. In this country, black people are a permanent minority and we will never have the numbers or the guns to stage a successful armed revolution. This is a hard reality, and it make it revolutionary cults little better than suicide cults.[48]

Simply because Wilkins rejected the use of violence as the Negro's path to liberation did not in any way make him a turn-the-cheek pacifist. In 1966, he wrote: "Today nonviolence is stridently challenged on the premise that Negroes must defend themselves when attacked. But the right of Negroes and of all others to self-defense is not truly an issue. The NAACP has always defended this right."[49]

Wilkins was always concerned with the perception of things, particularly among the white majority, which persuaded him to rule out the pursuit of change through violent means, not on any moral basis alone, but also and most importantly, on pragmatic grounds. Again, in 1966, at the apogee of national agitation for civil rights, when the guardians of Jim Crow found their backs to the wall and became even more dangerous, Wilkins counseled common-sense restraint.

> What we oppose, is the doctrine that Negroes should stand in armed readiness to retaliate and deal out punishment on their own. The record of unpunished murders of Negroes and civil rights workers makes this position emotionally understandable, but its fruit would be disastrous. As private vigilante vengeance, it would inevitably breed white counter-vigilantism and would furnish a pretext to any law officer wishing to "crack down" on Negro protest.[50]

In terms of practical politics, this philosophy impelled Wilkins to confront the Black Panthers and other purveyors of Black Power at a time when both were becoming increasingly popular with blacks in almost every locality, including many local NAACP branches. Referring to the slogan "Black Power," he warned:

> No matter how often it is defined, this slogan means antiwhite power. In a racially pluralistic society, "Black Power" has to mean that every other ethnic group is the antagonist. It has to mean "going it alone." It has to mean separatism. We of the NAACP will have none of this. We have fought unceasingly for genuine pride of race and for the inherent nobility of equal citizenship. We deny that racial dignity requires the ranging of race against race.[51]

Few of Wilkins' contemporary leaders and virtually none today were capable of such reasoned eloquence.

Not only did this closely held premise lead Wilkins to denounce every suggestion by blacks to take up arms as a path towards freedom; it also contributed to his near-obsession on behalf of the construction of coalitions, especially those that drew in powerful white organizations and institutions. Over and over again, he pounded home the need for working coalitions into the minds of his staff. He measured the effect of major initiatives on how they might help or hinder the growth of closer coalitions. He and Clarence Mitchell invested an enormous amount of time, energy, resources, and good will in the development of the greatest private coalition ever formed in our nation's political history—the LCCR—and he and Mitchell worked very hard to maintain control of this unprecedented "people's lobby."[52]

Sometimes, in the interests of keeping the coalition together, Wilkins tolerated temporary backsliding, for example, in holding the national trade unions together to lobby Congress for the Voting Rights Act, at the same time that some of their locals were simultaneously fighting the NAACP's efforts to open up their ranks to black apprentices and members. On the other hand, he never countenanced the sacrifice of poor blacks or other minorities simply to sustain such coalitions. After the health and growth of the NAACP branch structure and membership, which was always his first priority, the pursuit of coalitions was the runner-up during the Wilkins reign.

Although the staff trained, advised, provided technical information and legal knowledge, and offered encouragement, the gains registered by the NAACP for the most part were the product of the efforts made by its volunteer membership, an achievement without precedent in this nation's history. How much of this would have naturally occurred during the organization's evolution, it is difficult to judge. However, there is little doubt in my mind that Roy Wilkins, a conscious product of the enlightenment, a rationalist, and a humanist, convinced of the ultimate perfectibility of mankind and dedicated to the efficacy of education as the principal tool for enlightened change, raised the NAACP membership's level of training and knowledge to a height few others would have dared to attempt. His legacy was the army of thousands of militant change agents who stayed the course over three decades and carried on until the 1990s, some ready to fight any challenge within their communities, others rising to the fray only when a local development became a recognized threat.

13. The NAACP Develops Financial Muscle

Why do I rob banks? Because that's where the money is.
Attributed to notorious bank robber Willie Sutton, circa 1950s

By 1965, it was becoming clear to the insiders in the movement that the civil rights issues were less and less simply black and white. As political gains began to increase and federal laws broadened to cover most exigencies, supported by favorable Supreme Court decisions, the leaders of the movement, including those of the NAACP, came to realize that the economic and social problems of African Americans were less readily addressed by either court decisions or federal legislation, or by protest and confrontation. The new complexities—including the expanded legal definition of who constituted a member of a minority group—required more initial knowledge and data, greater research, and more nuanced strategies. Even during the early 1960s, Wilkins often lamented that the size of his current staff was inadequate to confront these new challenges.

At the same time, General Counsel Robert L. Carter was crafting a proposal to the IRS to obtain tax-deductible status for a new entity that could tap foundation, corporate, and large individual gifts competitively with sister agencies, and thereby support an expanded staff, including academically trained specialists. After the IRS decided affirmatively on Carter's submission, Wilkins insisted that the proposed entity be structured in such a manner as to guarantee its total control by the NAACP executive director and board. He was not in any mood to countenance another defection, as had taken place when the LDF, initially under Thurgood Marshall and later under Jack Greenberg, chose to strike out in new directions, formulating and executing new policies, without any serious discussion—much less prior agreement—with the NAACP.

Robert Carter's task, as NAACP General Counsel, had been to devise a model acceptable to the IRS that was neither independent of its parent nor incorporated in its own right, but that could receive tax-deductible gifts (the only kind made by foundations and corporations) to support programs that were either charitable or educational, the two principal categories for IRS designation of what are commonly known as 501(c)(3) agencies. In a series of memoranda, Carter persuaded the IRS that certain programs of the NAACP were inherently tax-deductible (that is, either charitable or educational, or both) and therefore automatically merited that designation. He proposed that the NAACP, as the parent, organize a wholly owned subsidiary whose trustees would be elected annually by the NAACP's National Board of Directors. Those trustees would guide the new entity's choice of programs, finances, staff appointments, and related matters, but it would carefully avoid any form of lobbying or political activity. The trustees would select their own officers, adopt budgets suggested by the national staff and the board's budget committee, and represent the new entity before potential donors, but it would not initiate new policies. Indeed, all of its substantive decisions were subject, directly or indirectly, to the approval of the NAACP national board. If these measures were not sufficiently structured to ensure total control by the national NAACP, the corporate secretary of the new entity was to be automatically the executive secretary (later executive director) of the NAACP itself. Thus, Wilkins held the key position in the new entity as well. So did his successors.

Carter's submissions to the IRS included the proposal for a separate set of books for the new entity to record both contributions and other income and all expenditures. Finally, this system permitted dividing allocations between the new entity and the NAACP national office both in respect to personnel and overhead.

The model created by Robert Carter became the prototype for scores of other activist agencies both in civil rights (CORE, ADL, SCLC, ADA) and other activist fields (NOW, Sierra Club, ACLU, AAUN, and so forth). It made possible the suddenly large and increasing flow of new support for these and other causes that had heretofore been supported, in the main, by individuals paying membership dues or making small nondeductible gifts. Within a few years foundation behemoths like Ford, Carnegie, and Rockefeller, as well as corporate giants like AT&T, General Motors, IBM, and Exxon, were recruited as supporters of civil rights, civil liberties, women's rights, ethnic group advancement, environmentalism, consumerism, urban development, and population control.

For the NAACP, the new entity—named the NAACP Special Contribution Fund (SCF)—opened the door to a totally new level of support that was inherently far more cost effective than that of the membership and branch operations, which had until then accounted for most of the NAACP's annual income. Because NAACP membership dues were so inexpensive—initially one dollar, raised to two dollars in the 1960s, then five dollars in the 1970s, $10 in the late 1980s, and modified in the early 1990s to deprive a regular member of *The Crisis* magazine unless he or she paid $15—the NAACP was unable to effectively utilize direct mail to either recruit or renew memberships. At each period, the cost of mailing and the rate of return were such that it would be impossible to break even, so long as the dollar unit most often requested was so low. As a result Roy Wilkins was wholeheartedly opposed to the use of direct mail by the NAACP. As the individual directing the development of the SCF staff, one of my first tasks was to dissuade him of this view.

A system begun under Walter White and refined by Gloster Current under both White's and Wilkins's leadership relied on face-to-face annual solicitations by the membership, especially during two membership-week drives at two different times during the year. The monetary cost to the organization of the time, energy, and transportation of the volunteer members who solicited renewed memberships and new memberships was relatively small—printing and transporting membership envelopes, some posters, and the staff time of a few executives and secretaries.

In 1965 the NAACP's sole financial reserves were comprised of life membership dues requiring a total contribution of $500, either at one time or in as many as 10 annual installments of $50. In practice, the NAACP used $50 of any larger dues amount, or the entire sum if the annual payment were $50 or less, for current operations. The remainder went into an interest-bearing account that served as a reserve against bad years. After several decades, the reserve had grown to a multi-million dollar cushion against more difficult financial periods, that is, periods when the Association operated at a deficit. (In 1965 and for all previous years, dues in any amount were not tax-deductible —thus, an individual could not list it as a charitable gift on his tax return and deduct it from gross adjusted income. Nor could a corporation or foundation purchase a life membership and deduct it as a gift. Some corporations evaded this restriction by purchasing life memberships or banquet tickets with funds from their promotional or public relations budgets.)

By the early 1960s, the large-scale assaults on Jim Crow in the South by CORE, SNCC, SCLC, and the NAACP resulted in widespread arrests, which increased as large numbers of volunteers from outside the South joined the demonstrations. The local magistrates would require bail bonds of $100 to $200 for the release the next day of those arrested, pending a trial some months hence. Most of the demonstrators were long gone by then and the cost of bringing them back, putting them up over night and feeding them, and then providing legal counsel, was usually far in excess of the fines imposed by the magistrates, whose rule of thumb was to ascertain the amount of the bail and then fine the absent accused the same amount.

Since the NAACP was the only civil rights organization with a substantial income (other than the National Urban League), it often provided the money required for bail. Very little of this sum—perhaps as much $3 million during the 1960s—was ever repaid. The effect on the NAACP's finances was significant; as its financial cushion deflated, it was compelled to juggle its resources precariously in order to overcome the valleys of income by marking time until the periodic peaks were achieved. Further, the needs of the branches and other demands upon the NAACP national office so greatly exceeded its financial resources that the board almost always voted to spend what appeared to be its last dollars on the immediate crisis in the firm belief that the

"Lord and the membership" would somehow find a way to carry on. He, or they, usually did, but even the tight-fisted Wilkins, who pursued the most conservative financial strategies, faced several large year-end deficits.

Into this mix arrived the SCF in early 1965, one year after the IRS made its historic ruling. The intervening 12 months had been employed in drawing up the by-laws and charter of the SCF, accompanied by some heated staff and officer discussions, as well as the search for someone to assume the responsibility for raising the funds and defining the nature of the SCF, which was still a paper entity. During 1964, the NAACP national office had raised a sum of slightly over $1 million, virtually all of it from its membership, which was overwhelmingly black. Indeed, the NAACP was then and remained for the next three decades the only national civil rights organization the majority of whose income came from African Americans. At the time, only the black churches like the African Methodist Episcopalians, the AME Zion, and storefront evangelicals, as well as the black sororities and fraternities and a few professional societies, were supported primarily by dues, tithes, and/or gifts from African Americans. On the civil rights front, neither LDF, CORE, SNCC, SCLC, PUSH nor the National Urban League ever relied in large measure on support from black members or contributors. Except for the National Urban League, which long enjoyed tax-deductible status, their annual income was a small fraction of that of the NAACP.[1] The Urban League relied almost exclusively on mainstream corporate support but once the NAACP, and Wilkins in particular, began to canvas the big foundations for support during the last five years of the 1960s, he helped open their doors for many other minority agencies, including the National Urban League, even though very few of those Wilkins visited actually decided to support the still-controversial NAACP.

On the other side of the coin, the left-of-center "activist" foundation leaders and boards, including the Field Foundation under Leslie Dunbar, the New York Foundation under John Heyman, the New World Foundation under Vernon Eagle, the Stern Foundation under Phil Stern, the Norman Foundation under Andrew Norman, and the Helen Rubinstein Foundation under Diane Goldstein, individually and collectively rejected the NAACP as too "middle-of-the-road" or "middle class" for their taste, designations that had gained prevalence in some of the most influential white-controlled press. Each the product of enormous family wealth, several of which were directed by millionaire scions, these vanguard foundations were seeking "true revolutionaries" who represented the "rural proletariat" of the South. For the most part, these foundations, like their media counterparts, viewed the NAACP as far too mainstream to seek the degree of societal change they believed necessary. With a few exceptions, largely in support of NAACP Labor Secretary Herbert Hill's initiatives, these foundations directed their grants to Dr. King, the Legal Defense Fund, CORE, and/or SNCC and their offshoots. A few, most particularly Field Foundation's Les Dunbar and New York Foundation's John Heyman, strongly criticized Wilkins's administration of the NAACP, particularly when they conversed with other foundation administrators.

Whereas the NAACP's net return over costs from mass memberships was chronically either negative or paper-thin, the surplus above the cost of generating and servicing NAACP Life Memberships had been substantial. That alone indicated one route for the new SCF's development strategy: attracting larger unit gifts at every level. The largest single gift ever received from an individual by the NAACP prior to 1960 was $10,000 and was highlighted in the 1959 *Annual Report.* For 95 percent of the membership fees, the average was between $5 and $10 in 1965. On the other hand, there was no way to measure how much in additional membership and contribution dollars these $5 dollar members generated during the course of a year from backyard barbecues all the way up the philanthropic ladder to black-tie formal dinners.

Although the strategy of soliciting larger-sized gifts from sources outside the Association—corporations, foundations, and wealthy individuals—may have appeared self-evident, it had been for the most part ignored until the formation of the SCF. One of the major reasons was the reluctance of Wilkins (and his predecessor) to ask for money outside of the organization. A peerless fund-raiser when directing his appeal to the branches, individual members, or large meetings at the annual convention, Wilkins felt inhibited when assigned the task of soliciting outsiders. Moreover, the rule of thumb for the period (1960s and earlier) was that organized labor was the NAACP's special friend, whereas corporations and big foundations were on the other side, if not the enemy. That posture emanated almost directly from the New

Deal era, which more than anything else shaped the political psyche of liberals, white and black, after World War II. The popularity of Marxist thinking among Communists, Socialists, and other "intellectuals" included a blanket condemnation of big business as *the* enemy. Most liberals avoided seeking nonliberal sources of money for liberal causes, including civil rights. But by the middle of the 1960s, it was becoming clear that grassroots resistance to change was highly virulent among the rank-and-file membership of organized labor. NAACP leaders, especially Labor Secretary Herbert Hill, were receiving hints from corporate executives that they were prepared to lower some racial barriers to employment but that the local labor unions prevented them from acting. Lockheed officials in Georgia were among the first to suggest that the NAACP target both management and labor in their plants in order to open the doors to Negro workers.

The school desegregation suits filed by the NAACP in major cities, beginning with Detroit and Boston, in the late 1960s, impacted heavily upon working-class neighborhoods inhabited largely by white union members. They and their families feared an invasion of black children attending the same schools as their children. The NAACP-led school desegregation campaign, which during the next decade spread to most of the major cities outside the South, partially contributed to the hardening of antiblack attitudes among rank-and-file union members. Irrationally, that racial bias carried over even to leading black trade unionists like A. Philip Randolph and Fred O'Neal, president of Actor's Equity, as well as to staunch trade union advocates like Bayard Rustin.[2]

Try as the national leadership of the AFL-CIO and some of the leading officers of its more liberal member unions might to move their followers in support of the civil rights struggle, grassroots resistance continued to grow. The increasingly aggressive use of Title VII of the 1964 Civil Rights Act, particularly by NAACP Labor Secretary Herbert Hill, who filed complaints faster than the NAACP legal department could process them, began to open doors for some Negro workers, at the same time contributing significantly to a white worker backlash.

These realities slowly sank into the mindsets of the NAACP leadership that, under Clarence Mitchell's deft diplomacy, was collaborating closely with labor's national leaders in Washington on a host of legislative matters. By chance, in early 1965 Wilkins happened to be a guest of the Schenley Corporation at a dinner honoring its founder, Lewis Rosensteil. The liquor magnate took the initiative in sitting down next to Wilkins to engage him in a lengthy conversation, after which Rosensteil handed Wilkins his card and urged him to phone for another meeting. A few weeks later Wilkins met again with Rosensteil at Schenley headquarters. After a few niceties, Rosensteil withdrew an envelope from his coat pocket and handed it to Wilkins with a smile. The envelope held a check for $50,000, the largest single gift to that date in the NAACP's 56-year history. Wilkins was stunned and almost lost his voice in expressing his appreciation. Aside from the obvious benefits, the event persuaded Wilkins that substantial sources of external support were possible, although in fact the NAACP did not actively target corporations for another four years. Even without a serious corporate campaign, some of the more enlightened corporations, guided by pioneering black executives like Harvey Russell of Pepsi-Cola, Abe Venable of General Motors, Tom Shropshire of AT&T, and Lee Archer of General Foods, began to make annual gifts to the NAACP SCF, now that tax-deductible status was available.

In 1969, Deputy Director John Morsell and I, as SCF's director of fund-raising,[3] decided to test the potential of corporate support by visiting five corporations that I selected. All were headquartered in New York City but represented different industries. We were both surprised and pleased with the reception we received from each of the corporations, whose staffs had done their homework thoroughly, using their own sizable research capabilities. They already knew far more about the NAACP than we knew about them. What the corporate research had uncovered appeared to be received quite favorably. Not only did all five commit themselves to support the new tax-deductible SCF; each asked the NAACP's advice and, if possible, assistance in helping to solve long-term personnel requirements. One company projected the need for 20,000 well-educated high school graduates by the end of the decade. The representatives actually asked if the NAACP could help identify such skilled individuals. Dr. Morsell, an educator himself, patiently explained that the prerequisite was to overhaul the public education system by starting with the youngest and moving upward in age. Only in that way, he explained, could the system ultimately turn out enough educated and skilled graduates at the end. Clearly, that was not the answer sought by the corporate executives.

The other side of the coin—African Americans as consumers—was also a major priority for these corporations. They had already recognized that black Americans, despite their lower salaries and higher rates of unemployment, constituted a potentially major market within the United States equivalent to the fifth or sixth largest foreign economy. Even in 1969, African-American purchasing power exceeded an estimated $175 billion.[4] It took no great imagination to conjure what this segment of our society might reach if blacks ever approached economic parity with whites.

For the next two decades, these two themes—the increasing number and improving status of African-American employees within each corporation and the black share of each consumer market—became the dominant criteria in persuading corporations to contribute to the NAACP. At Morsell's request, I drafted a plan to pursue corporate gifts systematically. Recognizing that virtually every corporate-giving officer in the NAACP's sphere of interest was at the time an African American, I recommended that the new initiative be organized within the NAACP headquarters staff and manned by African Americans, with advice and support from the professional fund-raisers. Wilkins approved the plan but the personnel selected never demonstrated the ability or the work ethic to extract more than a small percentage of the vast potential from the corporate world. The biggest problem was the absence of daily supervision; since the corporate solicitation staff was operating out of the national office and was on the SCF's payroll, they were reluctant to take orders from someone outside their realm of authority. With no senior staffer at headquarters responsible for watching over them, they seemed to work fewer hours than was necessary for the magnitude of the job. Some were overwhelmed with personal problems; others delved into outside projects while using their affiliation with the NAACP to gain access to resources. The problem under Wilkins was simply the absence of time or keen interest in following the corporate effort day to day.

Nevertheless, by 1976 the total annual income from corporations had risen to almost $436,000, a sum greater than the annual budgets of CORE, SCLC, or SNCC in earlier years. (A year after Ben Hooks succeeded Wilkins as the NAACP's CEO, a totally new approach would trigger a process leading to a level of corporate support never dreamed of under Wilkins. In fact, the annual income from corporations would eventually become the single largest source of income for the combined National Office and SCF.)

On the foundation front, the number of targets for civil rights support could be counted on the fingers of both hands. In addition to the five or six relatively small foundations identified earlier, which considered themselves in the vanguard of the civil rights struggle, four of the nation's largest foundations were enlisted in the struggle during the three-year period beginning in 1965. By mid-1965 I arranged a meeting between Wilkins and MacGeorge Bundy, the new president of the Ford Foundation. Bundy's already strong interest in and commitment to civil rights were stimulated by the meeting.[5] Under the direction of John Coleman, former president of Haverford College and at one time active in the local NAACP chapter in Pittsburgh, Pennsylvania, the generally liberal Ford Foundation undertook a lengthy evaluative study of the major national organizations comprising the civil rights movement. Besides the NAACP, the study included the National Urban League, the Legal Defense Fund, SCLC, CORE, and SNCC. The conclusions were highly beneficial to the NAACP. With the help of Ford Program Officer Leonard Ryan, my staff and I began to develop a series of presentations that resulted in six-figure grants to the SCF starting in late 1966. Of considerable importance was the establishment of a Ford Foundation precedent to make large annual grants in the form of general support, recognizing the difficulty that "cause" organizations had in obtaining sufficient funding for their overhead and for generating discretionary support.

As the 1970s opened, Thomas Cooney succeeded Leonard Ryan as the Ford Foundation's program officer for civil rights. Cooney played a critically important role in developing internal Ford staff support for a series of imaginative proposals. For the next three decades the Ford Foundation became the Association's largest annual donor through the SCF, as well as the largest cumulative donor. Ford grants over the years provided crucial assistance for voter education, legal initiatives, the first NAACP urban program officers, advanced computerized redistricting in the 1990 elections, improved management, executive search, and the expansion of the ACT-SO program.

The first important foundation grant, however, came from the Rockefeller Brothers Fund, which, because of its board composition could easily shortcut the bureaucratic systems that often slowed down the decision-making process in other foundations. The "Brothers Fund," as it was colloquially known, was comprised at the board level of the five Rockefeller brothers—Nelson, John, David, Laurence, and Winthrop—and their sister Abigail. Each had authority up to a certain level to initiate a grant to a recipient of their choosing. The top-flight staff of the Brothers Fund provided rapid but authoritative research and advice.

After Roy Wilkins had met formally with Nelson Rockefeller and informally with John Rockefeller III, the first grant was expedited in mid-1966 to support the initial phase of the school desegregation court campaign outside the South, only a few months after the large Schenley gift. The Rockefeller grant, though only $50,000, was still a major sum in the 1960s, and not only enabled the NAACP to launch the initial litigation but also sent an eloquent message to the other foundations that the highly professional Rockefeller Brothers Fund had determined that the NAACP merited serious support and that the Rockefellers themselves were "buying into the NAACP" as active backers. These grandchildren of John Rockefeller himself were according their seal of approval to the NAACP. Thereafter, Nelson Rockefeller's staffer working in the general area of Negro political activity—Evelyn Cunningham—was often seen at NAACP events, as were several of the Rockefeller "cousins," the fourth generation who were the children of Nelson, John, and their siblings. The effect this had on other wealthy individuals and families, especially in the Northeast, was salutary for the entire movement—the National Urban League, which already enjoyed Rockefeller support, and the Legal Defense Fund benefited over the long run even more than the NAACP.

Of even greater importance were the subsequent decisions of the Rockefeller Foundation (no longer controlled by the family) and the Carnegie Corporation to invest in the NAACP's school desegregation plan a few years later. (Earlier, Carnegie, which was regarded as the nation's premier foundation focused on education, had provided a grant to the NAACP education department for a small field staff carrying out its programs at the branch level.)

Meanwhile, a small comedy of errors accompanied the SCF's initial bid to the Rockefeller Foundation. From mid-1965 until late spring of 1966, that foundation declined to set up a meeting with Wilkins to discuss a request for support. At a trustee meeting of the SCF in February 1966, I reported on this with some emphasis, appreciating that one of the Rockefeller Foundation board members was Dr. Ralph Bunche, who also served as an SCF trustee. After the meeting, he took me aside and instructed me not to pursue the matter any further until he sent a letter stating that the moment was fortuitous for another approach. In June, he wrote that letter, noting that the Rockefeller Foundation had just approved a $2 million grant to the NAACP LDF and recommending that the NAACP now seek a grant from the Rockefeller Foundation. Though distressed to have been held back while a "rival" agency was seeking Rockefeller support, I immediately called for an appointment. The earliest that Rockefeller's second-in-command, Dr. Joseph Black, was available was mid-July 1967, when I would be on vacation. Wilkins, however, decided to accept the date. I wrote a detailed memo, explaining the background and underscoring the new grant to the LDF. The memo was delivered to Wilkins a week prior to the meeting. He was later reminded of the appointment, which he chose to attend alone.

Unfortunately, Wilkins either failed to read the memo or had forgotten its essential points. Thus, when Dr. Black thanked him for coming to the Rockefeller Foundation headquarters and suggested that he might want to know the details of the grant "the NAACP was to receive," Wilkins thought his own organization had been awarded the grant and not the Legal Defense Fund. He thereupon thanked Dr. Black and the foundation for their generosity, departed and, from a phone in the lobby, excoriated my deputy, Stacey Winter, for misleading him. When I returned the following week he, of course, had discovered that it was the Rockefeller Foundation that had been misled, since they failed to recognize that the LDF and the NAACP were no longer linked, nor had any of the LDF personnel bothered to clarify the matter. Thus, Dr. Black and his associates appeared to have honestly thought the grant to the LDF was a direct form of support to the NAACP. (This was neither the first nor certainly not the last time that the LDF's continued use of the NAACP initials had resulted in such confusion.)

After I reported the substance of the meeting to Dr. Bunche, he suggested that another appointment be made to explain to the Rockefeller Foundation senior executives that their grant to the LDF in no way assisted the work of the NAACP. Since Wilkins had already begun his vacation, an appointment was made for his deputy, Dr. John Morsell, and me in late August. Five senior Rockefeller executives, headed by Dr. Black, met with us in Black's office. John Morsell very carefully and clearly set forth the NAACP's dilemma: Since the staff of Rockefeller Foundation had made this sizable grant to the LDF, believing they were aiding the NAACP, and since the LDF and the NAACP had not been officially connected for almost a decade, he was hoping to initiate a new request for support from the NAACP itself. After some polite chat, Dr. Black responded by admitting their error, then stating in no uncertain terms that the grant to the LDF was made under a specific program interest, which was no longer in effect. In fact, he insisted, none of the foundation's current program interests related to the work of the NAACP. Therefore and regretfully, he concluded, there was no point in further discussions with the NAACP at this time.

At this point, Dr. Black rose from his chair to terminate the meeting. In doing so, his four colleagues and then John Morsell also rose to their feet. I, however, remained seated. I explained that, unfortunately, I was not as polite as my colleague and refused to accept this rejection amicably. If the Rockefeller Foundation declined to discuss a grant with the NAACP, I stated, I would have no reason not to convey the foundation's mistake both to Dr. Bunche and *The New York Times,* which I was certain would find it especially amusing that an error of such magnitude ($2 million) had been committed by so-called professionals.[6] Just as Morsell was gathering his thoughts to interject, Dr. Black spoke up and inquired whether the NAACP would be interested in a leadership training grant. Morsell cleared his throat and assured Black that such a grant would meet a major need of the organization. After they resumed their seats, and with surprising dispatch, Dr. Black commanded his subordinates to work out a project program with Morsell and me within a six-week time frame; he said he would brook no delay. Thus was born the grandest leadership training program experienced by any nonprofit organization during the 1960s.

With Althea Simmons, who would later head the project, the National Office created in the fall of 1967 the most elaborate leadership training program ever undertaken by a national grassroots organization. For $2.8 million over three years, the Association staff devised a program that began with the custom manufacturing of seven large motor home vehicles, redesigned to include the latest audio and visual hardware, as well as sleeping accommodations for two staffers, one of whom was also the driver. Each vehicle was assigned to one of the seven NAACP geographical regions where a carefully tailored curriculum would be offered to branch leaders in city and town after city and town. Elaborate scheduling was undertaken so that the vast majority of the NAACP's branch leaders received the training conducted by a senior training officer. For the first time, the national office provided simultaneous training within all seven regions directly to the local branches. Over the next three years, a generation of activists received the best the NAACP had to offer its local leaders. When the grant was used up, no other foundation would consider further support because none wanted a project in which the principal credit belonged to another foundation. Eventually, the vehicles were sold for a small fraction of their cost and the NAACP reverted to its traditional low-cost training methods at state, regional, and national meetings.

By 1969 the Rockefeller Foundation was searching for new challenges. The Association persuaded Rockefeller and Carnegie to join forces in supporting (for the next two decades) the NAACP's new campaign to fight for public school desegregation in regions outside the South. In the face of severe and continuing criticism, both foundations met the challenge handsomely, enabling NAACP lawyers under the SCF to confront the segregated school practices in almost every major Northern, Midwestern, and Far Western city.

In subsequent years a number of other important foundations supported specific NAACP programs, especially those that dealt with youth or education. However, very few invested in the other hard civil rights activities, despite the examples of Ford, Carnegie, Rockefeller, and Rockefeller Brothers. After the "big four," the most generous—usually for a year or two—were the Charles Stewart Mott, Readers' Digest, Joyce, Rosenberg, William Penn, Taconic, Field, Lilly Endowment, Pew, Babcock, Andrew Mellon, and Rosenthal Foundations.

In addition to the major corporate and foundation institutions, the newly formed SCF was obliged to consider how to generate support from individuals, especially the average American whose annual gift was likely to be modest. The goal was to devise methods that would attract large numbers of small-gift donors who, cumulatively, could become a new and major source of support. However, utilizing direct mail proved to be the most difficult component of fundraising on which to sell Roy Wilkins. He was stubbornly opposed to it and had never employed it on any sizable scale. Thus for more than a half century, the NAACP's approach to the acquisition of donor support rested on Dickensian values: One can't lose much money if one doesn't risk much.

To the NAACP leadership it mattered not that the LDF had mastered direct mail and that most of its support until 1965 came from donors through the mail. The same could be said for the ACLU, the March of Dimes, the Easter Seals, the Christmas Seals, and a host of other organizations. Some NAACPers believed that the tax-deductible status of the LDF had been the crucial factor in its direct mail success, but that factor only influenced large gifts, for the most part over $100. In any event, the SCF had attained tax-deductible status, negating that particular argument.

Walter White and Wilkins had both largely relied upon face-to-face solicitation of NAACP memberships during assigned weeks twice a year, not only for new members but also for renewals. They relied almost totally upon volunteers—the membership itself—that under the best of circumstances could not possibly provide total coverage of the existing membership; volunteers cannot be relied upon to fulfill every assignment given to them. They become ill, tired, hungry, out of sorts, distracted—the result is that long lists of members are not contacted for renewal. Nevertheless, low membership dues—in 1965 the basic membership was $5—make the use of direct mail unfeasible. There is no way the income from a mail solicitation can provide a decent net; indeed it may not cover its costs, when the basic dollar increment is so low. In 1965, an average contribution of $20 could provide a reasonable and possiblly significant net. With costs much lower than today—first-class postage cost three cents a letter in 1965 compared to 37 cents today—professional fundraisers were able to create and mail a full package for between 15 and 20 cents at the first-class rate. Today that same package costs between 70 and 80 cents each, including 37 cents for first-class postage, compelling most direct mail fundraisers to utilize the nonprofit rate of postage—about 12 cents a letter.

Extensive prior experience had convinced me that direct mail would work for the NAACP. Moreover, I saw the opportunity for the organization to benefit from the other important effect of direct mail—the exposure of its message at any given moment to hundreds of thousands of potential supporters, including media opinion molders and political and financial decisionmakers. Few nonprofessionals understood, especially in the mid-1960s, the positive public relations impact that effective direct mail letters and enclosures could have on a cause. The trick was to get the recipient to read the entire message, and that required effective writing, design, analysis, and the intelligent compilation of documentation, especially from third parties. The most effective accompanying documentation in that period and for at least another decade was a reprint of a news article from the *New York Times*. The latter's vaunted objectivity and professionalism favorably influenced a great many readers, excepting the extremes of left and right. With such backup from the *Times,* the letter writer was free to exercise strong rhetoric in the body of the letter, since the most important facts were verified by the enclosure from the *Times.* Rarely did a recipient take issue with the facts published in this illustrious newspaper. The other media, especially television, often decided to produce a news segment of their own after having read the NAACP's reprint of a *Times* article.

More often than not, when a professional undertakes a direct mail commission, he or she has a ready-made donor list with which to work. Since the SCF in 1965 had just commenced operations and the NAACP national office had never undertaken a mail campaign for contributions, I had no such list with which to work. It was also agreed to in advance that I would refrain from soliciting current NAACP membership lists, in order to try to avoid any diminution of income from the Association's membership, and, for similar considerations, I was prohibited from exchanging current membership names for the names of contributors to other organizations. (Later on I was granted permission to exchange life membership names and once a year to send them a solicitation letter for the SCF.)

Fortunately for the NAACP, I did possess a list of some 10,000 donor names from previous mail campaigns in other areas of interest, which I offered in exchange for the NAACP's use of active donors of other organizations. Often, professional counterparts in other organizations agreed that, since they trusted me and held the NAACP in such high esteem, they would accept repayment name-for-name later on from the names that responded affirmatively to the new appeal. Thus, one major concern was put to rest.

The second was obtaining the sum needed to pay for the mailing. There is never any credit offered by the U.S. Postal Service. In addition, since this was a new campaign by an organization without a track record in direct mail, the printers and mailers normally asked for their compensation in advance or on delivery. All in all, about $10,000 would be needed to cover the mailing of 50,000 test names. It's hard to believe, but that was a sizable sum in those days. Annual adult salaries were not much greater. In any event, I personally guaranteed the printing and mailing costs and wrote my own check—in the amount of $1,500, or more than a month's fee—to cover the required postage advance.

Now there was only one more hurdle to overcome—acquiring Roy Wilkins' approval of the letter drafted for his signature. Since he knew nothing of the arrangements described above, anticipating his reaction generated considerable anxiety for me. As an adept writer and former journalist, Wilkins had the reputation of being a tough critic and editor. As it turned out, all of the worrying was misplaced. His deputy, John Morsell, had the problem worked out when presented with the drafts and a design sketch of the entire package. Wilkins had just departed on an extensive trip to visit NAACP branches. Morsell, exercising his authority as the acting director, approved the text and package in Wilkins' absence because there was a specific time frame involved for the mailing dates. The entire mailing was out by the time Wilkins returned.

Within a week the results were streaming in. By the end of the cycle, the SCF had received $31,270, tripling its costs and generating more than 1,500 new donors. The new fund was off to a solid start. Over the next 30 years, the NAACP never experienced a year during which either the renewals or the test/acquisition mailings lost money. Every year for three decades the SCF derived a sizable profit from its test/acquisition mailings (renting or exchanging for the donor lists of other organizations) as well as from the SCF's renewal appeals. Ultimately, the SCF list exceeded 90,000 donors at its peak. During its first three decades (1965–1995), the SCF grossed $20 million from direct mail, most of it unrestricted as to purpose, thereby enabling the SCF to pay part or all of its overhead costs from this source (which meant that every dollar of many program grants was expended on those programs and their administration). The cumulative direct mail net was somewhat over half of the gross. Because overhead is rarely a category to which foundations and some corporations want their grants directed, it is the most difficult budget category for which to find donors.

Moreover, the process of mailing to other lists—testing and then acquiring new names—almost always results in several large gifts by individuals who are either personally wealthy or serve on foundation or corporate boards. Systematic research, for which the NAACP never had sufficient funding to undertake properly, will identify not only large givers on these boards but also smaller donors who are either board members or who possess sizable personal fortunes. Following up such leads with personal calls or notes from the CEO often produces much larger grants or gifts.

The contents of the direct mail packages by themselves greatly served the NAACP and its outreach. Many media decisionmakers produced their own stories from the appeals the NAACP sent them at home or at work. These appeals even generated editorials in the major newspapers. Hundreds of recipients wrote letters to the editors of their local newspapers based on the contents of the direct mail packages. Since whites were the overwhelming majority of the recipients of the direct mail campaign (successful mail campaigns directed to blacks did not materialize until 1981), the presentation of tough political and moral issues in a rational and convincing manner over Wilkins' signature served to raise his standing among whites and to gain greater acceptability of the NAACP and its policies as well.

Much as we would have liked to, however, my staff and I cannot claim that these superior results stemmed solely from our peculiar genius. The external events themselves were the decisive factor—in the early years all we needed to do was recognize that salient point and compose straightforward letters. The referenced events were a long string of assassinations and attempts on the lives of NAACP leaders throughout the Deep South. The frequency of these murders and maimings tended to cast a morbid pall on the early fundraising work.

Sometimes it was all one could do to gather one's inner resources and carry on as a professional with enough temporary detachment to complete the job. In those initial years—1965 to 1967—it was considered fortunate not to personally know each of the victims, and yet the task of exploiting each event was in itself emotionally difficult.

The most traumatic came in early 1966 when the NAACP branch president in Hattiesburg, Mississippi, was conducting a voter drive. His name was Vernon Dahmer and he managed to ignore the increasingly violent threats of the hatemongers who slithered beneath sight, until one night on January 10, 1966, while Vernon Dahmer and his wife were sleeping, a fire bomb was thrust into their bedroom window. As their wood-frame house exploded in flames, Vernon Dahmer leaped to his feet, grabbed a shotgun, and began firing through the front window at the Klansmen, while directing his wife to lead their three younger children through the rear door to safety. Dahmer succeeded in driving off the hooded marauders, but inhaled so much smoke that he died the next morning.

That afternoon, I learned that the Dahmers had four sons on active duty in four different branches of the military, two of them in Vietnam. They were all permitted to fly home for their father's funeral. The multiple ironies of this criminal act were self-evident. Here were four young men risking their lives to defend and protect their country's freedom while racists had assassinated their father and seriously injured their mother because they sought the fundamental right to vote. Arrangements were made for a wire-service photographer to attend the funeral in order to get that one photo alleged to be worth a thousand words—four young men in military uniform at their murdered father's grave. From my own experience, nothing I have ever produced for direct mail was as eloquent as that photo. Regrettably, such demonstrations of irony and appeals to decency proved ineffectual in reversing the overall course of the nation's racist history, even though they were successful as evanescent fundraising techniques. As a footnote to the Dahmer tragedy, it took Mississippi's criminal justice system some 35 years to convict the callow white perpetrators of this racial murder.

As the 1960s drew to a close, the issues became more complex. The direct mail messages were of necessity also complex. By then, however, the SCF had generated a sizable constituency of supporters and the direct mail medium was utilized every few months to explain in greater detail and effectiveness some of the Association's more controversial policies. The most memorable was the one that explained Wilkins' thinking in support of busing school children in Boston. Until the affirmative action controversies two decades later, no court suit initiated by the NAACP proved so difficult for the public to understand and accept as that school busing initiative, which was ordered by federal Judge Arthur Garritty, Jr. in 1970 as one of the few remedies open to him to overcome decades of racially segregating black school children. Earlier, Judge Garritty had ruled that this proven pattern of school segregation in Boston was unconstitutional. As a major remedy, he imposed upon the school system a mandatory busing plan in order to help desegregate the public schools in a timely fashion. Unfortunately, some white Irish-American children from South Boston were bused to predominantly black schools in a Roxbury, a black ghetto, whereas large numbers of Negro children were bused to schools in South Boston. The "Southie" response was years of violent and prolonged resistance.

Roy Wilkins' letter about the Boston school plan pleaded with the reader to remember that the NAACP has never been reckless or irresponsible, that the judge had no other meaningful alternatives, and that despite the divisiveness and disorder resulting from stubborn white resistance, this too would pass. Meanwhile, it asked the reader and other decent Americans to find some other aspect of the NAACP's work to support, if they were unable to go along with it on busing. The letter also made it clear that the NAACP would support the Court's remedy until the conflict was fully resolved; Roy Wilkins would not back down nor dream up an alibi. The letter stirred up hundreds of responses, virtually all of them positive. Many repeated Wilkins' own injunction that this time they agreed to disagree and would move on from there. The NAACP lost a few supporters during that prolonged and agonizing period, a period much longer than Wilkins or any of the experts had anticipated, but it gained a great many new ones. (Ultimately, the people of Boston, white and black, did succeed in working out a way to live with the court orders through which the public schools were largely desegregated.)

Besides providing much-needed overhead money, the new support from direct mail also helped greatly to make the Association's national income more predictable. Foundation grants took many months to develop and often as long as a year before the organization saw the first installment. It required almost a decade before the NAACP could annually project foundation income on a substantial level, largely as a result of sizable renewed support from the Ford, Carnegie, and Rockefeller foundations. However, almost none of these grants, except a healthy $500,000 annually from Ford, could be used for overhead—salaries of nonprogram staff, rent, postage, accounting, and general administration. Despite this, within a few years National Office Controller Dick McClain and I were able to project fairly accurately the pattern and size of the direct mail income, based on four or five renewal mailings to the entire donor file, plus a continuous and unceasing effort to identify new lists from which to acquire more names for that file.

For almost 30 years, Wilkins, Morsell, and later Ben Hooks took pains to understand how the process worked and to appreciate that any initiative that produced new income over costs was a contribution to the struggle. The NAACP staff comptrollers were equally knowledgeable in that regard. In 1995, however, when the NAACP faced its greatest crisis, those in command, fully ignorant of the facts, abandoned these strategies and propelled the civil rights organization into a downward spiral from which it never fully recovered.

In addition to these basic thrusts, which provided a healthy and diversified portfolio of income sources, combined with that derived from membership dues and contributions, the fundraisers initiated a large number of new income-producing methods. One of these was the traditional afternoon or early evening reception given by socially prominent hosts and/or hostesses at a desirable Manhattan address, honoring Roy Wilkins, Ralph Bunche, or other civil rights luminaries. Following a 30-minute report by the guest of honor, who normally focused on a few projects in need of support, another highly regarded individual—an Arthur Schlesinger Jr. or Joseph Rauh or Lloyd Garrison—would make the pitch, a 10- to 15-minute closer in which individuals were urged to contribute.

My development staff also produced some variations on this theme: musicales deliberately limited to 100 persons paying $100 each were much-talked-about events, held as they were in the homes of the wealthy. The most memorable was held on April 26, 1968, in the Park Avenue living room of Mrs. Lawrence Copley Thaw, daughter-in-law of the man who shot Stanford White, for a private, once-in-a-lifetime jam session by Ella Fitzgerald and her five-piece combo. Wilkins and Bunche cochaired this event, with another prominent friend, Mrs. Marietta Peabody Tree.

Mrs. Thaw's living room comfortably held 100 folding chairs, with plenty of room for the musicians and the buffet table from the Copenhagen Restaurant, which provided a postevent champagne supper. This elegant black-tie affair sold out so quickly that those individuals working on the event were placed under two weeks of relentless temptation from wealthy individuals who had failed to purchase tickets before the last ticket had been sold. That situation escalated when a number of single and divorced women learned that Huntington Hartford, scion of the A&P fortune, was attending—alone. Few guests arrived late that evening.

At the appointed time I waited outside for Miss Fitzgerald to arrive, helped her from her limousine, and presented my arm to lead her into the apartment. However, she grasped my forearm with such intensity that I was compelled to ask her what was disturbing her. She said: "I am so nervous—I never met Mr. Wilkins or Dr. Bunche before." As soothingly as I could, I explained to her that both Bunche and Wilkins were at this very moment pacing Mrs. Thaw's library, anxiously awaiting Madame Fitzgerald's arrival for the same reason. When they met, the ice broke instantly; the awe in which each held the other was obvious. Then Ella voiced her other concern: was this audience old enough to appreciate her classic jazz/swing style or did it expect her to venture into then popular country-western and rock-and-roll, neither of which had proven hospitable to her voice. We assured her that the audience was largely of the generation that grew up on a younger Ella and, as she walked into the living room, she beamed with confidence. The concert that followed was in itself the most rare of exquisite experiences.

A year later (May 11, 1969), the Fitzgerald musicale was followed with one of almost equal acclaim. Atlantic Record Company owner Ahmet Ertegun and his attractive wife, Mica, opened their well-appointed East Side town house to the NAACP for a night with Mabel Mercer and Bobby Short. Few New Yorkers have ever been treated to such elegance as those attending that event. Following the late supper, most of the 100 guests proceeded to take leave somewhat after midnight. Then, as a few of the remaining guests chatted in another room, piano notes floated by. They adjourned their discussion and followed the agreeable sound back to the living room, where Mabel and Bobby were entertaining themselves, while a dozen or so onlookers sat entranced—until 3:30 that morning. Each understood that he had been treated to the "real" concert.

As successful as these hothouse events had become, the most each could generate was $10,000 or $15,000. As the NAACP's program demands grew, we had to look for new avenues, such as the exhibition of black artists already described. Then one fortuitous day I met one of the most talented and genuinely involved human beings in my professional experience—Leonard de Paur.[7] During World War II, de Paur had organized an all-black male Army chorus, which broke down numerous racial barriers while entertaining civilians and troops alike. When I first met with de Paur, he was serving as director of community programs for Lincoln Center. The local dailies had been writing about the decline in the traditional (white) audiences necessary to support so many classical cultural institutions at Lincoln Center and Carnegie Hall—classical music, opera, ballet, theater—while the proportion of the city's minority population (black and Hispanic) continued to increase. The assumption had been that the latter would not become serious aficionados of high—or higher—culture, a concern of the Broadway theater owners and the midtown museum directors as well.

This pronounced dilemma provoked lengthy discussions with de Paur, following which I offered the seed of an idea. I suggested that the NAACP could help to develop an "uptown" following for these events by initially sponsoring its own concerts. Leonard de Paur expressed the view that few blacks felt comfortable in the recently completed Lincoln Center complex. A few weeks later, another meeting took place and, after further thought, he recommended that the NAACP sponsor a two-event concert series to be held in early 1975 at what is now Avery Fisher Hall, the first for Metropolitan Opera soprano Roberta Peters and the second for world-acclaimed pianist Andre Watts, an African American.

From the beginning, there were strong doubts about the NAACP's ability to attract an audience for the lovely Ms. Peters, but since de Paur was the professional in this area, we deferred to his views. After all, he also conducted the New York Philharmonic Symphony orchestra when it was on the road. Peters's following, he assured the NAACP, was substantial in New York. The advance sale, however, was lukewarm. The Lincoln Center box office personnel remained confident that the last-minute sales would prove successful. Scheduled to begin at 3 p.m. on a winter's Sunday afternoon, the sponsors' worst fear materialized when a snowstorm hit Manhattan two hours earlier. Less than half of the house was filled for what was otherwise a most enjoyable event. Two weeks later, however, the Andre Watts concert was totally sold out days before the event; scalpers were actually hawking tickets on Broadway and in the promenade—for a concert sponsored by the NAACP!

Several important lessons were learned from that experience. First, African Americans *will* attend classical musical concerts at the so-called downtown auditoriums. Second, avoid the winter if possible. Third, move the venue to a less expensive auditorium—we would have made a few thousand dollars on the Peters concert if the Lincoln Center hall had not been so expensive. The Watts concert provided net income to the NAACP, however. Fourth, if one wants to attract black concertgoers, try to give them a black artist of the first magnitude who will also attract white concertgoers. Over the next five or six years, my staff and I organized a half dozen concerts—at Carnegie Hall where the rental fee was less than half that of Lincoln Center and, in the view of some, afforded better acoustics. The most successful was performed on May 16, 1976, by grand diva Leontyne Price, who returned to 11 encores. Among the other artists sponsored by the NAACP in subsequent years were Shirley Verrett and Grace Bumbry, both lead sopranos at the Metropolitan Opera, as well as the contemporary diva Kathleen Battle.

We experimented with theater benefits but found that they were competing with several thousand local charities. Weighing the time and effort involved, it never seemed worth the effort. Then in 1972, an acquaintance of mine from other work, William Casey, was named chairman of the Securities and Exchange Commission (SEC) by President Nixon. A few years earlier the first black-owned Wall Street firm —Daniels and Bell—had been formed and one of the SCF's board members, himself a broker—Ira Haupt II—was assisting the new outfit. I spoke to Casey and he agreed to address a proposed benefit dinner for the NAACP SCF comprised of Wall Street firms honoring Daniels and Bell, giving the NAACP several dates from which to choose. Haupt visited William Salomon, senior partner of the investment banking firm of Salomon Brothers, who agreed to serve as chairman, and the publisher of *Institutional Investor,* Gilbert Kaplan, who agreed to serve as the master of ceremonies. The package was sure-fire—what Wall Street firm could resist attending such an event, especially when they were to hear and possibly meet the new head of the SEC? Held on May 22, 1972, the event was not only sold out in a matter of weeks; it also received broad media coverage and for the first time presented to the financial community the idea that the NAACP was a major player. Finally, it added to the awareness of and credibility for this new black brokerage venture.

These activities organized under the SCF's auspices increasingly involved the NAACP in the majority community to an extent never before experienced by this predominantly African-American organization. Beginning in the late 1960s, the events, including the concerts, dinners, and more intimate gatherings, offered white leadership in important fields like finance, industry, the mass media, and organized labor the opportunity to participate in the NAACP's affairs to an extent equaled only in the NAACP's earliest years, when the leadership was largely composed of white liberals, social workers, academics, and clerics. Socially prominent men and women began to accept leadership roles on the NAACP's benefit committees for the first time (though the LDF had attracted similar leadership almost from its inception in 1939). Some of these newly recruited figures joined the NAACP national board or, more likely, the trustees of the SCF.

The mass mailings, totaling more than one million letters annually in a typical year, were also largely directed towards white liberals and moderates during the 1960s and 1970s. Many of the recipients were well placed within the media, finance, foundations, and corporations. The cumulative effect of these letters, every word of which was written in-house and therefore maximized the Association's public relations posture, was to increasingly predispose the recipients to the NAACP's philosophy and programs, regardless of what emphasis the mass media might place on a given subject. The accompanying reprint of a news article or self-promoting folder was carefully selected to buttress this process.

Because there were virtually no lists comprised of Negro direct mail donors in those decades, the overwhelming majority of the SCF's direct mail letters were received by middle or upper-middle class whites, helping to mold a procivil rights constituency within the demographic heart of the white majority. These objectives were aided greatly by the demeanor and the sober rationality of Roy Wilkins, even at his angriest, as the NAACP's leader and spokesman. He frequently appeared on television, especially on the early morning network shows like "Today," "Good Morning, America," and "The Morning Show," each of which needed to fill two hours daily, as well as the increasingly popular evening network news shows that were beginning to replace the daily newspapers as the average American's principal source of news. These appearances broadened the understanding and heightened the popularity of Wilkins among whites in every region of the nation. The authoritative and popular news show anchors—Ed Murrow, Chet Huntley and David Brinkley, Eric Sevareid, Howard K. Smith, Harry Reasoner, and Edward P. Morgan—all of whom generally sympathized with the civil rights struggle, buttressed the public's regard for Wilkins and therefore for the NAACP. (During the decade before his death in 1968, this was even more true for Dr. King.)

By the end of the calamitous 1960s, however, the NAACP was confronting a renewed and concerted attack from the so-called left—the self-proclaimed militants, the nationalists and separatists, and the various breeds of Marxists, especially those who had decided to call themselves Maoists. Given the prolonged instability of political movements during that period, it was hardly surprising that some of these ultra-romantic expressions of arrested political development would find their way into the thinking and writing of younger reporters and television commentators, not to mention columnists and adherents of the "new journalism," which had developed its constituency by casting aside objectivity. Many of this newer breed covered, or commented on, the civil rights struggles of the period. Although enamored of the most reckless acts and those who spurred them, these individuals almost uniformly criticized the NAACP, the National Urban League, and the liberal leadership provided by Roy Wilkins, Whitney Young, Philip Randolph, Bayard Rustin, Charles Evers, Vernon Jordan, Clarence Mitchell, and other proponents of integration—each of whom sought to employ constructive tactics designed to bring people together rather than to separate them.

The mass popular culture began to assimilate the views of the so-called militants to such a degree that, with fewer and fewer exceptions, the voices of the more moderate and, in NAACP's view, responsible, black leaders were being passed over for loud and strident street corner "prophets" whose entire constituencies could fill a phone booth.[8] Not only the network television news programs, but more and more of the talk shows chose to air the views of such rabble-rousing speakers as Ron Karenga, Angela Davis, Stokely Carmichael, H. "Rap" Brown, and various representatives of the Black Panthers, affording them a degree of unearned (and undeserved) legitimacy. The program directors repeatedly told representatives of the NAACP that these esoteric "leaders" made better programming because of the sensational charges and comments one could expect from them. In fact, regarding these extremists, the media producers claimed, the more outrageous their manner and content, the bigger the radio or television audiences. Audience size had finally become the ultimate criterion of this pseudo-journalism. Ratings trumped content—and the truth. (Shades of Jerry Springer!)

For more than four years, at Wilkins' instruction, I regularly spoke to the producers of NBC's "Tonight Show," proposing a guest such as Wilkins, Young, Charles Evers, Rustin, or Randolph, without success. Then the highly popular nighttime show, hosted by Johnny Carson, began to book the Ron Karengas and Stokely Carmichaels, deeply influencing an important middle-of-the-road white audience. In the NAACP's view, these radical guests were alienating the American white majority in relations to the civil rights struggle.

As fate would have it, the producer of the "Tonight Show," at the time, was a man with whom I had served in the U.S. Army's Public Information Office at Fort Bliss, Texas, in the early 1950s. His name was Rudy Tellez and, given our past acquaintance, I felt free to speak with him directly. Tellez denied any particular political bias and argued that the individuals he had booked to speak about civil rights simply made "better television." (By this, he meant better ratings. Journalistic standards were hardly important to Carson or Tellez.) He insisted that he and his colleagues were not attempting to promote any particular agenda. On June 12, 1971, I decided to record my objections in a long letter to Tellez, accusing the "Tonight Show" of a bias that included both its opposition to the Vietnam War and its antipathy to those black civil rights leaders who are not actively opposing the war. I also suggested that the black leaders chosen for appearances on the show reflected a class-struggle view of the nation's ills, and were known solely for their militant rhetoric, which might attract a larger audience or make good copy, but which ignored the absence of a record of achievement in the field. I doubted whether Johnny Carson was afraid to interview a Wilkins or an Evers. In any case, I had thrown down the gauntlet, implying more to come. (By this time I had been authorized in writing to pursue the issue on behalf of Roy Wilkins, Whitney Young, Charles Evers, and Bayard Rustin.)

On June 15 Tellez phoned me, said he agreed with the letter, and urged me to wait a few more weeks before doing anything further. Two-and-a-half months later, when no further communication had taken place, I sent another letter to Tellez on September 8, 1971, but this time I sent copies of the correspondence to NBC Board Chairman Robert Sarnoff, NBC President Julian Goodman, and Johnny Carson.[9] On September 15, NBC's vice president for public information, Sydney Eiges, responded for Mr. Sarnoff and Mr. Goodman. He assured me, first, that Tellez had told him he was keeping the door open on booking one or more of the black leaders suggested by the NAACP, and two, Tellez asserted that three of the four—Wilkins, Evers, and Young—had in fact appeared on the "Tonight Show." (The correspondence was also passed on to Stuart Schulberg, the "Today Show" producer.)

The assertion that any of the three men—Wilkins, Young, or Evers —had ever appeared on the show was totally incorrect. I immediately transmitted Eiges' letter to each of the black leaders, who all wrote back that they had never appeared on the show. The same day, Tellez wrote that to me he was leaving the show in five weeks for another position, but that he thought we would have a better opportunity with the early morning "Today Show" (whose audience was far smaller and less influential).

In a new letter to Eiges, with the approval of Wilkins and the other three, I rejected both the assertion that any of the four leaders had appeared on the "Tonight Show," demanding a list of the dates for each alleged appearance, and rejecting the notion that the early morning show was an adequate substitute for the late night show. Eiges replied on October 7, admitting that neither he nor Tellez could document the earlier assertion that three of the four black leaders had already appeared on the show, in part because records for "some 18 months of the past five years are missing." He then argued that the "Tonight Show" is basically an entertainment vehicle and that opportunities for serious discussions are "rather severely limited." This, of course, begged the question of why the extremist black spokespersons had been invited to appear on the show. Again, he suggested that the early morning show was a more appropriate vehicle.

During the course of this odyssey, I met with two NBC officials, one of them Eiges, for lunch, and found them astonished that I was white. They could hardly hold up their end of the discussion. Though expected to attend, the show's producer failed to appear. The bottom line purpose of the meeting was to inform the NAACP that NBC was no longer responsible for the content of the "Tonight Show" with Johnny Carson because they had sold the show to Carson, whose producer, Freddie de Cordova, now had the final say. (Whether that would hold up in court remains a point of contention.) I concluded by stating that since NBC no longer owned the show, they would not mind if we publicly criticized Carson and his associates. Eiges expressed the hope that it would not come to that. Eiges was informed on January 7, 1972, that since no further progress had been recorded, we felt free to go public. He replied by letter, lauding his company's public affairs record in respect to civil rights. I then prepared a long summary of the events that had transpired and recommended to Wilkins that the NAACP release the memo with a press release criticizing NBC. Wilkins pondered it for several weeks and finally decided that an attack on NBC would alienate the rest of the media and might even be misconstrued as an attempt to censor the militants' views. He decided to file it. He was probably right.[10]

As a former newsman and an active public relations practitioner, I would venture to guess that Wilkins's style was more conducive to garnering white support than Dr. King's, which was often given to lavish Baptist sermonizing. More importantly, the local and regional NAACP leaders more often than not reflected the Wilkins style and philosophy, which the NAACP leadership went to great lengths to characterize as both constructive and responsible. These terms were so often repeated within the staff and membership meetings of the Association that they approached the status of mantras. But Wilkins and his colleagues were serious about adhering to them. The national director and his Board would unhesitatingly remove or suspend local leaders whose behavior they regarded as irresponsible and would admonish those whose public utterances were destructive in intent. The general public, white and black, could therefore come to their own conclusions as they witnessed the excessive remarks or behavior of some of SCLC's and SNCC's highly visible local or regional leaders. After James Farmer was supplanted by Floyd McKissack as CORE's national director and Roy Innes succeeded McKissack, the same could be said of that organization's leaders as well. A similar analogy is SNCC's replacement of John Lewis and Julian Bond with H. "Rap" Brown. Thus, between the mass media and the organization's controlled direct media, the NAACP was able to forge broad-based support among those whites sympathetic to the struggle. It also produced considerable respect among those in the middle who were motivated by a traditional sense of fair play. Even moderate conservatives, such as Republican Senators Everett Dirksen of Illinois, Thomas Kuchel of California, and Mark Hatfield of Oregon, publicly expressed their admiration for the NAACP.

The ultimate fund-raising events were the two testimonial dinners honoring Wilkins prior to his retirement in the spring of 1977, after a six-month celebration of his 75th birthday in September 1976.[11] The first was organized by the board chairman of General Motors, Tom Murphy, for April 2 in Washington, D.C. That year General Motors (GM) was the largest corporation in the world. The day-to-day organizer was one of the NAACP's most devoted friends, Abe Venable, who had single-handedly fought to obtain GM's annual support for the NAACP. With invitations over Murphy's signature, the cream of Washington's bipartisan political leadership, as well as many of America's most powerful corporate leaders, joined in the tribute to Wilkins. The dinner netted over $300,000 for the NAACP, at the time a record amount.

Wilkins's New York senior staff was determined to outdo the Washington gala by staging its own event. Mildred Bond Roxborough and I collaborated on what was to become the largest and most publicized dinner produced by the NAACP national office in its history. We engineered an event involving the cultural, intellectual, moral, and political leaders of the nation, as well as many of its most socially prominent. Mrs. Roxborough worked with renowned haute couturier Jeoffrey Beane to stage a dazzling fashion show, highlighting the work of African-American designers. I worked on the entertainment, recruiting Bobby Short and Geoffrey Holder to collaborate on the production of the entertainment for the evening. That too proved awesome. The cavernous Grand Ballroom of the New York Hilton Hotel was sold out, and, at show time, several hundred friends and staff were admitted as standing room attendees. Even the predinner reception was an event of extraordinary glamour, as the nation's leaders in so many fields came to pay tribute to Roy Wilkins. The evening failed to net as much as the General Motors's sponsored event, in part because so many corporations had already participated in the earlier event. But it did provide almost $300,000 for the Association after expenses.[12]

In a final bit of irony, therefore, Roy Wilkins' retirement and the testimonials marking it proved to be our watershed public relations achievement, propelling the NAACP into the nation's popularly accepted leadership ranks. The nation's decisionmakers and opinion-molders had finally accepted that the NAACP was one of the most important players on the national scene. For both fundraising and public relations work, it meant almost instant access to whomever one needed to reach by simply using the organization's well-known initials. It set the stage for a major advance in generating substantial business support. No longer a marginal change agent, the NAACP was accorded access to almost everyone who controlled an important lever. It was almost at the level of celebrity status.

Of greater importance was the nature of the NAACP's message. The Association's image-building from 1965 until Roy Wilkins' retirement in 1977 was greatly enhanced by the substance of the SCF's appeals, which most often dwelled on programmatic solutions or initiatives rather than on starkly drawn policy strokes. The very purpose of the SCF was to support the national programs of the NAACP, some of which predated the advent of the SCF in 1965, though most of the programs were totally new initiatives and directions in the decades following. The new and large sums of money that the SCF attracted, mostly from brand-new sources, enabled the NAACP to vastly expand its program staff and capabilities.[13] Within the first decade of operations, the SCF was raising enough money to support a program staff almost as large as the remainder of the NAACP's staff. Moreover, the SCF was able to take over such earlier programmatic responsibilities as those encompassed by the legal, education, labor, housing, and voter education departments—and in many cases to expand them significantly. That relieved the national office of a sizable financial obligation each year and enabled it to apply the freed funds to the expansion of the branch and membership structure and to its political action processes, including the Washington bureau. In addition, the SCF could be counted upon to pay for almost half of the Association's rent and overhead.

The new resources made it possible for the NAACP to take on tasks and court cases it would in earlier years have been compelled to pass up and to experiment with programs that had no prior history upon which to project success. The SCF was responsible for the NAACP becoming more than an advocacy and litigation engine; it was now conducting sizable national programs through its unequaled branch structure. Eventually, the SCF helped to generate significant funding for some of those programs at the local and state levels.

Most of the SCF's funding, as has already been stated, came from sources that, in the vernacular, were described as white. They consisted largely of gifts or grants from corporations, foundations, and individual white donors, both large and small. This in no way should lead one to conclude that the NAACP could not support itself without white generosity, or that African Americans were either unable or unwilling to support the NAACP, or that, in the weary cliché of recent years, "blacks refused to help themselves." The very opposite is true. Although the substantial support of white-controlled corporations and foundations, together with individual gifts by whites, made it possible for the NAACP to significantly expand its programs and litigation, the NAACP itself was never in terminal danger of closing down because its flow of income from African Americans had dried up. Without so-called white support, it would have had to depend less on professional staff and more on volunteers, but it would have survived during each era and through every crisis. That is because of a single overriding truth, factually verifiable by examining its annual reports to the IRS until 1995. That truth is that at *no time in any year between 1965 (when the SCF was launched to attract money from outside the black communities) and 1995 did these white sources of funding exceed or even equal the total generated by the overwhelmingly black membership and branches in dues, contributions, freedom fund dinner shares, and assessments, both local and national.*

It bears repeating that black men, women and children have historically provided the majority of the NAACP's income (and prior to 1965, contributions from white Americans to the NAACP were insignificant except for those that were directed to the LDF). No other national civil rights organization can now or could in the past make a similar statement. All the others depended largely or almost totally on the support of white contributors. The revisionist writings of those who questioned the NAACP's policy independence should realize that it was never in doubt from roughly 1915 until 1992, whereas the independence of those civil rights organizations that relied predominantly upon the largess of white individuals or institutions remains an open historic question.

Epilogue

The founders of the NAACP in 1909 set out to create a strong and effective organization of activists to advance the status of African Americans and to empower them to attain all of the benefits and responsibilities of full citizenship in American society. Sixty years later that vision was realized: the NAACP had become the strongest, largest, and most powerful civil rights organization the nation has ever known. Anchored firmly in thousands of local units with well over 400,000 paid members at any given moment, with several hundred youth councils and college chapters whose membership numbered roughly 40,000, with a staff whose intellect and capabilities were at the time unparalleled, and with a reputation among opinion molders for integrity and responsible action, the NAACP in 1969 had exceeded the wildest dreams of its founders.

As we have seen, in addition to becoming the foremost advocate of the aspirations of African Americans and the most despised foe of the KKK and the White Citizens Councils, the Association became the primary litigator on behalf of the civil rights of African Americans and other minorities. Black lawyers crafted the imaginative and groundbreaking strategies which overturned the noxious separate-but-equal doctrine and replaced it with a revolutionary new concept in *Brown v. Board of Education*—that racial segregation is inherently unconstitutional. Along the way, brilliant attorneys led by Charles Hamilton Houston, Thurgood Marshall, and Robert L. Carter devised new legal doctrines and innovative strategies. Not the least of their achievements was the Supreme Court decision guaranteeing "one man, one vote."

Under James Weldon Johnson, the NAACP cut its political eyeteeth seeking passage of an antilynching bill in Congress (which, to our nation's shame, has never been adopted). Then Walter White navigated the Association through its first challenge of a presidential nominee to the Supreme Court, helping to defeat Judge John Parker of North Carolina. That, in turn, whetted Walter White's political appetite and thrust the NAACP into opposing every senator who voted for Parker's nomination. In addition to defeating many of them (with the fortuitous assistance of Franklin D. Roosevelt's landslide in 1932 and his popularity thereafter), the heady experiences of political success led the Association to become an active player in almost every national election thereafter, institutionalizing voter education committees at the branch level in more than 1,000 communities and becoming the foremost nongovernmental agent of voter registration and vote pulling-in among minorities.

Well aware of the need for a 10 or 12 percent minority to build support among the white majority, White, Roy Wilkins, and Clarence Mitchell forged the most effective national coalition in modern times —the Leadership Conference for Civil Rights (LCCR), a coalition of more than 180 national organizations, including labor unions, religious denominations, black and other minority agencies, and groups representing women, the disabled, seniors, and immigrants.

That extended political power proved necessary during the turbulent 1960s, when CORE, SNCC, and SCLC were confronting specifically targeted violence-prone racists in parts of the South, when young blacks were employing sit-ins to desegregate retail stores and restaurants, when the NAACP and the LDF were leading unwelcome black children into court-ordered white schools, and when all of the civil rights forces were trying to register black voters.

Against this backdrop, the NAACP leadership pressed its strategy to overturn Rule 22 in the Senate. Then, under the leadership of Clarence Mitchell and Joseph Rauh of the marshaled forces of the LCCR's member groups, the NAACP gained passage of the most important civil rights legislation in the history of our republic—the 1964 Civil Rights Act, the 1965 Voting Rights Act, and the 1968 Housing Act.

The final piece of the puzzle came with the inauguration of the tax-deductible NAACP SCF in 1965. For half a century the NAACP had lived hand-to-mouth on the stingiest of budgets derived in the main from the meager dues of its mostly black membership. But during the last half of the 1960s, it became the recipient of sizable grants and gifts from some of the nation's foremost foundations and corporations, enabling it for the first time to significantly expand its staff and engage in programs nationwide to advance the status of African Americans. Its financial prospects were, for the first time in its history, salutary; it could anticipate a future during which it would not have to pinch pennies.

Thus, by the end of the six decades after it was founded, the NAACP had produced an arsenal potent enough to begin the dismemberment of the Jim Crow system in the American South and to ameliorate *de facto* segregation in the rest of the nation. Its weapons included the sweeping federal legislation and court decisions achieved during the decade which opened up the ballot box, elected office, public accommodations, education at all levels, the workplace and, in some instances, access to decent housing. The NAACP's organizational strength, with 2,500 local units and almost 450,000 members, was almost at its peak. Starting with Roy Wilkins, its staff was regarded generally among the most capable and effective in the cause field. The tax-deductible SCF produced a steady and growing stream of grants and contributions sufficient to drive the expansion of the Association's national programs. It no longer faced serious organizational competition with the demise of SNCC and the fading of CORE and SCLC, whose valiant leader, Dr. King, had been assassinated in 1968. Its closest ally and sister organization, the National Urban League, complemented the NAACP's activities as it too reached its apex.

As the decades of the 1960s closed, both houses of Congress were dominated by liberals and moderates who venerated the NAACP and respected its Washington lobbyist, Clarence Mitchell. Mitchell also claimed the regard and legislative support of the nation's trade union movement under George Meany, and then Lane Kirkland. The NAACP led the most powerful coalition on Capitol Hill—the LCCR—whose membership generally deferred to Wilkins and Mitchell. The U.S. Supreme Court, including Associate Justice Thurgood Marshall, was still sufficiently liberal to be counted upon, in most instances, as an ally of civil rights. The nation had experienced eight years of empathetic federal government under the Kennedy and Johnson Administrations. With the seating of the biracial Loyal Democrats of Mississippi at the 1968 Chicago convention, the Democratic Party, undergoing revolutionary changes, opened its doors, and welcomed African Americans, then Hispanics, Asians, and women. The political influence of the NAACP and blacks in general had never been greater, as unprecedented numbers became municipal mayors, federal judges, and even cabinet secretaries. With all of these forces in play, Wilkins and the NAACP leadership looked confidently into the next decade, fully expecting to implement the laws and court decisions that would effectively eradicate Jim Crow from the American landscape.

There were, without question, several signs of momentum in the opposite direction. The first and most frightening was the combustibility of the predominantly black inner cities in every region, as whites and middle class blacks fled to the outer rings and the suburbs.

That prolonged flight was followed by the migration of many inner city jobs either to the suburbs or to the newly developing Sun Belt. Left behind were the poorest and least skilled—the most vulnerable to despair, drugs, and crime. They became heirs to the grim physical deterioration of their housing and schools. The depth of their anger surprised almost every one, including the federal government and some of the leaders of the NAACP, which until the inner city riots, had invested most of its resources in the Jim Crow-oppressed and mostly rural South. Destitute African Americans (and soon enough Hispanics and other minorities) had little hope that their lot would improve through the ballot box or the desegregation of some schools. By the beginning of the 1970s a majority of African Americans felt isolated within the nation's inner cities. A large minority of blacks still remained in the rural South, which, after expensive and protracted court battles, was at last beginning to experience a measure of school desegregation.

Paradoxically, just as the NAACP was about to begin what its leaders believed to be an era of maximum strength to change the racial patterns of the nation, the American people were entering into an era of growing conservatism, in part a reaction to the life-style challenges of the Aquarius generation and the flaunting of drugs and sex. In part, it was a rejection of the passionate street demonstrations by the opponents of the Vietnam conflict, not the least of the televised burnings of the American flag. The rapid tempo of change throughout the 1960s seemed to threaten those in their adult prime. The latter lumped all of the challenges to the system and their culture together, stigmatizing the generally orderly and law-abiding civil rights movement. There is also no question that many white adults, and these were not only Southerners, had grown up believing in their own innate superiority and thus their automatic rights of privilege over Negroes. The rise of the new order was perceived by many—especially white men—as a direct threat to their very being and identity.

Another paradox was the rise of so many other mass movements, all challenging the status quo with tactics and strategies learned from the NAACP and its sister civil rights organizations. These movements —exemplified by the formation of Mexican-American, Asian-American, Puerto Rican, antiwar, feminist, environmental, senior citizen, and disabled advocacy and change agent groups—not only depleted the ranks of the civil rights movement but also competed for media coverage, funding, and seasoned professional staffers.

The reversal of the liberal doctrines that seemed to dominate the 1960s resulted in the election of a president in 1968 who was barely able to conceal his enmity towards the federally supported programs which, for almost four decades, had helped the least among us to improve their material status. However, now the least among us were rapidly becoming Americans of color, most compellingly African Americans whose legacy had been almost three centuries of slavery and another of brutally imposed Jim Crow. The Nixon Administration, dominated by its distaste for government programs, began the long process of rolling back the advances that had opened doors for poor white Americans since FDR's first term. Nixon's own paranoia and the scandal he sought to cover up led to a temporary break in the process which Ronald Reagan and the two Bushes would seek to continue. But the mean-spirited attitudes of so many white Americans, fed by callous and ideological leadership, would increasingly obstruct the NAACP's efforts to obliterate Jim Crow. Slowly, the federal courts and the Congress would follow the national trends among the white majority. The NAACP would learn that, despite all of its achievements between 1909 and 1969, it would not be able to count upon the Supreme Court or the Congress to keep the doors of opportunity open in most states.

Another paradox confronting the NAACP was the rise of black separatism throughout black communities in every section of the land, and most especially among urban blacks. So long as Roy Wilkins captained the NAACP there was no possibility that the nation's oldest and largest civil rights organization would abandon the ultimate goal of racial integration. Nevertheless, after decades of frustration and hopelessness, a growing number of black Americans, certainly a majority in the inner cities, had abandoned the dream of racial equality in an integrated society. Diverse leaders from Malcolm X to "Rap" Brown, from Floyd McKissack to Stokeley Carmichael, centered their appeals upon racial separatism, in the guise of Black Power or some other nostrum, like Black English. While the followers of Roy Wilkins stood fast against this reactionary trend, the inability of Wilkins and the NAACP to deliver more rapidly the jobs, the quality education, and the housing for which most black Americans yearned for themselves and their children began to nurture disenchantment even within the Association's rank-and-file.

None of what the future would hold, however, in any way diminishes the achievements of the NAACP. It was the foremost private change agent of the twentieth century—only the New Deal-Fair Deal-Great Society administrations produced greater change—and the role model for almost every citizens organization determined to reform the American system, from Common Cause to the Sierra Club to the American Association for the United Nations to the American Association for Retired Persons to the National Organization of Women. Equally important, virtually all of its achievements were the product of the courage, energy, and effort of African-American men, women, and children.

Because of the NAACP, today millions of African Americans are able to vote, to attend college and graduate school, to compete for most jobs, and to serve their government both as civilians and as military. Today racial lynching is so rare it is virtually unheard of. The majority of African Americans, on the other hand, still live in inadequate housing, send their children to inferior schools often in hazardous neighborhoods, cope with second-rate health care, and continue to fear a criminal justice system which is decades behind society in treating every citizen with respect and care. Many labor unions continue to resist the desegregation of their workplaces.

The NAACP, through its decades of militancy, has nevertheless opened a door that can never again be closed. Since the *Brown v. Board of Education* decision, Americans of color have refused to accept second-class status as a permanent given; they have come to realize that the U.S. Constitution guarantees their rights. They have also come to understand, in large measure because of the NAACP, that they must continue to fight for their rights because it is very rare that the privileged ever voluntarily surrender their inherent advantages to those whom they oppress or exploit. And for what it is worth—and it is worth a great deal—a large segment of white America—again in part as the result of the NAACP's effectiveness and reasoned demeanor—has come to support the rights of African Americans and other minorities to all of the benefits, rewards, and responsibilities of American citizenship.

Some day, hopefully, the majority of white Americans will support these noble goals.

Notes

Chapter 1

1. According to the *Boxing Almanac*, the first Negro champion was George Dixon, who held the bantamweight and featherweight titles from 1890 to 1892. He was followed by two of the greatest champions of the century, Joe Walcott (the original), welterweight champ twice between 1901 and 1906, and the all-time great lightweight champion, Joe Gans, who held the title between 1901 and 1908, the year Jack Johnson won the heavyweight title. The pugilistic successes of these three—Dixon, Walcott, and Gans—did not appear to inflame white Americans as much as Johnson's victory had, probably because Johnson never displayed the era's customary deference to whites. Today, Jack Johnson might well be accused by insecure whites of possessing a bad attitude. Blacks might also describe Johnson as "bad," and mean exactly the opposite *(Boxing Almanac*, 1996).

2. Between 1895 and 1915, Booker T. Washington was considered the nation's most politically powerful Negro because his message was reassuring to conservative and moderate whites, and he had gained direct access to the levers of power within the Republican party, for which he vigorously campaigned. Thus, he was accorded major patronage by Presidents McKinley and Theodore Roosevelt. This increased his power many times over and entrenched him with such white philanthropists as Andrew Carnegie, Jacob Schiff, William Lloyd Garrison, and his nephew Oswald Garrison Villard. As Dr. W.E.B. DuBois began to challenge Washington's philosophy openly, at least from 1903 onward, Washington grew increasingly apprehensive that a successful DuBois and later the NAACP would diminish his political and financial power and income. He did everything in his power to undermine the NAACP and DuBois, including personal and political attacks in newspapers beholden to him and the crafty use of patronage as a tool to garner opponents to DuBois. In addition to their philosophic differences, the two Negro giants also succumbed to personality conflicts. Oswald Garrison Villard, Albert Pillsbury, and other mainline NAACP founders were worried that an attack on the newly born NAACP would jeopardize their fund-raising potential. DuBois and Washington continued their public attacks on each other until Washington encountered a personal scandal in 1911, after which the NAACP and

DuBois came to his side and opened the door to an entente. Washington's death in 1915 interrupted the momentum toward rapprochement, but in 1916 DuBois engineered a private conference of about 50 of the nation's most important leaders on race, black and white, at the summer home of Joel Spingarn in Amenia, New York, which brought a measure of unity of purpose between the followers of Washington and DuBois, including agreement that Negroes should pursue all levels of education, that the acquisition of the right to vote was crucial to the liberation of Negroes, and that building a powerful organization—the NAACP—was essential for the Negro's advancement in the U.S. In the end, Washington's power was of minor importance to the future of the NAACP, though it loomed large in 1909 and 1910 Kellogg, C.F. *NAACP—A History of the National Association for the Advancement of Colored People, Volume I, 1909–1920,* Johns Hopkins University Press (1967), 72–75. There is no Volume II. Kellogg's Chapter 4 [67–88] is devoted to Washington and the rivalry with DuBois and the NAACP and contains numerous interesting details. The renowned scholar August Meier has written several articles on Washington and the NAACP, including one in the February 1954 issue of *The Crisis.*

3. *The Independent,* September 3, 1908, 529–534.

4. Ovington, Mary White, *The Walls Came Tumbling Down,* 100.

5. Villard later made *The Nation* independent of the *New York Post* (it remained a weekly). It became one of the most powerful progressive voices in the U.S. in the twentieth century.

6. Thus the NAACP in the 1970s and 1980s chartered branches that were predominantly Eskimo, Native American, Japanese-American, and Chicano. The full text of "The Call" and the complete list of the 60 signers can be found in Kellogg, *NAACP,* 297–299.

7. Hughes, Langston, *Fight for Freedom—The Story of the NAACP, 17–24; Ovington, The Walls Came Tumbling Down, 102–105;* Lillian Wald's Web site states that the initial NAACP meetings were held at her settlement house, which was later known as the Henry Street Settlement House. This may well be the same structure as the Charity Organization Hall identified by Kellogg.

8. Of particular interest is the statement by Herbert Aptheker, never one to disguise his sympathies for the Communist movement, that the founding of the NAACP and the decision of the founders to cast their lot with DuBois's supposedly radical views, as opposed to the admittedly conservative positions of Booker T. Washington, constituted the start of the modern civil rights struggle. With the advent of the NAACP, Aptheker wrote, "it had now become possible and necessary to commence a broadly based, black-white movement, dedicated—in the words of the 1906 address of the Niagara Movement—to achieving 'full manhood rights [for the Negro people] . . . every single right that belongs to a freeborn American, political, civil and social.' This was now the explicit aim of the National Association for the Advancement of Colored People. With its establishment began the modern Black freedom movement, and with its creation disappeared its outstanding harbinger, the Niagara Movement." Aptheker, Herbert. *Afro-American History: The Modern Era* 158.

9. Kellogg, *NAACP,* 18–19.

10. According to Kellogg, the founders' "three major objectives of the new organization (aside from legal aid) were to be mass meetings, investigations, and publicity." They also planned "to expand its membership and to seek funds wherever a foothold had been established—in Boston, Philadelphia, Chicago and Washington." 42).

11. *Ibid.*, 47–48.

12. *Ibid.*, 44–45. Among the celebrated speakers at the second conference in 1910 were Clarence Darrow (who received tumultuous applause when introduced), Ida Wells Barnett, Albert E. Pillsbury, John Haynes Holmes, Morefield Storey, the historian Charles Chesnutt, the financier Jacob Schiff, the philosopher John Dewey, the anthropologist Franz Boas, and Mary Church Terrell. *NAACP*, 45. Whereas the initial meeting in 1909 sought to refute scientifically the then-popular belief in Negro inferiority, the second conference in 1910 focused on the consequences of Negro disenfranchisement. The speakers urged Negro voters to support political candidates sympathetic to Negro rights and not to follow slavishly any political party. Other speakers developed the organic connection between disenfranchisement and segregated, third-rate public schools. Still others drew the connections between the absence of a powerful Negro vote, especially in the South, and unbridled lynching. On pp. 305 and 306, Kellogg lists the names of the officers, those of the members of the Executive Committee, and those of the one hundred members of the General Committee.

13. *Ibid.*, 91. Indeed, the special position accorded DuBois led him to believe he was accountable solely to the board of directors and not to the executive secretary. Moreover, he considered *The Crisis* his personal fiefdom and attempted to resist any editorial interference from Board Chairman Villard, a famous editor himself, or any other board member. In the Association's early years, as a result of DuBois's unique status, there was considerable internal dissension, especially over editorial positions taken by DuBois that had not been adopted by the NAACP (see *ibid.*, 99–101). By the following year—1912—the membership had grown only to 11,000, and there were only 11 local units, continuing the organization's precarious financial position (*ibid.*, 128).

14. *Ibid.*, 117–118.

15. Morton, Franklin, *Thirty Years of Lynching in the United States, 1889–1919*, New York, *NAACP*, 1919.

16. A newly published history of George Washington and slavery by Henry Wiencek asserts that Washington's Revolutionary Army "was more integrated than any military force until the Vietnam War." Wiencek, Henry, *An Imperfect God: George Washington, His Slaves and the Creation of America.*

17. The NAACP's Seventh Annual Conference, entitled "The Negro in Wartime," was held from December 27 to December 30, 1916 "to discuss freely the phases of the economic and civic relations of the colored peoples, especially the American Negro, to the war and the adjustment of those relations after the war." Delegates and members met in plenary sessions at Ethical Culture Hall in Manhattan to discuss the draft; "colored officers"; the racial practices of the Navy; voluntary work with the YMCA, the YWCA, and the Red Cross; the anticipated migration of Southern blacks to the North; and the wages blacks received during that era as well as postwar expectations. Delegates were offered rooms for the

four nights at between $4.00 and $6.00, breakfast for four days for between 25 cents and 50 cents, free lunch, and dinner for three days at 35 cents to 75 cents each, according to the NAACP pamphlet "The Negro in Wartime" (New York, 1917).

18. For the record, Negro soldiers distinguished themselves in every American war, in the Revolutionary War, the Civil War, the Indian Wars, and the Spanish-American War. American military leaders were quite aware of this record. George Washington paid pointed tribute to Negro soldiers, who constituted about one-fourth of the Revolutionary Army at the end of the conflict.

19. McNeil, Genna Rae, *Groundwork—Charles Hamilton Houston and the Struggle for Civil Rights,* 35–45.

20. Ovington, *Walls Came Tumbling Down,* 135–146.

21. According to a *New York Times* story almost eight decades later, "whites set fire to buildings and homes, looting and burning more than 1,200 structures. Klansmen reportedly raged through the streets shooting people. Survivors told of corpses stacked onto wagons and trucks . . . . In the years that followed, the promised rebuilding of Greenwood never happened. Instead, insurance companies refused to pay fire policies, citing special riot exemptions. Whites ultimately took over much of the land." These facts were gleaned from the report of a specially appointed riot commission established by the state legislature, which in 1998 and 1999 held hearings and conducted research into the events of the riot. *New York Times,* February 4, 2000, 1, 12).

22. A few of the most radical Negroes rebuked the NAACP because whites controlled both its policy-making apparatus and its finances. One of the original founders and himself an outspoken radical, William Monroe Trotter, resigned from the NAACP in 1914 and attempted, unsuccessfully, to found his own organization, largely on the ground that whites controlled the NAACP during its initial decade. Later both the Communist Party USA and the followers of Marcus Garvey made similar charges in generally unsuccessful efforts to discredit the organization.

23. Kellogg, *NAACP,* 133–136. Under James Weldon Johnson's tutelage, the first rural branch of the NAACP was founded in 1918 in Falls Church, Virginia, outside the nation's capital, by Joseph Tinner, its first president, and Dr. Edwin Bancroft Henderson, its first secretary. A stone monument to the two founders was erected 50 years later on Tinner Hill in Falls Church, *Jet* magazine reported in November 1999.

24. *Ibid.,* 136. In 1919 the NAACP's branches took the initiative in promoting the election of prominent local Negro leaders to the national board. That year as well the branches in Pennsylvania organized the first statewide organization. From then on the NAACP's state and regional groupings pressed their local units to monitor relevant state legislation and to report to the larger entity for follow-up and action, including lobbying.

25. Ovington, *Walls Came Tumbling Down,* 176–180. An NAACP press release dated February 14, 2000, announcing the performance of Johnson's musical, "God's Trombones," at a national board meeting, states that Johnson increased the organization's membership from 9,000 to 90,000 after being appointed the NAACP's first field secretary in 1916.

26. Johnson, Charles, "An Everlifting Song of Black America," *New York Times,* Arts and Leisure section, February 14, 1999.

27. Kellogg, *NAACP,* 135–136.

28. *Ibid.,* 106–107. In 1914, after five years of activity, the total membership barely reached 3,000 in 22 branches, according to the report given at the meeting in which Villard retired as chairman of the board. Kellogg, *NAACP,* 93. Yet one year later the membership grew almost threefold to 8,266, according to the board minutes of September 13, 1915. This was James Weldon Johnson's first year as a field organizer.

29. *Ibid.*, 137. It seems apparent that the organizing efforts of James Weldon Johnson contributed substantially to the growth of both the membership and the number of chapters.

30. While these distinguished Negro men were joining with hundreds of others in every aspect of the arts and humanities to produce the Harlem Renaissance, another Johnson—Jack—was being hounded from coast to coast until he finally relinquished his heavyweight title to an overweight white man with limited boxing skills, Jesse Willard, in Havana, Cuba, in 1919. Only seven years later, American sport had sufficiently progressed to permit another black man, Theodore "Tiger" Flowers, to defeat the legendary Harry Greb, long-standing middleweight champion of the world, on February 26, 1926. Roberts, James B. and Skutt, Alexander B. *The Boxing Register,* 82–83. As far as the white American public was concerned, no other black man participated in professional baseball, football, or hockey in that era. A minuscule few, such as Paul Robeson at Rutgers, excelled athletically at the college level, but they were considered aberrations. Twenty years later Americans would find it easier to accept Negroes possessing superb physical skills, but they were deemed not yet capable of serious cerebral challenges, even in sports.

31. Kellogg, *NAACP,* 51.

32. For these important reasons, it is difficult to explain why the NAACP leadership did not seek to broaden the number of magazine recipients among its membership or to subsidize larger printings for the youth and college members, few of whom paid high enough dues to be entitled to a subscription. On the other hand, historical anecdotes from elderly members often referred to the numbers of times each individual issue circulated from Negro to Negro reader. I remember in the early 1960s, when one of the nation's most popular weekly magazines boasted that its actual readership was three or four times greater than its subscription numbers, and an elderly black man recollected that in his younger days a single issue of *The Crisis* would be read by 15 or 20 individuals.

33. Kluger, Richard, *Simple Justice,* 1976. This is the definitive work on the history of the NAACP's campaign to desegregate the nation's public schools, which resulted in the Supreme Court's 1954 decision popularly referred to as *Brown v. Board of Education.*

34. As early as 1923, the Socialist Party of the United States addressed the issues of race and class in a tract by James O'Neal entitled "The Next Emancipation" (New York: Emancipation Press, 1923, 32 pp., including a membership form to join the Socialist Party). The tract's central argument is that there is an identity of interests between and among black and white workers, both of whom

are exploited by capitalists of both races. The cover carries a representation of black and white hands locked in a handshake with the words "Black and White Workers Unite." The opening sentences are "Fellow-member of the Negro race! Whoever you are, wherever you are, we greet you. Here is our hand. Give us yours!" It is interesting to note that many of the original founders of the NAACP, including William English Walling and Mary Ovington, openly considered themselves socialists.

35. *Encyclopedia of African-American Culture and History* Vol. 3, 1586).

Negro progress within the medical profession was no better: In 1893 Dr. Daniel Hale Williams, a Negro physician in Chicago, successfully performed the first open-heart surgery. This achievement enabled him to establish the first interracial hospital in the U.S.—Provident Hospital in Chicago—which trained more Negro doctors and nurses. The first Negro medical school was established at Howard University. According to *The Negro Almanac,* which was edited by Harry A. Ploski and James Williams, then public relations director of the NAACP, in 1987 only 3.4 percent of the nation's 707,000 lawyers and judges were African Americans. An even smaller percentage, 3 percent, of the medical professions were black. However, in other fields, the proportion of African Americans was higher and improving: among architects and natural scientists, 6.7 percent; among college and university teachers, 7.7 percent; among librarians and archivists, 6.8 percent; among writers, artists, entertainers, and athletes, 4.7 percent, and among business and professional managers, 6.2 percent (*Negro Almanac,* 627).

By the end of the twentieth century, seven decades after Howard University established a full-time law school, there were proportionately fewer minority members of the legal profession than of most other professions. A July 2000 study on diversity by the American Bar Association reported that blacks and Hispanics accounted for a total of 7 percent of American lawyers in 1998, whereas the two groups made up 14.3 percent of accountants, 9.7 percent of doctors, 7.9 percent of engineers, and 6.9 percent of natural scientists. Between 1995 and 2000, the same report noted, minority enrollment in law schools increased by only 0.4 percent, and in the same year, fewer than 3 percent of law firm partners were minority lawyers. Moreover, even these minority partners were, for the most part, at the low end of the compensation and management scales. *New York Times,* July 9, 2000, 22, from a Reuters dispatch.

An earlier study by the *National Law Journal,* as summarized by *Jet* in February 1999, reported that the number of full-fledged black law firm partners in 1996 was 247, only a 4.7 percent gain since 1994. The same report concluded that blacks were only 1.2 percent of the equity partners of the nation's 250 largest law firms, whereas the number of law firm partners for all minority partners grew by 8.4 percent during the same 2-year period. As if to underline the barely perceptible progress black lawyers have made among the premier American law firms, the growth in black law firm partnerships from 1994 to 1996 was 0.1 percent.

36. Ovington, *Walls Came Tumbling Down,* 108–111.

37. McNeil, *Groundwork,* 70–71.

38. McNeil, *ibid.*

39. In his memoir, *Crusaders in the Courts,* New York: Basic Books (1994), Jack Greenberg, successor to Thurgood Marshall as head of the NAACP Legal Defense and Education Fund (LDF), itemized the modest list of black civil rights

lawyers, state-by-state in the South, who were available to represent civil rights cases at mid-century. They included the following numbers: Mississippi, 3; Maryland, 5 or 6 (out of a pool of 30); Delaware, 1; Virginia, 4; Florida, 4; Arkansas, 2 or 3; Georgia, 1 (out of a pool of 13); North Carolina, 3 (out of a pool of 12); Tennessee, 3; and Kentucky, 2 (Greenberg, 37–41). Virtually all of these black civil rights attorneys were associated with the NAACP and/or the LDF.

Chapter 2

1. Ovington, Mary White, *The Walls Came Tumbling Down,* 108–109.

2. *Ibid.*, 113–115. The journalist was Albert J. Nock writing for *The American* magazine.

3. Hughes, Langston, *Fight for Freedom—The Story of the NAACP,* 115.

4. Until the appointment of James Weldon Johnson as the NAACP's first black chief executive, at least five white men and women served as the NAACP's executive secretaries between 1910 and 1920. They were, in chronological order, Frances Blascoer, Mary White Ovington, May Childs Nerney, Roy Nash, and John Shillady. Professor Joel Spingarn of Columbia University, whose field was comparative literature, was the first to be elected chairman of the board, the most powerful volunteer post, in 1914. Before then, Morefield Storey had served as president, then the most important lay post. Spingarn resigned as board chairman in 1917 to volunteer to serve in the U.S. Army during World War I. Ms. Ovington succeeded him at that time. Langston Hughes, *ibid., passim.*

5. McNeil, Genna Rae, *Groundwork—Charles Hamilton Houston and the Struggle for Civil Rights,* 116–117.

6. Hughes, *Fight for Freedom,* 57–62; Ovington, *The Walls Came Tumbling Down,* 154–167.

7. Kellogg, C. F. *NAACP—A History of the National Association for the Advancement of Colored People, Vol. I, 1909—1920*, 242.

8. See Cortner, Richard C., *A Mob Intent on Death: The NAACP and the Arkansas Riot Cases* for a full, detailed, and powerful narrative of the Negro farmers' rebellion and the attempts by the state of Arkansas judicially to lynch dozens of Negroes and of the successful efforts of the NAACP and its lawyers to gain their freedom.

9. Hughes, *Fight for Freedom,* 42–45; Ovington, *Walls Came Tumbling Down,* 198–213. The *Sweet* case appears to be the earliest fundraising model on record for the matching gift concept. The Garland Fund, headed by ACLU founder Roger Baldwin, announced that it would match every two NAACP dollars contributed for the Sweet case with one of its own. In response to this challenge, the NAACP national office raised a substantial sum of money, mostly from Negroes. Hughes, *Fight for Freedom,* 43.

Darrow's personal account of his defense of Sweet is recounted in his autobiography, Darrow, Clarence, *The Story of My Life*, Scribner's, 301–11.The reaction of African Americans to the *Sweet* case, and how it impacted on the NAACP, can be found in James Weldon Johnson's autobiography, *Along The Way.* New York: Viking Press (1933), 383–85.

10. In a 1963 poll by Louis Harris for *Newsweek* magazine, 81 percent of Negroes, North and South, affirmed that the United States was worth fighting for,

whereas 9 percent opposed the notion and 10 percent were not sure. The differences between North and South were insignificant. *The Negro Revolution in America.* New York: Simon & Schuster (1963), 61.

11. McNeil, *Groundwork,* 133, lists the members of the committee as Roger Baldwin, Morris Ernst, Lewis Gannett, James Weldon Johnson, James Marshall, Arthur Spingarn, Walter White, and Houston.

12. A detailed description of the political and personal conflicts within the Garland Fund's board over the NAACP grant, especially the strong disagreements between the NAACP's Executive Secretary Walter White and the American Civil Liberties Union's Director Roger Baldwin, over how the grant would be spent, appears in a book by Prof. Mark Tushnet, *The NAACP's Legal Strategy Against Segregated Education, 1925–1950,* 1–20.

13. Three decades later, NAACP General Counsel Robert L. Carter would develop a focused strategy based on the effect of segregation in public schools throughout the North, Midwest, and West.

14. McNeil, *Groundwork,* 150–151.

15. It is mistakenly, and perhaps gratuitously, argued by Prof. Mark Tushnet, *The NAACP's Legal Strategy*, that the NAACP had been politically motivated by the pressures of organizational and membership growth in the selection of those cases that form the building blocks for *Brown,* including *Sipuel, Sweatt,* and *McLaurin.* That hypothesis was effectively laid to rest by Judge Robert L. Carter, one of the principal architects of the long struggle to achieve *Brown,* in his review of Tushnet's book in the *Michigan Law Review,* May 1988, Vol. 86, No. 6, 1083–1089. "The key point that must be grasped concerning the relationship between organizational needs and legal strategy is not, as Professor Tushnet would have it, that NAACP litigators and local branches conformed their approach to the short-term desires of black Southern communities in order to increase the Association's organizational base among that constituency," Carter observed. "Rather, the organization's staff took the lead in setting an agenda at the local level. If organizational needs dictated legal strategy, that was because the legal strategy was *ab initio* the product of institutional necessities. After all, the organizational purpose of the NAACP was to secure equal citizenship rights for blacks, and among those rights was the right to equal educational opportunity. That litigation thus fulfilled one of the organization's basic functions," Carter concluded. Tushnet rather strangely second-guesses the strategic objective of the NAACP's school litigation, suggesting that the organization would have generated less white opposition if it had followed a strategy that merely sought to attain equal educational facilities, though still segregated by race. What Tushnet is saying, in effect, is that if the NAACP had trimmed its objectives to a goal of segregated but equal facilities, it would have provoked less white resistance—a highly self-evident alternative that Marshall, Wilkins, and Carter had faced and rejected five decades earlier.

16. NAACP 1943 *Annual Report,* 44. The NAACP's total expenditures in 1943 amounted to $149,912. The same annual report noted that 98 percent of the membership belonged to the branches, with Detroit the largest at 20,697, followed by Baltimore, Chicago, Philadelphia, and Los Angeles. Twenty-three branches had full-time secretaries, numbering 80,000 members in 1943. That same year, 93 new branches were organized and chartered (30–31). Total NAACP membership passed the quarter of a million mark in 1943.

17. NAACP 1943 *Annual Report,* 5.
18. Kluger, Richard, *Simple Justice,* 257–259.
19. Hughes, *Fight for Freedom,* 136–138.
20. Kluger, *Simple Justice,* 260.
21. Wilkins, *Standing Fast*, 196.
22. Kluger, *Simple Justice,* 264
23. Professor Redfield was my mentor in both college and graduate school.
24. NAACP *1947 Annual Report,* 4. Although they fell short of organizing an NAACP college chapter, many of the white students at the University of Oklahoma provided steadfast and enthusiastic support for the admission of Ms. Sipuel to their university.
25. Kluger, *Simple Justice,* 262.
26. *Ibid.*, 267
27. *Ibid.*, 268. Just as the Supreme Court was about to hear McLaurin's appeal, the state of Oklahoma partially relaxed the conditions restricting McLaurin's access to its facilities. Nevertheless, many white students, opposing the university's resistance to desegregation, refused to obey the rules set down by the university. Instead they treated McLaurin in the same manner in which they treated any other student attending the university, thereby undercutting the university's strategy to wear out McLaurin's patience and willpower.
28. Among the most outspoken critics of Marshall for accepting the McLaurin case was prominent Negro attorney and *Pittsburgh Courier* columnist Marjorie McKenzie Lawson. Greenberg, *Crusaders in the Courts,* 113. A decade later, she was part of the civil rights team in which I participated in John F. Kennedy's 1960 Presidential campaign. President Kennedy appointed her as the first Negro judge to a District of Columbia court. She was married to black attorney Belford Lawson, who successfully argued *Henderson* on the same day that NAACP attorneys argued *Sweatt* and *McLaurin.*
29. Interview with Carter (personal communication).
30. Kluger, *Simple Justice,* 276.
31. Greenberg, *Crusaders in the Courts,* 71.
32. Interview with Carter (personal communication).
33. Indeed, by 1952, nine Southern and border states had abandoned their prohibition of Negro students in their states' graduate schools: in addition to Oklahoma and Texas, the other states were Tennessee, Kentucky, Missouri, North Carolina, Virginia, Delaware, and Arkansas. Yet when the NAACP pressed for the entry of Autherine Lucy to Alabama's library school, the authorities led by Gov. George Wallace responded severely and sought to defame and destroy her. As the university stood by, a bloodthirsty crowd pinned Ms. Lucy in a classroom and thunderously shouted their desire to kill her. None of the mob was punished; instead the university suspended Lucy for causing the riot. Although the federal government took no action on her behalf, a federal judge reinstated her three weeks later. Almost immediately, she was expelled by the university on the ground that the judge had treated the trustees with disrespect.

Despite her courage, dignity and merit, she was blamed for the disorder by many, including such moderates as William Faulkner, who urged the NAACP to "Go slow now." Then the presidential candidate Adlai Stevenson joined the clamor, calling for a gradual approach. President Eisenhower had been counseling moderation. As social critic Mort Sahl was to observe sarcastically four years later at a civil rights gathering for the presidential candidate John F. Kennedy in New York City, "Stevenson's for gradualism and Ike's for moderation: between those two extremes most certainly lies the truth."

Stevenson's caution and verbal restraint in respect to racial issues was emphasized by one of his closest advisers, Harry S. Ashmore, executive editor of the *Arkansas Gazette.* In his 1982 memoir, *Hearts and Minds: The Anatomy of Racism from Roosevelt to Reagan* (New York: McGraw-Hill, 1982), Ashmore reveals the problems Stevenson had with those who were advocates of immediate racial change. When Harlem Congressman Adam Clayton Powell proposed a bill to withhold federal aid from school districts that refused to desegregate immediately, a bill warmly endorsed by Wilkins and the NAACP, Stevenson announced his fervent opposition. In April 1956, the NAACP's West Coast representative, Franklin H. Williams, escorted Stevenson around Northern California, and when Stevenson suggested that "those who were untouched" by *Brown* "should not be overzealous in condemning the South," Williams told him that "this kind of conciliatory talk was unacceptable," and that he would lose the black vote in the California primary if he failed to endorse the Powell amendment and if he declined to advocate "any other means necessary to root out Jim Crow." The quotes are all by Ashmore, paraphrasing Stevenson, pp. 228–231. Then, before an all-black audience in Los Angeles well covered by the press, Ashmore wrote, Stevenson revealed fully his core approach to race relations, concluding "I will do everything I can to bring about national unity even if I have to ask some of you to come about it gradually." (p. 231). As a veteran correspondent commented at the time, "He's blown it." The national press agreed. Ashmore, William Wirtz, Arthur Schlesinger, and others wrote numerous drafts of speeches attempting to reconcile Stevenson's views with those of the majority of liberals and civil rights leaders. Finally, Stevenson publicly declared that the race issue was, in the end, a moral issue that demanded a president's attention and participation. He scored Eisenhower for not taking leadership and for not calling together white and black leaders to discuss how to implement *Brown.* Although he seemed to have approached a commitment on the subject, he never really went far enough to offer concrete measures that the federal government and American society might take to resolve the claims of black Americans. In the end, he was a major disappointment to both liberals and civil rights activists.

Autherine Lucy, however, was persistent. In 1989, she went back to the University of Alabama and in 1991 obtained her Master's Degree in Elementary Education on the same day that her daughter received her Bachelor's Degree in Finance.

34. Shagaloff, Memorandum to Author, April 2000, 1–5.

35. Kluger, *Simple Justice, passim.* Also Shagaloff, "Memorandum," *passim.*

36. In 1970, June Shagaloff left the NAACP to get married.

37. Shagaloff, Memorandum to Author, April 2000, 3–4.

38. Hughes, *Fight for Freedom,* 138. Kluger, *Simple Justice,* 293–295.

39. Kluger, *Simple Justice,* 613–16. June Shagaloff pointed out in 1999 that, as early as 1946, the NAACP had filed an *amicus curiae* brief challenging the constitutionality of segregating Mexican-American children in public schools. The fed-

eral court in, *Mendez v. Westminister School District,* ruled in favor of the plaintiffs, the Mexican-American children. The court's decision declared straightforwardly that "equal protection of the laws regarding public schools is not provided by furnishing separate schools, the same physical facilities or curricula . . . A paramount requisite . . . *is social equality.* [emphasis added] It must be open to all children regardless of lineage." Shagaloff, Memorandum to Author, April 2000, 4. "This was the first case in which a federal district court held that segregation, *per se,* is a denial of equal protection of the laws," according to the *1946 NAACP Annual Report,* 4.

40. The NAACP published annual reports for the 1940s and 1950s, which document this assertion.

41. Interviews with Shagaloff, July-August 1998, and her Memorandum of April 2000, 3–5.

42. Shagaloff, Memorandum of April 2000.

43. The summary of the Clark study's recommendations is found in Shagaloff, Memorandum of April 2000, 4. Also see Kluger, *Simple Justice,* 717–723, for a more detailed picture of the various viewpoints regarding immediate versus gradual desegregation.

44. *Journal of Social Issues,* Vol. 9, No. 4, 1953. Clark presented evidence and conclusions bolstering the strategy that immediate desegregation of the public schools would be effective and in the long run would produce less opposition than gradual desegregation.

45. Kluger, *Simple Justice,* 641.

46. *Ibid.*, 640–641.

47. Harvard Law Professor Morton J. Horwitz, in *The Warren Court and the Pursuit of Justice,* (New York, 1988), called *Brown* "perhaps the most important judgment ever handed down by the U.S. Supreme Court." Book Review, *New York Times,* by Linda Greenhouse, August 5, 1998.

48. For readers desiring more details about *Brown,* I strongly recommend that they read Richard Kluger's authoritative and masterfully researched volume *Simple Justice.*

49. See note 44.

50. There have been several revisionist examinations of *Brown v. Board of Education* and of the NAACP's strategies and performance in bringing about this landmark decision. In a recent book, for example, James T. Patterson wrote that the civil rights leaders of the period (the 1940s and 1950s)—both black and white —were naive to believe that *Brown* would solve the problem of discrimination in the nation's public schools within a short time frame. Patterson, James T., *Brown v. Board of Education: A Civil Rights Milestone and Its Troubled Legacy,* New York, Oxford University Press, 2001. Prof. Patterson's *ex post facto* insight, what we used to term "Monday-morning quarterbacking," illustrates the problem of trying to divine what was in the minds of intelligent individuals two generations after the fact. It was certainly not naivete which clouded the reason of these sophisticated men and women of both races: they never relied on the decency of the U.S. people or some other sentimentality when they concurred, virtually unanimously, that school desegregation was inevitable. Instead, their optimism was based on an awesome and unshakable faith in the power inherent in the U.S. Constitution, a faith that prolonged the African-American commitment to racial progress long

after many white Americans had themselves begun to shed their own faith in the Constitution.

In the 1950s, the notion that large numbers of Americans would defy the Constitution and rulings of the Supreme Court was hardly conceivable. In modern times, there was simply no precedent for such behavior. And given the social dislocations and pathologies that have stemmed directly from America's failure to resolve its racial dilemma, those who believed that the nation's social and economic problems could be solved *without* successfully desegregating the nation's public schools and providing almost every child with a quality education are the truly naive.

Along these lines, Lewis M. Steel, a former NAACP legal staff attorney during the 1960s who has committed his adult life to civil rights causes, took direct issue with Patterson in a review of the latter's book in *The Nation,* Feb. 5, 2001. Steel took a diametrically opposite position by arguing that the nine justices of the Warren court sold out African-American children and, in effect, their own initial decision, by failing in *Brown II* to order immediate school desegregation or at least to order a firm timetable for compliance. This position has been argued before and has gained considerable acceptance. Steel adds a new fillip to it by suggesting that Frankfurter's religion (he was Jewish) was somehow related to the decision of the nine justices to agree on "all deliberate speed." Steel acknowledges the inhibitions of the court's only remaining Southerner, Stanley Reed, as well as the deep concerns among some justices over the potential for civil strife if the court ordered immediate relief. Nevertheless, he does not help his argument by his failure to explain the mind sets of nine middle-aged and older white males in the 1950s, all of them influenced by the events of the first half of the century, the majority either conservative or moderate, with a handful of liberals who were never close to becoming revolutionaries. The personal social and political philosophies of the justices in 1954 and 1955 made difficult the kind of decision that Steel sought five decades later. Steel offers no new research or documentation that would alter the pivotal role of Frankfurter, as described in enormous detail by Richard Kluger in *Simple Justice,* in guiding the justices to reach the desirable unanimous decision. There is no evidence that the formula Chief Justice Warren proposed a year later, having heard it from Frankfurter, who appropriated it from Justice Oliver Wendell Holmes, in any way swayed the justices in the initial 1954 decision. There should, of course, be no bar against reexamining the role of Frankfurter or any other justice in an analysis of *Brown*, but there is simply no call for raising someone's religion in an effort to suggest a sinister explanation for the formula of "all deliberate speed." The explanation for Steel's own feelings arise probably from his own inherited good fortune, together with his Jewish heritage, which have impelled him to commit to the civil rights struggle far longer than most activists, black or white.

Steel's mentor as NAACP general counsel, Federal Judge Robert L. Carter, has for more than a decade skillfully and passionately expressed his disillusionment with the implementation of the *Brown* decision, before the nation's legal establishment. (Ironically, no individual had done more to bring about that decision.) In his perorations, Judge Carter emphasizes the court's hypocrisy and its inconsistency for having made *Brown* and school desegregation the only important instance where the court found a serious violation of the Constitution and failed to order *immediate relief.* Anyone who doubts that race has been at the heart of the enormous legal and political failure to implement *Brown* is either naive or clueless in respect to the nature of American society.

Chapter 3

1. Ashmore, Harry S., *Hearts and Minds—The Anatomy of Racism from Roosevelt to Reagan,* 221–222.

2. Wilkins, Roy, Address before the Bar Association of St. Louis, November 15, 1973, as reprinted in Solomon, Helen and Wilkins, Aminda, eds., *Talking It Over,* a compilation of Wilkins's speeches and newspaper columns, 112.

3. Ashmore, *Hearts and Minds,* 222.

4. The 1957 NAACP *Annual Report* presents a detailed narrative of the events comprising the Little Rock confrontation between Gov. Faubus, the NAACP, the federal court, and the United States government, 9–13.

For a somewhat different perspective about the Little Rock events, especially as viewed through the eyes of the white establishment, see Harry S. Ashmore's memoir *Hearts and Minds,* Chapters 17 and 18, 251–286. These chapters shed light on the roots of Gov. Faubus' mercurial behavior, which, according to Ashmore, was the result of constant and effective pressure on the governor from racial extremists. A South Carolinian by birth, Ashmore was a seasoned journalist who served as executive editor of the *Arkansas Gazette.* He had more liberal views on race than most, and he gave editorial support for the peaceful desegregation of Little Rock High School. This made the paper a chronic target of the active racists and of the White Citizens Council, which sought to bankrupt it. The *Gazette* under Ashmore won twin Pulitzer Prizes for its coverage of the Little Rock showdown, and Ashmore himself became an icon to civil rights activists as one of the rare, extremely courageous white Southerners who stood up to the worst elements of the South, hardly wavering in the face of threats to his life and to his family. He later became chairman of the Ford Foundation's Center for the Study of Democratic Institutions.

5. Wilkins, *Talking It Over,* 249–254. Wilkins's summation of Eisenhower's behavior during the Little Rock crisis is devastating. In a letter to Rep. Adam Clayton Powell Jr., then chairman of the House Subcommittee on Education, Wilkins states: "I have great difficulty in speaking calmly about the role of President Eisenhower in this whole mess. He has been absolutely and thoroughly disappointing and disillusioning from beginning to end . . . . I still believe that any President of all the people would have at least issued a strong statement on the individual cases of violence that have occurred since the desegregation opinion, even if he did not issue a statement calling for overall observance of that opinion . . . . The situation has hardened not because the NAACP is insisting on obedience to the Supreme Court, but because the White House had abandoned its own Supreme Court and has abdicated leadership in a great moral crisis." Wilkins, *Talking It Over,* 251.

Friends of the late jazz immortal Louis Armstrong, mistakenly perceived as the most accommodationist of the Negro entertainers of his time, credit the immortal trumpeter with one of the most memorable comments in the history of civil rights. Armstrong is reported to have said of Little Rock: "If the U.S. government can't protect those children, then it can go to hell." No single act after *Brown* served to feed African-American anger more than the impotence displayed by the federal government in the initial showdown with Faubus. Armstrong, it should be noted, became the U.S. government's most successful artistic salesman abroad during the 1950s in the cultural rivalry with the Soviet Union as the Cold War heated up. However, because of President Eisenhower's failure to send in troops to protect the nine black children in the early months of the confrontation, Armstrong also canceled his first State Department–funded trip to Africa. This anecdote, in a slightly different form, is included in Ken Burns's nine-part history of jazz for the Public Broadcasting System in 2001.

6. Not every racist maneuver was grim. One humorous by-product of the school desegregation campaign surfaced during the struggle to desegregate the public libraries throughout the South. First, Florida segregationists attempted to ban *The Three Little Pigs* from library shelves because the children's book depicted pigs of differing color living together amicably. Then, in 1959, a publication of the White Citizens Council in Montgomery, Alabama, demanded that the libraries remove a children's book for ages three to seven by Garth Williams titled *The Rabbits' Wedding*. It seems the marriage in question took place between rabbits with white and dark fur. The author, in a statement issued by his publisher, Harpers, insisted the book held no "political significance." However, Emily W. Reed, the Alabama director of the Public Library Service, which lent books to local libraries, placed the book on the reserve shelves. This required the local librarians to request the book specifically. Ms. Reed denied in a newspaper interview that she had banned the book and, when pressed by a segregationist state senator in a public hearing, refused to indicate whether she believed in racial integration on the grounds that the question was not relevant to her responsibilities directing the library service. Her silence on this subject helped to rally the racist claque in the legislature, under pressure from the White Citizens Council. The state legislature prepared to pass a bill to require the head of the state library service to be born in Alabama and to have graduated from the University of Alabama or Auburn in an effort to remove Ms. Reed from her post, when she resigned to take a major post in Washington, D.C., as a coordinator for adult library services for the municipality. During the controversy, children's author Garth Williams admitted that he "was completely unaware that animals with white fur, such as white polar bears and white dogs and white rabbits, were considered blood relations of white human beings."

He added that his tale was not written for adults, who would not understand it because it was only about a soft, furry rabbit and had no hidden messages of hate." *New York Times,* Obituary, May 29, 2001, by Douglas Martin.

7. After the LDF split from the NAACP and Robert Carter had become the Association's leading lawyer as general counsel, Carter also resisted Wilkins's efforts to compel the general counsel to report to him and to clear his important initiatives with him. Carter believed that his authority, like that of Marshall, stemmed directly from the board and that he needed only to obtain approvals or clearances from the board or its legal committee. It was one of the chronic bones of contention between Wilkins and Carter throughout the 1960s until Carter chose to resign when a member of his staff was fired by the board. Neither Wilkins nor his deputy, John Morsell, made any effort to persuade Carter to reverse his position and stay as general counsel. Both appeared pleased that the Carter problem had been resolved by his departure.

8. Interview with Carter, July 18–19, 1998.

9. To this day, Carter is convinced that a few of his legal colleagues deliberately poisoned his relationship with Marshall by carrying tales and exaggerated quotes between the two men. Interview, July 18–19, 1998.

10. Interview with Carter, July 18–19, 1998.

11. Greenberg, *Crusaders in the Courts.* Jack Greenberg indicates in his autobiography only that Marshall had approved of his appointment. The political realities of the LDF board of trustees at that time made it virtually impossible for the board to choose Marshall's successor without honoring his recommendation. Marshall controlled the decisions of the trustees, most of whom were loyal to him and chose to be with the LDF instead of the NAACP after the IRS pressed the two entities to separate physically in 1957. Contrary to press reports of the period prior to Greenberg's appointment, no other names were ever placed in nomination nor was Robert L. Carter considered by the LDF Trustees as a candidate. According to Greenberg, in his memoir, the mistaken press reports misled proponents of Carter to believe he was "in the running," which added to their bitterness later. Greenberg, *Crusaders in the Courts,* 298.

The more important question is what was behind Marshall's rejection of Robert L. Carter in the years following the *Brown* decision; what led to the openly bad blood between them. So complete was their falling-out that staff members felt it incumbent upon themselves to take sides with one or the other before Marshall insisted that Carter remove his office from the LDF's headquarters on West 43rd Street and return to 20 West 40th Street, where the NAACP has long had its own offices. This partisanship was carried out to such an extent, June Shagaloff said almost a half-century later, that supporters of each sat with their leader—Marshall or Carter—during the lunch hour. (When I interviewed Carter in July 1998, he professed to have been totally unaware of this dichotomy.)

It is the writer's belief that Marshall grew more and more concerned about the recognition and attention accorded Carter, as more and more people learned of his crucially important role in the realization of *Brown;* he had been successful in persuading Marshall and others that nonlegal evidence, such as Dr. Clark's doll studies and social science data, could help to persuade the Supreme Court that the doctrine of separate but equal was inherently harmful to black children and therefore in violation of the Constitution. Though a legal genius, Marshall was as human as each of us, and his vanity caused him to suffer increasing anxiety as Carter's public recognition grew. Though there is absolutely no evidence to support Marshall's increasing suspicion that somehow Carter would do something to diminish Marshall's power or celebrity, it is likely that Marshall felt that such was actually happening. That suspicion, bordering on paranoia perhaps, was fed by several young staff members who carried unflattering comments from Marshall to Carter and back.

12. In his memoir, Jack Greenberg observed that nobody among the NAACP's leadership objected to Greenberg's appointment as Thurgood Marshall's successor. He also noted that the NAACP's Deputy Executive Director Dr. John Morsell, and its National Board Chairman, Bishop Stephen Gill Spottswood, attended the LDF board of trustees meeting at which Greenberg was formally elected to head the LDF. Greenberg added that Wilkins himself was of the opinion that the LDF's choice of a new CEO was not the NAACP's business and that

the only issue between them was that of "structure and not of personalities," because in 1957 the LDF chose to become a separate organization. Interview with Greenberg, 296–297.

13. In 1995 a federal courthouse in Youngstown, Ohio, was named after Nathaniel Jones (Youngstown was his hometown), after he had served as a federal appellate judge for almost three decades. Sharing the honor with Jones was his mentor, Federal Judge Frank J. Battisti. During the 1980s, a federal courthouse in Baltimore was named after Clarence Mitchell, the NAACP's stellar lobbyist and himself a lawyer. In the year 2000 a $30.1 million federal courthouse in South Carolina was named for Federal Judge Matthew J. Perry, who had been named to the bench by President Jimmy Carter. From the 1950s until then, Perry had been an important member of the NAACP's national board, an outspoken leader of the South Carolina NAACP State Conference, and the NAACP's acting general counsel between the appointments of permanent ones.

14. Interviews with Shagaloff, July–August 1998.

15. Shagaloff, Memorandum to Author, April 2000, 2–3, and interviews.

16. Interviews with Shagaloff, recalled later that she and her NAACP colleagues were so frightened by the outburst of violence that she immediately took lessons on how to shoot a revolver. While in Cairo, she also worked with several other communities in Illinois and Indiana, resulting in the cessation of segregated school systems in more than 15 communities in the fall of 1952, the largest being the school system in Evansville, Indiana.

17. The *Time* magazine quote of August 31, 1953, appears in the article by Dr. Kenneth Clark in the *Journal of Social Issues,* Vol. 9, No. 4, 1953, 52.

18. Shagaloff, Memorandum, April 2000, 3.

19. Shagaloff, Memorandum, April 2000, 5 and interviews.

20. *Ibid.*

21. *Ibid.*, 6.

22. Letter from Roy Wilkins to Rev. M.D. Bullock, president of the New Rochelle NAACP branch, January 27, 1961.

23. Resolution adopted by the delegates of the NAACP's National Convention in Philadelphia, July, 1961. See NAACP *1961 Annual Report,* chapter on resolutions.

24. Shagaloff, Memorandum, April 2000, 3, and interviews.

25. Greenberg, *Crusaders in the Courts,* 482–486. Also Shagaloff, Memorandum, April 2000.

26. He was Owen Beiber, who was serving his last months as UAW president in 1994. The other two white members were the national treasurer, Jerry Maulden, CEO of Arkansas Power and Light Corporation, a major player in the Southwest, and Rabbi David Saperstein, a Reform leader and head of a liberal Jewish activist center in Washington D.C.

27. Ford Foundation Vice President for Human Rights Lynn Walker (later Huntley), the program officer for the NAACP and other civil rights organizations, explained to Dr. Hooks and me in face-to-face meetings during the mid-1980s that the Ford Foundation had decided not to make an endowment grant to the NAACP, after having made substantial endowment awards to the National Urban League, the LDF, the Lawyers Committee for Civil Rights, and others, because, unlike these recipients, the NAACP "is a democratic organization ultimately ruled by its mem-

bership and therefore might some day change its philosophy or its policies," whereas the public interest law firms and other endowment recipients, being controlled by self-perpetuating boards, were unlikely to undergo such sweeping changes.

28. Interview with Carter, July 18–19, 1998.

29. The model devised by Carter to which the IRS accorded tax-deductible status was rapidly replicated by most of the activist nonprofit agencies in the nation, including the ACLU, CORE, Southern Christian Leadership Conference (SCLC), the National Organization of Women, and Americans for Democratic Action. At different times, I represented both the ACLU's Roger Baldwin Foundation and the NOW Legal Defense Fund in later years. Subsequently, centrist and conservative organizations followed suit, as did the Sierra Club and many other environmentalist organizations.

30. The NAACP proposals and activities described in these pages are summarized in a lengthy memorandum submitted by June Shagaloff Alexander to me in January, 2001, as a supplement to her original memorandum, in order to illustrate better the work of the NAACP education department during the 1960s and early 1970s.

31. The school systems in which the NAACP was most deeply involved during this period included, by state, the following: Arizona: Eloy, Phoenix, Tuscon; California: Banning, Berkeley, Garden Grove, Los Angeles, Oakland, Oxmaid-Ventura, Pasadena, Riverside, Sacramento, San Bernadino, San Diego, San Francisco, San Mateo, Sausalito, South Antelope Valley; Colorado: Denver; Connecticut: Bridgeport, Canbury, Hartford, New Haven, Norwalk, Stamford; Illinois: Alton, Centerville, Chicago, Fairmont Park, Joliet, Maywood, Mt. Vernon, Peoria, Robins, Springfield; Indiana: Fort Wayne, Gary, Indianapolis; Iowa: Davenport, Des Moines; Massachusetts: Boston, Springfield; Michigan: Benton Harbor, Detroit, Flint, Grand Rapids, Lansing; Minnesota: Minneapolis, St. Paul; New Jersey: Atlantic City, Bridgeton, Elizabeth, Englewood, Franklin Township, Jersey City, Linden, Montclair, Morristown, Neptune, Newark, Orange, Patterson, Plainfield, Rahway, Red Bank, Teaneck, Trenton, Union Township, Woodbury; Nevada: Las Vegas; New York: Albany, Bellport, Buffalo, Freeport, Glen Cove, Hempstead, Lawrence-Cedarhurst, Malverne, Manhasset, Mt. Vernon, New Rochelle, Niagara Falls, Nyack, Portchester–Rye, Poughkeepsie, Rochester, Roosevelt, Syracuse, Westbury, White Plains; Ohio: Cincinnati, Cleveland, Columbus, Dayton, Zenia; Oregon: Portland; Pennsylvania: Ardmore, Chester, Coatesville, Philadelphia, Pittsburgh, Willow Grove; Rhode Island: Providence; Washington: Seattle, Tacoma; Wisconsin: Milwaukee, Racine. During the 1970s and 1980s the NAACP legal department brought suit against the school systems of many of these cities to achieve racial desegregation. Shagaloff, Supplementary Memorandum to Author, January 2001.

32. Robert L. Carter argued from the very beginning of the controversy that the Internal Revenue Service had not compelled the NAACP and the LDF to separate. When that act took place, he informed his board members that the NAACP had lost control of one of its most important functions—the legal program—and of the fundraising that enabled it to carry on such a program. After Thurgood Marshall announced his departure in 1961 for the federal bench, Carter urged the NAACP board to reexamine rationally the split. When all of this proved futile, in

1961 Carter began informing Greenberg that the LDF was prohibited from meeting with NAACP lawyers, including volunteers. Further letters were sent in 1962 to a larger list of attorneys throughout the country. This time, the NAACP legal committee, which included such important LDF trustees as Bob Ming, who was also on retainer by the LDF, overruled Carter without in any way involving Wilkins, who had been ill during the period. Later, Ming and other LDF outside counsel who were board members of the NAACP were successful in blocking any legal move by the NAACP to prevent the LDF from using the NAACP's name. In 1964, when the NAACP finally received tax-deductible status from the IRS, Carter wrote Greenberg, insisting that the LDF desist from trying to represent NAACP branches. He wrote: "I want to make explicit the basic point of my telephone conversation with you on Tuesday, June 9, 1965 . . . . I am requesting that you cease any direct contact with any NAACP branches in regard to litigation." Greenberg, *Crusaders in the Courts,* 480. Overall, this note is based on Greenberg's own memoir, 478–481. Greenberg suggests that neither he nor the LDF heeded Carter's strictures in respect to LDF lawyers representing NAACP branches, or the later complaints of Wilkins and his board that the LDF was expanding into areas the NAACP considered its own jurisdiction. Greenberg argues that the only basis for the NAACP's objection to the LDF's continued use of its name was financial —that the NAACP coveted the LDF's larger tax-deductible income. In one note, he even suggests that the NAACP's complaints were based on "inept fund-raising" and "disappointed fund-raising." He denies, disingenuously, that the LDF had ever received gifts or grants meant for the NAACP, when each year a number of checks meant for the NAACP were transmitted to our headquarters from the LDF, whereas a tiny number of checks meant for the LDF were transmitted to the latter. The same note suggests that the story behind the initial grant from the Rockefeller Foundation to the NAACP, wherein the senior foundation staff was obliged to admit that it had mistakenly made a grant to the LDF, thinking it had helped the NAACP, was untrue. If Greenberg were not mistaken, then both Roy Wilkins and his deputy John Morsell would have been lying. Both had been deeply and personally involved in reversing this farcical enterprise. Greenberg also denies that the LDF ever received a grant from the Altschul Foundation, but the latter's staff told me that it had already made its regular gift to the LDF and would not therefore support the NAACP. It is possible that the staff of a small family foundation such as the Altschul also dispensed the personal gifts of the Altschul family, and that they made their gift from one of the individual Altschuls but considered it part of their overall giftmaking. This happened often with family foundations. In any event, Greenberg never denied that he received gifts from members of the Altschul family.

The lay leadership of the NAACP uniformly believed that the reason Greenberg and the LDF tenaciously hung onto the NAACP's name was because the use of the NAACP's initials substantially increased their receipts from their fundraising. There is little doubt this was true since, according to former LDF staff members friendly with me, virtually every experimental mail appeal undertaken by the LDF without the NAACP name association proved a failure. In an ironic twist, during the NAACP's scandals, which surfaced in 1993–1994, the organization was the victim of widespread disenchantment because of the behavior of several of its leaders and the misuse of funds. So broad was this disenchantment that the LDF spokesmen affirmed publicly that the LDF's income had also fallen off significantly during the same period and that if the decline continued, the LDF would probably drop the NAACP's initials, in order to avoid being victimized by Association. It seems that few of the LDF's supporters had any inkling that the LDF was "not part of the National Association for the Advancement of Colored People," as its disclaimer in very small type stated on its literature. The fact is that almost every literate American has heard of the NAACP, whereas only a tiny percentage of the population is familiar with the LDF. The monetary value is in the former.

33. After he defeated NAACP Chairperson Margaret Bush Wilson in a showdown with the NAACP board following Wilson's suspension of Hooks in 1982, NAACP Executive Director Benjamin L. Hooks made a serious effort to restore the relationship with the LDF, and though it did become noticeably warmer at the staff level, the majority of the NAACP board members remained combative over the LDF's continued use of the NAACP's initials. Eventually the suit that was filed in the late 1970s by the NAACP to compel the LDF to drop the initials was lost when the Supreme Court refused to review an appellate court decision denying the NAACP request, because it had waited too long to challenge the LDF's use of the name (*laches*, in legal parlance). Earlier, the federal district court had ruled in favor of the NAACP.

34. On September 10, 1999, a federal judge halted the desegregation program there, ruling that, according to one news report, "all vestiges of intentional discrimination had disappeared." *New York Times*, September 11, 1999, A1, A8. The LDF had defended the original desegregation plan in court and subsequently filed an appeal, which as of this writing has yet to reach the U.S. Supreme Court. Prior to the Charlotte decision, federal judges during the 1990s had voided desegregation plans involving busing in Nashville, Oklahoma City, Denver, Wilmington (Delaware), and Cleveland. Either the LDF or the NAACP legal department had been involved in each of these cases originally. Civil rights attorneys have asserted that these reversals are a direct result of the tidal wave of conservative bench appointments made during the 12 years of the Reagan and Bush Administrations. Despite the certainty with which the presiding federal judges have proclaimed that the aforementioned school systems had been desegregated, such experts as Professor Gary Oldfield of the Civil Rights Project of the Harvard School of Education have, for a decade, argued forcefully and with substantial documentation that, since the mid-1980s, the nation's schools have everywhere been steadily resegregating after two decades of progress in the South.

35. Although Vernon Jordan was considered by most civil rights professionals to have had the inside track as Roy Wilkins's successor, he was never actually offered the post. In an interview on April 27, 2000, Jordan told the writer that he had been urged by Wilkins to take a vacant post as deputy to Gloster Current, NAACP Director of Branches, in the early 1970s, as "a form of preparation" for the top post of the NAACP, as Wilkins had decided to depart several years thenceforth. After Jordan declined, Wilkins never brought up the subject again, Jordan recalled, until 1972 when news leaked that Jordan was about to accept the top post at the National Urban League. As Jordan remembers it, Wilkins phoned him to suggest that "Jordan was an NAACP man, not an Urban League man." Jordan, however, accepted the League's offer to become its president and CEO.

36. In his autobiography, Roy Wilkins described E.D. Nixon as follows: "He was straight as a ramrod, tough as a mule, and braver than a squad of marines.

When he took up the case, the white establishment of Montgomery didn't have a chance." Wilkins, *Talking It Over,* 226. A. Philip Randolph, for whom I had also worked during the 1950s, had an equally favorable opinion of E.D. Nixon.

37. Wilkins, *Talking It Over,* 228.

38. *Ibid.,* 227–229.

39. Garrow, David J., *Bearing the Cross—Dr. Martin Luther King Jr. and the SCLC,* 59.

40. Wilkins, *Talking It Over,* Introduction by Julian Bond to the 1994 revised edition, xiii.

41. According to numerous accounts, the most recent being *Freedom's Daughters—The Unsung Heroines of the Movement from 1830 to 1970* by Lynne Olsen, Dr. King, like most of the other African-American men of the period, was a prisoner of his sexist beliefs. He could not accept a woman in a staff role and passed over Ms. Baker by appointing Rev. Ralph Abernathy to the top staff position at the SCLC. There is reason to believe that Ms. Baker had similar problems at the NAACP. It is certain she encountered them when she put together the postlunch counter sit-in conference at Shaw University in Raleigh, N.C., which created a student alliance that resulted in the formation of the SNCC. At the time she persuaded the participants to remain independent of Dr. King's SCLC, as well as the other major adult movements. Dr. King had hoped the new group would become his youth division.

42. In an opinion poll for *Newsweek* in 1963, Louis Harris reported that the NAACP was overwhelmingly more popular among African Americans than any other organization. Among Negroes 91 percent held a positive view of the NAACP and of its leaders. Only 59 percent held positive views of CORE and 58 percent of SCLC, although 83 percent held a positive view of Dr. King and his associates. Of the remaining groups, 54 percent held positive views towards the National Urban League, 15 percent towards SNCC, and 10 percent towards the Black Muslims. Some 45 percent of those polled believed that the NAACP had done the most for civil rights, followed by 25 percent who held this view about Dr. King. (Nine percent felt this way about President Kennedy, the third highest total.) William Brink and Louis Harris, *The Negro Revolution in America,* 116–117.

Chapter 4

1. The 1876 election for president contributed significantly toward these events. Democrat Samuel Tilden, New York's governor, won the popular vote, but his Republican opponent, Rutherford B. Hayes, won the electoral majority. A deadlock ensued that was to be played out in Congress. The price the Democrats demanded for conceding a Hayes victory was the epitome of cynicism: the Republicans pledged that Hayes would withdraw the Union Army from the South, ending Reconstruction. In effect, the Army's withdrawal restored political power to the white landed class, which had so greatly benefitted from slavery, while canceling virtually all of the rights enjoyed for a decade by the newly-freed slaves. This grand betrayal led to the imposition of a new form of oppression that Negroes would endure for another century—the Jim Crow system.

For a detailed exposition of how Negroes were deprived of the vote after Reconstruction, see Lewinson, Paul, *Race, Class, and Party: A History of Negro Suffrage and White Politics.*

2. Numerous books have been written on the demise of Reconstruction and the rise of Jim Crow, including such a classic as C. Vann Woodward's *The Strange Career of Jim Crow.* Heather Cox Richardson's *The Death of Reconstruction* is probably the most recent work on the subject and explores the role of and attitudes toward labor, black and white, in the post-Civil War period.

3. Seventeen years before the founding meeting of the NAACP, Ida Wells Barnett, a 30-year-old Negro journalist, exposed the epidemic of lynchings in a series of articles in a newspaper in her adopted home town of Memphis. Her resultant celebrity catapulted her into national prominence. In her later writings based upon investigative reporting in the South, she was perhaps the first writer to expose the "big lie" of the racist propagandists—that lynchings were justified as a means of controlling the alleged sexual attacks by black men on white women. Her frank investigations of the sexual aspects of racism resulted in ominous innuendos and outright attacks on her own sexual behavior and alienated her from black male leaders. However, she was invited by the white organizers of the original "Call" in 1909, which resulted in the formation of the NAACP, of which Wells was an original founder. Her biography—*The Life of Ida B. Wells* by Linda A. McMurry, New York, Oxford University Press—was published in early 1999. It points out that Wells was one of the first activist American women to raise a family—in her case, of six children.

New York Times editorial writer Brent Staples, an African American, wrote an appreciation of Wells in a column on April 4, 2000. The occasion was the exhibition at the Museum of the City of New York of historic lynching photos. The exhibition was entitled "Without Sanctuary: Lynching Photography in America." (It originally opened at a small art gallery on Manhattan's East 70th Street.) Organized by James Allen, the exhibit consisted of several dozen vintage photos of actual American lynchings, all of them of Negro men except for one of a Jewish victim in Atlanta, Leo Frank. Many of the photos had been produced in multiples as postcards to permit spectators to send them to friends and relatives, boasting of their presence at such a dramatic event. The photos reveal that lynchings were occasions, not unlike parades and holiday picnics, for the entire family in their finery to attend as recreation. The faces of many of the spectators are etched with grins and smiles. The photos were published in an excellent book, also titled *Without Sanctuary,* which contains several important items of NAACP ephemera. For a moving and detailed account of numerous lynchings, see Leon F. Litwack's brilliantly written chapter, "Hellhounds," in the same book, pp. 8–37.

In his April 4, 2000, commentary, Brent Staples pays tribute to the figures in the antilynching movement "who eventually brought this horror to an end, among them James Weldon Johnson, W.E.B. Du Bois, and the heroine of the movement, Ida Wells Barnett." For some mysterious reason, which Staples declined to explain when I wrote him to question his oversight, Staples failed to mention the NAACP even once. While Wells began her antilynching work well before the founding of the NAACP, she continued it under the NAACP banner. Moreover, most of DuBois's efforts and all of James Weldon Johnson's were done as officers of the NAACP, which carried the fight to the highest corridors of the nation's power for almost a third of a century. Allen's book comprehends that notable fact, as did the inclusion of the NAACP items in the exhibit. Staples also ignores the strenuous and insightful efforts over two decades by Walter White, successor to James Weldon Johnson as the NAACP's executive secretary. This may have been a conscious omission since Staples, in a later column, published the inexplicable (and false) allegation that Walter White had seriously advocated the use of a "magic soap" for Negroes to transform them into whites in order to solve the nation's race problem.

Perhaps the saddest aspect of these events was the inability of the NAACP's contemporary leaders and staff, whom I informed of both matters, to respond in any manner whatsoever to correct or refute the two Staples articles; Staples, though African-American, clearly has a problem acknowledging the NAACP, its history, and its achievements.

4. In 1906 a Negro man, Ed Johnson, was falsely convicted of raping a white woman in Chattanooga, Tennessee, even though the victim had failed to identify him and he was threatened by a member of the jury. The judge sentenced him to death, but the Supreme Court, hearing his appeal, concluded that he failed to receive a fair trial and stayed his execution. Local Chattanoogans were incensed by what they considered unwarranted federal interference into their affairs, and they decided to take matters into their own hands. They broke into the town jail, tied him up, and dragged him through the streets to a bridge, where they hung him while a few men, not sated by the noose, riddled his swinging body with bullets.

In its only criminal trial in history, the U.S. Supreme Court convicted the town sheriff and some of his fellow participants of contempt of court for violating the court's order to keep the prisoner safe. They were thereby convicted of aiding in the lynching. Justice Oliver Wendell Holmes was outraged by the trial of Johnson, which he described as a "shameful attempt at justice." He also observed that "In all likelihood this was a case of an innocent man improperly branded a guilty brute and condemned to die from the start."

Almost a century later, Ed Johnson was cleared of the rape charge by Judge Douglas A. Meyers. Speaking in a Chattanooga courtroom, he set aside Johnson's conviction before a racially mixed crowd and a bank of television cameras, noting, "Something I don't believe the white community understands is that, especially at that time, the object was to bring in a black body, not necessarily the person who had committed the crime. And I think that's what happened in this case. There was a rush to find somebody to convict and blame for this." *New York Times,* February 27, 2000, 24, in an article by Emily Yelling beneath the headline, "Lynching Victim Is Cleared of Rape, 100 Years Later."

The judge's remarks a century later could have been applied to almost all of the lynching cases between the end of Reconstruction and the passage of the Civil Rights Act of 1964. It helps to verify the hypothesis that the pursuit of justice was rarely, if ever, a goal of mob lynching; instead, its purpose was to so terrify Negroes as to dissuade them from ever asserting themselves or their rights. No act better symbolized the defiance of this strategy than the twentieth century efforts by Negroes to register to vote.

5. The same conflicts in respect to issues and strategies that divided DuBois and Washington were to reemerge periodically during the ensuing nine decades of the NAACP's existence.

6. Between 1917 and 2000, the NAACP had publicly criticized every sitting president because of some civil rights deficiency in his policies and/or practices. However, with the exception of the 1964 election between Lyndon Johnson and Barry Goldwater, the Association has remained at least nominally nonpartisan until the presidential election in the year 2000. In that election the NAACP openly supported Democrat Al Gore and vigorously opposed his Republican opponent, George W. Bush. In order to oppose Goldwater in 1964, Roy Wilkins was compelled to obtain both a two-thirds majority of the 1964 national convention delegates and the approval of his national board. No such mechanism was employed in 2000, although the NAACP was governed by the same restrictions on political partisanship. Instead, the NAACP President Kweise Mfume and the board chairman Julian Bond established a subsidiary of the organization—the NAACP Voter Fund—made possible by a recent Internal Revenue Service ruling that promoted the generation of so-called soft money in politics. In the NAACP's case, one individual—a West Coast trial lawyer—contributed $9 million to this fund, enabling it to blanket the nation to promote African-American registration and to get out the vote for Al Gore.

7. Columbia Professor Eric Foner has noted that Wilson in 1913 had "dismissed many of the black employees of the federal government and imposed rigid segregation on the remainder. Three years later, he invited D.W. Griffith to show his film 'The Birth of a Nation,' which glorified the Ku Klux Klan and presented white supremacy as the underpinning of national unity, at the White House." Prof. Foner also observed that Wilson, who was the first Southerner elected president since Zachary Taylor, presided over a reunion at the site of the Battle of Gettysburg in 1913, attended by 53,000 veterans, "all of them white," which was cleverly transformed into a "festival of national reconciliation," as part of a systematic effort to erase the nation's collective memory over the major cause of the war—slavery—and of the treatment African Americans had received both during the three centuries of slavery and during the post-Reconstruction period in which Jim Crow laws and practices were imposed on the newly freed slaves. The book which deals with this collective brainwashing and which Foner reviewed is *Race and Reunion—The Civil War in American Memory* by David W. Blight. The Foner review appeared in the *New York Times Book Review,* March 3, 2001, under the appropriate title of "Selective Memory."

8. See James Weldon Johnson's autobiography, *Along This Way: The Autobiography of James Weldon Johnson,* 361–374, for a personal account of his efforts to gain passage for an antilynching bill. Of special interest are his pungent remarks concerning his efforts to persuade United States senators to support the bill already passed by the House.

9. Wilkins, *Standing Fast,* 53–54.

10. *Ibid.*, 54. Wilkins had left St. Paul for a key job with the Negro newspaper, the *Kansas City Call.* In Kansas City, he became more active with the NAACP and the growing movement for political change within many black communities in urban centers across the nation. James Weldon Johnson, who was the

first Negro executive secretary of the NAACP, served in that capacity from 1920 to 1931. His remarks to the 1923 conference continued to inspire Wilkins throughout his 36-year tenure with the NAACP.

11. Goings, Kenneth W., *The NAACP Comes of Age—The Defeat of Judge John J. Parker,* 18. Then in 1930, another residential segregation case came before Judge John J. Parker of the Fourth Circuit Court of Appeals. In this case, the city of Richmond had sought to establish residential segregation by employing the state's law against racial intermarriage, which had yet to be declared unconstitutional. The Richmond ordinance barred anyone from residing in a neighborhood in which the same individual could not legally marry its residents. In January 1930, Parker ruled that the ordinance was unconstitutional, and in May the Supreme Court upheld his ruling. Judge Parker and the NAACP would meet again at a historic turning point because earlier that year an associate justice of the Supreme Court (Edward Terry Sanford of North Carolina) died suddenly, providing President Herbert Hoover with an opportunity to appoint a new justice to the court.

12. *Ibid.*, 20.

13. *Ibid.*, 23.

14. *Ibid.*, 23.

15. *Ibid.*, 24–26.

16. Hughes, *Fight for Freedom,* 37–51; Goings, *NAACP Comes of Age,* 74–75; Wilkins, *Standing Fast,* 92–95. Among the senators opposing Parker were 17 Republican Progressives, including such stellar figures as Hiram Johnson, William Borah, George Norris, Robert LaFollette, and Arthur Vandenberg. A total of 10 Southern Democrats voted against Parker's nomination, among them Alabama's Hugo Black (later a liberal associate justice of the Supreme Court) and Kentucky's Alben Barkley, Truman's vice-presidential candidate in 1948 when he defeated the Dixiecrats, the Communist-controlled Progressive Party, and the Republicans. Three other Southern senators were listed as not voting but paired against Parker: Georgia's George, Alabama's Heflin, and Oklahoma's Thomas. Besides these three Southern Democrats, five Republicans were also paired against Parker. The reverse also obtained: three Republicans and five Democrats were paired in favor of Parker's nomination. Thus, the actual vote would have been 49 to 47 if the 16 paired absentees had been present. Once placed before the Judiciary Committee, the entire Senate fight lasted only 10 days.

17. In what must be either poetic justice or simply one more example of the ironies that run through the NAACP's history, President Hoover nominated another candidate for the Supreme Court near the end of his term. He was the noted jurist Benjamin Cardozo. Hoover's note to himself, according to Cardozo's biographer, Richard Polenberg, described his nominee as having three practical problems: "Jew," "Democrat," and "New York." In record time, the Senate approved Cardozo's nomination without debate or a roll call vote. Polenberg, Richard, *The World of Benjamin Cardozo; Personal Values and the Judicial Process.*

18. Goings, *NAACP Comes of Age,* 66–67.

19. *Ibid.*, 110–111. Goings provides DuBois's entire list of targeted senators as published in *The Crisis.* Those senators who were defeated in 1934 were Kean (NJ), Fess (NH), Hatfield (WV), Patterson (MO), Reed (PA), and Townsend (DE).

20. Wilkins, *Standing Fast,* 163.

21. *Ibid.*, 151–155.

22. *Ibid.*, 153. The same quotation contains an earlier passage laced with unmitigated anger by Hastie: "For fifty years, prejudiced white men and abject, boot-licking, gut-lacking, knee-bending, favor-seeking Negroes have been insulting our intelligence with a tale that goes like this: 'Segregation is not evil. Negroes are better off by themselves. They can get equal treatment and be happy, too, if they live and move and have their being off by themselves, except, of course, as they are needed by the white community to do the heavy and dirty work.'"

A version of the same events more sympathetic to DuBois may be found in an essay by a black historian, Dr. Lerone Bennett Jr. in the November 1994 issue of *Ebony* magazine, 104–106, under the title "The NAACP's First Revolt." Dr. Bennett quotes DuBois as deciding to reject the use of protests because they "would never end racism." Instead, Bennett allows DuBois to explain his radical shift from the strategy of integration to one of segregation as follows:

"By 1930 I had become convinced that the basic policies and ideals of the [NAACP] must be modified and changed; that in a world where economic dislocation has become as great as in ours, a mere appeal based on the old liberalism, a mere appeal to justice and further effort at legal decision, was missing the essential need; that the essential need was to guard and better the chances of Negroes, educated and ignorant, to earn a living, safeguard their income, and raise the level of employment. I did not believe that a further prolongation of looking for salvation from the whites was feasible. So far as they were ignorant of the results of race prejudice, we had taught them; but so far as their race prejudice was built and increasingly built on the basis of the income which they enjoyed and their anti-Negro bias consciously or unconsciously formulated in order to protect their wealth and power, in so far our whole program must be changed, and we must seek the power and particularly the organization among Negroes to meet this new situation." *Ibid.,* 106. Hardly a literary gem and notwithstanding its syntax problems, this explication by Du Bois demonstrates an apparently muddled economic view but one that helps to document his gradual slide in the direction of Marxism and the class struggle. The strategy proposed by DuBois directly conflicted with that of John L. Lewis, Walter Reuther, and the other leaders of the newly formed CIO, organized to compete with the racist AFL in attracting Negro members to fight side-by-side with white workers against their corporate employers.

Dr. Bennett also observes that the NAACP, in order to undercut the alleged appeal of DuBois's "radical" proposals, appointed a Committee on Future Plans and Programs, chaired by a "young radical economist," Abram Harris, who had earlier been proposed for the NAACP national board by DuBois himself. The committee's recommendations were, after some amendment, adopted at the 1935 national convention in St. Louis. The recommendations included a new program "for vigorous economic action and unification of Black and White workers." Local NAACP branches were instructed to become "centers of economic and political education," according to Bennett. However, Bennett quotes Dr. Ralph J. Bunche as stating that the recommendations were never carried out. According to Bennett, the NAACP did take steps to instruct local branches to take direct action on economic issues, and to organize youth councils throughout the nation.

The Bennett essay was written to provide a parallel with the crisis that NAACP Executive Director Benjamin Chavis had encountered earlier in that year and which resulted in his dismissal by the National board in August 1994. There was, however, not the slightest similarity between the ideological struggle that divided DuBois and Walter White during the Great Depression and the shady circumstances that resulted in Chavis's expulsion.

23. Wilkins, *Standing Fast,* 152–155. For a more detailed description of the struggle between DuBois and Walter White, see David Levering's second volume of his monumental biography, *W.E.B. DuBois—1919–1963,* 283–305. Levering also chronicles DuBois's evolving attraction with Marxism without in any way minimizing some of the great academic's questionable political judgment, such as his support of Japan in World War II.

24. *Time,* January 24, 1938, 9; 8–10 for the entire article.

25. *Ibid.* The *Time* article reports that Walter White had actually met with President Roosevelt as a result of the intervention of FDR's Negro valet, Irvin H. McDuffie. It also records that the Wagner-Van Nuys bill called for federal prosecution for sheriffs and peace officers who failed to give criminals and suspected criminals "reasonable protection from mobs." The bill provided for a $5,000 fine and/or jail time of up to five years for those convicted of this felony. It also provided for payment of $10,000 to the families of mob victims to be paid by the county whose officials had been responsible for failing to protect the victims. At the time, 12 states already had such a law.

26. Wilkins, *Standing Fast,* 129. Although Wilkins was convinced that FDR personally opposed lynching, in his autobiography he supports the view that Southerners, because of the seniority rule, dominated the committee chairmanships in both houses of Congress, producing a virtual stranglehold on legislation. Without their cooperation, no president, including FDR, had much of a chance to obtain congressional approval of his New Deal legislative agenda—an agenda that FDR and most of his colleagues believed was essential for the survival and restoration of U.S. society.

27. *Ibid.*, 168. See also Marian Anderson's autobiography, *My Lord, What a Morning.*

28. A full and detailed account of this important event can be found in an essay by Allida M. Black, entitled "A Reluctant but Persistent Warrior: Eleanor Roosevelt and the Early Civil Rights Movement,' which was published in *Woman in the Civil Rights Movement: Trailblazers and Torchbearers 1941–1965,* 234–243. Ms. Black notes that Interior Secretary Harold Ickes, a key player in this story, had early been the chairman of the NAACP's Chicago chapter.

Chapter 5

1. Wilkins, *Standing Fast,* 125.

2. The Scottsboro Boys were Charlie Weems, Ozzie Powell, Clarence Norris, Olen Montgomery, and Willie Roberson, all of Georgia, and Haywood Patterson, Eugene Williams, and Andrew and LeRoy Wright of Chattanooga. The oldest was Weems; Leroy Wright and Williams were thirteen at the time of their arrest.

3. Wilkins, *Standing Fast,* 157–158.

4. *Ibid.*, 158.

5. *Ibid.*, 159.

6. Four decades later Wilkins wrote in his syndicated column devoted to the subject of the Scottsboro case that Liebowitz, then a "famous criminal lawyer, volunteered to defend the men without fee. Liebowitz was given his transportation to Alabama and the insufficient sum of $3,000 for expenses. In the 1934 printed report of the NAACP, it is stated that the total 'so far expended by the Association [for the Scottsboro case] is $11,854.70.' This was in the same year that the total income of the NAACP, exclusive of special funds, was $44,176.91." That proportion—roughly one fourth of its income for the year, demonstrates how important the Scottsboro defense had been to the NAACP in 1934. Quoted from Wilkins, Roy, syndicated column of February 22, 1975.

7. Hughes, Langston. *Fight for Freedom—The Story of the NAACP.* It was especially ironic that Hughes was hounded in the post-war period by professional anti-Communists and political demagogues as a "Communist sympathizer."

8. Wilkins, Roy, syndicated column of February 22, 1975. In the same column he also stated, "It became apparent that, in spite of Judge Horton's ruling, the Scottsboro defendants would not be free as long as they were defended by the International Labor Defense, the legal arm of the American Communist Party."

9. The Meeropol-Holiday story has been told in several news articles, including "A Musical Chapter in the History of the Struggle for Civil Rights," by Chloe Vetlman, *The Forward,* March 31, 2000, p. 13; "A Song that Reverberates in the American Soul," by David Margolick, *New York Times* Arts and Leisure Section, July 2, 2000, pp. 1, 27; and, of course, Margolick's book, *Strange Fruit: Billy Holiday, Cafe Society and an Early Cry for Civil Rights.*

Meeropol and his wife adopted the two sons of Julius and Ethel Rosenberg, who were executed as Soviet spies in 1953. Meeropol had been a member of the CPUSA and a committed Zionist before and during World War II, a feat requiring considerable intellectual acrobatics.

The nightclub Cafe Society, which was located on Sheridan Square in Greenwich Village, had been founded by another left-wing Jew, Barney Josephson, as a venue for Negro performers such as Billy Holiday and Josh White. It opened its doors to both Negro and white customers, not common even in New York before World War II. The major Harlem nightclubs, such as the Cotton Club, which showcased the cream of Negro entertainment, refused to serve Negro customers.

In 1940, novelist Lillian Smith, a Southern woman, wrote a best-selling novel, also entitled *Strange Fruit,* which greatly contributed to the awareness among white Americans of the nation's racial injustices.

10. Wilkins, *Standing Fast,* 161.

11. Foster, William Z., "The Communist Position on the Negro Question," 12.This paperback pamphlet includes excerpts of speeches by William Z. Foster, Benjamin Davis Jr., Eugene Dennis, Nat Ross, James E. Jackson, Alexander Bittleman, William L. Patterson, and other CPUSA leaders, arguing the pros and cons of the new policy proposed in the resolution, which appears on pp. 9–12.The remarks of the party's leading Negro, Ben Davis, then a member of the New York City Council, in favor of the resolution, are particularly illuminating in terms of how effective was party discipline (pp. 19–23). For a later take on the CPUSA's policy toward the condition of African Americans, see Davis, Benjamin J., "The Negro People in the Struggle for Peace and Freedom," New York, 1951, a report

to the 15th convention of the CPUSA. Davis declares, "Wall Street's Negro reformist agents have converted the NAACP, the National Council of Negro Women, and, even the Brooklyn Dodgers, into a base for their warmongering subservience to imperialism and their undermining of the Negro people's unity and militancy. The central weakness of our work in the historic NAACP Washington Mobilization was the failure to introduce into this fight a revolutionary content, namely, the consciousness that this vast people's movement is part of the fight for peace and against American imperialism." The CPUSA had firmly allied itself with Stalin during both the war against Hitler and the Cold War, placing the struggle for Negro freedom well down on its list of imperatives.

12. So complete was the Kremlin's control of the CPUSA that each year until the mid-1940s it routinely shipped its annual files and records to the Comintern headquarters in Moscow. In 1993, John Hughes of the U.S. Library of Congress was informed by Russian officials that the complete and original CPUSA files were not only stored by the Comintern but were available for reproduction for American libraries. The Library of Congress paid the Russians $100,000 to microfilm the documents, almost 500,000 pages. Irvin Molotsky, *The New York Times,* Arts and Leisure Section, February 6, 2001.

13. The first quote comes from a resolution adopted by the NAACP's West Coast Regional Conference on March 8, 1947. The second appeared in a resolution adopted by the 38th Annual Conference (later called "convention") on June 28, 1947, in Washington, D.C.

14. Letter from Roy Wilkins to William L. Patterson, Nov. 22, 1949, as reprinted in a public flyer, "MEMO TO: NAACP Branches FROM: Roy Wilkins, Acting Secretary SUBJECT: The Communists vs. the NAACP's Civil Rights Fight, March 22, 1950." This widely distributed memo, the opening gun in the campaign to formally exclude the Communists from the NAACP, accuses them of increasing their efforts to take over local branches. It charges, "In recent years, these efforts on the part of the Communists have intensified. The shrillness with which they are demanding the right to infiltrate the NAACP requires explicit restatement of the Association's position and a warning to our branches to be alert to such attempts." In an interview with Herbert Hill in March 2000, Professor Hill revealed that he had provided Wilkins with an initial draft for the reply to Patterson.

15. NAACP, *1949 Annual Report,* 65 and 8. That year the NAACP staff consisted of 31 executives and attorneys as well as approximately the same number of secretaries and clerks.

16. During those stormy years, the Communists abroad, backed by the bayonets of the Red Army, seized control of the popularly based governments of Eastern Europe and of the global democratic organizations headquartered in the Soviet sphere of influence. Those organizations represented the world's students, youth, veterans, artists, writers, farmers, and other categories of humankind. Legitimate democrats were expelled, imprisoned, or executed by the Communists as the Cold War heated up.

17. Wilkins, *Standing Fast,* 210–211.

18. NAACP, *1950 Annual Report,* 49. In an interesting bit of revisionism, the mass media, including public television and the *New York Times,* have glorified the "civil rights" record and commitment of CPUSA members during the

1930s and 1940s, without ever referring to the vitriolic attacks the CPUSA made against the NAACP and its leaders during those decades or their historic abandonment of civil rights whenever the interests of the Soviet Union clashed with it.

19. Williams, Juan, "The Strangest of Bedfellows," *Newsweek,* September 14, 1988, 33. In this essay Williams speculates that neither Hoover nor Marshall believed that each was being used by the other. Marshall confirmed his FBI involvement in his later years during interviews with Williams and stated that he felt that by co-opting Hoover, he was able to be a more effective civil rights attorney on behalf of the NAACP.

Former NAACP Public Information Director Denton Watson, biographer of Clarence Mitchell, felt compelled to defend Marshall in a *New York Times* op-ed article, in which he emphasized the vulnerability of the NAACP's local branches to infiltration as a result of the "sophisticated techniques" utilized by the CPUSA. Watson observed that among the methods utilized by the Communists was the provision of women to "seduce NAACP members to convert them to their cause." *New York Times,* December 12, 1996, the year the Marshall FBI story first broke publicly.

For further background on the NAACP's firm opposition to the CPUSA and its Soviet directors during the 1950s, especially as articulated by Walter White, Roy Wilkins, and Thurgood Marshall, see Greenberg, *Crusaders in the Courts,* 102–106. Greenberg, who succeeded Marshall as the CEO of the Legal Defense and Education Fund, reports that in 1947 Walter White solicited a written testimonial from FBI Director J. Edgar Hoover regarding the civil rights organization's bona fides as a stalwart anti-Communist force (p. 105). Greenberg also notes that White suspended the NAACP's San Francisco branch when a "known member of the CPUSA became chairman of the Nominating Committee," (p. 104).

20. See Paul Robeson's pamphlet, "The Negro People and the Soviet Union," New York: New Century, 1950.

21. Until the 1980s the Communists kept alive the names of Robeson and DuBois, the latter's being applied to the post-war Communist-front youth groups. During the 1950s, Robeson's name usually headed the CPUSA's pro-civil rights and anti-colonialism fronts.

Chapter 6

1. The diluted Fair Employment Practices (FEP) order issued by FDR resulted from a threatened march on Washington conceived and organized by A. Philip Randolph in 1940. Randolph received the whole-hearted support of Walter White and the NAACP. With the latter's resources and grassroots base, Randolph scheduled a dramatic premarch rally at Madison Square Garden the night before the march to generate enthusiasm by the huge crowd for their long bus ride to the nation's capital early the next morning. At this juncture, FDR conveyed to Randolph his pledge to issue the executive order demanded by Randolph, as a result of which the march was called off. The rally, however, was used instead to demand the election of a Negro to represent Harlem in the New York City Council. Randolph expected to be the nominee by acclamation. However, a young, handsome and rapidly rising Baptist minister, Adam Clayton Powell Jr., usurped that honor on the Garden stage. Randolph, for whom I worked in 1955, never

forgave Powell. The latter, also a client of mine at that time, returned the favor to the august labor leader.

2. NAACP, *1943 Annual Report,* 3. In 1943, when the U.S. Army limited Negroes to 10 percent of the overall troops, the Army accepted 400 women as officer candidates for the Women's Army Corps (WAC), including 40 Negroes. Among them was Margaret Ellen Barnes Jones, who made the army her career, rising to the rank of major. Her husband was also an army major. She reported in her memoirs that most of the Negro female officers, including many with college educations, were "assigned to cleaning floors and latrines and working in the post laundry," until she protested as executive officer of her brigade and "persuaded [superiors] to reassign [them] to other duties," according to a history of the African American 6888th Battalion, "To Serve My Country, To Serve My Race," *The New York Times,* Obituary, April 27, 2000.

3. For an extensive contemporary discussion of the role of Negro servicemen and women and their treatment, and the campaign for defense industry jobs, as well as the global concerns of civil rights activists over the impact of American racism on the world's peoples of color, see the special issue of *Survey Graphic,* November, 1942, edited by Alaine Locke, with 21 articles written by such luminaries as Walter White, Earl Brown, Herbert Agar, Charles Johnson, A. Philip Randolph, John A. Davis, Sterling A. Brown, Lin Yutang, and Pearl S. Buck.

4. NAACP, *1943 Annual Report*, 4.

5. In December 1998, Lt. Gen. Benjamin O. Davis Jr., the original commander of the Tuskegee Airmen during World War II, was promoted to four-star general by President Bill Clinton. Davis, long retired, was then 85 years old. He was only the second African American to achieve four-star status, the first being General Colin Powell. President Eisenhower had appointed Davis as the first black general in the U.S. Air Force in 1954. His father, Benjamin O. Davis Sr., was promoted to Brigadier General on October 25, 1940, the first black general in U.S. history. He commanded Harlem's 369th Coast Artillery Brigade of the National Guard. The younger Davis had graduated from West Point in 1936, the first black to do so in half a century.

6. Current, Gloster B., "Walter White and the Fight For Freedom," *The Crisis,* March 1969, 113–119 and 134–135. White's book, *A Rising Wind: A Report on Negro Troops in the ETO, 1945,* Garden City, NY: Doubleday, Doran, 1945, details the long list of grievances expressed by the Negro troops he interviewed in the European Theatre. It also reveals the heightened political sensibilities of the Negro soldiers as a result of their wartime experiences. Page 119 of *Current's* article lists a number of post-war incidents involving violence against returning Negro veterans, which caused mounting concern among Negro civilians.

So widespread had the post-war violence become that White joined with such prominent figures as CIO Secretary and Electrical Workers President James Carey; Dr. Channing Tobias, President of the Phelps-Stokes Fund; AFL Civil Rights Director Boris Shiskin; and NAACP Washington Lobbyist Leslie Perry (Clarence Mitchell's predecessor) to form the National Emergency Committee Against Mob Violence. White and the aforementioned leaders visited President Truman in September 1946 to demand federal intervention to halt the violence and punish the perpetrators. As a result President Truman decided to establish by executive order a presidential committee, funded federally, to investigate not only mob violence, but also the entire spectrum of civil rights and civil liberties and to recommend action. The committee was chaired by General Motors CEO and Chairman Charles E. Wilson. Its report, released in 1947, covered a score of controversial subjects, from lynching and the use of the poll tax to prevent Negroes from voting, to the incarceration of Japanese Americans during the war and segregation throughout American life, including the military services. The recommendations mostly called upon the federal government to serve as the instrument for achieving racial justice and freedom in each of the subject areas investigated; it is recommendations, according to *Current*, were "hard-hitting" and "shook up the country with its declaration: '*the time for action is now.*'" *Current, Ibid.,* 119 and 134. *Current* concludes that "Practically all of its principal recommendations have since been achieved."

Registering to vote was not the only provocation that resulted in the lynching of returning black servicemen. On May 31, 1999, a memorial service was held in rural Bostwick, Georgia, for army veteran George W. Dorsey, who had returned from the war in the Pacific after four-and-a-half years in the service. On June 25, 1946, George, his wife, his sister, and her husband were murdered by a band of white vigilantes who had been angered by the release of Roger Malcolm, Dorsey's brother-in-law, after Malcolm had allegedly stabbed a young white man who was the son of his boss. The town talk was that the son had been having an affair with Malcolm's wife, who was also Dorsey's sister. The four victims had been shot more than 60 times. After six months of investigation by the FBI, no indictments were forthcoming. Forty-five years later a witness came forward who had seen the murders—he was then a frightened 10-year-old white boy, Clinton Adams, who believed the Ku Klux Klan had been behind the murders. The FBI reopened the case in 1991 but so far no arrests have been made. Adams had spent the ensuing years moving from place to place because he was afraid that the perpetrators were aware that he had witnessed the crimes. He told a reporter in 1999, at a time when local whites and blacks had formed a memorial committee to honor the victims, that when Dorsey was in the Pacific, "he was a soldier fighting .... But when he came back, he was just a nigger. Him being a veteran didn't enter anybody's mind. I know I'm not supposed to talk like that, but that's how it was then." *The New York Times,* June 1, 1999, A 18, in a story headed "1946 Killing of 4 Blacks Is Recalled—Veteran Is Honored In Georgia Service," with no byline indicated.

7. Eric Pace, Obituary, *The New York Times,* July 14, 1998, B10. Father Dunne, who died at age 92, also wrote a play in 1945, "Trial by Fire," which described the bombing of a Negro family that had moved into a white neighborhood. During 1948–1949 the play was performed in Los Angeles, Chicago, and New York. Coincidentally, its theme of a hostile white reception to the presence of a new black family was the basic story line of "A Raisin in the Sun" a decade later.

8. This passage was highlighted in the NAACP *1947 Annual Report,* 5–6. The NAACP was encouraged by President Harry S. Truman to seek redress of major problems faced by Negroes. The Association organized a protest by numerous voluntary agencies to demand a halt to racial violence and lynchings in 1946. In turn, the protest meeting led Truman to appoint the Presidential Committee on Civil Rights described in the note above, which together with his commissions on

higher education and military training, issued three vitally important reports forming the basis of Truman's civil rights policies. All three reports affirmed that "discrimination can never be abolished as long as there is involuntary segregation based on race, creed, color, or national origin." The higher education report called for the end of segregated education and the military training report urged the abolition of segregated military training, which ultimately led to Truman's 1948 order to desegregate the armed services.

Upon Truman's death in 1973, Wilkins wrote in his syndicated column (January 16, 1973) that Truman was no Johnny-come-lately to the cause of racial equality. According to Wilkins, Truman had declared in a speech in 1940 in Sedalia, MO, "I believe in the brotherhood of man, not merely the brotherhood of white men." Of Truman's presidency, Wilkins said, "Since the end of the Civil War, the cry from Negro Americans has been for a president in the White House who would speak out and act on the issues that affect black people. Harry S. Truman was such a president. Whatever errors he made in foreign and domestic policy, he gave attention to the special needs of black Americans. In this area he was not always right, but he was basically correct and as forthright as any president .... In the unforgettable 1948 campaign for re-election as president he issued his executive order on the use of Negro manpower in the armed services. It was the first step in completely desegregating the armed services. Those who belittle this should remember that HST was overturning a tradition that had ordained the separation of the races for generations. Negroes had two regiments of cavalry and two regiments of infantry in the entire armed forces. In the Navy they were only mess attendants. No pilots, no marines, no engineers, no entrance to special branches in any service." Reprinted in Wilkins, "Talking It Over," 94–96.

9. U.S. Congress, House of Representatives, Committee on the Judiciary, "Anti-Lynching: Hearings before Subcommittee No. 4 ... for the Better Assurance of the Protection of Persons Within the Several States from Mob Violence and lynching, and for other purposes." February 4, 1948, Washington: Government Printing Office.

10. Wilkins, *Standing Fast,* 196, 207–210. Watson, *Lion in the Lobby,* 162–173. *Encyclopedia,* 1591–1592.

11. A moving biography of Harry T. Moore was published in 1999. It is entitled *Before His Time—The Untold Story of Harry T. Moore, America's First Civil Rights Martyr.*

12. Wilkins, *Standing Fast,* 222–225.

13. In 1997, as a result of noteworthy investigative reporting by a Jackson newspaper, the state of Mississippi admitted that its Sovereignty Commission, founded in the 1950s, had actively orchestrated various widespread efforts, legal and otherwise, to thwart the civil rights movement and to violate the constitutional rights of speech, assembly and expression. In 1998 the state released more than 120,000 pages of documentation, revealing, among other things, a statewide conspiracy between officials and private leaders that included surveillance of citizens of the state as well as non-Mississippians, white and black. There was some inference that the commission "suggested" the "neutralization" of certain activists as well.

14. In the obituary of a former SNCC worker, Samuel Block, who was assigned to Greenwood, Missippippi to register Negro voters, it is reported that NAACP Field Secretary Medgar Evers had been obliged to revoke the charter of the local Greenwood chapter after Till's murder "because of its tepid response." Douglas Martin, Obituary, *New York Times,* April 22, 2000, C7. More likely, according to NAACP staff who remembered that period, it was the result of the pervading and all-encompassing fear inspired by an active KKK and a sheriff acting on their behalf. In any event, when Block arrived in Greenwood in 1963, he was able to sign up only five Negroes to vote during his first six months.

Emmett Till's mother, Mamie, and a collaborator wrote an historical drama based on Till's murder, which was performed in Chicago during 1998–1999.

15. NAACP, *1955 Annual Report,* 9.

16. Robert L. Carter, interview by author, July 18–19, 1998, in addition to his written comments on the draft text.

17. *Ibid.*

18. Wilkins, *Standing Fast,* 241.

19. NAACP, *1965 Annual Report,* 18 and 79; NAACP, *1964 Annual Report,* 11 and 91.

20. Wilkins, *Standing Fast,* 243–246. Wilkins observed that, following the passage of the watered-down bill, "Senator Russell went back to Georgia and claimed that by dropping Title III, Congress had repudiated *Brown v. Board,* and in a misguided way, he was partially right." Watson maintains that Mitchell also urged support of the weakened bill, despite the "pounding" Wilkins was taking from the militants within the NAACP. He also notes that the ACLU opposed the final bill as "worse than nothing." Watson, *Ibid.*, 395–397.

21. Wilkins, *Standing Fast,* 268–270.

22. Summary of *Gomillion v. Lightfoot* 364 U.S. 399 (1960), provided by Lexis legal service. Also see Parker, Frank R., *Black Votes Count.*

23. NAACP, *1964 Annual Report,* 7–8.

Chapter 7

1. The first Freedom Ride, a project of the Fellowship of Reconciliation and its sister agency, CORE, two pacifist groups with strong socialist underpinnings, and led by Rev. A.J. Muste, took place in 1947. A small contingent of 16 blacks and whites sought to implement the Supreme Court's decision that year prohibiting segregated seating on interstate busses. The ruling was largely ignored throughout the South. Known as the Journey of Reconciliation, the project involved more than a dozen Southern cities on Greyhound and Trailways buses, where the integrated group would challenge the local segregation laws. The group included Bayard Rustin, Rev. George Houser, Rev. Homer Jack, journalists William Worthy and James Peck, and attorney Conrad Lynn. The 1947 Freedom Ride petered out when more than six of its participants were arrested, found guilty and, after appeals to the North Carolina Supreme Court, forced to serve a month on North Carolina chain gangs. As soon as the project was announced, according to Rustin's biographer, Walter White offered the group the services of the NAACP's southern

attorneys. The same source quotes Rustin as stating: "The NAACP was absolutely necessary to our adventures in the South. Without the promise of support by the NAACP's legal team throughout the region, we didn't dare go in. Anything could happen to us if we didn't have NAACP lawyers coming to our assistance along the way." NAACP branches provided the group with food and shelter at each stop and, often, with physical protection. Thurgood Marshall, on the other hand, sharply criticized the "disobedience movement" because it "would result in wholesale slaughter with no good achieved." Marshall could in no way accept the utility of nonviolent tactics and seemed to hold little affinity for "well-meaning radical groups in New York" either. The overall background for this section can be found in Jervis Anderson, *Bayard Rustin: The Troubles I've Seen,* 113–124, 135–136; and Richard Severo, Obituary of James Farmer, *New York Times,* July 10, 1999, A 1 and C 10.

2. In an ultimate manifestation of historical irony, Southern Jews living in the Mississippi Delta were quoted in a 1999 PBS documentary as saving their harshest vituperation during the ferment of the 1960s for those "filthy Northern Jews" who aided Negroes during the civil rights struggle, alleging that the militant participation of the Northern Jews during the 1960s severely "embarrassed" the small number of Jews who had long resided in the Mississippi Delta towns.

3. Wilkins, *Standing Fast,* 237.

4. In my own experience, the more middle class the white reporter or foundation executive was, the more he or she vehemently supported the groups that appeared to be the most radical. Later on, the same response correlated well with middle-level black corporate executives, especially those whose homes were located in the predominantly white suburbs.

5. Wilkins, *Standing Fast,* 238.

6. Hughes, *Fight For Freedom—The Story of the NAACP,* 171–177; Wilkins, *Standing Fast,* 259–260. Wilkins observed: "The Oklahoma City sit-ins were the forerunners of the sit-ins that captured the attention of the country 18 months later in Greensboro, North Carolina. They were enormously successful, and by the end of the year, our young people had integrated 39 stores in Oklahoma City. We held workshops and seminars on tactics. The stage was well set for what was to happen later."

7. Hughes, *Fight For Freedom—The Story of the NAACP,* 186.

8. During the initial confrontation at the Woolworth's lunch counter, according to the *New York Times,* John Brown Erwin, a vice president of the Greensboro NAACP chapter, "walked the store aisles, quietly giving them [the sit-in participants] advice and support." He later received the "Unsung Hero Award" from the February One Society, which had been formed to permanently commemorate the date of the first Greensboro sit-in. Associated Press, *New York Times,* Nov. 28, 1998.

Many historians credit the example of the sit-ins for inspiring other students, Negro and white, to form SNCC. Former NAACP national staff organizer Ella Baker, who had helped Dr. King organize SCLC, is also credited with playing the key role in organizing SNCC. Early U.S. National Student Association (USNSA) activists also claim credit for a hand in the formation of SNCC, which, they believe, was a consequence of a major USNSA-sponsored student civil rights meeting in the South in 1964. It is of interest that the original founders of SNCC, who included John Lewis, now a congressman, and Julian Bond, initially welcomed participation by whites. However, as the larger Negro society gradually turned away from integration, SNCC leaders like Stokely Carmichael and H. "Rap" Brown led the organization to separatism, as did the leaders of the more radical Black Panthers, among them Huey Newton.

9. Hughes, *Fight For Freedom—The Story of the NAACP,* 173–175 and 194–197. The NAACP's annual reports during this period and the annual listings of the Thalberg Awards to local branches at the NAACP conventions are rich sources of details concerning the wide-ranging achievements of the adult branches, college chapters, and youth councils.

10. NAACP, *1965 Annual Report,* 82–85.

11. The men and women who comprised the NAACP's senior staff during the 1960s were each in their own right highly regarded senior experts and specialists and among the leaders in their respective disciplines. In addition to James Farmer and Bayard Rustin, who left the NAACP staff early in the decade, the most prominent were General Counsel Robert L. Carter, regarded as the leading civil rights attorney after Thurgood Marshall was appointed to the federal bench; Washington Bureau Director Clarence Mitchell, Director of Branches Gloster Current, Public Information Director Henry Lee Moon, Labor Secretary Herbert Hill, Education Secretary June Shagaloff, Housing Secretary William Morris, Youth Secretary Herb Wright (who was soon succeeded by Mark Rosenman), and, among the regional directors, an unsung heroine during the most dangerous years, Southeast Regional Director Ruby Hurley. Heading this array of talent was Executive Secretary Roy Wilkins, but much of his success was due to his wise, intelligent, and compassionate deputy, John Morsell, a Ph.D. in sociology who permanently postponed his budding career to serve Wilkins and the NAACP. Morsell held the operation together and was largely responsible for the follow through, though most of the individuals named above were self-starters who needed very little oversight; they often went further than their instructions permitted. Of these senior staffers, three were white and Jewish—Hill, Rosenman, and Shagaloff.

12. In his own memoir, Theodore Sorensen, JFK's special counsel, confidant, and speech writer, provided a detailed explanation of President Kennedy's resort to caution in implementing his pledged "stroke of the pen." Sorensen, Theodore C., *Kennedy,* 480–482.

13. As a staff member in the civil rights section of the Kennedy campaign in 1960, which was directed day-to-day by Harris Wofford under the overall authority of R. Sargent Shriver, I was able to observe Robert Kennedy's general antipathy to our efforts to attract Negro voters through, for example, a separate front group called the Ad Hoc Committee to Register One Million New Negro Voters, an entity largely funded by Kennedy supporters and headed by A. Philip Randolph, with Martin Luther King Jr. and Roy Wilkins as vice chairmen. I personally organized and directed this entity—quite possibly the first presidential candidate's mechanism targeting the registration of Negro voters. The Kennedy support for this device was hardly charitable or idealistic—JFK's polls indicated that nine out of ten unregistered Negroes would vote for Kennedy if they had the opportunity. I also wrote the basic strategy memo advising the Kennedy campaign on how to cement its relationship with Negro voters by, among other things, appointing Negroes with unique or specialized experiences to responsible campaign posts that

had nothing inherently to do with race, such as agriculture, housing, veterans and military affairs, and so forth. Most of my recommendations were regarded as too radical or advanced for the times, though they became almost commonplace later on. The memo was addressed to Wofford, who incorrectly refers to it as his own in his memoir.

The overall campaign division that sought to spur support for Kennedy among Negroes was the traditional Democratic National Committee Nationalities Division, which nurtured support among East Europeans, Italians, Irish, Jews, Germans, and other so-called ethnic groups. The director of the division in the Kennedy campaign was Angier Biddle Duke, a quintessential WASP whose lineage comprised three "old money" great fortunes (the third being the Drexels). However, as a politically active New Yorker and the former president of the International Rescue Committee, which resettled refugees from throughout Eastern and Central Europe, the Far East, the Caribbean, and Africa, he had developed a remarkably broad knowledge of ethnic groups and their interests and politics.

Robert Kennedy was much more agitated when he learned that Wofford and his staff had persuaded JFK to phone Dr. King's wife after King had been arrested on a traffic violation and later imprisoned in Georgia. Contrary to RFK's instructions, the Kennedy civil rights staff leaked the news to the press, which accorded it great national prominence. The impact upon Negro voters was substantial. King's father, a life-long Republican who had already endorsed Richard M. Nixon, publicly changed his mind and strongly endorsed Kennedy. Robert Kennedy feared that the campaign's tilt towards Negroes and civil rights would antagonize the moderate Southerners he regarded, in his own words, as "already in our pockets." During his term as attorney general, RFK would change his attitude towards Negroes and other minorities in response to powerful events.

14. Schlesinger, Arthur M. Jr., *A Thousand Days: John F. Kennedy in the White House,* 928–931; Garrow, David J., *Bearing the Cross: Martin Luther King, Jr., and the Southern Christian Leadership Conference,* 154–155 and 169–170. Peace Corps press release, May 13, 1962. Wofford records some of these events in his own memoir, *Of Kennedy and Kings.*

15. Wofford related the basic facts of this narrative to me at the time that he departed from the White House. Most accounts of the JFK White House are consistent with them as well. Nevertheless, four decades later, on March 17, 2001, during dinner in Chevy Chase, Maryland, Wofford recollected that he himself had agreed with President Kennedy's assessment at the time that the president was not politically strong enough to honor his campaign pledge of a stroke of the pen to desegregate federal housing nor was he in a position to present a civil rights bill to Congress.

16. A compelling account of Seiganthaler's beating and the permanent effect it had on Robert Kennedy can be found in Halberstam, David, *The Children,* 315–323. Halberstam's epic work is an exhaustive and sympathetic study of SNCC'S leaders and the impact they had upon events during the 1960s.

17. Garrow, *Bearing the Cross: Martin Luther King, Jr., and the Southern Christian Leadership Conference,* 153–157. Farmer is quoted by Garrow as stating: "We planned the Freedom Ride with the specific intention of creating a crisis. We were counting on the bigots in the South to do our work for us. We figured that the government would have to respond if we created a situation that

was headline news all over the world, and affected the nation's image abroad . . ." It is difficult for today's generations to comprehend the sheer courage required to place oneself at such risk physically, knowing with a reasonable degree of certainty that brute force would be the price for such sacrifice. CORE leader Jim Peck was beaten so badly on one ride that he never fully recovered from it. A few days after the Montgomery riot, I appeared on the Barry Gray radio show in New York City to discuss the Freedom Rides and the Kennedy Administration response. Without any foreknowledge, one of my friends, Marvin Rich, CORE's deputy director, arrived to participate in the discussion. More than half of his face was covered with blood-scabbed wounds from the Montgomery beatings. Needless to say, his appearance was deeply upsetting. As usual, Rich remained calm and deliberate in his presentation.

18. Ironically, Walker had commanded the federal troops dispatched by Eisenhower to Little Rock in 1957 for similar purposes. He candidly stated in 1962 that he was making up for his grave error in Little Rock by joining the rioting racists in Oxford. In 1963 Lee Harvey Oswald considered assassinating Walker but the plan went awry so he saved his venom for JFK.

Some 500 unarmed federal marshals were ordered by the attorney general to accompany Meredith, attorney Motley, and Medgar Evers of the NAACP. Of this number, about 200 were injured after they were stormed by an uncontrolled mob—estimated later by Theodore Sorensen to be approximately 2,500 "hooligans"—from which emanated gun fire as well as thrown rocks. The marshals kept in contact with the Oval Office through a local pay phone because the Pentagon had failed to establish a workable mobile communications unit. On the Oxford, Mississippi end of the pay phone was Deputy Attorney General Nicholas Katzenbach.

In 1999 William Doyle authored a book based on the White House tape recordings from FDR to Bill Clinton. Doyle's characterization of the conversations emanating from the White House to the Justice Department supervisor on the spot, Katzenbach, was that it bordered on panic. According to the transcripts, President Kennedy and his brother Robert were not only fearful for the lives of the unarmed marshals, but also were being led to believe that the mob was bent on assassinating James Meredith. Their helplessness is almost palpable in the face of Governor Barnett's refusal to restore order and protect Meredith, the marshals, and the Justice Department representatives. Doyle quotes President Kennedy as saying that Barnett wants him to remove Meredith, to which Robert Kennedy plaintively responds, "I can't get him out. How am I gonna get him out?" Meanwhile, the arrival of U.S. Army troops ordered by the president more than a day earlier to restore order continued to be delayed, resulting in the temporary impotence of the man holding the "most powerful office on the face of the earth." Doyle, William, *Inside the Oval Office—White House Tapes from FDR to Clinton,* as quoted in a review by Ron Rosenbaum in the *New York Times* Book Review, July 18, 1999.

19. Sorensen, Theodore C., *Kennedy,* 485–488. Governor Barnett of Mississippi was not exactly known for his intelligence. Attorney John Doar, a high-ranking Justice Department official during the period when Meredith was seeking entry into the state university, later related the episode when he accompanied Meredith to Jackson, the Mississippi state capital, to meet with Barnett. Doar is a tall, light-haired, light-eyed Caucasian. Meredith was relatively short and unmistakenly

Negro. They debarked from their plane, entered an official state limousine and, with lights flashing and sirens wailing, sped to the capitol building with a sizable police escort. On arrival they walked up the imposing stairs to the second floor, down a long carpeted corridor to a huge double door that was the entrance to the governor's office. The doors opened and Governor Barnett rose from behind his desk, and said, "Welcome to Mississippi, and which one of you gentlemen is Mr. Meredith?"

In 1971, then a lawyer in private practice, Barnett wrote a letter to the *Wall Street Journal* on behalf of a political client who was upset with the way a *Journal* correspondent had characterized him during a campaign in which Charles Evers was running for Governor. In his letter, Barnett demanded a retraction, absent which he threatened to sue the newspaper for "liable."

20. Schlesinger, Arthur M. Jr., *A Thousand Days: John F. Kennedy in the White House,* 940–949; Garrow, David J., *Bearing the Cross: Martin Luther King, Jr., and the Southern Christian Leadership Conference,* 154–157 and 167–168. Sorensen describes a White House reception for more than 1,000 Negro and civil rights leaders on Lincoln's Birthday, 1963, which, in the White House aide's mind, helped to alleviate the antipathy towards President Kennedy's civil rights "policies." "Their displeasure with his strategy," Sorensen wrote, "was in some measure alleviated because he treated them with dignity—not with condescension, and not as people deserving preferential status, but with the same respect and recognition that he offered to every American citizen." It is no doubt accurate that many individuals, Negro leaders included, were impressed by Kennedy's legendary charm; nevertheless, it hardly compensated for his refusal to act in any significant way during 1961 or 1962 to advance the civil rights agenda. He tried with all his heart and mind to make up for that deficiency during 1963, but was tragically interrupted by an assassin's bullet.

21. So steeped in Southern mores and racial practices was the nation's capital in 1962 that the venerable Washington Redskins of the NFL had chosen to wait until that same year to hire their first black player, Bobby Mitchell, who became a Hall of Famer. The late Shirley Povich of the *Washington Post,* generally acclaimed one of the nation's greatest sports writers, once chided the Redskins' racist policy by writing of an earlier game with the Cleveland Browns: "Jim Brown, born ineligible to play for the Redskins, integrated their end zone three times yesterday."

22. During this period Attorney General Robert Kennedy had urged CORE to postpone some of its planned Freedom Rides to permit all the parties to "cool off." James Farmer is reported to have rejected the Attorney General's plea, replying, "We have been cooling off for 350 years."

23. Schlesinger, Arthur M. Jr., *A Thousand Days: John F. Kennedy in the White House,* 950–953.

24. After Medgar Evers' assassination in June 1963, a delegation of black leaders, headed by Medgar's brother Charles and NAACP State Chairman Aaron Henry went to the White House to plead for federal support and assistance. According to both Charles Evers and Aaron Henry, black White House advisor Louis Martin, a highly experienced reporter, asked the delegation how many Negroes had they registered in the state of Mississippi. When Dr. Henry responded

with the meager figures, Louis Martin said, "Fellows, come back when you've got a mess of registered voters. This is politics, not tiddly-winks." They did return several years later with a "mess" of registered Negro voters.

25. Wilkins, Roy, "Talking It Over," Address to the Bar Association of St. Louis, November 15, 1973.

26. In his memoir of JFK, Theodore Sorensen described Wallace's "stand" before the front of the university's admissions door as "a knowingly empty and futile gesture," after which Wallace retreated from the political fray, having read his own statement to the press. Sorensen, Theodore C., *Kennedy,* 493. Sorensen also observed that Wallace had failed to object to further admissions of Negro students at the state university and its branches during successive weeks.

A four-term governor of Alabama, Wallace deftly manipulated the issue of race to build a national following that made him a serious candidate for president until he was shot and paralyzed for the next 16 years—the rest of his life. After trying a Populist Party line similar to that of Louisiana's infamous governor, Hughie Long, which appealed to the poor of both races, and losing by a wide margin, Wallace reversed course and based his 1962 gubernatorial campaign on his opposition to any concessions to his state's Negroes. He adopted a blatantly racist line. According to the *New York Times,* Asa Carter, a KKK leader, wrote Wallace's first inaugural address, in which he promised to protect Alabama's "Anglo Saxon people" from "communistic amalgamation" with blacks. His parting slogan, which was to be repeated mindlessly for the next two decades, was "Segregation now, segregation tomorrow, segregation forever." The same *Times* article, commenting on his publicity-generating gesture to "stand in the schoolhouse door" to block the entry of two black students, asserts that "Mr. Wallace, fearing jail for defying a federal court order, had privately promised President Kennedy that he would step aside if first allowed to make a defiant speech. These and other gestures made Wallace attractive not only to white Southerners still smarting over the changes wrought since *Brown*, but also factory workers and hard-hats whose jobs were in jeopardy in the Rust Belt because of global economic competition but who feared, more than anything else, black competition in the workplace as well as black students attending their children's schools." Wallace pandered to these fears with considerable success, garnering 13 percent of the national vote and the electoral votes of five states in the 1968 election in which Richard Nixon defeated Hubert Humphrey. Howell Raines, Obituary, *New York Times,* September 14, 1998, A1, B13. Raines covered the Southern civil rights beat and Wallace for many years.

Wallace became the perfect, archetypical ploy for the entire civil rights movement, the "big, bad, bogey-man of race," whose very existence prompted extra gifts of cash to the organizations from worried Negroes and liberals. Conversely, under the careful direction of right-wing fundraiser Richard Viguerie, the perpetual Wallace candidacy generated the creation of a massive direct mail constituency merging the goals of the white racists and the ultra-right conservatives. According to later news reports, Wallace was dismayed to learn that Viguerie—not he—owned the mailing lists of those who had contributed to him. He had to pay Viguerie a fee to use these lists; meanwhile, Viguerie successfully promoted a plethora of far-right causes based on mailings to the Wallace lists and others he secured from his previous employer, Marvin Liebman, including the membership list of Young Americans for Freedom.

The value of Bull Connor to the cause of civil rights cannot be exaggerated. The extreme brutality employed by his troops and his insensitive demeanor produced still photos and television news footage that galvanized a huge segment of American society to support the banner of civil rights. According to Theodore Sorensen, President Kennedy was especially aware of Connor's value to the cause. "The civil rights movement," the president is reputed to have said often, "should thank God for Bull Connor. He helped it as much as Abraham Lincoln" Sorensen, Theodore C., *Kennedy,* 489.

27. Schlesinger, Arthur M. Jr., *A Thousand Days: John F. Kennedy in the White House,* 955–963.

28. Schlesinger, Arthur M. Jr., *A Thousand Days: John F. Kennedy in the White House,* 963–968; Garrow, David J., *Bearing the Cross: Martin Luther King, Jr., and the Southern Christian Leadership Conference,* 268–282.

29. NAACP Controller Richard McClain, aided by Treasurer Alfred Baker Lewis, an elderly white democratic socialist, managed to avert financial disaster numerous times during the 1960s and 1970s, approaching the brink more often than the NAACP would have liked to admit. But their adept handling of funds, including transfers between accounts for short periods, kept the NAACP afloat. Black Memphis banker Jesse Turner succeeded Baker as treasurer and, because he was also an accountant, more closely managed the Association's finances, especially when McClain was succeeded by Hinton King as controller. Turner and King were as resourceful as McClain and Lewis in juggling funds during the fallow periods of income without in any way violating the law.

30. Multimillionaire J.M. Kaplan, founder of the Welch's Grape Juice Company and head of the J.M. Kaplan Fund, and Steve Currier, married to the "world's richest woman," Audrey Mellon Bruce, the heiress to the vast Mellon fortune, joined forces in a vain effort to forge a degree of policy and programmatic unity among the civil rights leaders and organizations by holding before them the prospect of very large financial support. Currier was the son of Mary Warburg, another civil rights activist and wife of financier E.M. Warburg. Neither the hoped-for unity nor the generous funding materialized. In January 1967, Steve and Audrey Currier died in a mysterious airplane crash in the Bermuda Triangle. The pro-civil rights Taconic Foundation was one of their most effective legacies.

31. Former NAACP staff members have told me that when Rustin joined the NAACP staff, Wilkins authorized a then substantial sum of the organization's funds to fix Rustin's teeth, which had greatly deteriorated, and to buy a new wardrobe for him. Until then, Rustin's appearance and clothing were known for their "tattered" appearance. Within a few years Rustin became one of the best-dressed figures in the civil rights movement, eccentric to some, somewhat dandyish to others, but without a doubt very stylish.

32. One reason it was not singled out by the members of the press who had been following Dr. King was that they had heard the speech, or components of it, on scores of earlier occasions.

Dr. King had not taken the time to write a new or original address, so he was compelled to give his then "standard" speech. Some of the civil rights veterans who had heard him numerous times before regarded the 1963 version as "hackneyed." It was not until King's assassination in 1968 that some of the television news organizations revived the 1963 speech and played it over and over again as part of the national mourning for the murdered leader. A film of the speech was also circulated widely by itself and as part of a powerful documentary that had been prepared under the direction of King's old Stalinist adviser, Stanley Levinson, to build support for King's memorial, so that the 1963 March on Washington speech was heard by a majority of Americans.

It has become a leap of egregious fiction to assume that, because King's speech had immortal segments eminently quotable, it was therefore Dr. King's march. As Roy Wilkins had observed, because the march organizers assigned King the "clean-up spot . . . the practice has grown among writers on King to call the August 28, 1963, gathering, 'his' march. It has been so stated in newspaper and magazine articles, on television and on radio. Nothing could be farther from the truth. Nothing could be more unfair to A. Philip Randolph . . . . Martin Luther King, with his matchless oratory, his mellifluous cadences, and his great charisma, was the star above the star-studded cast of civil rights speakers. But the man who dreamed the dream that brought 220,000 Americans to Washington on behalf of black and all minorities should have the acclaim that is rightfully his. Dr. King . . . would be the first to hail Randolph on his anniversary." Wilkins, Roy, "A. Philip Randolph," syndicated column, August 26, 1972, reprinted in "Talking It Over." Every behind-the-scenes account documents that Randolph, Rustin, Wilkins, and Walter Reuther were the key figures in realizing the march, with the principal participants coming from the NAACP's grassroots base and that of the UAW and allied unions. Rustin was paid from funds provided by the NAACP and UAW. His senior staff for the eight-week period were largely from the same two organizations and individuals on loan from sympathetic allies. NAACP branches generated most of the participants. The UAW and some other union locals organized the second largest source of marchers. In addition to the national publicity, the Rustin-directed headquarters for the march undertook the massive job of coordinating the dispatch and arrival (as well as the departure) of the 250,000 participants, most of whom arrived in buses; of the security for the entire six-hour event; and of the programs of speakers and music, both of which arrested the attention of the huge crowd. At the other end of the hierarchy, hundreds of professionals and volunteers from the NAACP and the trade union movement beat the drums for local participants, arranged for bus rentals and departure times, and kept order.

33. Farmer's speech was actually read by his deputy, Floyd McKissack, because he was in jail in Plaquemine, Louisiana, on the day of the march, for "disturbing the peace." He had been leading a protest against the massive and violent treatment of Negroes in that town and had learned that state troopers with dogs were searching for him house-to-house with tear gas and electric prods, determined, Farmer later said, to kill him when they found him. His speech to the march included a pledge not to cease the pressure on Jim Crow; McKissack read these words to the assemblage: "We will not stop until the dogs stop biting us in the South and the rats stop biting us in the North." Farmer, James, *Lay Bare The Heart: An Autobiography of the Civil Rights Movement.*

34. Sorensen, Theodore C. *Kennedy,* 504–505. President Kennedy marveled, as the world marveled, at the spirit and self-discipline of the largest public demonstration to that date ever held in Washington, D.C. Kennedy "felt that the march helped to unite the adherents of civil rights more closely; and merely the absence of violence in such a huge and restless throng had awakened new interest and won new adherents in white America." JFK's reaction, as described here by Sorensen in 1965, would today be regarded as dangerously approaching the borders of racial stereotyping.

35. The names of the four murdered young girls were Denise McNair, Cynthia Wesley, Addie Mae Collins, and Carol Robertson. This and other bombings touched off riots between the virtually all-black protestors and the all-white Birmingham police department. Like most other terrorist acts, this one served to expand support for the civil rights campaign, and to stiffen the resolve of those who wanted dramatic and strong federal intervention in the South, both to protect their civil rights activists as well as Negroes generally from the illegal violence of white racists, and to punish those who employed such violence in the hope of halting the advance of civil rights.

36. Watson, Denton L., *Lion in the Lobby: Clarence Mitchell Jr.'s Struggle for the Passage of Civil Rights Laws,* 592.

37. *Ibid.,* 592–594.

38. *Ibid.,* 595–602.

39. In his autobiography, John Lewis describes President Johnson's exercise of raw presidential power to crush the expectations of the Mississippi FDP to be seated in place of the regulars as "the turning point of the civil rights movement." Lewis argues that he and his fellow activists, having "played by the rules" within the system with right and morality on *their* side, "had the door slammed in our face." That rejection, in Lewis' view, led to a critical loss of faith, deepened by the assassinations of Robert Kennedy and Martin Luther King Jr., with whom, Lewis states, he remained on close terms despite their differences. He also records that he had become close to Robert Kennedy as the latter "discovered" his passion for social justice.

There is no question that each of these tragedies contributed to the loss of faith by increasing numbers of Americans, especially younger ones, in the American system and in the government itself. The Vietnam War was probably the major factor in this decline of confidence, including the hearings and revelations that emerged from it. However, Lewis overlooks the right of the president to exercise the power he holds in order to assure his reelection, which he felt might have been jeopardized by acceding to the Mississippi FDP, especially amongst his supporters in Southern and border states. Johnson unequivocally demanded a landslide in order to better legitimize his accession after JFK's assassination and also to bolster political support, especially in Congress, for his civil rights and antipoverty agenda. That he became the greatest civil rights president in American history is no longer in doubt.

Critics of LBJ's behavior towards the Mississippi FDP ought to recognize that more was gained by his second term as president in the civil rights arena than could have been extracted from the seating of a handful of FDP delegates of their own choosing at the 1964 convention. Further, four years later, with Johnson still president, a biracial delegation led by Charles Evers, Aaron Henry, Fanny Lou

Hamer, and white leaders successfully unseated the regulars (who by then had sprinkled a few safe blacks among their delegates) at the 1968 Chicago convention, while partial success was achieved by the Georgia delegation, one of whose leaders was Julian Bond. The four-year delay hardly equates with all of the legislative and executive branch progress made under LBJ (the Vietnam War and its dire consequences notwithstanding).

Lastly, the forced resignation of President Nixon and the Watergate scandal, the weak response of President Carter to the hostage-taking in Iran, the Iran-Contra episode under President Reagan with clear constitutional violations by Oliver North and others while the president and the vice president suffered from convenient memory lapses, the nomination of Clarence Thomas by President Bush as "the most qualified person in the nation," and the plethora of bizarre personal behavioral defects of President Clinton have, in my view, all contributed to the vast skepticism that dominates the American electorate. The inability (or lack of will) of America's political leaders to rein in the power of the wealthy, including huge corporate interests, who make the bulk of cash gifts to both political parties is perhaps the most recent contributor to the lack of faith in the efficacy of the system, except for those who can pay for their privileges. What LBJ did in Atlantic City in 1964 pales in comparison with most of these events. As for Representative John Lewis, I can affirm that he never truly lost faith in the system, to which his 16 years of exemplary service in Congress can attest.

Chapter 8

1. Garrow, David J., *Bearing the Cross: Martin Luther King, Jr., and the Southern Christian Leadership Conference,* 360. Garrow quotes these sentiments by SCLC Affiliates Director C.T. Vivian after a field trip to Selma to evaluate the climate for King's proposed initiative there. The general background for this and subsequent events in Selma is based on the highly detailed and extensive narrative by Garrow. Also Greenberg, Jack, *Crusaders in the Courts,* 355–361.
2. Garrow, David J., *Bearing the Cross,* 380–408.
3. *Ibid.*, 407.
4. Wilkins, *Standing Fast,* 307. In his autobiography, Wilkins relates that he was present in the congressional gallery for LBJ's civil rights speech. He reported that President Johnson's invocation of the civil rights mantra "we shall overcome" brought tears to the eyes of the civil rights leadership, including himself, that night. "I had waited all my life to hear a President of the United States talk that way." Wilkins confided, "and, at that moment, I confess, I loved LBJ."
5. Garrow, David J., *Bearing the Cross,* 407–410.
6. Meeting and interview with Dr. Benjamin L. Hooks, New York City, Aug. 31, 1997. Dr. Hooks served as treasurer and secretary of SCLC before becoming the NAACP's executive director in 1977. He said that most of SCLC's finances were chaotic because of incomplete or improper record keeping and that his task each year of attempting to produce an accurate financial statement was virtually impossible. Nevertheless, the supporters of King and the SCLC, for the most part, overlooked such transgressions in the interests of a "higher purpose."

7. In the 1980s the VEP was revived again, this time with two former SNCC leaders—John Lewis and Julian Bond—working as a team to proselytize on behalf of the need for voter registration throughout the South in those towns and cities that had failed to keep up with the rest of the region. By then approximately 90 percent of the VEP grants went to NAACP branches, according to VEP's own annual reports, about 5 percent to SCLC locals, and the rest to independent community efforts. By then SNCC and CORE were no longer in business in the South.

8. Much of the information and data appearing between pages 215 and 217 of this text have been gleaned from the annual reports of the NAACP between 1964 and 1990 and of the SCF between 1983 and 1990. Each of the NAACP reports (as well as the later SCF reports) carries sections on voter education, and many of the annual branch department sections also include interesting voter data. Lastly, each report carries accurate financial data for the respective calendar years (which were also the fiscal years) of both the NAACP and the SCF in respect to voter expenditures.

9. In Mississippi and other parts of the South, I witnessed at least six instances where elderly or crippled Negroes were literally carried into the voting booths by NAACP volunteers during the late 1960s and throughout the 1970s.

10. Watson, Denton L., *Lion in the Lobby: Clarence Mitchell Jr.'s Struggle for the Passage of Civil Rights Laws,* 644–646.

11. Wilkins, *Standing Fast,* 310–311.

12. *Ibid.,* 310.

13. Watson, Denton L., *Lion in the Lobby,* 647.

14. *Ibid.,* 647–649.

15. *Ibid.,* 649–650. The nine liberals were Democrats Bayh (Indiana), Burdick (North Dakota), Hart (Michigan), Kennedy (Massachusetts), Edward Long (Missouri), and Tydings (Maryland), together with three Republicans—Fong (Hawaii), Javits (New York), and Scott (Pennsylvania). The Southern Democrats who voted for the administration's proposal were Fullbright (Arkansas), Harris (Oklahoma), Bass and Gore (Tennessee), and Yarborough (Texas). Joining them were Republicans Cooper and Morton, both of Kentucky.

16. *Ibid.,* 653–656.

17. For further details on the NAACP's positions regarding the Voting Rights Act, see Clarence Mitchell's report in the NAACP *1965 Annual Report,* 12–14, as well as the introduction to the *Annual Report,* 5–6.

18. Watson, Denton L., *Lion in the Lobby,* 657.

19. As quoted by Roy Wilkins in his remarks at the Symposium on Civil Rights at the Lyndon Baines Johnson Library of the University of Texas, Austin, December 11, 1972, published in *The Crisis,* June/July, 1977, 318.

20. During the 1990s, the Republican congressional strategy, led by such extremists as Newt Gingrich, Tom DeLay, and Dick Armey in the House, and arch-conservatives Trent Lott, Strom Thurmond, Jesse Helms, Phil Gramm, and Orin Hatch in the Senate, has been to obstruct and confront on a narrowly partisan basis almost all progressive legislation proposed by the Democrats, not the least those bills pertaining to civil rights and the economic advancement of blacks and other minorities. In all likelihood, the 1965 Voting Rights Act could not have found the necessary political base to be enacted in the year 2002.

21. *Look Magazine,* June 29, 1965, 17–19.

22. Parker, Frank R., *Black Votes Count,* Foreword by Eddie Williams. Williams was the president of the Center for Political Studies in Washington, D.C., the principal think-tank on African-American affairs. Parker himself was a legendary civil rights attorney representing Negro individuals and groups against the full force of the Jim Crow system, especially in violence-prone Mississippi, where Parker worked for the ACLU and the Lawyers' Committee on Civil Rights.

23. Parker, Frank R., *Black Votes Count: Political Empowerment in Mississippi after 1965,* 1.

Chapter 9

1. Kellogg, Charles Flint. *NAACP: A History of the National Association for the Advancement of Colored People,* 35. Kellogg observes that in the early decades of the twentieth century, the AFL ignored the discriminatory practices of its member unions, so long as those unions' constitutions did not explicitly exclude Negroes.

2. Hill, *Black Labor and the American Legal System: Race, Work and Law,* 363–365.

3. *Ibid.*, 364–367.

4. Hill, Herbert, *Black Labor and the American Legal System: Race, Work and the Law,* 106. Senator Robert Wagner's aide, Leon Keyserling, later a renowned liberal economist, wrote this in a letter to Walter White in 1934 as an "explanation" for the provision's defeat, which Professor Hill quotes in his book.

5. In 1955 I was public relations counsel to A. Philip Randolph and directed his media campaign to be elected the first Negro vice president of the AFL-CIO when the two entities merged in December of that year. In late October, George Meany, embarrassed by the barrage of negative public relations his federation was receiving from Randolph's numerous radio, television, and press appearances, agreed to sponsor Randolph's election and to support a program of reform if Randolph promised to end the campaign that very day. Randolph agreed, but, as will be shown later, Meany resisted Randolph's efforts to combat racial discrimination within the unions and at the workplace.

6. During the 1940s most of organized labor was indifferent to the agenda of the NAACP and the aspirations of black workers. Indeed, a semi-official handbook of organized labor—"Labor in America" by Professor Harold U. Faulkner and International Ladies Garment Workers Union (ILGWU) Education Director Mark Starr—which was originally produced in 1944, reissued in 1949, and revised and published in a new edition in 1957—accords two paragraphs to Negro workers and their problems (pp. 324–325) out of a total of 330 pages. These two paragraphs are clearly an afterthought.

7. Unlike the nonprofit voluntary agencies that largely comprise the LCCR, most labor unions are well-funded nationally from the dues deducted from each monthly paycheck by the employers and forwarded to the national headquarters. In addition, many national unions (formally known as internationals because of their Canadian affiliates) also administer their members' pension plans, exacting a healthy commission for this service, which helps them to lower their overhead at

the very least. Some unions also profit from their members' health plans and other forms of insurance as well.

The typical voluntary nonprofit organization expends most, if not all, of its annual income during its fiscal year to carry out its programs; each January 1st, it must start all over again to renew its memberships and to raise other funds to sustain its operations. Many of the nonprofits are either nonmembership groups or with quite small memberships, thereby requiring more creative fundraising from outside sources, such as foundations, corporations, benefits, and the cultivation of large donors.

The relative wealth of national unions—as compared to nonprofits, but not as compared to the major corporations—permits them to field large and effective lobbying operations. Such lobbying often helps an individual legislator to translate what precise effect his votes for or against a specific piece of legislation will have on the union members in his jurisdiction. Labor lobbyists also have their fingertips on the exact number of union members who are registered to vote in each congressional district and each state. (In recent years, because of census bureau refinements, congressional legislators and their staffs also know the exact number of African Americans of voting age, registered or not, in their districts.) Just as the corporate world's influence is usually based on the millions of dollars at its disposal for the hard and soft contributions to campaign coffers, the influence of labor unions is based in part on such funds but even more on voter influence and turnout. With the introduction of less expensive computers three decades ago, a labor union was able to quickly reach every one of its members in a given district or state by a variety of demographics, the major one being party affiliation. This ability is almost total and rapid. Such electoral power constitutes significant clout and the NAACP's leaders, Mitchell among them, fully respected that clout.

8. As the NAACP executive who called upon the national labor leaders for assistance in fiscal emergencies, I can attest to the empathy and commitment to equality of many of them.

On the other hand, from my extensive experience in phoning local union locals on at least a dozen occasions to sell tickets for benefit dinners honoring Randolph, Rustin, Wilkins, Mitchell, and other blacks venerated by the AFL-CIO's national leaders, I can also attest to the largely hostile reception my calls received, not infrequently punctuated with racial and other epithets.

9. Journalist Joseph C. Goulden, in his biography of Meany, unequivocally concludes that the labor federation's efforts to eliminate racial discrimination were a failure between 1955 and 1963. He states: "For all the surface activity, however, there was little positive accomplishment. 'The sad fact of the matter was,' said an AFL-CIO staff member active in civil rights, 'many of the unions put together paper programs that meant nothing. George [Meany] used to talk about how the federal government used 1,000 troops and millions of dollars to get one Negro student [James Meredith] in Ole Miss. Hell, we had more than 60,000 local unions, and we didn't have any troops whatsoever.'" Goulden, Joseph C., *Meany—the Unchallenged Strong Man of American Labor,* 318.

10. During the one-year waiting period after which Title VII took effect (on July 3, 1965), Hill conducted dozens of meetings for NAACP branches and rank-and-file members to enable them to understand the provisions of the new Title VII law and how they could gather the necessary information and data to permit the

NAACP Labor Department to file employment complaints with the Equal Employment Opportunity Commission (EEOC). The branches and the grassroots membership became the primary source of the raw material that the NAACP labor department then utilized to fashion thousands of complaints, hundreds of which resulted in court cases conducted by the NAACP legal department, the Legal Defense Fund, and other, smaller public law offices, nationally and regionally. The magnitude of the complaints generated by the NAACP labor department largely exceeded the combined capacity of these civil rights law firms at any given moment. Only because of its vast grassroots structure was the NAACP able to generate so much activity in this area, in contrast to its sister agencies, which possessed very small grassroots bases.

11. Hill edited two books on the literature of Negro writers during his tenure at the NAACP. In addition to writing scores of articles on labor history, employment, economics, job training, jazz, and literature, he later wrote and edited several other books on some of these subjects. (See this volume's bibliography.)

12. Hill, Herbert, "Twenty Years of State Fair Employment Practice Commissions: A Critical Analysis With Recommendations," *Buffalo Law Review,* Fall 1964, 65–69.

13. Ibid., 66–67. The NAACP called upon the city and state of New York, in this article, to exercise sanctions against those unions that had been found guilty of racial discrimination, including canceling publicly funded construction contracts in which "the hiring of apprentices and journeymen is controlled by Local 28 and other AFL-CIO craft unions guilty of similar practices." Unsurprisingly, the wealth and political clout of the building trades unions insulated them from such hard-hitting acts on the part of Mayor Robert F. Wagner and Governor Nelson A. Rockefeller. Nevertheless, the action under SCAD against Local 28 was initiated by Republican Attorney General Louis Lefkowitz, who no doubt enjoyed placing the more liberal Democrats on the wrong side of the issue as far as their minority supporters were concerned. Lefkowitz went further, proposing an amendment to the state antidiscrimination law to forbid denying any individual entry into an apprenticeship program on any grounds other than objective qualifications. The proposal was adopted despite the "vigorous opposition of the AFL-CIO and the bitter objections of the Building Trades Unions," according to Hill.

14. Hill, Herbert, "The AFL-CIO and the Black Worker: Twenty-five Years After the Merger," *Journal of Intergroup Relations,* Vol. 10, No. 1, Summer 1982, 35–42.

15. *New York Times,* July 3, 1986, 1 and 13.

16. Hill, Herbert, "A Key Affirmative-Action Case," Op-Ed Article, *New York Times,* Feb. 18, 1986.

17. *Ibid.*

18. For background on the long journey traveled by Hill and the federal courts seeking to remove the racial barriers to membership in New York City's Local 46 of the Wood, Wire, and Metal Lathers Union, see Murray Kempton's column in the *New York Post,* October 8, 1977. A more recent update appeared in the May 1994, issue of *Union Democracy Review,* which noted that the union "was once dominated by the Westies gang, a murdering arm of organized crime. After the Westies were broken up by criminal prosecution, the local apparently fell into the hands of ordinary free lance toughs." A consent decree in 1970

"prescribed rules for admission of blacks and other minorities into the local's apprenticeship program and established an excellent referral system, which, if actually implemented, assured equal job opportunity for all members. A court-appointed administrator was assigned to police the agreement," the report continued, noting that, "despite initial progress during which one-fourth of the membership became minority, the agreement fell apart in a few years. The union's leaders and staff simply ignored the consent decree provisions and passed on virtually all job requests from contractors to their white cronies, who no longer bothered to appear at the hiring hall. Blacks and other minorities were passed over until they were financially broken and left the union. Physical intimidation was used against any minority member who protested. Eventually the minority members appealed to the EEOC, which returned the case to the courts, where it is now," the *Union Democracy Review* concluded.

19. Author interview with Herbert Hill, October 24, 1999, New York City.

20. *Ibid.*

21. Finkelstein, Katherine E., "Union Settles Bias Lawsuit on Hiring," *New York Times,* June 19, 1999. The article quotes the union's lawyer as maintaining that "Most job sites are 70 to 80 percent minority" at the time of the settlement, and that the union settled, in the words of the reporter, only "to avoid the trouble of litigation." According to a staff member of the EEOC, which brought a dual lawsuit at the same time, "Typically, the black and Hispanic guys were sitting in the hiring hall, while the white guys were out working."

22. Hill, Herbert, Interview of October 23, 2000. Hill stated that he usually sought to involve the NAACP's local membership and, if possible, the larger black community, in each confrontation with local unions. One of his most successful community demonstrations took place in the late 1960s, when Hill persuaded the leaders of local black street gangs to join the picket lines around federally financed public construction sites in Chicago. These led to widespread demonstrations that so alarmed Chicago Mayor Daley that he ordered the construction sites shut down because he feared that riots might ensue. Similar demonstrations with other community elements took place in Cleveland, Ohio where they shut down construction of a huge shopping mall and a federal court house; in Philadelphia, Pennsylvania where construction of a new U.S. Mint was halted; and in New York City, where progress on the new Harlem Hospital was interrupted.

Hill's ability to generate publicity caused consternation among leaders of the AFL-CIO and their international anti-Soviet arm, the International Confederation of Free Trade Unions (ICFTU). They frequently approached Hill to argue that his criticisms of American labor's racial practices harmed the West's efforts to counter Soviet propaganda. Hill says that his reply was always the same: "Instead of trying to shut me up, stop the unions from discriminating against blacks." Hill recalls that even the president of the AFL-CIO complained. "The scope of our publicity greatly annoyed George Meany, who no doubt felt that it affected the participation of American labor in foreign affairs, especially during the Cold War," Hill has observed.

23. NAACP, *1953 Annual Report,* 56–57.

24. Author interview with Herbert Hill, October 23, 1999.

25. NAACP, *1953 Annual Report,* 56.

26. NAACP, *1954 Annual Report, 52–53.*

27. NAACP, 1955 *Annual Report,* 47.

28. NAACP, *1953 Annual Report,* 60–63; and NAACP, *1954 Annual Report,* 57–60. For a detailed account of the NAACP's campaign on behalf of migrant workers, including graphic photographs by George Moffett, see Hill, Herbert, *No Harvest For the Reaper—the Story of the Migratory Agricultural Worker in the United States.* This publication led Edward R. Murrow and CBS TV's "See It Now" to produce the still-impressive award-winning television documentary on the subject, "Harvest of Shame," for which Hill served as a consultant. In 1957, Hill collaborated with Dr. Ernesto Galarza, leader of the National Agricultural Workers Union, in an investigation of migrant workers in California, which found that migrant Mexican workers had supplanted white and black farm workers, because the immigrants worked for less money and were more reluctant to fight for their rights as temporary or illegal workers. The NAACP then pressed public officials to insist that the farm owners hire more U.S. citizens, white and black, as migrant laborers.

29. In an adaptation of Yogi Berra's classic comment—"Deja vu all over again,"—the plight of migratory workers in New York State was exposed by two state legislators almost a half century later. In 1999, they charged that migratory workers—mostly from Jamaica and Mexico—were paid $210 for an 80-hour work week without any health or welfare benefits and were physically mistreated by their employers. The New York Farm Bureau, representing 30,000 farm owners, intensely opposed any changes in the existing laws, which New York Attorney General Elliot Spitzer, after hearing from the farm workers and the legislators, admitted were designed "to prevent you from getting the wages you deserve." Greenhouse, Steven, *New York Times,* October 28, 1999, Sec. B, p. 5, "Seeking New State Laws for Farm Workers."

30. Hill's book, *No Harvest for the Reaper—the Story of the Migratory Agricultural Worker in the United States,* recounts this trek northward with the migratory farm workers.

31. NAACP, *1954 Annual Report,* 53–56.

32. Nelson, Bruce, *Divided We Stand—American Workers and the Struggle for Racial Equality,* 235–238. Nelson examines this episode in detail. The realization among black workers in Local 2401 and elsewhere in Southern steelworker locals, as well as within the NAACP, that the steelworkers union had become the enemy was especially painful because of the esteem with which black workers had held the union's national president, Phil Murray, between the late 1930s until his death in 1952, and the warm manner in which Murray and his organizers had welcomed blacks into the union in the South during the first decade of the CIO. Indeed, blacks formed the core of many Southern locals in that period because of traditional white worker resistance to unionism and to Northern radicals who typified the first waves of organizers. However, after *Brown* and the election of a conservative bureaucrat, David McDonald, as the new steelworkers president, the union leaders determined that control of their Southern locals required a shift to the right, which included distancing the union from the civil rights momentum that was beginning to grow in the South. It was ironic, therefore, that the black union members who had been the majority of the founding members of these locals

were being brushed aside in order to satisfy the biases of the white workers, who originally resisted joining the union. Nor were the Steelworkers the only union to follow this pattern. *Ibid.*, 210–213.

33. NAACP, *1955 Annual Report,* 45–46.

34. Author interview with Hill, *Ibid.*

35. Hill, Herbert, "Black-Jewish Conflict in the Labor Context," a chapter in *African Americans and Jews in the Twentieth Century,* 265–267. Hill derived his facts from the hearings conducted by the Industrial Commission of Wisconsin in January, 1955, and from the brief and testimony relating to the law suit by Ross and Harris against the Bricklayers Local 8. His correspondence with AFL-CIO staff director for civil rights Boris Shiskin during the period was his basis for summarizing the labor federation's actual position in respect to Local 8's practices, as were statements by Meany and Zimmerman in official AFL-CIO publications, such as the *American Federationist,* December, 1957. There is an eerie dimension to the AFL-CIO's deployment of Zimmerman, a former Communist with whom they had struggled vehemently during the 1930s, as the repeated defender of racist practices by member unions of the labor federation. Also see *1957 NAACP Annual Report,* 49–51.

36. Interview with Hill, *Ibid.*

37. NAACP, *1959 Annual Report,* 54–55.

38. Nelson, Bruce, *Divided We Stand: American Workers and the Struggle for Black Equality,* 222–223.

39. *Ibid.*, 220. The paradox here is that the NAACP had been obliged to make a similar judgment in respect to the CPUSA's malleable commitment to racial justice in the 1940s as it now made in respect to the anti-Communist American labor movement in the late 1950s.

40. NAACP, *1956 Annual Report,* 54.

41. NAACP, *1959 Annual Report,* 52–53.

42. Hill, Herbert, "Racism Within Organized Labor: A Report of the Five Years of the AFL-CIO, 1955–1960," Address to the NAACP Annual Meeting, New York City, January 3, 1961, 13 (mimeographed text).

43. One of the most important studies of the intransigence of Southern local unions to racial change, and of the retreat from compelling such change by the national AFL-CIO is Alan Draper's *Conflict of Interest: Organized Labor and the Civil Rights Movement in the South, 1954–1968.* Draper cites numerous examples of local union participation, even leadership, of KKK or White Citizens Council activities. As for organized labor's support of civil rights, Draper observes, "It is also a story of stunning hypocrisy. At its first meeting in 1956, the AFL-CIO Committee on Civil Rights sanctimoniously threatened to stop cooperating with the National Conference of Christians and Jews unless it desegregated its local chapters. The committee must have had a perverse view of its jurisdiction because it took no action against AFL-CIO-affiliated unions that engaged in the same discriminatory practices it found so offensive in others. Some affiliated unions still barred blacks from membership, maintained segregated locals, and tolerated separate seniority lists. It is also a tale of willful ignorance." When the AFL-CIO's second-in-command in 1963 asked his Southern regional director "for a list of positive achievements in the area of civil rights," the regional director provided

the list, adding, "'You did not ask for a report on those organizations and firms where we still have a long way to go.'"

44. NAACP, *1957 Annual Report,* 48–49.

45. Braestrup, Peter, "NAACP Fights Big Jet Contract," *New York Times,* April 7, 1961, 1 and 17.

46. *Ibid.*

47. *Ibid.*

48. Braestrup, Peter, "Kennedy to Fight Curbs on Negroes in Federal Work," *New York Times,* April 8, 1961, 1 and 15.

49. My own response to the hard-line resistance of the machinists union as opposed to the more compliant attitudes of Lockheed management (as well as a half dozen other similar incidents) was to begin to reconsider just who "our friends" were, as well as identifying a new class of "enemies."

Chapter 10

1. Author interview with Hill, October 24, 1999, New York City.

2. *Ibid.* It will come as no surprise that all of the ILGWU's published materials either ignore the union's collision with the NAACP or deny the facts. Gus Tyler has been quoted as stating, years later, that the ILGWU had been vindicated by the court, which did not occur.

3. Seldin, Joel, *New York Herald Tribune,* July 2, 1962, 1 and 8, "ILGWU Condemned for Racial Barriers." The NAACP attorney on this case was a private cooperating attorney, Jawn Sandifer, who also represented McLaurin before the U.S. Supreme Court in the earlier railroad case. The 1962 case was formally known as *Holmes v. Falikman,* File 1963, NY State Commission on Human Rights. Moe Falikman was Local 10's manager. The same issue of the *Herald Tribune* profiled Ernest Holmes in a story by Fred Ferretti, "Crusading Negro Finds Road Is Rough," p. 8. The same day *The New York Times* ran a smaller article, headlined "Union Told to Get Job for Negro," p. 22.

4. *New York Herald Tribune, ibid.*

5. Wilkins' letter to Emanuel Muravchik, executive secretary of the Jewish Labor Committee, October 31, 1962. This letter is among the NAACP's archives in the Library of Congress.

6. *New York Times,* May 18, 1961, 27, "Garment Local Accused of Bias."

7. *New Politics,* Winter, 1963, Vol. 2, No. 1, 7. In Tyler's response to Hill's charges in the previous issue of *New Politics.*

8. Letter by Professor Herbert Hill of the University of Wisconsin to Adina Back, Exhibition Coordinator, The Jewish Museum, New York City, February 4, 1992. The writer is indebted to Professor Hill for the raw data he provided in 1992 regarding the history of this confrontation, including a copy of his seven-page letter to Ms. Back, to assist the NAACP staff in our efforts to present the NAACP's side to the general press.

I feel it incumbent on myself to note my long (44-year) association with the ILGWU, starting in 1948 in Perth Amboy, New Jersey, as a shipping clerk in a family garment factory, and including my direction of the 80th birthday celebration for David Dubinsky by the International Rescue Committee, my work with the International Labor Training Institute of the ILGWU in the 1950s and 1960s, my political collaborations in numerous local and national campaigns, my long association with the late Wilbur Daniels, the administrative vice president of the union, including a consultation initiated by Daniels for advice in the late 1960s on how the union should deal with the cheap garment imports that were then flooding the nation at a cost of tens of thousands of union jobs.

I cannot begin to express the disappointment I experienced as my research revealed the ILGWU's disgraceful behavior towards minorities, virtually all of them poor, which Hill's documentation unequivocally supports. Although these later abuses in no way cancel out the heroism and public spiritedness of the union's earlier decades and the stirring leadership provided by Dubinsky in those years, they cannot on the other hand in any way be justified in the racially motivated and power-preserving impulses that marked the ILGWU leadership's behavior from the mid-1950s onward. Of the many "gods that failed" in my political life, one of the most bitter was that of the ILGWU and of the social democratic movement it spawned.

9. NAACP, *1962 Annual Report.*

10. 1992 letter by Professor Hill, *Ibid.* Chasen is referring to Hill's initial letters to the ILGWU, listing the grievances of the minority union members.

11. Dubinsky, David and A. H. Raskin. *David Dubinsky: A Life With Labor.* In Dubinsky's "official" autobiography, there is not a single reference to either the NAACP or Herbert Hill. The book refers twice to the Powell subcommittee, describing the Harlem congressman as a vindictive opportunist, and falsely claiming that the ILGWU was vindicated in the hearings, citing as proof the fact that the hearings were halted and never resumed. There are two brief references to civil rights in which Dubinsky boasts about the union's estimable civil rights record without once citing an example. Nor does his biography refer to the court decisions ordering the union to admit black and Latino members into the housing projects and the home for the elderly it subsidized with membership dues.

12. U.S. House of Representatives, Committee on Education and Labor, "Report of the Subcommittee Investigating the Garment Industry," 87th Congress, 2nd Session, August 17–24 and September 21, 1962, 165–167. The woman who testified and then was barred by the union from employment in the industry was Florence Rice, who became an outspoken activist and chair of the Harlem Community Council.

13. Constitution of the International Ladies Garment Workers Union, New York: 1959.

14. One of Dubinsky's nastiest internal critics claimed that the principal difference between his style of dictatorship and that of the Communists whom he and the union vigorously opposed was the latter's use of the Red Army to enforce their bureaucratic tyranny. It was a significant difference, to be sure, but perhaps not as philosophically significant when one factors in the degree to which Dubinsky controlled the livelihood of his officers and staff. Their very ability to feed their children depended upon being on good terms with the ILGWU president. However, as far as we are able to tell, none of the anti-Dubinsky critics lost their lives or were imprisoned because of their views.

15. Hill, Herbert, "The ILGWU—Fact and Fiction," 3–23. In this article, Hill responds directly to Gus Tyler's rebuttal of his earlier article in the summer issue of *New Politics,* which was a refined version of his testimony before the House subcommittee on August 18, 1962. In the first article, entitled "The ILGWU Today —The Decay of a Labor Union," *New Politics,* Fall, 1962, Hill soberly exposes the union's policies of racial discrimination, the union's constitutional and by-law provisions that prevent any democratic challenge to the union president, much less any appearance of minority faces on the ruling boards, and the depressed wage scales and how they have been manipulated to assure a steady and sizable supply of low-income workers from the Negro and Puerto Rican communities for the garment manufacturers. The next issue of *New Politics* accorded Gus Tyler the opportunity to respond but the quality and nature of this response could not but deeply disappoint the union's partisans. Because Tyler's response was so flawed, the editors of *New Politics* accorded Hill the opportunity to respond point by point to the Tyler piece. In doing so, Hill destroyed both Tyler, and the union's case, noting over and over again where Tyler had failed to even respond to charges made by Hill or where he had distorted the facts to fit his arguments. It was such a revealingly disappointing response for the union that one of its old friends, Professor Daniel Bell of Harvard, wrote in *The New Leader,* a publication heavily financed by organized labor and especially by the ILGWU:

"The fact is—and this is the 'bite' in Hill's charges—that Negroes are under-represented in the leadership of many of the unions where they form a significant proportion of the membership. In the case of these unions, what the Negroes want is 'recognition' at the level of the top leadership and a growing share of the spoils of office . . . . The realistic process ... has been one of ethnic groups advancing themselves precisely in this fashion; by organizing on bloc lines, electing their own kind, and using the patronage system to enhance the wealth and status of the group . . . . In economic and educational opportunity, the Negro is in a position of inequality, and the government is bound to help him move ahead. But doesn't the trade union movement have a *special* obligation to help redress the balance?" (January 21, 1963)

16. Nelson, Bruce, *Divided We Stand: American Workers and the Struggle for Black Equality,* 233–235. Nelson quotes Charles Zimmerman, former leader of the Communist caucus within the ILGWU and later chairman of the AFL-CIO's Civil Rights Committee, as calling Hill's charges "demonstrably untrue ... malicious or tinged with anti-Semitism . . . . The fact that Mr. Hill is white and Jewish does not mitigate against this in the least." Emanuel Muravchik, executive director of the Jewish Labor Committee, in defending the ILGWU against the NAACP's charges, also suggested anti-Semitism and raised the serious question of whether "it is any longer possible to work with the NAACP." Since the Jewish Labor Committee's importance was never more than marginal, Muravchik's wondering aloud was no doubt supposed to suggest that if the NAACP continued on its campaign to desegregate the ILGWU, it would probably lose general Jewish support. This veiled threat never produced a moment's hesitation on the part of Wilkins or his colleagues. Also Hill, *New Politics,* passim.

17. Wilkins, Roy, Letter on NAACP letterhead, October 31, 1962.

18. *Ibid.*

19. *Ibid.*

20. This is not to say that it is impossible for a Jew to be anti-Semitic, or a black to be antiblack. Both are eminently possible. It simply did not occur in this case and the ILGWU's cynical use of the ploy remains unconscionable almost four decades later.

21. According to Hill's recollection, during this period he received a phone call from a conservative Republican congressman from Missouri, Thomas Curtis, with whom he was familiar, to report that the ILGWU's Dubrow had visited him (and many other congresspersons) solely to pass on the information that not only was Hill "a self-hating Jewish anti-Semite" but he was also a "Communist agent for the Soviet Union being paid by Moscow." The congressman, Hill recalls, told him that he roared with laughter at the allegations and then led the lobbyist to the door. Interview with Hill, *ibid.*

22. Near the end of Dubinsky's reign, E. Vogel, labor editor of *The Jewish Daily Forward,* showed up at Hill's office without warning one day and, without any preliminaries, launched into his remarks with this disclaimer: "I want you to know that nobody sent me here." A few minutes later he conveyed his real message to Hill: David Dubinsky will not move forward on union "reforms" if it appears that they were in response to pressure from the NAACP. Vogel advised Hill to "quiet down and lay low" in respect to any comments about the ILGWU.

23. I directed the 80th birthday dinner honoring David Dubinsky for the benefit of the International Rescue Committee on December 13, 1966, at New York City's Americana Hotel. The price Dubinsky exacted of me was to undertake the public relations assignment for the 70th anniversary of the founding of *The Jewish Daily Forward.*

The Dubinsky event itself proved extraordinary. A professionally-written and produced mixed-media biography of Dubinsky's long and colorful life, interspersed with live commentaries from national and world leaders, was the evening's highlight. ILGWU Assistant President Wilbur Daniels' wife, Pat, was commissioned to write the script. The honorary chairmen of the dinner were Harry S. Truman, Dwight D. Eisenhower, and Hubert H. Humphrey. Among the benefit officers were NAACP Vice Chairman Buell G. Gallagher, civil rights attorney Lloyd Garrison, AFL-CIO Vice President A. Philip Randolph, and Clothing Workers President Jacob Potofsky. The New York vice chairmen were U.S. Senators Jacob Javits and Robert Kennedy, Governor Nelson Rockefeller, and New York City Mayor John V. Lindsay. Among the long list of celebrities and statesmen who comprised the dinner sponsorship were Dr. Ralph Bunche, Rev. Martin Luther King Jr., Thurgood Marshall, Dr. Robert Weaver, and Whitney Young Jr.

24. Report of the General Executive Board, 32nd Convention, ILGWU, Miami Beach, Florida, May 12, 1965, 56–57. The report stated that the union-financed wing of the retirement home officially opened on June 11, 1961, and the ceremony was attended by political leaders, including New York Governor Nelson Rockefeller. Only then, after the public opening, did the union leadership become aware of the scandalous situation: "when the Workmen's Circle home refused to process several applications of non-Jewish members . . . [and] . . . when President Dubinsky was apprised of the refusal of the home to process a single non-Jewish application." At this point David Dubinsky ordered a halt to further applications "pending a review of the situation." The president's report

added: "We were shocked that the Workmen's Circle pension home, which had been built with ILGWU money, was not open to minorities and [we] immediately ceased our contributions." (In fact, the home was not open to any non-Jewish ILGWU members, including Italians, who comprised a sizable minority segment of the leadership.)

In effect, this pronouncement ended the union's financial support of the Workmen's Circle retirement home, more than three years after the NAACP had publicly exposed the practice. The union, however, continued to support the general work of the Workmen's Circle.

25. My professional association with the ILGWU began in 1955 when I worked with their International Labor Training Institute to recruit young Africans who might develop into free trade union organizers and leaders after an extensive stint with the union's New York-based institute. In those days I worked with the institute director, Arthur Elder, and his deputy, Maida Springer, one of the ILGWU's few black local executives. In the course of later associations through the International Rescue Committee, I had developed a close personal friendship with Wilbur Daniels, the union's administrative vice president. Daniels was a lawyer by profession with a sincere concern for civil rights, and a rabid opera lover who became a leader in the Metropolitan Opera Society. Robert L. Carter, then the NAACP's general counsel, was also a zealous opera fan. I therefore arranged a social meeting at Carter's home early in 1966 for both men and they soon because fast friends.

Moreover, at this meeting the ILGWU's racial problems and their antipathy for Herbert Hill were discussed at length. Carter sought to find ways in which the union could begin to open up its leadership ranks to blacks and other minorities. At one point Carter proposed that the union identify and appoint a small number of blacks as shop stewards. Daniels carried the proposal to Dubinsky and returned empty-handed. Daniels asserted that, "none of the black sewing machine operators would agree to stay several hours after work was completed to attend a steward's meeting." Carter then suggested that the union pay these stewards the differential to attend the required meetings. Daniels again returned empty-handed. This time the union response was that "singling out blacks for such special treatment would be regarded as discrimination against the other shop stewards."

As Carter and Daniels sought to find common ground in apparent futility, in December 1966, Dubinsky retired, following a gala celebration of his 80th Birthday benefiting the International Rescue Committee. The tributes were extensive and they came from prominent people in almost every segment of the population. Despite the acrimonious past, Roy Wilkins agreed to serve as a cochairman of the dinner, along with such luminaries as Walter Reuther, Mrs. Herbert H. Lehman, Reinhold Neibuhr, David Sarnoff, and Dubinsky's successor, Louis Stulberg. Because Wilkins would not break a long-standing commitment to speak before an NAACP branch that night, his deputy, John Morsell, attended the dinner in his place and was seated on the dais.

A few days after the dinner, I suggested to Daniels that we were now facing a new page in the NAACP/ILGWU relationship with the advent of Dubinsky's successor, a younger and more pragmatic individual, Louis Stulberg, who had served Dubinsky as his secretary-treasurer, and who had overcome the challenge to his succession from Dubinsky's son-in-law, Shelly Appleton.

Through Daniels, I arranged for Wilkins and Stulberg to meet for lunch at a Chinese restaurant half-way between the two headquarters, some three blocks separating them on Broadway. At the last minute, Stulberg's office phoned to allege that he was running late but would appreciate it if Wilkins could come by his office and pick him up. Wilkins looked at me with his patented skeptical half-smile, as if to say, "I know exactly what he is up to." Aloud, he said, "Let's go. We have to give him the benefit of the doubt. Especially if this leads to some form of cooperation between us." With that we marched off to 1710 Broadway, where the guards at the door had been fully prepped for our arrival. They whisked us to the top floor, and as the elevator opened, Stulberg was waiting to shake hands with Wilkins and parade him through the long aisles of clerical staff workers, many of them black or Puerto Rican, to his spacious office. Stulberg had achieved his initial goal: a stamp of approval from the NAACP that he could market with his own support staff, many of whom had walked picket lines to protest the union's refusal to allow *them* to organize their own union. Stulberg fully appreciated what Wilkins had done for him; indeed he read it as an expression of strength on Wilkins' part, enabling him (Stulberg) to consolidate his own newly won position. We proceeded to the Chinese restaurant, long a favorite of the ILGWU leadership, where the two leaders agreed to disagree on the role of Herbert Hill, but to find as many other areas of collaboration as possible. Every year thereafter for almost two decades, the ILGWU made a $10,000 contribution to the NAACP (roughly 10 percent of all the gifts collected from the labor movement during the 1970s and 1980s). Stulberg joined the Board of Trustees of the NAACP SCF, as did each of his successors, Sol "Chick" Chaikin and Jay Mazur. The ILGWU lobbying operation in Washington, headed by Evelyn Dubrow, became a stalwart ally of the well-oiled machine crafted by Clarence Mitchell and Joseph Rauh, also an NAACP Board member, through the LCCR, and its skilled executive director, Ralph Neas. ILGWU locals proved important mainstays in support of NAACP benefits, purchasing sizable blocks of tickets for their members.

At about this time, the union began to tap blacks and Puerto Ricans for some of its local and national board positions, a mark of progress but by no means to the extent that an observer could term it parity. Except for the top ranks, the union was fast becoming one of color, indeed of many colors, as Asian immigrants swarmed into the United States and found jobs in the needle trades. In 1998, I met with Jay Mazur, president of Unite!, which was the successor union to the ILGWU and two others, to introduce him to the leading Chinese dissident in exile. Mazur was accompanied by a Chinese-born, Chinese-speaking female vice president of the union.

26. In Dubinsky's autobiography, written with A.H. Raskin, he identifies the three greatest challenges to the union under his leadership: 1) the attempt by the Communists to take over the union; 2) the assault on the union's behavior towards its minority members that became the theme of the House subcommittee hearings chaired by Representative Adam Clayton Powell Jr. (on the initiative of the NAACP and Herbert Hill); and 3) the attempt to organize the ILGWU's headquarters staff members. Yet he could not bring himself to identify either the NAACP or Herbert Hill by name at any point in his autobiography.

Chapter 11

1. Tyler, Gus, *The Labor Revolution: Trade Unionism in a New America,* Viking Press, New York, 1966, 190–191, quotes the president of the plumbers' international union—Peter Schoemann—who stated candidly in the union's journal (April 1965) that this manifestation of nepotism was merely another form of patronage practiced in many walks of American life. His union, he proclaimed, "has not tried to conceal or apologize for the system of preferring sons in the building trades. We have campaigned openly for the right of our programs to select apprentices in the same way that any private business might select employees, or that an elected public official selects his political appointees. This extends all the way to a pure patronage system for those local programs that desire it."

2. Nelson, Bruce, *Divided We Stand: American Workers and the Struggle for Black Equality,* 232–234.

3. Jacobson, Julius, ed., *The Negro and the American Labor Movement,* 287–288, in article by Herbert Hill on the status of minorities in organized labor. Hill quotes Roy Wilkins as describing the AFL-CIO censure of Randolph as "an incredible cover up" in a statement on October 13, 1961. Goulden, Joseph, *Meany—The Unchallenged Strong Man of American Labor*, 307–318, describes the conflicts between Randolph and Meany in greater detail, including the moment when Meany publicly lost his temper with Randolph. Goulden claims that after Randolph was censured by the AFL-CIO Executive Board, Meany then capitulated to many of Randolph's demands privately, bolstering the pro-civil rights leadership and ordering a series of new initiatives, which shortly led to Meany taking the lead in pressing for a federal FEP provision in the draft civil rights bill being proposed by President Kennedy in 1963. According to Goulden, Kennedy's aides and the president himself opposed such a provision, predicting that it would lose the moderate congressional vote and destroy chances for the remainder of the bill to be passed. *Ibid.*, 319–323.

4. Hill, in Jacobson, *The Negro and the American Labor Movement,* 310.

5. One of organized labor's most effective public relations tools was a volume by ILGWU Assistant President Gus Tyler, organized labor's house intellectual, who wrote *The Labor Revolution,* as a paean to the AFL-CIO, Meany, and Dubinsky. Eligible for the "blindly optimistic" prize, this book insisted that organized labor was not in decline, despite the diminishing membership rolls and that it was on the verge of an enormous rise in power, influence, memberships and so forth. No doubt officially sanctioned by the AFL-CIO, Tyler's book found grounds to praise Meany's civil rights record and to blame Negroes for organized labor's historic antagonism because Negroes had allegedly so often served as scabs during strikes by white unionists. Besides their "history" of scabbing, Negroes were, according to Tyler, unable to obtain good jobs because they lacked the necessary skills and education, both of which would inevitably come in time, he added. Tyler, however, pronounced with confidence that the material wellbeing of Negroes rested with the trade union movement, including the craft unions, which would eventually open up the ranks to minorities because of strong federal fair employment laws. Tyler quotes Meany on the reasons why the AFL-CIO was justified in expelling corrupt or Communist-controlled unions but opposed expulsion of racist unions: "Corruption—like communism—seizes the leadership of a union and

works down to lower levels by perverting the union's democratic procedures . . . . Discrimination is resisted at the top but perpetrated below . . . . Would we be better off to cast out these misguided members and remove them from the influence of the mainstream of the labor movement; meanwhile expelling in the same action the national leaders who deplore and fight discrimination? I think not. I think we can do more to educating them if they are in the federation." This passage is based on two false assumptions: first, that the national leaders in the main actively opposed racial discrimination; and second, that the labor federation strongly pushed a program of persuasive education to overcome racially biased attitudes among rank-and-file unionists. Tyler is more candid in arguing that labor's political future depends in part upon the growth of the number of registered Negro voters who, he predicted, would vote for candidates supported by organized labor. Further, the more Negro workers belonging to the labor movement, Tyler suggests, the less likely it is that surplus labor, black or otherwise, will be used to lower the cost of labor, that is, wages.

6. Goulden, Joseph C., *Meany—the Unchallenged Strong Man of American Labor,* 318.

7. *Ibid.*, 317–319.

8. *Ibid.*, 319–321.

9. *Ibid.*, 320–321.

10. *Ibid.*, 320–322. The term employed by some civil rights activists during this period was superseniority. They sought to enable Negroes with long job histories in the lower paid, or semiskilled, categories to leap ahead of some whites who had greater job tenure in a specific position that would normally have qualified them for promotion whenever a higher position opened up. In short, Negroes who in the past had been barred from promotions to these higher positions because of their race would be given credit for their long work record in the lower paid positions, credit that would in some instances speed up their promotion over whites in higher positions.

"Superseniority," said Meany, "would throw into the street white workers who were in no way responsible for the previous discrimination against Negroes. Special treatment," he argued, "misses the point. There is not much future in a program for sharing misery." In both instances, Meany had become the impenetrable shield for white workers against any effort, either by the executive branch or by the courts, to penalize white workers by making up for past injustices to Negroes through preferences of any kind. *Ibid.*, 321–322.

11. *Ibid.*, 322.

12. Stetson, Damon, "Rights Act Helps Labor's Campaign," *New York Times,* July 3, 1965, 7. In one of the longest news articles written on employment discrimination, Stetson drew comments from civil rights activists and labor leaders regarding the activation of Title VII of the 1964 Civil Rights Act, which forbade racial discrimination both in respect to labor union membership and opportunities in the workplace. In general, civil rights activists evinced skepticism while organized labor's spokesmen attempted to present a picture of increasing racial progress. One unnamed New Jersey building trades leader was quoted as follows: "It's the law. We have to take the niggers in." That quote presaged how seriously the labor movement in general would accept enforcement of Title VII's provisions.

13. Hill, Herbert, "The New York City Terminal Market Controversy: A Case Study of Race, Labor, and Power," 361; Hill, Herbert, "The Judicial Perception of Employment Discrimination: Litigation under Title VII of the 1964 Civil Rights Act," 257. After four decades of dilatory tactics, Lather Local 46 finally agreed to a settlement in the spring of 1999, but refused to admit any wrongdoing. After a decade-long suit in the Southern District of New York by the Center for Constitutional Rights on behalf of 39 minority workers who regularly appeared at the hiring hall but rarely, if ever, were selected for jobs, the local union finally agreed to pay these workers a total of $500,000 in settlement of their claims. The local also agreed to comply with the renewed federal court order, originally filed in the 1970 consent decree, that provided minorities with intensive job training and rigorous reporting of the results of their efforts. To the last, the union insisted it had not discriminated against blacks and other minorities and had settled only "to avoid the trouble of litigation," following more than 40 years of its own obsessive litigation. It remains to be seen whether the union will actually comply with the court order and the settlement agreement, given its consistent refusal to do so since 1970. *New York Times,* June 19, 1999.

14. Herbert Hill disputes the claim by Jack Greenberg in his memoir that he turned over to the NAACP and Hill more than 850 employment complaints filed with EEOC by his staff in order to "moderate turf problems with the NAACP." Greenberg, Jack, *Crusaders in the Courts,* 413. Hill maintains that, quite to the contrary, Greenberg dispatched LDF staff attorneys to go through Hill's files at the NAACP, trying to identify as many complaints as they could utilize, especially after the LDF received a $300,000 grant from the Ford Foundation for a new and self-promoted employment program under the direction of Jean Fairfax. The LDF itself was chronically limited by its inherent design as a public interest law firm; without grassroots members it was unable to identify enough clients to represent. The NAACP's vast grassroots structure, with several thousand local branches and between 400,000 and 500,000 members, not to mention its activism among black members of labor unions, produced the vast majority of the black worker complainants, as already noted, in numbers far beyond the NAACP's staff and financial capabilities to represent before the EEOC or in court. The LDF carried an important part of that load, though NAACP staff members found it particularly ironic that the foundations, most especially the Ford Foundation, generously financed the LDF's employment programs, despite the fact that they had to scurry for cases, whereas they declined to finance the NAACP's cases that were well beyond the NAACP's financial and staff capacity. A few small liberal/left foundations, including Field and Stern, did, however, provide funding for Hill's labor department.

15. Hill, Herbert, "The New York City Terminal Market Controversy: A Case Study of Race, Labor, and Power," 45.

16. The initial membership of the NAAB constituted the first wave of Negro construction contractors during the 1970s, when the political climate, especially under President Richard M. Nixon, heavily favored advancement through entrepreneurialism. President Nixon appointed several key NAACP leaders to his administration, including National Board Member Samuel Jackson, who filled an important post at Housing and Urban Development (HUD) along with Samuel

Simmons, while former NAACP public information officer Stanley Scott became the deputy spokesman at the White House.

17. Plosky, Harry A. and James Williams, eds., *The Negro Almanac,* 68.

18. Hill, Herbert, "The New York City Terminal Market Controversy: A Case Study of Race, Labor, and Power," 46.

19. As late as December 1999, labor union executives associated with the AFL-CIO and the Randolph Institute during the 1970s continued to suggest that Hill fabricated his statistics, but have yet to produce any documented case against him or his work.

20. There is no evidence that Meany himself suggested to Rustin that he attempt to persuaded Roy Wilkins to distance himself from Herbert Hill's accusation. Phone conversations with Rustin's two closest aides during the 1970s—Norman Hill (November 9, 1999) and Rochelle Horowitz (December 1999)—confirmed that Rustin received no such marching orders from Meany. "Not that Rustin needed any such orders to decide to seek Wilkins' collaboration in repudiating Hill," observed Horowitz, now a retired vice president of the American Federation of Teachers (AFT). "Everyone in that circle back then was castigating Herb Hill," she recalled. However, both Horowitz and Norman Hill, Rustin's successor as president of the A. Philip Randolph Institute, believe that, in all likelihood, Rustin sought the meeting with Wilkins after consulting with Don Slaiman, the AFL-CIO's director of civil rights and the labor federation's watchdog (some have described him as the *apparatchik)* for the various "front" groups funded by the AFL-CIO, including the Randolph Institute. Norman Hill has been the latter's executive director or president for three decades. After his retirement form the AFL-CIO, Slaiman served as chairman of the Social Democrats USA, the right-wing American socialists stemming in large measure from the proselytizing of the late Max Schachtman, the renowned Trotskyite theorist and intellectual. A surprising number of AFL-CIO leaders and activists, in addition to Slaiman and Rustin, were dedicated Schachtmanites, including Sandra Feldman, president of the AFT; Horowitz and her colleague, Judy Bardacke, both of the AFT; Tom Kahn, George Meany's and later Lane Kirkland's special assistant; magazine writer and polemicist Josh Muravchik; Norman Hill; and Penn Kemble, who led several of the labor federation's front groups, like Frontlash. Most of the Social Democrats USA's annual funding came from the AFL-CIO and its constituent unions.

21. Telephone interview with Herbert Hill, November 7, 1999.

22. It was Herbert Hill's recollection, confirmed by Vernon Jordan by phone on November 9, 1999, that Jordan himself was not personally involved in any aspect of the meeting, including any prior planning. Jordan said his practice was to delegate all aspects of the Urban League's apprenticeship training program to its director, Napoleon Johnson.

23. Most of the details describing this meeting were reported to me contemporarily by both Wilkins and Hill. In addition, Hill added a few details in a phone interview, November 7, 1999.

24. Title VII was amended in 1972 to enable the Justice Department and the EEOC to file their own suits against unions and employers that discriminated.

25. Shabecoff, Philip, "Steel and Union to Adopt a Plan on Job Equality—Program Covers Racial and Sex Barriers—NAACP Aide Charges Flaws," *New York Times,* April 15, 1974, 1 and 21.

Hill's concerns proved accurate over the long run; the steel industry's settlement failed to wipe out the union's racial practices, sanctioned by the corporations, for many years, though the process had at long last begun. Fully implementing the settlement, however limited, especially in respect to the legally required cash awards, demanded the constant vigilance of the NAACP for almost a decade thereafter. For a detailed and insightful account of the black steelworkers' struggle for equality and recognition within the union, see Ruth Needleman's *Black Freedom Fighters in Steel: The Struggle for Democratic Unionism.*

26. During an annual corporate campaign chaired by a senior vice president of Rockwell Industries based in Pittsburgh, Pennsylvania and housed in the same office building as U.S. Steel, a Rockwell executive, in my presence, sought the participation of the steel company's CEO but was brusquely dismissed and told that he would never forgive the NAACP for its role in the campaign to eradicate racial discrimination in the steel industry.

27. By the early 1970s, the AFL-CIO's minions took to organizing serious campaigns against Hill's initiatives at the national NAACP conventions each July. They induced local labor unionists to run as chapter delegates to the national convention. At various times, as many as 20 percent of the NAACP convention delegates were trade unionists, most of whom attended with instructions to follow the line of organized labor on the key votes. Nevertheless, the overall delegate assembly, perhaps seeing through the organized labor smokescreen, continued to back Hill and his initiatives. At the NAACP's sixty-third annual convention in July, 1972, Hill charged that minority memberships were actually declining in the building trades unions despite the various federal home town plans promoted by the construction unions and supported by the Nixon Administration in Chicago, New York, Philadelphia and Pittsburgh, Pennsylvania.

28. *Washington Post,* June 2, 1974.

29. In late 1974, two federal appellate court decisions offered the NAACP and black workers a new degree of hope. In a case involving a California union before the National Labor Relations Board (NLRB), the District of Columbia Court of Appeals ruled that a union is not permitted to ignore racially discriminatory practices in the workplace. "The law," the decision pronounced, "does not give the union an option to tolerate some racial discrimination, but declares that all racial discrimination in employment is illegal." The Eighth Circuit Court of Appeals in St. Louis, Missouri ruled that the NLRB was obliged to investigate the racial policies of labor unions and was prohibited from certifying as bargaining agents any union found to be discriminating. For a relatively brief period, it seemed as if Hill's long-term assault on union bias using Title VII as his principal weapon was finally beginning to pay off. However, this too proved illusory.

Chapter 12

1. Wilkins, Roy with Tom Mathews, *Standing Fast: The Autobiography of Roy Wilkins,* 203–205. In this autobiography, Wilkins commented that, when learning of White's divorce and remarriage at the 1949 annual convention in Los Angeles, "half the delegates wanted to lynch Walter for leaving Gladys, and the other half wanted to string him up for marrying a white woman . . . . We had a very heated fight [on the National Board], but in the end cooler heads won. Our

argument was simple: how could an organization committed to integration fire its chief executive for marrying a white woman? It didn't make sense, and it wouldn't look good—not at all."

2. *Ibid.*, 218–220.

3. Garrow, David, *Bearing the Cross: Martin Luther King, Jr., and the Southern Christian Leadership Conference,* 343, including a quotation from Bayard Rustin describing King's fear of debating Wilkins. Also Anderson, Jervis, *Bayard Rustin: Troubles I've Seen—A Biography,* 245–247, confirming Rustin's observations. Rustin is quoted as saying: "Martin simply couldn't in-fight with Roy. Martin could stand up to the worst police brutalities in Birmingham, but he flinched from polemic exchanges with Roy."

The same pages contain a quote from Wilkins who, in responding to Dr. King's unconditional endorsement of Rustin as director of the 1963 March on Washington, said: "Martin, you're politically naive. And *you* need to dissociate yourself from some of the political people around you." This was no doubt a reference to the allegations by the FBI that King's close advisor, Stanley Levinson, retained his ties to the CPUSA, a bond which Wilkins would quite naturally, given his history, greatly deplore. Few today remember that in 1963, King had less than eight years of activism, counting all of his time leading the local Montgomery march, and he was in his early thirties, whereas Wilkins was then a mature leader in his sixties with more than 33 years of national experience as a high-ranking national NAACP executive.

4. Wilkins, Roy with Tom Mathews, *Standing Fast: The Autobiography of Roy Wilkins,* 147. To some extent, this proved to be the beginning of grassroots programs for the NAACP branches. Cash shortages prevented the National Office from immediately implementing his proposal.

5. When in 1965 I was assigned responsibility for directing the NAACP's national development campaigns, the departmental directors running their own workshops were June Shagaloff, public education; Herbert Hill, employment; William Morris, housing; Herbert Wright and later Mark Rosenman, youth and college.

6. Wilkins, *op. cit.,* 2–3. The entire first chapter of Wilkins' autobiography is devoted to his childhood and early years.

7. *Ibid.*, 26–34. In the June-July 1977 double issue of *The Crisis,* which celebrates Roy Wilkins' tenure at the NAACP on the occasion of his retirement, two photos of Wilkins' early years are published on page 210. The first is of his birthplace, a modest wood frame house. The second is of his early teenage St. Paul baseball team, which aptly illustrates the integrated milieu in which he was raised in Minnesota. In this case, as in many others, Wilkins was the only Negro in the picture.

8. *Ibid.*, 12.

9. The definitive work on the potential of the Negro vote during the 1940s was written by Henry Lee Moon. Much of it was distilled in his *Balance of Power —the Negro Vote.* Appendices II and III of Moon's book consist of tables of the number of citizens, of all races and of Negroes alone, by state and the percentage of the total vote that the Negro potential represented by state and by cities with populations over 500,000. Table IV is an analysis of the 1940 election that illus-

trates, state by state, what percentage change would be required to alter the electoral outcome in the 1948 election. Table V lists the voting requirements of each of the Southern states in 1946.

10. Wilkins, Roy with Mathews, Tom, *Standing Fast: The Autobiography of Roy Wilkins,* 123. In his autobiography, Wilkins described the entire Delta journey. Wilkins' own detailed report of the adventurous Delta journey was reprinted in the commemorative edition of *The Crisis,* 213–214, after originally appearing in the April, 1933, issue of *The Crisis.* George S. Schuyler's memoir, *Black and Conservative,* 198–205, describes in vivid terms the harrowing ordeal experienced by Schuyler during the Delta investigation.

11. Wilkins, Roy with Mathews, Tom. *Standing Fast: The Autobiography of Roy Wilkins,* 125. George Schuyler's memoir confirms many of the details regarding their Delta undercover investigation and adds a few others. By 1932, Schuyler was a vociferous and highly knowledgeable opponent of the Communists; it is therefore mystifying why his memoir does not mention the episode recalled so vividly by Wilkins at the Abyssinian Baptist Church, during which Wilkins' report was constantly heckled by the Communists. Possibly Schuyler did not attend that NAACP event.

During the 1930s, Schuyler was a prominent journalist for the *Pittsburgh Courier,* writing a weekly column and editorials. He also periodically held the post of *The Crisis* business manager while working for the *Courier*, and editing an NAACP newsletter during the period when Wilkins was the magazine's editor and the NAACP's public relations director. Midway through Franklin D. Roosevelt's second term as president, Schuyler joined H.L. Mencken as relentless conservative opponents of Roosevelt. Schuyler seems to have moved systematically to the right over the next few decades. In 1965, I debated him on radio programs over the independence struggle of Angola. Schuyler by then was in the pay of the Portuguese embassy and I was promoting the Angolan liberation movement headed by Holden Roberto. Angolan refugees were then being aided in the Congo by the International Rescue Committee, which I represented at the time.

12. *Ibid.*, 127.

13. One spring night some months later, I accompanied Wilkins to a late foundation gathering. At about 10:00 p.m. we left the meeting and Wilkins said he was heading for a subway stop on Fifty-first Street and Third Avenue, which took him a few blocks from his home in Queens. I pleaded with him to take a taxi (the entire ride in those days was under $5) but he adamantly refused, reminding me that he would be spending members' dues. Though about to say that I was certain no member would object, I realized that any further discussion was hopeless, so I walked with Wilkins to the subway stop, then took a cab for a mile-and-a-half to my own apartment. Almost an hour later, extremely anxious, I phoned Wilkins.

"Who is this?" Wilkins asked, somewhat groggy.

"It's me—Gil. I was worried and just wanted to make sure you got home all right."

"I'm fine . . . (long pause) . . . Don't *ever* do this again, do you hear me?"

"Yup . . . sure" was the chastened reply.

Thereafter, whenever I left Wilkins at night, I would return home, turn on the all-night news station and wait for an hour or so until I was confident there was no news about Roy Wilkins. But I never phoned Wilkins at night again unless it was a "real" emergency. As for Wilkins, he never mentioned it again. He rarely dwelled on matters that were no longer relevant.

14. I first met Wilkins in 1949 when—as assistant to Walter White—he visited Stanford University to counsel our newly-formed NAACP college chapter. I renewed that relationship when I entered graduate school at Columbia in 1951 and worked with him continuously thereafter until Wilkins died in 1981. For the next two decades I also worked closely with Wilkins' widow, Aminda, in her determination to memorialize Wilkins through a foundation in his name and a professorial chair at the University of Minnesota's Hubert H. Humphrey Institute.

15. Never, in a half century of involvement in the movement, have I ever heard any of the other major leaders or scores of lesser ones risk their popularity to lecture their constituency on what constitutes proper personal behavior. Rev. Jesse Jackson comes closest with his rhyming, often humorous, slogans. These injunctions do not constitute the kind of stern lecture that periodically came from Roy Wilkins.

16. In the late 1990s, black playwright David Barr collaborated with Mamie Till Mobley, Emmett's mother, to write a play dramatizing these events. It was entitled "The State of Mississippi vs. Emmett Till."

17. As one of a handful of whites present at the Abyssinian Baptist Church, I grew increasingly anxious with each speech, because those speaking from the pulpit were escalating the antiwhite sentiment. The day was also extremely warm and humid, and the tensions growing in the crowd raised the temperature even more, until Wilkins' remarks defused them.

18. Larsen, Ray, "NAACP Faces Forces of Change," *Newsday,* April 11, 1965.

19 . Unsigned article, "NAACP Board Does a Flip Flop," *Amsterdam News,* April 17, 1965.

20. Tanner, Jack, interview by phone, April 30, 2001. After leaving the NAACP's board in 1968, Tanner went on to become the first African-American federal judge in the American Northwest and was still serving in that capacity when I interviewed him. Though regarded as a maverick and somewhat to the left of center, he testified on behalf of the nomination of Clarence Thomas to the U.S. Supreme Court in 1991, along with former NAACP Board Chair Margaret Bush Wilson and Jimmy Carter's attorney general, Griffin Bell.

21. Powledge, Fred, "NAACP Rebels Seek Board Power," *New York Times,* December 8, 1964, p. 39, Section 1.

22. *Ibid.*

23. Handler, M.S., "NAACP to Help Implement Laws," *New York Times,* July 4, 1965, p. 25, Section 1.

24. Wilkins resisted efforts from his allies to end the largely one-sided debate until one of Wilkins' supporters managed to be recognized by the chair and to "call for the question." That proposition is not debatable; the delegates overwhelmingly approved it and then ended the debate. Wilkins then instructed me to inform the television teams to turn off their lights that were encouraging further comment by the opposition and interfering with the conduct of the meeting. Only

one television reporter, Lem Tucker of NBC, refused. I was compelled to pull the plug on the NBC lights while Tucker rode my back until removed by NAACP security personnel. Afterwards I explained again to Tucker that the NAACP had rented the hall, and also paid for the electricity. The press was present at the pleasure of the NAACP since the convention was a private meeting. As was anticipated, the networks used about 30 seconds of the Young Turks' protest in their coverage of the convention.

25. Larsen, *Newsday*.

26. White Americans are, for the most part, unaware of the caste system that has divided African Americans since the eighteenth century. The system is based upon the degree of skin lightness—the darker the skin the lower down the caste ladder one is. This probably stems from the early separation of slaves between field slaves and house slaves. The latter were often chosen for their appearance and the more comely women were frequently bedded down by the male plantation owners, who in turn gradually bred increasingly lighter-skinned progeny, for the most part still kept as slaves until the end of the Civil War. These lighter-skinned men and women made up most, if not all, of the servant staff within the great house, learning more refinements by their proximity to the slave masters. Some learned to read, write, and calculate math, though slaves evidencing these skills were punished by some owners, while others used the literate slaves to help conduct their businesses. Some of their descendants are today light-skinned enough to pass for white. It is believed that several million Americans with African heritage are now passing as whites. Others, like Walter White and Adam Clayton Powell Jr., chose to identify with their Negro brothers and sisters, rather than to pass.

It astounds whites to learn that some African Americans continue to denigrate individuals considerably darker than themselves, that a rigid caste system is still in effect in some places, especially in such cities as Washington, D.C. and Charleston, South Carolina, and on the campuses of some historically black colleges and universities. The talented filmmaker, Spike Lee, used the caste system as the theme of one of his earlier films, "School Daze," in 1988. More recently, an African-American writer, Lawrence Otis Graham, wrote a popular book on this subject, *Our Kind of People*. The book describes the growing black upper middle class, entrance to which requires education, money, several generations of cultured antecedents, and light skin. Graham emphasizes, however, that this self-described "elite" remains loyal to their African-American heritage while cultivating both black identity and responsibility for advancing other American blacks.

27. The text of Wilkins' entire address to the delegates is published in the NAACP *1976 Annual Report* 54–55, followed by the executive committee's response (55–56). The Board approved what it believed to be its arrangement with Wilkins after accepting a report from its Executive Committee at its annual meeting on January 12, 1976. That same meeting set up a search and screening committee to recommend Wilkins' successor to the Board.

28. I drafted this letter with guidance from Deputy Director John Morsell.

29. Wilkins, Roy, Address to the Youth Awards Dinner, NAACP National Convention, Jackson, Mississippi, July 3, 1969, published in Solomon, Helen, and Wilkins, Aminda, eds., *Talking It Over with Roy Wilkins: Selected Speeches and Writings,* 74, a collection of Wilkins' columns and speeches.

30. Wilkins' address to the 1970 convention is printed in the special issue of *The Crisis,* June-July 1970, 300–304. This long address details his objections to black studies programs, separate dormitories and eating facilities, etc. It also outlines the historical demands for separatism by Negroes since the early eighteenth century and compares the American racial system with that of South Africa and Rhodesia. "The siren of separatism has been sung again and again to Negro Americans," Wilkins observes. The same issue carries a statement, presumably from Wilkins, that remained a significant part of the NAACP's policies throughout his tenure and perhaps for a few years thereafter: "The NAACP does not exclude white Americans. The welcome mat, as far as we are concerned, is not being withdrawn. Unlike certain other groups, we are not asking for their money and rejecting their presence, their experience, and their talents."

31. Wilkins, Roy, "The Decade 1960–1970," Remarks to Symposium on Civil Rights at the Lyndon B. Johnson Library, University of Texas, Austin, December 11, 1972, Reprinted in *The Crisis,* June/July 1977.

32. Solomon, Helen and Wilkins, Aminda, eds., *Talking It Over with Roy Wilkins: Selected Speeches and Writings,* Column of February 3, 1974, 113–114.

33. So successful was the exhibition that for decades to come, I received invitations to commercial exhibits of the works of most of the participating artists. In 1972, for example, the Whitney Museum of American Art exhibited the works of Alma W. Thomas, who had been dubbed the "Black Grandma Moses."

34. I directed the entire project, including creation and production of the catalogue. Cultural projects such as this art show were welcome "therapy" from the day-to-day tensions of the life-and-death struggle taking place throughout the South.

The quote by Wilkins is from the Introduction to *1969: Twelve Afro-American Artists,* produced by the Gilbert Jonas Company for the NAACP SCF. The catalogue's publication was made possible because of two generous grants from Rockefeller "cousins"—that is, the children of the generation that included Nelson, David, John III, and Winthrop. The two cousins were Ann R. Pierson (now Roberts) and Hope R. Spencer.

35. In supporting liberation and reform movements globally, Wilkins was following the pattern established by W.E.B. DuBois during the first year of *The Crisis* magazine, when he published a powerful series of articles on women's liberation and personally spoke before a major peace conference as the NAACP's representative. DuBois also pioneered the collaborative role of the American Negro in African liberation struggles and became a world-wide voice against colonialism. From then on, DuBois, Walter White, Wilkins, and other NAACP leaders sought, in Charles F. Kellogg's words, "to bring the Negro movement in the main current of humanitarian reform." Kellogg, Charles Flint, *NAACP: A History of the National Association for the Advancement of Colored People,* 53.

36. When I was discharged from the Army in early 1955, I became involved with the ACOA and was elected to its Board the following year—joining Wilkins and Lester Granger as the only followers of mainstream politics on the Board at the time. Thereafter, I often carried Wilkins' views to the Board, and briefed him afterwards of the business conducted by it.

37. Wilkins did not stop there: On January 13, 1969, at Wilkins' behest, the NAACP National Board of Directors adopted a resolution in support of the "val-

orous efforts of the Catholic minority in Northern Ireland to secure political, economic, and social rights equal to those enjoyed by the dominant Protestant majority. From the perspective of our own experience of 60 years in a similar struggle in the United States, we can view the Ulster issue with understanding and sympathy and assure the Irish civil rights activists that they have our prayers and best wishes for success in their crusade for civil rights." *The Crisis,* March 1969, 140.

38. Solomon, Helen and Wilkins, Aminda, eds., *Talking It Over with Roy Wilkins: Selected Speeches and Writings,* Address to the International Conference on Human Rights, Teheran, Iran, April 20, 1968, 64.

39. Herman, Tom, "White Woodcutters in South Mississippi Turn to . . . NAACP?" *Wall Street Journal,* October 19, 1971, with a subhead "Strikers Drop Old Animosities to Accept Aid From Blacks; Is It an Evil Commie Plot?" *Newsweek* also featured the story with photos of the strikers receiving checks from Rev. Buford, November 8, 1971. The three television network news shows all covered the story as did many of the nation's leading newspapers.

40. This is not to say I was never given a hard time by some staff members. Branch and Membership Director Gloster Current riddled me with criticisms for more than a decade until he was convinced that my work was worthwhile. And Althea Simmons, who served in many posts including Education Secretary and chief of the Washington bureau, gave me (and almost everyone else) a great deal of difficulty for almost 20 years, at which point she came to the conclusion I was staying for a while. On the other hand, Clarence Mitchell, Bob Carter, Henry Lee Moon, and Ruby Hurley, among others, were especially warm and gracious. John Morsell became my closest personal friend until his sudden death in 1975. I accompanied Youth Director Herb Wright to a variety of events, including Friday night jam sessions at the Cliffside Park, New Jersey, home of Sarah Vaughan, whose basement was a mecca for visiting jazz musicians. In all the years I knew Roy Wilkins, a relationship that began casually in 1949 and ceased with his death in 1981, however tired or stressed Wilkins might be, I was never observed him to be rude or unprofessional.

41. In 1973, after a decade of enormous crises, Wilkins, in one of his syndicated columns, urged civil rights activists, especially college students, to "lighten up," to find the humor in the grim circumstances and, above all, think about "a pretty girl," he wrote. "In fact, a pretty girl is often just what the doctor ordered. Look around you. Try not to be turned off by the clothes (or lack of them) and see if the black Soul Sister is not neat—even pretty. The chances are that a well-built and good-looking girl is hiding beneath those ragged denims and those cloppy shapeless sweaters. Nowadays, of course, they don't leave much to one's imagination." Reprinted in "The Roy Wilkins Column," by the NAACP Special Contribution Fund, New York, 1974. The column was syndicated on July 21, 1973, under the title "Civil Lights."

42. Mildred Bond Roxborough, phone interview by author, August, 1998; June Shagaloff, phone interview by author, July-August, 1998.

43. Despite his middle-income salary, Wilkins managed to save a considerable sum throughout his career and, with the advice of several Wall Street brokers—most notably Palmer Webber—who were managing the NAACP's modest reserves, he invested with great shrewdness and success. When he died in 1981, he left Mrs. Wilkins with a sizable estate, considering his salary range, which,

together with her own pension, provided her with a comfortable life style until her death in 1995. She left most of the estate to charities and educational institutions, except for some gifts to close friends. (Phone conversation with Mildred Bond Roxborough, Feb. 12, 1998.) Ms. Roxborough had been secretary, then assistant to both John Morsell and Roy Wilkins, later one of three deputy directors of the NAACP under Ben Hooks, and executor of Mrs. Wilkins' estate. Unfortunately, most of Wilkins' executive staff did not fare anywhere as well in their later years.

44. Wilkins was not as self-controlled in the presence of Dr. King, for whom he occasionally adopted a sarcastic demeanor. Some of this was a result of Wilkins' life-long disdain for religion and men of the cloth. That bias compounded when Wilkins felt that Dr. King was behaving a bit sanctimoniously for Wilkins' taste, especially since Wilkins considered the achievements of *his* organization to be far more important and extensive than those of King's SCLC. In 1963, for example, Wilkins and King were involved in a heated exchange over the conditions for the 1963 March on Washington. According to Bayard Rustin's biographer, Wilkins taunted King, declaring: "In fact, Martin, if you have desegregated *anything* by your efforts, kindly enlighten me." "Well," said Martin, "I guess about the only thing I've desegregated is a few human hearts." Roy conceded that one and nodded." Anderson, Jervis. *Bayard Rustin: The Troubles I've Seen,* 246.

45. In his autobiography, LDF Director Jack Greenberg admits that the NAACP, and specifically its General Counsel Robert L. Carter, sought to prohibit the LDF from meeting with its branches and seeking to represent these branches and these members in litigation. Greenberg reports that Carter telephoned him after the SCF received tax-deductible status and then wrote him a letter, in which he stated: "I want to make explicit the basic point of my telephone conversation with you on June 9, 1965 . . . . I am requesting that you cease any direct contact with NAACP branches in regard to litigation." Greenberg, Jack, *Crusaders in the Courts,* 480. After the LDF repeatedly ignored the NAACP's demands, the NAACP launched its initial campaign to compel the LDF to drop its initials. This also failed.

46. Solomon, Helen and Wilkins, Aminda, eds., *Talking It Over with Roy Wilkins: Selected Speeches and Writings,* 51.

47. *Ibid.*, 126, in a syndicated column dated March 22, 1975, under heading "Integration the Only Way."

48. *Ibid.*, 72.

49. NAACP SCF direct mail appeal letter, November 25, 1966.

50. *Ibid.*

51. *Ibid.*

52. Meier, August and Bracey, John, "The NAACP as Reform Movement, 1909–1965: To Reach the Conscience of America," 22. The authors regard "Wilkins' adroit machinations as the prime cause of the ability of the NAACP to maintain control of the LCCR," a conclusion with which noted activist and scholar Julian Bond agreed in his introduction to the Wilkins autobiography, revised paperback edition, 1994, in which Bond cites the same quotation approvingly.

Chapter 13

1. For example, in 1960 the SCLC headed by Dr. Martin Luther King Jr. had a budget of $57,000 and a total of five employees. The NAACP's annual budget for the same year was substantially in excess of $1 million with more than 50 employees. "The SCLC Story," Atlanta, GA., 1964, 15. Also NAACP, *1960 Annual Report.*

2. My associates and I directed the planning, organization, and ticket sales of testimonial dinners honoring Randolph (on his 80th birthday) and Rustin (on his 70th birthday). Canvassing local New York City trade unions by phone, we encountered virulent anti-Negro sentiments among the officers of the majority of local unions.

3. From 1965 until about the mid-1980s, I often used the title of director of fund-raising or of development, even though some of my responsibilities included public relations. Then another senior staff member decided to use the title of director of fund-raising and, since my duties included generating material and specialist support, as well as developing new programs, in addition to directing the SCF's direct mail, corporate, and foundation campaigns, I was accorded the title of director of program support. Most of the NAACP's national programs were developed and funded by the SCF, as were many local versions of them. I held that post until 1995.

4. By 1999 African-American purchasing power was estimated to exceed $530 billion, according to a study by an economist at the University of Georgia's Selog Center for Economic Growth. That represented a substantial rise from the 1997 figure of $450 billion by the same source, itself a major increase of 54 percent over the 1990 figure of $305 billion. *Jet,* May 26, 1997, 4, "Black Buying Power Projected to Surpass $450 Billion in 1997: Study."

A more conservative estimate for 1997 of black purchasing power-—$392 billion—was released by Chicago-based *Target Market News,* based on a study of 3,000 African-American household interviews and diaries conducted by the U.S. Department of Commerce. The same study also reported a six-fold increase in 1997 spending among black families on the Internet over the previous year.

The 1999 University of Georgia study also identified the 10 states with the highest take-home pay for blacks in that year. They were: New York—$60.9 billion; California—$40.9 billion; Texas—$35.9 billion; Florida—$30.7 billion; Georgia—$30.4 billion; Illinois—$29.4 billion; Maryland—$27.9 billion; North Carolina—$24.1 billion; New Jersey—$23.4 billion; and Michigan—$22.9 billion. The University of Georgia 1999 study estimated that black purchasing power had increased from 1990 to 1999 by $225 billion, or 73 percent in less than a decade, compared with the overall national rise of about 57 percent. Such an increase is unprecedented for African-American economic growth in the modern era.

5. Bundy had been a senior White House advisor to Presidents Kennedy and Johnson. Following his death in 1997, his White House deputy, Harvard Professor Carl Keysen, observed at a memorial service that in Bundy's first report as president of the Ford Foundation, he asserted that "the struggle for Negro equality" was "the first of the nation's problems." His leadership and his actions at the Ford Foundation were responsible for a vast increase in the resources of the civil rights organizations, including the NAACP, and of related minority groups, not

only from Ford but also, because of Ford's commitment and example, from scores of other foundations.

6. To this day I am uncertain where these remarks came from because I had not planned them in advance. In fact, until that moment, I had sincerely believed that the Rockefeller Foundation's mistake would be rectified without the need for pressure. As John Morsell's eyes widened in disbelief, I attempted to convey to the foundation executives what might be described as my "best Bogart." All five foundation executives sat down simultaneously, leaving John Morsell standing for another few seconds. The room was very quiet for another minute. As Morsell told me later, he was on the verge of offering an apology and a diplomatic withdrawal, certain that I had simultaneously shot the NAACP and myself in the foot, when the Rockefeller Foundation vice president made his proposal. My best guess is that my response was purely instinctive, not cerebral, and I think I also sensed that Dr. Black was bluffing.

7. Long a fervent NAACP supporter, Leonard de Paur was himself a civil rights pioneer. A talented singer, conductor, and choral director, he created the outdoors programs of the Lincoln Center in 1970, programs that came to represent the diversity of the New York City's populace as well as of the arts. According to his obituary, de Paur conducted 2,300 performances between 1947 and 1968, from his own Infantry Chorus to the symphony orchestras of many major American cities, as well as the touring New York Philharmonic. He broke ground in so many ways that the *New York Times* Arts and Leisure Section, after his death, felt obliged to devote more than 50 inches, including photos, to a celebration of his life's work (August 1, 1999, 30, "Celebrating an Impresario"). That article, by Valerie Gladstone, included a quotation from de Paur's brother-in-law, civil rights leader and former Atlanta mayor Andrew Young, speaking about Leonard at a festival in honor of de Paur: "As a conductor," he said, "Leonard brought the American idiom, jazz and spirituals, to classical music, which was then largely European. Without him, there would be no Wynton Marsalis. In a sense, he was to classical music what Jackie Robinson was to baseball, except in baseball it was about color. In classical music, segregation went deeper, depriving us of a world of diverse rhythms and harmonies. At Lincoln Center he broadened the world for all the arts." Also de Paur's obituary, *New York Times,* November 11, 1998, "Leonard de Paur Dies at 83; Lincoln Center Administrator."

8. Another version of this phenomenon was the 1968 *Life* magazine issue that identified, as the "men who are speaking for black America," Jesse Jackson, Julian Bond, Eldridge Cleaver, Dick Gregory, and Bishop Albert Cleague. Inexplicably, the Luce flagship publication ignored Wilkins, Young, Randolph, Evers, Jordan, Rustin, John Lewis—and a host of others.

9. At the time I began to suspect that either Tellez had little or no voice in deciding the show's guest list, or he was stalling for time while he negotiated for a new position outside of NBC. I never learned which one was the accurate judgment, since Tellez left his post shortly thereafter for another position and we never spoke again.

10. A few months later I received an urgent phone call from a staff member of the "Tonight Show," asking if Roy Wilkins would be available the following day to appear on the show, which was taped in the late afternoon. It seemed that Sammy Davis Jr. was hosting the show and the staff felt that a Wilkins appear-

ance would be appropriate. I told them I would get back to them, knowing that Wilkins was on the West Coast speaking to branches. I reached Wilkins that evening, and told him the details, to which the NAACP leader replied with a firm negative. Noting that he had promised the Death Valley branch of the NAACP that he would speak at their annual dinner the next evening, Wilkins observed that since they paid his salary, he would honor that promise, even though the "Tonight Show" reached millions of the unconverted. I was not the least bit surprised and relished every second of the phone call in which I conveyed Wilkins's decision. Wilkins was never invited again by the Carson Show, nor were Young, Rustin, or Evers.

11. It is a measure of how much the nation's leadership venerated Roy Wilkins when one examines the testimonial letterhead assembled for these events. The honorary chairmen were President Gerald R. Ford, Nelson Rockefeller, Mrs. Margaret Truman Daniel, Mrs. Hubert H. Humphrey, Mrs. Lyndon B. Johnson, Mrs. Robert F. Kennedy, Mrs. Alice Roosevelt Longworth, A. Philip Randolph, and Mrs. Earl Warren. (There is an ironic flavor to this list, comprised of so many widows of the national leaders whom Roy Wilkins himself most admired—Harry Truman, Hubert Humphrey, Lyndon Johnson, Jack and Robert Kennedy, Franklin and Eleanor Roosevelt, and Earl Warren.) The dinner and birthday committee chairmen were Mrs. Ralph J. Bunche, Henry Ford II, John H. Johnson, George Meany, John D. Rockefeller III, and Dore Schary, a movie director and head of a major Jewish organization. They and the vice chairmen comprised a Who's Who of national leadership in government, industry, labor unions, philanthropy, and the arts. The program chairmen for these events were Bill Cosby, Sammy Davis Jr., Lena Horne, Sidney Poitier, and Bobby Short. Virtually every individual on the celebratory letterheads had a first-hand acquaintance, if not a friendship, with Wilkins. Many of the nation's governors and several mayors of large cities issued proclamations in honor of Wilkins' 75th birthday. They seemed to agree with Mrs. Ralph Bunche, who said in a widely-circulated letter to Americans in many stations of life:

[T]wo things cannot be denied: had Roy Wilkins not appeared on the scene, millions of black Americans would today be leading poorer, more frustrating lives. And in all his work Roy Wilkins has never wavered from the truth as he has seen the truth. In the era of Watergate, what more need be said?

"For almost 50 years Roy Wilkins has championed the cause of the common man in the halls of presidents and lawmakers. In an era shamed by the influence peddling and self-serving of national leaders, Roy Wilkins still comes to work each morning by subway. When he retires next year, his income will be an adequate but far from extravagant pension."

Letter signed by Mrs. Ralph J. Bunche, September 7, 1976, on the letterhead of the "Roy Wilkins 75th Birthday Celebration."

12. It became a source of continuous amusement throughout the seventies and eighties to find that our fund-raising and promotional ideas were so often copied by the NAACP SCF's competition, most especially the LDF. After General Motors and its chairman, Tom Murphy, announced their plan to pay tribute to Wilkins in Washington, the LDF recruited Ford Motor Company President Lee Iococca to chair a dinner in *its* honor in New York. When I set out to organize a committee for the New York event honoring Wilkins, I prepared an invitational

letter to Henry Ford II, CEO of Ford Motor, to serve as one of the leaders of the New York event. I wanted to avoid playing favorites, since both GM and Ford were generous NAACP supporters. However, after four months and several tries, including phone calls, I was unable to extract a response from Mr. Ford. I consulted with my colleagues at the NAACP and learned that Mrs. Ralph Bunche was a good friend of Henry Ford II. With her consent, I drafted a letter to Mr. Ford over her signature, which she approved, recounting our efforts and resubmitting the invitation. Three days later, Ford called Mrs. Bunche and revealed that he had never seen our earlier letters. It appears that someone, almost certainly someone associated with Iococca, had them intercepted, in order to avoid any competition within the Ford family over the LDF event chaired by Iococca. Needless to say, Mr. Ford agreed to serve as one of the dinner cochairs. Not too many weeks later, Iococca left the Ford Motor Company. This is not to suggest that the reason for his departure was the NAACP-LDF affair; it was alleged later, according to news reports, that it had more to do with other indfasdfasfasdfasdfation also withheld from Henry Ford II, who was still board chairman of the company.

13. The NAACP's *1968 Annual Report* lists 85 executive employees, no doubt the organization's record number for executive staff. The secretarial and clerical staff was probably almost as large at that time. This was the result of the SCF's rapidly increasing income, including major grants from Ford, Carnegie, and Rockefeller, as well as the first year of Ford's grant covering eight urban program directors. Since the SCF paid almost half of the National Office's overhead, the resulting savings enabled the latter to hire four regional directors, nineteen field directors, six youth regional directors, and seven membership staff executives. *1968 Annual Report,* 152–154.

Bibliography

"Ad Hoc Subcommittee Hearing on Investigation of the Garment Industry," pp. 165–167. U.S. House of Representatives, Committee on Education and Labor, 87th Congress, Second Session, August 19–24, September 21, 1962.

Archives of U.S. Library of Congress

Archives of New York Public Library

Allen, Robert L. *The Port Chicago Mutiny.* New York: Warner Books, 1989.

Allen, James, and Hilton Als, et al. *Without Sanctuary: Lynching Photography in America.* Santa Fe, NM: Twin Palms Publishers, 2000.

Anderson, Jervis. *Bayard Rustin: The Troubles I've Seen.* New York: HarperCollins, 1997.

Anderson, Marian. *My Lord, What a Morning: an Autobiography of.* New York: Viking Press, 1956.

Aptheker, Herbert. *The Negro People in America: A Critique of Gunnar Myrdal's "An American Dilemma."* New York: International Publishers, 1946.

Aptheker, Herbert. *Afro-American History: The Modern Era.* Secaucus, NJ: The Citadel Press, 1971.

Ashe, Arthur R., Jr. *A Hard Road to Glory: A History of the African-American Athlete 1919–1945* Vol. II. New York: Amistad, 1993.

Ashmore, Harry. *Hearts and Minds: The Anatomy of Racism from Roosevelt to Reagan.* New York: McGraw-Hill, 1982.

Baldwin, James. *The Fire Next Time.* New York: The Dial Press, 1963.

Baldwin, James. *Nobody Knows My Name.* New York: Dell, 1963.

Baldwin, Young, et al. *The White Problem in America.* New York: Lancer Books, 1965.

Ball, Howard. *A Defiant Life: Thurgood Marshall and the Persistence of Racism in America.* New York: Crown, 1998.

Barron, John. *Operation Solo: The FBI's Man in the Kremlin.* Washington, DC: Regnery Publishing, 1966.

Berman, Paul, ed. *Blacks and Jews: Alliances and Arguments.* New York: Delacorte Press, 1994.

Bogle, Donald. *Toms, Coons, Mulattoes, Mammies, & Bucks: An Interpretative History of Blacks in American Films.* New York: Viking, 1973.

Bontemps, Arna. *The Old South: "A Summer Tragedy" and Other Stories of the Thirties.* New York: Dodd, Mead, 1973.

Boxing Almanac and Book Facts. London Publishing Co., 1996.

Branch, Taylor. *Parting the Waters: America in the King Years 1954–63.* New York: Simon and Schuster, 1988.

———. *Pillar of Fire: America in the King Years, 1963–65.* New York: Simon and Schuster, 1998.

Brauer, Carl M. *John F. Kennedy and the Second Reconstruction.* New York: Columbia University Press, 1977.

Brink, William, and Louis Harris. *The Negro Revolution.* New York: Simon and Schuster, 1964.

Broderick, Francis L., and August Meier. *Negro Protest Thought in the Twentieth Century.* Indianapolis, IN: The Bobbs-Merrill Company, Inc., 1965.

Carmichael, Stokely, and Charles V. Hamilton. *Black Power: The Politics of Liberation in America.* New York: Vintage Books, 1967.

Clark, Kenneth B. *The Negro Protest: James Baldwin, Malcolm X, Martin Luther King Talk With Kenneth B. Clark.* Boston, MA: Beacon Press, 1963.

———. *Dark Ghetto: Dilemmas of Social Power.* New York: Harper & Row, 1965.

Cleaver, Eldridge. *Soul on Fire.* Waco, TX: World Books, 1978.

Conference on Jewish Social Studies. *Negro-Jewish Relations in the United States: A Symposium.* New York: Citadel Press, 1966.

Coon, Carleton S. *The Origin of Races.* New York: Alfred A. Knopf, 1963.

Cortner, Richard C. *A Mob Intent on Death: The NAACP and the Arkansas Riot Cases.* Middletown, CT: Wesleyan University, 1988.

Crawford, Rouse, and Woods, eds. *Women in the Civil Rights Movement: Trailblazers & Torchbearers 1941–1965.* Bloomington: Indiana University, 1993.

Darrow, Clarence. *The Story of My Life.* New York: Scribner's, 1934.

DeLaughter, Bobby. *Never Too Late: A Prosecutor's Story of Justice in the Medgar Evers Case.* New York: Scribner, 2001.

Dewey, John. *David Dubinsky: A Pictorial Biography.* New York: Inter-Allied Publications, 1949.

Dixon, Thomas. *The Clansman: Photo-Play Title—Birth of a Nation.* New York: Grosset & Dunlap Reprint, N.D. [1905].

Doyle, William. *Inside the Oval Office—White House Tapes from FDR to Clinton.* New York: Kodanshahm, circa 1999.

Drake, St. Clair, and Horace R. Cayton. *Black Metropolis: A Study of Negro Life in a Northern City.* New York: Harcourt, Brace, 1945.

Draper, Alan. *Conflict of Interests: Organized Labor and the Civil Rights Movement in the South, 1954–1968.* Ithaca, NY: Cornell University, 1994.

Duberman, Martin Bauml. *Paul Robeson.* New York: Alfred A. Knopf, 1998.

Dubinsky, David, and A. H. Raskin. *David Dubinsky: A Life With Labor.* New York: Simon & Schuster, 1977.

DuBois, W.E.B. *Black Folk Then and Now: An Essay in the History and Sociology of the Negro Race.* New York: Henry Holt, 1940.

———. *Color and Democracy.* New York: Harcourt, Brace, 1945.

———. *The World and Africa.* New York: Viking, 1947.

Durham, Philip, and Everett L. Jones. *The Adventures of the Negro Cowboys.* New York: Bantam, 1966.

Egerton, John. *Speaking Now Against the Day: The Generation Before the Civil Rights Movement in the South.* New York: Alfred A. Knopf, 1995.

Ellison, Ralph. *Invisible Man*. New York: Random House, 1952.

Falkner, David. *Great Time Coming: The Life of Jackie Robinson from Baseball to Birmingham*. New York: Simon & Schuster, 1995.

Farmer, James. *Lay Bare the Heart: An Autobiography of the Civil Rights Movement*. New York: Arbor House, 1985.

Farr, Finis. *Black Champion: The Life and Times of Jack Johnson*. London: Macmillan, 1964.

Faulkner, Harold U., and Mark Starr. *Labor in America: New Edition*. New York: Oxford Book Co., 1957.

Faulkner, William. *Intruder in the Dust*. New York: Random House, 1948.

Fishel, Leslie H., Jr., and Benjamin Quarles, eds. *The Black American: A Documentary History, Revised Edition*. Glenview, IL: Scott, Foresman and Co., 1971.

Fowler, Arlen L. *The Black Infantry in the West, 1869–1891*. Norman: University of Oklahoma Press, 1996.

Frazier, E. Franklin. *The Negro in the United States*. New York: Macmillan, 1949.

Franklin, Grant, et al. *African Americans and Jews in the Twentieth Century*. Columbia: University of Missouri, 1998.

Franklin, John Hope, and Alfred A. *Moss Jr. From Slavery to Freedom: A History of African-Americans*, 7th Edition. New York: Alfred A. Knopf, 1994.

Foner, Philip S., and James S. Allen. *American Communism and Black Americans: A Documentary History, 1919–1929*. Philadelphia, PA: Temple University, 1987.

Garrow, David J. *Bearing the Cross: Martin Luther King, Jr., and the Southern Christian Leadership Conference*. New York: William Morrow, 1986.

Genovese, Eugene D. *The Political Economy of Slavery*. New York: Pantheon Books, 1961.

George, Nelson. *Black Face: Reflections on African-Americans and the Movies*. New York: HarperCollins, 1994.

Ginzberg, Eli. *The Negro Potential*. New York: Columbia University, 1956.

Gitlin, Todd. *The Sixties: Years of Hope, Days of Rage*. New York: Bantam Books, 1987.

Goings, Kenneth W. *The NAACP Comes of Age: The Defeat of Judge John J. Parker*. Bloomington: Indiana University, 1990.

Golden, Harry. *Mr. Kennedy and the Negroes*. Cleveland, OH: The World Publishing Company, 1964.

Goulden, Joseph C. *Meany—The Unchallenged Strong Man of American Labor*. New York: Atheneum, 1972.

Graham, Lawrence Otis. *Our Kind of People*. New York: HarperColllins, 1999.

Green, Ben. *Before His Time: The Untold Story of Harry T. Moore, America's 1st Civil Rights Martyr*. New York: The Free Press, 1999.

Greenberg, Jack. *Crusaders in the Courts*. New York: Basic Books, 1994.

Gregory, Dick. *From Back of the Bus*. New York: E. P. Dutton, 1962.

Grimshaw, Allen D., ed. *Racial Violence in the United States*. Chicago: Aldine Publishing, 1969.

Hacker, Andrew. *Two Nations: Black and White, Separate, Hostile, Unequal*. New York: Charles Scribner's Sons, 1992.

Halberstam, David. *The Children*. New York: Random House, 1998.

Halliburton, Warren J., and William Loren Katz. *American Majorities and Minorities*. New York: Arno Press, 1970.

Hickey, Neil, and Ed Edwin. *Adam Clayton Powell and the Politics of Race.* New York: Fleet Publishing, 1965.

Hill, Herbert. *Soon, One Morning: New Writing by American Negroes, 1940–1962.* New York: Alfred A. Knopf, 1962.

———. *Anger and Beyond: The Negro Writer in the United States.* New York: Harper & Row, 1966.

———. *Black Labor and the American Legal System: Race, Work and the Law.* Madison: University of Wisconsin, 1977.

Hill, Herbert, and James E. Jones Jr., eds. *Race in America: The Struggle for Equality.* Madison: University of Wisconsin, 1993.

Hilliard, David, and Lewis Cole. *This Side of Glory: The Autobiography of David Hilliard and the Story of the Black Panther Party.* Boston, MA: Little, Brown, 1993.

Holt, Thomas C. *The Problem of Race in the 21st Century.* Cambridge, MA: Harvard University, 2000.

Hughes, Langston. *Fight For Freedom—The Story of the NAACP.* New York: Berkley Publishing, 1962.

ILGWU. *Constitution of the International Ladies Garment Workers Union,* New York: 1959

ILGWU. *Report of the General Executive Board.* 32d Convention, May 12, 1965.

Jacobson, Julius, ed. *The Negro and the American Labor Movement.* New York: Doubleday Anchor, 1968.

Johnson, James Weldon. *Along This Way: The Autobiography of James Weldon Johnson* New York: Viking Press, 1933.

———. *Negro Americans, What Now?* New York: Viking Press, 1934.

Kaiser, Charles. *1968 in America.* New York: Weidenfeld and Nicholson, 1988.

Kasher, Steven. *The Civil Rights Movement: A Photographic History, 1954–68.* New York: Abbeville, 1996.

Katz, William Loren. *Eyewitness: The Negro in American History.* New York: Pitman Publishing, 1967.

Kellner, Bruce. *The Harlem Renaissance: A Historical Dictionary for the Era.* New York: Methuen, 1987.

Kellogg, Charles Flint. *NAACP: A History of the National Association for the Advancement of Colored People,* Vol. I. Baltimore, MD: Johns Hopkins, 1967.

King, Martin Luther, Jr. *Where Do We Go From Here: Chaos or Community? New York: Harper & Row, 1967.*

Klineberg, Otto. *Negro Intelligence and Selective Migration.* New York: Columbia University, 1935.

———. *Race Differences,* 2d Ed. New York: Harper & Brothers, 1935.

Kluger, Richard. *Simple Justice.* New York: Alfred E. Knopf, 1976.

Koning, Hans. *Nineteen Sixty-Eight: A Personal Report.* New York: W. W. Norton, 1987.

LaFarge, John. *The Race Question and the Negro: A Study of the Catholic Doctrine on Interracial Justice.* New York: Longmans, Green, 1944.

Landis, Kenisaw M. *Segregation in Washington.* Washington, D.C: The National Committee on Segregation in the Nation's Capital, 1948.

Lardner, John. *White Hopes and Other Tigers.* Philadelphia, PA: J. P. Lippincott, 1951.

Lee, Alfred McClung, and Norman Daymond Humphrey. *Race Riot.* New York: The Dryden Press, 1943.

Lester, Julius. *Lovesong: Becoming a Jew.* New York: Henry Holt, 1988.

Lewis, David Levering. *W.E.B. Dubois: The Fight For Equality and the American Century, 1919–1963.* New York: Henry Holt, 2000.

Lewis, John. *Walking With the Wind: A Memoir of the Movement.* New York: Simon & Schuster, 1998.

Lewinson, Paul. *Race, Class, and Party: A History of Negro Suffrage and White Politics in the South.* New York: Oxford University, 1932.

Logan, Rayford, ed. *What the Negro Wants.* Chapel Hill: University of North Carolina, 1944.

Lomax, Louis E. *The Negro Revolt.* New York: Harper & Brothers, 1962.

Macolmsom, Scott L. *One Drop of Blood: The American Misadventure of Race.* New York: Farrar Straus Giroux, 2000.

Magat, Richard. *Unlikely Partners: Philanthropic Foundations and the Labor Movement.* Ithaca, NY: Cornell University, 1999.

Margolick, David. *Strange Fruit: Billy Holiday, Cafe Society and an Early Cry for Civil Rights.* Philadelphia, PA: Running Press, 2000.

Massey, Douglas S., and Nancy A. Denton *American Apartheid: Segregation and the Making of the Underclass.* Cambridge: Harvard University Press, 1993

McMurray, Linda A. *The Life of Ida B. Wells.* New York, Oxford University Press, 1999.

McNeil, Genna Rae. *Groundwork: Charles Hamilton Houston and the Struggle for Civil Rights.* Philadelphia: University of Pennsylvania, 1983.

Moon, Henry Lee. *Balance of Power: The Negro Vote.* Garden City, NY: Doubleday, 1949.

Morton, Franklin. *Thirty Years or Lynching in the United States, 1889–1918.* New York, NAACP, 1919.

Myrdal, Gunnar. *An American Dilemma: The Negro Problem and Modern Democracy.* New York: Harper and Brothers, 1944.

NAACP. Annual Reports 1939–1975.

NAACP. Special Contribution Fund Annual Reports 1983–1990.

Naison, Mark. *Communists in Harlem During the Depression.* Urbana: University of Illinois, 1983.

Needleman, Ruth. *Black Freedom Fighters in Steel: The Struggle for Democratic Unionism.* Ithaca, NY: Cornell University, 2003.

Neibuhr, Reinhold. Foreword to *Mississippi Black Paper.* New York: Random House, 1965.

Nelson, Bruce. *Divided We Stand: American Workers and the Struggle for Black Equality.* Princeton, NJ: Princeton University, 2001.

Norgren, Webster, et al. *Employing the Negro in American Industry: A Study in Management Practices.* New York: Industrial Relations Counselors, Inc., 1959.

Nossiter, Adam. *Of Long Memory: Mississippi and the Murder of Medgar Evers.* New York: Addison-Wesley Publishing Co., 1994.

Olsen, Lynne. *Freedom's Daughters: The Unsung Heroines of the Movement from 1830–1970.* New York: Simon and Schuster, 2001.

Osofsky, Gilbert. *Harlem: The Making of a Ghetto—Negro New York, 1890–1930,* 2d Ed. Harper & Row, 1971.

Osur, Alan M. *Blacks in the Army Air Forces During World War II*. Washington, DC: U.S. Government Printing Office, 1977.

Ottley, Roy. *Black Odyssey*. New York: Scribner's, 1948.

Ovington, Mary White. *Portraits in Color*. New York: Viking Press, 1927.

——— *The Walls Came Tumbling Down, The Autobiography of a Mary White Ovington: The Story of the National Association for the Advancement of Colored People Told by One of its Founders*. New York: Harcourt, Brace & Co., 1947.

Parker, Frank R. *Black Votes Count: Political Empowerment in Mississippi after 1965*. Chapel Hill: The University of North Carolina Press, 1990.

Patterson, James T. *Brown v Board of Education: A Civil Rights Milestone and Its Troubled Legacy*. New York: Oxford University Press, 2001.

Phelps, Shirelle. *Who's Who Among Black Americans*, 8th Edition. Detroit: Gale Research, 1994–95.

Pickens, William. *The Heir of Slaves*. Boston: The Pilgrim Press, 1911.

——— *Bursting Bonds: The Autobiography of a "New Negro."* Bloomington: Indiana University Press, 1991.

Ploski, Harry A., and James Williams, eds. *Negro Almanac*. Detroit, MI: Bellweather Publishing Co., 1989.

Ploski, Harry A., and Ernest Kaiser, eds. *AfroUSA: A Reference Work on the Black Experience*. New York: Bellwether Publishing, 1971.

Powell, Adam Clayton, Sr. *Riots and Ruins*. New York: Richard R. Smith, 1945.

Powledge, Fred. *Free At Last? The Civil Rights Movement and the People Who Made It*. Boston, MA: Little, Brown, 1991.

Rabinowitz, Howard N. *Race Relations in the Urban South, 1865–1890*. Urbana: University of Illinois, 1980.

Rampersad, Arnold. *The Art and Imagination of W.E.B. DuBois. 1976*. Reprint, New York: Schocken Books, 1990.

———. *Jackie Robinson: A Biography*. New York: Alfred A. Knopf, 1997.

Ransby, Barbara. *Ella Baker & the Black Freedom Movement*. Chapel Hill: University of North Carolina, 2003.

Reed, Christopher Robert. *The Chicago NAACP and the Rise of Black Professional Leadership 1910–1966*. Bloomington: Indiana University Press, 1977.

Richardson, Heather Cox. *The Death of Reconstruction*. Cambridge, MA: Harvard University Press, 2001.

Roberts, James B., and Alexander G. Skutt. *The Boxing Register*. Ithaca, NY: McBooks Press, 1997.

Roberts, Randy. *Papa Jack: Jack Johnson and the Era of White Hopes*. New York: The Free Press, 1983.

Rose, Phyllis. *Jazz Cleopatra: Josephine Baker in Her Time*. New York: Doubleday, 1989.

Rosenman, Samuel I. *Working With Roosevelt*. New York: Harper & Brothers, 1952.

Rowan, Carl T. *South of Freedom*. New York: Alfred A. Knopf, 1952.

———. *Breaking Barriers: A Memoir*. Boston: Little, Brown, 1991.

———. *Dream Makers, Dream Breakers: The World of Justice Thurgood Marshall*. Boston, Little, Brown and Co., 1993.

Sackler, Howard. *The Great White Hope*. New York: The Dial Press, 1968.

Saunders, Doris E., ed. *The Kennedy Years and the Negro*. Chicago: Johnson Publications, 1964.
Schlesinger, Arthur M., Jr. *A Thousand Days: John F. Kennedy in the White House*. Boston, MA: Houghton-Mifflin Co., 1965.
Schuyler, George S. *Black and Conservative: The Autobiography of*. New Rochelle, NY: Arlington House, 1966.
Shogan, Robert, and Tom Craig. *The Detroit Race Riot: A Study in Violence*. Philadelphia, PA: Chilton Books, 1964.
Smith, Lillian. *Strange Fruit*. New York: Reynal & Hitchcock, 1944.
Solomon, Helen, and Aminda Wilkins, eds. *Talking It Over with Roy Wilkins: Selected Speeches and Writings*, Norwalk, CT: M&B Publishing, 1977.
Sorensen, Theodore C. *Kennedy*. New York: Harper and Row, 1965.
Stampp, Kenneth M. *The Peculiar Institution: Slavery in the Ante-Bellum South*. New York: Alfred A. Knopf, 1956.
———. *The Era of Reconstruction, 1865–1877*. New York: Alfred A. Knopf, 1965.
Stewart, James Brewar. *Holy Warriors: The Abolitionists and American Slavery*. New York: Hill and Wang, 1976.
Stoddard, Lothrop. *The Rising Tide of Color*. New York: Scribner's, 1921.
Thomas, Hugh. *The Slave Trade*. New York: Simon & Schuster, 1997.
Tushnet, Mark V. *The NAACP's Legal Strategy Against Segregated Education, 1925–1950*. Chapel Hill: University of North Carolina, 1987.
Tyler, Gus. *The Labor Revolution: Trade Unionism in a New America*. New York: Viking Press, 1967.
Tyson, Timothy. *Radio Free Dixie: Robert F. Williams and the Roots of Black Power*. Chapel Hill: University of North Carolina, 1999.
Warren, Earl. *The Memoirs of Earl Warren*. Garden City, NY: Doubleday, 1977.
Warren, Robert Penn. *Segregation: The Inner Conflict of the South*. New York: Random House, 1956.
———. *Who Speaks for the Negro?* New York: Random House, 1965.
Washington, Booker T., and W.E.B. DuBois. *The Negro in the South*. Philadelphia, PA: George W. Jacobs, 1907.
Washington, Booker T. *The Future of the American Negro*. Boston, MA: Small, Maynard, 1899.
———. *Up From Slavery: An Autobiography*. New York: Doubleday, Page, 1901.
Watson, Denton L. *Lion in the Lobby: Clarence Mitchell Jr.'s Struggle for the Passage of Civil Rights Laws*. New York: William Morrow and Co., 1990.
Weaver, Robert C. *Negro Labor: A National Problem*. New York: Harcourt, Brace, 1946.
———. *The Negro Ghetto*. New York: Harcourt, Brace, 1948.
White, Theodore H. *The Making of the President 1960*. New York: Atheneum Publishers, 1961.
White, Walter. *A Rising Wind*. Garden City, NY: Doubleday, Doran, 1945.
———. *A Man Called White*. New York: Viking Press, 1948.
———. *How Far the Promised Land?* New York: Viking Press, 1955.
Wienceck, Henry. *An Imperfect God: George Washington, His Slaves and the Creation of America*. New York: Farrar, Straus and Giroux, 2004.

Wilkins, Roy, with Tom Mathews. *Standing Fast: The Autobiography of Roy Wilkins*. New York: Viking Press, 1982.
Williams, Juan. *Thurgood Marshall: American Revolutionary*. New York: Times Books, 1998.
Williams, Robert F. *Negroes With Guns*. New York: Marzani & Munsell, 1962.
Wills, Gary. *The Second Civil War: Arming for Armageddon*. New York: New American Library, 1968.
Wolfe, Tom. *Radical Chic & Mau-Maxin the Flak Catchers*. New York: Farrar, Straus and Giroux, 1970.
Wofford, Harris. *Of Kennedys and Kings*. New York: Farrar, Straus and Giroux, 1970.
Woodward, C. Vann. *The Strange Career of Jim Crow: A Brief Account of Segregation*. New York: Oxford University Press, 1955.
Wright, Richard. *Native Son*. New York: Harper & Brothers, 1940.
———. *Black Boy*. New York: Harper & Brothers, 1945.
Young, Andrew. *An Easy Burden: The Civil Rights Movement and the Transformation of America*. New York: HarperCollins, 1996.
Young, Whitney M., Jr. *Beyond Racism*. New York: McGraw-Hill, 1969

PAMPHLETS, SPEECHES and ARTICLES

Bunche, Mrs. Ralph. "Roy Wilkins 75th Birthday Celebration." Letter signed by Mrs. Bunche. September 7, 1976.
Clark, Dr. Kenneth. *Journal of Social Issues* Vol. 9, no. 4 (1953).
Davis, Benjamin J. *The Negro People in the Struggle for Peace and Freedom: Report of the 15th Convention, Communist Party*. New York: New Century Publishers, 1951.
DuBois, W.E.B., ed. *An Appeal to the World! A Statement on the Denial of Human Rights to Minorities in the Case of Citizens of Negro Descent in the United States of American and an Appeal to the United Nations for Redress*. New York: NAACP, 1947.
Foster, William Z., and Benjamin Davis et al. *The Communist Position on the Negro Question*. New York: New Century Publishers, 1947.
Hill, Herbert. *The Communist Party—Enemy of Negro Equality*. New York: NAACP, 1951.
———. *No Harvest for the Reaper—the Story of the Migratory Agricultural Worker in the United States*. New York: NAACP, 1955.
———. "Racism Within Organized Labor: A Report of the Five Years of the AFL-CIO." Address to the NAACP Annual Meeting, January 3, 1961.
———. "The ILGWU—Fact and Fiction," *New Politics* (Winter 1963).
———. "Twenty Years of State Fair Employment Practice Commissions: A Critical Analysis and Recommendations," *Buffalo Law Review* (Fall 1964).
———. "The Judicial Perception of Employment Discrimination: Litigation Under Title VII of the Civil Rights Act," *University of Colorado Law Review* (March 1972).

———. "The New York City Terminal Market Controversy: A Case Study in Race, Labor and Power," *Humanities in Society* (Summer-Fall 1981).
———. "The AFL-CIO and the Black Worker: Twenty-five Years After the Merger." *Journal of Intergroup Relations* Vol. 10, no. 1 (Summer 1982).
———. "A Key Affirmative-Action Case," *New York Times Op-Ed* (February 18, 1986).
———. Letter to Adena Black, Exhibit Coordinator, The Jewish Museum, New York (February 4, 1992).
Johnson, James Weldon. *The Practice of Lynching*. New York: Century Magazine, 1927, 65–70.
Locke, Alain, sp. ed. *Color: Unfinished Business of Democracy. Survey Graphic,* Special Issue, November 1942.
Media Studies Journal. *"1968."* Washington, DC: Freedom Forum, 1998.
Meier, August and John Bracey. "The NAACP as Reform Movement, 1909–1965: To Reach the Conscience of America," *The Journal of Southern History* 59, no. 1 (February 1993).
NAACP. *M is for Mississippi and Murder.* New York: NAACP, 1955.
———. *The Negro in Wartime.* New York: NAACP, 1916.
———. *Tenth Annual Conference.* Program, NY: NAACP, 1919.
NAACP Special Contribution Fund. *1969: Twelve Afro-American Artists.* New York: NAACP SCF, 1969.
Office of War Information, *Negroes and the War.* Washington, D.C.: Government Printing Office, circa 1943.
O'Neal, James. *The Next Emancipation: Black and White Workers Unite.* New York: Socialist Party Emancipation Publishing, circa 1922.
Robeson, Paul. *Forge Negro-Labor Unity for Peace and Jobs.* New York: Harlem Trade Union Council, 1950.
———. *The Negro People and the Soviet Union.* New York: New York Century Press, 1950.
Sancton, Thomas, ed. *Segregation.* New York: Survey Associates, January 1947.
School Money in Black and White. Chicago: Julius Rosenwald Foundation, circa 1934.
Shagaloff, June (Alexander). Memorandum to Author, April 2000, and supplemental memorandum, January 2001.
Time Magazine (Jan. 24, 1938): Cover, 8–10.
Wilkins, Roy. Letter to William Patterson, November 9, 1949.
———. *Memo to NAACP Branches: The Communists vs. the NAACP's Civil Rights Fight.* New York, NAACP, March 22, 1950.
———. Letter to Rev. M. D. Bullock, President of New Rochelle branch, NAACP (January 27, 1961).
———. Letter to Emanuel Muravchik, Executive Secretary, the Jewish Labor Committee (October 31, 1962).

Interviews

Judge Robert L. Carter
Gloster Current
Prof. Herbert Hill
Dr. Benjamin L. Hooks
Vernon Jordan
Michael Meyers
Dr. Eugene Reed
Mildred Bond Roxborough
June Shagaloff Alexander
Judge Jack Tanner

Periodicals and Newspapers

American Federationist
Amsterdam News
Buffalo Law Review
The Crisis
Ebony
The Forward
Humanities in Society
Jet
Journal of Social Issues
Journal of Southern History
Look
Michigan Law Review
The Nation
National Law Journal
The New Leader
New Politics
The New Republic
Newsday
Newsweek
New York Herald tribune
New York Post
New York Times
Time
Union Democracy Review
University of Colorado Law Review
The Wall Street Journal
The Washington Post

Photo Credits

Courtesy of Library of Congress, Prints & Photographs Division, Visual Materials from the NAACP Records: DuBois, Ovington, Joel Spingarn, J.W. Johnson, "A Man Was Lynched Yesterday," Howard Students Protest, Houston, Storey, Pickens, White, Wilkins as a Levee Worker, Mrs. Roosevelt, Wilkins, Marshall, Carter, Current, President Eisenhower, NAACP "Brain Trust," Wilkins & Marshall Counsel Autherine Lucy, President Johnson, Hill, Shagaloff, Medgar Evers, Rustin

Courtesy of Associated Press: 1939 Marian Anderson Concert, 1963 March on Washington

Courtesy of Hilton Clark: Dr. Kenneth C. Clark

Courtesy of Herbert Hill: Thurgood Marshall and Herb Hill, Moon, Wilkins, Hill, and Marshall

Courtesy of Gil Jonas: Jack Johnson, Marian Anderson, Charles Evers and Author, Ralph Bunche

Courtesy of Paul Robeson Jr.: Paul Robeson

Courtesy of Mildred Bond Roxborough: Dr. John Morsell

Courtesy of June Shagaloff: Moon, Shagaloff, and Walter White

National Park Service Photographs Courtesy of Harry S. Truman Library: President Truman, President Truman, Eleanor Roosevelt, and Walter White

LBJ Library Photos by Yoichi Okamoto: President Johnson and Wilkins, Joseph Rauh and Roy Wilkins, LBJ and Wilkins

LBJ Library Photo by Frank Wolfe: Clarence Mitchell and President Johnson

John F. Kennedy Library Photos by Robert Knudsen, White House: President Kennedy, President Kennedy

John F. Kennedy Library Photo by Abbie Rowe, White House: President Kennedy and civil rights leaders

Photos by Gil Jonas: NAACP leaders, Ruby Hurley, Leaders of Mississippi biracial delegation caucus at 1968 Democratic convention in Chicago

Index

A

C

D

E

F

G

K

L

M

O

P

Q

R

S

T

U

V

W

Y

Z